Real-life economics

Since the end of the Second World War industrial economic activity has been sought and generated on an unparalleled scale. Ever greater output and productivity have been the dominant policy objectives of practically every country in the world for the past 50 years. The cost of this kind of development has been and is being paid in widespread social and cultural disruption and potentially catastrophic effects on the global environment.

This book challenges traditional economic theories which have promoted this situation and constructs an economic framework within which it can be both understood and ameliorated. This framework is designed to illuminate and offer guidance about practical matters of an economic nature in the real world, in order to help in the construction of an economy more productive of human welfare. The book is divided into three parts. The first part defines the place of the economy in broader human culture. It begins with a clarification of issues of methodology, process and purpose. It goes on to develop a perspective of the whole economy and models the process of wealth creation. Part II presents a deeper discussion of economic progress and development and how they can be measured in practice. Part III discusses the relationship between the market, the state and non-monetary production. Despite its innovative interdisciplinary approach, *Real-Life Economics* remains recognisably economic in nature, incorporating many of the means and concepts from a variety of the schools of thought (including the neoclassical) which constitute the economics discipline today. The individual papers, from contributors many of whom are among the acknowledged leaders in their respective fields, are woven together by editorial comment into a powerful statement of an important new economic perspective.

Real-life economics

Understanding wealth creation

Edited by
Paul Ekins and
Manfred Max-Neef

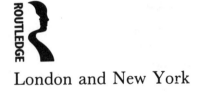

London and New York

First published 1992
by Routledge
11 New Fetter Lane, London EC4P 4EE

Simultaneously published in the USA and Canada
by Routledge
a division of Routledge, Chapman and Hall, Inc.
29 West 35th Street, New York, NY10001

© 1992 Paul Ekins and Manfred Max-Neef

Typeset in Baskerville
by Pat and Anne Murphy, Highcliffe-on-Sea, Dorset
Printed in Great Britain by
Mackays of Chatham plc, Chatham, Kent

British Library Cataloguing in Publication Data

A catalogue record for this title is available from the British
Library.

    ISBN 0-415-07976-4
    ISBN 0-415-07977-2 (pbk)

Library of Congress Cataloging in Publication Data
Real-life economics · understanding wealth creation /
  edited by Paul Ekins and Manfred Max-Neef.
    p.   cm.
  Includes bibliographical references and index.
  ISBN 0-415-07976-4. - ISBN 0-415-07977-2
  1. Economics. 2. Economic development - Sociological
aspects. I. Ekins, Paul. II. Max-Neef, Manfred A.
HB71.R34 1992   92-8827
330-dc20   CIP

All royalties from the sale of this book are payable to the
Living Economy Network.

Contents

Figures

Tables

Contributors

Mitchel Abolafia received his Ph.D. in sociology from the State University of New York at Stony Brook and now works in the Graduate School of Public Affairs at the State University of New York at Albany. He has written on market crisis, market regulation, opportunism and market rationality. He is currently working on a study entitled *Wall Street Culture* (Harvard University Press, forthcoming).

Peter Beresford and Suzy Croft have a long-standing involvement in issues of participation and empowerment as researchers, service users and community activists. Since 1987 they have worked with Open Services Project, a research and development project to increase people's say in social and other services. Their books include *Whose Welfare: Private Care or Public Services?* (Lewis Cohen Urban Studies Centre, Brighton, 1986) and *Citizen Involvement* (Macmillan, London, 1992).

Nicole Biggart received her Ph.D. in sociology from the University of California, Berkeley, and is now Associate Professor of Management and Sociology at the University of California, Davis. Her research has focused on the culture and organization of capitalism in both North America and Asia. Her book *Charismatic Capitalism: Direct Selling Organizations in America* (University of Chicago Press) was published in 1989.

Severyn Bruyn is Professor at the Department of Sociology, and from 1977–86 was Director of the Graduate Program in Social Economy and Social Policy, at Boston College. His books include *The Field of Social Investment* (Cambridge University Press, 1987), *Beyond the Market and the State* (co-edited with James Meehan, Temple University Press, Philadelphia, 1987) and *The Future of the American Economy: the Social Market* (Stanford University Press, 1990).

Robert Chambers is a Fellow of the Institute of Development Studies at the University of Sussex with practical and research experience in many countries of Africa and Asia. His best known book is *Rural Development: Putting the Last First* (Longman, Harlow, 1983).

Paul Ekins is a Research Fellow at the Department of Economics, Birkbeck College, University of London, and Co-ordinator of the international Living Economy Network. His books include *The Living Economy: a New Economics in the Making* (editor, Routledge, London, 1986) and *Wealth Beyond Measure: an Atlas of New Economics* (with Mayer Hillman and Robert Hutchison, Gaia Books, London, and Anchor Doubleday, New York, 1992).

Amitai Etzioni is University Professor at the George Washington University and Director of the Center for Policy Research. He was the initiator of the Society for the Advancement of Socio-Economics and his books include *The Moral Dimension: Toward a New Economics* (Free Press, New York, 1988).

Orio Giarini is Professor of Service Economics at the Graduate Institute of European Studies, University of Geneva, and former Head of the Industrial Economics and Services Division of Geneva's Battelle Research Institute. His books include *The Limits to Certainty* (with Walter Stahel, Kluwer, Dordrecht, 1989) and *The Emerging Service Economy* (editor, Pergamon, Oxford, 1987).

Tony Gibson is Director of the Neighbourhood Initiatives Foundation (NIF). As Director of Nottingham University's programme 'Education for Neighbourhood Change' he developed a variety of practical techniques and resources for enabling popular participation in processes of planning and development. His booklet describing these is *Making It Happen* (NIF, Telford, 1991).

Luisella Goldschmidt-Clermont is an Associate Member of the Free University of Brussels, in the Institute of Sociology and Centre for Economics. She is an independent consultant for *inter alia*, the International Labour Office, Geneva, which published her two studies: *Unpaid Work in the Household: a Review of Economic Evaluation Methods* (1982) and *Economic Evaluations of Unpaid Household Work: Africa, Asia, Latin America and Oceania* (1987).

Geoff Hodgson is Professor of Economics at Newcastle Polytechnic and General Secretary of the European Association for Evolutionary Political Economy. His recent books include *Economics and Institutions* (Polity, Cambridge, 1988); *After Marx and Sraffa* (Macmillan, London, 1991) and *Rethinking Economics* (co-editor with Ernesto Screpanti, Edward Elgar, Cheltenham, 1991).

Roefie Hueting is Head of the Department for Environmental Statistics of the Netherlands Central Bureau of Statistics (CBS). He is now working on the adjustment of the national accounts to arrive at a figure for Sustainable National Income, based on his *Methodology for the Calculation of Sustainable National Income* (with Peter Bosch and Bart de Boer, CBS, Voorburg, 1991). He is author of *New Scarcity and Economic Growth* (North Holland, Amsterdam, 1980).

Mario Kamenetzky, a US-based Argentine engineer and scientist with academic and entrepreneurial experience, retired in 1988 from his position of

Science and Technology Specialist with the World Bank. He is now writing and lecturing on consciousness-expanding work and its impact on business and the economy.

Tony Lawson is a lecturer in economics at the Faculty of Economics and Politics, the University of Cambridge.

Øyvind Lone works in the Department for Organisation and Environmental Economics at the Norwegian Ministry of Environment.

Mark Lutz is Professor of Economics at the University of Maine, Orono. His books include *Humanistic Economics: the New Challenge* (with Kenneth Lux, Bootstrap Press, New York, 1988), *Essays in Gandhian Economics* (co-edited with Romesh Diwan, Gandhi Peace Foundation, New Delhi, 1985) and *Social Economics: Retrospect and Prospect* (editor, Kluwer, Dordrecht, 1990).

Maureen Mackintosh is currently Reader in Economics at Kingston Polytechnic. She has also worked as an economist in British local government, and has done research on economic policy for the government of Mozambique. Her current teaching and research interests include the management and economic organization of gender. Her publications include: *A Taste of Power* (co-editor with Hilary Wainwright, Verso, London, 1987); *Development Policy and Public Action* (co-editor with M. Wuyts and T. Hewitt, Oxford University Press, Oxford, 1992) and *Gender, Class and Rural Development* (Zed Press, London, 1989).

Manfred Max-Neef is Director of the Development Alternatives Centre in Santiago, Chile. His publications include *Human-Scale Development: an Option for the Future* (Dag Hammarskjöld Foundation [DHF], Uppsala, 1989) and *From the Outside Looking In: Experiences in Barefoot Economics* (DHF, Uppsala, 1982).

Ian Miles is with PREST (Programme of Policy Research in Engineering, Science and Technology) at the University of Manchester, where he is researching a range of issues concerned with technological change. He has published widely, including the books *Social Indicators for Human Development* (Frances Pinter, London, 1985); *Home Informatics* (Pinter, London, 1988) and (with co-authors) *Mapping and Measuring the Information Economy* (British Library, Boston, 1990).

Geoff Mulgan is the author of *Communication and Control* (Polity, 1991) and *Saturday Night or Sunday Morning* (with Ken Worpole, Comedia, 1986). He has been a lecturer in communications at the Polytechnic of Central London and currently works as industrial policy adviser to the UK Labour Party.

Richard Norgaard holds a Ph.D. in economics from the University of Chicago and is a Professor of Energy and Resources at the University of California, Berkeley. He has published on resource scarcity, petroleum development, water development, pest management, biodiversity and tropical deforestation.

David Pearce is Professor of Economics at University College, London and Director of the Centre for Social and Economic Research on the Global Environment. His many books include *Sustainable Development: Economics and Environment in the Third World* (with Anil Markandya and Edward Barbier, Edward Elgar, Cheltenham, 1989); *Economics of Natural Resources and the Environment* (with Kerry Turner, Harvester Wheatsheaf, Hemel Hempstead, 1990); *Blueprint for a Green Economy* (Earthscan, London, 1989) and *Blueprint 2* (Earthscan, London, 1991).

Anisur Rahman has a Ph.D. in economics from Harvard University and taught economics at Dhaka University before going in 1977 to the International Labour Office in Geneva to co-ordinate a programme on Participatory Rural Development. In 1990 he returned to Bangladesh to work with popular initiatives. He is the author of *People's Self-Development: a Journey Through Experience* (Zed Press, London, 1992).

Wolfgang Sachs is presently a fellow at the Institute for Cultural Studies in Essen, Germany. His books include *For Love of the Automobile. Looking Back into the History of our Desires* (University of California Press, Berkeley, 1992) and *The Development Dictionary. A Guide to Knowledge as Power* (editor, Zed Books, London, 1992).

Alejandro Sanz de Santamaria is Professor of Economics at the Universidad de Los Andes, Bogota.

Peter Söderbaum is an Assistant Professor at the Department of Economics at the Swedish University of Agricultural Sciences. He has published on a wide variety of environmental economic issues, with an institutional economics approach.

Paul Streeten is Director of the World Development Institute at Boston University. He has also been Warden of Queen Elizabeth House, Oxford, and Director of the Institute of Development Studies at the University of Sussex. His books include: *Development Perspectives* (Macmillan, London, 1981) and *Beyond Adjustment: the Asian Experience* (editor, International Monetary Fund, Washington DC, 1988).

Hilary Wainwright is a Senior Simon Fellow at the University of Manchester. She was Assistant Chief Economic Advisor to the Greater London Council from 1982–6. Her books include *Labour: a Tale of Two Parties* (Chatto & Windus, London, 1987) and *A Taste of Power* (co-edited with Maureen Mackintosh, Verso, London, 1987).

Jane Wheelock has taught in the Business School of Sunderland Polytechnic since 1978. She is the author of *Husbands at Home: the Domestic Economy in a Post-Industrial Society* (Routledge, London, 1990).

Ponna Wignaraja is currently Adviser to the United Nations University on South Asian Perspectives. From 1980 to 1987 he was the Chairman of the

Participatory Institute for Development Alternatives (PIDA) in Sri Lanka. His books include *Towards a Theory of Rural Development* (co-author with G.V.S. de Silva *et al.*, Progressive Publishers, Lahore, 1988); *The Challenge in South Asia: Development, Democracy and Regional Cooperation* (co-editor with Akmal Hussain, Sage, London and New Delhi, 1989); *Women, Poverty and Resources* (Sage, London and New Delhi, 1990) and *Participatory Development: Learning from South Asia* (co-author with A. Hussain *et al.*, Oxford University Press, Oxford and Karachi, 1992 forthcoming).

Helen Wilkinson previously worked on policy at the National Consumer Council and currently makes foreign affairs programmes at the BBC.

John Oliver Wilson teaches in the Haas School of Business and the Graduate School of Public Policy at the University of California at Berkeley. He is also Co-Chair of the Berkeley Forum on Ethics and International Business and Chief Economist for Bank of America in San Francisco.

Acknowledgements

In any edited book, the editors' principal acknowledgements must go to those who have contributed to the work. This is especially so in this case, for *Real-Life Economics* was two years in preparation. While this extra time for reflection has made for a more integrated and coherent volume, it did mean that several paperwriters felt compelled to update their papers before the final draft. They undertook this extra work with patience and good humour for which we are most grateful.

This book is the principal output to date of the international Living Economy Network (see Appendix for address) of economists and other social and natural scientists who are interested in fostering the development of a new school of economic thought which recognizes as an axiom that all economic activity and behaviour is profoundly influenced by ecological, social and ethical realities and considerations; and that any attempt to divorce economics from these considerations, as much orthodox analysis seeks to do, is likely to be seriously flawed in itself and be equally flawed in its recommendations. More profoundly, if values, in terms of at least a pre-analytic conception of human nature and of fundamental ecological and social relationships, are always present, then masquerading as value-free, as positive economics seeks to do, serves at best to mask those underlying values; at worst it presents these values *de facto* as universal values and therefore becomes a vehicle for ideology.

It is thus to seek to promote a pluralistic and inter-disciplinary approach to economics, whether or not this comes to be called a 'living economics' or a recognizable school of thought by any other name, that the scholars and activists of the Living Economy Network have come together. Apart from the paperwriters, some of them are specifically cited in the editorial sections of the text, but many others have influenced the context of those sections and their contribution too needs to be gratefully acknowledged. If they remain anonymous it is because no specific influence can be traced, but nevertheless the book would not have been the same without them. The same is true for the three anonymous referees who made some invaluable suggestions at first draft stage, which resulted in considerable amendments for the second.

At the same time, it must be stressed that the book is not a manifesto with its contributors as signatories. The editorial context and conclusions are the responsibility of the editors only; the contributors can only be held to be in complete agreement with what they have actually written.

Even so, we will be disappointed if these contributions, the context in which we have placed them and the conclusions we have drawn, do not resonate widely and sympathetically within the economics and related disciplines and help progressive elements there to think and organize more effectively to meet the momentous economic challenges of the times.

At an administrative level, we thank collectively the original publishers of papers that have have been reproduced, though sometimes with considerable reworking. Individual acknowledgements are given at the beginning of the papers concerned. We must also thank Sally Howell for her patient secretarial work in getting a complex typescript into a presentable condition.

This is, therefore, very much a collective work, but the final responsibility for it is, of course, ours, who chose the papers and constructed the framework within which they are placed. Any shortcomings in this framework and the conclusions we have drawn should be laid at our door alone.

Paul Ekins
Manfred Max-Neef

Introduction

This book is the result of two convictions held by the editors: first, that economics in its mainstream neoclassical form is failing to provide an intellectually coherent explanation of economic reality, especially with regard to such issues as the nature of markets, environmental degradation, persistent poverty and household production, and is therefore responsible for much flawed policy advice; and second, that the many constructive, potentially complementary, alternative proposals on these and other issues, some originating in the economics discipline, others from outside it, are too often left standing in isolation from each other, so that the larger framework within which they could be accommodated, and which could help win them acceptance, is left unarticulated.

The first objective of this book, therefore, is to define the larger framework which can be built from insights from institutional, evolutionary and socio-economics; from ecological economics and the concern with sustainability; from an emphasis on development, including economic development, as a creative and participatory process; and from a perception of the economy that recognizes the productive role of households and the voluntary sector, as well as of business and government.

Within this framework neoclassical economics emerges as a useful but limited system of analysis; its use is limited by the extremity of many of its assumptions about human behaviour, social structure and the nature of the biosphere. These will be discussed in more detail in the text. Here it will suffice to say that, according to the framework to be presented, the use of neoclassical analysis should be confined to those situations where its assumptions can *a priori* be shown to be valid.

A second objective of the book was to present the new strands of economic thinking comprising the framework through the papers of some of those who have been most articulate in and responsible for promoting them. Thus many of the writers of these papers are activists as well as academic economists and other social scientists, who have sought either to organize around their ideas or implement them in the field or both, as well as write about them. They are pioneers, at the leading edge of some of the most exciting developments in economics.

The papers are deliberately varied in style and form. Many are more or less conventionally academic, others are discursive, others polemical; others still are autobiographical in tone. Such an approach seemed appropriate for an economic perspective that makes no claim to be value-free and which deals with issues that literally involve life or death for millions of people. Because economists exert a major influence on decision making, they have a responsibility to those whose lives they affect. Their personal experiences of coping with such responsibility are an important part of economics as a discipline.

The theme of Part I of the book is the nature of the economy and of economic science. The first chapter discusses the role of the economist and the place and purpose of economics: Wolfgang Sachs argues for economics to be kept in its place as a servant of wider cultural values rather than seeking to define them; Alejandro Sanz de Santamaria argues similarly that the economist engaged in development should be a partner and participant in the development process under study rather than just an external observer or manipulator of it; Tony Lawson argues for a realist as opposed to an instrumental orientation – the purpose of economics is to understand the real underlying forces and tendencies in the economy, as the only way to act or plan coherently within it.

Chapter 2 relates economics to social and ethical concerns, with Geoff Hodgson exploring the role of institutions, Amitai Etzioni postulating a moral dimension and John Oliver Wilson discussing different forms of justice. Chapter 3 introduces the ecological dimension, with papers from Roefie Hueting on environmental functions, David Pearce on equity and sustainable development and Richard Norgaard on coevolution. The ideas of these two chapters lead to the perception that most human situations have four dimensions – economic, social, ethical and ecological – all of which need to feature in social scientific analysis according to their relative importance in the situation in question. Chapter 4, with Mark Lutz, introduces humanistic economics, which shares many of the approaches and concerns of this book, and then briefly reviews some of the other broadly compatible intellectual and organizational strands within the economics discipline. By comparison with these, the book's distinctive position is clarified and is given a name: Living Economics.

Part II is about the nature of economic activity, progress and development. Jane Wheelock in Chapter 5 focuses on the household in a model of the total economy; Orio Giarini emphasizes the importance of services to a modern industrial economy, and the consequential change in the value of economic output. On the basis of these and previous contributions, a new model of wealth creation is constructed, entailing the combination of four kinds of capital (ecological, human, social/organizational and manufactured), multiple sources of economic welfare and multiple feedback effects.

Chapter 6 explores the genesis and nature of 'development' as a concept. Wolfgang Sachs sees it as a mono-dimensional, hegemonistic, economistic redefinition of human purpose, which institutionalizes poverty. Lutz interprets it in the light of humanistic economics. Rahman gives a creativist, participatory perspective. In both of these latter views the process of development is clearly related to the satisfaction of human needs. Chapter 7 reviews several related theories of needs, including those of Mario Kamenetzky and Manfred Max-Neef, the latter including a practical methodology for inducing self-awareness of needs. Robert Chambers also presents his concept of sustainable livelihood security which is clearly related to need-satisfaction.

Chapter 8 considers indicators relevant to the model of wealth creation and the concepts of progress and development which flow from it. An indicator framework with four components is developed. Øyvind Lone discusses environmental and resource accounts; Roefie Hueting recommends adjustments to national income accounts; Luisella Goldschmidt-Clermont shows how accounts of household production can be constructed; and Ian Miles presents the rationale for and an example of a set of social indicators. This four-component framework is suggested as a means of shifting the standards and targets of economies' performance from an excessive emphasis on production (with GNP as its measure) to a broader system that locates both monetary and non-monetary production in an ecological and social context. Finally in this chapter, Peter Söderbaum changes the focus from the macro to the micro level and adapts some of the chapter's ideas for use in that context, specifically suggesting positional analysis as an alternative to cost–benefit analysis.

Part III investigates the mechanisms of economic policy. Chapter 9 treats the market as a social construction. Mitchel Abolafia and Nicole Biggart view competition as a process both structured and mediated by social institutions. Paul Ekins shows how the market can be as responsive to and effective in expressing ethical values as more conventional consumer preferences. Chapter 10 moves to consideration of the state, at the global, national and local levels: Paul Streeten spells out some of the implications of global interdependence; Geoff Mulgan and Helen Wilkinson develop the concept of the enabling state; and Maureen Mackintosh and Hilary Wainwright describe some of the experiences of the Greater London Council in seeking to put a policy of enablement into practice. The chapter also contains a review of an important paper by Jean Drèze and Amartya Sen which argues for public action for social security.

Chapter 11 looks at the neglected third economic mechanism: that of direct provision through the household and community. Severyn Bruyn describes a possible new direction for community development in the United States. Three papers then focus on the theme of participation in different contexts: Peter Beresford and Suzy Croft on user control of welfare services; Tony Gibson on the regeneration of urban neighbourhoods; and Ponna Wignaraja on participatory rural development in South Asia.

The final chapter of Part III, and of the book, seeks to put the economic mechanisms in the context of environmental sustainability. An extensive quotation from Herman Daly's work establishes the importance of the overall scale of economic activity relative to the biosphere; David Pearce then outlines some of the practical implications of sustainable development; and Paul Ekins discusses how the concept of sustainability can be made operational.

For this brief overview it is clear that this book ranges over a most ambitiously wide terrain. Inevitably its coverage of the ground is uneven. Some issues are explored in considerable detail, others are dealt with in outline only, others still are only mentioned in passing. But despite this unevenness, it is our belief that what emerges is an original approach to economics that is well suited to many of the principal economic challenges of the age. Many of the elements of the approach are not original, of course. There is hardly an idea that was not already embedded somewhere in the literature. But the arrangement of the ideas and articulation of their interrelationships seem to us to provide new insights and opportunities to grapple with an increasingly complex and threatening economic reality. We hope that in time the approach may be further developed into a recognizable school of economic thought and be taught to economists as such. We do not imagine that the neoclassical mainstream will easily assent to becoming a mere subset of an approach that puts ethical, ecological and social concerns at least on a par with economic considerations. But we believe that such a multi-dimensional context is actually the only one in which an intellectually sound and practically relevant economics can be developed. If this book gives an impetus to establishing the context and promoting the development of such an economics, then it will have fulfilled its purpose.

Paul Ekins
Manfred Max-Neef

Part I

On the nature of the economy and economic science

1   Economics, knowledge and reality

The principal objective of this book is to further the understanding of real processes in the real world, especially as they relate to the economy, and especially as they relate to the more threatening or least satisfactory aspects of the human condition, with a view to enabling improvements in those aspects. That is to say, it seeks to define a framework of ideas through which useful knowledge can be generated that can be put to practical use in concrete situations.

The three papers in this chapter set down some ground rules for this endeavour, exploring:

- the relationship between the economy and the real world;
- an appropriate practical methodology for economists in the real world;
- an appropriate intellectual methodology for economists to employ in investigating reality.

The view of the subject-matter of economics to be adopted in this book is not controversial. It is based on Lionel Robbins's famous definition: 'Economics is the science which studies human behaviour as a relationship between ends and scarce means which have alternative uses' (Robbins 1984: 16). A further aspect is that 'the ends are capable of being distinguished in order of importance' (ibid.: 14). It is presumed here that this ordering takes place with a view to increasing human welfare.

The 'real world', however, is nowhere near as simple a concept as it sounds. It is actually experienced by different groups of people in radically different ways, to the extent that one might not know from their descriptions of it that they were talking about the same 'world' at all.

Anthropologist Richard Schweder (1984, 1986, 1989) has explored this issue in some depth. He identifies three responses to human diversity: universalism, developmentalism and relativism. He regrets that one of these three responses is so often posited as *the* true explanation of the human condition in contradistinction to the others:

The human mind is tripartite – it has rational, irrational and nonrational aspects: and comparing our ideas to the ideas of others, we will always be able to find some ways in which our ideas are like the ideas of others (universalism) and some ways in which our ideas are different. Sometimes those differences will suggest progress (developmentalism) and often they will not (relativism).

(Schweder 1984: 60)

While thus accepting the possible validity in specific instances of the universalist and developmentalist approach, Schweder elsewhere stresses 'the relativistic idea of multiple objective worlds' (Schweder 1989: 133). His argument can be presented in his words as follows:

> While reality is not something we can do without, neither can it be reached (for it is beyond experience and transcends appearances) except by an act of imaginative projection implicating the knower as well as the known. . . . An interpretive or hermeneutic or projective element (call it what you will) has long since been incorporated into philosophical conceptions of objectivity-seeking science. . . . Objectivity-seeking science portrays for us a really real external world so as to explain our reality-posits, but it does so by making use of our reality-posits in a selective, presumptive and partial way. . . . Since no reality-finding science can treat all appearances, sensations, experiences as revelatory of the objective world, and since, at least for the moment, no infallible way exists to decide which reality-posits are signs of reality and which are not, much is discretionary in every portrait of the objective world out there beyond our symbolic forms. . . . Yet it is possible for us to have important knowledge of the world, even if the objective world is subject-dependent and multiplex and even if we give up trying to describe the world independent of our own involvement with it or reactions to it or conceptions of it. . . . Accordingly, it is a core aphorism of the position advocated here that the objective world is incapable of being represented completely if represented from any one point of view and incapable of being represented intelligibly if represented from all points of view at once. The real trick and noble challenge is to view the objective world from many points of view (or from the point of view of each of several prejudices) but to do it in sequence.

(ibid.: 128–31)

The conception of 'multiple objective worlds', each with their own validity, is poles apart from the homogenizing thrust of western economism. The whole practice of economic development round the world bears witness to the imposition of a single 'development model' on widely disparate peoples and communities, which has resulted always in their disruption and transformation and often in their destruction. In a perceptive series of papers, three of which are included in this volume, Wolfgang Sachs has explored 'the archeology of the development idea'. The paper that follows deals explicitly with the hegemony of the economy on the world stage.

The economist's prejudice

Wolfgang Sachs

'Should India ever resolve to imitate England, it will be the ruin of the nation'. In 1909, while still in South Africa, Mohandas Gandhi formulated the conviction upon which he then, over a period of forty years, fought for the independence of India. Although he won the fight, the cause was lost; no sooner was independence achieved than his principle fell into oblivion. Gandhi wanted to drive the English out of the country in order to allow India to become more Indian; Nehru, on the other hand, saw independence as the opportunity to make India more western. An assassin's bullet prevented the controversy between the two heroes of the nation from coming into the open, but the decade-long correspondence between them clearly demonstrates the issues.

Gandhi was not won over to technical civilization with its machines, engines and factories, because he saw in it a culture which knew no more sublime end than that of minimizing bodily effort and maximizing physical well-being. He could only shrug his shoulders at such an obsession with gaining comfort; as if a good life could be built on that! Didn't India's tradition, undisturbed for thousands of years, have more substantial things to offer? Although far from being a traditionalist on many issues, Gandhi insisted on a society which, in accordance with Hindu tradition, gave priority to a spiritual way of life. An English style of industrialism is out of place wherever *swaraj*, the calm freedom to follow personal truth, is to rule; Gandhi pleaded for a renewal of the count- less villages of India and for a form of progress to be judged accordingly. In his eyes, India was committed to an idea of the good and proper life that contra- dicted the ideals prevalent in England during the age of automation. For this reason, a wholesale imitation of the west was simply out of the question; individual elements should be adopted only in so far as they could help give better expression to India's aspirations.

Nehru disagreed. He saw no choice other than introducing the young nation to the achievements of the west as soon as possible and taking the road toward an economic civilization. Even in the early days, and in spite of his great admiration for the man, he found Gandhi 'completely unreal' (letter of Nehru to Gandhi, 9th October 1945) in his vision. Though he intended to avoid the excesses of capitalism, he still viewed Indian society primarily as an economy, that is, as a society defining itself in terms of its performance in the provision of goods. From an economic viewpoint, however, human nature, the function of politics and the character of social reform assume a particular meaning. People are seen as living in a permanent situation of scarcity, since they always have less than they desire; the most noble task of politics is thus to create the conditions for material wealth; and this in turn requires the reorganization of society from a host of locally based subsistence communities into a nation-wide economy.

Nehru thus fostered precisely that western self-delusion which was also at the core of the development idea: the essential reality of a society consists in nothing else than its functional relations to achieve useful things; the rest is just folklore or private affair. In this view, the economy overshadows every other reality; the laws of economy dominate society and not the rules of society the economy. This is why, whenever development strategists set their sights on a country, they do not see a society that *has* an economy, but a society that *is* an economy. To take this conquest of society by the economy for granted is a burden inherited from nineteenth-century Europe which has been passed on to the rest of the world over the last forty years.

Production as a matter of secondary importance

Observing a group of Indios who work in their fields in the mountains around Quiche, and seeing the barren ground, the primitive tools and the scanty yield, one might easily come to the conclusion that nothing in the world is more important to them than increasing productivity. Remedies could swiftly be found: better crop rotation, improved seeds, small machines, privatization, and anything else the cookbook of business management might recommend. All this is not necessarily wrong; however, the economic viewpoint is notoriously colour blind: it recognizes the cost–yield relation with extreme clarity, but is hardly able to perceive other dimensions of reality. For example, economists have difficulty in recognizing that the land bestows identity upon the Indios since it represents the bridge to their ancestors. Likewise, economists often fail to note the central importance of collective forms of labour, in which the village community finds visible expression. The outlook of the Indios is incompatible with that of the economists: neither land nor work are for them mere production factors waiting to be optimally combined.

To put this in the form of a paradox: not everything that looks like an economic activity is necessarily a part of economics. Indeed, economics offers only one of the many ways of apprehending goods-oriented activities and putting them in a larger context. Obviously, in every society things are produced, distributed and consumed; but only in modern societies are prices and products, conditions of ownership and work, predominantly shaped by the laws of economic efficiency. Elsewhere different rules are valid, other models prevail.

One does not need to cite examples of ancestral beliefs, such as those held by the Bemba in Zambia, who see a good harvest or a successful hunting expedition as a gift from their ancestors and thus court their favour in the hope of higher production. Even the haggling and chaotic hustle and bustle in the souks of an Arabian medina have nothing to do with undercutting the competition; who pursues which of the many trades is determined by factors of social and geographical origin as well as by one's allegiance to a Sufi sect. (And of course by one's sex; trade is usually a man's job, but in Haiti, for instance, women have the say in such matters.) Likewise it is enough to consider the cycles of cultivation practised by farmers in Maharashtra, which neatly fit into the yearly round of weddings, festivals and pilgrimages. New methods of cultivation can soon disrupt this social calendar.

In societies that are not built on the compulsion to amass material wealth, economic activity is also not geared to slick, zippy output. Rather, economic activities like choosing an occupation, cultivating the land or exchanging goods are understood as ways to enact that particular social drama in which the members of the community happen to see themselves as the actors. That drama's story largely defines what belongs to whom, who produces what and how, and when what is exchanged with whom. The 'economy' is closely bound up with life and has not been isolated as an autonomous sphere which might stamp its rules and rhythms on the rest of society.

But in the West the economy alone dictates the drama where everyone must play their role.

An invention of the West

As late as 1744, Zedler's *Universal Encyclopedia* unwittingly gives a naive definition of the heading 'market': 'that spacious public place, surrounded by ornate buildings or enclosed by stands, where, at certain times, all kinds of victuals and other wares are offered for sale; hence the same place is also called market-place'. The market, heralded both as blessing and as bane over the last two centuries, this powerful idea – nothing more than a location! The author of the encyclopedia seemed only to be thinking of crowds, stands and baskets; there is no mention of 'market shares', 'price fluctuations' or 'equilibrium'. His concept of 'market' has practically nothing to do with the familiar concept of today; between then and now a far-reaching change has taken place in the self-image of society.

Adam Smith was the first thinker who, when using the term 'market', no longer envisaged a locally determinable outlet for goods, but that society-wide space throughout which all prices intercommunicate. The term, which until then had designated a specific place, subsequently acquired its generalized and abstract meaning: it now refers to the action of supra-individual equilibrium mechanisms.

This conceptual innovation was no accident, but mirrored a new social reality: an economy of national scope. Before then, a domestic market was not something to be taken for granted; even in Europe at the end of the seventeenth century one could hardly find trade between different regions of one country. Of course, there has always been trade – one need only think of the North German Hanseatic League or the splendour of Venice – but it was trade with distant countries, which remained limited to a few cities as bridge-heads. It is true that history knows markets in all shapes and sizes, but they were precisely local and temporary places of exchange, mostly between towns and the surrounding country with prices more a matter of custom.

In Adam Smith's century, however, the nation-state had drawn a web of trade relations over the whole of society and established the domestic market.

Like today's developing countries, the young states of that time pushed hard to make economic principles prevail everywhere, be it only to finance their own existence. That was the birth of the national economy, even on a lexical level: while the term 'economy' had formerly been applied to the 'domestic economy' of the prince, now the whole nation was transformed into a 'political economy'. And Smith became the theoretician of a society governed by the rules of the market.

Alternatives to the economy?

The transformation of society into a political economy was, of course, only achieved after a prolonged struggle demanding many sacrifices. After all, neither how people gained their livelihood or regarded property, nor their idea of good conduct or their sense of time, was shaped by a commercial ethos. The merchant was not yet an entrepreneur, land was not saleable, competition was frowned upon, usury disreputable, and those who worked for wages lived on the fringes of society. As a result, the progress of capitalism was punctuated by bitter disputes about whether and to what extent land and forest, grain and money, and workers themselves, could be treated as commodities.

In the last decades, similar radical changes have taken place in large parts of the Third World as economic ideology has tightened its grip. Traditions of sufficiency have been pushed aside, local exchange relations dissolved, collective forms of ownership broken up and subsistence economies wiped out. For a long time the guiding light of international development policy was to create societies of paid workers and consumers everywhere. Experts scrutinized countries to identify 'obstacles to development' which were hampering the free mobility of 'production factors'. No cost was too high, few sacrifices too great to turn societies into smoothly-running political economies.

Without any doubt, miracles were thus wrought, and a great tide swept through the countries of the southern hemisphere; history had taken an enormous leap. However, it becomes progressively clearer that a disaster is in the offing. At the very moment the economy has finally achieved dominion world-wide, social disruptions and environmental destruction have become rampant. The autocracy of the economy reveals its menacing head. Societies find themselves cornered: neither can they afford to surrender to this autocracy, nor can they escape from it. In fact, the economy, during its rise to the top, has stamped out the alternatives to itself and created a wasteland for modes to secure a livelihood which are not hazardous for man and nature. How is it possible to reinvent economic institutions that allow people to live gracefully without making them prisoners of the pernicious drive to accumulate? Maybe there will be more creative power in the Third World to meet this historical challenge. Simply because, in spite of everything, many people there still remember a way of life in which economic performance was not paramount.

The 'drive to accumulate', which Sachs calls 'pernicious', is, of course, at the heart of economic rationality as conventionally conceived. It is the explicit motive power of Adam Smith's butcher, brewer and baker, which both supplies our dinner and sets the invisible hand to work. In advocating alternatives to this rationality, one is either embracing the irrational or postulating the existence of different forms of rationality. The latter is precisely the position taken by Richard Schweder (1986) on the basis of his detailed researches into non-Western cultures:

> Rationality seems to have that peculiar bounded quality; it requires deductive and inductive logic, but deductive and inductive reasoning goes on within the framework of a third sort of logic that is bound to something neither uniform nor unitary. What we seem to need is a concept of divergent rationality. . . .
>
> Some rational processes are universally distributed across our species. As far as we know, all peoples respect certain elementary logical principles (negation, the law of the excluded middle) and adopt certain common patterns of hypothetical reasoning, means–ends analysis, causal analysis and experimental reasoning. Things that vary together are connected by the human mind. So are things that are contiguous in time and space, and so on. . . .
>
> At the same time, there are certain rational processes that are not universal. These include, for example, the presuppositions and premises from which a person reasons; the metaphors, analogies and models used for generating explanations; the categories or classifications used for partitioning objects and events into kinds; and the types of evidence that are viewed as authoritative – intuition, introspection, external observation, meditation, scriptural evidence, evidence from seers, monks, prophets or elders. The version of reality we construct is a product of both the universal and the nonuniversal rational process, but it is because not all rational processes are universal that we need a concept of divergent rationality.
>
> (ibid. 180–1)

One of the most powerful manifestations of Western hegemony is its universalistic attempt to present its 'presuppositions and premises, etc.' as the only human rationality, thus systematically seeking to devalue, undermine and supplant other 'types of evidence that are viewed as authoritative'. The acceptance of divergent rationality, on the other hand, acknowledges that there may be situations in which, for example, Western economics, the analysis of scarcity, is itself an alien or inappropriate form of enquiry and that 'development' in those situations may depend on quite different processes of action and reflection.

An illustration of this point is the Swadhyaya movement in India, described in Ekins (1992) and Rahnema (1990), which now involves some 3 million people. Swadhyayees are concerned to discover and serve God in themselves and other people. They do this in a way which produces significant wealth.

This wealth, they think, belongs to God and is distributed by the producers to the poor and disadvantaged. Swadhyaya villages are significantly better off than their neighbours but not as a result of economic analysis or a quest for economic development. Of course, their wealth and the process that produced it can be described in economic terms, not least using the framework to be developed in this book, but the essential point is that such an 'external' or objective description would be alien to the people involved, whose motivation is not economic enrichment but divine service. An economic analysis would simply fail to connect with their perception of what was happening. Moreover, and more importantly, if, through a desire to multiply the economic enrichment, a government or multilateral development agency sought to impose such an analysis on the people involved in the process, there would be a grave danger of disrupting the movement and reducing its present capacity for wealth creation.

Similar points could be made about India's Chipko Movement, which seeks to prevent deforestation of mountain areas and is described in Bandyopadhyay and Shiva (1987). Through its actions the movement prevents the destruction of many natural resources and saves thousands of hill people from destitution. But it is clear that its primary motivation is an ecological one. Chipko activists are deeply attached to the forests, regarding them as great living systems to be revered and protected. Although they know they would be impoverished without them, they do not view forests principally as resources, as an economist would. To them the forest is a mother to which they feel connected by a far more than economic relationship. Again, undue stress on the economic relationship would be more likely to hinder than help the Chipko process.

Such considerations have the profoundest implications for the practical work of economists, especially when it may impact on those people whose lives are ordered by a different rationality. Alejandro Sanz de Santamaria here gives an autobiographical account of how he felt impelled to change the whole basis of his practical methodology.

Economic science and political democracy

Alejandro Sanz de Santamaria

In their book *Order out of Chaos: Man's New Dialogue with Nature* (1984), Prigogine and Stengers make the following two statements:

> One of the problems of our time is to overcome attitudes that tend to justify and reinforce the isolation of the scientific community.

(ibid.: 22)

And,

The human race is now in a period of transition. Science is likely to play an important role at this moment of demographic explosion. It is therefore more important than ever to keep open the channels of communication between science and society.

(ibid.)

In this paper I want to show, through a critical analysis of some of my own personal experiences in economic research, that the particular forms in which economic scientific knowledges are produced and used today in Western societies enact a totalitarian (non-democratic) exercise of social power, obstructing the communication between science and society. I want to argue that the social processes whereby these knowledges are produced and used must undergo radical changes if economic scientific knowledges are to promote and support the development of democracy.

The two research projects I will refer to were both intended to produce an economic knowledge on the same Colombian peasant community, known as Garcia Rovira. This region comprised, in 1984, approximately 100,000 people distributed over an area of 500,000 acres. In the first project (1979–80) I had to produce a concrete knowledge on how the local labourers' migration patterns were affecting the regional economic development, with the corresponding recommendations on the economic policies that the government should enforce in connection with migrations. In the second (1984–today) I have had to evaluate the impact of a government economic development programme, which in 1984 had been under way in the region for eight years.

A central feature of these two experiences was that the knowledges and recommendations I had to produce had to be constructed based on primary information collected through in-depth fieldwork and surveys. Thus, in both projects the knowledge production process I had to carry out comprised, schematically, the following four 'conventional' steps: (1) a thorough analysis of the available literature on this rural community; (2) an in-depth fieldwork, in which different constitutive social agents of the community – peasants, land owners, merchants, state functionaries, local political, religious and military authorities and so on – were interviewed at length; (3) a survey, that had to be designed and implemented in the light of the results of the in-depth fieldwork; and (4) the knowledge construction process itself, using the information available in the existing literature and collected through the fieldwork and the survey.

My experience in the first project exerted a tremendous impact on my own underlying notions of 'knowledge' and 'science' – of which I was not fully conscious; on my understanding of the relationship between knowledge, science and social change (politics) and on my idea of the role of an academic researcher in economics in the context of the relationship between knowledge, science and politics. The experience was traumatic. This trauma led me to get involved in an intense study of certain philosophical and epistemological issues as soon as I finished the first project. Thus, when I started the second project

I was much better equipped to critically understand the 'origins' of that impact and, therefore, to conceive and practice alternative ways to produce and use economic knowledge.

The paper is divided into three parts. In the first part I will reconstruct the experience of the first project to show the kind of questions and issues it brought to the forefront. In the second I will describe briefly how I responded to these questions when I faced the second project. In the third part I will summarize some of the 'conclusions' I have derived from this whole process.

1 On the relationship between politics, the role of the academic economist and the social forms of producing and using scientific economic knowledge

The study of the available literature on Garcia Rovira, when I started the first project, was overwhelming: there was information on the agrological charac- teristics of the soil (soil qualities, steepness, altitudes over the sea level, etc.), on the local weather conditions (rainfall, humidity, winds, etc.), on the water availability (rivers, streams, dams and other irrigation facilities), on the regional population's size, growth rate and structure (urban, rural, age groups, etc.), on the most important crops grown in the region and the different labour processes practised to cultivate each one of them (amount of labour times required, constitutive tasks of these labour processes, production inputs needed, etc.), on the main characteristics of the markets (circuits) within which the different products circulated (local, regional, national and/or international markets), on prices per product, on the rural development programmes that had been enforced and were being enforced by the state and other institutions, on the land ownership distribution, on productivities and levels of production per product and so on.

The overview of all this information made it clear to me from the beginning that it was impossible to use it all in the production of the knowledge I was to produce; in fact, it was evident that I would have to abstract from most of it. Yet, at the same time, this overview made it clear to me that all of the aspects to which these informations related would have to be taken into account for the construction of any knowledge that aimed at becoming an effective instrument to procure the economic development of this community. A troubling contradiction indeed.

As I came into direct and close contact with many concrete individuals and households in the second step of this 'conventional' knowledge production process – the in-depth fieldwork – this contradiction became not only increas- ingly evident but also increasingly problematic. The richness and complexity of the information collected on the innumerable natural and social conditions under which each one of the individuals and households interviewed repro- duced themselves over time, as well as the impressive *differences* (heterogeneity) of such conditions among these social units – which are so often 'homogenized' under the concept of 'peasant' – progressively undermined, for me, the very possibility of producing a knowledge that I could legitimately claim to be a 'sound basis' for any kind of recommendation. 'Recommendations' of various kinds could be formally constructed. But I felt *a moral impediment* to doing so: in the name of what 'golden rule' was I to make an abstraction process *by myself* in order to produce *my* knowledge on the community and make *my* recommendations with respect to what 'ought to be done' to attain this community's 'economic development'?

But I had to do it: there was a legal contract to which I had to respond. Thus, I had 'to select a principle of organization', to design a rule of abstraction, that would allow me to determine what specific empirical information to look for in the interviews and the survey, and to use this information to construct my 'story' about the rural community of Garcia Rovira. I had to choose a specific set of concepts – a theoretical framework, a symbolic space – with which I could select and relate some of these informations to construct this story. And so I did.

Once these basic concepts were chosen, the in-depth fieldwork was carried out in a back-and-forth process between the data collection and the analysis of the collected information: the information collected in each visit would be carefully analysed and organized by means of our conceptual framework, and out of these critical analyses of the collected information new questions would always arise calling for additional empirical data. As an effect of each and every step forward in this back-and-forth process, the conceptual framework was further developed and enriched.

The complexity of the scenario I gradually perceived of the numerous intermingled social and natural processes in which the different individuals and households interviewed participated, turned the experience of going from the second step of my research – the in-depth fieldwork – to the third step, the survey, into the most valuable and forceful evidence of the arbitrariness of the abstractions economists have to make to construct any 'scientific' *economic* knowledge on any community: I was able to 'feel' it, to capture it in its full deepness, as I carried out each one of the three tasks that have to be accomplished when conducting a survey – the design of the sample, the painful process of constructing the survey questionnaire, and the even more painful process of collecting the information. The 'pain' one feels in this kind of research experience is, I think, directly proportional to how deeply concerned you are as a researcher about the future of the community under study, that is about the concrete *social effects* that the knowledge production process you are involved in will have on the community. How was I to design a sample survey of approximately 500 households that would be 'representative' of this community as a totality? I didn't have an answer then, and I still don't have it today.

After the extensive information (quantitative and qualitative) I had collected through the in-depth interviews with so many different households, it became a real *tour de force* to design a survey questionnaire of a reasonable length. Although the general structure of the questionnaire had to be defined by means of the basic concepts I had selected to construct this knowledge, these abstract concepts could not possibly provide an operational framework to make the minute but critical decisions on how to phrase the questions, on which questions to include and which to exclude, on how to construct the sequence of the questions, and so on. All these apparently 'small' decisions may very well affect drastically the resulting knowledge of the research process. Yet, most of them end up being made randomly – without one even being conscious that important decisions are being taken.

But the sample was designed, the questionnaire was constructed, the survey was carried out, and the collected information was 'ordered' in several computer files to be used as a 'raw material' to construct knowledges on the community. I proceeded then with the fourth and final step of this 'conventional' knowledge production process: to use all this information collected in the three preceding steps for the construction of such knowledge and the corresponding recommendations.

The effort I made to construct this knowledge comprised two successive steps. The first was to produce a *micro-knowledge* of the social and natural conditions of reproduction of approximately fifty households, selected with as many differences as possible among them. The main objective of this analysis was to see how far I could get in constructing my own 'understanding' (or knowledge) of the *differences* in the individual conditions of reproduction of these households, and also in figuring out, based on these analyses, the concrete 'economic policy' recommendations I would make so as to foster the 'economic development' of each household. The only definite conclusions I could get from this micro exercise, carried out at the 'simple' level of individual households, were to confirm my own 'technical' incapacity to unilaterally determine what policies would be actually effective in enhancing the 'development' of these households, and to strongly reinforce the 'moral impediment' I had felt throughout the whole process to make such 'policy' recommendations.

When I turned to the second step, the construction of a *macro-knowledge* on this community, my feelings of 'technical incapacity' and 'moral impediment' reached their peaks. How could I unilaterally construct 'a knowledge' on such a complex totality to recommend anything as to 'what to do' in order to procure its development? On what grounds could I claim that the specific 'options' I had taken throughout this long and cumbersome abstraction process to construct *my* knowledge on this specific community were 'the' correct options to effectively procure such development? I was unable to produce this macro-knowledge: for me it was technically and morally impossible.

In the light of this experience, the central question that led me into the fields of philosophy and epistemology was: if I was to *produce* an economic knowledge on the rural community of Garcia Rovira, and if this knowledge was to be *used* for the benefit (i.e. for the development) of this community, how was I to proceed as an 'academic economist', as a protagonist of this social process of producing such knowledge, to 'secure' that the specific knowledge I was to produce was 'adequate' for, and would be effectively and successfully used in procuring such a purpose?

In the process of doing this philosophical research I became increasingly aware of the problematic nature of two specific conditions under which my economic research in this first project had been conducted:

1. The radical separation in space and time between the economic knowledge production process I was carrying out and the social use that would be made of the resulting knowledges. This separation allowed for the social agents producing the knowledge to be *different* from the social agents responsible for taking action on the basis of that knowledge (which in this case was the state).
2. The radical separation between both of these two social agents and the people who were to be more directly and radically affected by the production and use of that knowledge: the 'investigated' community – in my case, the rural community of Garcia Rovira.

These separations led me to question the very political legitimacy of the 'conventional' social forms in which economic knowledges are produced and used. This posed a new problematique, which I had to face in carrying out the second research project: it was clear to me that in these social forms of producing and using economic scientific knowledges there was no communication whatsoever between science (myself as an academic economist) and society (the rural community of Garcia Rovira).

2 On new social forms of producing and using economic knowledge

This question about the political legitimacy of the 'conventional' social forms of producing and using economic knowledge was, to me, strikingly similar to the question Paulo Freire – the well-known Brazilian educator – had to face when he called into question the legitimacy of 'conventional' forms of education. Therefore a brief reference to Freire's work is very useful at this point.

For Freire (1970) the 'conventional' form of education, which he called 'banking' education,

> becomes an act of depositing, in which the students are the depositories and the teacher is the depositor. Instead of communicating, the teacher issues communiqués and makes deposits which the students patiently receive, memorize and repeat. . . . In the banking concept of education, knowledge is a gift bestowed by those who consider themselves knowledgeable upon those whom they consider to know nothing. Projecting an absolute ignorance onto others, a characteristic of the ideology of oppression, negates education and knowledge as processes of inquiry.

(Freire 1970: 58–9)

In sharp contrast with this scenario, in the new form of education Freire has constructed, which he calls 'problem-posing' education, the educator's efforts 'must be imbued with a profound trust in men and their creative power' (ibid.: 62); education must be 'the action and reflection of men upon their world in order to transform it', it 'consists in acts of cognition, not transferrals of information', it implies that 'the teacher is no longer merely the-one-who-teaches, but one who is himself taught in dialogue with the students, who in turn while being taught also teach' (ibid.: 68–9). For this educational process, 'the point of departure must always be with men in the 'here and now', which constitutes the situation within which they are submerged, from which they emerge, and in which they intervene' (ibid.: 72–3).

This critical analysis of the 'conventional' social forms of education is enlightening for a critical analysis of the 'conventional' social forms in which economists – unilaterally, not dialogically – construct knowledges: the separation between teacher and student that Freire criticizes is analogous to the separation between the production and the use of economic knowledges. In both cases 'knowledge' is transformed into a fetishized commodity whose 'production', 'circulation' and 'use' can be separated in space and time – and, therefore, can be effected by different people. In 'banking' education the teacher isolates him/herself from the students he/she educates; in the 'conventional' forms of producing and using economic knowledges the economists isolate themselves from the communities they investigate. In both cases communication between science and society is obstructed.

In problem-posing education teacher (science) and students (society) *communicate* because knowledge is not any more a commodity: it is a process constituted by a joint effort of students and teacher to understand the perception of reality that each one has, in order to transform the reality on which, to begin with, they have different perceptions. This communication requires then, as a precondition, an understanding-and-transformation of these perceptual differences. As Freire puts it:

> It is to *the reality* that mediates men, and to *the perception* of that reality held by educators and people, that we must go to find the program content of education. The investigation of what I have termed the people's 'thematic universe' – the complex of their 'generative themes' – inaugurates the dialogue of education as a practice of freedom. . . . Consistent with the liberating purpose of dialogical education, the object of the investigation is not men (as if men were anatomical fragments), but rather the thought-language with which men refer to reality, the levels at which they perceive that reality, and their view of the world, in which their generative themes are found. (Emphasis added.)

(ibid.: 86)

With this form of education Freire eliminated the teacher–student separation, in which 'the teacher presents himself to his students as their necessary opposite'.

In the 'conventional' forms of producing and using economic knowledges the investigated community's perceptions of their realities are always abstracted by the economist. Such a crucial abstraction is legitimized in the name of an 'objective scientific' knowledge. This is the basis to legitimize the space and time separations between the production and use of knowledge – together with the separations between the producers-and-users of knowledge from those who suffer the consequences of that knowledge.

These separations produce in turn a political effect of utmost importance: the exercise of the totalitarian power that is consistently exerted by social researchers on their 'investigated communities'. How right is Feyerabend (1982) when he denounces that intellectuals – in this case economists –

> have so far succeeded . . . in preventing a more direct democracy where problems are solved and solutions judged by those who suffer from the problems and have to live with the solutions and . . . have fattened themselves on the funds thus diverted in their direction. It is time to realize that they (the intellectuals) are just one special and rather greedy group held together by a special and rather aggressive tradition equal in rights to Christians, Taoists, Cannibals, Black Muslims but often lacking their understanding of humanitarian issues.
>
> (Feyerabend 1982: 85–6)

My challenge in the second project was then to develop alternative social forms of producing and using economic knowledge, in which these separations were superceded – as Freire did in education. This meant, among other things, that my responsibility as a 'development economist' in front of this community could not be limited to the conventional 'academic' task of producing an economic knowledge and making a set of formal recommendations. I had to be also responsible for the use – or lack of use – that would be made of this knowledge and for the concrete social effects that the knowledge I was to produce would have (or would not have) on the community over time. In other words, my responsibilities as a 'development economist' comprised the political problem (in the broadest sense of the concept) of how my 'activities' as a social (economic) researcher would ultimately affect the living conditions of this community, and not just the academic/technical problem of constructing a knowledge to justify, in front of social agents different from the investigated community (like the state), a set of formal 'economic policy' recommendations; it meant abandoning the comfortable position of being accountable only for 'analyzing and recommending', to be held responsible in front of the concrete individuals and households which constitute the community for the concrete social effects that the produced knowledges might have on their living conditions.

But I could not assume this new responsibility unilaterally – as it would have to be assumed in the context of the 'conventional' forms in which economic knowledges are produced and used. Thus, if I was to assume this new responsibility, I had to develop radically new forms of knowledge production and use.

Inspired by Freire's pathbreaking work in the realm of education, as well as by my own experience in the first project, I decided to start the second project working intensely at the micro level: meeting with members of the communities where the state development programme that was to be evaluated had been implemented. The explicit objective of these first meetings was to start a collective reflection process to identify and thoroughly analyse (understand) a few concrete problems – Freire's 'generative themes' – on which we would carry out a collective action to transform them; and the implicit objective was to start constructing the communication that was required between the academic economist (science) and the community (society) for a collective and integrated (non-separated) process of knowledge production and use to be possible.

The crucial contribution of this reflection–action process around very concrete problems has been to provide us – by 'us' I mean the 'new community' of peasants *and* academic economists that this process has been progressively engendering – with a collective experience, within which a collective knowledge on the numberless complexities of these concrete problems has been constructed (reflection) and used (action). New channels of communication between science (academic economists) and society (the communities *with* these economists are doing the impact evaluation of the government development programme) are being constructed, out of which 'new' knowledges are being produced.

Two central differences between these 'new' knowledges and the 'conventional' knowledges have to be underscored:

1. The *social process* whereby this 'new' knowledge was constructed: the conventional separation between subjects and objects in the production-and-use of knowledge was superceded. Thus, no totalitarian power is being exerted by science on society.
2. The *knowledge itself* that is being produced is not anymore a commoditized 'finished' product: it is now a permanently changing *process*, that is increasingly becoming a constitutive element of the daily life of this 'new' community.

3 Some provisional 'conclusions'

The broader, most profound implication of this research experience as I have lived it – and made sense of it – is political: it has revealed to me the totalitarian form of exercise of social power that is ingrained in the conventional forms of producing-and-using economic knowledges. This totalitarian form of exercising social power is embedded in the radical separation between, on the one hand, the few individuals who participate as *subjects* in the production and use of economic knowledges, and, on the other, the masses of people who, in spite of being the most deeply affected by these processes, are maintained as non participant *objects* of the production and use of these knowledges.

A second crucial teaching I have obtained has to do with the crucial importance of the *collective participation* by academics *and* the 'investigated' communities in the processes of production and use of those economic know-ledges that will affect the living conditions of these communities. Attaining this participation requires tremendous efforts in the construction of communi-cation channels between science (economists) and society (the 'investigated' communities). These communication channels can be constructed only if economists are willing to stop ignoring (abstracting from) in their concrete research practices the cultural complexity of how the communities they 'investigate' perceive their own realities. Communication between economic science and society will not be possible unless economists understand and fully accept in their research practices Feyerabend's striking proposition: 'I am not looking for new theories of science, I am asking if the search for such theories is a reasonable undertaking and I conclude that it is not: the knowledge we need to understand and to advance the sciences does not come from theories, it comes from participation' (Feyerabend 1987: 283–4).

As for the role of the academic economist, this experience has taught me that it cannot be any more that of an 'external' agent in charge of the limited and comfortable task of 'producing' knowledges to justify 'recommendations'. Such a role has to lead to one of the two following – and undesirable – scenarios: the production and circulation of useless knowledges and recom-mendations that nobody takes seriously; or the use of these knowledges and recommendations as weapons to exert the subtle, but extremely violent totali-tarian forms of exercise of social power that science has exerted on society. This second scenario – the worse of the two – is eloquently described by Michel Foucault in the following passages:

> In fact we know from experience that the claim to escape from the system of contemporary reality so as to produce the overall programs of another society, of another way of thinking, another culture, another vision of the world, has led only to the return of the most dangerous traditions. . . .
>
> I prefer very specific transformations that have proved to be possible in the last twenty years in a certain number of areas that concern our ways of being and thinking, relations to authority, the way in which we perceive insanity or illness; I prefer even these partial transformations that have been made in the correlation of historical analysis and the practical attitude, to the programs for a new man that the worst political systems have repeated throughout the twentieth century.
>
> (Rabinow 1982: 46–7)

In the first paragraph Foucault refers to the effects of what he somewhere else describes as the 'universal' intellectual's work (see Foucault 1980), and in the second he is describing the effects of what he calls the 'specific' intellectual's work.

One of the conditions of existence of 'universal' intellectual work is the two-fold assumption that (1) any kind of object can be defined as an 'object' of knowledge and (2) there are always essential elements where the truth is to be found, no matter what the object of analysis may be, whose discovery is the intellectual's function. This 'universal' assumption allows for the definition of 'society' as a *totality* as a legitimate object of scientific knowledge. Now, as soon as 'society' as a totality becomes a legitimate scientific 'question' (object of knowledge), constructing 'answers' to this 'question' must also become a legitimate task: it is, in fact, the answer that the 'universal' intellectual is expected to provide: it is – as it were – the answer that an economist is expected to provide in order to secure (!) the economic development of the communities – like Garcia Rovira – he/she investigates as totalities. It is the legitimacy of this 'question' and of this 'answer' that makes of the 'universal' intellectual such an arrogant and totalitarian figure.

For the 'specific' intellectual such a 'question' is *not* politically legitimate for the reasons I have expounded in this paper. Totalities like 'society' cannot be defined as objects of knowledge in the way 'conventional' science allows; therefore, it makes no sense to even think of ascribing to someone – that one who would be the 'universal' intellectual – *the* responsibility to produce a knowledge on such an object. Thus, in its 'new' context – a very complex context indeed – the 'specific' intellectual has to be a humble figure, an individual who has to be ceaselessly and collectively constructing and deconstructing his/her role, because his/her 'specific' role can never be 'universally' defined.

Economic science has produced mostly 'universal' intellectuals. I think it is time for economists to start transforming themselves – and to do it fast – into more 'specific', humble intellectuals.

Santamaria's conclusions require for the economist a new ethic and imperative of participation, communication and mutuality. In similar vein, Manfred Max-Neef (1988) has stressed the difference between describing and explaining phenomena, especially in the social sciences, and understanding them. Describing and explaining are the stuff of desks and books and seminars, in short part of the academic round. They are important, but they do not by themselves make for understanding. Understanding is at a different, higher order of complexity and, Max-Neef says, it demands participation in the situation or process that is to be understood.

In the light of Schweder's concepts of multiple objective worlds and divergent rationality, the imperative of participation is seen to be valid not only on moral democratic grounds but also with regard to simple effectiveness. Where the 'objective world' of study is different from that of the economist, which is the case in the vast majority of economic project and development work, a failure to participate effectively will result in the most relevant view of reality, that of those whose situation is being studied, being either misunderstood by the expert or missed completely. Effective action is most unlikely to be the result. Rather, the outcome will almost certainly be the totalitarian imposition of the economist's 'reality' against which Santamaria was arguing.

A practical methodology based on participation is not the only criterion for an economist's effectiveness in the real world. It must be complemented by an explicit commitment to a realist approach to economic analysis. The next paper describes the elements of such an approach in some detail.

Abstraction, tendencies and stylized facts†

Tony Lawson

A realist approach to analysis

In the context of a scientific activity such as economic analysis (scientific) *realism* asserts the existence of the objects of research as independent of the enquiry of which they are the objects. In other words, according to this doctrine, there is a material and social world that exists independently of any individual consciousness and which is knowable by consciousness – true theories of real entities can be obtained. And a methodological doctrine that is here subsumed under the general heading of realism is that such knowledge, or true theories, should be pursued. It is necessary to emphasize the last step because, in economics, it is not unusual to find accounts which implicitly suppose both that real entities or structures exist and that the truth status of relevant theories can be determined, and yet which argue that theories useful for predictive purposes – including theories acknowledged to be false – are *all* that is required. Indeed in the context of economics the philosophical doctrine most frequently opposed to realism is this peculiar form of 'predictive instrumentalism', and consequently some explicit comparisons of the two doctrines will be made below. Outside economics, however, it is more usual to find adherence to instrumentalism taking an essentially idealist form, whereby theories are not to be regarded as true or false but merely as (better or worse) instruments of prediction. For the purposes of what follows, however, there seems to be little harm in conflating these two versions of instrumentalism. (The significance of the differences between these two versions is discussed in Lawson 1989.) Thus, unless an explicit qualification is made, the term instrumentalism is used here to denote the methodological doctrine that all that is required of analysis (whether or not it is all that is considered to be possible) is a theory that is consistent with the given set of data in question. Clearly these distinctions require some further elaboration in the context of economics and in doing this I draw significantly on some recent contributions

†For helpful comments on an earlier draft of this paper I am very grateful to Lilli Basile, Geoff Hodgson and John Lovering. This is an edited version of an article which originally appeared in *Cambridge Journal of Economics* (13, 1989: 59–78). Permission from the publishers, Academic Press Inc. (London), to reprint it here is gratefully acknowledged.

in the philosophy of science and social theory, and especially Bhaskar (1978). (In recent years there has been a growth of, and of an interest in, essentially realist contributions, not just in the domain of the philosophy of science, but also in general social sciences or humanities – see for example, Bhaskar 1978; Cartwright 1983; Chalmers 1978; Giddens 1976; Gregory and Urry 1985; Hacking 1983; Hesse 1974; Keohane 1986; Leplin 1984; Levy 1981; McMullin 1984; Sayer 1984; and Sayers 1985. The present paper owes much to this general literature and most especially – and significantly – to the contribution of Bhaskar).

Realism and tendencies

Consider, first, three conceptual stages or aspects of a possible research analysis. The first involves the identification of some empirical phenomenon of interest, the second involves the construction of a 'model' or 'explanation' which entails (at least 'part' of) the empirical phenomenon in question – clearly these two stages can proceed in any order or simultaneously – and the third stage of the analysis entails subjecting the entities postulated at the 'modelling' or 'explanatory' stage to further continuous scrutiny.

For the instrumentalist the first two stages are sufficient. The empirical phenomenon in this case is always a presumed empirical regularity. And all that is required is a model that can accommodate it. To the extent that more than one model is sufficient for this task, conventionalist criteria (such as simplicity, parsimony, etc.) can be introduced for choosing between models. There is not even a necessary requirement that a chosen model be plausible – convenient fictions suffice. All that is required is an instrument for the job at hand. A model is accepted by the instrumentalist *merely* if the phenomenon in question is 'as if' it had been generated according to the constructed model.

For the realist, by contrast, while the empirically identified phenomenon may itself warrant reconceptualization and further examination (see below), the third stage of analysis is essential. The realist does also use the 'as if' form of reasoning, but is committed to the view that the entities posited at the modelling stage are or may be real, and are to be further investigated. According to the (essentially Aristotelean) version of realism that is considered here, it is such entities, things or structures that lie behind and actually govern the flux of observed phenomena. The object is to construct explanations for (i.e. to produce knowledge of the mechanisms that generate or govern) some observed phenomenon of interest. If several explanations are put forward and found to be consistent with the phenomenon in question, then these have to be selected amongst on the basis of their power to illuminate a range of empirical findings. In turn, some explanation is to be provided as to how any identified mechanism is maintained and so on. In short, for the realist the objective of economics, as indeed with all scientific activity, is to identify and understand real structures or mechanisms that govern the (equally real) phenomena that are experienced.

Now, according to the version of realism being defended here, given things can have powers to act in certain ways in appropriate circumstances by virtue of certain enduring intrinsic structures, or constitutions, or, more generally, natures. In other words, a given thing will have the power or disposition to act in a certain way by virtue of being the sort of thing it is. Often we will have knowledge only of causal powers of something and not of its nature. But if we do have knowledge of what a thing is, then we can deduce its causal powers. Thus once we understand the natures of copper, trade unions and private enterprise, for example, we can deduce their respective powers to conduct electricity well, defend conditions of workers, or seek profits and so on. Central to this realist view is the notion that powers may be exercised without being (precisely) manifest in actual states of, or happenings in, the world. In recent realist literature this notion of a power that may be exercised and yet unrealized in manifest phenomena is designated a tendency. It is the ascription of a tendency to a certain kind of thing that is interpreted as a statement of a law.

Why, then, should realists place such emphasis upon notions of generative structures and tendencies (so conceived)? And why, in doing so, should they reject the more orthodox, including instrumentalist, conception of laws as, or as necessitating, regularities amongst events (under some description), in favour of enduring tendencies of things? These questions can be straightforwardly addressed through a consideration of Bhaskar's (1978) illuminating analysis of the role of experiment in science. Experimental work, of course, is an often central aspect of scientific research – at least in subject-areas where it proves to be possible. Yet, on the whole, it remains relatively unanalysed as a form of scientific activity, despite being frequently emphasized as the ideal to which science, including economics, should aspire. Bhaskar's contribution is to draw out the significance of two readily available observations concerning it. The first observation is that most of the constant conjunctions of events that constitute important results in science, in fact, *only* occur in experimental situations. That is *closed systems* – those in which constant conjunctions of events hold – do not, in general (outside astronomy, at least) occur spontaneously. The second observation is that laws supported in experimental activity are frequently successfully applied outside experimental situations.

Now, these observations pose difficulties for accounts which view event regularities as necessary to significant results or laws. If laws are interpreted as necessitating regularities of the kind 'event (of type) X is *invariably* accompanied by event (of type) Y', then most of the accepted laws of physics, for example, do not hold – for they only hold in conditions of controlled experiment. If, however, this account of laws is then qualified so that laws take the form 'event (of type) X is invariably accompanied by event (of type) Y, under circumstances E', where E is typically those circumstances that obtain only in experimental situations, then other problems follow. First there is the consequence that any actual regularities of events (that the empirical law denotes) do not, in fact, generally occur independently of human intervention

– a somewhat counterintuitive result with regard to the notion of laws of *nature*. But, more seriously, the problem of what governs events outside the experimental situations is left completely without an answer and even unaddressed. And yet, as noted above, experimentally established results *are*, as a matter of fact, successfully applied outside experimental situations – an observation that is apparently without explanation.

As Bhaskar emphasizes such problems can be avoided – experimental activity and the application of experimentally determined knowledge outside experimental situations can be rendered intelligible – through invoking an ontology of generative structures and causal mechanisms that lie behind and govern the flux of events. Laws, for the realist, as noted above, are ascriptions of tendencies to certain kinds of things; they describe how generative structures behave. Now, such tendencies do not, in general, lead to regularities at the level of events because they will typically be juxtaposed with tendencies of other structures. Thus a breakaway leaf does not fall to the ground in strict conformity with an empirical regularity, for its actual path is influenced by aerodynamic, thermal and other tendencies. Yet its path is still recognized as being subject to the law of fall understood as a tendency, and this explains why the leaf eventually ends up on the ground (when it does). As J. S. Mill put it:

> If indeed every phenomenon was generally the effect of not more than one cause, a knowledge of the law of cause would, unless there was a logical error in our reasoning, enable us confidently to predict all circumstances of the phenomenon. . . . Effects [however] are commonly determined by a *concurrence* of causes. If we have overlooked any one cause, we may reason justly from all the others, and only be the further wrong. . . .
> . . . [A person's] error generally consists . . . in making the wrong *kind* of assertion: he predicated an actual result, when he should only have predicated a *tendency* to that result – a power acting with a certain intensity in that direction.
>
> (Mill 1844: 160–1)

Or, in the words of J. N. Keynes: 'As a matter of fact, in the instances that actually occur of the operation of a given cause, counteracting causes sometimes will and sometimes will not be present; and, therefore, laws of causation are to be regarded as statements of tendencies only' (Keynes 1890: 218).

On this account, then, experimental activity can be rendered intelligible not as an attempt to effect a law but as an attempt merely to *identify* it. In other words the objective of experimentation is to intervene in order to isolate a causal mechanism of interest by 'holding off' all other potentially interfering causal mechanisms. The intention is to engineer a closed system in which a one-to-one correspondence between actual outcomes and relevant tendencies can be expected. And, of course, the application of experimentally supported knowledge in an open system – that is outside the conditions of the experimental situation – can also be rendered intelligible through the realization that, once they are activated, relevant tendencies must necessarily be operative whatever else is going on. Thus, even as I hold a leaf in the palm of my hand, it is subject to the gravitational tendency. The context of milieu under which any mechanism may be operative is not a relevant condition for the law's specification. Once activated the mechanism is operative whatever empirical pattern ensues.

In short, if certain widely accepted features of scientific activity are to be rendered intelligible, the orthodox (empiricist and idealist/rationalist) conception of laws as necessitating a constant conjunction of events should be abandoned. And in place of it, clearly, something like the realist ontology of generative structures and tendencies, that lie behind and govern the flux of observable phenomena, needs to be invoked. On this realist view, the objective is to identify and understand generative structures and the ways in which they can act, in order that events in, and states of affairs of, the world might ultimately be explained.

Social structures and economic analysis

Perhaps some comments need to be made with respect to the possible existence, in the economic sphere, of causal powers and tendencies other than, or in addition to, the powers of human agents. Economists do generally appear to acknowledge human agency as a causal power but often conclude that, because everything that happens in the social world consists of changes in, or brought about by, people, all causal forces are essentially reducible to individual agency. The point is, of course, that, although dependent on human agency in general, social structures, relations, practices, conventions and so on exist prior to any individual act (at a given point in time and space) and govern it (i.e. make a difference to it) by providing limiting and enabling conditions (that are necessary for action to take place). In this sense social structures have causal powers. For example, the highway code, while certainly a social form, exists prior, and is given, to current motorists, and consequently makes a difference to how a person drives from A to B. At the same time, of course, it does not determine the actual trip taken – this conception of generative structures allows the status of human agency to be preserved. Similarly current rules of grammar impose limits upon, and facilitate, speech acts, but do not determine what is said. Usually, numerous different causal structures will bear upon some manifest phenomenon – work-place activities, for example, will be governed by all sorts of norms and conventions as well as male/female, skilled worker/unskilled worker, employer/worker relations (Lawson 1981). Thus the operation of any given generative structure will be offset by the action of others and is best understood, therefore, as a tendency. But even such a collection of work-place structures as that just noted will not, in combination, determine *all* that goes on; the status of human agency need not be undermined.

Now, as noted, it is true that social structures, in turn, exist only by virtue of human activity, in total. Of course, the contribution of individual agency to the reproduction and transformation of these structures will often (perhaps usually) be unintended, while the bearing that these structures have on individual action will perhaps be only tacitly and incompletely understood – although agents will always have some conception of what they are doing. But the point remains that for any individual action there are social structures that are given to it. In other words, individual agency presupposes social structure just as the latter presupposes individual agency – neither can be reduced to, identified with, or completely explained in terms of, the other. Generative structures, then, whose ways of acting are generally non-empirical (the world is open) and best interpreted as tendencies, are equally at work in the social, as in the natural realm – although, because of their dependence upon human agency, they are likely, amongst other things, to be relatively less enduring than natural tendencies.

Theory development and stylized facts

So far it has been argued that, on the realist view, tendencies may be regarded as powers or liabilities of a thing or structure which, because numerous countervailing mechanisms may be operative at the same moment and place, may be exercised without being manifest in the actual economic outcomes. Usually it is only under the sort of closed conditions striven for in experimental situations that a one-to-one correspondence may hold between the exercise of a tendency and its manifestation in actual phenomena. And in economics such a situation typically does not arise. Even so, if certain tendencies or combinations of tendencies are persistently activated over a significant span of time and/or space (or 'time-space'), or if some significant tendencies dominate others, it is not impossible that their effects will be detectable in actual phenomena to some extent. That is, although their effects will frequently be modified or hidden by the operation of irregular countervailing mechanisms and so forth, their persistency coupled with the irregular operation of the countervailing influences may allow their effects to 'shine through'. Thus, to the extent that any manifest phenomenon appears to reveal some degree of uniformity, generality, or persistency, albeit by no means complete in such respects, it would seem to provide a *prima facie* case for supposing that some enduring generative mechanisms are at work. Consequently, such partial regularities – with completely irregular details ignored – are often essential for initiating searches for operative causal mechanisms. Following Kaldor (1978: 2), amongst others, I shall refer to conceptualizations of such partial regularities as 'stylized facts'.

On this view, then, a stylized fact is a conceptualized phenomenon – typically a broad but not universal generalization about an event regularity – that is interpreted to hold in a way, or to a degree, such that the researcher regards as significant enough, given the context, that *prima facie* an explanation is called for. Thus, to use Kaldor's own examples, a stylized fact may be of the *form*: 'UK productivity growth is usually less than that of otherwise comparable industrial economies'; or 'when output increases in industrial economies so too do both employment and productivity'; or 'over different economies the variation in the capital/output ratio is significantly less than the variation in the capital/labour ratio'; or 'productivity is procyclical'; and so on. Such 'facts', once identified, can give rise to search for causal explanations.

The significance of the notion of a stylized fact in this framework, then, is that it may often provide a starting point for the analysis of enduring structures and mechanisms. In short, stylized facts can provide an access to enduring things as indications of possible manifestations of the effects of (possibly a combination of) causal tendencies. As such, stylized facts have a significant role in the realist framework, as marking a point of entry.

Theory development

Perhaps it will be objected, here, that by starting with a 'stylized' view of economic events or manifest phenomena, we are accepting a preconceived idea of – and therefore unnecessarily committing ourselves to the possibility of a false or inadequate conceptualization of – the particular phenomenon of interest. In fact, all human activity can be thought of as work on, and the transformation of, some given objects. Indeed, transformational activities represent the sort of manifest phenomena of social life that economics sets itself to explain. But the significant point to emphasize here is that this transformational view of human activity is no less relevant for scientific analysis, including economics. All analysis must start somewhere, with some materials to work on – with some stock of theories, methods, hypotheses and facts, etc. A recognition of this necessity facilitates an avoidance of the reductionist illusion, typically associated with empiricist (and also with some rationalist) accounts, of believing it to be possible to obtain some absolute and immutable foundations for knowledge through something like perception, intuition or direct experience alone (see Lawson 1987 on this). Some degree of epistemological relativeness then is always involved – knowledge has both an absolute and a relative dimension (Bradley 1914; Eaton 1965; Lawson 1987; Sayers 1985). In the first instance (for any social science) the social activity in question will be conceptualized (albeit possibly inadequately) by the relevant agents concerned – as the hermeneutic tradition has continually emphasized. Specific economists, however, will usually be confronted with theoretical redescriptions of these individual experiences – both as produced through the work of 'data collectors' and through the labours of other economists and social scientists in general. Now, the point is that there is scope for criticism and redevelopment whatever the level of conceptualization and redescription, and this, in itself, does not obviate the claim that 'stylized facts', while obviously preconceptualized, can mark a relevant point to begin the analysis. Perhaps the first step will *usually* involve some redefinition of the activities and categories involved – what, after all, is typically meant by skilled labour, semiskilled work, industrial decline, capital, unemployment and so forth? But to acknowledge this possibility, while it clearly suggests that scientific activity must be a demanding process of human labour, is only to be fallibilist about knowledge – which is part and parcel of being realist about events and causal things. In short, then, stylized facts may indeed provide a useful point of entry for analysis. The observation that claims about social phenomena are stylized does not, in itself, indicate capricious or suspect intent on the part of the conceptualizer – although, to repeat, as with all conceptualizations, stylized facts may be susceptible to immediate conceptual criticism.

Modes of inference

A remaining issue to address is the mode of inference whereby generative structures or mechanisms are 'inferred' from a conceptualization of some social phenomenon – or stylized fact – in question. Now, induction and deduction are both necessary to realist analysis although each alone is insufficient. The essential moment of realist analysis, the movement from a conceptualization of some manifest phenomenon to a hypothesis about the possible structures which give rise to or govern it, is one neither of induction nor deduction, and is usually captured in economics only by reference to the 'as if method' of reasoning. A discussion on what is involved with this form of inference, however – which following recent contributions in the philosophy of science I shall term 'retroduction' – is not taken up until the following section.

To sum up so far, on the realist view, science is concerned with enduring structures, with what kinds of things there are and with what they are able to do. It is by reference to these that the flux of phenomena can be explained. In economics, in particular, such structures may be only relatively enduring. Certainly, once identified, the conditions of their reproduction and transformation will also need to be assessed. But the object of science is above all to identify and understand structures that do endure to some extent. And in this endeavour, stylized facts, as conceived above, can play a contributory role, by providing a point of entry.

For the realist, then, the object of science is to come to grips with the generative mechanisms, with the ways of acting of relatively enduring economic structures, that govern the flux of phenomena that we experience. In an open system observed phenomena will typically be governed by numerous, often countervailing, causal tendencies, and so must first be resolved into their separate causal components. At the same time most economic structures or entities that give rise to or govern such phenomena will also be complex things possessing an ensemble of tendencies, liabilities and so forth. Analysis, then, must proceed by way of abstraction, by looking at something in a one-sided manner, by focusing on certain aspects of something to the neglect of others. On this realist view abstractions are made both in the initial analysis of economic phenomena and in the examination of mechanisms which give rise to them. If economic phenomena are conjuncturally determined they can be resolved into their causal components; that is resolved into the different effects of various causal mechanisms. To isolate one or a few such components is to abstract from the original phenomenon. Economic structures too can be abstracted by isolating certain powers or tendencies possessed amongst others. In each case, the abstraction achieved is intended to be *real* – it is not ideal, a convenient fiction, or some such. The aim is to obtain knowledge of *real* structures or mechanisms which give rise to or govern the flux of *real* phenomena of social and economic life.

That which is abstracted *from* – whether conjuncturally determined events or economic structures/systems and so on with causal powers – is the *concrete*. The concrete is a combination of diverse features, components or determinations and so on. The point of abstraction is to isolate or individuate these components or attributes and their relationships in order to come to understand them (better). Once such abstractions have been successfully achieved they can then be synthesized into a unity that reconstitutes the concrete, although at this point with the object of analysis more clearly and essentially understood.

Now, non-mainstream economists are prone to referring to forms of abstraction found in mainstream economics as 'inappropriate', the 'wrong kind' or 'highly artificial' and so on (see e.g. Kaldor 1978: 2, 202; 1985: 13). But when exactly a form of abstraction is appropriate, or of the right kind, or non-artificial, rather than the converse, is not something that is usually elaborated upon. From the realist point of view set out above, however, some kind of guiding or necessary principles can be set down. Thus from the realist perspective:

1. For an abstraction to be appropriate in the sense of non-artificial (or for a conception to be appropriately termed an abstraction) it must be concerned with the real rather than some ideal, or convenient fiction.
2. For an abstraction to be appropriate in the sense of the right kind, it must be concerned with the essential rather than merely the most general.

These suggested 'principles' are now considered in turn.

The abstraction as real

The view that abstraction is concerned with isolating that which is real follows straightforwardly from the account set out above. Realism, by definition, involves a commitment to identifying that which exists. Thus abstractions obtained are held to obtain not only in thought but also in the real world. Thus retroduction – the mode of inference from manifest phenomenon to possible causes – represents an attempt to identify the real, if abstracted, structure or set of structures that actually governs the phenomenon in question. Now retroduction by itself may well lead to a plurality of hypotheses of possible causal mechanisms – if there is one possible explanation consistent with the relevant aspect of the manifest phenomenon in question there will usually be others. Thus, and as noted above, the elimination of some of the various contending hypotheses must now ensue until only one remains – empirically justified through the explanatory power of the hypotheses that can be deduced from it. In other words, the reality of any posited structure or mechanism must itself be subject to empirical scrutiny. In turn, the conditions supporting an identified generative mechanism need also to be examined and explained and so on. In short, although the mechanism ultimately identified is an abstraction, the intention is that it should be real for all that.

Although this account of abstraction follows easily from a realist perspective, it represents an interpretation that appears to be in sharp contrast to the way the term is usually used in mainstream economics in general. According to the latter, the process of abstraction seems mainly to mean something like forming artificial constructs, or fictionalizing. Friedman's well-known methodological essay, at least in certain places, provides a case in point (Friedman 1953). Thus Friedman sets up an 'abstract model' (ibid.: 24) which posits consciously deliberating, 'rapidly or instantaneously' mobile, sunlight-maximizing, leaves as a putative mechanism to explain the (obviously stylized) phenomenon of a greater density of leaves on the (sunnier) southern sides of trees. Clearly, if we did not know the constructed hypothesis to be false – the mechanism posited to be fictitious – Friedman's reasoning could be considered a valid form of retroduction. Certainly the phenomenon in question – the greater density of leaves on the sunnier side of trees – appears, at first sight, to be broadly consistent with the hypothesis, so that the latter could, perhaps, explain why the observed pattern of leaves arises. But on the realist account, as noted, the reality of the posited mechanism must now be further checked. Its explanatory power, or ability to illuminate a range of empirical phenomena, must be examined, and eventually the identified mechanism itself must be explained in terms of other causal mechanisms. Now, Friedman's attitude towards such matters is clearly very different. Suppose, for example, that some phenomenon for which the hypothesis bears implications cannot be explained by the hypothesis. Suppose, say, that the sunnier side of a tree is trimmed, but that the remaining leaves fail to adjust 'rapidly or instantaneously' to the newly created spare positions. For the realist this would be reason to question the hypothesis. For Friedman, however, it seems clear that the causal mechanisms that actually govern the density of leaves is not at issue, for the sort of contradictory observation just noted is to be treated as merely indicative of qualifications that must be appended to the hypothesis – the object being (as Friedman notes in the context of a further example) to specify the conditions in which the hypothesis is found to hold:

The important problem in connection with the hypothesis is to specify the circumstances under which the formula works [or empirical regularity holds] or, more precisely, the general magnitude of the error in the predictions under various circumstances. Indeed, . . . such a specification is not one thing and the hypothesis another. The specification is itself an essential part of the hypothesis, and it is a part that is peculiarly likely to be revised and extended as experience accumulates.

(Friedman 1953: 18)

And what about further checking the reality of the posited mechanism through examining the structures which, in turn, govern it? In other words, what is Friedman's attitude to the issue of trying to understand the structures which govern the 'deliberating' and 'seeking' capacities of leaves? Once again Friedman rules out such endeavours by stipulating that his supposedly abstract conception is only to be assessed as empirically adequate with reference to a certain set or *class of phenomena* – in this case with those associations that the hypothesis was explicitly designed to entail:

> Is the hypothesis rendered unacceptable or invalid because so far as we know, leaves do not 'deliberate' or consciously 'seek', have not been to school and learned the relevant laws of science or the mathematics required to calculate the 'optimum' position, and cannot move from position to position? Clearly, none of these contradictions of the hypothesis is vitally relevant; the phenomena involved are not within the 'class of phenomena the hypothesis is designed to explain'; the hypothesis does not assert that leaves do these things but only that their density is the same *as if* they did. Despite the apparent falsity of the 'assumptions' of the hypothesis, it has great plausibility because of the conformity of its implications with observations.

(ibid.: 20)

In short, real abstractions are not the objective. For Friedman no independent or further assessment of any merely 'as if' hypothesis is being sought over and above its consistency with a typically very restricted set of phenomena that itself falls within an already restricted 'class of phenomena' that the hypothesis is explicitly designed to entail (see Lawson 1989 for a fuller discussion).

Perhaps not all theorizing in mainstream economics is as restrictive as this – or so explicitly so. Nevertheless, economic analysis abounds with acknowledged artificial constructs and even fictions (e.g. universal perfect competition, rational expectations, perfect foresight, etc.) which play consequential roles in supposed explanatory contexts. As such, the conclusions to be drawn concerning the limitations for serious analysis of theories positing such constructions are essentially just the same. For the realist, the construction of fictions is to be avoided. The object, through abstraction, is instead to identify the *real* causal mechanisms and necessary relations that govern the flux of *real* phenomena of the economic and social world.

Abstracting the essential

The second suggested 'principle' – that abstraction is concerned with identifying that which is essential rather than merely most general – also follows easily from the sketch of realism so far set out. Realism is concerned with the identification and understanding of real structures and mechanisms that govern some phenomenon of interest. The aim is to identify connections and relations essential to the existence and efficacy of some structure of interest – to gauge the identification and internal complexity of some significant entity. The aim, as Sayer puts it, is to obtain an abstraction 'which isolates a significant element of the world which has some unity and autonomous force, such as a structure' (Sayer 1984: 26). (If certain structures generating social phenomena combine in a 'system' – involving organic totalities of intra-acting structures or externally related interacting ones – then an abstraction, to be adequate, must both identify any necessary connections and avoid isolating a necessary relation from others essential to its existence.)

Now a widely subscribed to alternative approach, in economics, aims instead to seek formal relations of similarity, rather than to abstract the essential. As Dobb, distancing himself from this alternative approach, says of it, the aim is to base 'abstraction, not on any evidence of fact as to what features in a situation are essential and what are inessential, but simply on the formal procedure of combining the properties common to a heterogeneous assortment of situations and building abstraction out of analogy' (Dobb 1972: 40). Of course, generality of some kind is also a realist objective – to determine non-empirical invariances at the 'deeper' level of necessary relations and tendencies of things. These, however, are unlikely to be uncovered just by adopting the aim of seeking broad generalizations. As Dobb concludes, what this form of 'abstraction gains in breadth it more than loses, as it were, in depth – in relevance to the particular situations which are the focus of interest' (ibid.).

It is a characteristic of economic structures, for example, that much of what is essential to the explaining of a form of human activity is highly context-related. Thus, through a process of seeking merely wide generalizations, economic structures can easily be emptied of their context-related, but often essential, content. The employer–worker relationship, for example, may be identified as a transhistorical, pancultural feature of human society. But this observation, in itself, abstracts from the numerous variations in the nature of this relationship across time and space, and it is certainly insufficient, for example, to any understanding or explanation of work practices and activities that exist at a specific stage of human evolution in any particular region or place. Similarly, to note such generalities as that humans have preferences, or beliefs, or the ability to make choices, is to provide insufficient detail of these generative structures or causal powers for explaining any form of human activity they govern.

Perhaps the greatest danger of seeking merely broad generalizations, of pushing the abstractions so far that they are almost devoid of substantive content, arises from the fact that they then need to be supplemented by other propositions in order to have any explanatory value; for this opens the door to the inclusion of 'highly artificial' or 'bogus abstractions', to the sort of convenient fictions already noted above. In other words, almost contentless abstractions can easily, if unwittingly, be manipulated or 'strengthened', in illegitimate ways to yield conceptions that really are no longer abstractions at all. In orthodox or mainstream economics, for example, such 'assumptions', which may creep in unnoticed, are usually designed to achieve mathematical tractability, system closure or some such thing, rather than an understanding of the real causal mechanisms at work. Now if the original abstractions alone possess little explanatory content then it is the additional 'strengthening' assumptions that do all the work and determine the upshot. And a failure to appreciate this can lead either to an unthinking and erroneous presumption that these assumptions can eventually be replaced with accounts of essential aspects of real generative mechanisms without the whole construction collapsing entirely, or to a misguided attempt to extract more meaning from the constructions than can possibly be legitimate. The latter, again, is a point that Dobb has emphasized:

> There is the danger of introducing, unnoticed, purely imaginary or even contradictory assumptions and in general of ignoring how limited a meaning the corollaries deducible from these abstract propositions must have and the qualifications which the presence of other concrete factors (which may be major influences in this or that particular situations) may introduce. All too frequently the propositions which are products of this mode of abstraction have little more than formal meaning and at most tell one that an expression for such-and-such a relation must find a place in any of one's equational systems. But those who use such propositions and build corollaries upon them are seldom mindful of this limitation and in applying them as 'laws' of the real world invariably extract from them more meaning than their emptiness of real contents can possibly hold.
>
> (Dobb 1972: 41)

In sum, on the realist view, while abstract and concrete analysis always, in practice, accompany each other, abstract analysis is primarily concerned with attempting to understand real causal objects at their own level of being, in terms of their constitutive structures and causal powers, while concrete analysis is an endeavour to examine how the relevant abstractions combine. In this, abstraction is concerned with the real rather than the ideal or fictitious, and with what is essential in any situation rather than what is merely the most general. On this view, abstraction represents a way of understanding some domain of reality rather than a device for avoiding such endeavour. And in this it involves both theory and empirical observation as equally vital elements in the same scientific process.

Realism and economic theory

The branch of economics currently considered to be the most prestigious, that commands most respect, is, without doubt, formal 'economic theory' including, and indeed as exemplified by, general equilibrium theory in particular. It is, then, perhaps of some interest, finally, to bring relevant insights of the realist approach to bear briefly upon it. It is, of course, impossible to provide a complete and uncontentious statement of what economic theory consists of here. However, an important, informative and unusually explicit account of the sort of reasoning that is involved has recently been set out by Hahn in his Jevons' Memorial Fund Lecture, entitled 'In Praise of Economic Theory' (Hahn 1985), and it is this account that will be mainly considered.

According to Hahn, economic theorizing attempts 'to gain understanding of the particular by reference to generalizing insights and in the light of certain abstract unifying principles' (ibid.: 3). Interestingly, the reference to 'understanding' in this phrase is in part intended to indicate that, like the realist, Hahn perceives economic analysis to be 'not directly related to positivist prediction' (ibid.: 3). An equally interesting part of this phrase, however, is the reference to 'abstract unifying principles' or 'abstractions' for short. Hahn proceeds to label these as 'axioms' and to distinguish them from assumptions. The difference between axioms and assumptions is that the former, but not the latter, are thought to be claims about the real world that are universally agreed upon: 'Axioms are not plucked out of thin air and far from distancing the theorists from what somewhat mysteriously is called the 'real' world they constitute claims about this world so widely agreed as to make further argument unnecessary' (ibid.: 5).

Now, the axioms that Hahn cites, like, for example, 'agents have preferences', are so general as to fall into the category, noted above, of relatively contentless abstractions. As such, they may indeed be widely held as true, and may even be uncontentious. The problem, of course, is that because these axioms are effectively devoid of content very little can be explained by them alone. For the realist, any move from the abstract to the concrete always involves empirical study, as different abstractions are combined and synthesized in the light of knowledge of contingent relations and conditions. But for the practitioner of 'economic theory' the axioms, instead, are to be 'idealized and strengthened' through the addition of extra formal 'assumptions' (ibid.: 7). And as noted above, if relatively contentless abstractions are combined with powerful assumptions it is the latter that do much of the work. And a significant and consequential feature of economic theory is that the additional assumptions that tend to be made can be regarded as no more than convenient fictions. Consider the examples mentioned by Hahn:

> That people have preferences and try to satisfy them we treat as an axiom while universal perfect competition, for instance, must count as an assumption.
>
> (ibid.: 10)

> That managers have preferences is an axiom; that they take a particular form, for instance that they are linear in expected profit, is an assumption.
>
> (ibid.: 11)

If you want more out you have to put more in, that is you must supplement the axioms with assumptions, e.g. that production functions are Cobb–Douglas.

(ibid.: 13)

Clearly assumptions such as universal perfect competition, linear expected profit functions, Cobb–Douglas production functions, and so on, are not intended to capture the mode of operation of real economic mechanisms – indeed they appear, in the main, to be designed merely to achieve mathematical tractability. To put it mildly, and as Hahn on occasion acknowledges, 'at the end we shall have to agree that the genuine axiom: persons have some preferences, has been idealised and strengthened by theorists beyond the point at which it commands universal consent' (ibid.: 7).

Now, it should be clear that economic theory, so conceived, has little to commend itself to the realist. Hahn, more astute than most economic theory practitioners, expressly acknowledges this, observing that for 'economic theory' the 'aim is not realism' but to understand where it is that the axioms and assumptions that are made logically lead (ibid.: 13). And to the extent that the axioms are almost contentless, to repeat, it is the additional assumptions that do most of the leading. A failure to appreciate this point, however, easily gives rise to the two, apparently widespread, errors already noted above. Thus, first of all, there appears to be a common misconception that, sooner or later, the assumptions can be removed, just as scaffolding is from an otherwise stable construction, leaving the basic results of economic theory intact. This observation, in fact, seems to lie behind a persistent criticism that Kaldor levels at general equilibrium theory in particular. Thus, Kaldor writes in this connection:

[The] authors [of general equilibrium theory] were motivated by the belief that they were only laying the foundations of an explanation of how a market economy works, an initial stage of the analysis which is in the nature of 'scaffolding': it has to be erected before the permanent building can be built, but will be removed step by step as the permanent building nears completion. However, since Walras first wrote down his system of equations over 100 years ago, progress has definitely been backwards not forwards in the sense that the present set of axioms are far more restrictive than those of the original Walrasian model. The ship is no nearer to the shore, but considerably farther off, though in a logical, mathematical sense, the present system of derived tautologies is enormously superior to Walras's original effort.

(Kaldor 1985: 13)

And second, associated with a misconstrual of the aims and nature of economic theory, and in particular with a failure to recognize the significant role of assumptions, is a generally held supposition that, because the original, relatively contentless abstractions, or axioms, are intended to capture some domain of reality, the same is also true of the final conception, so that it can therefore be justifiably used for purposes of explanation and policy analysis. Such a supposition, of course, is incorrect. If a general equilibrium, or any other, model is derived in the manner of economic theory, it can be regarded as no more than something like an ideal fiction. It can, of course, be confronted with data and, with suitable qualifications, may even be found to be data-consistent. But this can tell us very little of value. Indeed it tells us no more than what we learn from the example of Friedman's 'deliberating', 'mobile' leaves – that the particular, highly restricted, set of data employed in the relevant exercise are *merely* 'as if' they had been generated according to some version of the particular fiction in question, Or, perhaps more accurately, we should learn that the nature of the data, the criteria of fit, the degrees of freedom in model specification, and so on, are such that a total fiction can be found to 'fit' the specific set of data to hand. We could deduce little more. Certainly such a result does not help us to explain or understand mechanisms or events in the non-equilibrium world in which we live. On this point, in fact, Hahn – in apparent contrast to many other practitioners of economic theory – seems, to a significant extent, to agree:

> [Certain] economists . . . might be taken to be engaged in the following programme: to enquire how far observed events are consistent with an economy which is in continuous Walrasian equilibrium. Such a programme would be of considerable value. For we might find that events which we had explained as due to disequilibrium or indeed to Trade Unions and monopolists could be accounted for without these. That surely would be valuable for understanding. But it would not be true that we understood the events. For we would not understand how continuous equilibrium is possible in a decentralised economy and we do not understand why a world with Trade Unions and monopolies behaves like a perfectly competitive one. Theorising in economics I have argued is an attempt at understanding and I now add that bad theorising is a premature claim to understand.
>
> What has happened in this instance is that 'as if' prediction methodology has taken over. Recall Friedman's example. . . .
>
> (Hahn 1985: 15)

In sum, the methods of economic theory in general, and general equilibrium theory in particular, *may* have their own rationale even if, as Hahn critically notes, many of their proponents do not carry them through coherently. If a commitment to realism is accepted, however, the whole basic approach seems misconceived. In particular, the two 'guiding principles' set out above are neglected. Thus, by starting from that which is merely most general, that which is essential is lost. By incorporating a layer of assumptions designed mainly to achieve mathematical tractability, that which is real is emasculated. From this perspective, then, the resulting conceptions, as 'abstractions', can indeed be seen as 'inappropriate', 'artificial' or the 'wrong kind'.

Final comments and conclusion

On the realist view, science, including economics, is concerned with what kinds of things there are and what they are able to do. The aim is to identify and understand real, relatively enduring generative structures and mechanisms, their powers and tendencies, which govern the flux of actual economic and social events, and by reference to which the phenomena of the world are explained.

Typically, economic structures will be highly complex possessing an ensemble of powers and tendencies. Similarly, empirical phenomena will be the resultant of numerous causal effects. Thus *abstraction* of the real and essential is a necessary feature of coming to grips with significant causal *tendencies* while *stylized facts* may provide a pointer from which to start. Both deduction and induction are essential to analysis, though each alone is insufficient, for retroduction – the movement from manifest phenomena to the mechanisms relations that govern them – is also essentially involved.

Because of the importance of basic conceptions and methodology to any analytical framework, the principal themes of this chapter bear recapitulation. First 'the economy' is a culturally specific notion. Economic analysis may not be appropriate at all outside this specificity. It is also possible that, in so far as elevation of 'the economy' to dominance in human life has contributed to contemporary problems, economics will not be able to solve these problems and solutions must come from elsewhere.

Second, the human experience of reality is diverse, based on multiple objective worlds and divergent rationality. To understand such experience, economists must be prepared to participate in the 'worlds' into which they are enquiring. Third, underlying the multiple objective worlds of human experience there is an independently existing reality. While this can never be comprehended directly and can only be approached through one of the worlds of human experience, it is nevertheless the purpose of scientific activity to understand this underlying reality. It is therefore relevant to speculate briefly as to its nature.

In an article calling for the restructuring of science, Willis Harman wrote: 'The medieval metaphor was of the universe as a "great organism". After the scientific revolution, the metaphor was replaced by one of a "great machine". . . . The emerging root metaphor appears to be that of a universe as a "great thought" ' (Harman 1988). Harman's point is not to advocate choice between these metaphors, but to recognize that reality is probably a combination of all three. Different forms of scientific analysis are therefore appropriate, depending on the aspect of the reality being investigated.

Following Popper and Eccles (1981), Harman has suggested a four-level hierarchy of science, comprising, starting from the bottom, physical sciences, life sciences, human sciences (including economics) and spiritual sciences.

The pure objective, reductionist and positivist characteristics of what is some-times called 'the scientific method' is in fact *a* scientific method that is only appropriate to the physical sciences. Ascending the hierarchy of sciences, the method needs to become progressively more participatory, holistic and intuitive or consciousness-directed if reality is to be apprehended.

This way of approaching reality is also in line with Sarkar's redefinition of science. According to one recent commentator: 'Sarkar, speaking from the Indian episteme, can divide science into [the] intuitional and material, thus allowing more ways of knowing the real' (Inayatullah 1991: 14). Specifically, these 'ways of knowing the real' were through reason, sense inference, intuition, authority and devotion/love. Sarkar's goal was a 'rational intuitional science', in which 'science and technology are important but are now placed in an evolutionary social model' (ibid.: 14). It is in the context of this general approach to science that the next two chapters explore the place of the economy in human life, especially emphasizing the importance of a holistic approach.

2 Economy, society and ethics

The first task for an economics focusing on real life is to place the economy in the context of the total human condition. The next two chapters will develop a model of that condition in terms of four fundamental dimensions: the economic, social, ethical (this chapter) and ecological (the next).

The ethical dimension is conceptually relatively straightforward, though its implications for economics are profound, as will become apparent. It is here taken to comprise a concern with *right* or *good* actions, as opposed to those which are merely useful or pleasurable (see Ross 1930 and Brandt 1979 for further discussion).

The conceptual separation of the economic and social dimensions is more problematic. Indeed, there is a vast literature exploring the relationship between the two from different viewpoints: the work of Marx and Marxian political economy; Veblen and the American institutionalists; Karl Polanyi (1944, 1977) and the school of economic anthropology; Max Weber's *Wirtschaft und Gesellschaft*, published in 1978 in English translation as *Economy and Society* (Weber 1978); and the work of Talcott Parsons and Neil Smelser (Parsons and Smelser 1956; Smelser 1963). In their commentaries on Weber and Parsons, Holton and Turner have reviewed many of the ideas in the above streams of thought (Holton and Turner 1986, 1989).

Here the economic dimension is taken to refer to those human activities and relationships involved in the allocation of scarce resources between competing uses, as per the earlier definition of economics; the social dimension relates to the rest of social life and culture, including the political domain. The next three papers explore some of the key interactions between the economic, social and ethical dimensions, the first focusing on the relative importance of individuals and the institutional frameworks within which they act; the second making explicit the practical implications of the moral dimension of economic life; and the third introducing the concept of socio-economic justice.

Rationality and the influence of institutions

Geoff Hodgson

Although orthodox economic theory has developed a great deal in recent decades, it has retained at least one enduring feature: the tastes and preferences of economic agents are normally taken as given. Just as orthodox economic theory has failed to address adequately the question of technological change, it tends to take the individual 'for granted' (Lukes 1973).

Of course, this basic approach is in line with the highly individualistic ideology of eighteenth- and nineteenth-century liberalism which still permeates economics and is reflected in the politics and economics of the modern New Right. In addition, however, it has philosophical roots in the Cartesian division of the world into two spheres of mind and matter, and the conceptual separation of the individual from his or her natural environment. Just as economists often ignore the environmental context of production and growth, the individual is taken as immanently conceived; he or she is delivered into the world with mind, tastes and so on, completely formed. Taking the individual for granted seems to deny the fact that individuals too are products of, and interact in and with, a natural and social world. A result of this inter-action is continuous change both within and without the individual.

It is proposed here that the Cartesian idea of the individual divorced from a social and natural environment has outlived its time. It should be replaced by a more complex and non-dualistic conception. One consequence of such a revised view is to qualify the idea of rationality which pervades orthodox economics. It should be recognized that there are multiple levels of decision-making and that the tastes and preferences of individuals are affected by the social and natural environment, including, in particular, the influence of social culture and institutions.

Fortunately, the basis for such a theoretical shift already exists. One of the most significant developments in modern economic theory has been the increasing attention to problems of information. Although the assumption of perfect knowledge is still widely adopted in the textbooks, among advanced theorists there is now a greater regard to situations of risk or uncertainty. It will be shown here that such considerations lead first to cognitive issues and thereby to the influence of culture and institutions upon the framing of decisions and the selection of information. Furthermore, informational con-siderations lead us to consider the role of habits and routines in both cognition itself and in dealing with the informational complexities of decision and action.

Informational issues in economics

Whilst orthodox economics is paying increasing attention to issues of informa-tion, the treatment of information is often open to criticism. Typically, in orthodox economic theory information is treated in a positivistic manner, flowing as an undifferentiated fluid from our senses to our brain. It is nevertheless essential to distinguish between sense-data, information and knowledge. Sense-data consists of the vast jumble of aural, visual or other signals that reach the brain. We have no other contact with the outside world and our fellow humans other than through this sense-data.

Whilst sense-data is necessary to provide us with information, it is by no means sufficient, and the two are not the same. To derive information it is necessary to impose a prior conceptual framwork on the jumble of neurological stimuli, involving implicit or explicit assumptions or theories which cannot themselves be derived from sense-data alone. In other words, there has to be a process of cognition of the sense-data, to select from and convert it into a form that is in some sense meaningful and has informational content for the agent.

There are further important distinctions to be made, such as between information itself and varieties of knowledge. For instance, information that may be 'understood' in one way can have a different significance in a different context, or when the theoretical or conceptual framework is changed. There is also the vital question of 'tacit knowledge', such as that relating to acquired skills, which cannot be readily codified in the form of information that can be passed on to others (Polanyi 1957, 1967).

These cognitive and epistemological considerations are familiar to many psychologists, philosophers and social scientists. But their profound implications are not always taken on board. Consideration of them is especially important for economics, because whilst it has begun to address problems of information and knowledge with some seriousness in recent years, discussion of the cognitive and epistemological questions is still relatively underdeveloped and is confined to a small number of theorists.

Cognition, culture and institutions

In part, the contemporary interest by economists in problems of information and knowledge is the result of the persuasive endeavours of the Austrian School. While correctly bringing these issues to the fore, and with a critical effect on much of conventional theory, Austrian theorists such as Friedrich Hayek have insisted on the subjective character of knowledge and expectations, and used such arguments to support ultra-individualistic policy conclusions.

However, whilst this line of argument moves initially in the right direction, it takes an unacceptably subjectivist turn. It can be accepted that information and knowledge have important subjective and individual features, but the concepts and theories that are used in their acquisition are not – and cannot be – purely subjective, as if they resulted from an isolated individual. Concepts and theories are always created in a social context. Given that no information or knowledge is concept- or theory-free, none is purely subjective in its essence.

Consequently, cognitive theory does not lead to the exclusion of the social dimension but to its reinforcement. Whilst living and acting in the world we are continuously in receipt of a vast amount of sense-data. The attribution of meaning to this apparently chaotic mass of data requires the use of acquired concepts, symbols, rules and signs. We cannot hope to create a conceptual framework capable of handling this on our own. We have to rely on inter-action with others to develop our cognitive skills, to form judgements about the world and to acquire guidelines for action. Perception is an act of categorization, and in general such categories are learnt. For instance, our education and socialization in early years helps us to develop our innate perceptual equipment and form a conceptual basis to understand and act in a complex and changing world. Furthermore, for cognition we rely on a language and linguistic structure which is socially formed.

Cognition thus has cultural specificity. The acquired conceptual framework reflects the culture, the social norms and rules which we have assimilated (Douglas 1987; Lloyd 1972). Just as our knowledge of the world does not spring out alive from the sensory data as it reaches the brain, only through the acquisition of a complex and culturally specific conceptual framework can sense-data be understood.

In sum, cognitive processes are social in the sense that they involve the use of social language and concepts, and that they reflect ideas and practices which relate to a social culture. We are all individuals, and the totality of our knowledge and experience is unique, but the mechanisms of our perception and acquisition of knowledge are unavoidably social and unavoidably reflect social culture and practices. For this reason the stress on matters of informa-tion and knowledge should not lead to a subjectivist outlook, but directly to the study of the cognitive and practical functions of institutions.

As an example, consider how economic agents learn from experience and attempt to reduce their mistakes. This, of course, has become a highly fashion-able topic for both mainstream and avant-garde economic theory. Contrary to some of the crude theoretical presentations of this process (e.g. in the rational expectations hypothesis), learning is not simply the acquisition of raw information as it is signalled by economic indicators in the real world. Any such data has to be interpreted before agents can learn. The interpretative framework, and indeed the individual's 'model' of the economy that may be used to evaluate the data and make estimates of the future, is not 'learnt' from the sense-data alone. Thus any model of the learning process is inadequate if it takes agents as responding in a straightforward, automatic and uniform manner to given economic indicators, as if no differing or concept-specific individual process of cognition were involved. In short, once questions of information and knowledge are brought to the fore, consideration of the cognitive processes is unavoidable. Whilst cognitive theory complicates matters to a great degree, it is still possible to make general statements about economic life. This is partly because of the close relationship between social culture and institutions, on the one hand, and cognitive activity and cognitive development, on the other. As a consequence, institutions and culture bestow a degree of stability, regularity and predictability upon economic behaviour, even if unforeseen events and surprises remain possible.

Unconscious processes

More detailed considerations of the processes of learning and action have further fundamental consequences. Just as 'information' is not like an undifferentiated fluid entering the brain, the processes relating cerebral activity and action are varied and complex, and do not all occur at one level.

This may seem to be a fairly obvious point but it has deep implications which are rarely taken on board. Even those economists who place great emphasis on the processes of learning in the theory of economic activity most often assume high standards of rationality and high levels of computational ability for the individual. It is assumed that the large quantity of complex sense-data received by the individual can be processed in such a manner that no significant parts are ignored, and they all play a role in the calculations of purpose or preference by the agent.

In part it is a habitual response by mainstream economic theorists, who, having been taught that a key feature of economic life is that all commodities are scarce, deem information to be generally scarce as well. Accepting that crucial information is usually scarce, the problem is, however, more complex. In general, sense-data is not in shortage but in over-abundance. The brain faces the difficulty not only of ignorance in regard to some pertinent facts, but also of dealing with an overwhelming wealth of other signals which are being received all the time.

Rational choice theorists continue to claim that each level of consciousness and action can be explained by a single, overall, 'rational' mechanism. Habits, for example, are regarded as repeated acts that are pefectly 'rational', given the lack of information in the hands of the actor that could lead to a change of behaviour. Thus Anthony Downs (1957) suggests that habitual voting for one party, despite some ignorance of its policies, is 'rational' because of the difficulty and 'cost' to the citizen of obtaining the appropriate information to reconsider or adjust voting behaviour. Similarly, Gary Becker claims that there are stable underlying preferences that encompass not only simultaneous action at all levels but also what appear to be 'changing' preferences through time (Becker 1976).

However, what is common to all these responses is the lack of an explicit differentiation between degrees of consciousness in the decision-making model, and an assumption that there is an underlying, or long-run, stable preference function that governs behaviour overall. True to the Cartesian paradigm, there is a Chinese Wall between the realm of mind and decision, on the one hand, and the material world, on the other. In reality, however, there are a number of levels of consciousness and decision, from full, deliberative reason to autonomic (but sometimes controllable) acts.

In fact a diversity of levels and forms of calculation and cognition, and an associated hierarchical structure, are necessary for the mind to function adequately in a complex world. A fundamental argument against the idea of a single, underlying preference function is that the computational limitations of the human mind make full conscious deliberation at all levels of decision-making impossible.

The limitations of rationality

It is highly implausible to assume, like orthodox theorists, that all action is equally rational, at all levels of consciousness and intentionality. Yet it is precisely the assumption of global rationality and maximizing behaviour that causes orthodox economists to fail to distinguish between different types of act or decision. In orthodox economics all action is at the same level of conscious-ness – the level of a utility-maximizing machine.

The argument here against global rationality is very close to that of Herbert Simon and his emphasis on 'bounded rationality' (Simon 1957). The fundamental idea here is that the mind has limited computational capacity. Even if all the information was available, such as in a game of chess or with Rubic's Cube, it is difficult or impossible to draw out all the logical implica-tions and derive an optimal solution. Simon's so-called 'behaviouralist' position is much superior in this regard to that of orthodoxy.

However, there is no clear and sustained differentiation of substance in behaviouralist works between conscious and unconscious processes. Further-more, Hubert and Stuart Dreyfus have argued that Simon's research programme has underestimated the intuitive aspects of human decision-making (Dreyfus 1986). Whilst there is a strong and necessary emphasis on the existence of imperfect information and bounded rationality in behaviour-alism, there can be insufficient recognition that information does not enter raw into the decision-maker's mind. The perceptive, cognitive and conceptual processes are sometimes downgraded or ignored.

As I have argued elsewhere (Hodgson 1988), cognitive and cerebral processes are best regarded as a complex and multi-tiered system. Actions themselves take place in regard to different levels of thought. Thus, as a simple case, there is a distinction between actions which are the result of extensive deliberation and computation by the agent, and those, on the other hand, which are habitual or even reflexive. Cognitive and other cerebral processes are so complex that they are not simply 'bounded' or limited, they also have to take place on different levels. Consequently, we cannot be comprehensively rational or deliberative even concerning the data which can, in some sense, be handled by the brain.

Of course, it was Freud who popularized the concept of the unconscious. But we do not have to tie ourselves to all the details of the Freudian theoretical framework to retain this notion. The fundamental idea of there being processes at work in the human mind that are not fully conscious or deliberative has a following that is much wider than those of strictly Freudian persuasion.

One reason why economists have failed to embrace this twentieth-century innovation in psychology is not difficult to find. Freud and the Post-Freudians suggest that our actions are not all determined by rational calculation or conscious deliberation. To put it bluntly, this flies in the face of the widespread assumption in economics that we are masters and mistresses of our fate. If we are not sovereign over all our mental processes and actions then how can such an idea as 'consumer sovereignty' over the economy be entertained? How can an agreed contract between two agents be regarded as a fair expression of their needs if it results in part from motives or drives that are not fully conscious? The central idea of the inviolability of individual judgement is placed under threat. Post-Freudian theory undermines some of the main nineteenth-century liberal assumptions with which orthodox economics is often so keen to associate.

Yet the world of advertising has a different view of consumer behaviour which is all too well known. The appeal is not predominantly to reason but to the subtle symbolic significance or 'image' of the product. Sex, glamour, anxiety, escapism and envy are used to full effect. The analysis of advertising and purchasing has become fertile ground for the Freudian psychologist, the semiologist, the anthropologist and the sociologist of culture. But mainstream economics, with its obsession with rational choice, has very little to offer. Instead, it prefers to believe in an unreal world that conforms to classic liberal theory.

The argument for conceiving the mind and consciousness as multiple-levelled and hierarchical is compelling. The argument about whether 'economic man' is entirely rational or non-rational is a false dichotomy. Human agents are both rational and sub-rational at the same time.

At higher levels of consciousness and deliberation we do make a limited number of rational calculations upon which we base plans for future action. But it is a 'common mistake', as John Searle points out, 'to suppose that all intentional actions are the result of some sort of deliberation, that they are a product of a chain of practical reasoning' (Searle 1984: 65). For example, deliberation is not always present in the act of everyday conversation. 'In such cases, there is indeed an intention, but it is not an intention formed prior to the performance of the action' (ibid.). Searle calls this 'intention in action' (ibid.).

The concept of 'intention in action' is at a level similar or slightly higher than 'practical consciousness' as defined and used extensively by Anthony Giddens: 'Practical consciousness consists of all the things which actors know tacitly about how to "go on" in the contexts of social life without being able to give them direct discursive expression' (Giddens 1984: xxiii).

Furthermore, with flashes of intuition and insight we may sometimes exhibit what could be described as super-rationality. As well as calculative rationality, there is intuition 'above' and practical consciousness 'below'.

Arguably, human decision-making relies on all these levels and types of reason.

Importance of habits and routines

Somewhere below intentions in action lie habits. These are themselves of different kinds. There is the habitual twitch or nervous response. Other habits cover acts that are complex and were formerly planned, such as the daily habit of driving to work that becomes so deep rooted that we switch, as it were, to 'autopilot' and think consciously of other things, arriving at our destination being unable to remember any incident on the journey. Below habits could be classified a variety of reflexes, and automatic actions such as breathing.

In emphasizing habits we are making a link with other writers such as Giddens (1984), Nelson and Winter (1982), Oakeshott (1962), Polanyi (1957, 1967) and Veblen (1919), who have emphasized the function of the habitual, and only partially deliberative, actions in retaining knowledge and skills and promulgating them through society. 'Practical knowledge' and 'practical consciousness' are embedded in economic life. Through structured action in a social context they function as a kind of transmission belt for much of society's productive expertise and technique.

One of the functions of habits is to deal with the complexity of everyday life. They provide us with a means of retaining a pattern of behaviour without engaging in global rational calculations involving vast amounts of complex information. The processes of action become organized in a hierarchical manner, facilitating monitoring at different levels and rates, and with different degrees of response to incoming information.

We should expect hostility to this idea of the nature and role of habits from both positivists and classic liberals. Positivism fails to find empirical support for the very idea of consciousness; whereas classical liberals eschew the idea that the individual is not fully purposive in his or her actions. In a place where positivism and classic liberalism meet, in orthodox economic theory, we find a doubled hostility and a categorical rejection of the concept of habit as it is understood in daily life. Indeed, some twentieth-century theoretical developments have led to the unwarranted eclipse of the notion of habit in social science (Camic 1986).

We acquire habits in various ways. Sometimes it is through the imitation of others. This does not always result from full, conscious choice, as all animal species are born with some capacity to imitate. The development of the intellectual and practical skills of young children is based largely on imitation, and we retain this faculty in later life, often without conscious thought about what we are doing.

In other cases habits may result from open, conscious choice. Thus after consciously choosing to purchase a car, the result may be its habitual use, normally without much deliberation or comparison of the marginal costs of alternative means of transport. We may initially use the car because we see it as more comfortable, and choose it on that basis, but on later occasions any such rational deliberation does not take place. We simply 'get into the habit' of using the one rather than the other, even if conscious deliberation was crucial at the start.

Whatever their origin, repeated acts tend to congeal into habits, and become removed from the sphere of rational deliberation in the mind. This should not necessarily be regarded as some kind of mental defect. As suggested above, habits, like some other forms of non-deliberative thinking, can have an important positive function. In fact, the capacity to form habits is indispensable for the acquisition of all sorts of practical and intellectual skills. At first, whilst learning a technique, we must concentrate on every detail of what we are doing. It takes us a great deal of time and effort to learn a new language, or to play a musical instrument, or to type, or to become familiar with a new academic discipline. Eventually, however, intellectual and practical habits emerge, and this is the very point at which we regard ourselves as having acquired the skill. When analytical or practical rules are applied without full, conscious reasoning or deliberation then the technique can be said to have been mastered.

On the negative side, however, mechanical habits can remove important actions from the due exercise of deliberation and creative skill. This limitation is likely to be more serious with the more complex, higher-level activities. Any effective organism, and indeed any successful social organization, must contain the right mix of habitual and routinized behaviour, on the one hand, and capacity to change and develop, on the other.

Precisely because many actions are not fully flexible and deliberative, and are habitual in the context of a given structure, it is important to examine social institutions to see how habits and routines are formed. The study of institutions offers a means of examining the basis of routinized action from the viewpoint of the system as a whole.

A social institution can be defined in the broad sense of a social organization which, through the operation of tradition, custom or legal constraint, tends to create durable and routinized patterns of behaviour. It is this very durability and routinization, in a highly complex and sometimes volatile world, which makes social science with any practical applicability possible at all.

The durability of institutions, and the value of institutional analysis in economics, can be assessed in regard to empirical work which demonstrates that institutional factors can explain much of the productivity growth of the major OECD countries (Hodgson 1989, 1991c). To some extent, this line of enquiry has been explored by theorists such as Mancur Olson (1982) who are closer to orthodoxy. Other theorists, particularly Nelson and Winter (1982), have begun to develop a formal framework for incorporating habits and routines, in which their role is regarded as roughly analogous to the gene in biology, thus providing a basis for evolutionary rather than equilibrium modelling in economic theory. Evolutionary ideas have also become particularly important in the treatment of technological change (Dosi *et al.* 1988). It should be pointed out, however, that modern evolutionary models in economics, unlike those of Herbert Spencer and the Social Darwinists, do not generally support the *laissez faire* conclusion that given evolutionary outcomes are the best of all possible worlds (Hodgson 1991a, 1991b).

Conclusions

To conclude, there are many philosophical and practical reasons why the utility-maximizing models of the globally rational individual in orthodox economic theory should be abandoned. First, such models propose a given individual, with autonomous preferences and beliefs, formed apart from the social and natural world: a 'globule of desire', to use Veblen's famous phrase. This dualistic approach, dividing individuals from their social and natural environment, is incompatible with philosophical realism (Bhaskar 1975, 1979), which sees the person as inseparable from a social and natural environment, which is both a precondition for, and in part an outcome of, human action.

Second, modern economic theory is beginning to recognize that if information is to be taken seriously then severe limitations must be placed upon the concept of rationality. We may go further by suggesting that the problem is not simply with the idea of global rationality but with rationality itself, that is with the idea that all actions are subject to reason and deliberation in regard to pertinent and available information. We are drawn to a hierarchical model of the human mind in which habits as well as more deliberate actions play an important role.

Third, the treatment of information itself is also worthy of theoretical scrutiny. All sense-data has to be interpreted in some way, and if the individual is not to be taken as given then his or her cognitive framework must itself be explained. Work by social anthropologists suggests that culture and institutions are crucial in the cognitive processes through which sense-data is perceived and made meaningful by the agent.

Finally, the key ideas of habits, routines and social institutions provide a basis for an alternative type of economic theory, utilizing an evolutionary analogy (Hodgson 1992). Such a theory does not only provide a more dynamic and non-equilibrating type of analysis, but it reminds us more directly of the links between the human and the natural world.

The I & We paradigm

Amitai Etzioni

In this paper I summarize some of the key themes from my recent book *The Moral Dimension* (Etzioni 1988). The themes are, of course, developed much further in the book than here and illustrated by a wealth of empirical evidence. The essential message of the book is that the old neoclassical paradigm is not so much being replaced as encompassed by a new paradigm, one that draws on many critical works and partial alternatives of the past decades. As with most paradigms, the new I & We paradigm is not born in maturity, but its basic structure is apparent. The new paradigm arises from the old one on three axes: the assumptions about the goals people pursue, the ways they pursue them (the means-selection) and the characterization of the acting unit – is it a solitary person or a person embedded in a community?

Selection of goals: the deontological position

The neoclassical paradigm assumes that people have one overarching goal: the satisfying of their wants. Historically, these wants were depicted as materialistic; more recently, satisfaction derived from other sources has been added, such as the pleasure gained from helping the poor, but the core concept remains self-centred and hedonistic and Me-istic: people are propelled by *their* wants, *their* self-interest, *their* profits. Research in this tradition further assumes that a person's various 'tastes' can be neatly ordered into one unitary pattern of desire, with a common denominator to 'trade-off' various items (apples for oranges, etc.), a notion at the heart of economics. In contrast, my finding is that people have several wants, including the commitment to live up to their moral values, and that these wants cannot be neatly ordered or regulated by prices. This finding provides a starting point that is fundamentally different from that of the neoclassical premises. From this different starting point we can launch a fresh study to understand individual behaviour, economic and otherwise, to study society and the economy within it.

The I & We paradigm assumes a divided self, which *does* have the hedonistic urges assumed by the neoclassical paradigm (albeit those too are affected by the values of the society in which the person lives). However, far from mindlessly pursuing these desires, the person is viewed as a judging self which examines its urges and evaluates them by various criteria, the most important of which are moral/social values. (Aesthetics is another source of criteria.) A struggle ensues: under some conditions urges win out; in others, morals triumph.

There are many ways of classifying ethical positions. That explored in *The Moral Dimension* is moderately deontological, where a deontological position is the notion that actions are morally right when they conform to a relevant principle or duty. Deontology stresses that the moral status of an act should not be judged by its consequences, the way utilitarians do, but by the intention. Moderate deontologists take consequences into account but as a secondary consideration.

The significance of incorporating this moral dimension into the concept of human nature is that it is perhaps the most important feature that separates us from animals. Our moral commitments and our urges do not often pull us in the same direction. Much of human life is explainable as a struggle between the two forces, and a study of the conditions under which one or the other prevails. Much evidence to this effect can be found in *The Moral Dimension* and need not be repeated here (Etzioni 1988: 52–63); however, even a modicum of introspection provides first-hand evidence of this significant, perpetual inner conflict. Those who never experience such conflict are either born saints – or utterly debased.

Selection of means: values and emotions

Having resolved the conflict and decided upon a goal, how does a person go about selecting a course, the means to the goal? Neoclassicists say, *rationally*, that is by using empirical evidence and logical inference. Hodgson in the previous paper has discussed some of the problems with this approach, but it is also contradicted by the observation that most choices are influenced heavily by normative/affective (N/A) factors, that is by people's values and emotions. These factors shape to a significant extent the information that is gathered, the ways it is processed, the inferences that are drawn, the options that are considered and the options that are finally chosen.

Entire categories of means, whether 'efficient' or not, are judged to be unacceptable and *automatically* ruled out of consideration. Thus, most reasonably competent daughters and sons of the American middle class consider it unthinkable not to attend college. About a third of those entitled to collect welfare refuse to apply, because 'it's not right'. Furthermore, emotions (e.g. impulse) cut short deliberation (when it does occur). While emotions and values have often been depicted as 'distorting rationality', which they can do, they also agitate against using means that may be efficient in the narrow sense but are indecent or hurtful to others or the community. Furthermore, Pieters and Van Raaij show that N/A factors can often play a positive role in decision-making, especially by mobilizing or inhibiting action or generating or communicating information (Pieters and Van Raaij 1987). In short, the moral order deeply affects not merely what we seek to accomplish but also the way we proceed.

The individual in community

The neoclassical paradigm draws on and contributes to the Whiggish tradition of investing all moral rights in the individual; the legitimate decision-maker is assumed to be the individual. All attempts to modify the person's tastes are viewed as inappropriate interventions (hence the term 'consumer sovereignty'). Moreover, the government is usually blamed for attempts to redirect individuals, and such redirections are treated as intrinsically coercive. In contemporary terms, the neoclassical paradigm is essentially libertarian.

A recent philosophical trend, the communitarian movement, attempts to correct this radical individualism. Communitarianism builds on the observation that individuals and communities are mutually dependent, and that certain 'public goods', not just the individual, are fundamentally of merit – for example, defence, basic research, public education. Some extreme communitarians entirely neglect individual rights in the name of societal virtues, the motherland or some other such cause. A much more defensible position may be found in recognizing that both individual rights *and* duties to the community have the same basic moral standing, hence, the I & We paradigm. It follows, for example, that we need to both recognize the individual *right* to a trial by a jury of peers, and the individual's *obligation* to serve on a jury; to be defended, and to pay for defence; to benefit from the savings of past generations, and to save for future ones.

The voice of the community is typically moral, educational, persuasive, that of peers and leaders. If coercion is relied upon, this indicates that the community has been weakened, with too many members engaged in activities previously considered unthinkable. The more effective policy is not to enhance the government but to rebuild the social and moral community. This shift starts with a change of paradigms, from the neoclassical to a new approach that encompasses rather than ignores the concept of community, one that balances (*not* replaces) individualistic tendencies with concern for community, and one that reaches beyond the realm of material incentives and sanctions to the role of values, particularly shared values, as long as they are *freely endorsed and not imposed*.

Empirical work on the role of community has shown unequivocally that social collectivities are major decision-making units, often providing the context within which the individual decisions are made. Moreover, in many areas collectivities, if properly structured, can both render more rational decisions than their individual members (though not necessarily highly rational ones) and account for more of the variance in individual decision-making than do individual attributes (see Etzioni 1988: 186–98 for discussion and references).

Another crucial function of community is to contain the conflict and limit the scope of market competition. This social context is not merely a source of constraints on the market but a precondition for its ability to function. Three types of elements encapsulate and sustain market competition in this way:

- Normative factors, such as a commitment to fairness in competition and trust that this commitment will be shared by others.

- Social bonds, reflecting the fact that competition thrives not in impersonal calculative systems of independent actors unbound by social relations, as implied by the neoclassical paradigm, not in the socially tight world of communal societies, but in the middle range where social bonds are strong enough to sustain natural trust and low transaction costs, but not so strong as to suppress exchange orientations.

- Governmental mechanisms as the arbiter of conflicts, where normative factors and social bonds have proved insufficient constraints, and the enforcer of judgements. These crucial governmental roles illustrate the need to move beyond the conceptual opposition between 'free competition' and 'government intervention', which implies that all interventions are by a government, that all interventions are injurious and that unshackled competition can be sustainable.

The essential capsule of competition is thus best considered an intertwined set of normative, social and governmental mechanisms which each have a distinct role but also can, within limits, substitute for one another.

Implications of the I & We paradigm

Once the foundations of the I & We paradigm are in place numerous implications follow. I provide here a few examples, derived from the fuller list in *The Moral Dimension* (Etzioni 1988: 237–51). Many of the implications have yet to be worked out.

1. *Research implications*: It is productive, for explanatory and predictive purposes, to take into account *both* hedonistic urges and moral commitments, when studying human behaviour. For instance, to understand the level of compliance with tax laws we need to know how high the tax rates are (a neoclassical factor) and the extent to which people consider the tax system unfair. To understand why people conserve energy, we need to know both of changes in oil prices, and if people believe that conservation helps their country and the environment, and so on.

2. *Policy implications*: How might the I & We paradigm lead to developing public policy? Take the widely agreed upon observation that Americans save too little. Economists recommend various public policies to enhance savings and reduce consumption. One policy in the United States is to curtail Federal expenditures (a major source of consumption), another is a tax on consumption. Both policies have a cost. The first may cause a recession, which exacts huge human and economic costs. We have had four induced recessions since 1970. The second policy is regressive; it beats up on the poor. That these policies have costs does not mean that they are necessarily undesirable but it points to the merit of at least also drawing on other measures. A fuller policy would emphasize being in debt as socially undesirable behaviour, one that undermines our collective well-being and threatens our future – this was the way debt was perceived until the 1950s. The President, community leaders and educators would all play a role in changing the community's perspective.

3. *Education and public implications*: More is at stake than criticism of a paradigm of science; there are educational effects on the youth and on the public. Neoclassicists teach each year millions of high school and college students a paradigm that, as economist Robert Solow puts it, 'underplays the significance of ethical judgements both in its approach to policy and [in] its account of individual and organizational behaviour' (Solow 1981: 40).

Neoclassical textbooks are replete with statements such as 'the rational thing to do is to try to gain as much value as I can while giving up as little value as I can' (Dyke 1981: 29). They discuss the Bible and dope as two interchangeable consumer goods (Kamerschen and Valentine 1981: 82), and view children as 'durable consumer goods' (Becker 1976: 169). One wonders about the effect on the attitude of potential parents toward children, if they are taught systematically to think of their offspring as a trade-off to other 'goods', such as cars?

As Brennan and Buchanan wrote, 'the economist's way of thinking . . . involves, in many cases . . . a sort of cultivated hard-nosed crassness towards anything that smacks of "higher things of life" ' (Brennan and Buchanan 1982: 6). This orientation is illustrated by studies that suggest duelling is an efficient way of settling disputes, question whether the costs of preventing hijacking are worth the expenditures, and 'show' that it is more efficient to buy and sell babies on an open market than it is to regulate adoption, with its attendant black market (Wermeil 1984: 64).

A study of the educational effects of neoclassical teachings shows that students become more self-oriented, just as they may become more rational in their decisions. Such effects are evident in a series of free-ride experiments conducted by Gerald Marwell and Ruth Ames (1981). In eleven out of twelve experimental runs most participants did not free-ride and contributed from 40 per cent to 60 per cent of their resources to the 'group pot'. However, a group of economics graduate students contributed only an average of 20 per cent.

Beyond the effects on students are those on the general public. Here, too, the prevailing neoclassical approach to moral values tends to debase them. All societies set aside certain areas as 'sacred'. To make the public think about these sacred areas in cost–benefit terms 'secularizes' them, strips them of their moral standing and ultimately causes them to be treated as neoclassicists say they are. For example, to create a market for rights (e.g. selling permits to pollute) undermines taboos against certain behaviours; it normalizes them, hence makes them less costly and more common.

All this points to the fact that more is needed than the documentation of the role of moral values and community. We need also to include these factors in our teaching and public philosophies. In so doing, we are not opening the door to the imposition of a unitary set of values but strengthening those individuals who are committed to moral values and to developing public policies that are caring and decent.

Socio-economic justice[†]

John Oliver Wilson

Economists have traditionally equated justice with distributional issues. The primary problem is one of distributive justice, in particular a question of the ideal or desirable distribution of income and wealth. As Musgrave has stated:

> The distribution of income and wealth in a market economy depends on a number of factors including the laws of inheritance, the distribution of innate talents, the availability of educational opportunities, social mobility, and the structure of markets. As a result of these factors, a state of distribution, with a given degree of equality or inequality, comes about. This state will seem appropriate to some, while others will prefer a greater, and still others a lesser, degree of equality.
>
> (Musgrave 1959: 17)

When it comes to defining what is a desirable degree of equality in the distribution of income and wealth, or an acceptable degree of inequality, economic theory is woefully inadequate. The issue is viewed as a trade-off between efficiency and equality; a problem of determining the appropriate distribution of income and wealth through the political system and then allowing the economic system to achieve maximum efficiency in the production and distribution of commodities. Given the limitations of the traditional economic understanding of justice, we must turn to the literature of philosophers and others who have dealt with this issue in far more depth. We begin with the meaning of commutative justice, then examine productive or social justice, and conclude with distributive justice.

The concept of commutative justice was first asserted by Aristotle. The philosophical basis for commutative justice is rooted in the fundamental moral prohibition against harm, and in economic exchange harm is avoided when there is equivalence of exchange. Therefore, the issue of commutative justice is to determine the meaning of equivalence of exchange (Gunnemann 1986). It was this problem that Aristotle attempted to answer in discussing the relationship of a 'just price' and 'value in exchange' for a commodity that is exchanged in an economic market. In raising these issues, Aristotle set the stage for all future philosophic and economic thinking on the matter of commutative justice.

Thomas Aquinas identified fraud as a sin that arises in the course of voluntary transactions, and quoted Cicero that 'contracts are to be free of lies' (Aquinas 1975: 215). Adam Smith argued that a competitive market will determine a fair market price for all exchanges, but implicit in such a market is a world 'of shared meanings and mutual knowledgeability' (quoted in Gunnemann 1986: 103). It is a world that involves trust and credibility. In

---

[†] This essay forms a section of a much larger study of human values and economic behaviour (Wilson 1989: 25–32).

one of the more current statements on the issue, the National Conference on Catholic Bishops states that commutative justice 'calls for fundamental fairness in all agreements and exchanges between individuals or private social groups. It demands respect for the equal human dignity of all persons in economic transactions, contracts, or promises' (NCCB 1986: 35–6).

Productive justice relates to the fairness of participation by individuals in the economic system. It considers the impact of the methods of production on 'the fulfilment of basic needs, employment levels, patterns of discrimination, environmental quality, and sense of community'. Furthermore, productive justice includes 'a duty to organize economic and social institutions so that people can contribute to society in ways that respect their freedom and the dignity of their labor' (ibid.: 37).

The roots of the concept of productive justice can be traced back to Aristotle, although it was Thomas Aquinas who is credited with formulating the basis for the modern understanding of productive justice. This basis is rooted in the acceptance of the essentially social nature of human beings. Justice 'can be neither specified nor understood apart from the web of social interdependence which entails mutual obligation and duty' (Hollenbach 1977: 210).

Roman Catholic theologians have built upon the base of Aquinas and his legal justice, and expanded that base during the past century into a well-developed concept of social or productive justice that has the following major characteristics. First, the philosophical basis of productive justice is the view that the individual is essentially a social being. It is through our interaction with other individuals in society that we actualize our true being. Second, labour defined in the broadest sense of productive participation in an economic system is the most important means that we have of realizing productive justice. Third, productive justice is determined in the institutionalized process of integrating the individual into the economic system. As a socio-economic process of integration, productive justice differs significantly from commutative justice and distributive justice which are primarily concerned with the nature of individual economic relationships.

When most people think of justice, they are referring to distributive justice. In the most general terms distributive justice concerns the issue of allocating the benefits of a society or an economic system among all the members of that economic system. But how to define those benefits and how to determine a just criterion for allocation are highly debatable issues. A survey of the vast literature on distributive justice suggests that there are four primary criteria that contend with each other in these regards: (1) to each according to merit; (2) to each according to rank; (3) to each according to essential needs; and (4) to each the same (Perelman 1963: 1–29).

To each according to his or her merit is generally interpreted to mean work or labour effort. Therefore, distributive justice is achieved when the benefits of an economic system accrue to individuals in proportion to their own efforts. If one individual works longer and harder than another individual, then that individual should receive a greater portion of the benefits available in an economic system.

Implicit in this understanding of distributive justice are the requirements of just wages and prices, and a system of exchange that is fair along with equality of opportunity. Given these conditions, then one could argue as does Nozick that whatever arises from a just situation (an equal distribution of basic entitlements) by just steps (equality of opportunity, just wages and prices, and a fair system of exchange) is just (Nozick 1974).

To each according to his or her rank requires that the members of a society or economic system be divided into different classes, and that the members of each class be treated according to some notion of equality while those in different classes may not be accorded equal treatment. Rank-ordered justice has a long tradition, and is most frequently associated with a view of society that rank has its privileges up to such a point that this creates stability and certainty in the nature of things. Rank may be viewed as the best means of achieving equity in the treatment of individuals within an institutional setting, such as the case where rank-ordered justice is applied to the principle of seniority in employment. For example, many American corporations and government institutions practice the principle of 'last hired–first fired', particularly those where labour unions are strong. This is clearly a case of rank-ordered justice.

To each according to his or her essential needs requires that an economic system determine a certain level of basic human needs that must be satisfied, either through direct participation in the economic system (productive justice) or through a redistribution of resources sufficient to satisfy those needs (distributive justice). Traditionally, essential needs are defined in terms of certain basic requirements to sustain life and enable the individual to live at some minimal standard of living. That standard could be expressed in terms of income or certain levels of food consumption, housing standards, and legal, daycare and other family support services. Clearly, the difficulty with this approach is how to define essential needs.

To each the same thing is the final concept of distributive justice. When the same thing is defined in terms of income, and assuming that every individual has an identical and known marginal utility function of income, then this concept requires equality in the distribution of income. Such an extreme position has never been achieved by any economic system, but there are less absolute versions that fall into this general concept of distributive justice.

In conclusion, we can consider socio-economic justice as consisting of three different concepts: commutative justice, productive justice and distributive justice. Associated with each of these concepts are specific outputs as shown in Figure 2.1. Thus, socio-economic justice is defined by a matrix (J) of relevant outputs $(y_1, \ldots, y_9)$. A particular economic system can be characterized by those outputs which are dominant in that society.

For instance, Economic System I might integrate the following outputs into its legal system and institutional structure: $J_I = (y_1, y_2, y_3, y_6)$. Such an

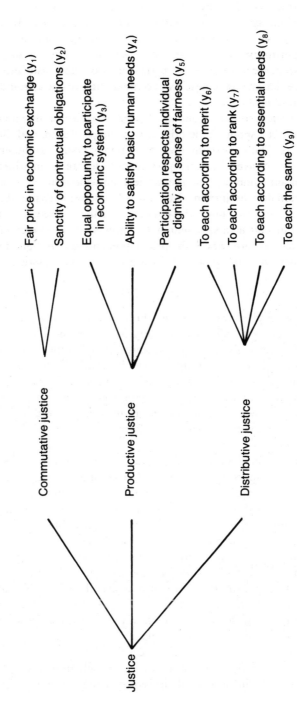

Fair price in economic exchange (y_1)

Sanctity of contractual obligations (y_2)

Commutative justice

Equal opportunity to participate in economic system (y_3)

Ability to satisfy basic human needs (y_4)

Participation respects individual dignity and sense of fairness (y_5)

Productive justice

To each according to merit (y_6)

To each according to rank (y_7)

To each according to essential needs (y_8)

To each the same (y_9)

Distributive justice

Justice

Figure 2.1 Socio-economic justice and associated outputs

economic system would reward all individuals on the basis of merit, while ensuring that all individuals have an equal opportunity to participate in the economic system. Alternatively, Economic System II might integrate a different set of outputs: $J_{II} = (y_1, y_2, y_4, y_5, y_7)$. This economic system would attempt to maintain equality in access to socio-economic practices through rank-ordered justice, while structuring its public and private institutions to ensure that the basic needs and sense of dignity and fairness of each individual are satisfied.

Whether or not Economic System I is better or worse than Economic System II cannot be determined by simply comparing the two matrices of outputs. There is no universal definition of justice, and therefore the issue can only be resolved by introspection and debate as to which best reflects the dominant morality of the society in question. For instance, with an individualist, utilitarian view, this will involve analysing the impact of a given system of justice upon the happiness of the individual. An alternative view might involve an assessment of the fairness or equity with which all individuals are able to share in both the production and distribution of the total social and economic benefits generated by a given economic system.

The general thrust of these three papers is clear and is in substantial agreement with all the main approaches in the economy/society literature listed at the beginning of this chapter. It is that the operation of the economy, and the behaviour of its agents, cannot validly be considered except as part of a wider social reality. It simply is not tenable to restrict the focus to individual agents and interpret their economic activity as if it proceeds autonomously from their own impulses which are in turn powered by asocial, immanently formed individual preferences formulated at a single, 'rational' level of consciousness.

Parsons and Smelser express a far more realistic view, in line with this chapter's papers, of the economy/society interaction: 'The whole society is in one sense part of the economy, in that all of its units, individual and collective *participate* in the economy. Thus households, universities, hospitals, units of government, churches etc. are *in* the economy. But *no* concrete unit is "purely economic" ' (Parsons and Smelser 1956: 14).

If no concrete unit is purely economic, then any purely economic analysis is a simplification of reality, an abstraction, which must be justified *a priori* according to the criteria for realist analysis laid down by Lawson in Chapter 1 – that the abstraction is of the real and essential. Conversely, in focusing on some essential elements it should not distort the analysis by ignoring others.

Perhaps there are some human situations so dominated by the issue of competing uses for scarce resources that 'pure economic' analysis is justified, although intuition suggests that it is precisely in such situations that the social and moral dimensions of decision-making become most pressing. But in general the economic, social and ethical are inextricably intertwined, and an economics that seeks to remain 'pure' is of very limited use. Parsons and Smelser believed that 'We have been able to place economic theory within the general theory of social systems with considerable accuracy' (ibid.: 308). However successful their attempt, it is clearly desirable on theoretical grounds that economics be related to and informed by the other social sciences. It is also a practical prerequisite if economics is to be relevant to real-life.

The economy is not only, to quote Parsons and Smelser again, 'a functional sub-system of the more inclusive society' (ibid.: 306), it is also a functional sub-system of a more inclusive ecology. If this chapter has been concerned to ensure that economics gives due weight to relationships between people, it is the people–nature relation that is the subject of the next.

3   Economy and ecology

Before describing in theoretical terms the economy/ecology interaction, it is worth emphasizing the current context of discussion of this issue. The sorry fact is that despite twenty years having passed since the Stockholm Conference on the Environment and despite the Brundtland Commission's explicit warning that human activity was disrupting ecological life-support systems to the extent of approaching 'thresholds of human survival' (WCED 1987: 33), policy-makers have not even begun to address the issue in its full gravity. Some 25 per cent of the world's people, those in the industrialized countries, are responsible for 80 per cent of its annual resource use and a similar proportion of its emissions and toxic wastes. Their systems of production and consumption, combined with the environmental impacts of poverty in non-industrialized countries, have resulted in a variety of patently unsustainable and threatening effects, including global warming, depletion of the stratospheric ozone layer, acid rain, deforestation, soil erosion and desertification, species extinction, water depletion and toxic pollution.

The consequences of these effects are still massively uncertain, but scientific opinion is now generally agreed that they will entail enormous costs and potentially catastrophic irreversibilities. Meanwhile, the principal aspiration of the other 75 per cent of the world's people is to emulate the life-styles and therefore the resource use and pollution generation of the rich 25 per cent. Eastern Europe and the republics of the former Soviet Union plead for aid and co-operation to finance their reindustrialization. India and China, with 40 per cent of the world's population, are similarly geared to huge industrial expansion.

Faced with such a situation, one of the few hopeful developments has been a greatly increased understanding both of the economy/ecology interaction and of the necessary conditions for a development process that is not environmentally destructive, now widely called 'sustainable development'. These are the topics of the next two papers. Their measured, reasonable tone should not be allowed to obscure the enormity of the challenge with which they deal, which has to date barely started to be addressed. The third paper builds on Hodgson's earlier reference to 'an evolutionary analogy' and places many of the ideas of this and the previous chapter in a dynamic context through the concept of coevolution.

The economic functions of the environment

Roefie Hueting

Externalities

The growing severity of the problem of environmental deterioration, including depletion of resources, has caused a great increase in interest in the concept of external effect. This concept was introduced amongst others by Marshall (1969: 221ff.), Pigou (1962: 131–5, 183–96) and Scitovsky (1954: 143ff.) at a time when the environmental issue did not play a major role. Mishan (1971) reviews the more recent and extensive literature on external effects. According to Hennipman, in modern welfare theory the term 'external effect' is generally defined as 'the positive or negative influence operating outside the market which, as a side-effect of economic actions, is exerted on the conditions of production or the level of satisfaction of other households' (Hennipman 1968: 250). These side-effects are considered to be 'unintended or unintentional'.

From the descriptions and the examples given it appears that externalities cover a much wider field than the impacts on the environment by human activities. They also include a whole range of other effects such as the interdependence of consumer satisfaction, for example envy when others have more goods to consume; productivity-increasing inventions becoming available without charge to producers; advantages and disadvantages accruing to a producer as a result of activities of other producers, for example economic obsolescence of machines, the availability of well-trained labour, supplies of raw and auxiliary materials and of specialized semi-finished products at lower prices.

On the other hand, according to the definitions given in economic literature, the concept of external effect or external economies and diseconomies does not cover all impacts on the environment. Thus the description of an external effect as an influence operating outside the market implies that this effect can occur only if a market does in fact exist. These are evidently effects on 'outsiders' who do not belong to the parties constituting the market, the buyers and sellers of goods and services. Since government services are not performed by way of the market mechanism, no external effect can occur here. Moreover the government is assumed to take into account the interest of all citizens when making its decisions. This implies that all parties are represented in a government decision. Consequently there can be no question of influence on 'other households' which remain outside the considerations in the decision, as in the case of decisions made by individual firms or citizens, and nothing is external. Naturally the government is also supposed to express in its decisions both the wants of the citizens and its own preferences for a livable environment for generations to come. Particularly for this reason, which is of more fundamental importance than the absence of a market, there can be no questions of influence on 'outsiders' for whom no allowance is made in the decisions. However, effects on the environment can almost certainly be caused by the government.

Thus, when a road is built through a nature area or a sewer is laid to discharge into a river, sea or estuary, important effects on the environment are caused, however accurately the government has weighed the various interests. Moreover, in such a case it does not matter whether others than the users of the road or the sewer suffer the damage through the effect. Even if every citizen makes equal use of the road or sewer, a number of functions of the environment are nevertheless lost wholly or partially for the same citizens.

In a somewhat different form the same thing occurs with goods and services produced by the market: the government decides about circumstances in which goods and services are produced and consumed, and whether or not effects on the environment are internalized in the price of the products whose production and consumption burden the environment. In the final instance the statutory framework determines the degree of burdening of our environment. The conflict between the quantity of goods and services produced and the quality of the environment is therefore not confined to the 'market economy' but continues to apply fully if production is collectivized partially or even wholly. The heart of the conflict lies in the finite carrying capacity of the environment.

The environment defined as a collection of scarce goods

On account of the reasons mentioned above, among other things, the present author has introduced the concept of 'function' (Hueting 1980, 1970). The reasoning is briefly as follows. For an economic approach the environment can best be defined as humanity's physical surroundings, on which people depend for all their activities, such as producing, consuming, leisure, breathing, travelling. In everything people do, they use their environment in one way or the other. Consequently, as a first step towards systematization, possible uses of the environmental components water, air and soil are distinguished. These possible uses are called 'environmental functions' or, in short, 'functions'.

As a result of more activities being undertaken by more and more people, the possible uses of the environment are increasingly falling short of meeting the existing demands. This situation is manifested when the use of an environmental function by a given activity is at the expense of the use of another (or the same) function by another activity, or threatens to do so in the future. We call this competition between functions.

When competition of functions occurs, the environment acquires an economic aspect. Economics boils down to the problem of choice with regard to the use of scarce alternatively applicable means for the satisfaction of classifiable wants. A good is scarce if the demand for it exceeds its availability, or, which amounts to the same, when something else we would like to have (an alternative) has to be sacrificed to acquire it. Environmental functions meet this definition fully as soon as they compete. Competing functions are scarce goods. Losses of function form costs, irrespective of whether or not they are expressed in monetary terms. Economics deals with the problem of choice among scarce goods; the terms 'money' and 'market' do not occur in the definition of its subject matter. From this it follows that when no such competition occurs, functions are free goods, without an economic aspect: they can then be used without sacrifice.

A distinction is made between three kinds of competition of functions: spatial, quantitative and qualitative. When spatial and quantitative competition of function occurs, the amount of space and the amount of matter respectively are deficient in respect of the existing or future needs for them. This kind of competition is absolute. Withdrawal of matter or attachment of space on behalf of a certain function excludes the use of other functions. Thus in cities there is not enough space for walking *and* private cars *and* cycling *and* public transport *and* children playing. Outside the cities competition prevails in the use of space for roads, suburbanization, recreation, farming and the survival of plant and animal species. An example of quantitative competition is the insufficiency of the amount of ground water for the growing requirements of industrial water, water for agriculture and water for domestic use. The same holds true for many other resources; their amount falls short in respect of existing demand, or threatens to do so in the future.

In qualitative competition the function 'dumping ground for waste' (or 'addition or withdrawal of species and matter') of the environmental components water, air or soil is in competition with other possible uses, such as 'water as a raw material for the drinking water supply', 'air for physiological functioning', 'water or soil allowing the existence of natural ecosystems' (plant and animal species of the aquatic and terrestrial ecosystems). An agent is introduced into or withdrawn from the environment by an activity as a result of which the quality of an environmental component changes; this may disturb other use or render it impossible. An agent is defined as a constituent or amount of energy (in any form whatever) which may cause loss of function by its addition or by its withdrawal from the environment by people. Agents could be chemical substances, physical phenomena (e.g. heating, noise, radiation) and the addition or withdrawal of plants or animals.

Tracing the competition between functions exposes the conflicts. This can be done with the aid of matrices, for elaboration of which see Hueting (1980).

With the concept of environmental function the environment acquires a central place in economics, as the basis of man's existence, and environmental losses are no longer considered as externalities or unintentional side effects of economic activities. Losses of function are often deliberately allowed for in decisions, notably decisions by the government, the only body that can influence the degree of availability of competing functions. When competition occurs between environmental functions, the functions are always used at each other's expense. In this process it is not possible, in analogy with external effects, to distinguish between 'main functions' and 'secondary functions'. Such a distinction would be pointless, because it cannot be established *a priori* which use is the most important one, economically speaking.

The concepts of function and loss of function are on the one hand connected with the matter of the environment and on the other are determined by the demand for the function, which makes possible measurement in physical units (see below). Thus the function 'drinking water' is coupled to the matter of the water and its quality and also to the need for drinking; the quality of the water is determined by biological processes. In this way the link between ecology and economics is made.

Competition between functions may occur in all kinds of forms. But in by far the majority of cases one can speak of the use of the environment by current and consuming activities which is at the expense of other desired uses or (with a certain degree of probability) of future possible uses. Roughly speaking, we have now reached a situation in which the use of an environmental function is always at the expense of one or more other functions (now or in the future). Of course our environment is material, as are the things that we produce and consume with the aid of it, whether these are wheat, music (vibrations of the air), medical aid, or books. In this situation the subject matter of economics can be described as the study of the problems of choice that occur when arranging the dead and living matter of our surroundings in accordance with people's wishes. Such a definition does justice to the fact that the environment is the basis of our existence, the foundation of our production and consumption and, in view of the competition of functions, finite.

The problem of shadow prices of environmental functions

On account of the obvious conflict between use of the environment for stepping up production and conservation of the environment for other use and for the future, calculations of shadow prices for environmental functions that are directly comparable with the market prices of goods and services would be most welcome. However, only in a few cases can such shadow prices be calculated. To find them, supply and demand curves have to be constructed.

The supply curve can, in principle, always be constructed. It consists of estimates of the costs of measures for various degrees of eliminating the causes of the loss of function, as a result of which the function is partly or wholly restored. The measures will often be a mix of technical provisions, such as add-on technology (treatment plants and the like) and changes in process, and reducing or halting the burdening activities (which also can be expressed in monetary terms). The supply curve is called an elimination cost curve.

Constructing a demand curve is much more difficult. The reason for this is that only in exceptional cases can the intensity of the individual preferences for environmental functions be entirely expressed in market behaviour or other behaviour that can be translated into market terms (money). Loss of function can sometimes partly be compensated by provisions which act as a substitute for the original function. In some other cases it causes financial damage. When, for instance, water is polluted by chemicals, compensation of the function 'drinking water' or 'water for agriculture' is possible to a certain degree and during a certain period by purifying the intake of the polluted ground or surface water. In the long run, however, elimination of the pollution is necessary, because of the cumulative effect. An example of financial damage is the damage by floods to crops and properties resulting from loss of the function 'regulation of the water management' of a forest.

Both compensation and financial damage can be interpreted as revealed preferences for a given function. As regards compensation, this will be immediately clear: after all, provisions are made to replace the function originally present. However, amounts of damage can also be conceived as revealed preferences, since they are losses suffered as a result of the disappearance of the function. In practice one can often choose between accepting damage and taking compensatory measures. Thus in the case of corrosion of steel by air pollution there is a choice between accepting the additional damage from corrosion and better production of the material.

Opposite the costs of elimination we naturally have the benefits of restoration of the function. The decrease of compensation costs and financial damage constitute the part of the benefits resulting from restoration of the function by elimination measures which can be manifested via the market. As stated above, preferences can seldom be manifested entirely via the market. It is clear that only a very small proportion of the losses of environmental functions are compensated, while in addition they are not always reflected in financial damage. Often, too, the possibility of compensation does not exist. Thus double-glazing may reduce the nuisance of traffic noise inside the house, but not outside; it continues to be impossible to open windows in fine weather without being disturbed by noise. Stench is practically inescapable. A compensatory measure like moving to a clean area is feasible only for the happy few. Moreover it evokes new traffic streams causing new losses of function. Financial damage through noise nuisance and air pollution is very incompletely reflected in the fall in value of the house, as a result of the tightness of the housing market and the immobilization caused by ties to work and the neighbourhood (Jansen and Opschoor 1972). The construction of new forests and lakes is pointless as long as the process of acidification is not halted by elimination measures. The loss of soil by erosion cannot be compensated. Most important of all, much of the damage caused by losses of function will occur in the future, such as the damage caused by loss of the stability of the climate, by loss of the functions of tropical forests ('gene reserve', 'regulator of the water flow', 'preventer of erosion', 'supplier of wood', 'buffer for CO_2 and heat', 'regulator of the climate' and the like), and by the disruption of ecosystems resulting from the extinction of species. Calculating the net present value (NPV) of future damages, the current extent of which can be established via the market (e.g. damage by flooding resulting from loss of the function 'regulator of the water flow'), breaks down on the unsolvable problem of the level of the discount rate in environmental costs and benefits (Hueting 1991). Also, the risks of future damage and the resulting poor prospects for the future cannot manifest themselves via the market of today. Yet there is obviously a great need for unvitiated nature and a safe future.

Because of the limited possibilities for preferences for environmental functions to be manifested in market behaviour, efforts have been made to trace these preferences by asking people how much they would be prepared to pay to wholly or partially restore functions and to conserve them. Quite a lot of research is going on in the field of willingness to pay for the environment and willingness to accept environmental losses (Johansson 1987; Kneese 1984; Pearce *et al.* 1989). It is questionable, however, whether this method can provide reliable figures for a number of reasons (argued in detail in Hueting 1989). Five of the most important reasons are, in brief:

1. Information on the significance of environmental functions is deficient in many cases. This is especially true for the functions which determine the future quality of the environment. With respect to these (life-support) functions it is often a question of the risks of interrupting complicated processes versus the chances that technologies, that have not yet been invented, may cope with those risks. Many people may not be able to weigh these risks and chances. In all cases in which individuals are not aware of the importance of an environmental function, the questioning method is pointless. These cases constitute the most important part of the environmental problem.

2. In many cases the only sustainable solution is a shift towards environmentally non-burdening activities. This mostly saves rather than costs money. Thus cycling is cheaper than driving. People who realize this may refuse to answer because the question is not relevant.

3. A number of people will probably have their doubts about the participation of others (the Prisoner's Dilemma from game theory) or prefer to wait and see (the Free Rider Principle from the theory of collective goods). Thus in developing countries, where the tropical forests are, the view is widespread, for a number of good reasons, that people from the rich countries should pay for their conservation.

4. In cases where the whole community is involved, the willingness-to-accept approach is pointless. For who is paying whom to accept the loss?

5. There is a considerable difference between saying that one is willing to spend money on something and actually paying for it.

The willingness to pay (or to accept) approaches might be justified insofar as people are directly affected by environmental losses. Many such losses, however, constitute part of a process which may lead to the disruption of the life-support functions of our planet and endanger the living conditions of generations to come, and therefore cannot be considered separately. In all these cases the approach is pointless.

A practical solution: shadow prices based on standards for sustainable use of functions

Environmental functions are connected with specific human wants: environmental components (water, air, soil) derive their functions from the possibilities to meet these wants. The functions are also coupled to the specific demands made on the matter of the environment for the fulfilment of the function. Consequently the availability of the function and the occurrence of losses of function can be established objectively. For instance, the degree of availability of a function such as drinking water can be established by measuring the concentrations of matters which determine the fulfilment of this function. This opens up the possibility of providing information in physical units on behalf of economic choices regarding the use of the environment, even when information in monetary terms cannot be given. The data in physical units constitute economic information because they can be used for choices among scarce goods.

However, as the choice is mostly between the use of functions for the production and consumption of goods and other possible uses, the need for information in monetary terms remains urgent. Therefore the present author has made the obvious proposal to base the shadow prices on the sustainable use of the functions (Hueting 1986b, 1989).

With regard to the concept of sustainability points of application can be found in ecological literature. Thus Odum states that through human activities a development is increasingly taking place which results in mature, stable ecosystems being replaced by more recent, less stable stages (Odum 1971). As fewer stable stages remain, restoration of impaired systems becomes increasingly difficult and of ever-longer duration, and the number of potential and actual possible uses falls steadily. An irreversible situation can come into being when harm is done on a large scale to predators, substantial numbers of species are lost or general biological activity is suppressed. This is a disruption of food chains that may lead *inter alia* to disruption of the life-support functions of our Earth. The process of the decline and disappearance of species can be seen as an indicator of the extent to which we are already on the way to disruption of the life-support functions. The chance of severe disruption can be minimized if human activities, through the use of recycling processes, (again) become part of the biological cycle, whereby the height of the level of activities is limited by the condition that the degree of stability of this cycle does not decrease. A sustainable activity pattern will amount to recycling of natural resources, changing to non-polluting sources of flow energy and a use of land that leaves sufficient room for natural ecosystems to function.

In any case the emission to the environment of accumulating chemicals, such as heavy metals, PCBs, CFCs, CO_2, nitrates and phosphates, is incompatible with sustainability. Depletion of non-renewable resources is not sustainable and has to be compensated by developing renewable substitutes, and bringing them into practice. One discussion of such compensation is El Serafy (1989). As for erosion, only an erosion rate equal to the natural rate of increment of the top soil is sustainable.

For over ten years politicians and all kinds of organizations all over the world have been expressing their preference for a sustainable use of the environment. Especially since the publication of the Brundtland Report sustainable use of the economic functions of the environment is generally

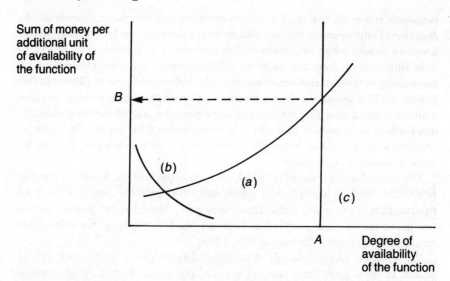

Sum of money per
additional unit
of availability of
the function

The degree of availability is measured as the value of one or more parameters, such as the concentration of harmful substances or oxygen in water on the degree of erosion or fragmentation of the countryside. About a unit of availability one can only say that the costs of its acquisition change along with the parameter, generally progressively.

Key:

(a) Supply curve of the function, or elimination cost curve.

(b) Demand curve of the function based on individual preferences derived from market behaviour such as compensation costs. As these preferences can manifest themselves only very partially in market behaviour, the intersection of curve (a) and curve (b) does mostly not reflect the shadow price of the function.

(c) Demand curve of the function based on preferences for a sustainable use of the function, voiced by society.

A   Standard for sustainable use of the function.

B   Shadow price of the function based on the standard for its sustainable use.

Figure 3.1.   Supply and demand curves for environmental functions

accepted as one of the main goals of the development of world society (WCED 1987). Therefore standards for sustainable use of functions can be conceived as preferences for the degree of availability of the economic functions of the environment, voiced by society. In 1990 the demand curve for functions founded on individual preferences, which mostly remains unknown because of the impossibility of knowing these preferences, can be replaced by a demand curve based on preferences voiced by society. Because demand by society is defined as being completely inelastic (namely, as a standard) this curve is a perpendicular straight line. This 'degenerate' demand curve can be viewed as the limit of curves which become more and more perpendicular as the demand becomes more and more inelastic.

In conclusion the above can be illustrated with the aid of Figure 3.1 (given more completely and with a mathematical derivation in Hueting 1980: 118ff.).

This whole approach is developed further, for the purpose of correcting the national income statistics, in the present author's contribution to Chapter 5 of this book.

Economics, equity and sustainable development[†]

David Pearce

'Sustainable development' and 'sustainability' were the fashionable catch-words of the 1980s, which have provided a large and sometimes nebulous literature. The focus is on sustainable agriculture, sustainable industry, sustainable economic development (e.g. see Carr 1988; Conway and Barbier 1990; Glaeser 1988; WCED 1987) and sustainable societies. At its simplest sustainability means making things last, making them permanent and durable. What is being sustained can be an object of choice – an economy, a culture, an ethnic grouping, an industry, an ecosystem or sets of ecosystems – but sustainable *development* implies that the object of concern is the whole process of economic progress in which economies contribute to improvements in human welfare, however defined. For how long it is being sustained is an open question – few would dispute horizons of concern of a hundred years, many would be indifferent to a thousand years. How sustainability comes about is the subject matter of most of the debate, but one theme is constant to all the discussions: sustainability means sustaining and augmenting natural environmental systems, or is a condition for sustaining economic development.

This common environmental theme is suggestive of an economic interpretation of sustainable development. *Sustainability requires at least a constant stock of natural capital, construed as the set of all environmental assets.*

Once it is interpreted in this way, sustainable development turns out to serve goals which would command wide, though not universal, assent. Sustainable development (hereafter 'SD') is then consistent with:

- justice in respect of the socially disadvantaged;
- justice to future generations;
- justice to nature; and
- aversion to risk arising from:
    our ignorance about the nature of the interactions between environment, economy and society; and

[†] This paper was first published in *Futures: the Journal of Forecasting and Planning* 20/6 (Dec. 1988). Reproduced by permission of Butterworth & Co. (Publishers) Ltd.

the social and economic damage arising from low margins of resilience to external 'shock'.

The rest of this article explores the idea of SD as requiring constant natural capital stock, which could be interpreted in several ways: constancy of the *physical* stock; constancy of the *economic value* of that stock; or constancy of the *'price'* of the stock. They are not the same: constant values are consistent with the price of an environmental asset going up and the quality going down, or *vice versa*. Constant physical stocks pose formidable problems of finding homogeneous units for measurement. Economic measuring rods – values and prices – involve imputing prices to environmental assets which are not marketed. Lastly there is the issue of whether it should be the constancy of the total stock or the stock per capita. Clearly, the per capita concept is the relevant one, which raises the spectre that rapid population growth could easily destroy sustainability prospects. These issues are not explored here.

The natural capital stock

The idea that man-made capital – machinery, infrastructure, factories, technology – is a critical ingredient in economic progress is familiar to everyone. Economists formalize this by saying that capital is contained in the *production function* which links inputs – capital, labour, technology – to the output of goods and services. More generally, human welfare is in part a function of economic output, and therefore of the inputs.

Natural environments can be thought of as a stock of natural assets serving economic functions. These assets act as:

- a supply of natural resource inputs to the economic production process – soil quality, forest and other biomass, water, genetic diversity, and so on;
- a means of assimilating waste products and residuals from the economic process – oceans and rivers as waste-receiving media, and so on;
- a source of direct human welfare through aesthetic and spiritual appreciation of nature; and
- a set of life support systems – biogeochemical cycles and general ecosystem functioning.

Both man-made capital (K_M) and natural capital (K_N) contribute to human welfare. The former operates mainly through the economic process, but can directly affect human welfare through built structures and heritage. The latter operates through the economic process and directly. Figure 3.2 illustrates this.

Sustainability and constant capital stock

The idea that human welfare flows from the stock of capital, widely construed, rather than the flow of services from it (income or throughput), owes its origins to Kenneth Boulding (1966). But Boulding's conception embraced all capital including the stock of knowledge and 'spiritual capital'. Modern SD literature tends to focus on the maintenance or enhancement of natural capital, K_N. Constancy of natural capital, or, more strictly, the non-negativity of the rate of change in natural capital, relates probabilistically to sustainability because it is not inconceivable that societies can endure and progress with a declining K_N. We can say only that it is more likely that declining K_N will be correlated with reductions in sustainability. Moreover, as we shall see, the correlation is likely to be stronger for some societies than for others, and is perhaps highest in the poorest, resource-dependent societies and lowest in the richest K_M-intensive societies. At the global level, however, reductions in K_N mean probable economic impairment for all societies. Global warming, ozone layer depletion and ocean pollution are all examples of natural capital reductions that reduce global welfare. In the economist's language they are 'global bads'.

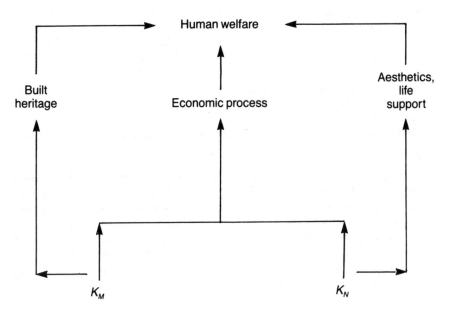

Figure 3.2 Capital and the economic process

Why, then, is a constant or increasing natural capital stock likely to be associated with sustainability? If sustainability is equated with *durability* then there is a basic reason for linking constant K_N to sustainability; namely, that K_N increases the *resilience* of the economy to major shocks such as climatic change, war and pestilence, and to 'cumulative shock' in which economies are destabilized by chronic processes. But the sustainability literature tends to treat SD more normatively by implying that a sustainable economy serves the interests of *justice*. The three types of justice involved are:

- justice to people within a generation: 'intragenerational' justice;
- justice to people between generations: 'intergenerational' justice; and
- justice to non-human sentient beings: 'justice to nature'.

Lastly, the SD literature tends to imply that improvements in human welfare are also served by a sustainable development path. The three goals that are therefore allegedly served by SD are:

- equity (within and between generations, and to nature);
- survival (durability as resilience); and
- welfare improvement (raising average standards of welfare).

The resulting classification is similar to that proposed by Conway and Barbier (1990). Moreover, these objectives may only be complementary up to a point. That is, there may have to be trade-offs between them. Thus we have no particular reason to associate egalitarianism with durability as a fact of history, nor egalitarianism with efficiency (welfare improvement). None the less, the idea that there are complementarities between basic social objectives on a sustainable developmental path is fundamental to the SD literature, as stressed in WCED (1987). I return to this point shortly.

How, then, does a constant or increasing K_N serve these goals? That is, why should the pursuit of environmental quality be especially relevant to sustainability? I look at each of the linkages in turn.

Natural capital and the poor: intragenerational equity

The basic role for stressing the role of K_N in serving the interests of intragenerational equity is that the poor are often more affected by environmental damage than the rich. This assertion runs directly counter to most of the conventional wisdom whereby the environment is assumed to be the concern only of the rich – 'environmental élitism'. There are two contexts in which the environment – poor linkage can be investigated.

The clearer context is that of developing countries where direct dependence on the natural resource base is conspicuous. An example is fuelwood dependence. In many African countries, in Haiti or in Nepal, the ratio of fuelwood use to total energy use is of the order of 90 per cent. Many households are totally dependent on fuelwood and charcoal for energy. Other biomass such as agricultural residues and animal waste is of additional importance. It follows that environmental quality is not a luxury but a basic necessity for these nations.

The case against environmental élitism is more complex for the developed world where direct dependence on natural resources is less obvious. In a survey of the available literature, I found that the physical incidence of pollution was higher the poorer the community at risk (Pearce 1980). The way the valuation of that incidence relates to income is less certain, but the evidence does not favour the widespread view that the rich are willing to pay more for environmental quality in general (see Baumol and Oates 1988, for the conventional view).

Natural capital and future people: intergenerational equity

John Rawls's (1972) theory of justice has been invoked as the moral basis for arguing that the next generation should have access to at least the same resource base as the previous generation (Page 1977). Rawls's 'maximin' strategy suggests that justice is to be equated with a bias in resource allocations to the least advantaged in society. Such a rule would emerge from a constitution devised by people brought together with a 'veil of ignorance' about their exact position in society. Risk aversion dictates that the constitution makers would avoid disadvantaging specific groups for fear that they themselves would be allocated to those groups. The intergenerational variant of the Rawls outcome simply extends the veil of ignorance to an intertemporal context in which each generation is ignorant of the time which it will be allocated.

Interpreted in this way, there would appear to be no particular reason to focus on K_N as the instrument for achieving intergenerational equity. It might apply more to K_M, or to some composite of K_N and K_M. How might the emphasis on K_N be justified? One might argue that K_N is somehow 'basic'. In Rawls's terms, it might be a candidate for a 'primary good' – a good with the characteristic that any rational being would always prefer more of it to less. The life support functions of natural environments seem to fit this category since less of them would remove the capability of choosing and preferring. If the ability to make a choice is given higher status than the act of choosing, then there is another argument that favours emphasis on K_N. This is that K_M is always readily changed up or down, but K_N is subject to *irreversibilities*, in that reductions in it can result in extinction. Extinction removes the capability to choose.

These 'primary' and 'irreversibility' characteristics suggest that K_N and K_M are substitutes only up to a point. This is evident in Figure 3.2. K_N supplies some functions not supplied by K_M. I develop the point further below.

Natural capital and non-human rights

The rights of sentient non-human beings figure prominently in the SD literature. Indeed, it is significant that the first publication to elevate sustainability to the status of a social goal was the World Conservation Strategy (IUCN and WWF 1980). The link to K_N is simple – the greater stock of natural capital the greater the habitat occupiable by wildlife is likely to be and the more consistent it is likely to be with genetic diversity. The exact relationship, however, could be complicated. For example, the physical biomass of the standing tree stock could grow and diversity become less if the trees are monocultural. Such complications are reflected in the continuing debate about forest plantations.

Natural capital and survival

Both K_M and K_N permit resilience to the impairment of the economic system by external or cumulative shock. At its starkest, the more K_N there is in a poor developing country, the more likely it is that resources can be mobilized to withstand drought and pests. K_M might permit resilience as well, but the SD literature stresses that sustained resilience requires the adoption of technologies suited to ecological conditions in the relevant area. Draught animals may be better than tractors in this respect. Organic fertilizer secures soil enrichment and 'body' whereas artificial fertilizers secure only nutrient increase and risk run-off problems for water supplies. K_N may therefore be preferred on resilience grounds. In the poorest societies solutions involving K_M are frequently not feasible on cost and logistical grounds. Natural capital augmentation then becomes the only route to sustainability. This much underlies the current emphasis in development programmes on agroforestry, simple water-harvesting techniques, afforestation and socially relevant technology.

How far the same presciption holds true for the developed world is more difficult to determine. In many African countries margins of resilience are low, with even comparatively minor perturbations causing major distress. By contrast, margins of resilience in the developed world appear high. But the effects of chronic, cumulative environmental degradation can have serious impacts in terms of reducing resilience margins, as with issues of global and transboundary pollution. There is no need to offer doomladen predictions in this respect. Since the basic common features about such margins is uncertainty, and since errors imply irreversible consequences in at least some cases, a risk-averse strategy is to elevate K_N augmentation to a priority in the developed world.

Natural capital and economic efficiency

A superficial view of the comparative economic rates of return to expanding K_N and K_M suggests favouring the latter. If the two forms of capital necessarily trade off against each other, then the rate of return argument would imply an expansion of man-made capital at the expense of natural capital. But is such a trade-off necessary?

Figure 3.3 suggests a way of looking at what sustainability advocates are saying on this issue. The vertical axis shows K_M and the horizontal axis shows K_N. The trade-off view is characterized by the curve AB – we cannot have more environmental capital without less man-made capital, and *vice versa*. This has echoes of the 'growth versus the environment' debate of the 1970s. Some of the SD literature, however, argues that K_N and K_M are *complements*. This idea is shown by line 0CD. Which is correct? One suspects that both extremes are false. A possible compromise is to argue that complementarity characterizes economies in the early stages of development, and trade-offs characterize later stages. An ecological economic history then has the challenge of explaining how the complementarity/sustainability switch takes place.

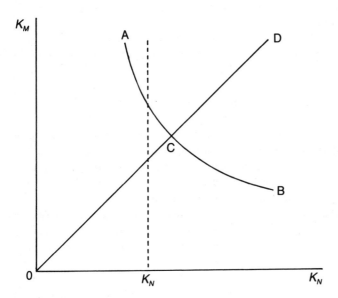

Figure 3.3 Capital complementarity and sustainability

Notice in Figure 3.3 that the existence of a trade-off does not entail a prescription about a development path, C to A rather than C to B, for example. A movement from 0 to C might then typify an arid zone in need of grazing land rehabilitation and soil and water conservation. A move from C to A might be more relevant to an industrialized nation choosing between land development and habitat conservation. Figure 3.3 offers no guidance on choosing the development path – it does not say what ought to happen. For that some form of social evaluation is required. Even here, however, more insight can be obtained from the SD debate.

It is clear, for example, that past development has been wrongly biased in favour of K_M for several reasons. K_M tends to be a marketed product, but the inputs from K_N are generally unpriced, there being few markets in environmental services. The presence of a zero price for K_N means that, relative to the positive prices of K_M, more of it will be used. It appears not to be scarce. At the same time, zero prices mean that there is no incentive to augment natural capital – there appear to be no real benefits. It is only in the last two decades that environmental economics has corrected this fundamental error of thinking.

Another reason for the K_M bias has been the failure to understand the pervasiveness of the benefits of augmenting K_N. Natural environments are multi-functional and hence the valuation process has to be preceded by a detailed analysis of the various functions. Efforts to do this on a case study basis have demonstrated that economic rates of return to investments in natural capital are directly comparable to the 'harder' investments such as factories and power stations. In the African context, an example of this is given in Anderson (1987).

Thus the economic efficiency argument does not automatically favour K_M. We need a more comprehensive valuation of environmental functions. Choice might be constrained by some 'boundary' in Figure 3.3. There might be some minimum stock below which no nation should go if it is to avoid a major disruption. This 'safe minimum standard' certainly has an empirical dimension in poor countries. A measure of carrying capacity indicates the maximum number of people that can exist, sustainably, at a certain level of per capita environmental impact, on the basis of existing or projected resources. It is a limit, not an optimum. The stock corresponding to the carrying capacity offers one definition of the safe minimum standard. Alternatively, an extra margin for uncertainty would make the safe minimum standard stock somewhat higher than that corresponding to carrying capacity. Carrying capacities are variable. Above all they can be increased by augmenting natural capital, or reduced by increasing per capita resource use or other environmental impacts.

Thus sustainable development is a catalytic concept. The definition advanced here suggests that sustainable development is based on constant or augmented natural capital stock. This approach appears to have directly derivable linkages to the social objectives of equity within and between generations, economic efficiency, and resilience. It appears also to be consistent with rights in nature. The challenge to advocates of SD lies in justifying the emphasis given to natural environments as a means, an instrument, of achieving SD.

Coevolution of economy, society and environment
Richard Norgaard

The western world-view

The dominant western view of the world as a machine was well developed before Darwin provided key ideas to evolutionary thinking. Early western scientists set out to know a static world as God had created it. Philosophers envisioned the acquisition of knowledge as a process whereby individual minds try to decipher nature. In this sense, people and the natural world were juxtaposed right from the beginning. The mind has been thought of as an independent entity that perceives and interprets. Like the mind, nature in the dominant world-view just exists. Mind and nature are independent of each other. Asking questions, thinking, and acting change neither the underlying principles which govern the external world nor the mind itself. The world just is and the mind perceives and interprets it. The emphasis in the modern world-view on the objectivity of knowledge stems from this static juxtaposition of mind and nature.

The modern world-view has several other important characteristics. First, the world is conceived of as consisting of many atomistic parts which can be known independently. Second, systems consist of mechanistic integrations of the parts whereby the influence on the system as a whole due to a change in a part can be formally modelled. The formal model must be tractable so that predictions and prescriptions can be derived. Newton was the first to make substantial breakthroughs toward this end, and was so admired that the dominant world-view can be described as having been Newtonian ever since. Third, knowledge is, or at least 'should' be, about universal phenomena. Knowledge is desirable because it is useful. Knowledge is more useful if it can be used anywhere. For this reason, universal truths are sought and given the most respect in the modern world-view. Fourth, truths which can be stated simply are more useful than truths which are complex and difficult to apply.

This modern, or Newtonian, world-view can be presented diagrammatically. Whereas the coevolutionary world-view has everything connected to everything else and evolving together over time, Figure 3.4 shows a ring. We observe nature, derive theories about universal characteristics of natural parts and relationships in nature, test theories against nature, design alternative technologies and social organization based on theories, select new technologies and social organization for implementation according to our values, and thereby modify nature. But we only modify the relative proportions and importance of nature's parts and relations; the universal nature of the parts and relations remains unchanged.

The nineteenth-century image of development was based on this western understanding of knowledge and action. Given the assumption that both natural and social systems consisted of unchanging parts and relations, development consisted of adjusting the relative numbers of the parts and the relative strengths of the relations. Action did not change the underlying nature of the systems. Since the nature of the parts and relations of systems were presumed not to change, knowledge could be presumed to be universal over time. Furthermore, differences in natural and social systems across regions could also be thought of as differences in the proportions of parts and strengths of relations. Thus the idea of underlying univeral truths could be maintained across diverse environments and cultures.

The barrier drawn between the changing proportions of the parts and strengths of the relations and the nature of the parts and relations is a key aspect of the Newtonian epistemological stance. No such barrier, of course, separates the reality from which we draw theories and design technologies from the reality we affect through our use of technologies. The existence of this barrier in our public understanding of science helps explain why development has been unsustainable. Action changes the nature of parts and relations, typically in an irreversible manner. The introduction of totally new parts – agrichemicals and industrial wastes into ecosystems, and televisions and fax machines into social systems – creates brand new relations. Basing action on science girded by false beliefs in universals, in unchanging parts and relations, continually results in 'unforeseen' changes in social and environmental systems. Thus the unsustainability of past development has an epistemological explanation.

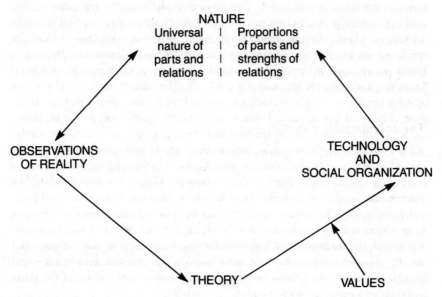

Figure 3.4   The dominant (or Newtonian) world-view

Neoclassical economics as used in capitalist countries and the analogous optimization techniques used in socialist countries epitomize the modern world-view. Early economists explicitly acknowledged their philosophical debt to Isaac Newton while the mathematizers of economics – Cournot, Jevons, Pareto and Walras – formalized economics along the mechanistic models of Newton. The neoclassical model is atomistic in the assumption that land, labour and capital are separate components. These components are like individual atoms. They are combined but not changed during the production of goods and services and are only related to each other through their relative values determined in exchange. Neoclassical economics is mechanistic in its assumption that economic systems can operate in equilibrium at any position along a continuum and move back and forth between positions. If more labour becomes available, the system adjusts so that more labour intensive goods are produced and are sold at lower prices relative to capital intensive goods, the returns to labour fall, and the returns to capital increase. If the quantity of labour returns to its previous level, the economy produces the previous mix of goods at the same prices and the earnings of labour and capital return to their previous levels. Atomistic-mechanistic models are characterized by a range of stable equilibria and the reversibility of system changes.

Thus economics incorporated atomism and mechanism, the two most productive assumptions of western natural science. The parts of the economy as well as the relations between the parts do not change their characteristics. The only thing that changes in the basic world-view is the relative numbers of different parts and the relative strengths of different relations. The imaginary barrier of Figure 3.4 is clearly in place. The economists' knowledge of the economic system can be used to change the relative numbers and strengths without changing the characteristics of the parts and relations themselves. Thus the theories of economics about the parts and relations still hold after using the theories to design interventions in the economy to make it behave more like we would like it to behave.

The coevolutionary challenge

As is now accepted in the natural sciences, our biosphere did not just come into being all put together and working like an intricate clock. It evolved over some three and a half billion years. People became a part of this global evolutionary process beginning about three million years ago. While this is a mere one tenth of one per cent of the earth's total history, it is sufficient in biological time for people to have influenced the evolution of the biosphere. Early people put selective pressure on the species they hunted and gathered. At the same time, hunting and gathering selected for effective hunters and gatherers, people who were more likely to survive and to support a larger number of offspring. Later people put selective pressure on the biosphere through the agricultural practices of deforesting and clearing land, weeding out some species and encouraging others, selecting the varieties that most consistently produced well, enriching soil and eventually irrigating. These transformations facilitated the evolution of species unable to survive without people. Agriculture, in turn, selected for different perceptive abilities and physical strengths among humans than had hunting and gathering. People and their environment have coevolved.

The process of coevolution was not limited to mutual genetic selection. People survive as members of groups. Group success depends on culture: the system of values, beliefs, artifacts, artforms and structures which sustain social organization and rationalize action. Cultural traits which fit the ecosystem survive and multiply; less fit ones eventually disappear. And thus they are selected much like genetic traits. At the same time, cultural traits influence how people interact with their ecosystem and apply selective pressure on species. Not only have people and their environment coevolved but also social systems and environmental systems have coevolved.

This coevolving of parts and relations can be portrayed at any level of complexity. Consider the coevolution of the ecological system, values, knowledge, social organization and technology as illustrated in Figure 3.5, an intertwining of the elements which is more or less symmetrical. No system dominates another, none provides a more obvious starting point for understanding the whole, and each can only be understood in the context of the others.

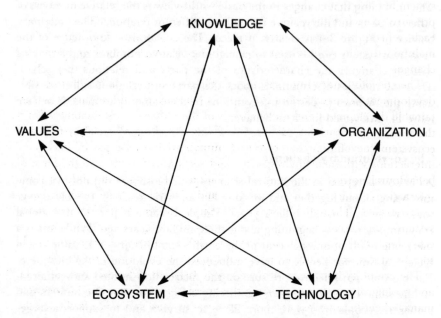

Figure 3.5   The coevolution of knowledge, values, social organization, technology and the ecosystem

The coevolutionary process was geographically patchy because of natural barriers such as mountains, deserts, rivers, and seas and because people lived in clusters. For these reasons, the world can be thought of as having been a patchwork quilt of loosely interconnected, coevolving social and ecological systems. Within each patch the ecological system evolved in response to cultural pressures and tended to reflect the values, world-view and social organization of local peoples. At the same time, the cultural system in each patch evolved in response to selection for fitness with respect to the ecosystem and hence tended to reflect the fertility, species composition, stability and management options presented by the ecosystem. The reflections of each system in the other also evolved. Through this process, each patch took on unique characteristics particular to the random biological and cultural mutations of the patch and the introductions from other patches which proved fit. What can be known about coevolved systems is particular rather than universal.

The emerging coevolutionary world-view is dynamic. Not only is each subsystem related to all the others but each is also changing and affecting the evolution of the others. Deliberate innovations, chance discoveries and random changes occur in each subsystem that affect the distribution and qualities of components and relations in the subsystem. Whether these new components and relations are maintained depends on whether they prove fit with respect not only to the other components and relations within the sub-system but also to the other subsystems. With each subsystem putting selective pressure on each of the other subsystems, they coevolve in a manner whereby each reflects the others. Thus the coupling illustrated in Figure 3.5 is maintained even while everything is changing for the coupling selects the change.

The coevolutionary interpretation of Figure 3.5 gives us insight into how development occurred before the use of hydrocarbons, the nature of unsus-tainable development and the challenge of the return to sustainability. Until the use of hydrocarbons, development was a process of social system and ecosystem coevolution that favoured human welfare. People initiated new interactions with their environment, and social institutions – in the form of behavioural norms, myths and organization – developed to reinforce those interactions which were favourable and discourage those which were unfavourable. Through the coevolutionary process of development social systems increasingly reflected characteristics of the human-influenced ecosystems they inhabited, while ecosystems reflected characteristics of the social systems which affected how individuals interacted with the ecosystems.

The era of hydrocarbons drove a wedge between the coevolution of social and ecological systems. Capturing the energy of the sun through ecosystem management became less and less important as western science facilitated the capture of fossil energy. Social systems evolved around the expanding means of exploiting hydrocarbons and only later adopted institutions to correct the damage this coevolution entailed for ecosystems. Hydrocarbons freed societies from immediate environmental constraints but not from ultimate environ-mental constraints – the limits of the hydrocarbons themselves and of the capacity of the atmosphere and oceans to absorb CO_2. Our value system, knowledge system, social organization and technologies coevolved to fit the opportunities which the exploitation of fossil energy provided. Our social systems reflect these medium-term opportunities rather than the long-run opportunities of coevolutionary development with the renewable resources of the global system. The policy challenge of sustainable development consists of finding a path towards a positive social and ecological coevolution.

Sustainability does not imply that everything stays the same. It implies that the overall level of diversity and overall productivity of components and relations in systems are maintained or enhanced. It implies that existing traits are deliberately maintained as options until after new ones have proven superior. Of course, it is not possible deliberately to monitor or manage every trait. The shift towards sustainable development entails adopting policies and strategies that sequentially reduce the likelihood that especially valuable traits will disappear prematurely. It also entails the fostering of diversity *per se*. This definition of sustainable development applies to belief systems, environmental systems, organizational systems and knowledge systems equally well. And necessarily so, for the sustainability of components and relations in each subsystem depend on the interactions between them.

From this broader perspective of sustainable development we see that development has been unsustainable, not simply because the use of hydrocarbons has been destroying the environment, but because there has been a cultural implosion. Value systems have been collapsing. Knowledge has been reduced to western understanding. Social organization and technologies have become increasingly the same around the world. The cultural implosion and environmental transformation have been closely interconnected. The switch to hydrocarbons allowed cultures to stop coevolving with their unique environments and adapt the values, knowledge, technologies and organization of the west.

Two examples can clarify the difference between the western and coevolutionary world-views. Imagine that economists accepted that economic systems evolve over time, that the national economies and global economy of the late twentieth century are fundamentally different from the economic systems of one hundred years ago when neoclassical economic theory began to crystallize. Assume that economists accepted that a limited number of multinational corporations in the late twentieth century producing and assembling the components of vehicles through a network of suppliers around the world with the backing of financial and management networks, behave differently from either the state trading monopolies of the dying colonial empires or the relatively many firms run by industrial barons in the late nineteenth century. Assume that economists accepted that the monetary systems and relations between government and private enterprise had evolved substantially. Furthermore, assume that economists accepted that many of the changes that had taken place in the economy were designed directly or stemmed indirectly from their very own way of thinking about economic systems. Economists would then have to concede that their theory needed to evolve as economies evolved and furthermore that their theory at any point in time influenced the evolution of economies. Economics would no longer emulate Newtonian mechanics.

American agriculture a century ago was dominated by small farmers producing multiple products in small plots using limited capital equipment, considerable family labour, and few purchased inputs such as fuels, fertilizers and pesticides. Farmland, buildings and equipment were largely owned by the farmers themselves and, to the extent they were not, credit was provided by a local bank. Some products were consumed great distances from the farm, but most were consumed within a hundred miles. Today American agriculture is dominated by large farmers producing one or two crops each in large plots using large implements, hired labour and considerable purchased inputs. Government lending programmes, banks and stock-holders now have a significant claim on the assets of farmers. Agricultural products are now consumed at great distances from the farm, and many farm enterprises are subject to the vagaries of world markets, government price support and credit programmes, and international lending policies. While these changes are typically attributed to new agricultural technologies, many are related to changes in incentives induced by agricultural policies designed by economists in the Economic Research Service of the US Department of Agriculture. Economic thinking has changed agriculture and nineteenth century economic models of agriculture have become obsolete. The barrier of Figure 3.4 does not exist in the long run.

The subdiscipline of environmental economics, in particular, is in an awkward position. Knowing the basic assumptions of the neoclassical model helps us understand why we have environmental problems when we pattern our economic policies around this approach to thinking. The model assumes that environmental systems are divisible and can be owned. It fails to acknowledge linkages within environmental systems that cannot be matched with a market feedback. It assumes that both the economic system and the environmental system can operate along a continuum of equilibrium positions and move freely back and forth between these positions. Reminding ourselves of these basic premises leads to the following insight. Markets fail to allocate environmental services efficiently and consequently environments are not managed properly because environmental systems are not divisible, because environmental systems rarely reach equilibrium positions and because changes are frequently irreversible. One can readily deduce that the use of economic theory to design economic systems, or at least the use of economic theory to justify economic design, over the past century has contributed to environmental destruction. Nevertheless, many environmental economists have ignored this feedback as if the barrier of Figure 3.4 were in place. Furthermore, the policy response of these environmental economists to the environmental problems generated by patterning our economic organization in the past after the neoclassical model is that we should try harder. Environmental systems, according to economic logic, should be brought under the influence of Adam Smith's 'invisible hand' by dividing the indivisible and assigning the unownable ever more finely. To the extent this approach is working, it is through the destruction of the more highly inter-connected portions of ecosystems, a process of breaking nature down into the parts that survive the process to fit the neoclassical model (Norgaard 1985).

Thus one of the important points emphasized by the coevolutionary paradigm is that it is extremely important for us to realize that we are inside the causal loop of Figure 3.4. While physics and chemistry progressed initially by assuming unchanging parts and universal relations, the environmental systems as a whole cannot be successfully treated as if the barrier of Figure 3.4 exists. The coevolutionary framework presents a way of illustrating this while emphasizing the interrelatedness of values, knowledge, social organization, technology and ecosystems. How we understand natural and social systems affects how we act on these systems, the evolution of these systems and consequently what is important to know in the future. The modern world-view and its incorporation in neoclassical economics has prevented us from observing, understanding and acting upon problems which would be understood better using frameworks which acknowledge we are inside the system we are trying to understand and change (Norgaard 1988).

Values are an important part of everything that is inside the system. Contrary to the modern view, values cannot be separated out and then called upon at distinct times as needed. The coevolutionary view emphasizes how knowledge, social organization, technology and even the environment have long coevolved with human values. In this sense, values are embedded in everything with which we work. Problems cannot be broken down into the objective, scientific parts and the subjective, value parts. 'Problems' are always problems to some extent because of a mismatch between old values which historically selected the dominant traits of our knowledge, social organization, technologies and environment and new values applying new selective criteria.

Similarly, the dominance of current patterns of thinking and what are accepted as facts have been selected by the historical dominance of specific values, forms of social organization, types of technologies and characteristics of environments. To some extent, all problems are problems of how we have known, for how we have known has helped select for the qualities of all of the components of any problem. The same is true for our social organization, our technologies and our environments.

Implications of coevolution for sustainable development

If sustainable development is to be achieved, we will have to devise institutions, at all levels of government, to reallocate the use of stock resources towards the future, curb the pace and disruption of global climatic changes, reverse the accumulation of toxins in the environment and slow the loss of biological diversity. These are the key resource and environmental issues that must be addressed. Sustainable development implies switching from the use of stock to flow resources, especially from the use of energy from fossil hydrocarbons to current energy from the sun.

The management of flow, or renewable, resources for sustainable development must extend from the vitality of the smallest microbes in farmers' fields to the functioning of the atmospheric system that surrounds us all. Furthermore, these extremes are closely linked. The services of soil microbes affect the atmosphere through nitrogen fixation, the decomposition of organic material to carbon dioxide and the facilitation of nutrient uptake for the vegetation cover that affects both the stock of organic hydrocarbons and the Earth's albedo. The atmospheric system, in turn, affects the climatic conditions upon which vegetation and soil microbes depend. Flow resource systems must be understood and managed, both locally and globally, as mutually determined systems.

The differences between agro-ecosystems have steadily declined. Regionally unique ecological processes have been increasingly overridden by the use of fertilizers and pesticides. Under sustainable development these regionally unique processes will have to be restored and managed to capture solar energy and conserve nutrients. New agricultural technologies and institutions will be more specifically tailored to the features of the region and goods being produced than have been agrichemical technologies and institutions. We will have to pay more attention to the details of technical and institutional possibilities and limitations for specific regions. Ecosystem-specific technologies will probably be management intensive rather than capital intensive. Poor regions needing assistance will need more than simply the financial means to acquire capital equipment and technologies and to adopt institutions from other regions. Appropriate knowledge, inputs and forms of organization will have to be developed for each area.

Facilitating the adoption of technologies and institutions which support the management of the global system of renewable resources will be a major challenge. Our economies and social structures have evolved over the past century to take advantage of the medium-term opportunities provided by fossil fuels. New legislation, regulations, agencies and incentives to private action to capture the gains of ecosystem management will constitute significant economic and social changes. While institutions have to be locally tailored to support ecosystem-specific technologies, local institutions, none the less, will still have to mesh with regional and global institutions designed to capture the gains of ecosystem management on a larger scale and to prevent untoward broader consequences of local decisions.

Sustainable development, broadly conceived, addresses the sustainability of cultural systems as well as environmental systems. The idea of progress through technical mastery of nature has been central to western culture for several centuries. Belief in technical progress also provides the enticement for the transfer of values, knowledge and modern forms of social organization to other cultures. Widespread belief in technical progress has been key to the public consequences behind change in the developed and developing world. But technical progress is increasingly in doubt. As we push our technologies to exploit more and more resources, we now recognize that both the direct devastation and the unforeseen consequences are becoming increasingly global in nature. Independent of the side-effects, people are increasingly recognizing that the products of new technologies do not necessarily increase happiness.

Belief in progress also entailed the idea that we were progressing towards pure, universal values and one right way of knowing. Given this belief, non-western cultures were obviously seen as irrational, not on the path of progress, hence their demise could be rightfully hastened. Well into the nineteenth century westerners thought it was acceptable to exterminate cultures in the way of progress. While many non-western cultures have been destroyed through direct violence and the introduction of disease, most met their demise through the loss of a positive image of their future.

Something new has taken place in recent years. Increasingly we believe that traditional peoples not only have a right to maintain their cultures but also a right to influence how their cultures might evolve. Minority and alternative cultures within the United States and in Europe are also maintaining their identity much more openly than before. Cultural survival is also being enhanced not only as the western idea of progress wanes, but also through new interest in the knowledge of other peoples. Western scientists, for example, are beginning to look at traditional agricultural systems in order to understand how agro-ecosystems, management techniques and cultures can coevolve sustainably. Thus non-western cultures are beginning to be given respect.

In conclusion, it can be noted that neoclassical economics readily yields predictions and prescriptions within the context of the existing system by ignoring interrelatedness. The coevolutionary paradigm does not so readily yield predictions and prescriptions, but it does help us understand why neo-classical predictions and prescriptions are inevitably wrong. Sustainable development will entail a return to the coevolutionary development process with the diversity that remains and the deliberate fostering of further diversity to permit adaptation to future surprises.

Despite differences in emphasis, the central message of the three papers in this chapter is clear: the correct appraisal of the ecological dimension of economic activity is of vital importance not just to realist analysis but also in terms of achieving overall economic efficiency and sustainability. Pearce also stresses the ecological dimension's ethical implications; while Norgaard has internalized in his coevolutionary model social organization, human values and a scientific method, in line with the arguments in Chapter 1, that stresses change and interrelatedness as opposed to equilibrium and individual autonomy.

Four-dimensional human space

The arguments of this and the previous chapters can now be drawn together into a common analytical framework, based on the four dimensions funda-mental to human life: the economic, social, ecological and ethical.

The chosen representational form for the four dimensions is shown in Figures 3.6 and 3.7, a regular tetrahedron with the four keywords at its corners. They are equivalent – there is no implied hierarchy in that one corner is drawn as an apex of the pyramid – any of the keywords could have been in this position. Each point of the space inside this pyramid can be imagined as having four co-ordinates corresponding to one of the dimensions. The closer a point to any particular corner, the greater the co-ordinate, meaning that the stronger is the influence of that dimension relative to the others. The corners themselves are the points of pure economy, society, ecology and ethics. It is as if each of these points radiates an influence within the figure which diminishes

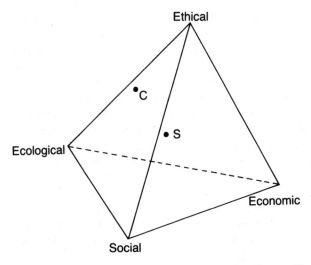

Figure 3.6   Four-dimensional human space: Swadhyaya (S) and Chipko (C)

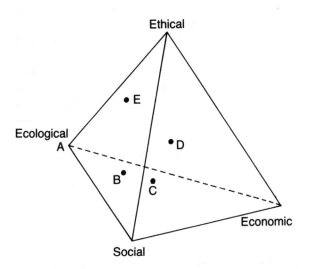

Key:
A – Ecological materialist
B – Self-maximizer
C – Planet management environmentalist
D – 'Realo' Green politician
E – Deep Green ecologist

Figure 3.7   Four-dimensional human space: attitudes to environment and resources

in intensity with distance from the point. Each corner has a triangular plane opposite it, where the dimension represented by that corner is taken to have no influence, that is its co-ordinate is zero. The point at the centre of the pyramid is where all the dimensions are equally influential or balanced.

It must be stressed that all that can be indicated in this way is the *relative* strength of the four dimensions. It says nothing about the intensity of those strengths. If one dimension is perceived as more influential, then *de facto* this diminishes the relative importance of the others, even though they may still be extremely important. Thus the pyramid's centre point could equally apply to a condition of passionate ecological, social, ethical and economic commitment, or to one of total apathy. Conceiving of the space in this way allows it to be used for a rough and ready but quite insightful analysis of human affairs in many different ways.

Thus, consider social movements such as Swadhyaya or Chipko (mentioned in Chapter 1). Both are concerned with values, social relations, economic resources and conservation of nature. But locating them in the four-dimensional space as in Figure 3.6 (about which locations there may of course be disagreements) shows quite graphically a difference between the movements. Thus this picture conveys that Swadhyaya's main concerns are ethical and social, with their attitudes to the economy and ecology largely deriving from these concerns. Chipko's main concerns are ethical and ecological with their economic and social positions largely deriving from these.

Or the space can be used to analyse different attitudes to environment and resources, as in Figure 3.7. A pure concern with through-puts of energy and materials, which gives no weight to social, economic or ethical considerations is located at point *A*. Someone concerned with maximizing their share of this through-put, however, would need to give attention to both the economic and social dimensions, still perhaps discounting ethical concerns, and this attitude would be located at *B*, remaining on the base of the pyramid as here drawn. The planet-management environmentalist, giving nearly equal and great weight to ecology and economy, with perhaps a lesser (but some) commitment to social and ethical matters, might be at *C*, now off the base of and inside the pyramid. The 'Realo' green politician will probably try to maintain a balance close to the centre of the pyramid *D*. The Deep-Green ecologist will probably tend to move away from social and economic considerations and take up a strongly ecological/ethical position at *E*.

The use of the tetrahedron should now be clear. Far more important than the actual location of any point is the process of positioning it there, the explicit consideration and justification of which aspects of the human condition are being given weight and why. In the next chapter, in order more precisely to define 'living economics', this technique will be applied to different modes of economic analysis. Before that, however, it is necessary to explore some of the precursors to, and similar contemporary expressions of, the living economic approach, with special reference to their normative assumptions and objectives.

4 Living economics in perspective

Much of the analysis thus far has been positive, concerned with what *is*, rather than normative, concerned with what *ought be*. Once it is accepted that, as argued by Lawson, economics should adopt a realistic approach, should endeavour to identify and understand real-life generative structures and tendencies rather than merely 'as if' instrumental reasoning, no matter how well it predicts, then the arguments of Hodgson, Etzioni, Hueting, Pearce and Norgaard largely follow: people are not uni-dimensionally rational; they are influenced by socially determined cognitive and institutional structures; they do have strong moral convictions on a different level to consumer preferences; the environment does perform vital economic functions; natural capital is being unsustainably consumed; economy, society and environment do coevolve, and so on.

Of course, these 'facts' are not uncontentious. Rational Economic Man maintains his grip on mainstream thought not only as a convenient predictive fiction. He is also justified as a legitimate abstraction in Lawson's terms: that is, he is taken to embody the real and essential elements of human behaviour.

These two different *positive* views of reality – the four-dimensional 'living economic' and the one-dimensional 'rational economic' – generate quite different *normative* concerns. If society consists simply of rational, atomistic individuals, if initial economic distributions are taken to be just, and if the conditions for the efficient operation of the market, that social institution most oriented to individuals, are taken to be satisfied: then the logical implication is that markets should be allowed to operate freely, to the obvious benefit of those with most effective demand, the rich. If, on the other hand, there is much social mediation of individual cognition and, therefore, preferences; if individual choice does not necessarily yield social welfare; and if power relations are important determinants of economic outcomes: then, even if initial distributions are taken to be just, there is a *prima facie* case for inter- vention in markets, implying less market freedom for the rich. The case for intervention is strengthened if some people are perceived to be suffering from unmerited social disadvantage.

Moreover, from the living economic standpoint, there are also dynamic implications in the respective views, for the initially dominant view will tend to reinforce the behaviour and motivations that are compatible with it. Thus, if it is acknowledged that human nature in general contains a wide spectrum of motivations from the highly individualistic to the highly communitarian; then the dominant social choice of an individualistic rationality will encourage and reward individualistic behaviour causing society to become more atomistic. A more social orientation, however, provided that it is freely articulated and espoused and not imposed, will tend to generate more social values and greater community cohesion.

Whether the former is viewed as 'freedom' or 'fragmentation' and 'breakdown'; and whether the latter is viewed as 'coercion', 'rigidity' and 'inefficiency' or as 'social security' depends largely on the viewpoint and on the balance between the individual and social dimensions in the society and at the time in question.

The living economic and rational economic world-views therefore yield two quite different basic policy orientations, the latter stressing individual self-interest, the former insisting that this be placed in a social context. But policies do not only derive from views of reality. They are also inevitably based on ethical considerations, on wider perceptions of value and justice, of economic purpose and of the intrinsic worth, or otherwise, of the human person. With regard to these questions, the living economic approach draws heavily on the long and distinguished tradition of economic thought which Mark Lutz in the next paper describes as 'humanistic economics'.

Humanistic economics: history and basic principles
Mark Lutz

'Humanistic economics' is a new label, used to describe economic thought that is explicitly centred around the human being with all his/her needs and higher aspirations; in Theodore Roszak's words, 'a nobler economics that is not afraid to discuss spirit and conscience, moral purpose and the meaning of life, an economics that aims to educate and elevate people, not merely to measure their low-grade behaviour' (Roszak in Schumacher 1973: 9). In what follows, I venture to offer a sketch of this tradition by pointing to some of its major proponents and some of the linkages between them.

The first 150 years: from Sismondi to Schumacher

The history of what we now call 'humanistic economics' starts with the Swiss historian and political economist Jean C. L. S. Sismondi (1773–1842), who was born in Geneva. At the age of 30 he published his first book on political economy: *De la Richesse Commerciale* (1803), a work that gave him a reputation as a stout follower of Adam Smith. It was also in that context that he was a decade later invited to pen an entry on 'political economy' for the prestigious *Brewster Encyclopedia* in Edinburgh. Yet it was in accomplishing this very task, in 1815, that Sismondi broke with the reigning classical tradition by presenting in skeleton fashion a new type of economics that a few years later he fleshed out in his book, *The New Principles of Political Economy* (1819, English translation 1991).

Sismondi's reorientation is as simple as it is far-reaching, as can be seen by taking note of the book's very first sentence where he introduces political economy as a branch of a science of government. As such political economy: 'has, or ought to have, the purpose of striving for the welfare of all people united in society. It pursues this highest end by exploring all means and opportunities compatible with human nature; at the same time it aims at securing the greatest possible sharing of all persons in this welfare' (Sismondi 1991: 21).

The difference from his old master is quite apparent when we remember that the scope of the new science was said to consist of 'an inquiry into the nature and causes of the wealth of nations'. Instead of focusing on wealth, Sismondi centred his *New Principles* on human welfare, boldly transforming economics into an explicitly normative discipline. For the rest of his life he asked the fundamental question as to what constitutes the very object of human society. For example:

> Is it to dazzle the eyes by the immense production of useful and elegant things; to astonish the understanding by the empire which man exercises over nature, and with the precision and rapidity with which inanimate machines execute human work? Is it to cover the sea with vessels and the land with railways, distributing in every way the productions of an ever increasing industrial activity?
>
> (Sismondi 1966b: 140–41)

Sismondi's own response runs otherwise: what really counts is how an economy serves the happiness of the people. Does it provide 'abundance, variety and wholesomeness of nourishment', 'sufficiency of clothes', 'convenience and salubrity of lodging' and 'the certainty that the future will not be inferior to the present' for both the rich *and* the poor? He observes that 'subsistence is necessary to life, to all the moral developments, all the intellectual developments, of which the human race is susceptible'. Therefore, 'society, as well as individuals, must consider bodily wealth before anything else, must provide in the first place for its wants', otherwise 'the health of the mind is impossible'. Material satisfaction of these needs will give rise to new wants, such as the search for aesthetic, moral and intellectual beauty. In short, for Sismondi the ultimate aim of political economy is 'to secure the development of man, and of all men' (ibid.: 141). (We may add 'and all women too'.)

One might wonder what may have provoked a scholar well established in one set of principles to abandon them in order 'to place Political Economy on a new basis' investigating 'what distribution of income will spread the most happiness throughout the nation, and consequently attain the end of the science'. The answer is simple. Sismondi had travelled repeatedly to industrializing England, the site of 'a great experiment for the instruction of the rest of the world', and what he saw there frightened him: 'I have seen production increasing whilst enjoyments were diminishing. The mass of the nation here, no less than philosophers, seem to forget that the increase of wealth is not the end in political economy, but its instrument in procuring the happiness of all. I sought for this happiness in *every* class, and I could nowhere find it'. England, to him, 'by forgetting men for things, [had] sacrificed the ends to the means' (ibid.: 115).

Sismondi's concern for the overly fragile welfare of the poor led him to spend much of his time analysing the recurring slumps and financial crises of the newly emerging business cycles. In the process, he developed what might very well be the first attempt at formulating a macro-economic theory of underconsumption based on income distribution and disequilibrium adjust-ment paths. In this context, he argued and debated with the leading economists of his time, with Ricardo, with Say and Malthus and above all with McCulloch. Nevertheless, it is probably fair to say that except for the case of Say, who is said to have made some important additions to the fifth and final edition of his *Traité*, his influence on political economists was nil.

Sismondi was strongly opposed to slavery and colonization, and one of the first to see the threat of an incipient consumerism. He also threw himself against the reigning gospel of *laissez faire*, he advocated government regulation of working hours, of child labour, progressive taxes for capitalists and employers, employer financed unemployment and accident insurance for workers.

More generally, he looked upon political economy as an instrument of public policy needing concrete institutional information rather than 'intellec-tual systems'. In his own words, 'political economy is not founded on dry calculations, nor on a mathematical chain of theorems . . . ; [it] is founded on the study of man and men, . . . societies in different times at different places' (quoted in Sherbourne 1972: 98). No wonder he was particularly critical of David Ricardo and his followers whom he denounced as having 'totally dis-regarded the human being and fixed only one goal for political economy: an unlimited growth of wealth'. To the extent that people did enter the equations, they did so as uprooted day labourers with no participation in property or decision making. Sismondi warns that 'the state of suffering and disequietude' of this new proletariat (a label first coined by Sismondi) is such that 'it is not easy to preserve the feeling of human dignity, or the love of freedom', and then goes on to compare this modern institution to slavery as performed by ancient civilizations.

But above all else, Sismondi was an early prophet pointing out the immense human costs of industrialization. As one scholar put it so well:

> Sismondi remains in the history of modern economic thought as the first author who denounced the costs of industrial development, and who saw it as a forced phenomenon which works by uprooting men and capitals from one occupation to channel them into another, causing the bankruptcy of

entrepreneurs and poverty for workers who at this point are complete prisoners of the need to offer work under any condition whatsoever.

(Barucci 1975: 990)

Similarly, he clearly understood the connection between population growth and material insecurity of the new wage labourers 'who bring into the world many more children, precisely because they know less distinctly how those children are to be established' (Sismondi 1966a: 124).

Quite obviously, ideas such as his did not fit his times any better than they would ours. During the 1830s and 1840s the pace of industrialization and urbanization accelerated in France and Switzerland as elsewhere, and in 1842 Sismondi died in intellectual isolation, as an unhappy and frustrated pioneer of the 'new economics' he had started to unveil and defend decades earlier. (Sowell 1972 and Parquez 1973 represent a new interest in Sismondi's work since 1970, with the advent of post-Keynesian economics.)

What Sismondi did not know was that his books, although never translated into English, were to be read by several subsequent key economists, including J. S. Mill. Similarly, and perhaps more importantly, he must have inspired the English Thomas Carlyle, who as a young man at Edinburgh was ordered by Professor Brewster to translate Sismondi's submitted article for the Encyclopedia. Carlyle's attacks on orthodox political economy, calling it 'the dismal science', 'pig philosophy', and so on, are well known and must have had a decisive influence on at least one of his students: John Ruskin, the first great humanistic economic philosopher on British soil.

John Ruskin (1819–1900) was a well-known art historian, a brilliant writer and a skilful lecturer. He was not an economist. Yet he was unable to keep himself from entering into polemics against political economy during the second half of his life. The reason, he explained, was that failing effectively to teach art appreciation to the working class made him realize that the problem was not with the workers but with a system that had been degrading and stunting their aesthetic needs and sensibilities. At the age of 40, equipped with a most rudimentary knowledge of the teachings of political economy, he swung himself fearlessly against its foremost representative, John Stuart Mill.

Before we go on, it is useful to remind the reader that Mill had successfully changed somewhat the direction and thrust of political economy. Rather than following the classical emphasis of enquiring into the nature and causes of national wealth, Mill preferred to approach the subject more as a science of human behaviour postulating an abstract 'man' who desires to possess wealth and who, by necessity of his nature, will prefer a greater portion of wealth to a smaller one. Mill had no illusions that wealth-seeking was an assumption adequately portraying a flesh-and-skin human person, even admitting that 'no political economist was ever so absurd as to suppose that mankind is really thus constituted'. The method of abstracting and reducing the whole person to an asocial and amoral being was necessary due to his new way of conceptualizing political economy as a science that reasons from hypothetical assumptions and not from facts. And he cautioned that such an 'arbitrary definition of man' may lead to conclusions that are only true in the abstract but *not* in the concrete real world full of 'frictions' and 'disturbing causes'. Such warnings, of course, have not stopped later economists from applying their abstractions to real-life situations.

It is generally acknowledged that John Stuart Mill was the first to conceive what Alfred Marshall decades later was to call Homo Oekonomicus, or economic man. It was against this newly invented abstraction of Mill that Ruskin threw himself with heart and soul when he writes:

> Among the delusions which at different periods have possessed themselves of the minds of large masses of the human race, perhaps the most curious – certainly the least creditable – is the modern *soi-disant* science of political economy, based on the idea that an advantageous code of social action may be determined irrespective of the influence of social affection.
>
> The social affections, say the economist, are accidental and disturbing elements in human nature; but avarice and the desire of progress are constant elements. Let us eliminate the inconstants, and considering the human being merely as a covetous machine, examine by what laws of labour, purchase and sale, the greatest accumulative result in wealth is attainable. Those laws at once determined, it will be for each individual afterwards to introduce as much of the disturbing affectionate element as he chooses, and to determine for himself the result on the new conditions supposed.
>
> (Ruskin 1888: 17–18)

So much for the set-up, certainly not unfairly characterizing Mill's method, but now Ruskin attacks, holding that the 'disturbing elements in the social problem are not of the same nature as the constant ones; they operate not mathematically, but chemically, introducing conditions which render all previous knowledge unavailable'. In effect, what Ruskin is saying is that pleasure or 'wealth' utility is fundamentally and incommensurably different from social or moral utility. Introduce a little bit of one into the other and everything takes on a radically different look: previous conclusions derived from some abstract economic man-based analysis are rendered simply irrelevant. Ruskin offers an illustration from the employer–employee relationship where self-interested men confront each other without any sense of a work ethic, fairness or loyalty; in Ruskin's words, both sides are held to be actuated 'by no other moral influences than those which affect the rat or swine', thereby totally missing the human 'motive power of the soul' and so incapacitating the economist to reckon with the effects on productivity resulting from cooperative action. Imprisoned in his framework, the political economist cannot see what Ruskin could, namely that here, as elsewhere, a peculiar agent, the human soul in action, enters into the economists' equations without their knowledge, 'falsifies every one of their results'. Ruskin logically concludes: 'I neither impugn nor doubt the conclusions of the science, I am simply uninterested in them' (Ruskin 1988: 18).

Ruskin, after concluding that orthodox economics is dangerously irrelevant for public policy purposes, embarked on constructing a 'new economics' where 'moral animation' has its place and where Mill's wealth is redefined from exchange value and subjective utility to *'life'*, the objective and life-sustaining property intrinsic to goods and services. Commodities have value to the extent that they 'avail life' in the sense of satisfying vital wants or basic human needs. In the process, he wants to judge production to the extent that it also produces the capacity to use the products effectively. Logically, he ends up focusing on the quality of work, asking whether it recreates the labourer as it ought to, or whether it corrupts him, 'breaks him in pieces', and in a sense 'kills him'. So much work, he deplored, is nothing but mechanical toil that blinds the eyes, blunts the hopes, steals the joys and blasts the soul of workers. What a waste of human creativity, what a blow to personality! Needless to say, Ruskin was no friend of machine production, a process geared more to the accumulation of endless riches than to the enhancement of the quality of life.

There is no need to elaborate here further on Ruskin's reconstruction of a new political economy of life aiming at prescribing 'socially advantageous action'. That task has been undertaken in a far more promising fashion by some of his avowed disciples, particularly John Hobson and Mohandas Gandhi who were both midway into their own lives when John Ruskin died at the turn of the century.

John Hobson (1885–1940) studied classical literature at Oxford during the 1870s and was soon exposed to the influence and writings of Ruskin which at that time he regarded more as an expression of passionate rebellion than as useful social theory. It was only towards the end of the century that he systematically re-examined Ruskin's work and found him to be not only 'the most enlightened political economist', but also a 'most brilliant' and effective of social reformers whose mind 'seized with incomparable force of vision the cardinal truth of human economics, namely that every piece of concrete wealth must be valued in terms of vital costs of its production and the vital uses of its consumption' (Hobson 1914: 9–10). Yet at the same time Hobson felt that he pursued his vision with a lack of clarity and rigour that blunted his effectiveness. In the words of Hobson, 'From a Pisgah height his mind's eye swept in quick penetrative glances over the promised land, but he did not occupy it, or furnish any clear survey' (ibid.: 10). To make a more scholarly contribution towards articulating that vision became the leitmotiv of Hobson's work for the rest of his life.

We may also mention here as a side note that Hobson's life was not always an easy one. His career as a (self-educated) economist started most promisingly when in 1889 he published, together with A.F. Mummery, a businessman, his first book, *The Physiology of Industry*. That work challenged Say's Law of Markets in a similar spirit as did Sismondi seven decades earlier. In it, recessions and depressions were attributed to a tendency inherent in market economies towards excessive savings, or 'underconsumption'. The book got a very negative review from Professor Edgeworth, the founding editor of the *Economic Journal*. It did not take much for *The Physiology* to be branded as heresy, so leading to Hobson being fired from London University where he had been permitted to lecture on the topics of literature and political economy. Embittered, he was driven into a 'mixed life of lecturing, controversial politics and journalism' which he felt may have been 'damaging to orderly thinking', but on the other hand allowed him to get a more direct grassroots level of understanding of economic reality. It was only during the 1930s with the work of J.M. Keynes that he felt rehabilitated and suddenly more recognized. At the same time, the belated respectability granted to him on this issue did not translate into a more general reassessment of his work in human economy.

Hobson's attempted reconstruction of economics along humanistic lines fills many books and cannot be properly conveyed here. Rather, we will limit ourselves to point to some of its basic elements. The bottom line of his socio-economic thought is his embrace of a hierarchy of values. Human beings have material needs of food and shelter; above that are the higher needs of personality or self-rationalization with a context of 'an enlightened sense of community'. This, in short, is Hobson's 'human standard' against which an economic system needs to be assessed. It is a standard of 'organic welfare' in the sense that it allows for the interaction of social industrial life and consumption patterns and in that it implies a growth of the social economic structure in which the civilizing impulses of mutual aid shall work 'with a clearer consciousness of their human value' (Hobson 1914: 304). The social consciousness he had in mind was not mere mechanical 'like-mindedness' generated by similar cultural upbringings, but rather an active awareness of the common good and a willingness to freely contribute to it.

In his *Work and Welfare* (1914), Hobson proceeds to apply this norm in analyzing production, consumption and distribution. He faults conventional economics for assuming that costs only occur in production while consumption consists only of utility, a value measured by the buyer's willingness to pay. In contrast, Hobson assigns costs and utilities according to how they affect the growth in personality. Artistic production, for example, when truly creative has little or no cost. Similarly, the creative work of the independent craftsman has much less wear and tear than the monotonous and narrow toil of the industrial worker, especially if we also consider the heavy human costs of anxiety in insecure work pregnant with uncertainty about layoffs and unemployment. In fact, he repeatedly argued the effect of economic security on 'steadiness of character', observing that 'irregularity of employment is the most destructive agency to the character, the standard of comfort, the health and sanity of wage earners, [since] it takes out of a man that confidence in the fundamental rationality of life which is essential to the soundness of character' (ibid.: 199). Workers exposed to such powerful illustrations of unreason and injustice can hardly be expected to have much sympathy for religion, ethics and education.

In this context, we may also mention one of Hobson's greatest insights that was only decades later rediscovered by humanistic psychologists such as Abraham Maslow:

When moralists talk of altering human nature they are often misunderstood to mean that instincts and desires deeply implanted in our inherited animal outfit can be eradicated and others grafted on. Now, no such miracles are possible or needed. But substantial changes in our environment or in our social institutions can apply different stimuli to human nature and evoke different physical responses. For example, by alterations in the organization and government of business and industries, so as to give security of employment and livelihood to workers, and some increased 'voice' to them in the conditions of work, it seems reasonably possible to modify the conscious stress on personal gain-seeking and to educate a clearer sense of social solidarity and service. . . . *Security is, therefore, the first essential in any shift of relative appeal to personal and social motives.*

(Hobson 1929: 234, emphasis added)

Such a dynamic view of human nature is both penetrating and almost trivial once proclaimed. Its significance for anybody interested in a new 'living' economics can hardly be underestimated. Above all, it tends to curb our enthusiasm for relying excessively on competition as a means to coordinate economic resources, to stimulate labour productivity and to resolve conflicts.

Hobson also emphasized the feedback effect of unearned income and other property-related injustices on social attitudes. 'So long as property appears to come miraculously or capriciously, irrespective of efforts or requirements, and so long as it is withheld irrationally, it is idle to preach "the dignity of labour" or to inculcate sentiments of individual self-help' (Hobson 1914: 298).

In addition to elaborating the research programme started by Ruskin five decades earlier, a programme of building a new economics centred on the whole person with an inborn capacity for self-fulfilment, a social economics that counts both economic and non-economic costs and benefits in the assessment of alternative institutions and policies, Hobson was also a life-long political activist pushing for legislative implementation of his ideas. Being a member of the Independent Labour Party, he led government commissions recommending the establishment of a national minimum wage as well as others discussing the implementation of worker participation. As the 'intellectual godfather' of the Labour Party, he was also an effective spokesman for the nationalization of monopolies and the introduction of progressive income taxes. Last, but not least, he was a vocal Internationalist occupying an important place in the British peace movement.

It was also in this latter context that we should briefly dwell on his outspoken opposition to imperialism, a movement led by his country during the last few decades of the nineteenth century, when some 5 million square miles of tropical territory were added to the British Empire. Hobson wrote various works, including a book, *The Psychology of Jingoism* (1901) and an article on the 'Economic Taproot of Imperialism' (1902). The latter was fleshed out in one of his most famous and controversial books, *Imperialism: A Study* (1902). The book presents a coherent economic theory rooted in his underconsumption perspective explaining the international scramble for colonies from an economic point of view.

For Hobson, imperialism was based on the notion that

> there exists one sound, just, rational system of government, suitable for all sorts and conditions of men, . . . and that our duty was to impose this system as soon as possible, and with the least possible modifications, upon the lower races, without any regard to their past history, and their present capabilities and sentiments.
>
> (Hobson 1902: 245)

To this kind of view Hobson was a vocal and early dissenter, observing that 'there may be *many paths* to civilization, that strong racial and environmental differences preclude a hasty grafting of alien institutions, regardless of continuity and selection of existing agencies and forms' (ibid., emphasis added). Yet at the same time it is important to note that Hobson is more pluralist than cultural relativist. When talking about 'many paths to civilization', he does imply that there is a common destiny to be pursued, there is such a thing as civilization. Elsewhere he defines it as 'the art of living together comfortably in large numbers' and consisting in 'harmonizing the needs of a standardized community with those of a freely self-expressive personality' (Hobson 1929: 311). In other words, Hobson's concept of civilization is intrinsically connected with his human standard of organic welfare. The higher this welfare, the higher the civilization. As we will see, he thereby lays the groundwork for a humanistic development policy.

In conclusion, let us part from Hobson by quoting a passage from Richard Tawney, an economic historian who was very much influenced by Ruskin. He comments in one of his reviews of a book by Hobson back in 1930:

> The essence of humanism, perhaps, is the attitude which judges the externals of life by their effect in assisting or hindering the life of the spirit. It is the conviction that the machinery of existence – property and material wealth, and industrial organization, and the whole fabric and mechanism of social institutions – is to be regarded as means to an end, and that this end is the growth towards perfection of individual human beings. In this sense, Mr. Hobson is the greatest of economic humanists. Undisturbed by the roar of the wheels he approaches with questions most of us are too clever, or too superficial, to condescend to ask. What is the thing for? In what way do its gyrations minister to the dignity and happiness of mankind?
>
> (quoted in Smith 1980: 228)

Richard Tawney (1880–1962), too, embraced a humanistic economic doctrine in the same sense Hobson had done. He, too, insists that 'externals' such as property rights and other social institutions are not to be regarded as ends. Rather, they are 'instruments of life' which are 'to be maintained when they are serviceable and changed when they are not'. What counts are institutions which are primarily compatible with the liberation and cultivation of human powers and only secondarily with economic efficiency or social equality (Tawney 1964: 85–6).

One of the 'externals' that Tawney fingered as illegitimate was the large-scale investor-owned stock corporation. Private property, originally legitimized as providing security to enjoy the fruit of one's labour, increasingly has become just another form of absentee ownership 'thereby undermining the creative energy which in the early ages [it] protected' (Tawney 1920: 117). As remedy, Tawney prescribed nationalization combined with administration by employee associations.

Tawney wrote almost a dozen books, three of them very well known: *The Acquisitive Society* (1920), with its early assault on consumerism and materialism; *Religion and the Rise of Capitalism* (1926) exploring the emergence of modernization in Europe; and *Equality* (1931), a critical account of British socio-economic institutions in the 1920s; the last one having been motivated by the incompatibility of inequality with the marks of a truly civilized society: 'the spirit of humanity and the sense of dignity of man as man' (ibid: 1964: 33).

Given the absolute centrality of the notion of human equality in humanistic social thought, it is useful to quote Tawney on its meaning:

It is obvious that the word 'Equality' possesses more than one meaning, and that the controversy surrounding it arises partly, at least, because the same term is employed with different connotations. Thus it may either purport to state of fact, or convey the expression of an ethical judgement. On the one hand it may affirm that men are, on the whole, very similar in their natural endowments of character and intelligence. On the other it may assert that, while they differ profoundly as individuals in capacity and character, they are equally entitled as human beings to consideration and respect, and that the well-being of society is likely to be increased if it so plans its organization that, whether their powers are great or small, all its members may be equally enabled to make the best of such powers as they possess.

(ibid.: 46–7)

It is, of course, the latter meaning which he accepts in preference to the egalitarian ethic. True equality is the hallmark of civilization: a society 'is civilized in so far as it uses its material resources to promote the dignity and refinement of the individual human beings who compose it' (ibid.: 81). Note again that for Tawney, as for the other exponents of the humanistic tradition before him, 'civilization' is understood normatively rather than merely reflecting a particular level of material and technological accomplishments.

Both Hobson and Tawney are no doubt central figures in advocating the humanistic perspective to Europeans and westerners, but there is a third person in the 'holy trinity' moving on from where the footsteps of John Ruskin ended. This time, however, the message was to be carried to more remote parts of the British empire: South Africa and India.

This brings us to Mohandas Gandhi (1869–1948). In his autobiography, Gandhi acknowledges the 'magic spell' that Ruskin's *Unto This Last* exerted on him back in 1904 when he read it non-stop on a long train trip in South Africa. 'The book was impossible to lay aside, once I had begun it. It gripped me. Johannesburg to Durban was a twenty-four hours' journey. The train reached there in the evening. I could not get any sleep that night. I determined to change my life in accordance with the ideals of the book.' After admitting that 'after I launched into active life I had very little time for reading' of the few books he did manage to read, 'the one that brought about an instantaneous and practical transformation in my life was *Unto This Last*. I translated it later into Gujarati, entitling it *Sarvodaya* (the welfare for all).' Gandhi concludes, 'I believe that I discovered some of the deepest convictions reflected in this great book by Ruskin, and that is why it so captured me and made me transform my life. . . . I arose with the dawn, ready to reduce [Ruskin's] principles to practice' (Gandhi 1968: 445, 446).

Following Ruskin, Gandhi saw economics as meaningful only if it pursued the right end: the welfare of society, by which he meant an economic system providing the basic necessities for all in a manner that respected the higher values of human dignity, non-violence and creative labour. Much of his thoughts on a development economics aiming at strengthening the rural village economy in terms of greatest possible self-reliance could be understood in the context of the British domination of the Indian economy during the 1920s and 1930s. But beyond that, we can find in his voluminous teachings scattered here and there in outline form one of the first systematic critiques of modernization with its tendencies towards urbanization and immiserization of the masses, particularly in the vast rural hinterland. He focused on the growing problem of structural unemployment and emphasized the need for revitalizing the labour-intensive traditional sector. This, according to one Gandhian scholar, Amritananda Das, is the very kernel of Gandhian economic thought: 'the fundamental insight from which the rest of Gandhian economic thought can be derived by a series of elaborations' (Das 1979: 4–5). It is probably fair to say that much of what Gandhi had pointed to became enshrined in the work of modern development economists disenchanted with either the neo-classical or the Marxian approach (e.g. Mehta 1978).

Gandhi is of course more generally known for his attack on modern civilization in the west. He did so in 1908 in the columns of a paper he edited in South Africa. Subsequently available in book form under the title *Hind Swaraj* (1984) it had a rather profound impact on Indian public opinion. Modern secular 'civilization', where bodily comfort is made the object of life, he refers to as 'a civilization only in name' taking note 'neither of morality nor of religion', observing that 'under it the nations of Europe are becoming degraded and ruined day by day'. Elsewhere he equates this *soi-disant* civilization of the British with what the Moslems call 'satanic civilization' or the Hindus' 'Black Age of humanity'. In contrast, Gandhi defined 'true civilization' as that mode of conduct which points out to people the path of duty. By that definition he finds Indian civilization with its ancient roots much more civil than the modern counterpart imported from the west: 'The tendency of the Indian civilization is to elevate the moral being, that of the Western civilization is to propagate immorality. The latter is godless, the former believe in God.' At the same time, it is important to note that Gandhi readily grants that Indian civilization has its own defects and mentions child widows, polyandry and Niyoga ('where in the name of religion girls dedicate themselves to prostitution') (Gandhi 1984: 34, 61, 63).

Such is Gandhi's view on civilization. He measures it like Tawney and Hobson by the ethical canons of humanity and human dignity and adding in the process a spiritual element as well.

We now come to E.F. Schumacher (1911–77), who studied economics in Germany under Joseph Schumpeter, and had a long and successful career in England, moving freely between the biggest names in academia and the establishment. During the 1940s when at the Oxford Institute of Statistics, he was involved with J.M. Keynes and his famous 'Proposal for an International Clearing Union' (1943). At the same time, he is said to have also been the main author of Sir William Beveridge's *Full Employment in a Free Society* (1944). In 1950 he joined the National Coal Board. Thereafter he gradually developed the outlook expressed in his best-known work, *Small is Beautiful* (1973), a book that has, probably more than any other, served as the principal source of inspiration for the contemporary alternative economics movement. The book is too well known to need any description here. Instead we will limit ourselves to pointing out some of its aspects that may in the context of the present paper be seen as deserving to be highlighted.

First, anybody familiar with the book will have noticed the background presence of Gandhi, especially when Schumacher criticizes the modern secular mind and when he outlines his new strategy for development stressing human needs, rural development and appropriate technology. In the final part of the book, when discussing questions of ownership appropriate for the industrialized north, the strong influence of Tawney, particularly his *Acquisitive Society*, can also hardly be missed. Perhaps at the peril of oversimplification, we may postulate that Schumacher succeeded in rearticulating essential premises and principles of the long humanistic economic tradition in a manner that caught the fancy of almost a whole generation of students, at least in the United States. Needless to say, he raised new issues such as environmental depletion and degradation, and added to that many of his own insights, as, for example, the important problem of unit size or 'scale', an issue that was more implicit than explicit in the works of Sismondi, Ruskin and Gandhi. Schumacher's logic here follows directly from the emphasis on people, not production of goods. 'But people can be themselves only in small comprehensible groups. Therefore we must learn to think in terms of an articulated structure that can cope with a multiplicity of small scale units' (Schumacher 1973: 70). His explicit concern for smallness, of course, also underlies his ideals of a more human technology and a village-centred approach to development.

Second, one should take note that Schumacher, when discussing education in the context of building the human resource, is openly opposed to the modern belief system imprisoning the modern educated intellect with almost dogmatic force. In this context, he not only mentions evolutionism, Marx, Freud and positivism, but is also sharply critical of *relativism*, the general idea 'denying all absolutes, dissolving all norms and standards, [and] leading to the total undermining of the idea of truth' (ibid.: 81). He saw it as a foremost task of education to dislodge all these 'large' ideas of the modern mind which 'educated' people had inherited from the nineteenth century. According to Schumacher, education can help us only if it produces the 'whole person' with a 'centre' or a soul. The task at hand was to reintroduce ethics into the economic discourse. So, for example, the farmer is not merely a 'factor of production' but, before anything else, he (or she) is 'an end-in-itself, meta-economic, and in a certain sense sacred' (ibid.: 99). So is also the land he or she works.

Third, and intrinsically related to the second point, Schumacher holds dear the notion of hierarchical 'levels of being'. He explains, 'it is only when we can see the world as a ladder and man's position on that ladder, that we can recognize a meaningful task for man's life on earth' (ibid.: 89). The human being, as the highest of God's creatures, 'was given "dominion", not the right to tyrannize, to ruin and to exterminate' (ibid.: 100). In fact, he links the very concept of human dignity to this acceptance of *noblesse oblige*.

Finally, Schumacher was not against development, only against (the prevailing) misguided development efforts emphasizing goods and growth of production of goods rather than people. Indeed, he saw rural poverty as perhaps the greatest challenge to economics. As its practitioners, we have to provide for basic need satisfaction, 'above all the elimination of rural poverty by bringing into existence millions of new workplaces in the rural areas and small towns' (ibid.: 164). Elsewhere we can read:

> The crucial task of this decade [i.e., the 1970s] is to make the development effort appropriate and thereby more effective, so that it will reach down to the heartland of world poverty, to the two million villages. If the disintegration of rural life continues, there is no way out.
>
> (ibid.: 180)

He adds that 'genuine development' will only ensue if we can help the rural people in the Third World help themselves (ibid.: 192).

With such penetrating observations, constituting, as they do, the very bedrock of a humanistic strategy for socio-economic development, we can end our somewhat sketchy treatment of Schumacher and with it also of the entire historical survey. Figure 4.1, originally published elsewhere (Lutz and Lux 1979: 52), summarizes in graphical form the history of humanistic economics within the context of the neoclassical and the Marxist schools of thought, two traditions, along side which it proudly stands and to neither of which it can be reduced.

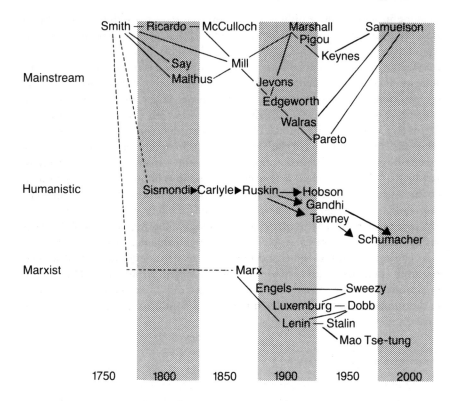

Figure 4.1 The historical flow of humanistic economics

Basic principles of humanistic economics

Our historical survey will now permit us to present in some distilled manner what might be called the 'first principles' that underly the work so far presented and therefore accounts for its distinct unity. We will attempt to show that the present perspective shares four interrelated cardinal elements or foundational cornerstones on which much of the various superstructures securely rest. They are (1) a normative orientation rejecting pure positive economics, (2) a welfare standard explicitly expressed in terms of *human* welfare rather than 'economic' or 'social' welfare, (3) the *a priori* ethical assumption of human *equality* and (4) an epistemology that rejects naturalism, understood as the doctrine holding that natural science can account for all relevant phenomena.

Humanistic economics as a normative discipline

Economic activity, meaning the activities of production, distribution and consumption of material goods and services, is seen as carried out for some end, that it is only meaningful if it serves a purpose. All activities are meaningful and valuable only to the extent that they serve this purpose. The ultimate purpose of economic activity is to solve real problems in the socio-economic system. In other words, real problems are the *raison d'être* of humanistic economics. In this sense it is an applied science, very much the same kind as medical science which seeks to cope with medical problems. Just as medicine operates under the overarching value of health, so, too, humanistic economics has its overarching value which permits the identification of any 'problems' in the first place. Humanistic economics, therefore, is a value-directed discipline. At the same time, it should be emphasized that such a value-directed basic approach does not rule out empirical or logical analysis that helps describe, explain and predict the socio-economic actual world that we find ourselves in. Once again, just as medicine relies heavily on chemistry, physiology and biology, so humanistic economics will draw on relevant laws or regularities surfaced by psychology, sociology, history, anthropology and positive economic analysis, as well as philosophical and logical deductions.

In conclusion and at the cost of potential oversimplification, we may say that ever since Sismondi, economics can no longer be seen as the theory of maximum possible production with consequent effects on welfare, but rather, in the opposite manner, as the theory of maximum possible welfare with consequent effects on production.

The criterion of human welfare

In light of the fact that humanistic economics exhibits not only a characteristic unity over time but also claims a validity across cultures at any point in time, it is logically necessary to subscribe to a value standard that is seen as universally applicable and therefore also objective and rational in the sense of claiming to be grounded in good reasons.

From Sismondi to Schumacher such a standard was explicitly assumed in the form of human welfare, or the material and psychological well-being or health of the person. So much we can claim without anticipating much controversy. The more tricky next step consists in an articulation of some more specific aspects of this standard. Quite obviously, it gets us involved in an account of a universally valid image of human nature.

The humanistic school approached the challenging task by defining the person as a being with certain basic material needs and 'higher' (social and spiritual) aspirations which define 'desirable' desires. On the one hand, an individual has to survive and maintain an adequate level of health by meeting the 'lower' biological needs dictated by its biological organism: the needs for clean water, food and shelter. As Hobson, the most secular representative, put it, values 'that rank lowest in clear consciousness (though highest if they fail) [being] served by things and processes that satisfy our ordinary daily needs, our material requirements' (Hobson 1929: 48). From a more social point of view, we may add that survival of the species also dictates a biological need for procreation. In this sense, a man needs a woman and *vice versa*.

So far, the needs enumerated are shared by animals, and if we substitute 'habitat' for shelter, they also go for many other living organisms. It is the additional recognition of 'higher' aspirations that gives the humanistic vision its characteristic distinction. These are seen to be specific to our own species constituting the distinctive human element par excellence. In other words, beyond striving to meet our natural needs of survival, we also share a human need for a meaningful world-view, for 'individuation', self-realization in (and through) authentic community. All our humanistic economists surveyed adhere to this notion of a 'hierarchy of values' implying a 'vertical dimension', a duality of 'lower' and 'higher' aspects of life. Moreover, they associate these distinctly human 'higher reaches' of personality with Man's 'inner' or spiritual nature. The animal-transcending quality of our nature can be defended as did Schumacher in the unique capacity of self-awareness and the 'need to know our self' or, as Hobson did, in terms of organic evolution. Hobson, indeed, was led to hazard the following welfare criterion:

> If nature makes so much 'nisus' (directive activity) towards the preservation and growth of species, and if social cooperation plays the distinctive part it seems to do in human survival, then it may be argued that the highest value attaches to the conduct and the emotions which sustain society in the elaborate structure it has attained, and assists it to further useful modes of cooperation. This will seem to furnish a criterion for human welfare in its higher reaches by stressing the feelings, beliefs, interests, activities and institutions, which bring men into closer, conscious, willing cooperation for as many different sorts of work as possible, or, put otherwise, which enrich the human personality through the largest measure of sociality.
>
> (Hobson 1929: 73)

There is a direct connection between the 'higher' elevated status of the human being with the human capacity of free will and the intrinsic worth of the person – that is, human dignity. Therefore we may render the 'human standard' somewhat more simple by assessing to what extent the meeting of basic material needs is consistent with the personal claim demanding respect for one's dignity.

The presupposition of human equality

We have already mentioned the intrinsic connection between humanism properly understood and the notion of equality as defined by Tawney. It is also the cornerstone of the Jeffersonian doctrine of 'all men are born equal'. Its underpinnings are typically metaphysical or spiritual, holding that all men and women were created in the image of God. Even Hobson admits that 'Probably it remains true that all men are equal in the sight of their Maker, the little divergences on which they pride themselves shrinking into insignificance'. Whatever the reason, the assumption of essential equality regardless of race and gender is absolutely paramount. According to Hobson and the entire tradition, it is 'in this real equality of men [that] we find the basis of a valuation and a standard of welfare' (Hobson 1929: 52). The human standard applies to *all* members of society. It is Gandhi's (and Ruskin's) *sarvodaya*, meaning 'welfare for all', rather than the utilitarian 'greatest good for the greatest number'.

We can now formulate in more complete form the human standard: the norm for human well-being within a reference population demands clearly *material sufficiency and dignity for all*.

The limits of the scientific method

Humanistic economics does not mix well with scientific abstraction. Such was recognized already by Sismondi, who early on protested against 'dry calculations' and 'mathematical abstractions' and instead preferred the study of men, women and their social institutions. Ruskin, too, ridiculed Mill's soulless Economic Man as a 'covetous machine' and was contemptuous of the 'economist's equations'. Hobson, Tawney, Gandhi and Schumacher all echoed this sentiment. The latter devoted an entire book to this general issue. In it he throws himself against Vilfredo Pareto's claim that 'there is not the slightest difference between the laws of political economy and sociology and the laws of the [physical] sciences', as a manifestation of a thinker 'who refuses to acknowledge the hierarchy of levels of being and therefore cannot see any difference other than the difference in "complexity" between a stone and a man' (Schumacher 1977: 101–2). Schumacher grants that a scientific framework based on physical cause and effect works well for inanimate matter. But already at the plant level there are also more subtle causes operative in the form of 'stimuli' as when light acts as a stimulus for growth. At the animal level, we encounter 'motives' and at the human level we enter the domain of 'will', meaning and purpose. In contrast to Rational Economic Man, the picture presented by 'modern materialistic Scientism', the Whole Person is not only equipped with reason but also the higher intellectual faculties, supra-rational and supra-logical wisdom.

As a result, natural science methods based on mathematical logic have their limitations when dealing with life in general and self-consciousness in particular. Life is bigger than logic, Schumacher muses. It deals with existential questions, with the description of living experience, including the 'inner experience' of persons. For the purpose of truly understanding human nature, therefore, we have to rely also on what is called 'philosophical anthropology', meaning a philosophical account of human actions and aspirations. In other words, humanistic economics is as much economic philosophy as it is economic science.

Closely related to the question of method is the problem of incommensurability between the different levels of being and the values they recommend. (For a discussion, see Hobson 1929: 71–2 and Schumacher 1977: 23.) This goes to the heart of denying the modern economist's practice of assuming the

axiom of comparability and the related notion that morality can be accommodated within an expanded framework of an 'overarching utility function' (see
Lutz and Lux 1988, ch. 6).

There is another implication to all this. Once we refuse to reduce the person
to the one-dimensional clod of naturalistic science, there now arises the possibility for 'disinterested action' being free in the sense of self-determination.
According to Schumacher, 'the power of self-awareness gives [the person] an
additional motivation for movement: will, that is the power to move and act
even where there is no physical compulsion, no physical stimulus, and no
[external] motivating force actually present'. It is for this basic reason that
Schumacher, Hobson and the others can recognize definite limits to socialization and enculturation. We can learn from society and tradition, internalize
the knowledge and then 'sift it, sort it, keeping the good and jettisoning the
bad' (Schumacher 1977: 28, 135). In other words, the humanistic tradition,
believing in the 'higher intellectual faculties', in the need to be developed,
affirms 'individuation', while their naturalistic counterparts are unable to go
beyond 'socialization'.

In conclusion, we postulate that all the spokesmen of the humanistic
tradition surveyed have been employing the human standard and a humanistic methodology in their work on socio-economic problems. Of course, the
problems and the social context in which they lived have been changing over
the last two centuries and so we find a different kind of emphasis with each
one. Table 4.1 presents in summary form the evolution of the humanistic
problems emphasized. At the bottom of the table, we take the liberty of also
indicating the contemporary scene as it has been developing since
Schumacher.

Summarizing, the humanistic approach emphasizes first and foremost the
meeting of the material needs of all members of society, including the basic
needs of the future generations, thereby fully endorsing the contemporary
concept of sustainable development. But the story does not end here. The
other ingredient of the humanistic perspective is the explicit recognition of
legitimate higher needs and aspirations that must be respected when making
economic prescriptions. It is here where humanistic economics really becomes
'humanistic'. It explains the preoccupations of Hobson with security, the
central focus on work, a prime catalyst in human development from Ruskin to
Schumacher. Moreover, it underlies Tawney's critique of functionless
property and Gandhi's and Schumacher's special emphasis on dencentralized,
participatory, local decision-making. Finally, as we shall see, it will also
provide the underpinnings for our treatment of socio-economic development
in Chapter 6. To conclude the present section, we will compare humanistic
economics with the 'new welfare economics', the normative offspring of
positive economics used by conventional economists engaged in public policy
analysis to recommend reasoned solutions to social problems. We will do so by
means of Figure 4.2 featuring a chart comparing both types of normative
economics.

Table 4.1 Humanistic economics in a changing world

	Key historical events	Predominant economic doctrines	Humanistic problem
Sismondi	Industrialization of France and Switzerland	Smith, Ricardo and followers	Amelioration of material privation. Study of what makes for recurrent slumps. Need for government intervention. Need to slow down industrialization
	First business cycles	Economics becomes increasingly abstract and fixated on wealth	
Ruskin	Increasing marketization of British society. Growing industrial conflict	J. S. Mill, Senior, Cairnes	Need to study increasingly alienated preferences of people. Focus on alienation centres on quality of labour and work
		Economics becomes centred on abstract economic man	
Hobson and Tawney	Growing consumerism, i.e. England turns into an 'acquisitive society'. Increasing inequality. Growth of the corporation.	Marshall, Wicksteed, Clark	How to cope with the 'Social Question', with poverty, insecurity and meaningless work
		Advocating 'marginalism' in consumption, production and distribution. Money as the measuring rod in economics	The question of 'functionless property' in the form of corporate absentee ownership
	British imperialism		The reasons and effects of imperialism
	Russian Revolution		
Gandhi	British occupation of India.	'British utilitarians'.	Increasing dependency of Indian economy. Modernization versus Indian culture. Combat growing rural impoverishment, urbanization and secularization
	Soviet Revolution in Russia. Growth of Fascism in Europe		

Schumacher	Growing materialism in west	Influence of Keynes, Kaldor, Harrod and Domar	Dehumanization and depersonalization of European civilization
	Independence for colonies	Growing preoccupation with economic growth, measured in GNP	Economics blind to ecological destruction
	Beginning of energy crisis (Club of Rome Report)		Imposition of inappropriate technologies destroys Third World economies
Post-Schumacher	Globalization of economy	Decline of Keynesian economics. Growing aversion to government intervention	Provision of material sufficiency for all
	Debt crisis	Development as global Reaganomics	Respect for human dignity in the provision of material sufficiency
	Threat of environmental destruction (Brundtland Report)		Sustainable development in both South and North
	Perestroika in eastern Europe		

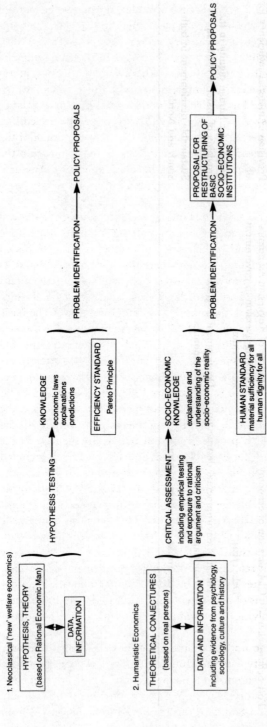

Figure 4.2 Two types of normative economics: neoclassical versus humanistic

1. Neoclassical ('new' welfare economics)

HYPOTHESIS, THEORY (based on Rational Economic Man) → HYPOTHESIS TESTING → KNOWLEDGE economic laws explanations predictions → PROBLEM IDENTIFICATION → POLICY PROPOSALS

DATA, INFORMATION

EFFICIENCY STANDARD Pareto Principle

2. Humanistic Economics

THEORETICAL CONJECTURES (based on real persons) → CRITICAL ASSESSMENT including empirical testing and exposure to rational argument and criticism → SOCIO-ECONOMIC KNOWLEDGE explanation and understanding of the socio-economic reality → PROBLEM IDENTIFICATION → PROPOSAL FOR RESTRUCTURING OF BASIC SOCIO-ECONOMIC INSTITUTIONS → POLICY PROPOSALS

DATA AND INFORMATION including evidence from psychology, sociology, culture and history

HUMAN STANDARD material sufficiency for all human dignity for all

The upper half of Figure 4.2 representing orthodox normative economics welds together two separate diagrams (slightly amending one of them for clarity) which appear in a recent introductory text (Frogen and Greer 1989). Moving from the left to right we are faced with two boxes signifying the scientific method of confronting hypotheses with raw data. Such a juxtaposition is carried out by means of empirical testing, the result of which contributes to our accumulated knowledge of economic phenomena (e.g. laws, explanations and predictions). All of this goes under the heading of scientific, or 'positive' economics and prepares the reader for the right-hand half of the figure describing normative economics. The latter starts by juxtaposing the accumulated economic knowledge with the box labelled 'efficiency standard' with the additional specification of 'Pareto principle'. Let us pause here for a moment.

The efficiency standard, as anybody familiar with economic theory will know, is the very heart of normative economics. It serves as its touchstone sorting out the good from the bad. 'Efficiency', of course, is a rather loaded term with strong positive connotations and therefore appearing offhand as eminently acceptable. Yet it represents a very strong value judgement: resources ought to be allocated in accordance with market demand since market demand expresses value in the sense of 'willingness to pay'. The basic problem with this norm is, of course, that 'willingness to pay' not only reflects 'urgency of want' but also 'ability to pay'. What differentiates the old Pigovian welfare economics from the 'new' is the latter's refusal to grant interpersonal utility comparisons and the strong reliance on the Pareto principle, characteristics strongly criticized in Lutz and Lux 1988, ch. 7, and Lutz 1986.

Proceeding with our chart, the juxtaposition of factual knowledge and the dictates of efficiency allows us to identify 'problems'. In response, the scientific economist would then propose remedial policy. In the case of the International Monetary Fund, for example, such policies have often included the removal in the name of efficiency of government subsidies for vital goods.

In the lower half of Figure 4.2 we entered the picture of humanistic economics. It, too, builds knowledge by means of testing conjectures against reality. But there are certain basic differences. The agent in humanistic economics is not abstract Rational Economic Man but a real person with body, heart and soul. As a result, the data and information used is more broadly conceived relying on relevant knowledge from outside of economics. Finally, the conjectures are tested in a broader manner allowing, besides econometric tests, other means of assessment, particularly the ability to withstand rational criticism involving, for example, appeal to shared but unobservable experience.

Once we have gained some understanding about how the social economy works, we juxtapose that reality with the Human Standard. As before, we can now identify problems and recommend remedial action. There are two basic differences in this half of the story as well, one being, of course, the radically different nature of the Human Standard (also believed to be objective) from the Efficiency Standard discussed above. The other variation consists in the insertion of an extra box labelled 'proposals for restructuring of basic institutions'. Neoclassical welfare economics, in contrast cannot feature such a box, simply because it operates under the constraining assumption that the prevailing institutional framework is to be taken as given. It would seem, therefore, that humanistic economics is of a normative economics where we are allowed, even encouraged, to discuss the merits of basic institutions such as property relations and the wage system.

Enough has been said to demonstrate the essential differences of the two normative alternatives. Both claim to be objective and universally applicable. The view presented here of orthodox welfare analysis as a normative body of thought too deficient to be taken seriously has been a primary motivating force in the development of the humanistic alternative.

Humanistic economics is by no means an isolated attempt to articulate an explicitly ethical alternative to the supposedly 'value-free', but actually rich-market-economy orientated, neoclassical mainstream. Mark Lutz sees humanistic economics as one of four strands of a social economics movement in the United States, which he defines as follows:

> Social economics is an economics centred around and directed by certain basic value premises or ethical postulates. It critically examines the mutual interaction between economic valuations (including observed preferences), economic activity (work, consumption, technological innovation, etc.) and economic institutions (markets, property relations, employer/employee relations etc.) in light of those basic premises. It can be seen as a kind of 'social' or 'human' welfare economics with a strong orientation towards identifying and solving social problems through ameliorative action consisting of economic policy proposals or, when necessary, a more radical restructuring of social institutions. In the process the market is rejected as a final arbiter of social values and instead priority is given to a non reductionistic, holistic ethos intrinsically related to a conception of society as an organic whole.
>
> (Lutz 1990a: 416–17)

In addition to humanistic economics, Lutz sees social economics as composed of 'the so-called "solidarist school" of social catholicism, neo-institutionalists [and] adherents of neo-Marxism' (Lutz 1990b). It was the Catholics who started the social economics movement as the Catholic Economic Association during the Second World War. In the 1960s it became more diverse and secular, changing its name in 1970 to the Association for Social Economics (ASE). ASE has a journal, *Review of Social Economy*. Lutz (1985) compares the institutionalist thought in social economics, and outside it, with its other elements, and Lutz (1990a) is a general review of social economics as a whole.

A recent book by Goodwin (1991) has also sought to build a social economics, starting from the principles of Alfred Marshall. Humanistic economists are organized in addition through the Human Economy Center at Mankato State University, Minnesota, which publishes a newsletter *Human Economy*. Related to but distinct from the humanistic economists is a small group of Indian economists in the United States organized in the Association of Indian Economic Studies who explore the economic implications of Gandhi's teachings. (Their principal publication to date is Diwan and Lutz 1985.)

Institutionalists, also called evolutionary economists, have their own distinguished tradition based on the work of economists such as Veblen, Myrdal and Galbraith. In the United States this group is organized in the Association for Evolutionary Economists (AFEE), whose journal is the *Journal of Economic Issues*. In Europe there is the European Association of Evolutionary Political Economy (EAEPE), with close links to the *Review of Political Economy*, which is also reflective of a post-Keynesian economic approach.

The latest organizational initiative in this general field is the Society for the Advancement of Socio-Economics (SASE), which was founded at a conference at Harvard University in 1988. Lutz (1990b) compared socio-economics with social economics, concluding:

> Socio-economics sees itself as primarily a new and better tool of analysis in positively explaining social reality, while social economists, in general, favor a more normative framework that can help identify and solve social problems. . . . I can think of no reason a normative social economics cannot advantageously use new evidence resulting from positivistic analysis of a socio-economics. Similarly, a socio-economics might only be greatly enriched if its results can also be applied in a ready apparatus that allows for the identification and potential solution of social problems.
>
> (ibid.: 1990b: 318)

It may be that SASE, with its *Journal of Socio-Economics*, will serve as a general umbrella for various inter-disciplinary social scientific groupings such as those on economics and sociology or economics and psychology.

Social and institutional economics and socio-economics tend to focus on the ethical, social and economic dimensions of the four-dimensional framework presented in the last chapter (see pp. 86ff), although interest in the fourth dimension, the ecological, is growing within them. This fourth dimension has been partially treated by environmental economics, which has for some decades at least been a subdiscipline of mainstream thought. As such, however, it is included in many of the criticisms of the mainstream made earlier. In contrast to environmental economics, Martinez-Alier's researches have unearthed a little-known tradition rooted explicitly in matter and energy which he calls 'ecological economics'. In his book of that name he asks, 'One of my most persistent questions is why the recognition of the school of ecological economics, which has objectively existed since the 1880s, is unacknowledged even by its own members' (Martinez-Alier 1987: 3).

However, this concern with matter/energy does not at all lead Martinez-Alier, or the majority of the natural scientists whose economic work he is describing, to overlook the ethical or social dimension in their analysis. Towards the end of his book he writes:

> If economics is to be of use in the study of economic history, then economics, defined as the study of the human allocation of scarce resources to present and future alternative ends, cannot be separated from either the study of the social distribution of moral values concerning the adequate path of depletion of exhaustible resources, or from the history of science and technology.
>
> (Martinez-Alier 1987: 191)

> Economics should not be reduced to human ecology. Economics should be human ecology, and should also be the study of the cultural, social and ethical influences on production and consumption. Such ecological political economy bridges some of the gaps between the natural and the human sciences, and tends to integrate them.
>
> (ibid.: 207)

A similar concern is evident in the important book by Daly and Cobb (1989), an economist and theologian, which is revealingly (if lengthily) entitled *For the Common Good: Redirecting the Economy Towards Community, the Environment and a Sustainable Future*. The multi-dimensional approach of Daly and Martinez-Alier is embodied in the International Society for Ecological Economics (ISEE), set up in 1988, and its journal *Ecological Economics*. The approach was described in a recent ISEE Newsletter by ISEE's Executive Secretary:

> Ecological economics takes a pluralistic transdisciplinary approach encompassing aspects from ecology, economics and other disciplines. It has a pragmatic problem focus, with a comprehensive perspective that views a problem from a holistic, long-term and contextual point of view; a concern for sustainability and equity; a tolerance of uncertainty, including a willingness to ask questions we do not yet know how to answer; a concern for dynamics, process, non-equilibrium, heterogeneity and discontinuity; a social as well as an individualistic point of view; and a concern for the process of institutional change.
>
> (Hagan 1991: 4).

This ecological economic agenda was explicitly compared with both conventional economics and conventional ecology in the book *Ecological Economics: The Science and Management of Sustainability* (Costanza 1991) which derived from the ISEE international meeting of May 1990. The comparison is given in Table 4.2.

Another sub-discipline of mainstream economics is that concerned with 'development'. Because the capitalist industrialist countries are considered 'developed', development economics tends to focus on the economies of the

Third World, almost always with the objective of instructing these countries in how to follow in the footsteps of the 'developed'. In terms of achieving this objective, and with the exception of a few special-case Asian economies, development economics, on the basis of nearly four decades of experience, must be accounted a monumental failure. Furthermore, the policies it has advocated have resulted in untold social, cultural and ecological disruption, the effects of which have, of course, been omitted from the balance sheets of development programmes, which are therefore even more of a failure than their often abysmal financial performance seems to indicate.

The whole issue of development is explored in Chapter 6, so further discussion of the issue here will be limited to mentioning two organizations which, in different ways, are in the forefront of efforts to redefine development theory and practice. The Society for International Development (SID) acts in some ways much like the professional association for development economists, and one does not have to look far within it to find examples of the orthodox thinking that is criticized in this book. But it is also a diverse and pluralistic organization. Among the keynote speakers at its large triennial conferences are always some of the most unorthodox, challenging thinkers. Its journal *Development* is genuinely representative of the ferment in development thinking today. If the so-called 'core' economics journals were half as open-minded editorially, the economics discipline would be far more vibrant intellectually.

If SID acts as a broad forum for development thought, the People-Centred Development Forum (PCDF), aims to root such thought securely in activism. Founded in 1990, its objective, in its own words, is to

encourage and strengthen voluntary action toward the realisation of a people-centred development vision. It is a values driven voluntary network of activist-intellectuals who are helping to shape the directions of an emerging people's development movement. This movement envisions a just, sustainable and inclusive society that celebrates the richness and diversity of life, enhances personal freedom, lives by non-violence, and enables the growth of community and the human spirit.

(PCDF 1990)

There are many other organizational impulses that are seeking either to broaden the mainstream of economic analysis or to establish a multi-dimensional alternative to it, among which can be cited the International Network for Economic Method, with its bulletin *Methodus*, based in Hong Kong; the Karl Polanyi Institute organized out of Concordia University, Montreal, Canada; the European Association for Bioeconomic Studies, based in Milan and founded on the work of Nicholas Georgescu-Roegen; and the UK New Economics Foundation, together with the independent groups in France and North America that have organized the series of TOES (The Other Economic Summit) conferences. Contact addresses for all the initiatives or organizations mentioned above are given in the Appendix.

The nature of the living economics that is being developed in this book, and

Table 4.2 Comparison of 'conventional' economics and ecology with ecological economics

	'Conventional' economics	*'Conventional' ecology*	*Ecological economics*
Basic world-view	Mechanistic, static, atomistic Individual tastes and preferences taken as given and the dominant force. The resource base viewed as essentially limitless due to technical progress and infinite substitutability	Evolutionary, atomistic Evolution acting at the genetic level viewed as the dominant force. The resource base is limited. Humans are just another species but are rarely studied	Dynamic, systems, evolutionary Human preferences, understanding, technology and organization coevolve to reflect broad ecological opportunities and constraints. Humans are responsible for understanding their role in the larger system and managing it sustainably
Time frame	Short 50 years max., 1–4 years usual	Multi-scale Days to eons, but time scales often define non-communicating subdisciplines	Multi-scale Days to eons, multi-scale synthesis
Space frame	Local to international Framework invariant at increasing spatial scale, basic units change from individuals to firms to countries	Local to regional Most research has focused on smaller research sites in one ecosystem, but larger scales have become more important	Local to global Hierarchy of scales
Species frame	Humans only Plants and animals only rarely included for contributory value	Non-humans only Attempts to find 'pristine' ecosystems untouched by humans	Whole ecosystem including humans Acknowledges interconnections between humans and rest of nature
Primary macro goal	Growth of national economy	Survival of species	Ecological economic system sustainability

Primary micro goal	Max. profits (firms) Max. utility (individuals) All agents following micro goals leads to macro goal being fulfilled. External costs and benefits given lip service but usually ignored	Max. reproductive success All agents following micro goals leads to macro goal being fulfilled.	Must be adjusted to reflect system goals Social organization and cultural institutions at higher levels of the space/time hierarchy ameliorate conflicts produced by myopic pursuit of micro goals at lower levels
Assumptions about technical progress	Very optimistic	Pessimistic or no opinion	Prudently sceptical
Academic stance	Disciplinary Monistic, focus on mathematical tools	Disciplinary More pluralistic than economics, but still focused on tools and techniques. Few rewards for integrative work	Transdisciplinary Pluralistic, focus on problems

Source: Costanza, Daly and Bartholomew 1991: 5

the purpose of its articulation, and thus of the Living Economy Network that is undertaking it, can now be more clearly explained. First, the four-dimensional tetrahedral framework of Chapter 3 can be used as a means of locating all modes of economic analysis with regard to their relative considera-tion of ethical, ecological, social and economic issues. This is illustrated in Figure 4.3. Thus the pure neoclassical position would be at A, abstracting from ethical, social and ecological concerns with an emphasis on rationality, utility and self-interest. The neoclassical environmental economist might be at B on the line joining economy and ecology but still giving no weight to the other two dimensions. As, perhaps, intergenerational equity came to be perceived as important, the position would shift upwards towards the ethical corner (C), but would still have a zero social component. Only as intragenera-tional equity took on importance would social relations enter the picture, with the point moving fully inside the space (D). The Marxist economist is hard to locate in this framework because of the perception that the social dimension is dependent on the economic (i.e. there are only three linearly independent dimensions). The institutionalist or socio-economist who discounts the environment might be at E on the society–economy–ethics plane. Anti-economists, those who reject the notion of scarcity, might be at point F, on the ethics–ecology–society plane. The economism of someone like Gary Becker causes the tetrahedron to collapse into a straight line, with economy and ecology at its two ends, because of his perception that all human behaviour can be analysed economically, as in the Preface to his *A Treatise on the Family*: 'The [neoclassical] economic approach provides a framework applicable to all human behaviour – to all types of decisions and to persons from all walks of life' (Becker 1981: ix). As Schor notes, 'This approach effectively obliterated the idea of "an economy". . . . [The economy] is everywhere and everything, because it is just a way of behaving' (Schor 1989: 18).

Living economics, perceiving the four-dimensions to be of equal import-ance *a priori*, is located at the centre of the tetrahedron. In the language of Lawson's paper in Chapter 1, its initial assumption is that the 'generative structures' influencing human action have independent ethical, ecological, social and economic dimensions. In some situations the influence of any particular dimension may be weak, when it might be acceptable in the process of abstraction to ignore it, without losing, in Lawson's words, 'the real and essential'. This in turn would permit the utilization of the tools or method-ologies of another school of economic thought, the assumptions of which are based on such abstraction. But the procedure would have to be justified on each occasion. In this sense living economics is encompassing, seeking always to start from a comprehensive perception of reality, but simplifying as appropriate in particular circumstances. While such a procedure may seem long-winded, it has the great advantage of making values and assumptions explicit and therefore running less risk of using tools or methodologies where they are patently inappropriate.

Second, living economics seeks to bring within a single frame of reference,

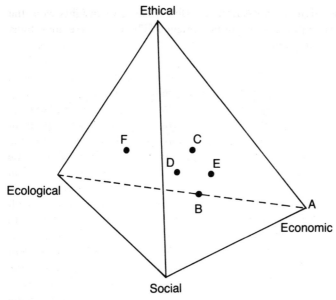

Key:
A – Neoclassical
B – Neoclassical environmental
C – B with intergenerational equity
D – C with intragenerational equity
E – Institutionalist (with no ecological concern)
F – Anti-economist

Figure 4.3 Schools of economic thought

in a mutually compatible way, some of the more significant streams of thought briefly reviewed earlier: the evolutionary economic approach of Hodgson and Norgaard's coevolution; Etzioni's socio-economics; Lutz's humanistic economics; the ecological economics of Hueting and Pearce; and, in future chapters, new approaches in development economics. This frame of reference provides a rich context for economic analysis in comparison with any of these streams in isolation, or compared to mainstream economics as a whole.

Third, living economics also seeks to emphasize areas of the economy which tend to be marginalized. Most important among these are still the environment, which has already been discussed, and the non-monetary economy, especially the household economy, the routine ignoring of which so devalues and insults the economic activity of half the world's population – women. Living economics seeks to give value to family and community activity with regard both to material output and their crucial role of social integration and cohesion.

On the basis of this holistic, enriched economic discourse, living economics is able to derive a new conception of wealth and how it is created. Thence it can evolve a perception of what constitutes economic progress and indicate how that progress might be measured. Finally, it can give insights as to the policies by which such progress might be achieved. These steps are the subject matter of the rest of the book.

Part II

On economic activity, progress and development

5 Seeing the whole economy

Having located the economy in a four-dimensional human space which makes explicit social, economic, ecological and ethical interaction, one can now proceed to identify the specific institutions through or in which all human activity, economic or otherwise, is expressed. These fall into four groups: market institutions, involved in the exchange of commodities, often mediated by money; government institutions, sanctioned by formal political processes, the rule of law or state power; households, normally comprised of families; and civic society, the voluntary groupings of citizens based on issues, interests or locality.

All these institutions are involved in economic activity, and all four groups are significant sources of wealth creation. As economic sectors, there is no hard and fast division between them. Rather they interact, some sectors growing, others shrinking, for economic, social, political, ethical or cultural reasons.

Conventional economic analysis tends to focus overwhelmingly on the market and the state, to the effective exclusion of the non-monetary sectors of the household and civic society. This is most unfortunate, for a moment's reflection reveals that, in real life, the non-monetary economy is and always has been fundamental both to human life and to the operation of the formal economy, whereas the converse is not true. Many human societies have got along well without states and markets. None have without families and voluntary, productive structures of interpersonal relations (i.e. voluntary organizations). By ignoring the domestic and voluntary sectors, such conventional economic analysis only sees that part of the iceberg that is above the water of monetization. Maps based on such perceptions are likely to be dangerously inaccurate. Real-life economics seeks to keep its eyes firmly on the total reality.

The household in the total economy

Jane Wheelock

The household at the heart of total economic activity

The significance of the unpaid, unmeasured, sector of the economy – much of the work of which is undertaken within the household – still remains largely unexplored. This paper is about those economic processes which are not encompassed by money or commodity relations, and their interrelationship with the recorded economy. The holistic analysis of the economy that I shall be presenting here places the family at the centre of its analytical framework. I shall be arguing that the family in particular, and the economically unmeasured sector in general, are not an alternative society. They enact sets of activities which are *complementary* to the formal, money economy: 'An analysis of the relationship between the family and the labour process must be central to any account of the mode of production as a whole' (Redclift 1985: 94).

In the next section, I shall be discussing why it is that the whole economy has rarely been looked at by economists, and explaining the advantages of a holistic approach. The analysis will concentrate on the domestic sector. This is justified on the one hand by the sheer size of the household economy, estimated at around 40 per cent of GNP as conventionally measured (Smith 1986); on the other, it is justified by its analytical significance. This is in contrast to Harding and Jenkins (1989), who started their analysis of total economic activity from the most sensational unmeasured part: the 'black economy'. Whilst they reach valid and useful conclusions on 'The Myth of the Hidden Economy', they thereby fail to develop the relationship between the family and the labour process. It is also important that starting from the family presumes an interdisciplinary approach, and a focus on the domestic sector places ethical and social considerations squarely on the economic agenda.

The third section will develop a typology of total economic activity. Fourth, I will ask how a system which sees the whole economy – and the families within it – is regulated, arguing that the work strategies that households adopt provide the link between the reproductive cycle of the family unit and the general process of accumulation and development under capitalism. This is of particular importance given the process of de-industrialization and the decline of full employment that has occurred under advanced capitalism. Since activities not subject to the pricing mechanism have regularly been excluded from the concerns of economists, the effects of economic restructuring on such economic processes have not been fully explored, nor has the social impact been integrated into the framework of economic understanding. Lastly, I will indicate the importance of family self-respect and its contribution to the formation of values in a post-industrial society.

Including the domestic sector

Despite the substantial weight of the domestic sector within the economy as a whole, it has rarely been adequately incorporated within economic models. Much of this inadequacy can be understood in terms of the way that economics has been concerned to maintain its position as 'queen' (*sic*) of the social sciences by taking an aggressively separatist stance in relation to other disciplines. To be able to incorporate the sort of gender issues included in the domestic sector into the discipline would require economists to acknowledge the importance of taking an interdisciplinary approach to their subject matter, something that only Marxists and Institutionalists have been prepared to do to date.

True, the household has long been seen as one of two basic units of analysis in economics. The firm is the other. Yet the focus of attention has been on the individual male earner, even though the stereotypical family unit, made up of a male breadwinner, his non-working wife and their two to three children, comprises only 15 per cent of all households. It is further surprising how consistently economists have regarded those entering the labour market as individuals rather than as members of a household unit; whilst at the same time regarding the household as an undifferentiated individual and not as a group.

By and large the household has been regarded as a 'black box' by economists, making it unnecessary to examine the gender pattern of either consumption, or of expenditure within this basic unit. Similarly, the significance of the household in terms of production has been largely ignored, as for example its role in the rearing of a future labour force. 'Economists hardly recognise that [the household] exists, caring little beyond that it consume an adequate number of dishwashers and continue to save at an appropriate rate' (Burns 1977: 3). In contrast, academic sociologists, as a response to the womens' movement, have taken the initiative in raising questions about what constitutes 'work', looking at work more widely and making connections between paid and unpaid work. Gender was also introduced as a significant factor, both in the labour market itself and within the household. The issue of women as dual workers both in the home and in the job market became incorporated into academic thinking.

The boundary between the formal economy and the household sector is established in how production decisions within the household are made. The crucial question becomes: 'On what basis do people choose to do some things themselves (household production), and to have others done by someone else (formal economy)?' (Smith 1986: 162). This can alternatively be put in terms of the choice individuals and families make about how to earn their income and whether they choose to work for self-consumption or for income.

These concerns do not merely throw light on the conventional constructs of employed, unemployed, and people not in the labour force as used in labour-market analysis; they are also steeped in considerations where gender is of fundamental importance. In addition, it is not appropriate to explain the basis on which the complementary economy functions simply in terms of economic gain. When we consider the full range of economic institutions, both informal and formal, it becomes imperative to look beyond the stereotyped assumption of 'rational economic man' (*sic*) to gain a proper understanding of people's motivation. The work strategies that households choose are based on diverse and conflicting motivations which incorporate not only economic evaluations but also traditional perceptions of gender roles and a concern for dignity and self-respect.

It is important to realise that the household is a productive economic institution, which like the firm, produces goods and services with a tangible economic value and employs labour and capital. In order to specify the relationship between the household and the formal economy it is essential to have a more precise understanding of the nature of the non-formal economy. The latter is a very diverse sector, which has been seen to include not just housework but also voluntary work, DIY, white-collar crime and the 'black economy', to name but a few of the other elements that have been put under its rubric. There is also a confusing variety of names, both for the sector as a whole, and for its component parts. Let me therefore turn to developing a typology for the institutional structure of the economy as a whole, so that the household economy can be clearly located in relation to the rest of the economy.

An institutional model: the household in the complementary economy

Economics already pays considerable attention to the institutional structures of the formal economy. Orthodox economics focuses on market structure, its effects on competition and on the prices charged by firms and their levels of output. Within the Marxist paradigm, the emphasis is on the institutional form taken by accumulation. During the accumulation process, the form taken by 'many capitals' in competition changes. Under modern capitalism there is not merely competitive, or non-monopoly, capital but also monopoly capital, financial capital, international capital and state capital. Both paradigms have similarly paid considerable attention to the institutions of the labour market. Again the orthodox focus is on the determination of prices, which in this case are wages. Marxists are concerned with the labour process and its role in accumulation. There has been little attention paid within either paradigm to the institutional structures relating to the reproduction of labour power or those which lie on the margins between this and the accumulation of capital. It is precisely this gap in the attention to institutional structures that the typology in Figure 5.1 attempts to address.

To take account of total economic activity within a developed economy, the formal sector of that economy can be contrasted with the complementary economy. Broadly speaking, the division between the formal and the complementary economy follows the line between measured and unmeasured

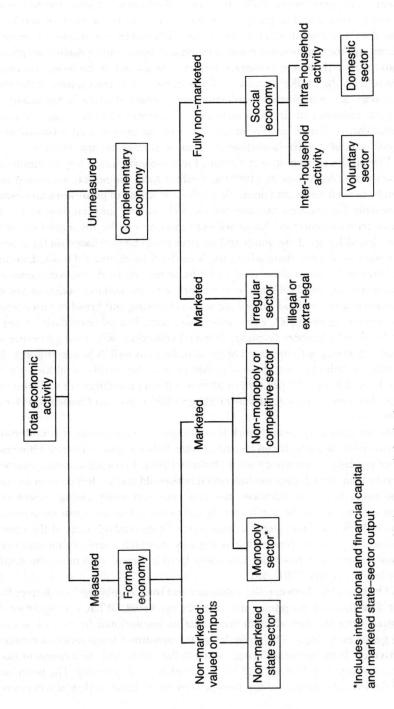

*Includes international and financial capital and marketed state–sector output

Figure 5.1 A typology of productive economic institutions

economic activity. Formal economic activity is recorded in the national income accounts (Smith 1986). But just as the formal economy has two sectors – one marketed and largely private, the other a non-marketed state sector – so too does the complementary economy. These are the marketed irregular sector and the non-marketed social economy, which can be further subdivided into the household and voluntary sectors. The output of the social economy is not sold on the market and its labour is unpaid. The institutions of the social economy are self-generated informal ones, which operate independently of regular economic institutions and can be characterized as personalized institutional forms. There are essentially two sorts of institutional relations in the social economy: intra-household relations and inter-household ones.

Within the household sector, work for self-consumption for the family unit takes place. As Mingione (1985) and others have suggested, household work can be broken down into domestic work – consisting of housework and caring, especially for children but also for the sick, elderly and handicapped – and extra self-consumption. Extra self-consumption can be distinguished by the fact that although these goods and services could be purchased on the market, the work is actually done within the household on an unpaid basis. Examples of extra self-consumption tend to be quite limited in developed economies, consisting largely of DIY and home improvements, making clothes or knitting and some forms of food processing such as brewing and bread or jam making. In developing countries, extra self-consumption is a more extensive category and can include water fetching, firewood collection, wild food gathering and food-processing activities such as grain milling, as well as house-building. It is perhaps worth realizing, however, that even in the world's wealthiest nation, the United States, 20 per cent of all single family dwellings are self-built, and that there are high rates of self-building in Germany and Canada too (Henry 1981, ch. 6).

In the voluntary sector, work is also unpaid, but this time it is undertaken between households. It can consist of what Bulmer aptly calls 'neighbouring', or of self-help or voluntary work (Bulmer 1986). Extra self-consumption may also be transferred from the individual household and undertaken on an inter-household basis. In addition, the childcare and other caring functions of domestic work may be partly transferred to the voluntary sector on an unpaid basis. As Stuart Henry sees it, this sector 'is the embodiment of the counter culture. . . . More generally it is the way in which people come together to satisfy needs that have not been met by the formal system of the regular economy' (Henry 1981: 19).

The boundary between the voluntary and the irregular sectors derives from the fact that the output of the latter is marketed. What distinguishes this output from the formal economy is that its institutional framework is either illegal or extra-legal. The irregular sector contains a huge range of economic activities, from corporate crime, white-collar crime and the evasion of tax or bureaucracy, to pilfering, fiddling and working and claiming. The boundaries of the irregular economy are flexible over time, because they are defined by changing social attitudes as codified in changes in the law. Historically, for example, what had been wood gathering, grazing and game rights became wood theft, trespassing and poaching respectively (Henry 1981: 14). Within the irregular economy a distinction can be made between illegal and extra-legal activities, where the latter avoid paying taxes, bypass required bureaucratic procedures or establish false entitlements to state support.

I have contrasted the formal economy with the complementary economy because the latter plays precisely that role. The complementary sector is neither parasitic nor residual. It operates not as an alternative society but as a complementary economic activity to the formal. So, for example, while the state and the private sector within the formal economy may have taken on some aspects of the production and reproduction of labour power (such as education, training, pension provision and health), the household sector still retains much of its responsibility here. Harding and Jenkins put this in a historical context, when they suggest that history can be seen as the progressive encroachment of the formal; yet 'along with greater scope for formality comes, of necessity, increased scope for informality' (Harding and Jenkins 1989: 136).

Similarly the irregular sector can be seen as a mirror of the free market capitalist spirit, indeed a caricature of it. In a rare study of corporate crime, Clinard and Yeager assert that 'Corporate crime is indicative of the distribution of power in our society' (Clinard and Yeager 1980: 21) and that it provides an indication of society's degree of hypocrisy by countenancing upper-class deception and calling it 'shrewd business practice'. What is more, 'the desire to increase or maintain current profits is the critical factor in a wide range of corporate deviance, from refusal to install pollution control equipment to well planned decisions to make a shoddy product that will wear out and need replacing' (ibid.: 47). On the other hand, the irregular sector can also be seen as complementing the role of the state as a redistributor of income; this is the case when the irregular economy provides an alternative or additional source of employment for people, and acts as a form of income support, as in many developing countries.

The family and the household sector can be seen to derive from sharply differing motivations. On the one hand they can embody an extension of choice, whereby families choose for example between consumption and self-consumption alternatives, or whether to have children and how many they will have. Pahl and Wallace can point to a process of domestication as the 'production of a value system which puts home-centred activities as the central focus of a distinctive life style' (Pahl and Wallace 1985: 219). On the other hand, the household economy can become a strategy for economic survival (Bradley 1986) with informal institutions acting as a mask for the failures of the official economy and an excuse for governments to offload responsibilities. The social economy then provides goods or services which are either hard to obtain, or too expensive, given the price mechanism or levels of taxation. An example of the former type of provision is self-help; of the latter, home improvements.

The same types of activities are to be found in the irregular sector, where the size and scale of activity is generally small with direct distribution and little specialization of labour. Levels of investment are low, and activity is often intermittent. Levels of return for work vary widely, and pricing is idiosyncratic, in part because the relations between providers and users are often grounded in personal ties. In addition it is often not easy to distinguish the irregular from the social economy for 'Many exchanges that are irregular involve an unrecorded exchange of money and are virtually indistinguishable from similar transactions that do not involve overt payment' (Ferman and Berndt 1981: 30).

The complementary economy therefore has an intermediate status in the social reproduction processes of capitalism: on the one hand, it performs a major role in producing and reproducing labour power; on the other hand, it can reproduce – in the irregular sector – non-monopoly capital, or even monopoly capital, in the case of corporate crime. So, for example, formal work reflects the fundamental cost of labour in the reproduction process, together with monetary consumption capacity, and it contributes to the state fiscal system. When individuals combine work in the formal and the irregular economy, this is a source of income, but it does not reflect the full costs of labour, and it cheats the fiscal system in part. Work undertaken entirely in the irregular sector is not detected and so cheats the fiscal system.

The balance between work for self-consumption and for income (whether formal or informal) is determined by the qualitative and quantitative structure of labour demand, including its gender structure and the role of state intervention. A classification system for the economy as a whole provides a framework for analysing the relationship between changes in the structure of the formal and complementary economies, together with the process of accumulation and economic growth.

The domestic economy and capitalist restructuring

Let me then sketch out a framework within which the effects of national and international changes in the nature of monopoly capitalism on household work strategies can be considered. How, in other words, is an economic system within which the domestic and voluntary sectors are to be incorporated, regulated? To undertake this, I should like to elaborate the typology already developed rather further. This will help to highlight the interrelations between the social and formal economies. Figure 5.2 summarizes the role that the different sectors of the economy play in structural economic change. The social economy plays a primary role in the production and reproduction of labour, with its responsibility for the care of children, the elderly, the sick and the disabled. The domestic sector also accumulates substantial amounts of household capital (Burns 1977; Gershuny 1978). The state sector of the formal economy plays a far smaller role in the reproduction of labour through its health and education services, and accumulates capital in the form of state

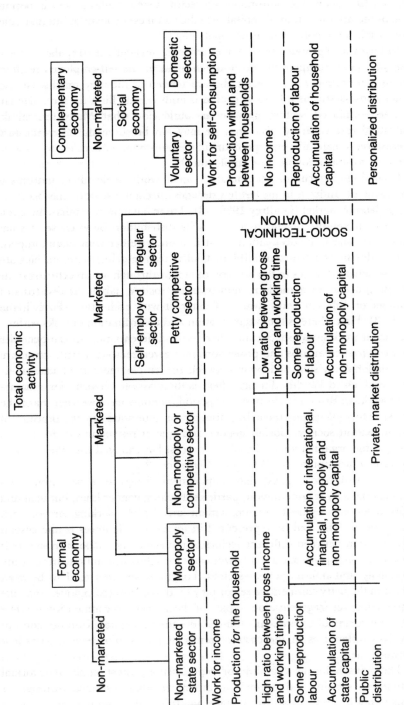

Figure 5.2 Selected characteristics of economic sectors

capital. Monopoly and non-monopoly sectors together play a very important role in the accumulation of capital, whether it takes the form of international, fincancial, monopoly or non-monopoly capital.

In terms of reproduction, it makes sense to consider the irregular sector as part of a petty competitive sector which includes the self-employed sector of the formal economy. This sector is characterized by the very small scale of its units whose status as a form of capital is ambivalent. Both the irregular and the self-employed sectors provide an outlet for what Marx termed the industrial reserve army, who may or may not be successful in establishing themselves as capitalist entrepreneurs in the non-monopoly sector, so avoiding a return to unemployment or employment.

Changing patterns of accumulation on a world scale affect patterns of employment. Indeed, in the last few decades the capitalist world has become a single labour market (Godfrey 1986: 23). There have been gender changes in the overall volume of employment, in its distribution between sectors and industries, and in its occupational distribution, together with spatial implications (Martin and Rowthorn 1986). Global restructuring of capital has also meant radical changes in the division of labour through a restructuring of the labour process. In a modern industrialized society, labour is divided in a number of different ways, which all interact with each other (Purcell *et al.* 1986: 3). First, there is the fragmentation and co-ordination of tasks within a particular work situation. Second, there is the differentiation and co-operation between particular jobs and professions in a given society. Third, there is an international division of labour between the employment structures of the First and Third Worlds. Finally, there is the division between domestic and paid work. In Britain in the post-war period, not only have we seen changes in the structure of employment but also radical alterations in the divisions of labour within society. Social, gender and spatial restructurings have taken place as the organization of the labour process has changed with the changing patterns of accumulation (Wheelock 1990a, ch. 2).

It is possible to suggest that employment structure is becoming more characterized by fragmentation, particularly along gender lines, but including rises in self-employment, unemployment and flexible working for both men and women. This can be represented in terms of differences in the costs of reproduction between different sectors of the economy. Labour in the social economy is not paid, since it involves work for self-consumption. In the state, monopoly and non-monopoly sectors, hourly wage rates tend to be high, whilst in the petty competitive sector they tend to be low (Mingione 1985: 30). Labour-market fragmentation is part of the process of competition between different forms of capital, including international capital. Competition also involves differences in the costs of reproduction within sectors, as well as between them.

The household, as the unit of reproduction, must apply its working activities to earning and to supplying directly goods and services through self-consumption. Individuals who make up this unit negotiate or otherwise decide a balance between work for income and for self-consumption. These decisions will be made in the light of social changes brought about by the process of international economic restructuring, which may alter the gender divisions of labour within the household. For example, empirical work undertaken on Wearside showed that pressures to change the household division of labour are likely to be particularly great in regions where male unemployment is high and where opportunities for female employment are relatively buoyant (Wheelock 1990a).

Families and self-respect: values in a post-industrial society

Any rearticulation of work strategies within the household is subject to four major constraints: economic rationality, pressures from the state benefit system, traditional ideology and the desire for self-respect (Wheelock 1990b). Women and men have different perceptions of economic rationality. On the one hand, economic rationality must take account of employment opportunities, levels of pay and access to state benefits for both husband and wife. On the other, economic rationality will also be coloured by the unequal access that women and men have to the family wage. In Britain the Keynes–Beveridge framework for state intervention in the labour market has proven poorly suited to the changing structure of employment since the Second World War (Cutler *et al.* 1986, ch. 4; Ekins 1986). It was based on an assumption that a husband could earn an adequate wage to support his family, a possibility undermined wherever de-industrialization has progressively reduced job opportunities for male manual workers. This assumption has done much to buttress concepts of a continuing traditional gender division of labour within the household, while economic restructuring has done much to invalidate it.

My own study of families where husbands are unemployed whilst their wives remain in paid work undertaken in an area characterized by extensive de-industrialization has shown that families may decide household work strategies on the basis of self-respect, involving a desire to be free both from the constraints of the market and from the state benefit system – a self-respect which may also fly in the face of traditional rationalities (Wheelock 1990b). Under these circumstances, wives may decide to work in the formal economy, whilst their husbands become more involved in the social economy.

A household work strategy based on dignity and self-respect can be understood in terms of a reconceptualization of the labour process. The labour process within the household involves the adoption of a personalized life-style. Indeed, one of the hallmarks of the social economy is that it permits the development of a personal life-style based on home-centred values, which may be at variance with economic rationality. In contrast, the marketed sectors of the economy satisfy needs which are directly circumscribed by market based values.

Thus different sectors of the economy satisfy different needs as Figure 5.2 shows: the state provides for collective needs, the market for private needs and the social economy for personal needs, corresponding to different systems of distribution. A distribution system depends upon differing levels of commodification between sectors: in the social economy there is a personalized system of distribution, which can be contrasted with the private, market-based system of the monopoly, non-monopoly and petty competitive sectors, and the public distribution of the state sector. The boundaries between the institutional mechanisms by which the three types of needs – collective, private and personal – are met are of course porous and variable. For example, the collective need for education or health can also be supplied through the market, or indeed within the domestic or the voluntary sectors. Personal needs can be and are transformed into private needs through the medium of advertising by the market sectors.

It is worth noting also that the petty competitive sector is unique in that a combination of private and personal needs can be met here. Whilst many might regard this sector as exploited by those forms of capital which have accumulated into larger units, individuals may choose to work in this sector, not merely as a survival strategy, but because they prefer the life-style that this work incorporates, particularly, perhaps, in terms of 'being their own boss'. Household work may also constitute a survival strategy as well as contribute to the development of a personalized life-style.

Institutionalists argue that value theory is a study of the process by which judgements about values are made. It is important to realize that such judgements are made in the context of the dynamic process of technological accumulation.

> The innovation and use of the better and more desirable technologies is a process that occasions changes in the structure of institutions and in their behaviour norms, which those institutions are imposing on individuals. And those institutionalized behaviour norms are the values of institutions and in turn are affecting the values of individuals.
>
> (Adams 1980: 37)

Gershuny puts forward a theory of socio-technical innovation which provides a framework for linking the domestic sector to the formal economy (Gershuny 1978, 1983). He points out that the connection between needs and economic demand is not a direct one, but rather mediated by technology. A socio-technical innovation is one where the means by which a need is satisfied change, so that households' demands for commodities change too. There are new modes of provision for particular needs; so instead of catching the bus to work, people buy cars which they drive themselves. Socio-technical innovations like the private motor car, television, video recorders, washing machines, freezers and microwaves, have a twofold effect. First, the new modes of provision for particular needs affect the structure of the economy through final demand, while, second, they influence the division between paid and unpaid time and thus household activity patterns. Gershuny's theory suggests not merely an interrelation between the household sector and the formal economy, but that the domestic sector may well be a causal factor for economic development. Such a shift to the domestic provision of services also has important gender implications, of which Gershuny is aware, although he does not develop them. They have been briefly discussed here.

There are thus some very important implications for economic theory arising from a holistic approach which places the family at the heart of the whole economy. It is not possible to separate either the domestic sector or the social economy from the formal economy. The social economy is neither at the margins of reproduction nor of accumulation. Indeed the complementary and the formal economies combine in provisioning society. The boundary between the formal and the social economy is established by how production decisions within the household are made, but households use multiple work strategies, so that this also provides the link between the complementary and the formal economy. However, the decisions that households make are not necessarily on the basis of economic maximization. So whilst the regulatory system within the social economy cannot be independent of that within the formal international capitalist system, it does have a separate pole. Work for self-consumption within the social economy may be a coping response to inadequate resources and entirely a function of economic constraints. But there may also be work for self-consumption which allows a personalized life-style and a sense of creativeness and dignity.

In terms of regulation of the total economic system, there is thus an enigmatic interaction between the social and the formal economy. This is because, on the one hand, work within the social economy may be the result of the market constraints of increasing poverty; on the other hand, it may be the result of increasing affluence and a relative separation from economic constraints represented by the adoption of a personalized life-style. As already mentioned, the interaction is rendered all the more ambivalent by the fact that even some of the least well off may choose to base their work strategies and their life-style on self-respect (Wheelock 1990b). The intimate relationship between the formal and the complementary economies means that the mode of regulation of monopoly capitalism is modified by the personal wishes and aspirations put into effect within the social economy.

Wheelock's classification of the economy into six sectors (state, monopoly, competitive, irregular, voluntary, domestic) is clearly congruent with Ross's identification of nine sectors: big business, public sector, small business, collectives and co-operatives, community enterprises, voluntary activity, barter and skills exchange, mutual aid and the household (Ekins 1986: 155). Both typologies spring from a perception of the necessity of including within economic analysis the non-commercial sectors of the economy, a theme which is taken up again by Goldschmidt-Clermont in Chapter 8 of this book.

If it is important always to remember that it is only part, and perhaps not the most important part, of the economy which produces goods and services through the state or for exchange on the market, it is equally important to be aware of the dramatic shift towards services which has occurred in all advanced industrial economies in recent years. This trend is difficult to document statistically and undoubtedly some of the numerical growth of the service sector is as much due to service functions which were previously in-house to manufacturing companies now being contracted out to specialist service firms as to any basic shift of activity. But this does not account for anything like the whole of the observed trend and analysts are now generally agreed that the service sector is of much greater intrinsic importance than used to be the case. This change has great implications not just for sectoral analysis but for the whole conceptualization of economic value and wealth creation.

The modern economy as a service economy: the production of utilization value

Orio Giarini

The transformation of the industrial economy into a service economy

The traditional industrial society can be described as a situation in which the privileged and by far the most important way to produce wealth and welfare is through the manufacturing process, whereby raw materials are transformed into final useable products sold on the market.

In this situation, where the main preoccupation is to produce goods, services, although sometimes recognized as important, are none the less secondary. In other words, they are not as important as and generally not essential to, production. John Stuart Mill stated explicitly that the economic process was aimed exclusively at producing 'utilities fixed and embodied in outward *objects*' (Mill 1968). In other words, even if material objects had finally a destination and a practical use value, there was no need to consider that the process of utilization of these material objects needed any further economic activity. It is therefore with a good conscience that the industrial revolution concentrated on the production of material goods as the essential process to further the wealth of nations.

But if we now look at all sectors of contemporary economic activity, we can easily find out that services of any sort represent the essential part of the production and delivery system of goods and services. A first fundamental fact to be taken into consideration is that for each product we buy, be it an automobile or a carpet, the pure cost of production or of manufacturing is very seldom higher than 20 to 30 per cent of the final price of these products. More than 70 or 80 per cent is represented by the cost of making the complex service and delivery system work, which means that service functions have become the greatest part of concern and investment even within the most traditional industrial companies.

It must therefore be clear that the service economy is not in opposition to the industrial economy, but is a development of it. In the same way, at the beginning of of the Industrial Revolution, agricultural production was not eliminated. On the contrary, it remained a fundamental economic activity, but it was through industrialization, directly or indirectly, that agriculture increased in productivity. Now both agriculture and manufacturing industry have more and more to rely on the development of services in order to improve their economic performance in production and distribution.

The service functions intervene at several levels in the production and use of wealth. We can broadly classify them in five categories:

1. Services performed long before any production starts such as research and development. It should be noted that it is only after 1930 that this function has become a specific, professional one deserving separate budget accounting. In some high-technology sectors, this pre-production service function can go as far as representing more than 50 per cent of the total cost of a full production series. Service functions such as investment programmes and market research studies also often intervene before any production process of any sort has started.
2. Concentration and specialization of production have required a greater and greater emphasis on service functions like planning, maintenance, storage, quality control and safety measures.
3. Distribution is already *per se* essentially a service function of great complexity and is obviously essential for the efficient organization of systems making products and services available.
4. A very specific characteristic of the service economy is the growth of service functions related to the utilization of any sort of products during their period of useful life. Users are more and more called upon to invest in their education in order to transform the potential value of any product or service into something of practical use. Users very often become part of the production system ('prosumers'), in order to make things work and yield their potential value.
5. Services now come into action more and more to manage both the waste and the pollution produced at all levels of the manufacturing process, as well as at the end of the useful lifespan of products, when they become waste themselves.

Figure 5.3 depicts the increased complexity of the economic system. During the Industrial Revolution, the transformation process from raw materials to the final product was the key feature of the economic system. Today, the larger part of economic resources is absorbed by functions parallel to this process on the right and on the left of the figure. On the one side an increasing number of services are needed before and during production: research, development, investment planning, storage and distribution

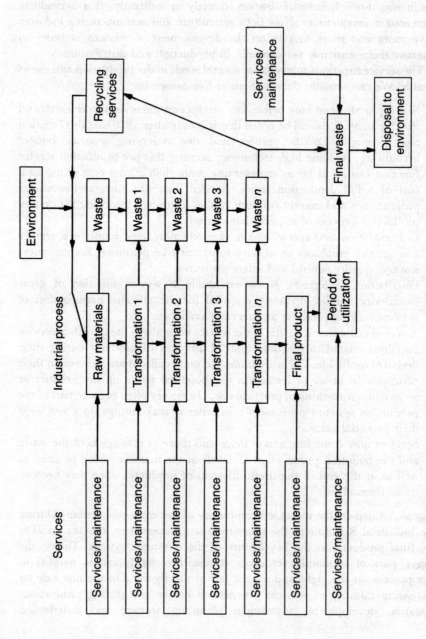

Figure 5.3 The role of services in the economy

systems, maintenance and repair, security measures and insurance, market research, and so on. On the other side, costs of disposal of waste accumulated during production and after utilization of products are clearly growing. It is obvious that agriculture and manufacturing industry are essential and strongly influence the nature of available services; but today it is also true that any sort of product which does not rely on the functioning of services is simply not in a condition to be used or even produced. Products of any sort can only exist economically through the service system.

We can therefore say that a key difference between the industrial economy and the service economy is that the first one gives value essentially to products which exist materially and which are exchanged, whereas value, in the service economy, is more closely attributed to the performance and real utilization (in a given time period) of products (material or not) integrated in a system. Whereas during the classical economic revolution the value of products could be identified essentially with the costs involved in producing them, the notion of value in the service economy is shifting towards the evaluation of costs incurred with reference to obtaining results in utilization.

The first approach considers the value of a washing machine *per se*, the second one evaluates the actual performance of the washing machine, taking into consideration not only its cost of production, but also all other sorts of costs (learning time of the people using the machine, maintenance and repair costs, etc.). The applicability of the two approaches depends in most cases on the technological complexity of the products: in the case of simple products and tools, the assessment of the value can be limited to the tool or the product *per se*. Nobody buying a hammer would think it necessary to take courses to learn how to use it. In the case of a computer, however, the cost of learning how to use it tends to surpass the purchase cost of the machine, especially if the costs of all the necessary software are added.

Similarly, people buying tools such as dishes or even a bicycle will not consider signing a maintenance contract. With the purchase of electronic typewriters, photocopying machines or even television sets, however, maintenance contracts – even for individual consumers – are more and more common. In the service economy, the functioning of a tool is being purchased (therefore, including costs of maintenance and repair); people are buying more and more functioning 'systems', not just products.

The real change towards the service economy stems precisely from the fact that services are becoming indispensable to make products and services fulfilling basic needs. Services are no longer simply a secondary sector, but they are moving into the focus of economic action, where they have become *indispensable production tools* to satisfy the basic needs and to increase the wealth of nations.

Reconsidering the notion of economic value given by John Stuart Mill, we can therefore safely say that in the modern service economy the value of the material objects cannot be considered anymore as limited to their mere existence. The utilization of all material objects requires more and more the functioning of services. Services have become, contrary to the Industrial Revolution, real production factors, which are indispensable for the creation of the wealth of nations on the same level as the material production itself. In quantitative terms, again, the allocation of resources to services is greater than to the agricultural and manufacturing processes together.

The evolution of the insurance industry in the last two decades is a typical example of the relevance of the service economy concept: until a decade ago, everybody, including people in the insurance industry, accepted that insurance policies covering, for example, life risks or material damages, were a typical secondary product in the traditional economic sense and that they could only expand once the basic needs were satisfied by material production. However, during the ten years following 1973, when the growth of GNP in the world dropped from an average of 6 per cent to less than 3 per cent per year, the overall sales of policies continued to grow at a rate of 5 per cent per year. If insurance consumption were of secondary importance, the slowdown in other activities and in particular in manufacturing would have produced more than a proportional reduction in the sales of insurance, according to Engels's Law.

The explanation for the continuous growth of insurance activities, even in periods of declining overall growth, lies precisely in the nature of the modern production system which depends on services as key tools to guarantee its proper functioning. At a very advanced technological level of production, where risks and vulnerabilities are highly concentrated and represent an essential managerial challenge, insurance has become – increasingly so in the last decades – a fundamental precondition for investment. Similarly, at a more general level, social security, health and life insurance have by now achieved the status of a primary need in most industrialized countries.

The very process of development of technology in the modern economy has led to a more and more complex system, where logistics, organization and information have become fundamental issues. Considering the economy as a 'service' economy also allows a better appreciation of the contributions made by contemporary technology: the latest technological advances have their greatest impact on systems concerned with the communication and organization of information, which is exactly what is needed in order to improve the management of change in present-day economies. All this is quite different from the direction which technology had taken during the classic Industrial Revolution, when all that appeared to matter was how to investigate and improve the stages of production which transformed raw materials into finished goods.

The management of waste and the environment: integrating economics and ecology

All the services which we have mentioned are essential in planning and in supporting production up to the point-of-sale, and during the products' period of utilization. Further on, the process of industrialization has put in evidence another important service: the management of waste.

Waste has always been a by-product of any type of human activity and production: by peeling a banana we produce waste; by cutting an arrow from a piece of wood we produce waste. When the Industrial Revolution stimulated a large movement towards the concentration of production and its specialization, waste inevitably also started to be concentrated and accumulated. Furthermore, the fact that more new products were derived from a manipulation of matter benefiting from a deeper knowledge of physics and chemistry resulted in an increased complexity of waste and a higher level of potential hazards such as poisoning by a greater number of products. Parallel to the increase of industrial waste, the extension of conspicuous consumption to an increasing number of people has also meant an enormous increase, quantitatively and qualitatively, in the waste-burden produced by millions of consumers. A plastic bottle cannot always be burned similarly to a piece of wood or paper: it may produce smoke of a corrosive or even poisonous nature. This requires today even more investment to organize an efficient and appropriate disposal system.

Every product finally becomes waste. Most materials, including our bodies, become waste at the end of their production and utilization cycle and some waste is transformed into new raw material. This transformtion process happens in some cases naturally, as with organic waste, sometimes only after a delay involving a recycling intervention by man. The recycling of waste is in most cases limited, either by 'economic entropy' (when the cost of full recycling would be prohibitive) or by physical (absolute) entropy (when full recycling cannot be done for physical reasons).

Waste handling and disposal is therefore one of the key subjects of the service economy.

Figure 5.4 indicates that, in a situation typical of the industrial economy, the production process was considered as terminated at the moment when a product or tool was available and sold on the market. In the service economy, the real issue – in terms of economic value – appears to be the maximization of the utilization of products and services together during their life time, taking into account a series of costs which first precede, then accompany production and finally follow it.

The above considerations on the management of waste help us in reconsidering once again the notion of value, and in particular of utilization value. On the one side, the traditional notion of economic value is linked to the existence and marketability of a product. On the other side, the notion of economic value in the new service economy is extended to include the period of utilization. By consequence, the notion of value in the service economy is in essence not only linked to the factors used in the phase of production, but much more to the value of any product (or service) as looked upon in terms of its performance or result over time. It is the utilization value during the utilization period of time which is the point at stake: the effective performance

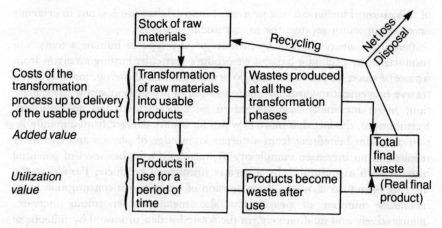

Figure 5.4   The real final outcome of the production process
Source: Giarini 1980: 31

(value) of an automobile as a transport system has to be accounted in terms of its period (and frequency) of utilization, and the effective benefit (value) of a drug has to accounted in terms of the level of health achieved. Whereas in the industrial economy the key question was, what is a product's 'monetarized' value?, the service economy asks another question, what is a product's 'utilization' value – what function does its serve, how well and for how long?

The service economy as a system and the management of vulnerability

The notion of system has become essential in the service economy. Systems produce positive results or economic value when they function properly, through real time and under the dynamics of real life. Whenever real time is taken into consideration, the degree of uncertainty and probability which conditions any human action becomes a central issue. The economics of the Industrial Revolution could, in contrast, rely on the fiction of a perfect equilibrium theory (outside real time and duration), based on the assumption of certainty.

The importance of the notion of utilization in the service economy has another consequence in terms of appreciation of economic value. Utilization is a process which takes place during a period of time. The duration of the utilization periods of products and services becomes therefore an important element to assess in order to optimize economic activity. Cost–benefit analysis has to be conducted more and more with reference to different possible periods of utilization, with the cost of waste after use needing to be integrated into the cost-calculation at the planning stage. The optimization of duration and also of durability is *de facto* taken more and more into consideration when products are marketed and sold, for instance, through leasing systems. In these cases, what is sold and bought is the utilization of a product including all the costs which are linked to make it function through its lifespan.

Any system working in order to obtain some future results is by definition in a situation of uncertainty, even if different situations are characterized by different degrees of risk, uncertainty or even indetermination, where risk here represents the probability of an occurrence, uncertainty measures the degree of confidence one can have in a given probability, and indetermination refers to systems or situations which lack any possibility of being defined. But risk and uncertainty are not a matter of choice: they are simply part of the human condition.

Rationality is therefore not so much a problem of avoiding risk as eliminating uncertainty to acceptable levels in given situations. Furthermore, the very systematic nature of the modern economy and the increasing degree of complexity of technological developments require a deeper and deeper economic understanding and control of the vulnerability of these systems, which increases with their technological quality and performance. The higher level of performance of most technological advances involves a reduction of the margins of error that a system can tolerate without breakdown. Accidents and management mistakes in such a system may happen less frequently, but their effects are more costly.

Quality and the measurement of service productivity

If we accept that economic value in a service economy is determined by the performance of a system, we can propose the idea that good quality performance has better value than lesser quality performance. A performance which is very bad can even produce negative or destructive results, which we have called 'deducted values' (Giarini and Louberge 1978). The two notions of quality and performance are in fact identical. What we are lacking is a system of measurement of economic value which can actually and effectively quantify the variations in wealth production generated by all types of economic systems.

We can also observe that the more modern economies become high-technology service economies, the more complex the relationship between quantity and quality tends to become. Even mass production, when using high technology, must incorporate more and more qualitative aspects simply to be economically functioning. For the more advanced systems and technologies, the notion of gaining in quantity at the expense of quality (performance) makes less and less sense.

The problem of measuring productivity of services puts well in evidence how far an economy essentially based on service functions cannot anymore rely on the traditional productivity measures developed for the industrial economy. Many scholars have tried to go as far as possible in the direction of exploiting traditional ways of measuring services output with some modest results (Ascher and Whichard 1987; Trogan 1988).

The key issue is the possibility of defining what is the product, what is an output of a service activity as compared to an industrial activity. In both cases, it is relatively easy to quantify the cost of the production factors and the inputs. In the case of the industrial economy, the product is identified by a material object sold on the market. Normally, productivity means the capacity of the production factors to produce in a given period of time more and more units of these material products.

In the case of services, we have to do with a performance, and therefore the traditional measurement of productivity leads in most cases to erroneous conclusions. The methodological difficulty is that, traditionally, economic theory is based on the assumption of a price of equilibrium between supply and demand. Thence, the cost of production is easily equated with the value of demand. The result is that, in the case of services, the measurement of their value and productivity is often based on the value of the production factors. In this way, for example, a public administration which doubles its employees or doubles the salaries of its employees with no additional performance whatsoever, would be considered as doubling its value in terms of gross national product. In the same way, an inefficient administration, badly paid, as is the case for one country in the European Community, has been considered as having an above average productivity because its relative costs to other public national administrations is lower, and they are all supposed to fulfill basically the same functions. Once again, no measurements of the *real performance or quality* of the services produced are taken into account and integrated into the traditional economic evaluation.

The extension of the service functions in the modern economies will increasingly oblige economists and all those involved with economic issues to decide:

- either to maintain their evaluation on the basis of the traditional accounting of value added as proposed by the classical and neoclassical industrial economics; this will diminish constantly the relevance and significance of such measurements;

- or find practical, as well as theoretical ways, to integrate measurements of services' performances, or (which is the same) measurements of the *quality* of outputs, in order to re-establish a significant and useful possibility of measuring the real wealth produced by the economic system.

This implies for instance that the measurement of the costs and productivity of health-related activity is not done in terms of the value added produced, but in terms of the level of health achieved for a given population and/or for a given individual. Once more, these quality indicators have to be integrated into a system of evaluation including of course also the traditional measurement of the added value.

All these considerations lead us to look closer at the problem of integrating monetary and non-monetary economic values. The industrial economy side-stepped this question by considering the non-monetary values outside the economic realm.

In fact the substitution of a non-monetary activity by a monetarized activity, even though entailing certain specific sacrifices, has been in practice considered as desirable in the belief that the productivity of the monetarized sector will more than compensate, in the long term, and often also in the short term, for any loss in the traditional, essentially non-monetarized sector. The industrial economy itself has stimulated the process of monetarization of a larger and larger part of the human wealth-producing activities. In the classical economic theory, the debate on the use of value implicitly admitted that economic, material welfare may also be produced by the traditional, non-monetarized sector, so that material welfare (TW) can be defined in general as:

$$TW = V_{NM} + V_M$$
where:
V — value
NM — non-monetarized
M — monetarized

But in practice non-monetarized values were kept outside the dominant economic model, because if not priced they were considered either outside the exchange system or outside the world of scarcity. A relatively high degree of non-monetarized values has however persisted, even in the most industrialized nations, for example non-remunerated work (housewives, benevolent activities), non-remunerated goods and services (unpolluted air and water).

What should be emphasized here is that in so far as V_M is the really dynamic part of the process in adding to TW (where V_{NM} is particularly static and/or irrelevant), then the economist could and did normally assume that $TW = V_M$ or, at least, that $dTW = dV_M$ (i.e. that any change in total welfare was only due to changes in V_M). However, V_{NM} is not independent of V_M; increasing V_M in fact reduces the field of the NM economy and/or transforms it. It is normally assumed that any loss in the NM sector will be more than offset by the M-substitutive activity, that in terms of value gain in V_M will be greater than any loss in V_{NM}. But it is only under such conditions that TW will, in fact, increase. The difficulty of analysing such an equation is due not only to the problem implicit in evaluating non-monetary activities but also to the price-based concept of value in traditional economic theory, when this is equated with welfare.

If the notion of value is limited to the monetarized production process we discover that, in fact, it implies that any priced production, and only priced production, is producing welfare. If the notion of value is based on utilization, however, then it is the total net contribution to welfare of the non-monetarized and the monetarized economic system that is relevant.

In other words it is the basic value paradigm of traditional economics, which equates value with price, be it the Smithian cost-of-production concept, or the demand-based one, which represents an obstacle to assessing the true net contribution to welfare by non-monetarized economic activity. The following remarks may clarify this:

- a closer look at any production process reveals that, among the production factors, there are many inputs which are not monetarized: the cost of the air for a company producing nitrogen through the liquefied-air process, is nil, as are the large quantities of river water used by a paper or an aluminium mill;

- if this air or water is highly polluted, costs will be incurred in returning these 'free' raw materials to their initial purity so that they can be used in the relevant production process.

Consequently, in the initial industrialization phase, the industrial system will have many essential production inputs 'free of charge'. Subsequently they will have to be paid for: this transfer into the monetarized system does not indicate that a process is increasing total welfare, but simply that it is first of all increasing the total costs for producing the same quantity of welfare.

The same examples can be drawn at the level of the individual: swimming in a non-polluted sea or lake for free is an element of welfare. Invention of the automobile led to an increase in total welfare by among other things, adding to the choice of places to go swimming. There is an obvious increase in total welfare (based on services available from the non-monetarized economy and from the monetarized one). In a third phase, the same industrial system which makes possible the production of automobiles, leads to the pollution of seas and lakes. Thus there is diminishing welfare (utilization value): costs entailed in re-establishing utilization value of the water, will be 'catching-up' costs and not costs adding to total welfare (or utilization value). We encounter here, once again, the concept of value deducted.

Starting from the traditional notion of value, it can be said that, in current economic accounting, a certain number of production phases (and a number of products) are not produced in order to increase added value but in order to restore at some cost previously destroyed utilization values. If the rise in national income in recent years is due increasingly to the development of the anti-pollution industry (detection systems, chemical products, incinerators, compacting machines for domestic use, etc.), this production is not adding to the initial level of welfare but it is being used more and more to fight the negative effects of industrial expansion.

The resultant added value is not a measure of added welfare: it represents the cost of previous consumption which now has to be paid in order to restore utilization possibilities. It is, in fact, a deducted value. The indicator of GNP as a sum of added values is in fact diverging more and more from an indicator of welfare: it is increasingly clear that it is rather only an indicator of cost. If, in the golden era of the industrial economy, it could also be assumed as an indicator of material/economic welfare, it is because in a period of no real diminishing returns of technology, almost all the production costs become net real wealth. Now, an even greater part of those costs represents a negative feedback loop effect on the overall trend of the total monetarized cost indicator – the GNP.

It is at the moment when more and more resources have to be used to restore utilization values destroyed, when the traditional value is less and less relevant as a measurement of welfare, that we need to measure performance to identify wealth creation. Measuring performance is a formidable task, as many economists have found, but there is no ducking the challenge. At a time when 70 per cent of the working population in the advanced economies (and more than 50 per cent in the rest of the world) perform service functions; and at a time when the global environment is coming under unprecedented stress from economic activity, it is high time to seriously redefine what is the type of wealth these functions and activity produce in real terms, and how they can be realistically quantified – in other words, how the quality of the performance can be measured in economic terms in such a way that we can find an updated answer to the old question of identifying and quantifying 'the wealth of nations'.

Giarini's concept of utilization value with regard to the environment is clearly compatible with Hueting's identification of environmental functions. The utilization value is what the function produces. Giarini's critique of GNP, and a broader framework of economic, social and ecological evaluation, are developed later, in Chapter 8.

Now, however, we are in a position to pull together various threads from the discussion of preceding papers to construct a model of wealth creation which is located in four-dimensional human space, keeps the total economy in view and focuses on performance, as utilization value, rather than prices.

A four-capital model of wealth creation

Paul Ekins

Conventional economic analysis usually depicts the process of wealth creation as in Figure 5.5, Model 1: land, labour and physically produced capital are judiciously combined in an economic process which produces goods and services, some of which are consumed to give utility to the consumers, and some of which are invested to enhance the capital stocks (or make up for depreciation). This model has the advantage of simplicity and perhaps it is adequate for uncomplicated economies.

For an industrial service economy, however, such a model misses most of the important parts of the story, as can be seen by consideration of the encompassing and considerably more complex Model 2 (Figure 5.5). Major differences between the two models are as follows:

- The redefinition of land as environmental capital, with the identification of its three economic roles: provision of resources to the economic process

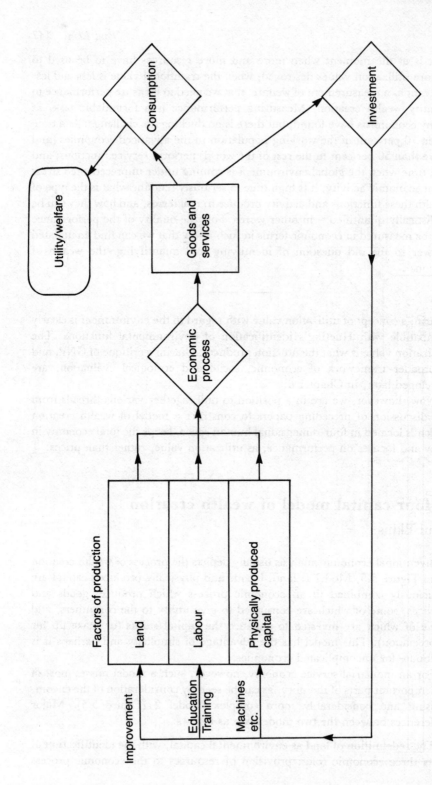

Figure 5.5 Model 1: The creation of wealth and utility

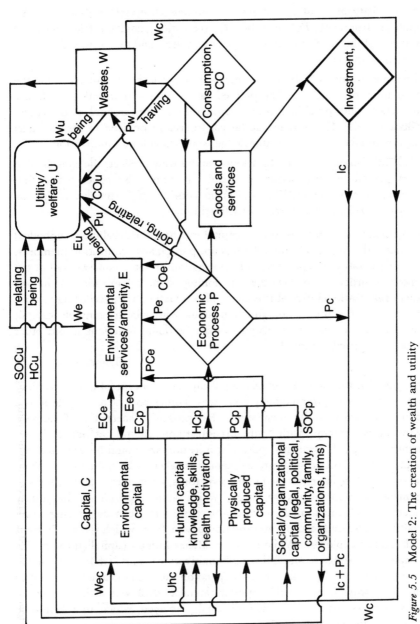

Figure 5.5 Model 2: The creation of wealth and utility

Note to Model 2: Upper case denotes source; lower case denotes destination quantities

(*ECp*), provision of direct environmental services (*ECe*, e.g. climatic control, beauty, recreation), and the absorption of wastes (*Wec*).

- The addition of wastes from the economic process and consumption which affect utility (*Wu*), the environment (*We*) and feedback into the capital stock (*Wc*).

- Acknowledgement of the direct environmental services provided by the built environment (*PCe*, e.g. beauty, recreation), and the effect on those services of the economic process (*Pe*, e.g. noise), and of consumption (*COe*, e.g. mass tourism).

- The subsumption of labour into an expanded concept of human capital, the formation of which Becker defined as 'activities that influence future monetary and psychic income by increasing the resources in people' (Becker 1964: 1). Human capital can therefore be seen to include such aspects of labour-power as knowledge, skills, health and motivation.

- The addition of social/organizational capital which reflects the considerable part played by institutions in wealth creation. The concept was first developed by Tomer (1973: 267–81) and considerably expanded in his book *Organizational Capital*, where it is defined thus:

Organizational capital is human capital in which the attribute is embodied in either the organizational relationship, particular organization members, the organization's repositories of information or some combination of the above in order to improve the functioning of the organization. It follows that organizational capital is a factor of production and, accordingly, is an element in the production function along with labour, tangible capital, human capital that is unrelated to organizational functioning and other types of intangible capital.

(Tomer 1987: 24–5)

From his identification of organizational capital as 'a type of human capital' (ibid.: 25), it is not immediately clear why Tomer sees fit to include it as a production factor in its own right. He posits a 'spectrum of human-organizational capital' with 'pure organizational capital' at one end, but whether he regards even this 'pure' form as human capital he does not say. For present purposes organizational capital is taken to be quite distinct from human capital, being embodied in the structures, rules, norms and cultures of organizations and society at large, which enable people to be jointly productive. Organizational capital is therefore here seen as residing in all social structures and institutions (and not just the firm, which is the only locus which Tomer explores). While it clearly affects human capital (through, for example, its impact on individual motivation) and while the actual performance of an organization will depend on the human capital within it as well as the ways in which this human capital is deployed, it is the *ways* of deployment, as distinct from the individuals deployed, which are taken to be the organizational capital itself.

- Acknowledgement of the generation of utility by many other sources in addition to consumption. Broadly these can be classified according to the four modes of experience:

Being – affected by the quality of the environment (Eu), the nature and level of wastes (Wu) and the quality of human capital itself (HCu)

Having – this is the mode that derives from consumption (COu)

Doing – this is the mode that derives from the work process (Pu)

Relating – this is the mode that derives from social and organisational structures ($SOCu$) as well as from the work process (Pu)

- An emphasis throughout on feedback effects. Two that have not yet been mentioned are the effect of utility ityself on human capital (Uhc, a happy worker is more motivated); and the way in which the environmental services themselves affect the natural capital stock (Eec). In a stable ecosystem, E and EC will tend to be symbiotically balanced.

There are two resources – space and time – that are crucial to all economic activity which have not been explicitly included in the model, although space can be considered as an aspect of environmental capital. The important difference between these resources and the four capitals that are included is that space and time are absolutely scarce and cannot be increased by investment, although investment in the other factors of production can make both space and time more productive, for example, miniaturization in electronics, time-saving domestic appliances. But no investment can increase the volume of a cubic metre or make a day more than twenty-four hours. The focus of the model is confined to those production factors that can be augmented or depleted.

It must be stressed that the complexities and feedbacks of Model 2 are not simply glosses on Model 1's simpler portrayal of reality. They fundamentally alter the perceived nature of that reality and in ignoring them conventional analysis produces serious errors including:

1. The environmental crisis, due to ignoring the direct benefits (including survival) of ecological capital and the negative feedback effects on the environment of many products and wastes.
2. The toleration of poverty, due both to the inadequate pursuit of economic justice and to an inadequate perception of the extent to which poverty is economically inefficient, impacting adversely on all forms of capital.
3. The undervaluing of the voluntary and domestic sectors, due to the false perception that economic wealth and money are the same thing, thus ignoring a large part of the contribution to wealth creation of social and organizational capital and the considerable quantity of non-monetary produced goods and services.
4. A view of work as an unfortunate necessity for income-generation, which ignores its direct role in generating welfare.

It is simply impossible properly to analyse the total economy of Figure 5.1 (p. 127) using Model 1, for it ignores the important role of institutions, especially in the social economy, lays exclusive stress on having at the expense of the other modes of experience and misses vital feedback effects, quite apart from its utterly inadequate depiction of the environment's economic contribution. For a sophisticated and practically relevant approach to current economic affairs, only Model 2 will do.

The extra complexity of Model 2 is also necessary to treat the concept of environmental sustainability. In Model 1 the implicit assumptions are that 'Land' acts as an infinite source of resources, while the wastes from production, consumption and depreciation are absorbed by an unspecified infinite sink. Given the infinity of source and sink, sustainability, of course, is inevitable and unproblematic.

It is clear from the earlier discussions of Hueting and Pearce, as well as from the most superficial contact with the real world, that the environmental source and sink are not infinite and can no longer be considered to be so, if they ever could. Modelling this fact needs the feedback effects of Model 2.

Building on Pearce's association of sustainability with constant or increasing natural capital stock, Model 2 enables one to express a few simple sustainability constraints relating the various environmental inputs and outputs, redrawn in Figure 5.6 for clarity, which shows the economy from an environmental point of view, i.e. only with regard to material throughputs.

For resources:

$$ECp < \text{ or } = Iec + Wec1$$

where ECp is the total outflow of renewable and non-renewable resources into the economic process, Iec is the generation of new environmental resources by investment and $Wec1$ is the addition to the resource stock achieved by recycling. The renewable component of Iec includes the replenishment of natural resources by human intervention or non-human processes (e.g. the sun). The non-renewable component of Iec implies new discoveries or the development of new technologies, materials or processes to substitute for those faced with depletion or exhaustion. It is certainly possible for renewable resources (e.g. for energy: sun, wind or waves) to substitute for non-renewable ones, but more problematic the other way round, because of the multiple and complex functions of many bioresources.

For wastes the relevant sustainability constraint is

$$Wec2 < \text{ or } = Aec2 \qquad \text{and}$$
$$We \quad < \text{ or } = Ae$$

where $Wec2$ and We are waste emissions into the environment which potentially affect the services it provides and $Aec2$ and Ae are environmental absorptive/neutralizing capacities. It is important to emphasize that not all wastes or emissions cause pollution. They only do so when they exceed the extent to which the environment can absorb, neutralize or recycle them. In the

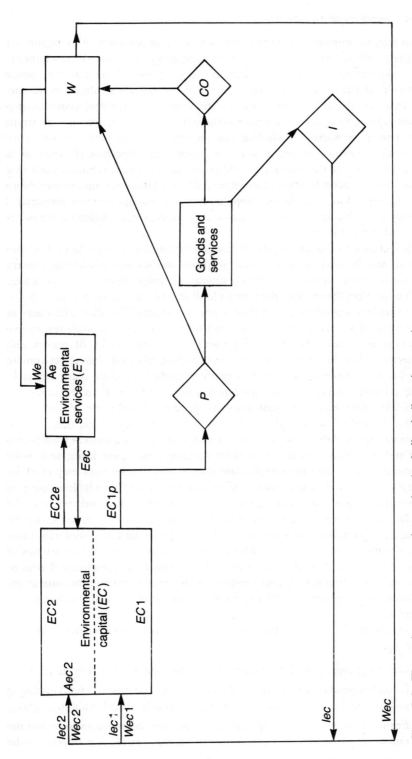

Figure 5.6 The environment–economy interaction (excluding built environment)

non-human bioeconomy there is no such thing as pollution. All emissions or waste products from one process are transformed into resources for another in a multitude of interlinked cyclical processes powered by the sun, which provides the necessary external energy input to decrease entropy in the bio-system overall, as life forms become increasingly varied and complex. It is hard to imagine a greater contrast to the industrial human economy by which low entropy resources, including vast amounts of fossil fuels, are converted into high entropy wastes in a linear process the objective of which is to maximize overall through-put, called economic growth. It is hardly surprising that such a process has run into sustainability problems as soon as more than a small proportion of the Earth's population seeks to adopt it. The conversion of linear to cyclical economic processes will be an important guideline for policy to be discussed later.

Returning to Figure 5.6, the distinction between *Wec2* and *Aec2* on the one hand, and *We* and *Ae* on the other, is important. Wastes *Wec2* impact on the environmental capital stock which produces environmental services; wastes *We* may affect the services themselves (and thence, of course, *EC* through *Eec*, but that is a secondary rather than a primary effect). The distinction may be exemplified as that between emissions which cause fundamental atmospheric and climate change (*Wec2*) and those which cause smog (*We*). Both ultimately interfere with the climatic experiences of those affected, but effects on the capital stock itself tend to be less easily remedied. Against that, it may be argued that the capital stock itself is less easily affected than the services it provides (*Aec2 > Ae*). The emissions that produce a local smog are lower than those needed to cause a global change in climate. One of the more serious characteristics of the present environmental crisis is that it derives from funda-mental degradation of the basic stock (atmosphere, ozone layer, soil, forest systems) rather than the simple interference with the services they produce. Regenerating this capital stock is likely to prove more formidable a task than removing interference with its services. It may not be humanly possible.

Having constructed a model of wealth creation that can serve for real-life analysis, it is now possible to address the difficult notions of economic growth, development and progress. In Model 1 it can be seen that, with consumption the sole source of utility, an increase in welfare becomes identical with an increase in consumption and production, leading directly to the use of the gross domestic product (GDP) as a welfare indicator, a practice still in almost universal use.

In Model 2 it is possible to distinguish easily between the following concepts:

- *Material growth*, growth in the economy's throughput of matter and energy.
- *Production growth* (increase in GDP and non-monetary production) leading to an increase in consumption and, therefore, *COu*'s contribution to welfare.
- *Environmental growth*, leading both to an increase in resources for consump-tion (e.g. fuelwood) or for environmental services (*E*, e.g. forests). This

generation of biomass leads to the concept of Gross Nature Product, which is not a mere subset of GDP for two reasons. First, a considerable portion of the Nature Product may not enter into money transactions. Second, it generates utility (through Eu) independently of its consumption. This kind of consumption is currently experiencing two powerful conflicting trends. Positively, genetic manipulation and chemical inputs have greatly increased outputs of foodstuffs in some areas, though not without fears for the future due to soil erosion and the negative effects associated with chemical intensive agriculture and biotechnology. Negatively, environmental degradation (deforestation, desertification) and harvesting beyond sustainable yields (e.g. overfishing) have greatly reduced biomass production. The future net outcome of these trends is uncertain.

- *Economic growth*, here defined as an increase in utility or welfare. Consumption contributes to this (COu), but so do many other factors, as has been seen. It is quite possible for the negative feedbacks from production growth (more wastes, environmental destruction, erosion of community) to produce negative utility effects that outweigh COu and so for GDP-growth to result in a decrease in welfare. It is still very much an open question as to how much production growth, if any, especially in industrial countries, is possible without engendering utility-cancelling negative feedbacks.

The common assumption, based more on wishful thinking than economic evidence that 'growth' in the long term can be 'green', the persistent confusion of production growth with economic growth, and the lack of understanding of the relationship of both concepts to the environment, all point to the desirability of the treatment of these issues in greater detail, which is done by Hueting in Chapter 8 and Ekins in Chapter 12. In Chapter 8 too, suggestions will be made as to how economic growth, as defined above as an increase in welfare, can be measured, in keeping with the previous discussion about the nature and creation of wealth. However, different societies may well arrive at different evaluations of what constitutes welfare, and therefore economic growth, and so will need different systems of welfare-indication. The predominant practice of using GNP as *the* welfare indicator is indeed an expression of just such an evaluation, whereby everything except market-orientated production is discounted.

Where evaluation is required to be more sophisticated, inevitably more complex value judgements will be required on economic and non-economic issues, such as distributional equity or community autonomy. These judgements in turn will draw on perceptions of the overall objectives of human life, as well as those of economic activity. If the society in question envisages a process of change over time, then such judgements will involve a conception of progress or development, to which we now turn.

6 Progress and development

What is one to make of the concept of 'development', now into its Fourth United Nations Decade while social and ecological disruption mushrooms round the so-called 'developing' world? The first four papers in this chapter will give some answers to that question from different perspectives, yielding a synthesis from which practical conclusions can be drawn.

Bygone splendour
Wolfgang Sachs

Fallen-down buildings hide their secrets under piles of earth and rubble. Mental structures are often erected on foundations covered by years or even centuries of sand. Archaeologists, shovel in hand, work through layer after layer to reveal underpinnings and thus discover the origins of a dilapidated monument. But mental constructs might also turn out to be ruins. How did they come about? What does the towering conceit mean? How does it fit what we know? These questions arise, then, accompanied by surprises and sorrows, a tale of bygone splendours slowly emerging.

The idea of development stands today like a ruin in the intellectual landscape. Its shadow, originating in a past epoch, nevertheless obscures our vision. It is high time to set about the archaeology of this idea and to uncover its foundations, along with the numerous constructions above them to see it for what it is: the outdated monument to an immodest era.

A world power in search of its mission

Wind and snow stormed over Pennsylvania Avenue on 20 January 1949, when in his inauguration speech before Congress, President Harry Truman defined the largest part of the world as 'underdeveloped areas'. There it was, suddenly, a permanent feature of the landscape, a pivotal concept which crams the immeasurable diversity of the globe's South into a single category – underdeveloped. For the first time, the new world-view was thus announced:

all the peoples of the earth were to move along the same track and aspire to only one goal – development. The road to follow lay clearly before the President's eyes: 'Greater production is the key to prosperity and peace.' After all, was it not the United States which had already come closest to this Utopia? According to that yardstick, nations fall into place as stragglers or lead runners. 'The United States is pre-eminent among nations in the development of industrial and scientific techniques.' Clothing self-interest in generosity, Truman outlined a programme of technical assistance designed to 'relieve the suffering of these peoples' through 'industrial activities' and 'a higher standard of living'. Looking back after forty years, we recognize Truman's speech as the address inaugurating the race for the South to catch up with the North. But today we also see that the field of runners has been dispersed, some competitors having fallen by the way, some beginning to suspect that they are running in the wrong direction!

The idea of defining the world as an economic arena was completely alien to colonialism; such a designation originated in the time of Truman. True, colonial powers did see themselves as participating in an economic race. Overseas territories were to serve as a source of raw materials and market entry. But it was only after the Second World War that they had to stand on their own and compete in a global economic arena. For England and France during the colonial period, dominion over their colonies was first of all a cultural obligation which stemmed from their vocation to a civilizing mission. Lord Lugard had formulated the doctrine of the 'double mandate': economic profit of course, but above all the responsibility to elevate the 'coloured races' to a higher level of civilization. The colonialists came as masters to rule over the natives; they did not come as planners to push the spiral of supply and demand. Colonial empires were perceived as political and moral spaces in which relations of authority set the tone, not as economic spaces articulated around trade relations.

Development as imperative

According to Truman's vision, the two commandments of the double mandate converge under the imperative of 'economic development'. A change in world-view had thus taken place, allowing the concept of development to rise to a standard of universal rule. In the Development Act 1929, still influenced by colonial frameworks, development was seen only in a transitive form: the concept applied exclusively to the first duty of the double mandate and represented the economic exploitation of resources such as land, minerals and wood products; the second duty was defined as 'progress' and 'welfare'. Only resources could be developed, not men or societies. It was in the corridors of the State Department, still during the war, that the conceptual innovation ripened: 'cultural progress' was absorbed by 'economic mobilization', and development was enthroned as the crowning concept. And so, a new world-view had found its succinct definition: the degree of civilization in a country could be measured by the level of its production. There was no longer any reason to limit the domain of development to resources only. From now on, people and whole societies could, or even should, be seen as the object of development.

To define economic exploitation of the land and its treasures as development was a heritage of the productivist arrogance of the nineteenth century. Through the trick of a biological metaphor, a simple economic activity turns into a natural and evolutionary process, as though hidden qualities would be progressively developed to their final state. The metaphor thus says that the real destiny of natural goods is to be found in their economic utilization; all economic uses are a step forward to direct inner potential toward that goal.

Western hegemony included

It is this metaphorical background which permeates Truman's imperative to develop and allows the universal 'developed/underdeveloped' axiom to be transformed into a teleological creed: societies of the Third World are not seen as diverse and incomparable possibilities of human living arrangements, but are placed on a single 'progressive' track, more or less advanced according to the criteria and direction of the hegemonic nations. Such a reinterpretation of global history was not only politically flattering but also epistemologically unavoidable: no development thinking can escape a sort of retroactive teleology, since underdevelopment can only be recognized in looking back from a state of maturity. Development without predominance is like a race without a direction. Therefore the hegemony of the West was logically included in the proclamation of development. It is no coincidence that the preamble of the UN Charter ('We, the peoples of the United Nations . . .') echoes the Constitution of the United States ('We, the people of the United States . . .'). To talk about development meant nothing more than projecting the American model of society onto the rest of the world.

Truman really needed such a reconceptualization of the world. European powers losing their colonial subjects signified a world which had fallen apart. The United States, the strongest nation to emerge from the war, was obliged to act as the new world power. For this it needed a vision of a new global order. The concept of development presents the world as a collection of homogeneous entities, not held together through the political dominion of colonial times, but through economic interdependence. Therefore, US hegemony had nothing to do with the possession of territories but everything to do with their openness to economic penetration. In this scenario, the independence process of young countries was allowed to proceed, in that they automatically fell under the wing of the United States when they proclaimed themselves to be subjects of economic development. Development was the conceptual vehicle which allowed the United States to behave as the herald of national self-determination, while at the same time founding a new type of world-wide hegemony, namely an anti-colonial imperialism.

Regimes in search for a raison d'état

The leaders of the newly founded nations – from Nehru to Nkrumah, Nasser to Sukarno – accepted the image that the North had of the South, and internalized it as their self-image. Underdevelopment became the cognitive foundation for the establishment of nations throughout the Third World. Some of the new leaders, during their struggles against colonialism, had learnt their lesson about the hegemony of western productivism from Russia or through the Third International. But essentially, that did not make much difference. Nehru (incidentally, in opposition to Gandhi) made the point in 1949:

> It is not a question of theory; be it communism, socialism or capitalism, whatever method is most successful, brings the necessary changes and gives satisfaction to the masses, will establish itself on its own. . . . Our problem today is to raise the standard of the masses.

Economic development as the primary aim of the state, the mobilization of the country to increase output, beyond all ideological skirmishes – this beautifully suited the western concept of the world as an economic arena.

As in all types of competition, this one also rapidly produced its professional coaching staff. The World Bank sent off the first of innumerable missions in July 1949. Upon their return from Colombia, the fourteen experts presented apodictic final conclusions: 'Short-term and sporadic efforts can hardly improve the overall picture. The vicious circle . . . can only be broken seriously through a global relaunching of the whole economy, along with education, health and food sectors' (IBRD 1950: xv). Increased production at a constant level implied nothing less that the overhauling of entire societies. Had there ever existed a more zealous state objective? From then on, an unprecedented flowering of agencies and administrations came forth to address all aspects of life – to count, organize, mindlessly intervene and sacrifice, all in the name of the construct, underdevelopment, 'guided' by numerous theories. Today, the scene appears more like collective hallucination. Traditions, hierarchies, mental habits – the whole texture of societies – all dissolved in the planner's mechanistic models. But in this way the experts were able to apply the same blueprint for institutional reform throughout the world, the outline of which was most often patterned on the American Way of Life. There was no longer any question of letting things 'mature for centuries', as in the colonial period. After the Second World War, engineers set out to develop whole societies, a job to be accomplished in a few years or, at most, a couple of decades.

Shocks and erosion

In the late 1960s, deep cracks began to appear in the building – the announced promises of the development idea were built on sand! The international elite, which had been busy piling one development plan on another, knitted its brow. At the ILO and the World Bank, experts suddenly realized that growth policies were not making it. Poverty increased precisely in the shadow of wealth, unemployment proved resistant to growth, and the food situation could not be helped through steel factories. It became clear that the identification of social progress with growth in production was pure fiction.

In 1973 Robert McNamara, then President of the World Bank, summed up the state of affairs: 'Despite a decade of unprecedented increase in the gross national product . . . the poorest segments of the population have received relatively little benefit. . . . The upper 40 per cent of the population typically receive 75 per cent of all income.' (McNamara 1973: 10).

No sooner than admitting the failure of Truman's strategy, he immediately proclaimed another development strategy with its new target group – *rural* development and small farmers. The logic of this conceptual operation is obvious enough. The idea of development was not abandoned; indeed, its field of application was enlarged. Similarly, in rapid succession, unemployment, injustice, the eradication of poverty, basic needs, women and, finally, the environment, were swiftly turned into problems and became the object of special strategies. The meaning of development exploded, increasingly covering a host of contradictory practices. The development business became self-propelling: for whatever new crisis, a new strategy to resolve it could be devised. Furthermore, the background motive for development slowly shifted. A rising chorus noted that development was not meant to promote growth, but to protect against it. Thus the semantic chaos was complete, and the concept torn to shreds.

A concept full of emptiness

So, 'development' has become a shapeless amoeba-like word. It cannot express anything because its outlines are blurred. But it remains ineradicable because its diffusion appears benign. He who pronounces the word denotes nothing, but claims the best of intentions.

Development thus has no content, but it does possess a function: it allows any intervention to be sanctified in the name of a higher, evolutionary goal. Development has been emptied out, but a curious plus remains. Watch out! Truman's assumptions travel like blind passengers under its cover. However applied, it always implies that there are lead runners who show the way to late-comers; it suggests that advancement is the result of planned action. Even without having economic growth in mind, whoever talks of development evokes notions of universality, progress and feasibility. He shows that he is unable to escape Truman's influence.

This heritage is like a weight which keeps one treading in the same spot. It prevents people – in Michoacán, Gujarat and elsewhere – from recognizing their own right to refuse to classify themselves according to the ahead/backward schema, and their freedom to rejoice in their diversity and wit. 'Development' always suggests looking at other worlds in terms of what they lack and obstructs the wealth of indigenous alternatives which could inspire.

The contrary of development, it must be emphasized, is not stagnation. From Gandhi's *swaraj* to Zapata's *ejidos*, we see that there are striking examples of change in every culture. Distinctions such as backwards/advanced or traditional/modern have in any case become ridiculous given the dead end of progress in the North, from poisoned soils to the greenhouse effect. Truman's vision will thus fall in the face of history, not because the race was fought unfairly, but because it leads to the abyss.

The idea of development was once a towering monument inspiring international enthusiasm. Today, the structure is falling apart and in danger of total collapse. But its imposing ruins still linger over everything and block the way out. The task, then, is to push the rubble aside to open up new ground.

Poor not different

Wolfgang Sachs

I could have kicked myself afterwards. At the same time, my remark had seemed the most natural thing on earth. It was six months after the catastrophic earthquake in 1985, and we had spent the whole day walking around Tepito, a dilapidated quarter in the centre of Mexico City, inhabited by ordinary people but threatened by land speculators. We had expected ruins and resignation, decay and squalor, but our visit had made us think again: there was a proud neighbourly spirit, vigorous activity with small building cooperatives everywhere; we saw a flourishing shadow economy. But at the end of the day, indulging in a bit of stock-taking, the remark finally slipped out: 'It's all very well, but, when it comes down to it, these people are still terribly poor.' Promptly, one of our companions stiffened: 'No somos pobres, somos Tepitanos!' (We are not poor people, we are Tepitans). What a reprimand! Why had I made such an offensive remark? I had to admit to myself in embarrassment that, quite involuntarily, the clichés of development philosophy had triggered my reaction.

The discovery of the low-income bracket

'Poverty' on a global scale was discovered after the Second World War; before 1940 it was not an issue. Of course, everybody knew even in colonial times that Zapotecs live in bamboo huts, Tuaregs eat mainly millet gruel or that Rajasthanis are often threatened by drought. However, frugality and misery in the regions of the South were attributed to a secular lack of civilization. For the colonialists the natives were immature and ignorant; with the patronage of the 'white man' they might some day enjoy the fruits of higher culture, but their 'economic development' was pointless. Societies which see themselves in the light of the 'civilization' ideal find other peoples 'uncivilized', just as Christianity saw 'heathens' everywhere outside its domain. Indeed, every imperial society sees in the Other the negation of the ideal it itself strives to attain. It is consistent with this logic that an economic society like the United States, as it rose to the status of a world power, perceived the Other as the negation of its own ideal of affluence and wealth.

In one of the first World Bank reports, dating from 1948/9, the 'nature of the problem' is outlined:

> Both the need and potential for development are plainly revealed by a single set of statistics. According to the UN Bureau of Statistics, average income per head in the United States in 1947 was over $1,400, and in another four-teen countries ranged between $400 and $900. For more than half of the world's population, however, the average income was less – and sometimes much less – than $100 per person. The magnitude of this discrepancy demonstrates not only the urgent need to raise living standards in the under-developed countries, but also the enormous possibilities to do just this.
>
> (World Bank 1949: 1)

Whenever 'poverty' was mentioned at all in the documents of the 1940s and 1950s, it took the form of a statistical measurement of per-capita income whose significance rested on the fact that it lay ridiculously far below the US standard.

When size of income is thought to indicate social perfection, as it does in the economic model of society, one is inclined to interpret any other society which does not follow that model as 'low-income'. This way, the perception of poverty on a global scale was nothing more than the result of a comparative statistical operation, the first of which was carried out only in 1940 by the economist Colin Clark. As soon as the scale of incomes had been established, order reigned on a confused globe: horizontally, such different worlds as those of the Zapotecs, Tuaregs and Rajasthanis could be classed together, whilst a vertical comparison to the 'rich' nations demanded relegating them to a position of almost immeasurable inferiority. In this way 'poverty' was used to define whole peoples, not according to what they are and want to be, but according to what they lack and what they are expected to become. Economic disdain had thus taken the place of colonial contempt.

Moreover, this conceptual operation provided the cognitive basis for inter-vention. The nature of this intervention followed logically, after the individuality of each country had been reduced to the quantifiable criterion of living standards: wherever low income is the problem, the only admissible answer can be 'economic development'. There is hardly a mention of the idea that poverty might also result from oppression and thus demand liberation. Or that sufficiency might represent a strategy of risk-minimization which is essential for long-term survival. Or even less that a culture might be directing its energies towards spheres other than the economic. No, as was the case in the industrial nations since the rise of the proletariat and, later, of the welfare state, poverty was diagnosed as a lack of spending power crying to be banished through economic growth. Under the banner of 'poverty' the enforced reorganization of many societies into money economies was subsequently conducted like a moral crusade; who could seriously refuse to sanction such a well-founded call for economic expansion?

Descent to the biological minimum

Towards the end of the 1960s, when it was no longer possible to close one's eyes to the fact that 'economic development' was patently failing to help the broad mass of the population achieve a higher standard of living, a new conception of 'poverty' was required: 'We should strive,' McNamara stated in 1973, 'to eradicate absolute poverty by the end of this century. That means in practice the elimination of malnutrition and illiteracy, the reduction of infant mortality and the raising of life-expectancy standards to those of the developed nations.' (McNamara 1973: 27) Whoever lives below an externally defined minimum standard is declared 'absolutely poor'; the yardstick of per-capita income was thrown onto the trash heap of developmental concepts. Two shifts in the focus of the international discussion of poverty were responsible for this. On the one hand, attention switched to yawning social gulfs within societies, which had been completely blurred by national averages. On the other, income revealed itself to be a rather blunt indicator of the actual living conditions of those not fully integrated into a money economy.

Efforts to apprehend poverty in terms of qualitative criteria emerged out of disappointment at the results of the mechanical stimulation of growth, but they too entailed a new form of reductionism. Since the first attempts in England at the turn of the century, the calculation of an absolute poverty line has essentially been based on a formula involving nutritional values. The absolute poor are those whose intake of food does not exceed a certain minimum of calories. The trouble with such definitions is not that they have led to a confused juggling with norms, but that they have reduced the living reality of hundreds of millions of people to an animalistic description. In an attempt to find an objective and meaningful criterion, the ground was cleared for a conception of reality which ignores the rich variety of what people might hope and struggle for, and factorizes infinitely varied human situations to one bare piece of data about survival. Is a lower common denominator at all conceivable? No wonder, with such atrophic categories, that the measures taken – ranging from deliveries of grain to people who eat rice to literacy campaigns in regions where the written word is altogether uncommon – have all too often been insensitive and shown no regard for the population's self-esteem.

Reducing life-worlds to calorie levels, to be sure, greatly facilitates the international administration of development aid. It allows a neat classification of the clientele, without which world-wide strategies would be pointless, and serves as permanent proof of a state of global emergency, without which doubt might be cast on the legitimacy of some development agencies. This readjusted conception of poverty enabled the development paradigm to be rescued at the beginning of the 1970s, especially since, in its official version, the fulfilment of basic needs strictly called for growth, or at least growth 'with redistribution'. The link to the previous decade's dogma of growth was thus established.

Poor is not necessarily poor

Binary divisions, such as healthy/ill, normal/abnormal or, more pertinently, rich/poor, are like steamrollers of the mind; they level a multi-form world, completely flattening anything which does not fit. The stereotyped talk of 'poverty' has disfigured the different, indeed contrasting, forms of poverty beyond recognition: it fails to distinguish, for example, between frugality, destitution and scarcity.

Frugality is a mark of cultures free from the frenzy of accumulation. The necessities of everyday life are mostly won from subsistence production with only the smaller part being purchased on the market. In our eyes, people there have rather meagre possessions; maybe the hut and some pots and the Sunday costume, but appliances are few and money plays only a marginal role. Instead, everyone usually has access to fields, rivers and woods, while kinship and community duties guarantee services which elsewhere must be payed for in hard cash. Despite being in the 'low-income bracket', nobody goes hungry. What is more, large surpluses are often spent on jewellery, celebrations or grandiose buildings. In a traditional Mexican village, for example, the private accumulation of wealth is subject to social ostracism; prestige is gained precisely by spending even small profits on great deeds for the community. 'Poverty' here is a way of life maintained by a culture which recognizes and cultivates a state of sufficiency; sufficiency only turns into demeaning poverty when pressurized by an accumulating society.

Destitution, on the other hand, becomes rampant as soon as frugality is deprived of its foundation. Along with community ties, land, forest and water are the most important prerequisites for subsistence without money. As soon as they are taken away or destroyed, destitution lurks. Again and again, peasants, nomads and tribals have fallen into misery, after they had been driven from their land, savannas and forests. Indeed, the first state policies on poverty, in sixteenth-century Europe, were a response to the sudden appearance of vagabonds and mendicancy provoked by enclosures of the land, while it had traditionally been the task of communities to provide for widows and orphans, the classical cases of the unmaintained poor.

Scarcity, however, derives from modernized poverty. It affects mostly urban groups caught up in the money economy as workers and consumers whose spending power is so low that they fall by the wayside. Not only does their predicament make them vulnerable to the whims of the market, but they also live in a situation where money assumes an ever-increasing importance. Their capacity to achieve through their own efforts gradually fades, while at the same time their desires, fuelled by glimpses of high society, spiral towards infinity; this scissor-like effect of want is what characterizes modern poverty.

Commodity-based poverty, still described as 'the social question' in the nineteenth century, led to the welfare state and its income and employment policy after the world economic crisis of 1929. Precisely this view of poverty, influenced by Keynes and the New Deal, shaped the development discourse in the post-war era.

More frugality, less destitution

Up till the present-day development politics has viewed 'poverty' as the problem and 'growth' as the solution. It has not yet admitted to the fact that it has been largely working with a concept of poverty fashioned by the experience of commodity-based need in the northern hemisphere. With the less well-off *homo oeconomicus* in mind, it has encouraged growth – and often enough produced destitution by bringing multifarious cultures of frugality to ruin. For the culture of growth can only be erected on the ruins of frugality; and so destitution and commodity dependence are its price. Is it not time after forty years to draw a conclusion? Whoever wishes to banish poverty must build on sufficiency. A cautious handling of growth is the most important way of fighting poverty.

It seems my friend from Tepito knew of this when he refused to be labelled 'poor'. His honour was at stake, his pride too; he clung to his Tepito form of sufficiency, perhaps sensing that without it there loomed only destitution or never-ending scarcity of money.

A humanistic approach to socio-economic development
Mark Lutz

The term 'development' seems to imply by its very nature 'values'. There is something latent believed to be essentially worthwhile and good that needs to be 'drawn out' or 'unwrapped', and the degree of that good having been realized constitutes the degree of development. If we are willing to grant that the latent good is being truly human, realizing the authentic self, then it follows, of course, that socio-economic development and 'human development' emerge as two sides of the same coin.

Moreover, since development refers to a global concept applicable to all nations and peoples although its experience and manifestation may differ widely between them, it would seem that it has to be grounded in a source of value that transcends culture (or subcultures) and thereby allows us to evaluate not only the different cultures at one point in time, but also the historical evolution of a particular culture over time, that is in terms of progress or decline. Humanistic economics either explicitly or implicitly operates under the assumption that such an ethical standard does, in fact, exist. As already discussed, it is grounded in the presupposition of a common humanity with a common organic nature (essentially common basic needs of sustenance) and essentially common aspirations allowing us to postulate the welfare rule which also serves as the norm of socio-economic development: 'material sufficiency and human dignity for all'. This norm consists of two key elements of meaningful progress: material progress and ethical progress. Let us look at each in turn.

Authentic development: the material progress dimension

How do we define material progress for all? The answer here is both simple and relatively uncontroversial. It consists in meeting the basic material human needs of all, meaning access to clean drinking water for all, an adequate nutritional diet for all and adequate shelter for all, where 'adequate' is primarily defined by the standards of modern science within a particular culture-specific context. The needs are objective, dictated by nature, but the means of satisfying these needs is definitely cultural. Similarly, and in following the humanistic tradition, we may want to specify a basic need for security by moderating psychological anxiety of potentially impending material deprivation. This can be provided for in very different ways, ranging from the maintenance of traditional kinship and extended families, to modern social security or 'income maintenance' systems. Here, too, the particular mode of coping with this particular need is left to the preferences and capacities of the peoples involved. In all cases, the emphasis is on adequacy or sufficiency, leaving absolutely no room for the notion of maximum individual accumulation as long as there is material deprivation for some.

Finally, when talking about the social priority of meeting basic human needs, we also have to include the needs of unborn future generations, implying therefore an environmental 'sustainability' constraint on development (WCED 1987). Once again, a normative consideration such as this has to be seen as universally or 'absolutely' binding regardless of the cultural differences.

Authentic development: the ethical progress dimension

The need for universality here rules out any ethical norms based on social construction, such as utilitarianism, emotivism and pragmatism. Similarly, it would also have to disqualify neo-Aristotelian ethics centring on virtues. It appears, therefore, that the only possible ethics is 'deontological' and grounded in moral personality. Such a cross-cultural ethics, ever since Immanuel Kant and here following Panikar (1984), can be derived from the following set of interconnected axiomatic assumptions:

1. Human nature is knowable.
2. It is knowable through reason, a cross-cultural organ of knowledge.

3. Human nature, because of the capacity of reason, self-awareness, and free will, is essentially 'higher' than nature and cannot be comprehended as within nature.
4. Every human being as person has a unique and intrinsic worth and can therefore claim respect for his/her human dignity.

The bottom line of human dignity sets the stage for a kind of ethical or 'civil' society that signifies respect for others in social intercourse. It condemns using, manipulating and exploiting others for the sake of individual advantage or gain. Intrinsic to this view is, of course, the idea of certain inalienable human rights that need to be guaranteed and protected. If there are cultures or social practices within cultures where some are systematically exploited, degraded or otherwise used, whether for social reasons or spiritual purposes, a routine disregard of this kind for the claims of human dignity clearly indicates a serious problem.

Therefore, we can say that meaningful progress or development implies not only the progressive meeting of the basic material requirements of all, but also conditions and institutions consistent with respect for *basic human rights*. In Chapter 8 a means of measuring such development is suggested.

People's self-development

Anisur Rahman

During the time I worked with the Bangladesh Planning Commission (1972–4) I learnt two great lessons. One was the utter inadequacy of our professional training as economists to suggest a viable path for the country's development. The other was that the best promise for development lay with the initiatives of the ordinary people.

Our failure as planners may perhaps be summed up as follows. The reasonings and calculations which we had learnt inevitably ended up with a huge resource deficit which could only be met, if at all, by massive foreign assistance. This implied some surrender, at least, of our autonomy as a sovereign nation; the country's economic structure also gets locked into a large import-dependence; this along with the debt burden would perpetuate the overall continued dependence on foreign assistance; the country's indigenous knowledge, skills and culture would be humiliated in the hands of the alien knowledge and culture embodied in foreign expertise and resources coming in on such a scale; and a beggar mentality rather than a spirit of dignified hard work would dominate the psychology of the society. As economists we were trained mainly in this kind of deficit and dependent 'development' planning. We had not learnt how to plan the mobilization of the human energy of the people, to plan to develop with what we have, not with what we do not have.

This paper is about *people's self-development*, which is emerging as a new urge and vision of elements of concerned intelligentsia, social activists and people's own ranks. I propose to discuss the perceptions and premises of this urge and vision, and contrast these with two major trends in development thinking – one to be called the 'liberal' trend and the other the 'socialist' trend – which have dominated the scene until now.

Popular perceptions and initiatives

Deepest popular urges

Some years back the programme concerning Participatory Organizations of the Rural Poor (PORP) which I was co-ordinating in the ILO facilitated the coming together of a number of forest-based people's movements in India, to visit each other and reflect together in a series of workshops over a period of one year, to articulate a common position on the question of 'forest, ecology and the oppressed'. The result was a revealing statement (Dasgupta 1983: 93–5) in which, among other things, there was a poignant commentary on the notion and actions of 'elites' on development. In essence, the commentary was the following:

> We lived with the forest as one organic whole – there was no separation between us and the trees, physically, culturally, emotionally, in a daily living and growing together. Then you came, with your notion of 'development', and separated us. To you the forest was a 'resource', and you could not even develop this resource as the forest is disappearing. We on the other hand did not count to you, and started becoming slum dwellers. We reject your notion of development and we want our life with the forest back. But we do not know how to achieve this. Your notion of development and your attempt to develop whatever it was, have destroyed even our hopes.

Where such elite efforts to promote 'development' have not yet matured so that hope still exists, and the people have mobilized themselves for self-development, one finds glimpses of the people's perceptions and urges which embody what could be interpreted as their own vision of development.

A study of a popular movement for self-development in the Matabeleland region in Zimbabwe – the Organization of Rural Associations for Progress (ORAP) – presents the following insightful observation:

> Significantly, the translation of the concept of development into Sindebelle (local language of Matabeleland) is 'taking control over what you need to work with'. The names of most of the ORAP groups also reflect these concerns. A few chosen at random are: Siwasivuka (we fall and stand up), Siyaphambili (we go forward), Dingimpilo (search for life), Sivamerzela (we're doing it ourselves), Vusanani (support each other and get up).
>
> (Chavunduka *et al.*1985: 1)

In apparently simple-minded words these popular articulations of people's collective self-identity reflect deep conceptualizations of popular aspirations. We have seldom been even interested in a genuine dialogue with the people to understand what their aspirations are, and in seeking *their* contribution to a social articulation of the notion of development in which the people themselves must be considered as the most important actors.

What do the people do, when they get mobilized for self-initiated action? This depends, of course, on the situation in which the people find themselves.

The primacy of human dignity

The Bhoomi Sena movement of Adivasis in Maharastra, India, which we studied in 1976/7 (Rahman *et al.* 1979) gave primacy to liberation from bonded labour – a question of human dignity, achieving which was the first step in their self-development. The Adivasis then fought for land rights and implementation of the minimum wage law. With an intense self-reliant spirit the movement since then has focused on cultural and political assertion of the Adivasis, and assertion in particular of their autonomy of action in all spheres – that is their self-determination. The movement is avoiding getting into any kind of dependence on outsiders for their 'development', even if this means a slower pace of *economic* development. To these Adivasis development is, indeed, moving forward authentically, in the search for their own life.

In a different setting, human dignity has featured as a primary urge in some grass-roots mobilization in Bangladesh also. Organizations of landless men and women created by the intervention of Nijera Kori, a rural development agency which does not offer any financial assistance to the people and promotes their self-organization, have not progressed much economically. But these landless groups consider their organization to be a solid step forward in their lives. Among other results, as some of these landless groups told me when I visited them in 1984, 'The jotdar ("kulak"), the officials and the police can no longer humiliate us – they have to treat us with respect, because we are now organised' (Rahman, personal diary).

For some organized women's groups in the landless categories with utterly meagre economic resources, the perception is even more telling:

> We know that there is no easy and quick solution to our problem of food and clothing. But we as women did not even have the right to speak. In our organisation we can now meet and speak, and share and discuss our problems. We feel that we are now human beings. We look forward to our weekly meetings where we stand up and speak – we can thereby release ourselves as we have never been able to do before, and we now have the courage to speak the truth.

> (Rahman, personal diary)

Experiencing humanhood thus is a great leap forward, the first necessary step in anybody's development. But other mobilized people's groups have had better access to economic resources, some with small productive assets of their own, some acquiring rights to economic assets such as land or fishing water by collective struggle after getting mobilized, and some amongst them being also able to mobilize external resources like bank credit or donor finance. With these, they have taken initiatives to promote their socio-economic livelihood as well.

Development philosophy

The above, and numerous other cases that are known, indicate that the mobilization of the people's collective energy generates imaginative solutions to the economic problem alone – production, distribution, marketing, skills training, promoting social welfare and social security and, along with all these, the problem of *employment* – which are not conceived in or available to professionally designed and managed economic development projects and programmes. However, my point is not to highlight in particular the economic dimensions of people's self-development. Some of the popular efforts which have found ways of significant economic betterment within relatively short periods may be *the more fortunate ones*, and many countries may not have such possibilities to reduce economic poverty significantly in the short-to-medium run, as discussed below.

The problem of mass poverty

As a Member of the Bangladesh Planning Commission I had made some calculations on the kind of improvement we could most optimistically expect to have in the incomes of the masses of the country's population over the medium-to-long term. I quote below from a submission I had made in March 1972 to the then Prime Minister:

> Bangladesh remains one of the world's poorest countries, and will take a long time to meet the aspirations of its people for a decent economic life. The possibility of meeting the aspirations of the people in the short run does not exist, and this is not the problem the government is facing today in any meaningful sense. The problem is how to carry the suffering people of Bangladesh through a long and extremely hard journey to the realisation of their aspirations within the framework of a stable social order.
>
> (Rahman 1972: 2)

The basic problem that we faced was not special to Bangladesh. For many countries in a state of mass economic 'poverty' and 'unemployment' there may not be an early enough 'cure', in terms of technological and/or social management possibilities with available resources, except for a specially small country which can be 'lifted' quickly by external assistance coupled with its own resources. For any given country it should be difficult to predict or promise a significant reduction of mass poverty in the new future in view of many factors which are not within the control of the society no matter how mobilized its people are, including internal and external resistances, that should be expected, to the very effort to promote people's mobilization and self-determined development. In this respect, the women's groups in Bangladesh referred to earlier may have shown a better perception of the problem than those development professionals who theorize about reduction of mass poverty, and political forces who promise so generously. We have seen three 'decades of development' and for most of such countries the problem of mass 'poverty' and 'unemployment' has been aggravated, or in any case appears to be intractable.

In this sense, viewing the 'development' problem as many quarters do in terms of eradication of (economic) 'poverty', providing to the population ('entitlements' to) the 'basic needs', and so on, is liable to raise aspirations more than can be fullfilled for any given generation. This raises an operational question of social motivation to work constructively for the realization of such a goal. As suggested above, the *first step* towards a possible solution of the problem requires a constructive co-operation of those – the 'present generation' – who may hardly be a significant material beneficiary of the solution. But the operational development problem concerns this very generation, which has to be motivated to participate in a social endeavour towards what may be at best a gradual eradication of poverty from which this generation itself may benefit very little.

I suggest that a focus on economic needs and economic 'poverty', a culture of development discourse that becomes preoccupied with what the people *do not have*, gets trapped in the negative thinking and dependence orientation that this generates, rather than motivating the society to become constructively engaged in moving forwards. With a constructive engagement, the people show imaginative ways of progressively fulfilling their needs and urges. This includes, naturally, their need and urge for economic betterment. However, in view of what has been said above, it is the constructive engagement rather than economic achievements *per se*, which is the more universal aspect of popular initiatives – the fact that the people are mobilized, *engaged* in tasks set by themselves and going about them together, pooling resources and energy whereby they can do better than walking alone, drawing strength and sustaining power from a shared life and effort. Sometimes they succeed and sometimes they fail (in their own terms); but through all this they move forward in the evolution of (search for) their lives. It is such a positive evolution that is possible, and this is important in its own right, both for the involved people themselves as well as for the future generations to whom they can pass on the heritage of constructive social engagement to move through life with all its odds, showing their creativity and a spirit of tackling challenges, developing thereby as a *human personality*.

Consumerist view of development

Philosophically speaking, there are two opposing views of development. One is a *consumerist* view, which regards the human being primarily as a consumer of goods and services. Basically, 'development' is seen in this view as an expansion of the flow of consumption. As a means to bring this about, an expansion of the productive capacity of the country is needed, but the primary logic of development remains a progressive increase in consumption. For a time, development was identified with aggregate economic growth to bring about a progessively higher flow of aggregate consumption irrespective of its distribution (the 'reactionary' view). Gradually, the interpersonal distribution question was raised, in terms of who *benefits* from such development *as consumers* (the 'liberal' view). The development debate then focused on questions such as growth first or distribution first, or can we have growth with distribution simultaneously, and how can 'entitlements' (command over goods and services) be truly ensured for all and so on. This debate continues to this date; but the basic consumerist view prevails, concerned with who gets what as a consumer, and what is the intertemporal and interpersonal trade-off in this question. The question that this view does not ask is who in the society are able to take the needed initiative to produce the goods and services, and what happens to the different sections of the population as *creative beings*, that is *the distribution of the power and opportunity to fulfil oneself by creative acts.*

The theoretical height of the consumerist view is the notion of maximizing the 'intertemporal utility function', which is primarily concerned with the time-stream of consumption, considering saving as a necessary sacrifice to maximize this function, rather than being a positive strategy to develop one's creative powers. Likewise labour is considered to have a disutility to be minimized, rather than as the expression of human creativity.

The notion of 'poverty' follows the same viewpoint. The concern here is whether a person has the necessary income or access or 'entitlement' to, the bundle of goods and services postulated to be the needs of human beings as consumers. 'Poverty' in terms of *lack of an 'entitlement' to develop as a creative being* is, again, not expressed as a concern. The problem of 'poverty' in this sense is a consumer's rather than a creator's problem, focused on the 'poor' not being able to consume the things desired (or biologically needed) rather than not having the opportunity of producing (or commanding) them through their creative acts.

Sen, who introduced the notion of 'entitlement', goes beyond entitlement to what he calls 'capabilities', converging with the creativist view of development:

> When we are concerned with such notions as the well-being of a person, or standard of living, or freedom in the positive sense, we need the concept of capabilities. We have to be concerned with *what a person can do*, and this is not the same thing as how much pleasure or desire fulfilment he gets from these activities ('utility') nor what commodity bundles he can command ('entitlements'). Ultimately, therefore, we have to go not merely beyond

the calculus of national product and aggregate real income but also that of entitlements over commodity bundles viewed on their own.

(Sen 1983: 755, emphasis added)

It is worth reflecting on how the 'development' problem might have presented itself to our foreparents – let us say the earliest human communities. They *had to* create what they wanted, and, moreover, had no external standards to consider in deciding what they wanted. Given this situation, I should think, they could not have had any static set of 'wants' – their wants, to be meaningful, had to be defined and redefined continuously in the dynamic context of evolving possibilities of what they themselves could create. In this sense, a difference between wants and creative urges did not exist for them. They were not 'poor' – it was the beginning of their life to move forwards, by applying their creative powers.

The two, however – wants and creative urges – got separated as a result of, first, class separation between people by which the control over productive resources got polarized, giving the dominant class the power also over the lives of others. Second, the dominant class and its allies (together, the 'elites') developed certain consumption standards and were able to influence by their social power the culture and aspirations of society so that to attain these standards came to be regarded widely as the purpose of life itself. This has resulted in *aspirations and urges dissociated from the immediate creative possibilities of the people.* In turn this is causing pointless frustration among the masses besides strengthening mass dependence on the elites, and submission to a view of development as the fulfilment of such aspirations, and hence to submission of the initiative for development to the more 'successful' in the hope that such 'development' could possibly be 'delivered' by those who have attained this themselves. Even many 'class struggles', of local as well as of wider scales, retain this consumer consciousness, with material aspirations which are way beyond the creative possibilities of the working class; implicitly, such struggles retain a dependency orientation, cherishing the hope that some other power (class) will deliver the kind of material development needed to satisfy such aspirations.

Basic human need: the creativist view

In recent times, the concept of satisfaction of 'basic needs' of the population has emerged as a primary objective of development in liberal development thinking. Interestingly, the five 'basic needs' which have been identified – food, clothing, housing, medical care, education – are in some form or other the needs of *animals* as well, who typically do not create (materially, socially, culturally) except at a very elementary and static level (e.g. creating the bird's nest). But the distinctive *human-ness* for us is not in needing these elementary means of survival, but what the combination of our distinctive brain and the limbs can do and, therefore, the urge we must have as human beings to fulfil this power. This urge is often for the sake of creation itself, but in the process of satisfying this urge this also creates the means of satisfying whatever other needs, 'basic' or 'non-basic, that we wish to and can satisfy, *according to our own priorities*. Through such creation we evolve – *develop* – as creative beings. This is the basic *human* need – to fulfil our creative potential in ever newer ways – although this may not be expressed or asserted by all because of the conditioning resulting from structural social and cultural domination mentioned above.

As opposed to the consumerist view of the liberal school, there exists a *creativist* view of development which regards the human race primarily as a creative being. In recent times this view is explicit in the articulations of activist-intellectuals working directly with the people to promote their self-development (Fernandes 1986; Tilakaratna 1987). But the underlying philosophy is not new. At the level of scientific discourse this view was, perhaps, first suggested in the philosophy of Karl Marx.

The philosophy of Marx

Marx viewed human beings primarily as creators who because of their class situation either fulfil or become alienated from their creative power. Looking at the development of capitalism Marx was excited by its spectacular creativity; the central focus of his analysis of capitalism was the revolutionary development of *productive* forces in this phase of human history. Likewise, the central argument in his theory of revolution was the need, and what he considered the inevitability, of the overthrow of capitalism as its creative phase comes to an end, and as a further development of the productive forces would be possible only in the hands of the 'working class'. In tracing the development of capitalism Marx observed the phenomenon of 'exploitation' as the primary means by which the capitalist class appropriates the resources needed for the development of the productive forces in its hands; Marx's primary concern here was to explain the process of capitalist accumulation rather than condemn it. In fact, he praised the capitalist class for the practice of *thrift* which he observed in them, as a necessary virtue to obtain a high rate of investment and hence development of the productive forces.

While he was thus excited by the creativity of capitalism in its 'glorious' days, Marx saw the working class alienated from its own creative potentials and power, the free exercise of which alone could give it fulfilment as labour. The working class *as a producer* and not as a consumer must, therefore, revolt and take over the means of production, to fulfil itself as producers. The history of 'Man' (as unalienated workers) would then truly begin. This implied that, through the revolutionary development of the productive forces in its hands, labour would eventually produce (and control) enough for everyone to have according to one's 'need': but such (material) needs satisfaction would follow human creativity and does not appear in Marx as the primary motive force for human effort.

Experiments in socialism

Marx's writings, of course, shift from the philosophical to the political-economic to the polemical, and are separated by time and contexts, so that they may not necessarily give the same message always. However, the greatest followers of Marx have also been inspired by a creativist vision of the working people. Lenin had conceived of socialism as a social construction in which 'the majority of the working people engage in independent creative work as makers of history' (Lenin 1918: 646). But unfortunately Lenin's political theory of the party of professional revolutionaries led by intellectuals as the 'vanguard of the proletariat' with an 'advanced consciousness' contained the seeds of major distortions (Rahman 1988).

What emerged in the Soviet bloc under the rule of such parties was far from the above Marxist vision of the working class as the principal architect of socialism. On the contrary, the notion of 'advanced consciousness' of the 'vanguards' was invoked to justify stifling dictatorship by the Party over the working people. This great distortion of socialism was accompanied by official interpretations and articulations of the ideology which had little relation with Marxism. Initiatives by the workers and peasants were hardly ever encouraged, and in glorifying the achievements of 'socialism' such initiatives and achievements if at all they were taken, were hardly ever highlighted (after Lenin). Resistance to such distortions of socialism and dictatorial policies surfaced from time to time, coming from Marxist intelligentsia as well as from the working class, only to be ruthlessly suppressed. Finally, the sheer incompetence in economic management coupled with the corruption of elements in the Party leaderships has resulted in 'socialism' of this variety being dismantled fast throughout the Second World, its moral appeal quite spent.

The other great revolutionary leader of this century, Mao, encouraged people's initiatives more passionately, challenging the people to 'be fired with great, lofty proletarian aspirations and dare to break paths unexplored and scale heights yet unclimbed' (Han Suyin 176: 213). In this way Mao was able to keep the vast 'poor' Chinese masses engaged in a sustained process of development with considerable (shared) austerity, building the economic base of a possible 'modern' China through an accumulation rate of the order of 30 per cent over 1951–78, the highest sustained rate any 'poor' country has shown in recent history (Ghose 1984: 258, Table 3), in the process also advancing significantly in meeting the material 'basic needs' of the population, by a self-reliant mobilization of the people which inspired progressive forces all over the world. I suggest that this, one of the two greatest economic developmental feats of this century (the other being Japan), could not have been achieved if instead of appealing to the creative spirit of the Chinese people Mao had highlighted their 'poverty' as the main problem to be solved. This is a basic question of what motivates the human spirit to move forward: one cannot move forward thinking of what one does not have; one can only move forward thinking of what one can accomplish with what one has.

With the seizure of power by anti-Maoists as soon as Mao died, the Chinese revolution also started to unwind. Among the reversals on so many fronts it is pertinent to note that, while the people's creativity rather than their 'wants' were highlighted in Mao's time (something never highlighted in post-Lenin Russia or for that matter in the Soviet bloc), the new leadership in China started talking more of the 'poverty' and 'unemployment' of the masses rather than their initiatives and innovativeness to take on challenging tasks. Both undoubtedly existed and exist both in Mao's China and in today's China; but from what one chooses to highlight is revealed one's basic philosophy (ideology) of social life and purpose. However, the shift in the ideology of China has been limited to the economic sphere and remains to be complemented by a parallel shift in the political sphere, thus creating a tension of the first order whose final resolution is still to be seen.

Collectivism and structural change

Among those who are working to promote people's self-development, whether they have had association with formal left trends or not, two debates stand out as of prime importance.

Collectivism

Marxism has been identified with collectivism as one of its principal visions, and indeed this has been a major bone of contention in the great confrontation between two rival ideologies of the present era. Marx himself saw in collectivism the final emancipation of labour from a state of alienation from one's supposedly true self – the collective man or woman.

Socialist experiments of this century do not demonstrate that human beings can transcend their individualism and become fully collectivist men or women. In this sense Marx's vision of collectivism as the final emanicpation of labour remains questionable independently of the logic of his specific model of transition from already associated labour to full collectivism.

Those who are working with the people to promote their self-development do not, by and large, have a dogmatic position on the question of collectivism. The people when they are mobilized and deliberate themselves to set priorities and tasks, do a lot of pooling of resources and talents, and co-operation, and engage in a lot of collectivist initiatives. They do so as they see the objective advantage of doing so, and as they feel inspired from working together to identify and solve problems and develop greater trust in each other. The poorer and the more oppressed the people are, the more, other things equal, are they likely to see the advantage of such co-operation and solidarity among themselves for material improvement as well as for emotional security and resisting oppression. The development of such co-operation among the people may be enhanced by sensitive 'animation' work, but cannot be forced, without alienating them, by some ideological principle external to the organic evolution of their life, a principle to be applied mechanically (e.g. collective ownership of land or such other 'means of production'). It may not be guaranteed that full collectivism may be attained some day, or even that there will be no shift back toward some more individualism, in a possible permanent movement of dialectical tension between these two identities of the human species. There cannot be people's self-development with any ideological dogmatism external to the people's evolving life and consciousness.

In any case, with the turning around of the great socialist experiments of the century towards greater individualism, the ideological debate over individualism and collectivism is weakening. At the same time it is being witnessed that rule in the name of the people and 'democracy' in the (so-called) 'free world', and in the name of 'dictatorship of the proletariat' and 'socialist world', actually represents rule of some or other category of elites over the people. This is clarifying the real ideological issue to be the question of real social power – whether the working people could have the power to determine their own destiny within a framework of horizontal social interaction with other classes, as equals and not as inferiors. This, ultimately, is the question of real *democracy*, not the democracy merely of periodic elections and the freedom to express the verbal word on what should be done, but the freedom and opportunity of the people to take the initiative to do it themselves.

Structural change

As I have suggested, people's self-development can start even under conditions of extreme resource shortage – mobilizing themselves for assertion of human dignity and self-determination, and to co-operate to accomplish collectively determined tasks, in the process developing in capabilities and in human personality. In fact, some conditions of the acutest resource shortage (e.g. under natural calamities) are known to have produced the most impressive popular mobilizations with such self-developmental elements. The possibilities and pace of self-development, however, are naturally constrained by the availability of physical resources to work with, and as observed before, people's self-mobilizations themselves have often been directed towards achieving greater access to such resources by collective negotiation and struggle. In countries where the bulk of physical resources are controlled by elites, a redistribution of the control over such resources in addition to redistribution of the social power to take development initiatives is, therefore, necessary. *This* distribution question – rather than the question of distribution of 'incomes' *per se* or 'benefits from development', and so on – is the basic question of equity in the creativist view of development.

While thus calling for radical structural change in societies with polarized control over physical resources, this viewpoint questions the identification of *people's ownership* with *state ownership* which, as we have noted, may actually separate the people from the means of production (and thus inhibit rather than promote their self-development). The distribution question is therefore one of giving the people (individually and/or collectively) real control over resources to work with to develop their own potentials, not to be dictated by a state-appointed managerial technocracy. The concept of 'socialism' defined as 'social ownership' of the means of production which has often been identified with state ownership needs in this light a thorough re-examination.

There is need for rethinking also on the tasks *before* such structural change is accomplished, and on the prerequisite for such change to truly liberate and promote people's creativity rather than stifle it with new forms of domination. Most left quarters have been preoccupied with the macro-question of capturing state power to initiate 'socialist' development before action is initiated to animate the people in self-developmental mobilization. But micro-level initiatives to promote people's self-development are showing that this need not await a redistribution of resources even for physical resource-poor communities who can start developing today at least in human personality, social values and social organizations, and *who themselves consider such advancement to be a positive gain*; on the other hand, the question of macro-structural change for most societies where this is desired remains uncertain and often intractable; it is not very convincing to suggest that generations should keep on waiting for the elusive 'revolution' before mobilizing themselves to move forward with what they have and what they can acquire through local struggles. There is, furthermore, another profound need for working to promote micro-level people's self-development right now, to enhance the very possibility that a macro-level social change, if it does occur some day, may truly release and promote the people's creativity. I suggest that a *political leadership which is not involved in people's self-development now, will not be able to promote this after coming into power, because it will not know what this means, nor how this can be animated.* This – what a leadership can do after coming into power – is also a question of organic logic resting on what it has done, and hence learnt, previously. As a corollary, the hope of a macro-level structural change to promote people's self-development rather than to suppress the popular initiatives we are witnessing today at local scales, lies in the emergence of an 'organic vanguard' which is rooted in such popular movements and does not claim itself to be above (and unaccountable) to the people.

———

These papers clearly reveal both the shortcomings and continuing usefulness of the concept of development. First, in accordance with Sachs's critique, development is not a prescribed, linear journey on universal tracks from 'poverty' or 'underdevelopment' to 'affluence' or 'developed' status. Any definition of development that envisages a universal outcome of the development processes, inevitably involving a hierarchy with those closest to that outcome identified as 'developed' and those furthest from it as 'undeveloped', can be seen as hegemonic and dependency-creating. Nor is development necessarily an economic process, but one whereby innate human potential is creatively and constructively realized by those concerned, on both the individual and collective levels. The form of expression of this potential is not predetermined but is culturally specific. Development is a journey from where oneself or one's society happens to be to a new state which involves greater individual and social fulfilment and capability. This new state is and can only be the product of endogenous creative effort.

Development *is* creative activity to the extent that such activity realizes creative potential. *Per se*, it does not lie in meeting the basic needs of food, clothing, housing, good health or education or any other external objective. However, in so far as these *are* felt needs, one may expect that people's creative activity will be orientated towards meeting them. The form in which they are met, however, will be culturally specific. Thus there is no presumption, for example, that a felt need for education will be met by schooling, or that good health will be promoted through allopathic medicine. In the terminology to be employed later by Max-Neef (pp. 197ff.), although all people may have the same fundamental needs, their satisfiers, or ways of satisfying these needs, may vary greatly across cultures.

From this perspective the external interventions that can be made in favour of development are limited to those that liberate the creative potential of people to achieve their own development. They will involve helping people to dismantle structures of injustice that oppress them; to gain access to the resources they require for their development; and to overcome the debilitating effects of past injustice and oppression which may have diminished their perception of their creativity. In practice, of course, these objectives are likely to be pursued simultaneously. Lutz's development criteria of material sufficiency and human dignity for all fit into this perspective in the sense that enduring material deprivation, regarded as such by the deprived rather than by externally-imposed criteria, is clearly a sign of development failure in so far as people are unable to realize their creative potential to overcome it; and the violation of human dignity is equally clearly likely to inhibit their realization of that potential.

This sort of reasoning exposes the invalidity of development as a 'league table' concept with countries or any other social entity ranked in some order of notional attainment. Classically, of course, the order was GNP per capita. In UNDP (1990) the measure is the Human Development Index, comprising a combination of purchasing power, life expectancy and literacy. But the competitive comparative thrust is the same, forcing diversity into channels of uniformity. For social scientists to proceed in this way is a recipe for cultural uniformity, the world-wide relentless drive towards which is only too apparent.

This is not at all to say that there are no objective indicators of welfare which can, over time, throw light on the sort of developmental process undergone. Because human societies all have certain characteristics in common, there are likely to be some generic similarities in different societies' indicator systems, corresponding at least to the four dimensions of the human condition posited in Chapter 3. Chapter 8, indeed, discusses indicator frameworks in some detail and arrives at some very positive practical conclusions. The crucial point about such frameworks is that they should be generated by the society intending to employ them. For them to be valid for creativist development they must indeed represent the considered expression of the goals the society is trying to achieve. If they are not thus valid, people will simply not try to achieve them. This touches again the crucial issues of motivation, aspiration and human needs, to which we now turn.

7 Human needs and aspirations

Human needs are ontological facts of life. They can be clearly distinguished from wants in that continuous failure to satisfy needs results in progressive, and sometimes irreversible, human malfunctions, whereas unsatisfied wants lead to little worse then frustration. Because needs are *needs*, they are the most potent source of human motivation, when people know whence their satisfaction is to be sought.

The most obvious needs are those of subsistence and they are also the most obvious source of motivation. Millions of people in the Third World perform heroic feats day after day simply to stay alive. That is not to say that it is always obvious, especially to outsiders, how even subsistence needs should be satisfied, as witness the vast number of 'development projects' which sought to contribute to subsistence, but which quite failed in that objective.

In so far as there can be said to be a mainstream economic theory of human needs, and it can only be said with regard to that branch of the discipline called 'development economics', it focuses exclusively on the so-called basic needs of food, clothing, shelter, health and education. In the rest of economic theory, people tend not to have needs; they have wants or, more precisely, they have potentially infinite, insatiable wants based on commensurable, continuous and transitive preferences. For a real-life economics this will not do.

The economics of the satisfaction of needs†

Mario Kamenetzky

In the search for fulfilment and development we have explored the universe and the atom, toyed with the genes and experimented with different political and economic systems. Much less have we experimented with and explored the human mind and body, the sources and patterns of the energy deployed by human beings in their struggle for survival and the effort to perfect their

† This is a revised version of an article which originally appeared in *Human Systems Management* 2, 1981: 101–11. Permission to reprint it here is gratefully acknowledged to the journal's present publishers, International Organisations Services B.V., Amsterdam, the Netherlands.

lives. The suggestion offered in this paper is that the underlying cause of the development crisis with its multifaceted expressions may well be the centuries-old repression of some psychological, biological and socio-cultural needs. When the natural channels of satisfaction are blocked, the repressed needs find spurious bypasses for their unfoldment with pervasive negative effects on society and nature.

These negative effects elicit a fundamental question: will our economies and societies continue to narrowly focus on the satisfaction of the *needs* for food, shelter, clothing, health, and education, and of the *desires* promoted by the marketplace, keeping the other *needs* unsatisfied, or will instead social and economic organizations progress towards a multi-dimensional approach that enhances everyday life through the satisfaction of all *needs*?

Needs and desires

Carlos A. Mallmann (1973) has defined needs as those requirements that are always found when the behaviour of human beings is analysed irrespective of culture, race, language, creed, colour, sex or age. Needs do not depend on the value system of specific social structures, nor are they conditioned by the natural environment in which a community evolves or by its degree of technical and social development.

Needs cannot be programmed by society or modified by the will of the conscious mind. They stem from the unconscious which is like a *read-only-memory* provided by nature and from which nature speaks to us for as long as we do not consciously and subconsciously block the communication channels. Desires can instead be modified, even suppressed, by acts of will because they are products of the interaction of the conscious mind with subconscious behavioural programmes. The subconscious is like a *random-access-memory* where we store both the systems of values and beliefs received from society during the acculturation process and the records of personal experience which introduce individual modifications in those social systems of values and beliefs.

Desires not only differ from one society to another and among individuals in the same community, they also change within a given society as the technologies, and with them the cultural patterns, of that particular society change. Moreover, desires are different for each individual at different stages of life. On the contrary, needs are the only characteristic common to human beings in all societies at any time of their individual and social evolution. They are like the base material of a photographic film, which will produce different pictures depending on the nature and intensity of the beams of light to which it is exposed. Like beams of light on a photosensitive material, values and beliefs modify the simple and replicable structure of human needs to produce more complicated sets of desires.

Human beings always need shelter and always need food, but they may prefer owning luxurious homes to eating good food or *vice versa*. The need for a dialogue with the spirit may be satisfied through various forms of meditation, contemplation of nature and prayer that follows different rituals. Human beings need clothes to protect themselves from cold weather, but this need should not be confused with either the urge to wear clothes – even in hot climates – in order to avoid the social taboo against nudity or the desire for clothing which is associated with certain social groups and status.

A holistic view of human needs

Figure 7.1 suggests the minimum set of independent needs, derived from my original proposal that was published in 1976. The satisfaction of needs at any given level above the biological level is supported by the satisfaction of the needs from the levels below it. At the same time satisfaction at a higher level enhances satisfaction at lower levels. The scheme is purposely designed as an egg in order to convey the ideas of simultaneity, wholeness and interaction.

The *biological needs* are those which, if not satisfied, lead either to the physical disappearance of the individual – energy-renewing requirements – or to an imbalance in the individual's life-supporting systems – energy-balancing requirements. Among this group of needs, sexual activity is unique in that while it is always deeply rooted in the biology of the individuals and contributes to their energetic equilibrium, it may also contribute to the reproduction of the species and satisfy the psychological need for recreation and the socio-cultural need for communication.

The *bio-psychological needs* also result from physical requirements, but they are often intertwined with desires which respond to mental requirements related to the satisfaction of the other needs. Clothing and shelter protect the body against the rigours of the weather, but clothes are also accessories of the erotic games that satisfy recreational needs, and houses afford the privacy often associated with the satisfaction of the biological needs of sleep, excretion and sexual activity. Care and protection of the body and mind have the purpose of keeping individuals in good health, allowing their full physical and mental development, and preserving them from destruction by other members of their society or by natural forces.

The *psychological needs* for knowledge, recreation and a dialogue with the spirit aim at perfecting life and relaxing the stress produced by the efforts that survival entails.

The *socio-cultural needs*, although still anchored for satisfiers in the individual unconscious, require a society in order to be satisfied. The search for satisfiers of all the other needs can be undertaken by one individual alone. Communication, participation and autonomy speak instead of activities that involve at least two persons. In a captivating re-creation of Robinson Crusoe's adventure, the French novelist Michel Tournier (1967) describes the whole process by which a person left alone on an isolated island survives – satisfaction of biological needs – and slowly perfects his life – satisfaction of bio-psychological and psychological needs. But it is only when Friday joins him that he becomes a complete human being once again.

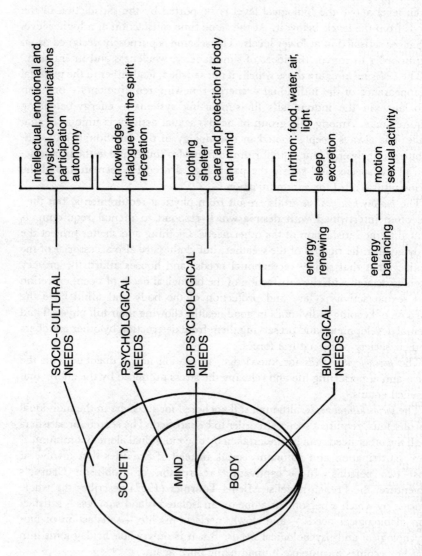

Figure 7.1 Set of needs

SOCIO-CULTURAL NEEDS
- intellectual, emotional and physical communications
- participation
- autonomy

PSYCHOLOGICAL NEEDS
- knowledge
- dialogue with the spirit
- recreation

BIO-PSYCHOLOGICAL NEEDS
- clothing
- shelter
- care and protection of body and mind

BIOLOGICAL NEEDS
- nutrition: food, water, air, light
- sleep
- excretion
- motion
- sexual activity

energy renewing

energy balancing

SOCIETY

MIND

BODY

The repression of needs

When one need or another goes unsatisfied, human beings frequently find distorted paths for reducing the pain associated with the deprivation of the corresponding satisfiers. It has been shown that under conditions of sexual freedom and scarcity of food, images of food appear in people's dreams and in the arts as frequently as erotic arts and dreams are found in sexually-repressed societies (Holmberg 1969). It has also been shown that the lack of satisfaction of the need for emotional and physical communication may give rise to strong drives for power, domination, violence and the possession and consumption of goods. This may explain the explosion of consumption among rich, but emotionally starved people. It may also be the root of the blind violence that is threatening both developed and developing societies through such diverse manifestations as the arms race, terrorism, drug abuse, torture, kidnapping, rape, guerrilla activity, harrassment, sabotage, martial law, concentration camps, genocide and massacres.

Individuals instinctively react with violence to a threat of being destroyed – a response to the biological need of protecting the body. Individual violent behaviour may also result from nutritional deficiencies and metabolic disorders. But when either rulers or some of the ruled groups intentionally organize violent efforts, they introduce in the mind of the people three kinds of programmes whose effectiveness in instigating violent behaviour has been proved. One group of programmes promotes aggressive competition and makes each competitor at home, school, church, playground and market-place neglect the subjectivity of the others (Kohn quotes Eisenhower as saying 'The true mission of American sports is to prepare young people for war' – Kohn 1986: 145); another family of programmes, by handicapping the development of affectional bonds of trust in the parent–child relationship and in the intimacy of youthful and adult sexual relationships, generates subconscious records of deprivation of emotional well-being for which violent behaviour tries to compensate (Montagu 1974, 1978; Olsen 1975; Prescott 1975); and the third group is related to the programming by political and religious groups that leads people to hate other people and believe that their destruction is necessary for their own salvation. This programming transforms human beings into automatons, suppressing their instinctive needs for intellectual, emotional and physical communication, participation, autonomy, knowledge and a free, unhindered dialogue with the spirit. When these needs are not satisfied, humans cannot unfold their humaneness.

This is precisely what has happened during most of human history, and is still happening. Since early history human beings began to develop socio-economic institutions of various kinds in order to reduce risks and increase efficiency and effectiveness in obtaining satisfiers for their needs. The management of these institutions was soon appropriated by elite groups whose power was further reinforced by their appropriation of the means that humans kept inventing for the production of satisfiers. These elites imposed rules upon society by which they allowed themselves to acquire more satisfiers of more needs than those allowed to the majorities under their authority. They specially repressed the satisfaction by the latter of the needs for communication, participation, autonomy, and knowledge.

When technologies for the production of satisfiers, and for warfare, were based almost exclusively on human energy, the elites thought that any diversion of this energy from productive and re-productive uses towards 'unfruitful', 'sterile' purely recreational and relational activities had to be avoided. It was feared that an expenditure of energy for these purposes would decrease both the labour force required for production and the level of aggression required to make war. A modern example is the Chinese *A Barefoot Doctor's Manual* which stated: 'If young people talk about love, marriage and having children at too early an age, then their energies will be dissipated, affecting their work and their study' (1977: 173). At the same time, wanting to have clear and secure channels through which to transfer their accumulated wealth and acquired power to their own descendants, and unable or unwilling to repress their own sexual drives, the elites programmed patrilineal cultures where women were divided into three groups: the privileged family-guardians of the upper classes, the reproductive machines and economy-keepers of the lower classes and the pleasure-giving courtesans and prostitutes.

The elites knew that, despite repression, an analysis by the masses of the programmes that were guiding their behaviour would lead to revolts. Hence they controlled the sources of knowledge that could empower people for this self-analysis of the interactions between a person's development and the surrounding environment. One of the controlled sources, often plainly barred to the masses, was education, because it may teach people how to access knowledge through sensorial experience and logical processes. The other controlled source was religion because it may help people in gaining intuitive knowledge by establishing a fruitful inner dialogue with the spirit that breathes in all of creation and guides its evolution.

Because of the multifarious forms that repression assumed, both repressors and repressed ended suffering from a lack of awareness and acceptance of the real, total person and a confused perception of the role of human beings in nature and society. To develop as a fully human and fully alive person became a difficult, and sometimes risky, endeavour. The elites themselves frequently became victims of the repression of the socio-cultural needs: on the one hand they created rigid intragroup hierarchies and engaged themselves in destructive competition, all of which deprived them of communication, participation and autonomy; on the other hand they either denied themselves the achievement of relations and self-expressions which were forbidden by the severe codes of conduct of their making, or paid the psychological price of feeling guilty of violating their own commands. The deprivation of socio-cultural needs at all levels of society created unstable violent environments around and within the elites which frustrated their enjoyment of the accumulated wealth and acquired power.

During the last 200 years, many societies have attempted to shake off repressions and correct inequities in the satisfaction of needs. In the free-market societies that emerged after the British industrial revolution and the American and the French social revolutions, the attempts mainly pointed towards securing freedom for commercial exchanges, intellectual communications and the dialogue with the spirit; and extending the rights of participating in the political decisions and of accessing knowledge to all in the body politic. But, because the reformers in these societies were still operating under the influence of values and beliefs from old behavioural programmes, emotional and physical communications were – and to a large extent still are – kept under close control, a control that often goes well beyond the granting of protection against the brutality of imposing one's will and desires over the other's non-consent. On average, women benefited less than men did from the efforts towards increased religious, political and commercial freedom, and suffered more than men did from the intervention by the state in the domain of interpersonal communications. Although the availability of and easy access to modern contraceptives have lately increased the freedom in these societies for *private* sexual activity, the *social* expression of emotional and physical tenderness and care and the *social* recognition of people's ownership over their bodies are lagging behind. Hence, the freed sexual activities became competitive, scoring and performing. Behaviour in the market-place was mimicked in the bedrooms: people became money-seekers in the former and pleasure-seekers in the latter. In both cases success is measured by the ratio of *how-much-one-gets* over *how-much-one-gives*. Along this process both Eros and Agape are often killed, and the quest for gratuitous erotic recreation and unselfish communications – which can never stop because it is unconsciously driven – begins to wander along the path of successive unfulfilling relationships.

In the centrally planned societies that emerged after the Russian revolution, the Marxist bureaucratic elites adopted the same old behavioural programmes that repress emotional and physical communications and further tyrannized people with oppression by not allowing free intellectual communications in the fora, free dialogues with the spirit in the temples, or free commercial exchanges in the markets.

The private realm, in which many needs can be satisfied without either the exchange of money or the protection of laws, was invaded everywhere. In the free-market societies, this domain was invaded by both the products marketed by an efficient productive system and the states unwilling to relinquish their control over the satisfaction of socio-cultural needs. In the centrally planned societies, the state was the sole powerful invader with its absolute control over everything and everybody. In both societies, the task of becoming fully human and being fully alive remains troublesome. However, in the free-market societies those who became aware of the intrusion, the Thoreaus, the Whitmans the Krishnamurtis, the people who live in intentional communities (McLaughlin and Davidson 1985), manage to create private spaces which are better prepared to resist market encroachment and state intervention. In centrally planned societies, people would until recently not have dared to think, let alone exercise, these kinds of options.

The economics of the satisfaction of needs

It is the main suggestion of this essay that no narrow political approach that would deny the possibility of an integrated satisfaction of all needs should be accepted. Two facts support this suggestion:

- first, the satisfaction of the needs for intellectual, emotional, and physical communications, autonomy, participation, recreation, knowledge, and the dialogue with the spirit do not require large amounts of marketable goods and services, they can often be satisfied without any;
- second, thanks to technological progress it is now easier to simultaneously satisfy all the needs of entire populations than was the case when production was based on primitive technologies whose operation required large amounts of human energy.

Political economy has traditionally been concerned with the production, distribution, use and consumption of goods and services. The economics of the satisfaction of needs will replace this narrow approach by an integrated analysis of the production, distribution, use and consumption of satisfiers for the whole set of human needs. This analysis will consider as potential satisfiers a broad spectrum of entities: goods, services provided to people by both the economy and the ecosystems, knowledge, relations and self-expressions. It will also differentiate *productive activities*, in which human energy is spent to produce tradable goods and services, from activities in which the investment of human energy yields a direct satisfaction of needs. To qualify the latter I propose to use the adjective *libidinal* because the scientific concept of libido includes all forms of human energy that, through a complex set of forces characterized by an intense somatic persistence and reserve of power, strive continuously to preserve and improve life. Hence, an *economics of the satisfaction of needs* cannot ignore the *economy of the libido*; it should deal with it and satisfy its requirements. Among *libidinal activities* the analysis will further distinguish *wealth-consuming activities*, which satisfy needs by consuming, or using goods, services, and knowledge supplied by the productive system, from *gratuitous activities*, which satisfy needs through self-expressions and relations among individuals and between individuals and nature.

Some activities can simultaneously be productive and libidinal. For instance, improvements in production processes may allow the workers to obtain gratuitous libidinal rewards directly at the work-place as a result of fruitful intellectual and emotional communications with the others who participate in the task, and of an efficient physical communication with the materials under process. Fishing provides a good example of an activity that can be practised according to any of the three modalities described above: it is a libidinal wealth-consuming activity when it is performed only for pleasure, using goods, such as reels and boats, and consuming services, such as the dredging of rivers and meteorological information; it becomes a productive activity when the catch is sold in the market; and it is a libidinal gratuitous activity when a person catches fish by using only his body and elements obtained from nature, and does it in order to satisfy his hunger. Similarly, a banjo may be played to express joy or sorrow – a libidinal wealth-consuming activity – or to produce musical messages and distribute them to audiences – a productive activity. Alternatively, music can be made by whistling or snapping the fingers, and feelings can be expressed by singing – libidinal gratuitous activities.

Economists and technologists usually focus their analyses on the technical patterns of productive activities, on the availability and cost of the resources that those activities use and consume, and on the requirements from libidinal wealth-consuming activities as they are expressed in the markets. Economists and technologists often fail to recognize the role of libidinal gratuitous activities in the economies and the effects of the social programming of the minds on the attitude that humans adopt towards these kinds of activities and towards nature. Only a few practitioners of the arts, the humanities and psychology, and the sages that all walks of life spontaneously produce, have explored the way in which libidinal gratuitous activities, which include relations with nature, are performed under a given set of patterns of production; of legal, social and political institutions; and of systems of values and beliefs.

In his interpretation of everyday life in Thailand, Niels Mulder says that he concentrates on *how a person who operates within the contemporary Thai system perceives his situation and expresses it through language, arts, rituals, thoughts and writings* (Mulder 1979: x). What Mulder brings out are the ways by which Thailanders consciously adjust to the requirements of both their social programming and the subconscious records of experience with the Thai social and physical environment. What I propose is to take one further step and introduce into techno-economic and social analysis the feelings and suggestions that arise from the unconscious with its instinctual drives for the satisfaction of needs that are universal and unchanging, and its deep intuitions. An economic theory that would relate economic and social behaviour with the complex workings of the totality of human consciousness would take account of the costs involved in becoming fully human and being fully alive in a particular society and physical environment. It would also take account of the benefits that society and nature derive from economic activities undertaken by people who, because they feel fully human and fully alive, have the consciousness of being in unity with the rest of humankind, and with nature, and thoroughly develop the creativity with which the spirit has endowed them.

The application of such a theory requires efforts to expand the consciousness of the people who will participate in the construction of the economic system. They ought to become aware of the obstacles that programmes stored in the subconscious of their minds interpose in their way towards becoming fully human, develop their potential ability to change those programmes, and heighten their creativity by clearing the channels of communication with the spirit that speaks from the unconscious (Kamenetzky 1989).

Micro-economic activities and macro-economic policies both change in scope and nature when decision-makers and operators are endowed by an expanded consciousness with wide-angle lenses for the perception of reality, and with an enlarged capacity for processing the obtained data in an integrative way. I will illustrate this with a brief discussion of the different approach that an expanded consciousness could introduce in technological design and project implementation, and in the design of a new macro-economic framework for the satisfaction of needs. The few examples that follow, which show the difference that an expanded consciousness could make in micro-economic activities, have been taken from my own experience with technological design and project implementation. Similarly, the suggestions on the steps in developing an economics for the satisfaction of needs, with which this paper ends, are based on my witnessing of experiments with socio-economic structures designed and operated by people with an expanded consciousness (Kamenetzky *et al.* 1986, vol. II: 1–21).

Technological design

When choosing the technology for a productive investment the libidinal rewards that the workers can obtain from the production process should not be neglected. The provision of these rewards becomes as important as the optimal allocation of capital, labour, land and knowledge for the successfully humane operation of an enterprise. Responding to the libidinal forces that preserve and improve life, human beings provide labour to the economy in order to produce satisfiers for the entire society and obtain satisfiers for themselves and their families. But the libidinal forces demand more than just the satisfaction of the basic needs for survival, and work can provide these additional satisfiers when it is appropriately organized.

The above statements can be illustrated by the example of the design of cheese factories. These have evolved from small rural plants processing 2,000 to 5,000 litres of milk a day to huge, highly automated urban plants processing 300,000 litres of milk or more a day. Economies of scale were reported as a result of these changes, but when workers at the modern cheese plants were asked about their feelings, they said that they found the urban plants alien-ating because their working time was spent pushing buttons in a healthy, polished, air-conditioned environment, while the rest of their time was often spent in poverty-ridden, ugly slums. The workers would like to return to rural areas and work in smaller factories where modern technology would reduce the time and physical effort required at certain steps of the process, such as when removing the curd from the cheese vats, but would still make it possible to obtain libidinal rewards from manually sensing and controlling the gentle process of curdling milk and slowly transforming it into cheese. The workers foresee in their dreams rural environments where good education for their children and themselves is made possible, and social and cultural constraints that oppose freedom in recreation and interrelations, and bridle creativity, are lifted.

Appropriate technological design can fulfil those dreams. It is easier to transport cheese to large urban distribution centres than to transport milk to huge urban processing plants. It also is easier to control the waste produced by small plants in rural areas than to dispose of the effluents of a large urban plant without either taxing the city's system of waste disposal or hurting the plant's neighbourhood, or transferring the problem to another area. An appropriate design of the operational hardware and the organizational and marketing software may take the total costs of a system in which small rural cheese factories are integrated with large urban storage and distribution centres to figures that compare well with those from a system in which milk is collected at the farms and processed in a large urban plant.

Project implementation

The implementation of a large investment project often involves the mobilization of a huge army of labour for remote underdeveloped areas. The provision of adequate facilities and services for the satisfaction of all the needs of the initial population is however neglected during the design of the project and mishandled during its implementation.

Typically, workers and supervisors are all male and are discouraged from bringing their families; hence, a concentration-camp environment soon develops. Only the engineers and administrators are provided with somewhat comfortable housing and means of rapid transportation to the nearest recreation areas for periodical relief from tension and boredom, relief that is not fully satisfying, and even these who are in the upper echelon of the work force become restless. For the rest of the working population a lumpen prostitution often develops in neighbouring villages, and venereal diseases are spread. The establishment of emotional and physical communications among the workers introduces additional tensions: they have then to cope with the prejudice against homosexuality that persists in many societies. At the end, intoxication by alcohol and drugs becomes the preferred way of escaping from the harsh reality. Even when they are well fed, the workers are often badly nourished, and if all things are taken together, practically none of their needs is found to be fully and adequately satisfied. Then, it should be no matter of wonder that computer-designed, critical-path construction schedules cannot be maintained and implementation is delayed because of absenteeism, social unrest, increased accidents and even open strikes and violent revolt.

In one instance, in a Latin American country, the well-engineered project of a large steel mill become a model of success in getting local technicians to master sophisticated technology through an effective transfer of knowledge by foreign experts, but its implementation was severely procrastinated by human problems of the type described above.

Steps in developing an economics of the satisfaction of needs

Economic systems should be designed by people for satisfying people's needs and supported by the ecosystems which provide raw materials, energy and cleaning services. The journey towards such a system progresses through consciousness-expanding efforts which aim at freeing the mind from obsolete subconscious behavioural and belief programmes with their encoded messages of greed, dominance, divisiveness, fears that the autonomy and diversity of the others will affect our own stability, rigid gender roles and contempt for instinctive drives. These messages distort the conscious perception of inner and outer reality and, by disabling the communications between the conscious mind and the unconscious, sever the links of humans with nature. After overcoming these handicaps, the restructured minds can adopt policies and practices that simultaneously promote freedom, equity and efficiency in the economy and reunite humans with nature. Examples of those policies and practices are the following:

- The design of educational systems that increase people's awareness of the constraints and opportunities for their development produced by nature and society; lead to the discovery of the potential for creation, production and playfulness that is in each mind and body; and facilitates the inner dialogue with the spirit, which guides the works and the evolution of nature and which speaks to humans from the unconscious of their minds.

- The promotion of the participation of all people, men and women, old and young, in the guidance of the economies, transcending through their expanded consciousness the inequalities that the invisible hand of the markets often creates and the oppression and inefficiency that the heavy hand of the state usually generates.

- The building of the circular flow of money, goods and services through successive levels of complexity, from the community to the bio-region and from there to the nation and the world, the economic activities at each level taking place within the constraints and opportunities produced by nature and being supported by and supportive of the activities at the next level.

- The promotion of businesses that are clean in their use of nature, honest in their dealing with the consumers, disciplined in their financial management and a joyful place where owners and employees feel they are being treated with fairness and compassion.

- The creation of markets in which producers and consumers have full access to information and financial resources.

- The organization of communities that support free exchange of physical, emotional and intellectual communications among people, protect them from brutality and violence and oppose all types of social and individual coercion into particular systems of behaviours and beliefs.

Experiments with socio-economic structures designed and operated by people with an expanded consciousnes prove that such objectives are feasible. These consciousness-expanding efforts, although still too few, are breaking new ground for a truly evolutionary process. In contrast to a revolution, which initially seems to sharply turn away a society from the direction in which it was moving, but soon after rolls back to near the starting point, an evolutionary process keeps constantly rolling out, opening new paths and unfolding new stories. A revolution can be the work of overpowering leaders and submissive, fearful followers; an evolutionary process requires instead the full and free participation of all social groups and the work of facilitators that help people expand their perception of the ever-unfolding reality.

Thomas Jefferson wrote in 1776 that

> laws and institutions must go hand in hand with progress of the human mind. As that becomes more developed, more enlightened, new discoveries are made, new truths disclosed, and manners and opinions change with the change of circumstances, institutions must advance also, and keep pace with the times.
>
> (Peterson 1987: 553)

Two centuries have passed and this advice goes still unheeded. Power elites must awaken to the conviction that by introducing repressive programmes in the mind of the populations whose acculturation they control, they have generated violence and destabilization. Now, these negative effects are not only returning as a boomerang to impact on the businesses and the personal lives of the elites, they are also threatening to destroy the fabric of society and the intricate patterns through which all of life is webbed in nature. It is time to step out of those obsolete legal and political patterns which are hindering the integrated satisfaction of all needs. To do so will require that laws and institutions be adapted to technological change and, at the same time, that technology and economics be humanized. Any political decision to make possible for all the enjoyment of libidinal wealth-consuming activities by increasing the production of wealth and equitably distributing the income it will generate must involve two other decisions: first, the decision to create a social environment in which all may freely engage in libidinal gratuitous activities; and, second, the decision to protect the physical environment that supports all human activities.

Kamenetzky's system of human needs goes well beyond the five 'basic needs' on which economic analysis normally focuses. However, it has intriguing similarities to three of the other major theories of needs that have been specifically proposed for, or adapted to, an economic context: those of Max-Neef, Maslow and Doyal and Gough.

Max-Neef's theory will be presented below. Maslow's (1954) theory has been pressed into service by Lutz and Lux (1988) to provide the motivational underpinning for their humanistic economics. Figure 7.2 reproduces their representation of Maslow's famous hierarchy (Lutz and Lux 1988: 10). Doyal and Gough's theory of needs was expounded by them in Ekins (1986: 69–80). The schematic illustration of their theory is reproduced here as Figure 7.3.

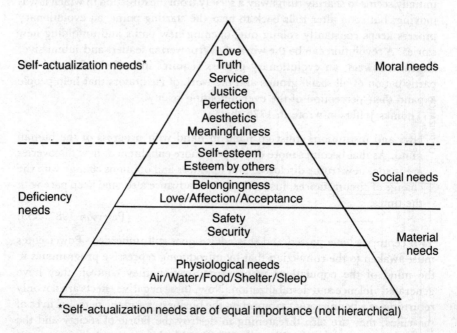

Figure 7.2   Maslow's hierarchy of needs (values)
Source: Lutz and Lux 1988: 10

Maslow's theory is the only one here considered explicitly to postulate a hierarchy of human needs, with people progressing from the deficiency to self-actualization needs as the former become increasingly satisfied. Lutz and Lux argue, however, that Maslow's later work moves away from this strictly hierarchical progression towards a 'dual self' theory, which recalls Etzioni's 'I & We paradigm', in which people try simultaneously to satisfy their deficiency and self-actualization needs. Where these needs conflict, choice based on some ethical system is necessary.

Doyal and Gough give more emphasis than the other theorists to the way in which individuals are socially formed. They stress the interdependence between individual and societal needs, while also making it clear that 'we do not accept forms of functionalism which presuppose that individuals simply mirror the structural properties of their social environment' (Doyal and Gough 1986: 72). In their theory the basic human need is for individual capability of action. This in turn requires physical and mental health and autonomy. Such health and autonomy in a social context are acquired rather than innate and, to some extent at least, need to be taught. Apprehending the

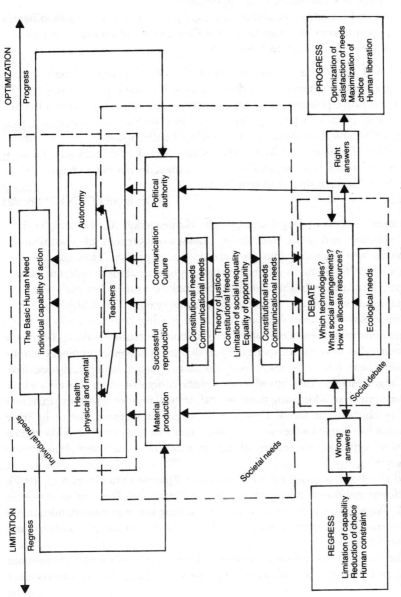

Figure 7.3 Schematic illustration of Doyal and Gough's theory of human needs
Source: Doyal and Gough 1986: 77

skills of material production and successful reproduction, and the forms of communication, culture and political authority, needs teachers. What is taught about these subjects depends on individuals' perceptions, the debate over alternatives and the social context within which this debate is conducted. If the dominant social objective is human liberation – understood as the achievement of a basic individual capability by all – then this context will require an explicit theory of justice, constitutional freedom, limitation of social inequality and equality of opportunity.

Doyal and Gough's conclusion strikingly prefigures, from a quite different starting point, some of the arguments in Chapters 9 and 10 about the relationship between the market and the state:

> We end up with an apparent paradox: that some type of central state responsibility, control and provision is a necessary prerequisite for the redistributive policies which are in turn preconditions for basic individual needs to be met in practice. However, in principle, the human need for liberation and the societal need for political authority are in no way incompatible. The question is not whether or not there should be a state. It is what sort of state it should be, and how it could meet the needs and rights of those it should serve rather than dominate.
>
> (Doyal and Gough 1986: 78)

The need-systems of Doyal and Gough, Kamenetzky, Maslow (in the dual-self version) and Max-Neef have obvious differences of classification, emphasis and approach. But they are not incompatible. They can co-exist, with each being useful in different situations or appealing to different people. If one is regarded as 'right', that does not make the others 'wrong'. They can perhaps best be regarded as facets of the same reality. The difficulty is not in choosing between these alternatives, but in making any reasonably complex formulation of human needs relevant to economic decision-making. Given the problems that have been experienced in designing strategies to meet even the so-called basic human needs of food, clothing, housing, health and education, one might imagine that introducing greater complexity into this area would not help much in addressing the very real, critical problems with which a large part of humanity is faced. However, Max-Neef's recent initiative in Latin America has proved otherwise and done more in four years to make operational an expanded conception of human needs than any other development undertaking.

What follows is based on a document in Spanish (Max-Neef *et al.* 1986), which was published in English in 1989 as *Human Scale Development: An Option for the Future*, and the experience since in putting the recommendations in the document into practice throughout the Latin American subcontinent and further afield.

The document was a response to the chronic sense of social and economic crisis perceived by the authors to be pervasive in Latin America today.

Development and human needs

Manfred Max-Neef

Latin America: crisis and perplexity

In creating the future, there is either the risk of making errors of perception, or of making errors of action. Concerning perception, two serious mistakes are often made. The first is to believe that the Latin American crisis can be ascribed principally to an external crisis. The second, stemming from the first, is to assume that our depression is just a passing historical circumstance. Although it is true that external conditions do considerably influence dependent and vulnerable economies like ours, it is, none the less, also probable that a recovery of the capitalistic economy in the North will not affect significantly our own recovery.

It would be a delusion to base a strategy for future development on the expansion of exports of primary products. Very simply, indicators suggest that the bulk of primary products will be affected, for different reasons, by unfavourable terms of trade. Moreover, others are already being replaced by more efficient substitutes. Another strategy based on the diversification of exports, that is, of manufactured goods, would inevitably come up against the protectionist policies of the powers in the North. Also, to assume a type of development which is nurtured by external contributions of capital is ruled out altogether on account of the serious and insoluble condition of indebtedness in which we are forced to live.

In our opinion, the future lies in mustering all our energy to design imaginative but viable alternatives. The conditions for these alternatives seem to be quite clear. The two schools of economic thought which have prevailed in the Latin American setting, neo-liberal monetarism and the more interventionist state-centered developmentalism promoted by the Economic Commission for Latin America, these have not been able to satisfy the legitimate needs of the Latin American masses. A new perspective is called for which aims at an adequate satisfaction of human needs. Furthermore, if future development cannot be sustained through the expansion of exports or through substantial injection of foreign capital, an alternative development must generate a capacity for greater self-reliance.

We are proposing an orientation which would enable us to create conditions for a new praxis based on Human Scale Development. Such development is focused and based on the satisfaction of fundamental human needs, on the generation of growing levels of self-reliance, and on the construction of organic articulations of people with nature and technology, of global processes with local activity, of the personal with the social, of planning with autonomy, and of civil society with the state, where 'articulation' is taken to mean the construction of coherent and consistent relations of balanced interdependence among given elements.

Human needs, self-reliance and organic articulations are the pillars which support Human Scale Development. However, these pillars must be sustained on a solid foundation which is the creation of those conditions where people are the protagonists in their future. If people are to be the main actors in Human Scale Development both the diversity as well as the autonomy of the spaces in which they act must be respected. Attaining the transformation of an object-person into a subject-person in the process of development is, among other things, a problem of scale. There is no possibility for the active participation of people in gigantic systems which are hierarchically organized and where decisions flow from the top down to the bottom.

Human Scale Development assumes a direct and participatory democracy. This form of democracy nurtures those conditions which will help to transform the traditional, semi-paternalistic role of the Latin American State into a role of encouraging creative solutions flowing from the bottom upwards. This is more consistent with the real expectations of the people.

I wish to emphasize at this point the democratic nature of the alternative proposed. Instead of relying on stereotyped ideological options, this document advocates the need to: develop processes of economic and political decentralization; strengthen genuine democratic institutions; and encourage increasing autonomy in the emerging social movements.

The creation of a political order which can represent the needs and interests of a heterogeneous people is a challenge to both the state and civil society. The most pressing question, not only for a democratic state but also for a society based on a democratic culture, is how to respect and encourage diversity rather than control it. In this regard, development must nurture local spaces, facilitate micro-organizations and support the multiplicity of cultural matrixes comprising civil society. This type of development must rediscover, consolidate and integrate the diverse collective identities that make up the social body.

Processes which nurture diversity and increase social participation and control over the environment are decisive in the articulation of projects to expand national autonomy and distribute the fruits of economic development more equitably. Hence, it is essential to prevent the increasing atomization of social movements, cultural identities and communities. To articulate these movements, identities, strategies and social demands in global proposals is not possible through the programmes of homogenization which have characterized the Latin American political tradition. It requires, on the part of the state, new institutional mechanisms capable of reconciling participation with heterogeneity. It also requires more active forms of representation, and greater translucency in the practices of the public sector.

It is not the purpose of this document to propose a state model that promotes Human Scale Development. Rather, our emphasis is on empowering civil society to nurture this form of development. This is not to minimize the importance of the state but to develop further the potential role of social actors, of social participation and of local communities. Our preoccupation is a 'social democracy' or rather a 'democracy of day-to-day living' which does not imply a lack of concern for 'political democracy' but a firm belief that only by rediscovering the 'molecular' composition of the social fabric (micro-organizations, local spaces, human-scale relations) is a political order founded on a democratic culture made possible. We believe that in order to avoid the atomization and the exclusion of people – be it in political, social or cultural terms – it is absolutely necessary to generate new ways of conceiving and practising politics. Thus, this document attempts to open up a space for critical reflection on the way we live and, more importantly, on the urgent need to develop a new political praxis.

Development and human needs

This new praxis starts from a theory of human needs for development. Human needs must be understood as a system; that is, all human needs are interrelated and interactive. With the sole exception of the need of subsistence, that is, to remain alive, no hierarchies exist within the system. On the contrary, simultaneities, complementarities and trade-offs are characteristics of the process of needs satisfaction.

Needs and satisfiers

As the literature in this area demonstrates, human needs can be classified according to many criteria. We have organized human needs into two categories: existential and axiological, which we have combined and displayed in a matrix (see Table 7.1, pp. 206–7). This allows us to demonstrate the interaction of, on the one hand, the needs of Being, Having, Doing and Inter-acting; and, on the other hand, the needs of Subsistence, Protection, Affection, Understanding, Participation, Creation, Leisure, Identity and Freedom.

From the classification proposed it follows that, for instance, food and shelter must not be seen as needs, but as satisfiers of the fundamental need for Subsistence. In much the same way, education (either formal or informal), study, investigation, early stimulation and meditation are satisfiers of the need for Understanding. The curative systems, preventive systems and health schemes in general are satisfiers of the need for Protection.

There is no one-to-one correspondence between needs and satisfiers. A satisfier may contribute simultaneously to the satisfaction of different needs, or conversely, a need may require various satisfiers in order to be met. Not even these relations are fixed. They may vary according to time, place and circumstance. For example, a mother breast-feeding her baby is simul-taneously satisfying the infant's needs for Subsistence, Protection, Affection and Identity. The situation is obviously different if the baby is fed in a more mechanical fashion.

Having established a difference between the concepts of needs and satisfiers it is possible to state two postulates: first, fundamental human needs are finite, few and classifiable; and second, fundamental human needs (such as those contained in the system proposed) are the same in all cultures and in all historical periods. What changes, both over time and through cultures, is the way or the means by which the needs are satisfied.

Each economic, social and political system adopts different methods for the satisfaction of the same fundamental human needs. In every system they are satisfied (or not satisfied) through the generation (or non-generation) of different types of satisfiers. We may go as far as to say that one of the aspects that define a culture is its choice of satisfiers. Whether a person belongs to a consumerist or to an ascetic society, his/her fundamental human needs are the same. What changes is his/her choice of the quantity and quality of satisfiers. In short, what is culturally determined are not the fundamental human needs, but the satisfiers for those needs. Cultural change is, among other things, the consequence of dropping traditional satisfiers for the purpose of adopting new or different ones.

It must be added that each need can be satisfied at different levels and with different intensities. Furthermore, needs are satisfied within three contexts: (1) with regard to oneself *(Eigenwelt)*; (2) with regard to the social group *(Mitwelt)*; and (3) with regard to the environment *(Umwelt)*. The quality and intensity, not only of the levels, but also of contexts will depend on time, place and circumstances.

Poverties and pathologies

The proposed perspective allows for a reinterpretation of the concept of poverty. The traditional concept of poverty is limited and restricted, since it refers exclusively to the predicaments of people who may be classified below a certain income threshold. This concept is strictly economistic. It is suggested here that we should speak not of poverty, but of poverties. In fact, any fundamental human need that is not adequately satisfied, reveals a human poverty. Some examples are: poverty of subsistence (due to insufficient income, food, shelter, etc.), of protection (due to bad health systems, violence, arms race, etc.), of affection (due to authoritarianism, oppression, exploitative relations with the natural environment, etc.), of understanding (due to poor quality of education), of participation (due to marginalization of and discrimination against women, children and minorities), of identity (due to imposition of alien values upon local and regional cultures, forced migration, political exile, etc.). But poverties are not only poverties. Much more than that, *each poverty generates pathologies*. This is the crux of our discourse.

In the Latin American context examples of persistent economic pathologies are unemployment, external debt and hyperinflation. Common political pathologies are fear, violence, marginalization and exile. Our challenge consists of recognizing and assessing these pathologies generated by diverse socio-economic political systems, with every system creating in its own way obstacles to the satisfaction of one or more needs. A further challenge is to develop and fulfil dialogue in pursuit of a constructive interpretation of the issues and solutions raised here. These challenges form the basis for an ongoing programme of participatory action research which has blossomed in hundreds of communities in Latin America since *Human Scale Development* was published.

Deprivation and potential

The very essence of human beings is expressed palpably through needs in their twofold character: as deprivation and as potential. Understood as much more than mere survival, needs bring out the constant tension between deprivation and potential which is so peculiar to human beings.

Needs, narrowly conceived as deprivation, are often restricted to that which is merely physiological and as such the sensation that 'something which is lacking is acutely felt'. However, to the degree that needs engage, motivate and mobilize people, they are a potential and eventually may become a resource. The need to participate is a potential for participation, just as the need for affection is a potential for affection.

To approach the human being through needs enables us to build a bridge between a philosophical anthropology and a political option: this appears to have been the motivation behind the intellectual efforts of, for example, Karl Marx and Abraham Maslow. To understand human beings in terms of needs, that is, conceived as deprivation and potential, will prevent any reduction of the human being into a category of a restricted existence.

Human needs and society

If we wish to define and assess an environment in the light of human needs, it is not sufficient to understand the opportunities that exist for groups or individuals to actualize their needs. It is necessary to analyse to what extent the environment represses, tolerates or stimulates opportunities. How accessible, creative or flexible is that environment? The most important question is how far people are able to influence the structures that affect their opportunities.

Satisfiers and economic goods

It is the satisfiers which define the prevailing mode that a culture or a society ascribes to needs. *Satisfiers are not the available economic goods.* They are related, instead, to everything which, by virtue of representing forms of Being, Having, Doing, and Interacting, contributes to the actualization of human needs. Satisfiers may include, among other things, forms of organization, political structures, social practices, subjective conditions, values and norms, spaces, contexts, modes, types of behaviour and attitudes, all of which are in a permanent state of tension between consolidation and change.

For example, the availability of food is a satisfier of the need for Protection in much the same way that a family structure might be. Likewise, a political order may be a satisfier of the need for Participation. The same satisfier can actualize different needs in different time periods.

The reason that a satisfier may have diverse effects in various contexts is due to the following: the breadth of the goods generated; how they are generated; and how consumption is organized. Understood as objects or artifacts which make it possible to increase or decrease the efficiency of a satisfier, goods have become determinant elements within industrial civilization. In industrial capitalism, the production of economic goods along with the system of allocating them has conditioned the type of satisfiers that predominate.

While a satisfier is in an *ultimate sense* the way in which a need is expressed, goods are in a *strict sense* the means by which individuals will empower the satisfiers to meet their needs. When, however, the form of production and consumption of goods makes goods an end in themselves, then the alleged satisfaction of a need impairs its capacity to create potential. This creates the conditions for entrenching an alienated society engaged in a productivity race lacking any sense at all. Life, then, is placed at the service of artifacts, rather than artifacts at the service of life. The question of the quality of life is overshadowed by our obsession to increase productivity.

Within this perspective, the construction of a human economy poses an important theoretical challenge, namely, to understand fully the dialectic between needs, satisfiers and economic goods. This is necessary in order to conceive forms of economic organization in which goods empower satisfiers to meet fully and consistently fundamental human needs.

This situation compels us to rethink the social context of human needs in a radically different way from the manner in which it has been approached by social planners and designers of policies for development. It is not only a question of having to relate to goods and services but also to relate them to social practices, forms of organization, political models and values. All of these have an impact on the ways in which needs are expressed.

In a critical theory of society, it is not sufficient to specify the predominant satisfiers and economic goods produced within that society. They must be understood as products which are the result of historical factors and consequently, liable to change. Thus, it is necessary to retrace the process of reflection and creation that conditions the interaction between needs, satisfiers and economic goods.

The vindication of subjectivity

To assume a direct relation between needs and economic goods has allowed us to develop a discipline of economics that presumes itself to be objective, a mechanistic discipline in which the central tenet implies that needs manifest themselves through demand which, in turn, is determined by individual preferences for the goods produced. To include satisfiers within the framework of economic analysis involves vindicating the world of the 'subjective', over and above mere preferences for objects and artifacts.

We can explain how needs are met: our own and those of others in our milieu, family, friends, members of the community, cultural groups, the economic system, the socio-political system, the nation and so on. We can try to understand how satisfiers and predominant economic goods are related in our environment to the manner in which we emotionally express our needs. We can detect how satisfiers and the availability of goods constrain, distort or enhance the quality of our lives. On this basis, we can think of viable ways to organize and distribute the satisfiers and goods so that they nurture the process of actualizing needs and reduce the possibilities of frustration.

The ways in which we experience our needs, hence the quality of our lives, is, ultimately, subjective. When the object of study is the relation between human beings and society, the universality of the subjective cannot be ignored. Any attempt to observe the life of human beings must recognize the social character of subjectivity. It is not impossible to advance judgements about the subjective. Yet there is a great fear of the consequences of such a reflection. Economic theory is a clear example of this. From the neoclassical economists to the monetarists, the notion of preferences is used to avoid the issue of needs. This perspective reveals an acute reluctance to discuss the subjective-universal. This is particularly true if it is a question of taking a stand in favour of a free-market economy. Preferences belong to the realm of the subjective-particular and, therefore, are not a threat to the assumptions that underlie the rationale of the market. Whereas to speak of fundamental human needs compels us to focus our attention from the outset on the subjective-universal.

The way in which needs are expressed through satisfiers varies according to historical period and culture. The social and economic relations, defined by historical and cultural circumstances, are concerned with the subjective and the objective. Hence, *satisfiers are what render needs historical and cultural, and economic goods are their material manifestation.*

The evolution of human needs

Owing to the dirth of empirical evidence, it is impossible to state with absolute certainty that the fundamental human needs are historically and culturally constant. However, there is nothing that prevents us from speaking of their socio-universal character because people everywhere want to satisfy their needs. In reflecting on the nine fundamental needs proposed in this document, common sense, along with some socio-cultural sensitivity, surely points to the fact that the needs for Subsistence, Protection, Affection, Understanding, Participation, Creation and Leisure have existed since the origins of *homo habilis* and, undoubtedly, since the appearance of *homo sapiens*.

Probably at a later stage of evolution the need for Identity appeared and, at a much later date, the need for Freedom. In much the same way, it is likely that in the future the need for Transcendence, which is not included in our proposal, as we do not yet consider it universal, will become as universal as the other needs. It seems legitimate, then, to assume that fundamental human needs change with the pace of evolution. That is to say, at a very slow rate. Therefore, fundamental human needs are not only universal but are also entwined with the evolution of the species. They follow a single track.

Satisfiers behave in two ways: they are modified according to the rhythm of history and vary according to culture and circumstance. Economic goods (artifacts, technologies) behave in three different ways: they are modified according to episodic rhythms (vogues, fashions) and diversify according to cultures and, within those cultures, according to social strata.

In summary, perhaps we may say that fundamental human needs are essential attributes related to human evolution; satisfiers are forms of Being, Having, Doing and Interacting, related to structures; and economic goods are objects related to particular historical moments.

Evolutionary, structural and episodic changes take place at different paces and rhythms. The movement of history places the human being in an increasingly unrhythmical and unsynchronized domain in which human concerns are neglected more and more. In the present moment, this situation has become extreme.

The speed of production and the diversification of objects have become ends in themselves and as such are no longer able to satisfy any need whatsoever. People have grown more dependent on this sytem of production but, at the same time, more alienated from it.

It is only in some of the regions marginalized by the crisis and in those groups which defy the prevailing styles of development, that autonomous processes are generated in which satisfiers and economic goods become subordinated once again to the actualization of human needs. It is in these sectors that we can find examples of synergic types of behaviour which offer a potential response to the crisis which looms over us.

A matrix of needs and satisfiers

The interrelationship between needs, satisfiers and economic goods is permanent and dynamic. A dialectic relationship exists among them. If economic goods are capable of affecting the efficiency of the satisfiers, the latter will be determinant in generating and creating the former. Through this reciprocal causation, they become both part and definition of a culture which, in turn, delimits the style of development.

As Table 7.1 indicates, satisfiers can be organized within the grids of a matrix which, on the one hand, classifies needs according to the existential categories of Being, Having, Doing and Interacting, and, on the other hand, according to the axiological categories of Subsistence, Protection, Affection, Understanding, Participation, Creation, Recreation, Identity and Freedom. This matrix is neither normative nor conclusive. It merely gives an example of possible types of satisfiers. In fact, this matrix of satisfiers, if completed by individuals or groups from diverse cultures and in different historical moments, might vary considerably.

An examination of the different fields in the matrix with their possible satisfiers demonstrates clearly that many of the satisfiers can give rise to different
economic goods. If we take, for instance, field 15, showing different ways of
Doing to actualize the need for Understanding, we see that it includes
satisfiers such as investigating, studying, experimenting, educating,
analysing, meditating and interpreting. These satisfiers give rise to economic
goods, depending on the culture and the resources, such as books, laboratory
instruments, tools, computers and other artifacts. The function of these goods
is to empower the *Doing of Understanding*.

Examples of satisfiers and their attributes

The matrix presented is only an example and in no way exhausts the number
of possible satisfiers. Because satisfiers have various characteristics, we suggest
for analytical purposes five types that may be identified, namely (1) violators
or destroyers, (2) pseudo-satisfiers, (3) inhibiting satisfiers, (4) singular satisfiers, and (5) synergic satisfiers (see Tables 7.2 to 7.6).

The first four categories of satisfiers are exogenous to civil society as they
are usually imposed, induced, ritualized or institutionalized. In this sense,
they are satisfiers which have been traditionally generated at the top and
advocated for all. On the other hand endogenous satisfiers derive from
liberating processes which are the outcome of acts of volition generated by
the community at the grass roots level. It is this that makes them anti-
authoritarian, even though in some cases they may originate in processes
promoted by the state.

One of the important aims of Human Scale Development is to affect change
in the nature of the Latin American State. It should move from its traditional
role as a generator of satisfiers which are exogenous to civil society, to a
stimulator and creator of processes arising from the bottom upwards.
Particularly, given the tremendously restrictive conditions which the current
crisis imposes on us, an increase in the levels of local, regional, and national
self-reliance should be deemed a priority. This objective can be met through
the generation of synergic processes at all levels of society.

The fact that several of the satisfiers offered as examples do not appear in
the matrix is due to the fact that the tables are more specific. It must be borne
in mind that the matrix is merely illustrative and not normative.

Application of the matrix

The schema proposed can be used for purposes of diagnosis, planning, assessment and evaluation. The matrix of needs and satisfiers may serve, at a
preliminary stage, as a participative exercise of self-diagnosis for groups
located within a local space. Through a process of regular dialogue – preferably
with the presence of a facilitator acting as a catalysing element – the group
may gradually begin to characterize itself by filling in the corresponding

Table 7.1 Matrix of needs and satisfiers*

Needs according to axiological categories	Needs according to existential categories			
	Being	Having	Doing	Interacting
Subsistence	1/ Physical health, mental health, equilibrium, sense of humour, adaptability	2/ Food, shelter, work	3/ Feed, procreate, rest, work	4/ Living environment, social setting
Protection	5/ Care, adaptability, autonomy, equilibrium, solidarity	6/ Insurance systems, savings, social security, health systems, rights, family, work	7/ Co-operate, prevent, plan, take care of, cure, help	8/ Living space, social environment, dwelling
Affection	9/ Self-esteem, solidarity, respect, tolerance, generosity, receptiveness, passion, determination, sensuality, sense of humour	10/ Friendships, family, partnerships, relationships with nature	11/ Make love, caress, express emotions, share, take care of, cultivate, appreciate	12/ Privacy, intimacy, home, spaces of togetherness
Understanding	13/ Critical conscience, receptiveness, curiosity, astonishment, discipline, intuition, rationality	14/ Literature, teachers, method, educational policies, communication policies	15/ Investigate, study, experiment, educate, analyse, meditate	16/ Settings of formative interaction, schools, universities, academies, groups, communities, family

	Being	Having	Doing	Interacting
Participation	17/ Adaptability, receptiveness, solidarity, willingness, determination, dedication, respect, passion, sense of humour	18/ Rights, responsibilities, duties, privileges, work	19/ Become affiliated, co-operate, propose, share, dissent, obey, interact, agree on, express opinions	20/ Settings of participative interaction, parties, associations, churches, communities, neighbourhoods, family
Leisure	21/ Curiosity, receptiveness, imagination, recklessness, sense of humour, tranquility, sensuality	22/ Games, spectacles, clubs, parties, peace of mind	23/ Day-dream, brood, dream, recall old times, give way to fantasies, remember, relax, have fun, play	24/ Privacy, intimacy, spaces of closeness, free time, surroundings, landscapes
Creation	25/ Passion, determination, intuition, imagination, boldness, rationality, autonomy, inventiveness, curiosity	26/ Abilities, skills, method, work	27/ Work, invent, build, design, compose, interpret	28/ Productive and feedback settings, workshops, cultural groups, audiences, spaces for expression, temporal freedom
Identity	29/ Sense of belonging, consistency, differentiation, self-esteem, assertiveness	30/ Symbols, language, religions, habits, customs, reference groups, sexuality, values, norms, historical memory, work	31/ Commit oneself, integrate oneself, confront, decide on, get to know oneself, recognize oneself, actualize oneself, grow	32/ Social rhythms, everyday settings, settings which one belongs to, maturation stages
Freedom	33/ Autonomy, self-esteem, determination, passion, assertiveness, open-mindedness, boldness, rebelliousness, tolerance	34/ Equal rights	35/ Dissent, choose, be different from, run risks, develop awareness, commit oneself, disobey	36/ Temporal/spatial plasticity

* The column of BEING registers *attributes*, personal or collective, that are expressed as nouns. The column of HAVING registers *institutions*, *norms*, *mechanisms*, *tools* (not in a material sense), *laws*, etc. that can be expressed in one or more words. The column of DOING registers *actions*, personal or collective, that can be expressed as verbs. The column of INTERACTING registers *locations* and *milieus* (as times and spaces). It stands for the Spanish ESTAR or the German BEFINDEN, in the sense of time and space. Since there is no corresponding word in English, INTERACTING was chosen *à faul de mieux*.

Table 7.2 Violators and destructors*

Supposed satisfier	Need to be supposedly satisfied	Needs whose satisfaction it impairs
1. Arms race	Protection	Subsistence, Affection, Participation, Freedom
2. Exile	Protection	Affection, Participation, Identity, Freedom
3. National security doctrine	Protection	Subsistence, Identity, Affection, Understanding, Participation, Freedom
4. Censorship	Protection	Understanding, Participation, Leisure, Creation, Identity, Freedom
5. Bureaucracy	Protection	Understanding, Affection, Participation, Creation, Identity, Freedom
6. Authoritarianism	Protection	Affection, Understanding, Participation, Creation, Identity, Freedom

* Violators or destructors are elements of a paradoxical effect. Applied under the pretext of satisfying a given need, they not only annihilate the possibility of its satisfaction, but they also render the adequate satisfaction of other needs impossible. They seem to be especially related to the need for protection.

Table 7.3 Pseudo-satisfiers*

Satisfier	Need which it seemingly satisfies
1. Mechanistic medicine: 'A pill for every ill'	Protection
2. Over-exploitation of natural resources	Subsistence
3. Chauvinistic nationalism	Identity
4. Formal democracy	Participation
5. Stereotypes	Understanding
6. Aggregate economic indicators	Understanding
7. Cultural control	Creation
8. Prostitution	Affection
9. Status symbols	Identity
10. Obsessive productivity with a bias to efficiency	Subsistence
11. Indoctrination	Understanding
12. Charity	Subsistence
13. Fashions and fads	Identity

* Pseudo-satisfiers are elements which stimulate a false sensation of satisfying a given need. Though they lack the aggressiveness of violators, they may, on occasion, annul, in the medium term, the possibility of satisfying the need they were originally aimed at.

Table 7.4 Inhibiting satisfiers*

Satisfier	Need	Needs, whose satisfaction is inhibited
1. Paternalism	Protection	Understanding, Participation, Freedom, Identity
2. Over-protective family	Protection	Affection, Understanding, Participation, Leisure, Identity, Freedom
3. Taylorist-type of production	Subsistence	Understanding, Participation, Creation, Identity, Freedom
4. Authoritarian classroom	Understanding	Participation, Creation, Identity, Freedom
5. Messianisms (Millennarisms)	Identity·	Protection, Understanding, Participation, Freedom
6. Unlimited permissiveness	Freedom	Protection, Affection, Identity, Participation
7. Obsessive economic competitiveness	Freedom	Subsistence, Protection, Affection, Participation, Leisure
8. Commercial television	Leisure	Understanding, Creation, Identity

* Inhibiting satisfiers are those which by the way in which they satisfy (generally over-satisfy) a given need seriously impair the possibility of satisfying other needs.

Table 7.5 Singular satisfiers*

Satisfier	Need which it satisfies
1. Programmes to provide food	Subsistence
2. Welfare programmes to provide dwelling	Subsistence
3. Curative medicine	Subsistence
4. Insurance systems	Protection
5. Professional armies	Protection
6. Ballot	Participation
7. Sports spectacles	Leisure
8. Nationality	Identity
9. Guided tours	Leisure
10. Gifts	Affection

* Singular satisfiers are those which aim at the satisfaction of a single need and are, therefore, neutral as regards the satisfaction of other needs. They are very characteristic of development and co-operation schemes and programmes.

Table 7.6 Synergic satisfiers*

Satisfier	Need	Needs, whose satisfaction it stimulates
1. Breast-feeding	Subsistence	Protection, Affection, Identity
2. Self-managed production	Subsistence	Understanding, Participation, Creation, Identity, Freedom
3. Popular education	Understanding	Protection, Participation, Creation, Identity, Freedom
4. Democratic community organizations	Participation	Protection, Affection, Leisure, Creation, Identity, Freedom
5. Barefoot medicine	Protection	Subsistence, Understanding, Participation
6. Barefoot banking	Protection	Subsistence, Participation, Creation, Freedom
7. Democratic trade unions	Protection	Understanding, Participation, Identity
8. Direct democracy	Participation	Protection, Understanding, Identity, Freedom
9. Educational games	Leisure	Understanding, Creation
10. Self-managed house-building programmes	Subsistence	Understanding, Participation
11. Preventive medicine	Protection	Understanding, Participation, Subsistence
12. Meditation	Understanding	Leisure, Creation, Identity
13. Cultural television	Leisure	Understanding

* Synergic satisfiers are those which, by the way in which they satisfy a given need, stimulate and contribute to the simultaneous satisfaction of other needs.

fields. A method of accomplishing this is described in some detail elsewhere (Max-Neef *et al.* 1989: 40–3).

The outcome of the exercise will enable the group to become aware of both its deprivations and potentialities. After diagnosing its current reality, it may repeat the exercise in propositional terms; that is, identifying which satisfiers would be required to fully meet the fundamental needs of the group. As the satisfiers are selected with increasing levels of specificity, they should be discussed critically by the group in terms of their characteristics and attributes, in order to determine if they are – or should be – generated exogenously or endogenously, that is by the community itself. Such an analysis will demonstrate the potential capacity for local self-reliance. The same analysis of proposed satisfiers will enable the group to assess not only whether their positive effects are singular or synergic, but also whether the negative effects are violators, inhibiting satisfiers, or pseudo-satisfiers. The next stage of reflection of the group is to determine whether access exists to the necessary economic goods and material resources.

The proposed exercise has a twofold value. First, it makes it possible to identify at a local level a strategy for development aimed at the actualization of human needs. Second, it is an educational, creative and participatory exercise that brings about a state of deep critical awareness; that is to say, the method is, in itself, a generator of synergic effects.

The technique described is not restricted only to an analysis of local spaces. It is likewise applicable at regional and national levels. In local spaces it can be a broad based participation process where those representing the interest of the economic, political and social domains of the community may express their ideas.

At a regional level the exercise should be undertaken by a carefully chosen team which not only represents the different domains of endeavour, but also, by virtue of its representative nature, combines both public and private interests. At the national level it is essential that the task should be approached in a transdisciplinary manner because of the complexity of the issues.

Development geared to the satisfaction of fundamental human needs cannot, by definition, be structured from the top downwards. It cannot be imposed either by law or by decree. It can only emanate directly from the actions, expectations and creative and critical awareness of the protagonists themselves. Instead of being the traditional objects of development, people must take a leading role in development. The anti-authoritarian nature of Human Scale Development does not involve making the conflict between state and civil society more acute. On the contrary, it attempts to prove, through the method proposed, that the state can assume a role which encourages synergic processes at the local, regional and national levels.

Implications for development

From the linear to the systemic approach

Fundamental human needs must be understood as a system, the dynamics of which does not obey hierarchical linearities. This means that, on the one hand, no need is *per se* more important than any other; and, on the other hand, that there is no fixed order of precedence in the actualization of needs (that need B, for instance, can only be met after need A has been satisfied). Simultaneities, complementarities and trade-offs are characteristic of the system's behaviour. There are, however, limits to this generalization. A pre-systemic threshold must be recognized, below which the feeling of a certain deprivation may be so severe, that the urge to satisfy the given need may paralyse and overshadow any other impulse or alternative.

The case of subsistence may serve to illustrate this clearly. When the possibilities of satisfying this need are severely impaired, all other needs remain blocked and a single and intense drive prevails. But such a situation does not hold true only in the case of subsistence. It is equally relevant in the case of other needs. Suffice it to say, that total lack of affection, or the loss of identity, may lead people to extremes of self-destruction.

Whether to follow the assumptions of linearity or the systemic assumptions is such an important choice that it will determine the resulting style of development.

If linearity is favoured, the development strategy will most probably establish its priorities according to the observed poverty of subsistence. Programmes of social assistance will be implemented as a means of tackling poverty as it is conventionally understood. Needs will be interpreted exclusively as deprivations and, at best, the satisfiers that the system may generate will correspond to those identified here as singular. Last, but not least, linear assumptions will stimulate accumulation regardless of people's human development. Paradoxically this option results in a circular cumulative causation (in the sense of Myrdal) and, thus, the poor remain poor inasmuch as their dependence on exogenously generated satisfiers increases.

If one opts for the systemic assumptions, the development strategy will favour endogenously generated synergic satisfiers. Needs will be understood simultaneously as deprivations and potentials, thus allowing for the elimination of the vicious circle of poverty.

It follows from the above that the way in which needs are understood, and the role and attributes ascribed to the possible satisfiers, *are absolutely definitive*, in determining a development strategy.

From efficiency to synergy

To interpret development as here proposed, implies a change in the prevailing economic rationale. It compels us, among other things, to undertake a critical and rigorous revision of the concept of efficiency. This concept is often associated with notions such as the maximization of productivity and of profits, the ambiguity of both terms notwithstanding. If we stretch economic criteria to the most alienated extreme of instrumental reasoning, productivity appears quite inefficient. In fact, by overemphasizing the need for Subsistence, it sacrifices other needs and so ends up threatening Subsistence itself.

The dominant development discourses also associate efficiency with the conversion of labour into capital, with the formalization of economic activities, with the indiscriminate absorption of the newest technologies and, of course, with the maximization of growth rates. In the eyes of many, development consists of achieving the material living standards of the most industrialized countries, in order for people to have access to a growing array of goods (artifacts) which become increasingly more diversified.

Human Scale Development does not exclude conventional goals such as economic growth, so that all persons may have access to required goods and services. However, the difference with respect to the prevailing development styles lies in considering the aims of development not only as points of arrival, but as components of the process itself. In other words, fundamental human needs can and must be realized from the outset and throughout the entire process of development. In this manner the realization of needs becomes, instead of a goal, the motor of development itself. This is possible only inasmuch as the development strategy proves to be capable of stimulating the permanent generation of synergic satisfiers.

To integrate the harmonious realization of human needs into the process of development gives everyone the possibility of experiencing that development from its very outset. This may give rise to a healthy, self-reliant and partici-pative development, capable of creating the foundations for a social order within which economic growth, solidarity and the growth of all men and women as whole persons can be reconciled.

The exercise described here has, as already stated, received an enthusiastic response from hundreds of different communities in Latin America, from local grass-roots groups working in a specified locality (the majority), to seminars of academics, to meetings of government officials. For the grass-roots especially the process permits a clarification of the realities of their socio-economic-cultural situation. It gives an opportunity to free the creative imagination, similar to the 'Future Workshops' devised by Robert Jungk (Jungk and Mullert 1988). Thence the required bridges between the (negative) present and (positive) future can be identified. Finally the group, which will by then have engendered a considerable degree of self-knowledge, can proceed to a consideration of specific self-reliant development strategies and projects, resources that can be mobilized and outside support that can be enlisted. Although the HSD exercise was developed with a Third World context in mind, there is nothing that invalidates it for use in any society. In an industrial context the need of subsistence will be less pressing, of course, and one can expect many other differences across different cultures and situations. However, because the 'development crisis' is perceived as most acute in the Third World, one can expect the methodology to be most employed there, as indeed is the case with the take-up in Latin America. Most importantly, it defines a frame within which the relatively recent explosion of self-organized community action in Third World countries, as identified in, for example, Schneider (1988) or Pradervand (1989), can orient itself towards holistic, need-satisfying endeavour.

However, as Max-Neef, Elizalde and Hopenhayn recognize, 'grass-roots self-mobilisation is not enough', and the second half of their document is devoted to discussion as to how this can be related constructively to macro-social processes, which is also one of the subjects in the final part of this book. There is a need for all actors in the formal development process, from inter-governmental institutions to national governments to municipal authorities and all the economists, planners and officials whom they employ, and irrespective of whether their prime focus is environment, development or employment, to recognize the primacy of local wishes and realities and to find ways of helping them to be realized. This applies especially when the needs are being articulated by those whom development professionals characterize as 'poor'.

Sustainable livelihoods: the poor's reconciliation of environment and development
Robert Chambers

I shall argue in this paper that the thinking and strategies advocated and adopted with regard to problems of population, resources, environment and development (PRED) have largely perpetuated conventional top–down, centre–outwards thinking, and have largely failed to appreciate how much sustainability depends upon reversals, upon starting with the poorer and enabling them to put their priorities first.

The context of the interrelationships between population, resources, environment and development is well understood and generally accepted. A summary overview, with which most would agree can set the scene.

The context is the rural South, mainly but not only in the tropics. Three major processes stand out. These are population growth, 'core' (urban, industrial, rich) invasions of rural environments, and responses by the rural poor.

Population growth

Rapid population growth is the norm in the South. According to World Bank estimates (rounded), in the thirty-seven years from 1988 to 2025, populations will grow by 80 per cent in low-income countries and by the same 80 per cent in middle-income countries, in total from less than 4 billion to over 7 billion, while in Sub-Saharan Africa (SSA) taken on its own the increase will be over 180 per cent, from 464 million to over 1.3 billion (World Bank 1990: 228–9). As in much of SSA, it is often where the environmental base is most fragile and deteriorating, and where the rural population is a high proportion, that population growth is projected to be most rapid.

'Core' invasions and pressures

The second process – 'core' invasions and pressures – is shorthand for extensions into rural areas of the power, ownership and exploitation of central, urban institutions and individuals which include the richer world of the North, governments of the South, commercial interests, and professionals who are variously wealthy, urban and powerful. 'Core' also reflects the bias of language and thought which makes urban areas the centre, from which other areas, where many of the rural poor live, are 'remote'. Core invasions have mixed effects. They both generate and destroy livelihoods. They create conditions for population growth, and exercise pressure on the environment. The normal, core, centre–outwards view of these processes sees them as almost entirely benign; but the view from the periphery is radically different and a necessary corrective. In that view, the rich are seen as engaged on a massive scale in destroying and rendering less secure the livelihoods of the poor. The rich compete for and appropriate resources. Common land is enclosed and encroached by the wealthy. Forests, fisheries and ranching lands are appropriated by government and commercial interests. A common pattern is that logging and ranching interests, sometimes with corrupt forestry officials, contractors and politicians, come first and cut out the timber, and then poor cultivators come in their wake. It is the consumption of rich people and of the rich world which devastates tropical rain forests much more than encroachment by the poor which is so often blamed. There are many patterns and variations, but on a very wide scale, the core invasions of the rich North and of the rich in the South are appropriating and degrading resources on which the rural poor depend.

Responses by the rural poor

The third process is responses of poor rural people to population growth and core invasions. Patterns vary and exceptions are many. But a useful framework for discussion is a distinction between green revolution agriculture, in areas which are generally fertile, irrigated or otherwise well watered, uniform and flat, and low-resource or resource-poor agriculture in areas generally less fertile, rain-fed, diverse and undulating. In resource-poor areas, which are typical of most of SSA and of the hinterlands of Asia and Latin America, as populations grow and common property resources are appropriated, agriculture becomes more intensive, and for a time at least less sustainable as fallows shorten and/or livestock become more numerous. Core invasions and pressures, appropriations and exclusions by government and by the urban and rural rich, declining biological productivity, and rising human populations drive many of the poorer people to migrate.

This they do either seasonally or permanently, some to cities and towns, some to areas of green revolution agriculture, and some to forests, savannahs, steep slopes, flood-prone flatlands and other vulnerable or marginal areas. In these areas they may adopt sustainable forms of cultivation and pastoralism, but more often cannot, hindered and discouraged as they are by insecure tenure, lack of appropriate technology and poverty.

These three processes are linked in many ways, and are not sustainable. The policy questions are, then, how these pressures can be restrained, and how vastly larger numbers of people can be enabled to gain adequate, secure, decent and sustainable livelihoods in rural areas.

Normal professionalism: 'first' thinking and PRED

Normal professionalism means the concepts, values, methods and behaviour dominant in professions, and 'first' thinking refers to the ways of thinking prevalent in the urban, industrial and Northern cores of power and knowledge. In much normal professionalism and 'first' thinking (Chambers 1985, 1986), it is things, especially the things of the rich, which come first, while people come last, with the poorer rural people last of all. To caricature, the top–down view of 'the rural poor' sees them as an undifferentiated mass of people who live hand-to-mouth and who cannot and will not take anything but a short-term view in resource use. In consequence, it is held, their activities must be regulated and controlled in order to preserve the environment.

Such beliefs endure tenaciously, for four reasons. First, they are gratifying: it feels good to think that one knows better and that others are irresponsible. Second, they divert attention from the depredations of the rich, about which it is so much more difficult and uncongenial to do anything. Third, they justify the exercise of power against the poor, and that has its attractions. Fourth, these beliefs are self-sustaining because the official actions to which they lead provoke the poor to behave in ways which appear to justify the actions.

In the light of experience, though, beliefs have been modified. Population professionals now recognize that large families make sense to many of the poor, and see that eliminating poverty must usually precede or accompany the reduction of fertility. Professionals who start with resources and environment recognize that poor people are often behaving rationally, and sometimes rationally in desperation, when they exploit resources and the environment in ways which are not sustainable. Development thinkers now pay much attention to questions of political economy, of who gains and who loses in processes of economic growth or decline. All the same, for many professionals, and whatever their rhetoric, the rural poor, the remote, and women, still come late in processes of analysis and are sometimes relegated to terminal footnotes. They are not the starting point.

Sustainable livelihood security

The basic grounds for putting the poor first are ethical and not in serious dispute. For many that is enough in itself. But in addition, there are also overwhelming practical reasons. These apply even from the point of view of normal professional concerns with PRED. The argument is that unless the poor – the last – are put first, the objectives for environment and development will themselves not be attained.

Practical last-first analysis starts with what poor people want. Poor people have many priorities, and these vary from person to person, from place to place, and from time to time. Health is often, if not always, one. In addition a common and almost universal priority expressed is the desire for an adequate, secure and decent livelihood which provides for physical and social well-being.

This includes security against sickness, against early death, and against becoming poorer, and thus secure command over assets as well as income, and good chances of survival. Again and again, when they are asked, poor people give replies which fit these points. A phrase to summarize all this is livelihood security.

This line of strategic thinking was explored by the Brundtland Commission's Advisory Panel on Food, Agriculture, Forestry and Environment. The Panel developed sustainable livelihood security as an integrating concept, with these meanings:

> Livelihood is defined as adequate stocks and flows of food and cash to meet basic needs. Security refers to secure ownership of, or access to, resources and income-earning activities, including reserves and assets to offset risk, ease shocks and meet contingencies. Sustainable refers to the maintenance or enhancement of resource productivity on a long-term basis.
>
> (Food 2000 1987: 3)

Sustainable livelihood security integrates population, resources, environment and development in four respects: stabilizing population; reducing migration; fending off core exploitation; and supporting long-term sustainable resource management.

Stabilizing population

Part of the pressure on the environment comes from population increases, compounded by poverty and exploitation and displacement of the poor. For stabilizing human population, livelihood security may often be a precondition. The insecure and poor are sensible to have many children. It is rational for those who lack secure command over resources, and who expect some of their children to die, to have large families. This is both survival strategy and insurance. They need to spread risks and diversify their sources of food and cash, putting family members in different activities and places, and relying on surviving children for support in old age. The less they expect their children to live, the less they command a decent living, and the less they can look forward to a secure old age, the more sense it makes for parents to have more children.

Reasons for wanting and having lower fertility are not simple, and causality is complex and elusive. Good health and decent livelihoods, two major aspirations of the poor, are not in themselves necessarily sufficient for parents to want fewer children, but they appear as predisposing conditions. There is suggestive evidence that smaller holdings and secure tenure can combine to encourage lower fertility (World Bank 1984: 109).

A cautious statement which may understate the positive relationships is that in conditions where livelihoods are adequate, secure and sustainable, assets can be passed on to children, children are likely to survive and the benefits of child labour are limited, parents have less reason to want large families.

Reducing distress migration

Poor people rarely like to migrate. The suffering of migrants, whether rural (as recounted by Jan Breman (1985), a social anthropologist who accompanied rural migrants in Gujarat) or urban (as Dominique LaPierre's carefully researched 'novel' *City of Joy* testifies for Calcutta), is often appalling, and migrants further impoverish the poor in the areas to which they move by competing for resources, services and work. In many areas, migration into fragile marginal lands and into forests contributes to environmental degradation. But when people have secure control over resources which can provide them with adequate livelihoods they have incentives to manage them so that they do not have to migrate.

Fending-off core exploitation

Those with secure ownership of assets, or secure rights and access to resources, are often able to survive bad times without permanent impoverishment. They are better placed to resist exploitation, indebtedness, or the loss of productive assets through distress sale. It is where people are legally, politically and physically weak, and lack secure legal rights to resources, that they are most vulnerable. Fending off core exploitation or appropriation can mean that they and their children can stay where they are, and not join the ranks of those who have to migrate.

Taking the long view

Core interests tend to take a short-term view of resource exploitation. Conservationist rhetoric should not be allowed to mislead here. Government officials focus on the end of the financial year; politicians on the next election. Governments have often protected forests less well than have communities. Corrupt alliances of politicians, forest officials and contractors, if not universal, are still rather common: many have grown fat by felling, not protecting, forests. For its part, normal project appraisal by discounting future benefits and seeking high internal rates of return also takes a short-term view, while commercial interests concerned with profits take an even shorter one.

In contrast, poor people with secure ownership of land, trees, livestock and other resources, where confident that they can retain the benefits of good husbandry and pass them on to their children, can be, and often are, tenacious in their retention of assets and far-sighted in their investments. It is misleading to confuse the behaviour of those who are very poor and desperate with that of those who are poor but not desperate.

For the desperate poor, sheer survival is the priority, and, however much they may wish to, people find it difficult to take the long view. For the merely poor, though, once basic survival is assured, and given safe and secure conditions, there is evident a strong propensity to stint and save when the opportunity presents. What appears an inability to invest labour for the longer term is often a rational recognition of insecurity: who will plant a tree or invest labour in works of soil conservation who fears the tree will be stolen, or the land appropriated, or the household itself driven away? Tenants-at-will rarely plant trees or dig terraces. In contrast, long-term tenure and secure rights of usufruct encourage a long-term view and the investment of labour and funds in resource conservation and enhancement, as is shown by extensive tree-planting in countries as different as Haiti, India and Kenya (Chambers and Leach 1987; Conway 1988; Murray 1986) and by the largely overlooked long-term investments in concentrating soil, water and nutrients in stable and productive microenvironments (Chambers 1990). As such examples indicate, many poor people with secure ownership, rights and access to resources invest for the future once they can meet their basic needs.

The implication of these four points is that poor people are not the problem but the solution. If conditions are right they can be predisposed to want smaller families, to stay where they are, to resist and repulse short-term exploitation from the cores, and to take a long view in their husbandry of resources. The predisposing conditions for this are that they command resources, rights and livelihoods which are adequate, sustainable and above all secure.

Four modes of thinking

Against the background of normal professionalism, 'first' thinking, and the case for sustainable livelihood, it is now possible to separate out four modes of thinking concerning environment, development and poor people. These are:

- environment thinking (ET);
- development thinking (DT);
- livelihood thinking (LT); and
- sustainable livelihood thinking (SLT).

To sharpen and simplify the points, though with risk of caricature, the contrasts can be presented in a matrix (Figure 7.4). This is then a source of practical working hypotheses.

ET and DT are both forms of 'first' thinking, manifestations of normal professionalism. When challenged, many with ET or DT mindsets will concede that of course people, and poor people, should come first, should be ends not means; but will then revert to their normal professional patterns of thought. In other respects ET and DT differ. Traditional or normal biologists of the past have emphasized the negative effects on the environment both of development and of poor people's livelihoods. For their part, traditional or normal economists have valued positive contributions to economic development and production from both environment (land, water, trees, crops, etc.) and labour (as aspects of livelihoods). ET takes the long view and values the future more than the present, whereas the DT of normal economists takes only a medium-term view and discounts future benefits as in conventional cost–benefit analysis.

	ET	DT	LT		SLT
The people concerned	Traditional biologists and conservationists	Traditional economists and 'developers'	The very poor	The poor	The professionals
Primary focus	The environment	Production	Livelihood survival	Livelihood security	Enabling adequate, secure and sustainable livelihoods
Major criteria in decision-making and evaluation	Conservation of resources Maintenance of diversity	Economic growth Productivity and economic returns	Immediate survival needs	Basic needs plus security	Sustainable gains by the very poor Livelihood security for all
Time horizon Value placed on the future	Long Higher than present	Medium Lower than present	Short Lower than by the poor	Short and long Higher than by the very poor	Moving from short and low (survival) to long and high (sustainability)
Normal structure of thinking — Ends / Means	E at apex; −ve and −ve arrows to D and L; D ------- L	D at apex; +ve and +ve arrows to E and L; E ◄-----► L	L at apex; +ve and +ve arrows to D and E; D ◄---- E		SL at apex; +ve and +ve arrows to D and E; D ◄----► E, +ve

Key: E = environment, including natural resources
D = development
L = livelihoods
SL = sustainable livelihoods

Figure 7.4 Four modes of thinking compared
Note: The continuous arrows represent causal connections and directions emphasized in the way of thinking. The dotted arrows represent connections that are recognized but not stressed

A third mode of thinking, which can be called livelihood thinking (LT), entails reversals or 'flips' which at once alarm and exhilarate. When the priorities of the poor are the starting point, the elements in the analysis arrange themselves in a new pattern, and nothing is ever quite the same again. The first priority is not the environment or production but livelihoods, stressing both short-term survival and satisfaction of basic needs and long-term security.

On its own, though, LT does not provide a workable mode of analysis to enable professionals to see what to do. However valid, if neglected, we recognize the knowledge, perspectives and priorities of the poor to be, outsider professionals still have their own valid and powerful tools of analysis. The challenge is to synthesize the best in ET, DT and LT. Sustainable Livelihood Thinking (SLT) takes sustainability from ET, linking with the needs of the poor for long-term security for themselves and their children; productivity from DT, linking with the needs of the poor for more food and incomes; and the primacy of poor people's livelihoods from LT.

SLT centres on enabling very poor people to overcome conditions which force them to take the very short view and 'live from hand to mouth', or 'from day to day'. It seeks to enable them to get above, not a poverty line defined in terms of income or consumption, but a sustainable livelihood (SL) line defined to include abilities to save and accumulate, to adapt to changes, to meet contingencies, and to enhance long-term productivity. SLT reverses thinking which flows from core to periphery or from the top down, and substitutes thinking from periphery to core, or from the bottom up. It sees sustainable development as achievable by enabling the critical group of the very poor to gain livelihoods which are sustainable and secure. This will stabilize use of the environment, enhance productivity and establish a dynamic equilibrium, above an SL line, of population and resources. SLT seeks to create and maintain conditions in which very poor and poor people become less poor and insecure and see benefits for themselves in sustainable development.

In development there has been a succession of 'add-ons' to existing methodologies and analytical approaches: with project appraisal, in succession, we have had impact on the poor, impact on women, and now impact on the environment. It may be tempting to make sustainable livelihoods yet another 'add-on'. What I am proposing here is more radical: the exploration of SLT is not as add-on, but as alternative.

SLT looks intellectually exciting and practically promising. Strategies can seek various sequences of change. One of the more important is shown in Figure 7.5. In this model, a vicious downward spiral, as with soil degradation in parts of SSA, has people exploiting an environment which becomes less productive and in turn diminishes their livelihoods. A solution is sought not through unproductive conservation but through development. This can, for example, take the form of food or cash for work for productive conservation works, providing short-term livelihood support and long-term prospects for livelihood intensive and sustainable human use of the environment. This example raises the question of just how much potential there is for such sequences, and consequently how much direct scope there is, especially in resource-poor, fragile, vulnerable and degraded environments, for the application of SLT. For without biological and economic potential, applications of SLT would be rather limited.

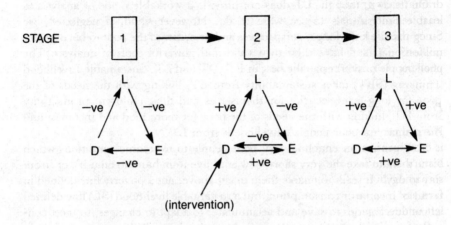

Figure 7.5 Applying sustainable livelihood thinking

Potential and opportunities

Sustainable livelihood thinking, putting poor people and their priorities first, leads to a search for potentials and opportunities. The question to be addressed, environment by environment, is how biologically, economically and in terms of social organization, more people can gain adequate, secure and sustainable livelihoods. Especially this means how people who are poor can avoid becoming very poor, and how people who are very poor can progress to becoming merely poor. When this question is the starting point, the potentials and opportunities for sustainable livelihoods for rural people appear as immense as they have been unrecognized. Two dimensions stand out here: bio-economic potentials, especially of resource-poor environments and agricultural systems; and professional error, biases and neglect which have left those potentials unrecognized and undeveloped.

Bio-economic potentials

Paradoxically, degradation often protects potential for the poor. Because land is degraded – deforested, eroded, waterlogged, saline, bare from overgrazing, flooded or unsustainably cropped – it has low value, especially where current management practices seem likely to persist. But again and again, when management practices are changed, remarkable bio-economic potential is revealed (see e.g. Bunch 1988; Conroy and Litvinoff 1988; Mishra and Sarin 1988). Some of these potentials are to be found in the livelihood-intensive creation and protection of micro-environments in which farmers, women and men, concentrate soil, water and nutrients (Chambers 1990). Others are for growing perennials, especially trees: in India, some 69 million hectares of degraded lands could be growing trees to produce annual biomass increments dramatically greater than those current (Chambers *et al.* 1989: 39–49), with at least tenfold increases in the production of most minor forest products. Since these are livelihood-intensive, the degraded forest land (36 of the 69 million ha.) has immense potential for supporting many more livelihoods for poor people on a sustainable basis.

Professional error, biases and neglect

Normal professionals have often been wrong in believing that they know what is best, and that poor rural people do not know. In consequence, the agrarian history of the South is littered with failed good intentions. By being wrong and so having little or nothing to offer, and by failing to encourage and support farmers' own innovations, professionals have unintentionally and unwittingly left undeveloped livelihood potentials for the poor.

Professional biases have also contributed to neglect. Normal professionals have accorded low priority to the 'last' things of the poor. Whatever is rural, agricultural, small, labour-intensive, used by or important for women, dirty, smelly and low status has received rather little attention from research or extension. So until the 1970s, multi-purpose trees, cassava, sweet potatoes, yams, bees, goats and organic manure were often not priorities; and donkeys, though valuable means to rural livelihoods, still seem beyond the professional pale.

Gaps between the normal central concerns of disciplines have also been neglected. This is illustrated in Figure 7.6.

Professions and the government ministries and departments which preserve and accentuate their specialization, focus quite narrowly, overlooking linkages which are often important for resource-poor farmers. Agroforestry, meaning the interaction of trees with crops, livestock and other elements in farming systems, has been a classic case where agronomists have been concerned with crops, not trees or livestock; animal husbandry specialists with animals, not crops or trees; and foresters with trees, not crops or animals, and moreover trees in forests rather than on farmers' lands. Fishpond aquaculture is similar. Once again, professional neglect presents opportunities for the poor. Precisely because the linkages have received little attention, their potential has not been much exploited; and because it has not been much exploited, it has not yet been appropriated by those who are richer and more powerful.

Policy errors have also concealed and protected potentials. Regulations prohibiting cutting trees on private land have deterred smallholders from planting and protecting trees; the other side of the coin is the potential for planting that can be released when the restrictions are removed, as happened on an astonishing scale in Haiti (Murray 1986). In many countries low agricultural prices have been inadequate incentives and rewards to induce and enable farmers to gain adequate livelihoods from cultivation and animal husbandry. When resource-based secure livelihoods are taken as the prime objective, it can be seen how changes in policy can release and realize such potentials.

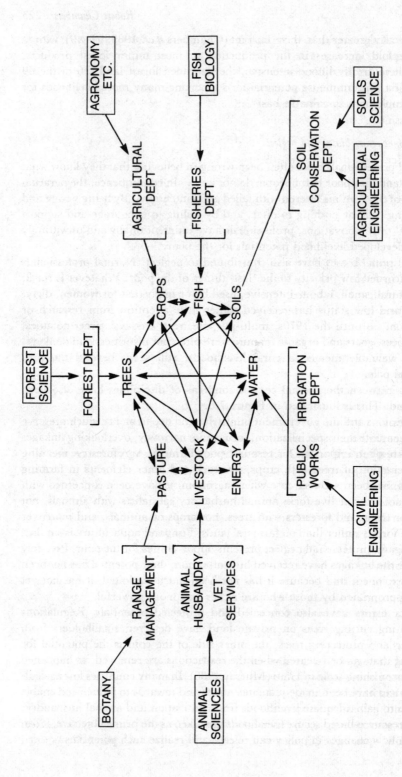

Figure 7.6 Disciplines, departments and professional gaps

Note: Gaps neglected by normal professionalism are represented by most of the lines in the centre, which often represent critical linkages in resource-poor farming systems

With all these neglected and protected potentials the opportunity for the poor depends on who gains from the new productivity. Because these gains have not yet been appropriated by the rich, there is a chance for the poor. But the closest commitment and attention are vital to ensure that those who gain most from change are the poorer, and not once again the less poor – the rich, businessmen, bureaucrats, politicians and the North.

Analytical and practical implications

This paper has analytical and practical implications, and generates an agenda for research. Five areas stand out.

The nature of secure and sustainable livelihoods

Normal professional analysis of deprivation tends to fix on 'poverty' which is defined in terms of flows. This originates in urban studies of wage earners, and in professionals' need to count and to make numerical comparisons (Chambers 1986). It sees the needs of poor people in terms of increasing those flows – of cash and of food, and often in terms of 'employment', meaning a single source of such income.

This view of deprivation is deficient in many respects. From a livelihood angle, two stand out. First, the urban and industrial concept of employment, with a single wage or salary, fits few rural realities. Most poor rural people have multiple sources of income and food as their livelihood strategy – cultivating, working as labourers, migrating, hunting and gathering on commons, artisan work, providing services, petty hawking, and so on. 'First' approaches to rural and agricultural development are often concerned with 'jobs' and 'employment', but this often does not fit rural needs and opportunities.

The second defect of the normal professional view of poverty is the neglect of vulnerability (IDS 1989) and the importance of security against impoverishment. Vulnerability to loss of assets and to indebtedness are persistent anxieties for many of the poor, who are concerned not just with increasing their consumption, but also with security and self-respect. One element, therefore, in a secure and sustainable livelihood will often be enough assets to be able to meet contingencies without becoming permanently poor, and to assure a degree of independence.

The policy implications of these two points are striking. First, SL approaches would often seek to strengthen and stabilize multiple source survival strategies. The strengthening of existing enterprises, or the introduction of new ones, especially if they fill in seasonal gaps in productive work, can enable households to move up above a notional sustainable livelihood line.

Second, as basic subsistence is increasingly assured, so priority shifts from flows to assets which can be used as buffers or banks to handle contingencies. The 'flow' approaches of normal anti-poverty programmes like the Integrated

Rural Development Programme in India do not include such provision. On the contrary, in attempting to raise incomes and consumption of the poor, they increase indebtedness. The security of the poor may be diminished by the debt and by a vulnerable asset like a buffalo which can fall sick, die or be stolen. Opportunities to gain more secure assets such as trees, which appreciate fast and which unlike buffaloes do not entail debts, may often be higher priorities for poor people.

Sustainable livelihood-intensity

Sustainable livelihood-intensity (SL-intensity) merits development as a practical concept. It can be argued that it should be a criterion in project identification and assessment wherever considerations of poverty, environment and development apply. It subsumes and amalgamates ET's sustainability, DT's productivity and LT's satisfaction of needs. SL-intensity is linked to political economy and to questions of who gains and who loses. If a notional SL line is adopted, the SL-intensity of a programme or project will be related to the numbers who are enabled to move above it. In project appraisal, the SL criterion can be expected to give different results to conventional cost–benefit analysis. A dam which displaces a large population may, in its direct effects, have a net negative SL score. Valued in net SL terms, activities of transnational corporations, and of logging contractors in particular, may quite often come out negative. The challenge now is to make the concept operational, as a complement or alternative to other criteria.

Types of action with high SL-intensity vary by environment, for example as between core poverty – where poor people are found in accessible areas of intensive agriculture and dense population, and peripheral poverty – where poor people are found in areas which are remote and marginal. SL-intensive approaches to core poverty are likely to include homestead gardening, rights to trees, access to common and private property resources, labour-demanding farming systems to generate work and wages, and irrigation to provide higher wages and productive work round more of the year. With peripheral poverty, SL-intensive approaches are likely to concern complicating and diversifying marginal farming, including crops, livestock and trees, and the creation, protection and exploitation of micro-environments which capture and concentrate soil, water and nutrients. With SL-intensity as a criterion, each human group and environment will generate its own diverse mix of actions which fit.

Policies for sustainable livelihood security

With that qualification, there are many policies and actions which contribute to sustainable livelihood security. Most basically, these are:

- Peace and equitable law and order
- Equitable and secure rights and access to resources
- Access to basic services

- Safety nets of support for the very poor and destitute, and for the poor at bad times
- Freedom from hassle and exploitation.

More specifically, and given the priority of enabling the very poor to become merely poor, and of enabling the poor to avoid becoming very poor, measures to be considered for their high SL-intensity include:

- Land reform, in which land is redistributed to the landless and near-landless, small-scale tenancy and sharecropping is transformed into inheritable rights to land, and insecure farm families are given secure title
- Sustainable livelihood forestry, in which poor people have secure rights to harvest the produce of diverse forest species
- Community management of common property resources for higher productivity equitably shared
- Agricultural research and extension to provide resource-poor farmers with baskets of diverse choice and to support and spread the results of their experiments and innovations
- High prices for what poor people produce and sell, including the crops and animals of small farmers, craftwork, and those physical assets (whether jewellery, livestock, wood, charcoal, honey, fish etc.) sold in bad years or at difficult times of the year
- Slack season income and food through irrigation, public works, and various forms of off-farm work
- Preventive and curative health services which are effective, accessible, and free or nearly free
- Community and group organization to resist exploitation and to make demands
- Abolishing restrictions which give officials power to extract payments from the poor.

Support for the new professionalism

The new professionalism (Chambers 1983, 1986) which is needed reverses many of the ways of thinking, values, methods and behaviours of normal professionalism. It starts not with population, resources, environment or development, but with poor people and their needs and priorities. To develop, strengthen and spread this new professionalism requires:

- Changes in curricula, training methods, professional rewards and incentives, the selection of technical assistance personnel, and criteria for promotion
- Changes in career patterns, with more time (especially early and late in careers) spent in the field working and learning with rural people

- Strengthening 'gap' institutions like ICRAF (the International Council for Research in Agroforestry, in Nairobi), and ICLARM (the International Centre for Living Aquatic Resources Management in the Philippines) which direct expertise to neglected gaps, linkages and potentials

- Sponsoring new initiatives and institutions to explore and exploit opportunities for the very poor and poor presented by other gaps, such as diversified livelihood forestry (Chambers *et al.* 1989), farming system intensification including the creation and use of micro-environments, and rural transport.

Appraisal, research and development by the poor

These implications concern professionals' own investigation and analysis, and their own actions on centralized structures. They are valid but only one side of the coin. The other, and once again neglected, side is where rural people, the poor and the very poor, themselves observe, analyse, research and act, and where it is their reality and their creativity which count. The normal professional belief is that only outsiders can effectively undertake these activities; but experiences with farmer participatory research (Amanor 1989; Chambers *et al.* 1989; Farrington and Martin 1988) and with participatory rural appraisal (IIED 1988; MYRADA 1990) have shown this belief to be at once false, damaging and self-validating.

Given the right conditions, farmers and poor people, whether literate or illiterate, whether women or men, have shown a greater capacity than outsider professionals have expected to map, model, observe, interview, quantify, rank, score, diagram, analyse, plan, experiment, innovate and implement and monitor change. Participatory mapping and modelling on the ground and on paper, multi-dimensional seasonal analysis with scoring and quantification, diagramming nutrient flows in farming systems, ranking village households for wealth or well-being, designing agricultural experiments – in activities like these rural people have shown an unexpected ability to present and analyse complex and diverse local systems and relationships.

The wonder is why it has taken so long for outsider professionals to learn this. The explanation seems to be that outsiders' attitudes and behaviour have validated their belief in the ignorance and incapacity of the poor: they have stood on pedestals and lectured; indigenous technical knowledge has been ignored and despised; and even more, the creativity of rural people has been smothered unseen. What has been missing is the combination of rapport, restraint, methods and materials for the expression and development of rural people's capabilities.

The opportunities now opened up look large and relevant. Agriculture is an example. Reductionist agricultural research has served industrial and green revolution agriculture by simplifying and standardizing through its high-input packages for uniform and controlled environments. But to generate more sustainable livelihoods in the fragile environments and through the risk-prone agriculture of much of the South requires that farming systems become more complex, more diverse, and more internally intensive. Fortunately, it is precisely with local complexity and diversity that, through the new methods, the knowledge and analytical abilities of rural people show strength and power.

To encourage and enable poor rural people to express and enhance their knowledge and undertake their own analysis, experiments and action, requires new roles for outsider professionals: to convene, catalyse, and facilitate; to search for what people want and need; to search for and supply choices and advice; to support small farmers' and pastoralists' own experiments; and to work with communities to enable them to devise and test new approaches for managing their common and private resources.

These modes of participation have three elements: participatory methods; a culture of sharing, in which ideas, insights and methods are freely exchanged; and above all, professional attitudes and behaviour which are not arrogant but humble, not inhibiting but facilitating, not standing high but sitting low, not lecturing but listening and learning. The most underdeveloped and most badly needed technologies are not biological or physical, but social and psychological to enable normal professionals and bureaucrats to change their behaviour and attitudes, so that their actions instead of disabling and weakening the poor, enable them and empower.

The paradox of reversals

The practical conclusion is a double paradox: that population control, sustainable resource exploitation, environmental conservation, and rural development are all best served not by starting with them as things or themes in a normal professional, disciplinary or departmental way, but by starting with people; and that the people to start with are not the rural poor, but ourselves. The start has to be with our changing and learning. We have to learn how to enable and empower the very poor and the poor themselves to appraise, analyse and plan, to command and manage resources, to organize, to make demands, and to resist invasions from the cores.

In doing this, sustainable livelihoods provide common ground and common objectives for professionals and the poor. What most poor rural people want is then not the problem but the starting point for shared solutions. For it is precisely secure rights, ownership and access, and people's own appraisal, analysis and creativity, which can integrate what poor people want and need with what those concerned with population, resources, environment and rural development seek. To reverse normal professionalism and to put first the very poor and the poor is the surest path to sustainable rural development; and to make that reversal, we, the professionals, have to start not with them but with ourselves, with quiet personal revolutions.

These chapters (5, 6 and 7) in Part Two have covered a lot of ground. The economy has been shown to be far broader than is often portrayed, with households and voluntary organizations making an important productive contribution. The increasing role of services in industrialized economies has brought into question the attachment of value to products at their point of sale rather than to their functioning over their useful lives. The implicit hegemony and explicit economism of the 'development' world-view has been challenged; instead it is the release of people's own creativity which has been argued to be the mainspring through which they improve their lives. This improvement has been rooted in a holistic theory of needs and their satisfaction; and an operational methodology has been outlined as to how the motivation and potential that are inherent in the urge to satisfy needs can be realised. Finally, Chambers has discussed the role of powerful outsiders in the development process with a striking confirmation, from a very different perspective, of Santamaria's conclusion (in Ch. 1) of the importance of professional reversals in favour of a form of participation that gives priority to the felt needs of those whose development is in question.

All these points are of considerable importance in themselves. But in order for them to be effective in practice, there need to be ways of evaluating progress towards the objectives they imply. What indicators and measures of success of this sort of development can be used? That is the subject of the next chapter.

8 Indicators of development

Constructing an indicator framework

Having arrived at some understanding both of the process of wealth creation and the nature of economic progress, it is possible to turn to the question of how that progress should be indicated: what measurements should be taken in order to show the health of the economy and give policy guidance?

At present, as has been mentioned, the erroneous identification of production growth (growth of output) with economic growth (increase of welfare) and the ignoring of the non-monetary sector have resulted in the use of GDP figures as the predominant indicator of economic success. Many economists now agree that this crude practice is in urgent need of replacement by a new indicator regime which is more theoretically coherent and practically relevant to the real state of the economy. Two of the papers in this chapter, those by Hueting and Miles, will take GDP as their point of departure in fleshing out a new approach.

Three broad types of reform would appear to be possible and there is now a considerable body of research experience with each:

1. The adjustment of GDP to take account of some of its worst shortcomings and omissions (e.g. environmental and health impacts, non-monetary economy), to move it closer towards being an indicator of sustainable production or income, or even welfare. It is worth noting that an enormous possible number of such adjustments could be made (discussed in Anderson 1991), but that each one reduces the usefulness of GDP as an indicator of the money flows through the economy. It is arguable that this is what GDP is in fact supposed to be and that any attempt to use it to indicate sustainable income, let alone welfare, is misguided. However, what the proponents of such an argument rarely then address is how to stop such use of GDP as a welfare indicator, given that it has unfortunately become so universal.

2. The second approach is to seek to construct an explicit index of welfare to replace the use of GDP in this role. Given the complexity of the concept of welfare, and the methodological difficulties of combining all its various components into a single index, this is an endeavour fraught with more or less

arbitrary assumptions and crude approximations. However, much the same criticism can be levelled at the System of National Accounts itself (e.g. on the definition of the production boundary) so they do not of themselves invalidate the concept of a welfare index. Nordhaus and Tobin were among the earliest to attempt to construct an alternative welfare index, to considerable academic interest (Nordhaus and Tobin 1973). Probably the welfare index which achieved widest use is the Physical Quality of Life Index (PQLI – Morris 1980), which combines statistics of infant mortality, literacy and life expectancy into a weighted composite.

The Appendix to Daly and Cobb (1990) comprises a recent ambitious attempt to construct a welfare index, the Index of Sustainable Economic Welfare (ISEW) and a survey of past efforts. ISEW consists of personal consumption, weighted by distributional inequality and adjusted: downwards for depletion of non-renewable resources, long-term environmental damage, expenditure on consumer durables and national advertising, defensive private expenditures on health and education, costs of commuting, urbanization, car accidents, water, air and noise pollution, and the loss of wetlands and farmland; upwards for services from household labour, consumer durables, and streets and highways, public current expenditures on health and education, net capital growth and net change in international financial position.

ISEW's authors freely admit the intractable nature of their task: 'Nothing is better calculated to make one realise the difficulty of estimating economic welfare over time than the effort to devise an index. . . . We have been forced to make some heroic assumptions in the process of compiling the ISEW . . .'' (Daly and Cobb 1990: 415–16). Such assumptions militate against a welfare index of this sort ever gaining wide enough consensus and support to be officially adopted. But it can be a powerful expositional device to show in graphic form the extent to which GNP and a welfare index such as ISEW now diverge. Figure 8.1 shows this comparison for the US economy since 1950. While GNP has risen almost continually, ISEW reached a peak in 1976 and has declined fairly steadily since. As Daly and Cobb say:

> Despite the year-to-year variations in ISEW, it indicates a long-term trend from the late 1970s to the present that is indeed bleak. Economic welfare has been deteriorating for a decade, largely as a result of growing income inequality, the exhaustion of resources, and the failure to invest adequately to sustain the economy in the future.
>
> (ibid.: 445)

3. The third approach is to abandon the idea of a single indicator in favour of a framework of indicators which show the various components of welfare individually. This approach obviously has fewer methodological problems in that the only choice now involves which indicators to include rather than having to weight their relative importance as well. This is the approach taken by Anderson, who chooses twenty indicators for his 'Global Report' framework, including secondary-school enrolment ratios for boys and girls, hours

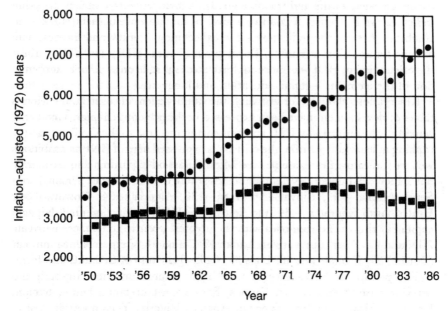

Key:
●   PC-GNP stands for per capita Gross National Product.
■   PC-ISEW stands for per capita Index of Sustainable Welfare.

Figure 8.1 Alternative measures of economic welfare
Source: Daly and Cobb 1990: 420

worked per week and the rate of unemployment, the income of and assets owned by the richest and poorest quintiles, statistics of species loss, deforestation and carbon-dioxide emissions and the energy intensity of GNP (Anderson 1991).

In similar vein, but without the environmental dimension, UNICEF lists among its Basic Indicators (UNICEF 1989: 94–5): the under-5 and under-1 infant mortality rates, the male and female adult literacy rates, life expectancy at birth, income shares of the lowest 40 per cent and highest 20 per cent of the population, as well as GNP per capita.

These three approaches are not mutually exclusive. It is perfectly possible to adopt a method which makes limited adjustments to GNP to arrive at an Adjusted National Product (ANP), which then incorporates ANP into an indicator framework, and which finally weights and combines the indicators of the framework to arrive at a single index.

All three of these steps are taken in the *Human Development Report* of the United Nations Development Programme (UNDP 1990), which adjusts the figures of national income per capita to account for national differences in exchange rates, tariffs and tradable goods; it then presents a variety of social indicators which reflect a country's level of human development; finally, it combines three of the indicators – life expectancy, literacy and the adjusted income figure – into a Human Development Index (HDI). (In UNDP 1991 the calculation of HDI was more sophisticated but still consisted of a combination of the elements income, education and longevity.)

Reservations about the desirability, the validity even, of constructing league tables of development have been expressed in the previous chapter. However, ranking 130 countries by HDI and comparing the rank to the GNP per capita ranking at least fully justifies the criticisms expressed here of GNP as an overall welfare indicator. For example, the Middle East oil-exporting countries have not achieved a human development comparable to their income: Oman – 56, Saudi Arabia – 43, Libya – 36, Iran – 36, Algeria – 34, Kuwait – 34, United Arab Emirates – 34 (the figures are HDI ranking minus GNP per capita ranking). The countries with the greatest positive differences between HDI and GNP per capita are Sri Lanka 45, China 44, Vietnam 40, Myanmar (Burma) 39, Kampuchea 38, Laos 37, Chile 34, Costa Rica and Cuba 26.

The picture in Africa gives a very bleak impression with Niger, Mali, Burkina Faso, Sierra Leone, Guinea, Somalia, Mauretania, Benin, Sudan, Central African Republic, Senegal, Angola, Nigeria, Yemen (Arab Rep.), Liberia, Côte d'Ivoire, Congo, Namibia and Cameroon all located in the bottom third of the HDI scale with an HDI rank at least ten points below their GNP per capita rank. Ethiopia, Zaire, Madagascar and Zambia, in contrast, though still in the bottom third, gave an HDI ranking at least ten points above their GNP per capita rank. Some of such results are counter-intuitive and should generate a rich research agenda.

One criticism of HDI is that the omission of any indicator of human rights can greatly overstate the quality of life in a repressive country whatever its economic, health and education achievements. This is acknowledged in UNDP (1991), the second *Human Development Report*, which supplements the HDI with a Human Freedom Index (HFI) based on *The World Guide to Human Rights* (Humana 1986). Lutz has also addressed these issues by advocating the combination of a human rights index with PQLI to generate an Authentic Socio-economic Development Index (ASEDI).

> Our earlier discussion of authentic development suggested two essential components of socio-economic development: material and ethical progress. The indicator of material progress selected here is the Physical Quality of Life Index (PQLI), which has already been briefly described. To show ethical progress a human rights index is used.
>
> Already three centuries ago, the idea of human rights had been enshrined in a British Bill of Rights and later adopted elsewhere. More recently, the crowning event of this long development was, of course, the Universal Declaration of Human Rights in 1948 by the United Nations. With its Manifesto serving as foundation, two covenants were hammered out, one on 'Civil and Political Rights, the other detailing 'Economic, Cultural and

Social Rights'. All countries being members of the United Nations have by virtue of the UN Charter (Article 5c) chosen to be bound by respect for these sets of basic rights and almost all have ratified both covenants. In other words, the universal application of these rights rests not only on a philosophical basis but on a positively accepted obligation as well.

More recently an attempt has been made to publish a comprehensive human rights index based on the very rights recognized by the United Nations. Published three years ago under the auspices of *The Economist*, it covers 120 countries and forty different human rights drawn primarily from the Covenant of Civil and Political Rights, but also containing some others, such as the rights of children to be protected from economic and social exploitation, the right to work, free job choice, protection against involuntary unemployment, equal pay for equal work and the right to own property either individually or in association with others. The index ranks the countries on a scale from zero to 100, a score of 13 for Ethiopia to 98 for Sweden, Finland, Denmark and the Netherlands.

The PQLI and Rights indices can be combined into a single one which will express in numerical (albeit approximate) manner the relative level of development of each country. Multiplying together the individual component scores of the two indices, the Authentic Socio-economic Development Index (ASEDI) can be expressed as the square root of that product.

Table 8.1 compares the ASEDI levels with the traditional GNP/capita alternative for seventy-five of the lowest GNP countries in 1985, omitting from the eighty-five countries listed by the World Bank as having a GNP/capita of less than $3,000 only those countries for which human rights data was inadequate. As can be expected, the two indices correlate quite highly, with a coefficient of correlation of .624. At the same time, there are some interesting and rather significant differences, as for example, in the cases of South Africa, Burma, Bolivia and Sri Lanka.

(personal communication 1991)

Comparing ASEDI and HDI shows how the human rights index has affected rankings. Several of the countries with high HDIs relative to GNP have much lower ASEDIs because of their human rights performance (e.g. Ethiopia, China, Chile). Several other countries for which this is also likely to have been the case do not feature at all in the ASEDI because of a lack of human rights data (Vietnam, Kampuchea, Laos).

Both HDI and ASEDI omit any consideration of the environment, perpetuating the myth that societies can develop while their supporting ecosystems decline. The new indicator framework to be outlined below starts with ecological indicators. It then adjusts the product figure of the formal economy and shows how a figure for household product can be calculated. These two product indicators are then embedded in an array of appropriate other indicators. The derivation of a composite index is not attempted, partly out of awareness of the difficulties involved, as discussed earlier with reference to the Index of Sustainable Economic Welfare, partly out of agreement with Miles:

Table 8.1 Level of development of seventy-five countries with GNP/capita less than $3,000 (1985)

According to GNP/capita (US$ 1985)	According to ASEDI (1985)	According to HDI (UNDP 1990) *Low human development*
1. Ethiopia 110	1. Ethiopia 18	(1) Niger
2. Bangladesh 150	2. Yemen, AR 24	(2) Mali
3. Burkina Faso 150	3. Yemen, PDR 28	(3) Burkina Faso
4. Mali 150	4. Central African Republic 29	(4) Sierra Leone
5. Mozambique 160	5. Mozambique 32	(6) Guinea
6. Nepal 160	6. Mali 37	(7) Somalia
7. Malawi 170	7. Niger 37	(10) Benin
8. Zaire 170	8. Guinea 37	(11) Burundi
9. Burma 190	9. Pakistan 37	(13) Mozambique
10. Burundi 230	10. Burkina Faso 38	(14) Malawi
11. Togo 230	11. Somalia 38	(15) Sudan
12. Madagascar 240	12. South Africa 38	(16) Central African Republic
13. Niger 250	13. Haiti 40	(17) Nepal
14. Benin 260	14. Zaire 41	(18) Senegal
15. Central African Republic 260	15. Sierra Leone 41	(19) Ethiopia
16. India 270	16. Liberia 41	(20) Zaire
17. Rwanda 280	17. Nepal 42	(21) Rwanda
18. Somalia 280	18. Malawi 43	(23) Bangladesh
19. Kenya 290	19. Bangladesh 43	(24) Nigeria
20. Tanzania 290	20. China 43	(25) Yemen Arab Republic
21. Sudan 300	21. Burundi 45	(26) Liberia
22. China 310	22. Sudan 45	(27) Togo
23. Haiti 310	23. Syria 45	(29) Haiti
24. Guinea 320	24. Rwanda 47	(30) Ghana
25. Sierra Leone 350	25. Indonesia 48	(31) Yemen, PDR
26. Senegal 370	26. Benin 49	(32) Côte d'Ivoire
27. Ghana 380	27. Togo 49	(35) Tanzania, United Republic
28. Pakistan 380	28. Côte d'Ivoire 49	(36) Pakistan

(continued overleaf)

Table 8.1 – continued

According to GNP/capita (1985)		According to ASEDI (1985)		According to HDI (UNDP 1990)	
60. Chile	1430	60. Colombia	68	59. (79)	Paraguay
61. Jordan	1560	61. Sri Lanka	69	60. (80)	Brazil
62. Syria	1570	62. Papua New Guinea	70	61. (83)	Sri Lanka
63. Brazil	1640	63. Botswana	72		*High human development*
64. Uruguay	1650	64. Hungary	72	62. (85)	Malaysia
65. Hungary	1950	65. Mexico	72	63. (86)	Colombia
66. Portugal	1970	66. Korea	72	64. (87)	Jamaica
67. Malaysia	2000	67. Brazil	75	65. (91)	Mexico
68. South Africa	2010	68. Dominican Republic	79	66. (93)	Panama
69. Poland	2050	69. Ecuador	81	67. (95)	Portugal
70. Yugoslavia	2070	70. Uruguay	83	68. (97)	Korea, Republic
71. Mexico	2080	71. Jamaica	85	69. (98)	Poland
72. Panama	2100	72. Panama	85	70. (99)	Argentina
73. Argentina	2130	73. Argentina	89	71. (100)	Yugoslavia
74. Korea	2150	74. Costa Rica	92	72. (101)	Hungary
75. Algeria	2550	75. Portugal	92	73. (102)	Uruguay
				74. (103)	Costa Rica
				75. (107)	Chile

Note: Numbers in brackets in HDI column are original HDI ranking when more countries are considered

'Insurmountable difficulties are posed by the search for a single, composite measure of welfare or quality of life. Perhaps we should be glad that human life remains too rich to be represented in one-dimensional terms' (Miles 1985: 56).

A new framework

In line with the discussion in earlier chapters, it is desirable that the new framework should incorporate social, ethical and ecological as well as economic issues; should cover the social as well as the monetary economy; and should take an explicit account of 'stocks' (the capitals discussed earlier) as well as flows. Ideally it would be desirable to construct a balance sheet and income/expenditure account for each of the four classes of capital across both the monetary and non-monetary economies. This is by no means as utopian a suggestion as it may at first sound, although it is probably true that such an indicator framework could never be made fully operational, nor should one expect excessive precision. Methodologically it is preferable:

- To have the right framework with omissions, because one is then aware of the omissions and can seek both to allow for and minimize them, rather than having the wrong framework which appears complete but actually excludes important variables.

- To have a framework the structure of which is accurate but which embodies imprecisions in its components, rather than one which achieves detailed precision but only at the cost of structural distortions or omissions.

Thus the indicator framework suggested here has the following components, which are developed in some detail by the contributors' papers:

Component 1: Environmental and resource accounts

These accounts are constructed to show both stocks and flows of environmental resources and substances that affect the environment.

Environmental and resource accounting
Øyvind Lone

Basic concepts

The report of the World Commission on Environment and Development recommends that sustainable development objectives are integrated in the policies, programmes and budgets of major central economic and sectoral agencies of governments, and that

Where resources and data permit, an annual report and an audit on changes in environmental quality and in the stock of the nation's environmental resource assets are needed to complement the traditional annual fiscal budget and economic development plans.

(WCED 1987: 314)

The basic ideas of natural resources accounting are:

- to provide an *integrated information system* for the whole resource process from natural resources stocks, through extraction and processing to end-use and disposal, including recycling, waste and pollution, and other environmental effects,
- to measure resources *in physical units* throughout and thus be able to provide material and/or energy flows and balances data, and
- to *connect these physical accounts* and measurements (wherever possible) *to economic valuations and aggregates*, above all to national accounts and economic statistics and econometric forecasting and analytic models.

Thus both physical and monetary units are used in the accounts. One may also develop aggregated environmental quality indicators.

The Norwegian experience

The origins of the ideas behind the shape resource accounting took in Norway are diverse but mostly to be found in the debate in the late 1960s and early 1970s about economics and the environment; about the weaknesses of GNP as a welfare measure, especially as a measure which positively includes much damage to the natural environment; and about the (alternative) ecological viewpoint, stressing energy and materials flow analysis, and, perhaps above all, the ideas of Robert Ayres and Allen Kneese (Kneese 1977) about combining economic analysis with data on the material and energy flow accounts (even if specifically concerned with environmental/pollution questions, not so much with natural resources).

There were several reasons for doing the accounts in physical units:

- to avoid complicated indexing (if economic values had been used)
- to reflect the original concern with physical scarcities
- to give an accurate physical description of production processes
- to ensure (physical) consistency and coherence in the accounts
- to provide for linkages to ecological analyses.

The decision to proceed with physical units entailed, as well, the use of *diverse* physical units (Joule, KWh, calories, etc. for energy, tons and volumes for materials, hectares and km^2 for land use, etc.). This leads into the question of resource classification, which was initially chosen largely to reflect renewability. Three main categories were used (all subdivided into two, giving six in all): renewable resources, conditionally renewable resources and non-renewable resources (the last two adding up to the category of 'exhaustibles', use of which *may* be irreversible).

Of course, the whole idea of ecological thinking would be lost if it is not emphasized that this classification to some extent cuts across the web of nature, and that all these categories are intimately linked together, for instance the second (1b) and the third (2a). Even more important, all life is ultimately dependent on inflowing resources (i.e. sunlight), which drives 1b, maintains 2a and produces 2b, not to speak of having produced the accumulated stock of fossil energy of 3b.

1. RENEWABLE RESOURCES

    1a Inflowing resources (solar, cosmic radiation etc.)
    1b Oceanic and atmospheric cycles (wind, waves, tides, hydrologic cycle)

2. CONDITIONALLY RENEWABLE RESOURCES

    2a Environmental resources (land, water, air)
    2b Biological resources (plant and animal species and populations)

3. NON-RENEWABLE RESOURCES

    3a Recyclable resources (minerals)
    3b Transient resources (fossil and nuclear fuels)

When the practical work on resource accounting started, this classification was modified, not in the way that the fundamental idea of different renewability categories was given up, but because it quickly turned out that there was a fundamental difference between the importance and use of what was called *material* (and energy) resources and *environmental* resources and between the structure and data requirements of material and environmental accounts.

Material resources for the most part provide humanity with *goods* that are mostly *traded* and to a large extent *substitutable*. Environmental resources, on the other hand, mostly provide *services* that are frequently *non-traded* and *non-substitutable*.

The description of a natural-resource accounting system above applies mainly to material (including energy) resources, whereas environmental resource accounting stresses questions concerning the state of this resource (air, water, land), what is put into it, how these inputs change its state, the effects of this change, including effects on human health and welfare. There is a strong link, however, between material and environmental resources, in that inputs to environmental media (e.g. atmosphere) are practically equivalent to outputs from material resource use processes (e.g. energy use). For all the environmental resource categories, locational and distributional data are essential.

Resource accounting (more precisely material accounting) should make it possible to answer questions concerning a country's natural resources such as

- How much is left (renewables: growing stock and annual increment, non-renewables: reserves)?
- How much is harvested (renewables) and extracted (non-renewables)?
- How efficiently (physical rates of recovery etc.)?
- How much is imported and/or exported?
- How much is processed (domestically)?
- How efficiently (physical input/output measures)?
- How much is used (domestically)?
- For which end-use purposes?
- How efficiently (first- and second-law energy efficiencies, physical input/output measures)?
- Where does it all end up (material balance of waste and by-products from extraction, harvesting, processing, end-product disposal)?
- How much is reused/recycled?
- How much is waste and/or pollution?
- How much will be available in the future and at what cost?
- How much will be demanded in the future and at which price?

These mainly physical data supply very important, even necessary, information, but should always be supplemented by economic data (on prices, costs, private and social profitability, etc.) in order to provide a sufficient basis for major policy decisions. Also, the physical data should be used with great caution, as they may, just as economic data, very easily lend themselves to simplistic misinterpretation.

As an example, the important and interesting data considering questions of relative scarcity of non-renewable resources are probably not the simple relations between reserves and annual extraction (the reserves/production or R/P ratio, much too easily misconstrued as the 'lifetime' of the 'remaining' stock of the non-renewable resource) in themselves. Rather, the annual changes in these ratios due to extraction, discoveries of new deposits, price and technological changes should be seen as the important indicator. Of course, this should be seen together with the long-term real-price trends of the resource, the extent of reserves given higher prices, changes in the rates of any reuse and recycling, and, finally, the rate of substitution and cost of substitutes in the end-use sectors.

These strictures of course apply as well to other purely physical measures: neither R/P ratios, MSYs (maximum sustainable yield), rates of recovery of minerals and fossil fuels, energy efficiencies nor recycling ratios should be seen as goals in themselves, but only as important data on resource use and trends.

This leads into the question of the relation between physical and economic units and between resource accounts and national accounts. The idea was from the very beginning to link the resource accounts to the national accounts. This turned out not to be too difficult, but an important modification of the original resource accounting idea should be noted.

The material balance aspect of the resource accounts are now most frequently contained in physical input–output tables (more precisely activity analysis tables: sector/commodity balances) as this greatly facilitates linkages to and use of economic (sector/commodity) data with the resource accounts. Comprehensive and total, if rough, mass balance exercises are accordingly carried out only in special cases (for example forestry, agriculture, quartz) and are not now included in the regular annual energy or fisheries accounts, for instance, though they are included in the forest accounts (updated, however, only every three years).

The resource accounts are thus run in parallel with the national accounts for the central part of the economic activities (extraction or harvesting, processing, import/export, consumption and investment), but in physical units and for resource commodities only, and may include non-traded materials/goods/residuals.

The amount of detail provided in the accounts reflects the importance and complexity of the resource in question at the different stages of the resource process. Thus, as an example, the fisheries accounts are highly differentiated in the stock accounts (reflecting the various species and populations and the importance of age classes in this short-cycle biological resource), but relatively simple in the processing and use stages, as there are relatively few processing industries or user sectors. The energy accounts are of course highly differentiated and detailed for most stages, and particularly for final energy use, energy being used by most or all economic activities.

There is no provision in the national accounts for the stock of natural resources (apart from agricultural land and livestock and forest land and standing timber volume), which is of course an essential element in the resource accounts. A few attempts have been made in the CBS to calculate the present value of selected natural resources, but on the whole, there is not a great deal of Norwegian enthusiasm for the attempts and arguments in some other countries to revise thoroughly the SNA (System of National Accounts) in order to include the capital stock of natural resources in economic values.

Finally, the attempts to include the environmental effects of resource use and disposal in the resource accounts do not, of course, have any parallel in the national accounts. These provisions for close linking of physical and economic data and accounts have, as will be discussed later, proved useful to modelling and analysing physical and economic trends, and has made it possible to produce highly valuable projections and forecasts concerning future resource use and consequences. The discussion above applies mainly to the material resources and material accounts. As noted the environmental resources are different in important ways, which may be seen also in the way environmental accounts have to be set up.

The important questions answered by environmental accounts are:

- What is the state of this resource (air, water, land)?
- What is put into it (air, water)?
- How does this change its state?

- What are the effects of this change?
- How does this affect human health and welfare?
- What is the present and potential use of the resource (land)?
- How does this land-use change?
- WHERE?

It should be obvious from this quite tentative and partial list that the character of environmental accounts is much more diverse and difficult to fit into one common concept than the material accounts. A few common features are, however, apparent. The first is the character of the environmental resources themselves, as noted above, mainly non-traded, non-substitutable services. The second is the essential need for both air, water and land for extremely disaggregated, local data, due to the particular *spatial* character of the resources. This applies above all to land and water, but is also true, if not to quite the same extent, for air.

The work on environmental resource accounts has thus been much more individualized than is the case for material accounting. The two major priorities have been on land resource accounting, and on air emission accounts (linked to the energy accounts). After some discussion, it was decided to postpone the development of water resource accounting, in part because of the very heavy data requirements, in part because of some doubt about which users and managers such accounts should aim for.

The general idea for the air (and possible future water) accounts is that each should be made up of two interlinked parts: an account showing the state of the resource, based on monitoring, and an account showing the emissions to the resource from resource-using sectors and households (in the air emissions case closely linked to the energy accounts).

Concerning land use accounting, a tremendous amount of work was done with getting an overview of the very different data sources: maps and other 'cartographic' information such as airphotos and satellite pictures; other localized data such as the raw data from forest inventories; statistics from population, housing, agricultural and forestry censuses; and regular administrative routines, and so on, and with developing classification systems at least potentially able to use and combine all these disparate data sources.

Development of environmental and resource accounting in other countries

Several other countries in the Economic Commission of Europe (ECE) have what now amounts to considerable experience with resource accounting. Short accounts and the experiences of the Federal Republic of Germany, Finland, France, Portugal and Spain are given below. Several other countries have also shown an interest in and worked with natural resource accounting (in different ways and to different degrees, e.g. Canada, the Netherlands, the United States and recently the United Kingdom). Of course, practically all ECE countries have wide experience of closely related activities within the field of environmental statistics. It must be emphasized that resource accounting is to a large extent a particular way of organizing resource and environmental data and not a whole new set of data (even if some new or special data are sometimes required, e.g. in order to complete a material balance account).

Outside the ECE region, Australia and New Zealand have both shown some interest in resource accounting, and the People's Republic of China plan to integrate natural-resource accounting in its new national accounting and planning system (with assistance from the World Resources Institute and Norway).

The *Federal Republic of Germany* has established physical accounts for energy supply and use linked with the input-output tables of the Federal Statistical Office (FSO). The Federal Republic plans to establish more comprehensive accounts for natural resources in both physical and monetary terms in the next few years, and recently announced that the FSO has started research work to find out the possibilities of supplementing the national accounting system with a satellite environmental accounting system.

In *Finland*, a preliminary study on natural resource accounting was undertaken by the Central Statistical Office (CSO), initiated and financed by the Ministry of Agriculture and Forestry, from 1984 to 1988. A basic model of materials and energy accounting applied to wood material, energy and nutrients accounting, and a system of land use accounting was developed, based mainly on the Norwegian model of resource accounting. The aim was to create a system of natural resource accounts suiting Finnish conditions which could be implemented in the most important natural resource sectors in the next few years. The report (in Finnish) was published in 1988. Social objectives of the proposed system included:

- economical and sustainable resource utilization
- environmental protection
- self-sufficiency and material security
- regional equilibrium.

The functions of natural-resource accounting were defined as follows:

- consistent and standardized resource and environment data
- identification of key variables and relationships
- monitoring, summarizing and presenting trends
- problem evaluation (at various spatial/management levels)
- inputs to other activities, such as modelling.

Since 1988, the work on natural-resource accounting has been financed jointly by the CSO, the Ministry of Agriculture and Forestry and the Ministry of the Environment, focusing on forest resource accounting and land-use accounting. Plans for the near future call for the development of energy and air emissions accounting.

In *France*, an Interministerial Committee on Natural Resource Accounts was set up in 1978 with the task of drawing up a programme of work for the phased introduction of a complete system of natural resource accounts. A major milestone in the work of this commission was reached in December 1986, when the French Ministry of Environment together with INSEE (Institut National de la Statistique et des Etudes Economiques) published the commission's report 'Les Comptes da patrimoine naturel', dealing with (1) the general principles and methodology of natural resources accounting, and (2) presenting the first pilot accounts for fauna and flora, forest resources and inland water (INSEE 1986).

The French system of natural resource accounts ('comptes du patrimoine naturel') is based on three types of accounts: *elements* accounts (minerals, water, atmosphere and soil as well as plants and animals), *agents* or *participants* accounts (the human use of natural resources and the environment) and *ecozones* accounts (territorial units; land use and ecosystems, based on statistical cartography and remote sensing). The principles indicated have already taken shape in France through the creation of participant accounts, in particular satellite accounts in monetary units (hunting accounts, environmental protection) as well as species accounts (animal life and forests) and elements accounts (continental waters). The next step is to apply remote sensing techniques on a large scale, in particular for the full-scale development of ecozone balances and accounts. But if the general methodology is now well established, the practical implementation of the whole accounting system is far from being reached.

In *Portugal*, and 'Experimental Matrix of Natural Resources Consumption' is being built for the manufacturing sector, covering energy and materials consumption of renewable (water, forest, energy, animal and vegetable) and non-renewable (fuels, minerals) resources. The basic information is collected from formal industry statistics (materials and energy consumption), and the methodology consists at present of simple aggregate material balances. Some data on wastes and re-use are also included (e.g. concerning paper and the forest industries). Important issues on which this matrix should provide information include environmental impacts, import and export flows of either raw materials or products (final and intermediate), and consumption and use of natural resources in relation to stocks and regeneration rates at the national as well as at local and regional levels. The intention is to use the results for both sectoral and regional analysis, trying to complement economic information with environmental aspects. The information from this matrix will also make possible interconnections, in the context of input–output analysis, with inter-sectoral flows information, which also exist at the regional scale.

In *Spain*, work on natural resource accounting started in an Interministerial Commission in 1986, with six working groups on rocks and minerals, water, marine resources, continental flora and fauna, land (territory) and wastes. The perceived need for resource accounting was for systematic and integrated information on the country's natural resources, particularly the physical stock and flow of natural resources used by man in his processes and industries, and the wastes generated, but bypassed by the existing economic accounting systems. The idea was to represent natural-resource-user systems, provide models for their operation, and forecast their effect on such resources. The final results in each case in this first stage have been uneven, because of administrative factors, such as the information available. There is at present no final statement on the matter, so that it is not possible to say what the future will be of natural resource accounting in Spain in the medium term. However, several of the working groups have developed concrete programmes, for example, the land (territorial) group with its work on the LANDCOVER programme in the CORINE context of the European Communities. Also, proposals of the fauna and flora working group have led to the creation of a major data base for this area. Finally, Spain has recently joined the countries of the European Community providing energy balances in physical and economic terms to EUROSTAT. The next stop on the road to natural-resource accounting in Spain should involve the approval of the different projects proposed by the interministerial commission, with the aim of systematically including resource accounting in economic decision-making.

A major part of the long-standing theoretical debate on resource accounting has concerned the need and methods to adjust national accounting, including gross national product (GNP) figures. Few countries have done much on this question, most of the work having concentrated on establishing physical accounts and linking these to (traditional) national accounts, even if the Federal Republic of Germany recently has announced that conceptual work has started on this (as noted above). Also, Japan has calculated an alternative measure of 'net national welfare' for the years 1955 to 1985, showing lower rates of growth than conventional GDP measures.

One weakness of the traditional accounting and planning systems of both market and centrally planned economies that has given rise to considerable criticism is that wealth concepts are given too little attention both in the accounting systems as such and in the identification and pursuance of national policy objectives. One possibility is to try express the stock of natural and environmental resources in economic as well as physical terms. Some work has been done on the value of stocks of petroleum, timber and soil resources in Indonesia and on petroleum, hydro-power and forests in Norway. Both these exercises demonstrated that adjustments in key macro-economic indicators, for example savings and investments rates or GDP growth rates may be significant in resource-based economies, whether developing or developed.

Environmental and resource accounting in international organizations

Apart from the individual countries mentioned, several international organizations have also shown some interest in resource accounting, for example the ECE, the Nordic Council (of Denmark, Finland, Iceland, Norway, Sweden) and the OECD, where projects aim to establish pilot accounts for forest resources by some five or six countries (lead by Norway) and for water resources (lead by France). Energy balances, in both physical and monetary terms, are established and delivered to EUROSTAT by members of the

European Community, such as Denmark, the Federal Republic of Germany, Italy, France, the Netherlands, Spain and the United Kingdom.

The United Nations Environment Programme (UNEP) has worked with the World Bank and the United Nations Statistical Office (UNSO) on how better to take into account natural resources and the environment in development planning (Ahmad *et al.* 1989). This has included work on physical resource accounts and on methods to adjust the System of National Accounts (SNA) or other macro-economic measures of a nation's economic activities and resources, some of which are identified later in this chapter.

Environmental and resource accounting: two examples

Energy and air pollution

Energy accounting was given top priority early on and has kept that priority throughout. In the early years, the emphasis was on projecting electricity demand, as a basis for decisions on development of hydroelectric power projects. This was both a major economic issue because of the costs involved, and an important environment issue, because of the strong environmentalist opinion in favour of preserving free-flowing rivers from further development.

The development of improved projections for energy and electricity demand was a major advance, both in improving communication between ministries concerning the most realistic demand forecasts, and for the Ministry of Environment (and the Ministry of Finance) in particular. Projections based on disaggregated energy accounts and macro-economic modelling proved to give lower, more realistic results than earlier crude energy/GDP per capita calculations. Such disaggregated accounts and projections also facilitate the analysis of the effects of different policy measures. This work has been organized since 1980 through an inter-ministerial committee chaired by the Ministry of Petroleum and Energy, with participation from the ministries of finance, environment, industry and transport, along with the CBS.

A second inter-ministerial committee, this one for pollution projections, chaired by the Ministry of Environment, with the same participants, was established in 1986, and collaborates closely with the energy projections committee. This committee has looked at air pollution projections, based on macro-economic modelling, the energy accounts and on air emission accounts partly derived from the energy accounts.

Since 1987, these modelling and accounting tools have been used to look into not just the energy demand and air pollution resulting from present policies but also to analyse the economic, energy and emissions effects of alternative economic and environmental policies. One example from the so-called SIMEN study (Bye *et al.* 1989) was that by changing the tax structure towards higher taxes on petroleum products (but keeping total tax revenue constant by reducing personal and business taxes) one could reduce emissions of carbon dioxide by 16 per cent, sulphur dioxide by 21 per cent and nitrogen oxides by

14 per cent in the year 2000 as compared to the base scenario. This would have only relatively minor macro-economic consequences, reducing gross domestic product and consumption by between 1 and 2 per cent, compared with the base scenario, even if some sectors would be more strongly affected.

Further work along these directions have confirmed the main points of the SIMEN study. One analysis in the 1989 CBS report reduces the three pollutants by between 23 and 25 per cent in the year 2000 with a GDP growth reduction of 1.8 per cent and private consumption by 0.8 per cent. Another analysis effects reductions of between 23 and 26 per cent in the year 2010 with concomitant GDP and consumption reductions of 2.7 and 1.0 per cent respectively. It should be emphasized that these figures are all compared to a base scenario, and not to current emissions or GDP levels.

In these analyses, efforts were also made to calculate the benefits of such reductions in air pollution. For both these exercises, such benefits in the form of reduced health and other damage costs were conservatively estimated as being of the same order of magnitude as the (small) relative loss of GDP and consumption.

A further development and refinement of this work has been done in connection with the work of the inter-ministerial committee on Norwegian climate policy.

All in all, the development and use of energy and air-pollution accounting, linked to economic modelling and analysis, has resulted in very useful tools for analysis and policy decision, not just for the Ministry of Environment but for integrating environmental policies and considerations in overall government policy, including economic and energy policy.

Water

As a resource category, water has a double identity; in the Norwegian system, water is both a *material resource* (with energy, minerals etc.) and an *environmental resource* (with air and land). The Norwegian proposed water resource account thus comprises both an account of the material flow of the water resources (such as energy and mineral resource accounts do) and an account of water as an environmental medium (such as the environmental accounts for air). The French system also includes both these aspects.

Another essential characteristic of water as a resource is that it is in the main a *localized resource*, in (almost) the same way as land. The predominantly local or regional management of water, often by river basins, thus requires that water resource accounting should be done on a local or regional level, while national-level accounting is probably not very meaningful unless supplemented with more detailed accounts, preferably on the basis of river basins and/or management districts. Moreover, this further implies that data ought to be given on a very precise geographical basis, such as is ensured by a detailed water-course register, used by as many producers and consumers of information as possible.

General structure of water resource accounts

In general, water resource accounting should include the basic hydrological information of *the water balance* (this concept is fortunately well known to water resource managers) for river basins/management districts and on the aggregated, national level. How much importance should be given to secure more detailed data on this balance would depend on national characteristics.

In countries such as Norway, with abundant resources in relation to quantitative water demand, both on a national level and regionally (withdrawals making up less than 1 per cent of annual national runoff), this is probably not a major preoccupation of the accounting system. In other OECD countries with these figures at some 20 to 30 per cent, this would obviously be different. In all cases, the water balance should include relatively detailed information on the withdrawals of different users (irrigation, households, industry, energy production, etc.) and on both *withdrawals* (gross) and *consumption* (net) of water and thus on the amounts of withdrawn water recharging the water cycle.

In some countries, detailed information on the parts of the water balance concerned with the role of (wild and cultivated) *plants and evapotranspiration* might be necessary and valuable. This is particularly the case when *climatic variability* (concerning both rainfall and temperature) might pose major management problems, which is the case even in countries such as Norway, if only for the use of water for the production of hydroelectric power.

It should be emphasized that there should be a close connection between the quantitative aspects of the water balance (or material) accounts and the environmental water accounts, even if withdrawals are practically negligible. This is because the amount (runoff, but also volumes of lakes and rivers) of water is often highly relevant to the amounts of discharges (biological and chemical oxygen demand, chemical elements, etc.) the system is capable of absorbing and dealing with in order to keep specified environmental quality standards.

The amounts of frequently polluted water discharged as the difference between withdrawn and consumed water is also an important connection in this respect, as, of course, the amounts treated in purification and treatment plants. The close connections between the 'resource' and the 'environmental' aspects of the accounts further emphasizes the importance of a basic geographical identification register on as detailed a basis as possible.

The second aspect of water resource accounting is the environmental water accounts. This should comprise both a monitoring system for the state of the (water) environment and an emission (or discharges) account, that is to say, both the current (quality) state of the resource ('stock') *and* the inputs to the system ('flow'). This is in order both to correlate and analyse better the connections between emissions and changes in the state and to analyse and forecast future emissions, based on (fixed or changing) coefficients such as are used in the resource accounts/forecasts (e.g. for forestry) based on results of economic forecasting models.

Main users and uses of the water-resource accounts

The main categories of users who might use such a system in order to ensure better integration between them would be national and regional authorities and groups and organizations involved with (1) water supply (including water for agricultural irrigation), (2) recipient use, (3) energy production (hydro-electricity, cooling), (4) river transport, (5) conservation, wildlife and leisure.

The main use of a water-resource accounting system would be to ensure consistency between different data, different claims on and projections of the use of the water resources in a region or a river basin. Either through one central authority or through some consultative mechanism or organization, depending on institutional arrangements, a basic reference account would be established, agreed to by all, and any major plans or changes in activities implying changes in the water regimes, water uses, or water quality would have to be discussed and cleared through a process clarifying its effects on future water resource accounts (resource budgets). It is difficult to exemplify this without getting involved in a long discussion, but a whole host of uses of such a system can easily be imagined, but at this stage are better left open, as individual countries' resource situations, national perceptions of challenges and problems, and institutional arrangements for managing water resources very soon would be central to the discussion.

Here are some purely illustrative examples, mostly drawn from Norwegian water-resources management experience. Future use of rivers not as yet touched by hydroelectric development (nor included in conservation areas to be spared such development) has been debated through a major project, classifying hydro projects by economic costs as well as by environmental implications of hydroelectric development for other users of the water resources and river basin. This methodology could easily be imagined as providing one basis of a Norwegian water-resource accounting system.

Some examples of cross-resource implications of water resource use that might be taken into consideration by a water-resource accounting (and a general resource accounting) system:

- The intensive work on reducing water pollution from existing industrial plants, among them pulp and paper plants, over the period from 1975 to 1984, has led to major changes in the forest industry's utilization of wood-based residues for energy use and by-products, and thus for the energy and forestry resource accounts, changes monitored and analysed through those accounts.

- The importance of hydroelectric power in Norway means that energy accounting and budgeting is central also to the use of water resources and river basins; thus the forecasts of future energy use from the energy accounting/budgeting plays a major part in the work with the future use of Norwegian water resources.

- Pollution control policies may in some cases (e.g. the United States, Japan) lead to major reductions in industrial water demand, reductions that could be monitored and forecasted more efficiently through an accounting/budgeting system, thus avoiding major over-investment or over-capacity in water supply.

Conclusions and recommendations

Potential advantages of resource accounting are:

- It ensures a comprehensive perspective of resource use and environmental considerations, above all on the relations between stocks and flows.

- It provides standardized definitions which facilitates the linking of physical resources and environmental data with economic data and analytic and forecasting models.

- It provides a framework for collection and data utilization so that data collected for one purpose can be used for many other purposes.

- This framework facilitates co-operation and co-ordination between different sectors and agencies using the same resource(s).

- It provides data for construction of indicators of the state of the environment.

However, very few governments have much experience in actually using such accounting systems in policy- and decision-making. Also, major unresolved problems remain, particularly concerning monetary evaluation of resources and environmental services.

In the light of the Norwegian experience (further discussed in Alfsen *et al.* (1986), some fundamental preconditions for (greater) success may be summarized in this way; when undertaking a national effort to develop and implement natural-resources accounting and budgeting (NRAB), it is essential to:

- IDENTIFY important resource and environmental problems, and the major decision-making institutions as users of NRAB (at the appropriate administrative/geographical level).

- CONCENTRATE on a few of the most important of these problems, where it is possible to reach some results in the relatively near future, and where managers are (or may become) willing and able to use NRAB in their planning and management.

- INVOLVE managers/users and political institutions as early and as closely as possible in the development of the NRAB system.

- DEVELOP the necessary integrated economic/ecological expertise in and around the central institutions responsible for natural-resource accounting and budgeting, to ensure the continuity of the necessarily highly specialized competence demanded in this field.

- EXPLOIT to the utmost existing data collection routines, management concepts and management tools capable of being integrated with and used as part of an NRAB system.

- AVOID ambitious theoretical system-building and resist the temptation to engage in large, indiscriminate data collection that very easily may emerge as an end in itself (though some work on fundamental concepts and structures is necessary to ensure coherence, and uncritical data collection may result, by serendipity, in new, unsuspected data and correlations).

Another recommendation based on the experience so far is that *environmental resources* and *conditionally-renewable resources* should be given priority in the development of resource accounting systems and procedures as more likely to be subject to irreversible over-exploitation and being in many instances non-substitutable. Problems of future scarcity, particularly of non-renewable resources, which were given great publicity in the 1970s, no longer seem to warrant such attention in the construction and use of resource accounting.

Component 2: an adjusted national product

This component comprises an adjusted national product (ANP), which would be net national product (NNP: GNP adjusted for depreciation of physical capital) adjusted further for the following:

Depreciation of natural capital: this would show up in the environmental accounts, where it would have to be given a monetary value in order to be deducted from (or added to if the environment had improved) GNP. Repetto *et al.* (1989) have discussed in detail the appropriate methodology for this task, and have applied it to forest, soil and petroleum resources in Indonesia.

Adjustments for 'defensive expenditures', which Leipert defines as:

> outlays with which the attempt is made to eliminate, mitigate, neutralize or anticipate and avoid damages and deterioration that industrial society's process of growth has caused to living, working and environmental conditions. They serve only to restore, reapproach, or defend a status (say, a specific environmental quality, secure income, or certain benefits of consumption) that has been lost or compromised by negative impacts of the economic and social process. Seen from a dynamic perspective, defensive expenditures are additional macroeconomic costs incurred by a specific growth and development pattern; they are costs of maintaining the quality of life and the quality of the environment and of ensuring production, consumption and livelihood. They ought to be identified as such in the GNP.
>
> (Leipert 1989: 28)

Leipert (1989) has computed these expenses in the Federal Republic of Germany in six areas:

- The environment: the costs of environmental damage and over-exploitation of resources.
- Transport: commuting costs due to the centralization of production and the negative effects of increased car transport such as accident repair.
- Housing: the increased costs of land and rents due to urbanization.
- Security: the increased risk incurred in industrial societies and/or increased associated costs of crime, accidents, sabotage and technical failure.
- Health: costs arising from car accidents, from unhealthy consumption and behavioural patterns and poor working and living conditions.
- Work: job-related costs not already counted.

Leipert's study found that defensive expenditures in the Federal Republic of Germany increased by 150 per cent from 5.6 per cent to 10 per cent of GNP from 1970 to 1985. GNP itself only increased by 39.4 per cent in the same period, drawing Leipert to the conclusion that:

> The genuine growth that was still achievable in terms of providing new economic options for private households, without simultaneously disadvantaging them in other spheres, is being bought at an ever higher price.
>
> (Leipert 1988: 114–15)

The deduction from NNP of natural capital depreciation and defensive expenditures follows the suggestion of Daly:

> Two adjustments to NNP are needed to make it a closer approximation of Hicks's concept of income and a better guide to prudent behaviour. . . . Let us define the corrected income concept . . . as Net National Product (NNP) minus both defensive expenditures and depreciation of natural capital. . . . This definition entails no interference whatsover with the current structure of the UN System of National Accounts. There is no loss of historical continuity or comparability. Two additional accounts are introduced . . . to gain a closer approximation of the central and well-established meaning of income.
>
> (Daly 1989: 8)

Daly's suggestion does indeed bring GNP closer to Hicks's concept of (sustainable) income, but it still excludes past environmental deterioration which may have crucial implications for environmental sustainability. The following paper not only gives some rigorous theoretical examination to some of the GNP/growth/welfare issues already briefly mentioned; it also develops the important concept of sustainability standards in relation to national income accounting.

Growth, environment and national income: theoretical problems and a practical solution

Roefie Hueting

In economic policy, the news media and, alas, also in some economic literature, the increase in production as measured in national income (or gross national product, GNP) is called economic growth, identified with increase in welfare and conceived as *the* indicator for economic success. Defining production growth as economic growth means defining economics as production. Such a definition excludes, among other things, the scarce environment from economics. Economic growth, defined in this manner, obtains the highest priority in the economic policy in all countries of the world. At the same time we see across the world growth of national income in accordance with the present pattern being accompanied by the destruction of the most fundamental scarce, and consequently economic, good at man's disposal, namely the environment.

From this simple observation three conclusions can be drawn. Society is sailing by a wrong compass, at the expense of the environment. It is a question of a wrong use of terms, at the expense of the environment. The belief in ever-continuing exponential growth in production, as measured in national income, is the heart of the environmental problem.

As this misconception of terms may reflect a wrong insight into the interrelationship between production, economic growth, welfare and environment, thus hampering fundamental solutions of the environmental problem, this article will (1) briefly outline the objections to using national income as an indicator of welfare, growth and economic success, (2) explore the interaction between conservation of the environment and the level of production as measured in national income and (3) make a practical suggestion for the problem of correcting national income for environmental losses.

Objections to using national income as an indicator for economic success

Economics boils down to the problem of choice with regard to the use of scarce, alternatively applicable means for the satisfaction of classifiable wants. Welfare is defined as the satisfaction of wants evoked by dealing with scarce means. So welfare, or satisfaction of wants, is a psychical category, an aspect of one's personal experience. Economic theory assumes that when dealing with scarce means we try to maximize our welfare (the opposite is non-sensical). Besides maximization of welfare with given means, the desire to raise the level of satisfaction of wants (welfare) in the course of time is also regarded as a motive of economic action.

It follows from this brief description of the subject matter of economics that economic growth and economic success can mean nothing other than increase in the level of welfare. Our economic actions have scored success when our satisfaction of wants has increased. Since satisfaction of wants is not directly observable 'from the outside' and thus not in itself a cardinal measurable quantity, it seems logical to look at factors that *are* measurable in figures and that can arguably be supposed to determine the level of welfare. Both in part of economic literature and in the practice of statistical measurement this has been confined to looking at the production of goods and services: the national income.

The objections to this could be classed in three categories, that will be summarized very briefly.

The *first category* is of a more or less 'technical' nature. It encompasses five points.

1. The consumer surplus which relates to the difference between the total utility of a good and the product of price (as the criterion of marginal utility) and quantity is not expressed in the height of national income.
2. In national income the value added by production is calculated at market prices. This means that the (marginal) utility of goods of different subjects is added. This is already unallowable with equal income distribution because it is impossible to compare utilities between individuals: some people attach greater value to goods than others. With the existing inequality of incomes this is not allowed *a fortiori* on account of the diminishing marginal utility of money as income grows. The impossibility of comparing utilities between individuals further implies that if part of the population of a country regresses and the rest progresses, no pronouncement can be made on the final result (this situation certainly occurs).
3. The law of diminishing marginal utility applies to individuals. However, the same tendency is noticeable for the whole economy, as has been shown by recent research (Van Praag and Spit 1982). It appears from this research that ever more extra goods are necessary for the attainment of the same increase in welfare as income rises. This relativizes the importance for welfare of an ever-growing production.
4. Real national income is obtained by expressing the income in current prices in constant prices with the aid of a composite price index. This can only be done correctly for a constant package of goods. Because of the constantly changing package of goods the calculated value of the price index varies, depending on the solution chosen (Hicks 1948; Kuznets 1948; Pigou 1949). This problem weighs especially heavily over a long period.
5. Not all production takes place in business enterprises or in government agencies. This may not only influence the level of national income but also the changes in it, if, for instance, the work of former housewives is taken over by paid domestic help, crèches, dishwashers and restaurants.

The *second category* of objections to identifying increases in national income with economic growth and economic success relates to the intermediate character of some elements of national income. In the calculation of national income in accordance with the present conventions, a number of activities which have a cost character and therefore ought to be entered as intermediate deliveries are designated as final consumption. S. Kuznets (1947, 1948) who deserves to be mentioned as one of the great theoreticians of the conception of national income, emphasizes this. Kuznets divides these activities into three classes: expenditure invoked by an urban pattern of living; expenditure inherent in participation in the technically and monetarily complex civilization of industrial countries; and the major part of government activity.

To this a fourth class can be added: the expenditure on measures that compensate or restore the losses of environmental functions, as defined in my earlier paper in this volume, or prevent losses of environmental functions from occurring. These expenditures are entered as intermediate deliveries in so far as the measures are taken and directly paid for by private firms, but as final consumption when the measures are paid for by private households or the government and also when they are taken by private firms but financed via levies imposed by the government. All these outlays should be entered as intermediate when a long time series such as that for national income is composed. For the losses of environmental functions are not entered as costs at the time they occur. It is therefore double counting to enter outlays for compensating these losses or for eliminating them as final consumption. Such outlays do not contribute to the quantity of consumer goods. They protect or replace scarce environmental goods that were already available. This double counting also makes income figures of different years incomparable, at least when they are used as a measure for economic growth and welfare. For the rest of this article 'production growth' will not only be used quite distinctly from 'economic growth', it will also be taken to mean production growth after correction to remove double counting.

The *third category* of objections to the identification of increase in national income with economic growth (increase in welfare) relates to the fact that production is only one of the factors that determine the level of welfare. At least eight factors play a role.

1. The package of goods and services produced by man.
2. The scarce environmental goods in the broad sense – that is, including space, energy, natural resources, plant and animal species.
3. (Leisure) time.
4. Income distribution.
5. Working conditions.
6. Employment.
7. Health.
8. The safety of the future in so far as this depends on our behaviour with regard to scarce goods (such as life support functions of the environment).

All these eight factors play a part in economic action. They constantly have to be weighed against each other whenever the desired quantity or quality of a given factor is at the expense of one or more other factors. When this is not the case, no economic aspect is at stake in the sense that no choice has to be made to deploy scarce resources between competing uses. Seen from the point of view of those who choose, citizens or politicians, there is thus an unbreakable link between all the factors influencing welfare.

The interaction between environment and production

One of the misunderstandings with regard to the environmental problem pertains to the relation between conservation of the environment and the level of production, as measured in national income. The notion that production should be increased in order to create scope for environmental measures is widespread and highly popular in official economic and environmental policy. The proposition is disputable, because environmental deterioration is to a large extent precisely a *consequence* of production growth.

GNP growth results from two factors: increase in labour productivity (LP) and increase in labour volume (LV). In one analysis of basic material of the Dutch national accounts, of which the sectoral composition does not differ appreciably from that of the UK nor, probably, of most other Northern countries, for the years 1965–79, it emerged that the growth of GNP amounted to 72 per cent, of which only 5 per cent was caused by LV increase (Hueting 1981). Thus the production growth in such an economy is mainly the result of increasing LP, without taking into account the loss of some environmental goods, that is by polluting, degrading and depleting the environment and its resources free of charge.

Preventing such loss, by levies or by regulations, means that, given the existing technology, more labour input is required for the production of a given number of goods. This reduces labour productivity and consequently checks production growth. Saving the environment without checking production growth (corrected, as already stressed, for double counting) is only possible if a technology is invented that is sufficiently clean, reduces the use of space sufficiently, leaves the soil intact, does not deplete energy and resources (i.e. uses energy derived from the sun and recycling) *and* is at least as cheap as current technology. This is hardly imaginable for our whole range of current activities.

The Hueting (1981) analysis shows that one-quarter to one-third of the activities making up national income (notably state consumption) do not contribute to its growth, because by definition no increase in LP can result from them. Other activities result only in slight improvements in productivity. The 3 per cent annual growth (a doubling of production in twenty-three years) desired by official policy, and also advocated in the Brundtland Report (WCED 1987), must therefore be achieved by much higher growth among the remaining activities. The analysis has been updated by the author to 1986 with the same result: 70 per cent of GNP growth is generated by 30 per cent of the activities making up GNP. Unfortunately, these are mainly the activities which, by their use of space or by the pollution they generate, in production or consumption, most harm the environment; notably the oil and petrochemical industries, agriculture, public utilities, road building and mining.

A shift in human activities to reduce the burden on environment and resources can be achieved in two ways: first, by dictating environment-saving measures for production and consumption and, second, by directly changing the production and consumption patterns.

The first method (e.g. applying end-of-line provisions or changing processes) mostly results in higher real prices of the products and thus in a decrease in the growth of national income. When such process changes do not result in higher prices or even result in lower prices, no environmental problem exists, as stated before: the market forces will bring about these changes 'automatically'. While it is possible that market imperfections such as ignorance or inertia delay for some time the introduction of processes that are both cleaner and cheaper, it is most unlikely that this situation will long persist, for as soon as one firm applies such processes, competition forces others to follow suit. Of course, the price increases resulting from the environment-saving measures cause a shift towards more environment-friendly activities.

Technical measures often do not really solve the problem, because the growth of the activity overrides the effect of the measure, or because, owing to the persistent and cumulative character of the burden, the measure only slows down the rate of deterioration. In these cases, in addition to the technical measures a direct shift in behaviour patterns (the second method) must ensue, forced by government regulations and levies. Thus it is estimated that to stop its contribution to the acidification of forests and lakes, apart from applying all available technical means, the Netherlands must reduce the number of car miles and its farm livestock by 50 per cent.

A direct shift in production and consumption patterns will usually also check the growth of GNP, as follows from the above mentioned analysis of the national accounts (the environmentally most burdensome activities contribute most to GNP growth). It probably will even lead to a lower level of GNP. This is because in terms of the national accounts environmentally benign activities represent a smaller volume than environmentally burdensome activities. Thus a bicycle-kilometer, a sweater, an extra blanket, beans and a holiday by train represent a smaller volume than respectively a car-kilometer, a hot room, heating the whole house, meat and holiday flights. This is mainly because the exhaustion of environment and resources is not charged to national income as costs. If it were, the differences would become much smaller or nil.

However, a shift to the former activities would increase our welfare and economic growth in the true sense if we value bicycling, more herbivory and safeguarding the future higher than we value traffic jams, extreme carnivory and increasing the risks of environmental disasters. Unfortunately there is no method to calculate whether or not this is the case as we shall see in the following section.

Two vital conclusions can be drawn from the above. First, it is unlikely that stimulating GNP increase in industrialized countries will solve the problems of developing countries. For such an increase will most likely be possible only by accelerating encroachment on the limited energy stocks and the limited carrying capacity of the environment, which would be at the expense of developing countries. As just described, if we try to avoid this encroachment, the growth would be checked. Second, growth of GNP and safeguarding the environment and resources are two conflicting ends. Sustainable use of our planet's resources requires a shift in priority from increasing GNP to saving the environment. This certainly does not mean 'Stop production growth', but rather a shift in production and consumer activities in an environmentally acceptable direction in order to arrive at sustainable economic development, and then to wait and see what the increase in production would be. Those who advocate both ends are apparently either blind to present-day reality or are speculating on as yet uninvented technologies while putting at risk the basis of our existence. Such advice may do more harm than good to the environment, because it strengthens the forces behind the increase of national income, which are already much stronger than those defending the environment.

The recommended shift in priority in economic policy would avoid both risks and future financial losses. For restoration after the event is usually much, often very much, more expensive than prevention, while a number of environmental losses are irreversible or may lead to overshoot. This shift would also stimulate the search for and application of environment-friendly technologies much more strongly than current policy.

Correction of national income: a theoretical dilemma, but a practical solution

It follows from the above that the environment constantly risks falling victim to the misconceptions of economic growth and welfare, and the resulting one-sided stress of economic policy on the increase of production as measured in national income. Therefore a correction of national income for environmental losses seems highly recommendable, provided that it is made clear in the presentation of the results that the figures found also do not constitute a complete indicator for society's welfare in the course of time. In view of the severe criticism and the pressure for carrying into effect such a correction, that has been going on now for decades, one might be surprised why up to now this work has not been completed, or even started. The main reason for this is the theoretical impossibility to construct shadow prices for environmental functions (and their loss) that are directly comparable with market prices of goods produced by man.

A correction for expenditure on compensatory, restoratory and preventive measures would be feasible without theoretical difficulties. This defensive expenditure, which only re-establishes or maintains environmental functions that would remain available without the negative impact of our activities on the environment, is, as already discussed, wrongly entered as value added, thus leading to an overestimation of the increase in national income and concealing what is going on in the environment. On the one hand, such a correction would be a step forward, as it would partly solve the well-known problem of double counting and provide more information about the relation between production and environment. On the other hand, it would express the environmental losses very incompletely and introduce the *pars pro toto* problem: part of the information is conceived as the total environmental effect. For, as is well known, most environmental losses are not restored or compensated.

National income is recorded in market terms. For confrontation of environmental losses with this figure it is therefore necessary to construct shadow prices for environmental functions that are directly comparable with market prices. For this a demand-and-supply curve has to be construed. In the period from 1969 to 1974, the Netherlands Central Bureau of Statistics attempted to do this with, very briefly, the following results (Hueting 1980).

As described in my earlier paper in this volume (see p. 68), the supply curve consists of an elimination cost curve. Elimination is defined as doing away with the burden on the environment, either by technical measures or by reducing (where necessary to zero level) the activity causing the burden. Both the expenditure on the measures and the drop in volume caused by reduction of activities are interpreted as costs. The construction of the supply curve as defined here may entail technical difficulties but not problems of theoretical economics.

The demand curve, for the reasons given in the earlier paper, usually cannot be calculated because in most cases it is impossible to quantify the intensity of the need for environmental functions, which led to the proposal, also described earlier, to replace the unknown demand curves by calculations based on standards for the sustainable use of environmental functions.

The feasibility of this approach is being investigated at the Netherlands Central Bureau of Statistics, based on the following procedure. Define physical standards for environmental functions, based on their sustainable use. Formulate the measures necessary to meet these standards. Finally, estimate the amounts of money involved in putting the measures into practice.

In technical terms this means that in the familiar diagram of the supply-and-demand curve for environmental functions we have to determine a point on the abscissa which represents the standard for sustainability. A perpendicular on this point intersects the supply curve; the perpendicular replaces the (unknown) demand curve. The point of intersection helps to indicate the volume of activities, measured in money, involved in attaining sustainable use of the functions. This can be summarized in Figure 8.2.

As Figure 8.2 shows, the investigation, in addition to establishing the point of sustainability on the abscissa, amounts mainly to formulating the measures that are necessary for bridging the distance *BD* and for estimating the costs of those measures. By so doing the size of the loss as already recorded in physical units in the year of investigation, for instance 1990, is then expressed in monetary units. This corresponds with the minimal costs that must be incurred to bridge the distance between the present situation and sustainable use of the environment. Comparison of this amount with the standard national income yields the sustainable national income.

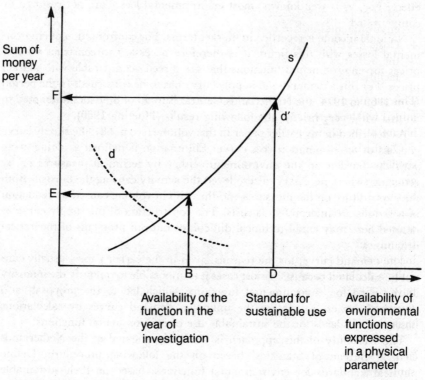

Key:
s = supply curve
d = incomplete demand curve based on individual preferences (emerging from expenditure for compensation of the function, etc.)
d′ = demand curve based on the sustainability standard
BD= distance that must be bridged in order to arrive at sustainable use of the environmental function
EF = costs of the loss of function, expressed in money

Figure 8.2 Translation of costs in physical units into costs in monetary units

Notes: 1 The arrows indicate the way in which the loss of environmental functions recorded in physical units is translated into monetary units

2 Figure 3.1 in my paper on economic functions of the environment (see p. 68) shows marginal curves while the above figure shows total curves

The curve is composed of four categories of measures:

1. Costs of technical measures and their introduction.
2. Costs of developing alternatives for depletable natural resources, such as replacement of fossil fuels by forms of energy derived from the sun and of copper wire by glass fibre.
3. Costs of the direct shift from environmentally burdening to environmentally friendly activities when technical measures are not sufficient to reach the point of sustainability. 'Shift' has been opted for, because the costs of reduction of the activities alone lead to an overestimation of the environmental loss in monetary units.
4. Costs of reduction of the population and the resultant drop in volume of the activities when categories 1 to 3 lead to an unacceptably low level of facilities per person.

This arrangement is based on the fact that the environmental burden is determined by the number of people, the amount of activity per person and the nature of the activities.

On the basis of the analysis mentioned in the previous section (a relatively small part of the activities, that are the environmentally most burdensome, generate the greater part of growth of national income), the following outcome has been derived (Hueting *et al.* 1991). Decreasing environment burdening activities by one percentage point has a negative effect on national income of at least 1.8 per cent; a shift from environment burdening to environment friendly activities by 1 per cent has on balance a negative effect on national income of at least 1.5 per cent. This outcome makes it possible to determine quite accurately the point on the supply curve where technical measures will have to be abandoned in favour of a direct shift (reallocation) of activities. At this point, per unit of prevented burdening the cost of this shift will be lower than that of technical measures.

The basic assumption of the exercise is that the transition to sustainable activities is made in every country in the world at the same time and in the same way. This assumption has to be made because the greatest environmental problems occur on a world-wide scale. As a result no allowance has to be made for among other things transfer of activities to other countries.

Often what is proposed above is criticized with the comment that no allowance has been made for the development of technology. This criticism is not relevant because the investigation is directed towards the concrete situation in one year in the past. For that year a sum of money is calculated completely statistically with the aid of data on the costs of available technology. The difference between the sustainable income and the standard national income will of course work out smaller when, in a repetition of the investigation, new technologies have meanwhile been developed.

Because of the central importance of adjusting GNP to give a better estimate of real income, and because of the fact that this importance is being increasingly perceived in governmental statistical offices round the world, it is worth drawing together and comparing the Daly and Hueting proposals covered in this chapter.

Daly advocates calculating natural capital depreciation and defensive expenditures across the whole range of subjects tackled by Leipert, and deducting these from NNP to arrive at a sustainable social net national product (SSNNP).

Hueting advocates concentrating on environmental issues by correcting for double counting of environmental expenditures and calculating a further correction to national income by the amount of the costs necessary to reach certain sustainability standards.

The adjustment recommended here combines the approaches of Daly and Hueting. It proposes the deduction of natural capital depreciation (after Daly) in an exactly analogous way to the derivation of net national product (NNP) from GNP by deducting the depreciation of manufactured capital. It further proposes the deduction of actually incurred environmental defensive expenditures (after both Daly and Hueting), as these should rightly be considered as intermediate costs. It proposes the deduction of the costs necessary to reach standards of sustainability (after Hueting). This overall proposal also broadly corresponds to that made by Pearce:

> We would support the measurement of *sustainable income*, [where]:
> Sustainable Income = • Measured Income (GNP)
>   • Household Defensive Expenditures
>   • Monetary Value of Residual Pollution
>   • Depreciation of Man-Made Capital
>   • Depreciation of Environmental Capital.
> (Pearce *et al.* 1989: 108)

It must be stressed that these proposals to adjust GNP are intended to construct a better indicator of production or income *not* of welfare. Welfare, in the approach taken here and as Hueting emphasized in his paper, is quite different from production. Therefore this process of adjustment is quite different, for instance, to that of Mäler (1991), who explicitly sets out to adjust GNP for environmental factors to arrive at a net welfare measure (NWM). Following an exercise in welfare optimization he calculates that NWM does not require that defensive expenditures be deducted from net national product, provided that current environmental damage and the value of the degradation of stocks, including natural capital, are so deducted. Mäler is unequivocal about the relation between welfare and consumption when he writes that NWM (the result of a standard utility optimization procedure) 'can be interpreted as the sustainable income, in the sense that it gives the maximum feasible constant flow of consumption' (Mäler 1991: 13).

It is precisely this identification of welfare with consumption (or production) that Hueting rejects so emphatically. His proposal to deduct defensive expenditures from GNP to improve it as an indicator of production was based on the perception that these expenditures were in the nature of intermediate costs that had been wrongly counted as final expenditure. They represented an overstatement of production. The relationship of such production to welfare is far more complex than that envisaged by Mäler.

It should, therefore, be clear that the adjusted national product advocated as the second component of the indicator framework being developed here is a production, and not a welfare, indicator. More specifically, it is a more accurate indicator than GNP (or NNP) of the final output of the formal economy.

Component 3: measurement of non-monetary production

The framework's third component considers the complementary economy (see Figure 5.1, p. 127), which consists of three sectors: the irregular, voluntary and domestic sectors. While there have been estimates of the size of the irregular sector, which have their uses, its nature precludes the systematic measurement that would be necessary for its inclusion in the national accounts. Voluntary sector activities are so diverse and unamenable to market comparisons that they largely defy monetary measurement altogether. The household sector is different, and the construction of a national account for this sector is well within the bounds of feasibility.

Measuring households' non-monetary production[†]

Luisella Goldschmidt-Clermont

Part of the goods and services consumed by the population are produced and consumed without undergoing monetary transactions. This is so, for instance, for the domestic services provided to the household by unpaid household members, for 'do-it-yourself' repairs of household premises and equipment, for water-carrying, basket making, weaving, knitting, sewing, and so on, for own-consumption. These non-monetized productive activities go unrecorded in labour statistics and in the national accounts.

How does this non-monetary sector of the economy compare with the recorded economy? How does it compare in size, in value, in contribution to human welfare? How do the monetary and non-monetary sectors interact; in other words, how, why and when do production and manpower leave the

† This paper is based in part on research supported by the International Labour Office Employment and Development Department and Bureau of Statistics, and the Fonds National pour le Recherche Scientifique (FNRS, Brussels). Opinions expressed herein are the sole responsibility of the author.

household for the market, and *vice-versa*? What do these transfers mean in terms of personal welfare and of the nation's extended income (monetary income plus non-monetary income)? How are these transfers affected by labour-market factors such as market rigidities, shortage of manpower in periods of economic growth or concern for unemployment and underemployment in periods of recession? Should we account for the non-monetary sector in economic statistics, in economic analysis, in economic and social-policy formulation? What is the impact of economic development and of increased monetization on household production, on the distribution of the nation's manpower between the market and non-market sectors? In industrialized economies, what would the impact be, for instance, of a reduction of working hours on the labour supply, on the production of goods and services for self-consumption, on the consumption of market goods, on time available for leisure, education and so on?

Many of these questions cannot be answered in the present state of the art. The non-monetary sector, historically the oldest, is new from the point of view of economic studies: it was until recently almost totally neglected. In this paper therefore the answers can only be indicative; directions are suggested for further work which would improve knowledge of the field. However, a concrete suggestion is made as to how household production can be incorporated into the national accounts.

1. Socio-economic context

Before discussing the economic measurement of non-monetary household production, the socio-economic context in which this production occurs has to be clarified as well as some of the assumptions underlying our approach.

Social, cultural and personal factors combine with economic factors in determining the structure and content of household activities; ideally an interdisciplinary approach should therefore be used for studying the non-monetary economy. It is not sufficient to isolate economic considerations when studying the household economy: the impact of tradition, of quality considerations, of social values soon shows in interviews of household members. When asked why a particular activity is performed in the household while market replacements are available, the answers often are: 'That is how my mother did it' or 'It would not be socially acceptable to do otherwise' or 'What is available on the market is not as good as what the household produces' or 'I enjoy doing it'. These social and psychological considerations are put forward along with economic considerations: 'We cannot afford to buy the market product' or 'No market replacement is available in our area'. (Goldschmidt-Clermont, unpublished data on interviews performed in Stanford, California in 1982 and in Geneva, Switzerland, in 1983).

Household studies are perhaps, in the social sciences, the area in greatest need of an interdisciplinary approach because the household is the place where economics, social values and personal characteristics converge towards the very end of human activity: the transformation of natural and human resources into something capable of meeting human needs and wants.

Family studies sometimes combine a sociological and psychological approach; to our knowledge, economics is rarely if ever present. A first step for integrating economics could consist of finding out, in a given social group, how household members perceive the 'value' of their non-monetary activities, the concept value being taken in its widest meaning, that is inclusive of economic, social and personal components. A qualitative inventory of such values could be established on the basis of case studies. A further step could then aim at assessing the respective weight of these values in decision making, and at studying their variation under the impact of external factors. Such a multi-disciplinary study would throw some light on the process by which social values permeate economic action.

Pending the performance of multi-disciplinary studies, economics need not remain idle. It can and should provide more economic data than presently available on households' non-monetary production.

2. Boundaries, size and economic significance of the non-monetary household sector

Households' activities can be grouped in three main categories:

1. Personal activities (non-economic).
2. Productive non-market activities (mostly for own-consumption).
3. Productive market-orientated activities.

The border between categories 1 and 2 is defined by the 'third-person criterion' which states that an activity is to be deemed productive (economic) if it may be delegated to a person other than the one benefiting from it (Reid 1934).

The border between categories 2 and 3 roughly corresponds to the 'production boundary' defined in the United Nations System of National Accounts (SNA) (United Nations, Statistical Office 1968). The accounts include a few non-monetary production items such as imputed rents from owner-occupied dwellings and agricultural product consumed by the producing farmer; they exclude others such as:

- domestic activities
- processing of primary commodities for own use (food preservation, making cloth or furniture, etc.) by households which do not produce the primary commodity
- production of other commodities for own use (clothes, shoes, etc.) by households which do not sell any part of them
- own-dwelling upkeep and repair.

The inclusion or exclusion of household production in the national accounts has been the subject of considerable debate, particularly in recent years in connection with the revision of the SNA. (The revised version should be available by 1992.) Inclusion or exclusion of households' non-market production raises fundamental questions of principle relating to the purpose of national accounting, to the range of activities to be covered, and to the organization of the data so as to serve the different uses to which data are put. It raises methodological questions as to the appropriate methods for imputing a monetary value to activities which are not the object of monetary transactions. It also raises practical questions: as statistical offices are already under pressure to produce more and better data about the market sectors of the economy, they find it difficult to embark on the entirely new data collection required for non-market household production.

From the revision preparatory work, it appears likely that only minor changes will be made to the production boundary. Some kind of agreement seems to have been reached by statisticians along the following lines. Household production is definitely recognized as a productive activity contributing to economic welfare. However, national accounts are not intended for measuring economic welfare and they cannot and should not claim to reflect the entire economic and social reality. The many purposes which national accounts have served so far (among others, analysis of the market sectors, of prices, of monetary flows, construction of econometric models, forecasting of economic trends) would be hindered by the inclusion of households' non-market production in the standard series and, in particular, in the GDP. Not only is it desirable to maintain the stability of time series, but also the inclusion of household production would require a high proportion of additional imputations, while the current trend is to reduce imputations as much as possible. (Imputations are a source of inaccuracy which may further increase the margin of error of GDP estimates.) It is proposed to record households' non-market production in a 'satellite account', that is in a supplementary system of the accounts.

The product of the non-monetary sector can be measured in physical units. For instance, so many tons of wheat transformed by households into edible food; so many millions of meals prepared by households; so many tons of clothes washed by households; so many siblings or aged persons cared for at home; and so on. Such data would be useful for studying trends in the availability of products for extended final consumption; they would permit comparisons with the monetary sector by showing the relative share of the monetary and non-monetary sectors in the provision of a specific good or service.

Physical units however do not permit larger comparisons: one ton of washed clothes cannot be compared to one ton of coal extracted by industry. In order to avoid this problem, it is common practice to use monetary units, that is to measure values. Values can be aggregated which makes them convenient to use; so convenient that there is a tendency to forget the complexity of price formation mechanisms and the tenuous links monetary values entertain with welfare. For lack of better approaches, this is the way the economy is measured at present; in order to assess the economic siginificance of the non-monetary sector and its relations to the monetary sector, one has to proceed in a similar way.

However, before embarking on such a task, one more general remark has to be made about economic measurements: volumes and values do not tell the whole story of economic significance. For instance, as demonstrated by the economic disorganization consecutive to truck drivers' strikes, the *strategic significance* of transportation by truck is larger than suggested by the relative contribution of this sector to GDP. Similarly, the strategic significance of barber shops appears very low for the functioning of the economy, whatever the amount of value added they generate.

The strategic significance of the non-monetary household sector is probably very high, not only for population welfare or even population survival (e.g. water carrying, in some areas) but also for the functioning of the entire economy. However, this strategic significance is difficult to assess because unpaid workers in the household sector are not likely to go on strike like truck drivers: the social values in all societies, the economic functions performed by unpaid household workers and their personal relations to the persons bene-fiting from their work prevent them from striking. In order to assess the strategic significance of say domestic services, let us imagine that a powerful wizard puts all females to sleep at the moment they start undertaking their domestic activities. (Time-use studies show that, the world over, females are the main providers of unpaid domestic services.) In such a scenario, males may take over the provision of food and of basic essentials for themselves, for the children and for the handicapped. While they will be performing these domestic services, crops will not be harvested, transportation services, mining, industrial production and so on will be disrupted and no monetary income will flow into the household for purchasing the goods and services the economy might still be able to provide.

This excursion into socio-economic fiction just aims at underlining a missing dimension in our economic measurements. Perhaps economics could borrow, from graphs' theory or from military science, the tools for measuring the strategic significance of economic sectors. In the meantime, we can only approach the measurement of the non-monetary sector with the traditional tools.

The *volume of labour inputs* absorbed by the non-monetary household sector is a good indicator of its size. The best data on such labour inputs are provided by time-use studies. Research data indicate that, in industrialized economies, *non-monetary household production requires about as many hours of work as all combined activities in the monetized sectors.* In other words, care of children, health care of family members, meal preparation, cleaning dwelling, care of clothing, own dwelling and equipment repairs, and so on, absorb as much labour time as agriculture, manufacturing, transportation, trade and so on combined (see for instance, among the most recent publications: As *et al.* 1986; Chadeau 1989; Gershuny and Jones 1986; Roy 1989a and 1989b). Anthropological observations reveal similar proportions in the rural areas of developing countries when water carrying, firewood collection and food processing for household consumption are added to domestic activities. (For a review of these observations, in relation to the economic assessment of non-monetary household work, see Goldschmidt-Clermont 1987a).

Defining the monetary value of non-monetary household production raises difficulties because both its labour inputs and its product are non-monetary. Values therefore have to be imputed from the monetized sector to unpaid household labour (input approach) or to household product (output approach). Several studies have been made, using either an input or an output approach. Because these studies vary not only in valuation methodology but also in population coverage and in activities included, their results are not comparable. They indicate that the value of non-monetary household production lies somewhere between 30 and 50 per cent of the gross domestic product (GDP), in industrialized and in developing economies. Within the broad input/output approach categorization, several variations can be distinguished. Their detailed description is not undertaken here as they were analysed and discussed at length elsewhere (Goldschmidt-Clermont 1982, 1986, 1987a, 1987b and 1987c).

Broadly speaking, the input-based valuations determine the *value of labour inputs* by taking the number of hours worked in, for instance, domestic activities and by imputing a market wage to this number of hours. In some studies, the imputed wage is chosen to be the same as domestic servants' wages; in other studies, it is chosen to be the wages of employees performing in commercial enterprises (restaurants, laundries, day-care centres, nursery schools, etc.) functions similar to those performed in the household; in others still, it is chosen to be the wages paid in the market for qualifications similar to those displayed by unpaid household workers. The selection of 'appropriate' wages is a major problem as the valuation will vary greatly depending on whether the selected wage is at the bottom of the ladder (housekeepers' wages usually are low) or whether the selected wage is high because well-equipped enterprises can afford to pay high wages. In the latter case, the values arrived at are related to enterprises' productivity and not to households' productivity: these values are sensitive to factors affecting market wages but extraneous to the household and they carry no relation to the value of the output in kind generated by unpaid household work. The hourly output of peeled potatoes by a housewife using a kitchen knife is less than the output of a cook-help using power driven equipment; the enterprise can therefore pay a higher wage to the cook than it could pay an employee using a kitchen knife.

Another input-based valuation method consists of imputing to the hours of work the wage forgone in the market by the household member who performs the household production. The method relies on a number of assumptions which are unrealistic in most strata of the population in industrialized countries and which are totally unacceptable in economies with a lower degree of market penetration. The most important of these assumptions are:

economically rational behaviour of utility-maximizing individuals, having choices and choosing freely in a competitive market; possibility of substituting market work for non-market work, and *vice-versa*, in units, until equilibrium is reached; and so on. The values computed with this method may, to a certain extent, represent a cost of household production; definitely not its value.

In addition to producing results which have limited significance from the point of view of economic analysis, the imputation of market wages to non-market time has the further drawback of producing results which are not compatible with national accounting procedures and are therefore not suitable for comparison with national accounting data.

Output-related valuations do not have these drawbacks and are therefore preferable on theoretical grounds. These valuations determine the *value added in household production* by taking as a starting point the quantities (in physical units) of goods and services produced in the household, by imputing to these quantities the price of similar goods or services available in the market and by deducting the value of intermediate consumption. From the point of view of the household, the value thus computed is a 'forgone expense'. The advantages of this approach are that it relates to household productivity circumstances, that it does not require hypothetical assumptions on households' behaviour and decision making, and that it is in line with national accounting practice. The main drawback of output-based valuations is pragmatic: they require data on the volume of household output which have only rarely been collected so far, although several relevant studies do exist (see section 4).

3. Obstacles to the valuation of households' non-monetary activities

The measurement and valuation of non-monetary activities is meaningful not only for the clarification of unpaid workers' status (as repeatedly requested by women's organizations during the last two decades), but also for the overall improvement of economic statistics. Transfers of production occur between the recorded and unrecorded sectors of the economy. For instance, in industrialized countries, a sizeable share of private laundering moved from the household to commercial enterprises in the 1920s and early 1930s; it then moved back to households in the 1940s and in the 1950s, as appropriate equipment became available. Such transfers between the recorded and unrecorded sectors generate effects in GDP figures causing them to increase or decrease while the actual amount of goods and services available to the population does not change. Economic measurements of non-monetary household production are also necessary in several fields of policy formulation: allocation of productive resources, economic policy, labour policy, income distribution, social policy, fiscal policy, population policy, common law. (See discussion in Goldschmidt-Clermont 1990: 281–5.)

In recent years, consensus has been steadily increasing among economists and statisticians about the need to measure and value the non-market sectors of the economy, including domestic activities; their estimated size and value are such that they cannot continue to go unrecorded. However, progress in achieving valuations appears to be slow; the reasons may be several and of different kinds. Only if we can identify the obstacles shall we be able to take action on them.

One first obstacle lies in the need to ensure continuity of definitions in statistical time series. In order to overcome this obstacle, it was proposed that households' non-monetary production be dealt with separately in national accounting: household production can be presented in a satellite account, without modifying the current structure of the accounts (Goldschmidt-Clermont 1987b). By measuring the value of the non-monetary sector by methods compatible with those used for the other sectors of the economy, it will be possible to achieve an overview of 'extended production', that is, of conventional GDP plus household production.

A second obstacle lies in the newness of the task. Statisticians carry out difficult measurements in fields where they now have gained more than half a century of experience; but experience is not available on the measurement of domestic activities and to start on this task may appear more difficult than it really is.

A third obstacle lies in the fact that emotional factors link people (including statisticians) to household production: living style, quality considerations and so on, may be extremely important elements in personal lives and one may tend to give them more weight when valuing 'grand mother's cake' than when determining the value of manufactured men's shirts (United Nations 1968, para. 4.56). Are we seeking to achieve more refined results for household production than for the agricultural sector or for manufacturing? At the present stage, when procedures for valuing domestic and related activities are still being developed, we should perhaps be satisfied with somewhat less precision, provided the measurement and valuation methods we adopt are sound. The criteria of 'soundness' being compatibility with national accounting and meaningfulness for economic analysis. Statistical refinements may be postponed to later endeavours.

A fourth obstacle lies in the pressure under which statistical departments are working in order to produce better or more complete results in the fields in which they are already engaged. Where then to find the resources for engaging in a new field? The answer here is of a political nature: resources become available if political pressure is sufficient. The corresponding choices will be made and decisions will be taken, only if the usefulness of the new data about the household non-monetary sector is clearly understood.

4. Valuing households' non-monetary production

In this section, proposals are put forward with three goals in mind:

1. Using an output-related valuation method for household level and aggregate level valuations because of its theoretical and analytical advantages (see section 2).
2. Lightening as much as possible the pragmatic difficulties inherent to output-related valuations, by starting with a minimal set of activities while leaving the door open to gradual expansions as expertise becomes available.
3. Taking stock of existing data while reducing to a minimum the new data to be generated.

The valuation method proposed combines time-use data with an output-related measure of household productivity, namely returns to labour in non-monetary production.

4.1 Returns to labour

The general procedure in national accounting for calculating value-added by non-market outputs such as, for instance, agricultural products consumed by the producer (United Nations 1968, para. 6.21) consists of:

- measuring the amount of output in physical units;
- valuing it at market prices;
- calculating value added.

This procedure can be applied to all non-market household output.

Measuring the amount of output Physical quantities of some of the goods and services produced by households were estimated in several studies in industrialized countries (Bivens and Volker 1986; Chadeau and Fouquet 1981; Chaput-Auquier 1959; Clark 1958; Sanik and Stafford 1983). The largest, most encompassing measurements of household output were performed in a national study in Finland (Finland 1980 to 1986). These studies indicate that it is feasible to perform such measurements; they provide guidance on how to proceed.

Valuing output Once measured in physical units, household output is assigned an imputed value (gross output value) on the basis of market prices for goods and services equivalent to those produced in the household. National accounting procedures provide guidance on price determination (prices differing between areas, seasons, rural and urban markets), on price adjustments for quality differences and on the use of producer or of consumer prices.

Value-added Once gross output value has been calculated, intermediate consumption is deducted in order to obtain value-added. Returns to labour are then obtained by deducting from value-added the consumption of fixed capital.

At the micro-economic level, returns to labour represent the saving (forgone expense) which accrues to the household for engaging in the productive activity. At the macro-economic level, these returns to labour correspond to what, in national accounting, would go under the headings 'compensation of employees' and 'operating surplus'. Returns to labour are an output-related measure of the value of labour expended in domestic activities; they are compatible with other economic measurements as they are obtained through the general national accounting procedure.

To undertake at once a large-scale valuation of domestic activities according to this general national accounting procedure, may be an undertaking which goes beyond the available means of the statistical offices or of the institutions responsible for it. The proposal here is to proceed gradually by

- starting with micro-level valuations of returns to labour performed on a limited sample of the population (perhaps only case studies as is done for household budgets) and on a limited number of activities, on the understanding that the sample and the coverage of activities can be extended at later stages as experience is gained (section 4.3);
- deriving macro-level valuations of households' non-monetary production from the micro-level data (section 4.4) and proceeding with the necessary data adjustments for the construction of a satellite account (section 4.5).

4.2 Time-use data

Time-use research started around the 1920s in academic departments and has been performed since in several countries. In some cases, it has been taken over by national statistical offices. An interesting amount of international co-ordination has been achieved, in particular under the auspices of the International Research Group on Time Budgets and Social Activities and, more recently, of the European Foundation for the Improvement of Living and Working Conditions in Dublin which funds the Multinational Longitudinal Time Budget Archive. A corpus of time-use data is thus available and is likely to be further developed as the many uses of such data are increasingly recognized.

The proposed valuation procedure takes advantage of time-use data for two reasons. First, because, measured in time units, labour inputs into household production can be compared to labour inputs into production for the market; this comparison provides *per se*, a direct assessment of the economic significance of domestic activities. Second, because given the availability of time-use data, part of the statistical effort required for valuing household production could be saved *if satisfactory values* could be imputed to the time inputs.

In order to qualify as satisfactory, these values should be established in accordance with national accounting practice; this is an absolute requirement if the data on households' non-monetary production should be comparable to national accounting data and should be usable in economic analysis or in policy formulation. A second requirement is that the household values be related to production circumstances in the household (household size and composition, household equipment, and other circumstances which influence household productivity) – that is, that these values be related to actual household output. These values should not be market wages (see the discussion in section 2). Returns to labour in household production qualify for this valuation.

4.3 Combining time-use data and returns to labour for micro-environment valuations

In order to perform the valuation, it is necessary to compute returns to labour on an hourly basis: that is to relate the returns in a particular activity to the time expended by the household under consideration for performing the activity.

This method was used in 1975–6 in the Philippines for calculating the economic contribution of children to household income (Cabanero 1978). Cabanero computes the hourly returns to labour in several activities by combining the gross output value of home-produced goods for household consumption and for sale (furniture and fixtures, home-sewn clothes, woven materials, food preparation, laundering for household and for others, etc.) with the time devoted to this production. She uses these returns to labour rates for valuing all home production by children including care of younger siblings and housework. (It is interesting to notice in passing one of her results: in general, when holding age constant, returns to labour are higher than market wages for children of all income classes.)

Returns to labour were calculated in Indonesia and Nepal in 1972–3 for several market-orientated activities some of which were identical to activities performed for household consumption: food preparation, handicrafts and so on (Nag *et al.* 1978). The values obtained for the few activities selected in the study ranged from 2.5 to 6 Rp./hour for food preparation and from 1.5 to 3 Rp./hour for handicrafts. (As a point of reference, agricultural wage labour ranged from 6 to 20 Rp./hour.)

Returns to labour were also calculated at the micro-economic level for a few activities in a limited number of households in Stanford, California, in 1982 (Goldschmidt-Clermont 1983). These case studies showed returns to labour ranging from a negative value (a loss of US $1.30 per hour for hand-knitting a cardigan) to a return of $29.80 per hour for making yogurt at home; intermediate values were obtained for other food preparation activities and for ironing clothes. (As a point of reference, housekeepers' wages ranged in that community between $6 and $8 per hour.)

Yogurt preparation may be used for illustrating the procedure followed in Stanford.

1. Household product: plain yogurt, prepared four litres at a time from low-fat milk. The monetary outlays were $2.41 for milk, yogurt culture, a

thermometer and gas fuel. The process required 20 minutes of 'active' preparation time (shopping for ingredients, pouring and mixing, cleaning up) and an estimated 4 minutes of 'passive' or 'secondary' time (watching the thermometer while performing other tasks).

2. Market product: all plain lowfat yogurts available at the local supermarket were acquired. After being removed from their containers in order to avoid identification, they were subjected, along with the home-made yogurt, to quality rating by the household members. Only one market product came out with the same rating ('excellent') as the household product. If purchased in economy-sized containers, the four litres of yogurt would cost $11.36. The time spent buying the selected brand, as part of the household's weekly shopping, was two minutes.

3. Net monetary saving due to household production: $11.36 – $2.41 = $8.95.

4. Net time cost of household production: 20 minutes – 2 minutes = 18 minutes.

5. Returns to labour: $8.95 in eighteen minutes corresponding to an hourly return of $29.83.

A few comments are required. In the industrialized economies, market penetration is large and market substitutes providing monetary values for the imputation are readily available. This situation does not exist to the same extent in Third World countries (Séruzier 1988: 42). However, in addition to the studies mentioned above, the prices of equivalent market substitutes were used for the valuation of some household products in Nepal (Acharya and Bennett 1981), in Pakistan (Alauddin 1980), in Botswana (Dahl 1979) and in Indonesia (Evers 1981).

The data collected in the Stanford case studies showed the impact of production circumstances on household returns; for example, the higher the number of persons for whom food is prepared, the higher the return rates. They also showed the impact on household returns of the availability and quality of market alternatives: the more time it takes to acquire a product on the market, the more it pays to produce at home; the more satisfactory the market alternative, the less it pays to produce at home; the poorer the quality of the market alternative, the higher the returns on good quality household production; and so on. These remarks deal with *productivity differences between the market and the household* which are reflected in the returns to labour; contrarily to a common prejudice, market production may, sometimes, be less efficient than household production. In such a case, the returns to household labour are high. The Stanford data also show the impact of some non-economic components of value (e.g. personal preferences) on time allocation to household production. For instance, although ironing trousers at home (after they have been dry-cleaned in a commercial machine) resulted in returns amounting to $18.50 per hour, one housewife continued to use the full dry-cleaning service (cleaning plus ironing) because she 'hated' ironing. By imputing to the household product the price of a market good that the household judges equivalent in quality to the one it produces, this method incorporates an indicator of welfare subjectively assessed by the household. This is the case, for instance, in the assessment of home prepared meals versus restaurant meals; some households have more stringent requirements than others about what they eat and about the environment in which they eat.

Returns to labour are interesting *per se* for economic analysis purposes as they yield information on the relative productivity achieved by households in the various domestic activities. They also make it possible to compare returns to labour in non-monetary activities to the returns achieved by the household for labour in the market sector (wages and other job-related benefits minus job-related expenditures, taxes, etc.). The calculation of returns to labour is a promising field which deserves further research.

4.4 Combining time-use data and returns to labour for macro-economic valuations

The method proposed for macro-economic valuation of households' non-monetary production consists of imputing data from micro-economic valuations to time-use data gathered from a representative national sample. The method is 'light' in the sense that it requires less statistical work than the general procedure. Statistical work is economized by:

- utilizing time-use data which are already available in several countries and which are collected from representative national samples;
- calculating hourly returns to labour on a limited sample and on a limited number of activities, and averaging them out for imputation to other activities.

The precision of valuations achieved through this method depends on the quality of the time-use data, on the nature of the sample and on the activities for which returns to labour are calculated. This precision can be adjusted to the resources available for performing the valuation.

Data sources

Commonly used data sources are:

- Official statistics (census and national surveys data on household composition, on dwelling characteristics, on consumer expenditures, on prices, on wages, etc.).
- Special studies conducted for business, policy or other purposes (on care of children, on meals taken at home and away from home; comparative quality tests of consumer goods performed by public bodies or by independent non-profit organizations; nutrition and food studies; trade bulletins, price lists, etc.).
- Special household surveys conducted for collecting data on time-use, on the volume of household production and on household expenditures; in some

surveys, questions are also added on the motivations for household production (forgone expense, quality preferences, conformity with social expectations, personal satisfaction, lack of alternatives, etc.).

- Sociological studies using participant observation or key informant interviews, and covering a satisfactory number of representative households (sociological studies can be combined with the special household surveys).

Successive steps

When applied at the national level, the procedure proposed here requires the following successive steps, steps 1 to 6 being performed on a limited sample of households.

1. Measurements of the *amount of household output*, by activity. The following are examples of such measurements which have been utilized in valuations:

   - Meal preparation: frequency and content of various types of meals prepared at home; sometimes information was also collected on origin of food and its level of processing, on number of persons consuming the meals and so on.
   - Food preservation: amount of fruit, vegetables, fish, and so on, preserved by various methods.
   - Care of dependent household members: number of children of various ages cared for at home (part-time or full-time) and kind of care given (physical care, general supervision, training in special skills, etc.); number and characteristics of persons receiving special care at home (elderly, handicapped, ill persons) and kind of care.
   - Upkeep of dwelling and of its surroundings: surface swept and cleaned on a routine basis; kind and frequency of repairs and maintenance of a periodic kind.
   - Care of clothing: frequency and amount of laundering, of mending and so on.
   - Manufacturing for household consumption: number of clothes home-made, by type (sewn, knitted or woven; skirts, dresses, trousers, socks, pullovers or other; for children, women or men); other.

2. Once measured in physical units, the output of each household is assigned an imputed value (*gross output value*) on the basis of the prices paid in the market for similar goods or services. The following are examples of prices which were used for calculating the imputed gross output value of household production in industrialized countries:

   - Price of various types of foods or of meals available commercially, comparable in content and quality to the home-prepared ones.
   - Price of processed, semi-processed or commercially preserved foods.
   - Price paid for the care of children in foster homes and of handicapped or elderly people in institutions.

- Price paid for laundering performed away from home.
- Price of market-produced goods (ready-made clothes, soap, furniture, etc.).

In cases where the household product is not available on the market, the price of a market product fulfilling the same function can be used. This method was used in Nepal (Acharya and Bennett 1981) to determine the value of dried vegetables which are hardly ever sold; they were imputed the value, in the off-season, of the cheapest vegetable which could be used for feeding the household.

3. *Value added* is calculated by deduction of the value of intermediate consumption (including the wages paid to domestic servants). When statistical data on consumers' expenditures are available, they can be used; alternatively they can be collected from the limited sample under investigation, a method which would produce more accurate returns to labour.

4. *Returns to labour* are then calculated by deduction of fixed capital consumption. The same comment on availability of statistical data and on the alternative of collecting data from the sample applies here as for consumers' expenditure (see item 3 above).

5. Returns to labour are then expressed on an *hourly* basis by relating them to the time expended by the household under consideration for performing the activity.

6. *Valuation* is achieved by combining the average hourly returns thus calculated on a limited sample, with time-use data collected on a larger statistical basis.

4.5 Constructing a satellite account of households' non-monetary production

In line with the forthcoming revision of the SNA, it is proposed to present households' non-monetary production in a satellite account. This has several advantages: it leaves untouched the existing time series and the purposes they serve. It enables statistical offices to build up their data bases gradually and to develop valuation methodology compatible with national accounting practice. Satellite accounts are flexible: they can present data in physical and monetary units. The satellite accounts need not be constructed anew every year: frequency can be adjusted to the statistical resources available, thereby reducing the burden of collecting the basic statistical data with sufficient topicality.

An important requirement of the exercise is to preserve the possibility of linking and combining data from the satellite accounts with data from the standard national accounts. Constructing a satellite account requires some adjustment of national accounts data: a further breakdown according to new criteria and reallocation of certain elements. For instance, all non-monetary production has to be presented in the satellite account under two headings: 'accounted for in GNP' and 'not accounted for in GNP'; in order to achieve this, it is necessary to show separately, in the traditional accounts, the non-monetary items they include. It is also necessary to identify separately, in the traditional accounts, the part of households' final consumption and the wages paid to domestic servants, which are to be treated as intermediate consumption in the satellite account. For computing the consumption of fixed capital, the purchases of consumer durables have to be identified separately in the national accounts for many years back (Lützel 1989). For satellite account data to be compatible with traditional accounts data, it is necessary to use in both the same categories and definitions. Further work is needed for matching the classification of activities used in time-budget studies with those used in macro-economic accounting (Chadeau and Roy 1986) or in household budgets (Aldershoff and Kasper 1986).

'All these problems should however not prevent further action', says Heinrich Lützel, Director of the National Accounts Department at the Federal Statistical Office of the Federal Republic of Germany. 'Statistics should react within the scope of its possibilities even if in this field the usual standards cannot be applied for the statistical foundation of the data supplied' (Lützel 1989: 16 – English version).

5. Conclusion

In the present state of the art, the economic measurement of households' non-market production requires action both at the national level and at the international level.

Action at the national level

At the national level, the action required is at first of a political nature. Political determination to include households' own-account production in official statistics and in policy formulation will gradually be achieved as a result of a combination of factors:

● Political pressure as, for instance, that exerted by women's organizations.
● A clear understanding of the economic nature of household productive activities, of their impact on the monetized sectors of the economy and *vice versa*.
● A clear understanding of the benefits to be derived in economic planning and in welfare planning from data on household production.
● The realization that evaluations of household production are feasible and can be achieved without unduly draining the financial resources available for statistical purposes.
● Clarification of miscellaneous items which unduly worry individuals or political circles on the possible consequences of these valuations. For instance, poor households or poor countries may be afraid of appearing less poor with regard to others if the value of their own-account production is

added to their monetary income. As a result, they may fear to lose some of the benefits which accrue from their low ranking in income classifications. The reality is quite different: if own-account production was added to the monetary income of both the rich and the poor, the income gap between them would show to be wider than what it now appears to be. This is because labour productivity in household production is higher in richer households (or in richer countries) because of larger capital investments and of the possibility for them to abandon to the market the least productive tasks (i.e. to buy the corresponding goods or services).

The efficiency of political pressure will be greatly increased if it can lean on solid economic analysis and economic data. Also, political determination may prove more easy to achieve if it is shown that to account for household productive activities will benefit not only women but the whole of society.

In order to go beyond lip-service recognition of household production, tangible commitments to this goal are needed. A first essential commitment is to provide the financial resources required for achieving technical expertise and for undertaking statistical field work. Perhaps some affirmative action would be required for ensuring that funding institutions' programmes include research and field work on the economics of household production.

Action at the international level

At the international level, there is a need for co-ordination. The review of some 110 economic assessments of non-monetary household production performed in industrialized countries (Goldschmidt-Clermont 1982 and 1987a), has shown that data collection and valuation methods used in countries with differing degrees of monetization are very similar, while these countries' differences highlight the weaknesses and advantages of the various methods. Because of such differences and similarities, experience gained in one country in the economic assessment of unpaid household work can be valuable to other countries.

Another outcome of the review is the observation that although several valuations are available, a lack of common definitions seriously hinders their comparability. As a field of research, the economic valuation of households' production suffers from a lack of communication between those involved: valuations were tackled sporadically over the past fifty years by researchers belonging to several disciplines (economics, national accounting, engineering, anthropology, sociology and home economics), by policy-makers, by women's organizations and so on. Their views and results were published in various languages, in numerous journals and reports, which, all too often, are not widely available. None of the standard documentation tools (abstract journals, documentation data bases) covers this wide range of sources. As a result, researchers cannot benefit from experiences made by others and progress is slow.

It would be desirable to maintain regular contact between countries and institutions involved in the economic valuation of households' non-monetary production. Such contacts have already been initiated in a few international workships organized occasionally by different institutions; they ought to be organized on a systematic regular basis.

In order to develop technical expertise in this field, two immediate actions are required at the international level:

- to create a *technical information network* that will facilitate the rapid exchange of experiences and ideas between those involved in the economic assessment of non-monetary household production;
- to convene a *working group of experts* for drafting guide-lines in order to reach common definitions (coverage and categorization of households' activities) and to make recommendations on methodological issues.

Who will pick-up the challenge and act on these two items? International bodies such as the UN Statistical Office, the International Labour Office or the World Bank which have already started showing interest in the field? Or will it be picked up by other bodies, international professional associations, academic institutions or research foundations?

The ball has been set rolling, the future will tell whether this is, once more, an ephemeral effort towards the economic assessment of non-market household production or whether, this time, the necessary steps will be taken for making it a full-member of the economic measurements family.

Component 4: health and social indicators

The first three components of the indicator framework being proposed here have been frankly economistic, components 2 and 3 dealing explicitly with production and component 1 analysing the environment strictly in terms of scarce resources. This fourth component of the framework has two distinct purposes. The first is to continue the economistic analysis by giving, through a Capital Report, as accurate an account as possible of the stocks of physical produce, human and social/organizational capital in order to complete the practical realization of the model of wealth creation which was developed theoretically in Chapter 5.

The second purpose of this section of the framework is to relate the economy to the wider society, to show through a Quality of Life Report the human, ethical and social consequences of economic processes, to fill in the ethical and social dimensions of the human condition that were discussed in Chapters 2 and 3. In a world of cultural diversity it is clear that different societies could choose very different indicators for this part of the framework but, whatever the choice, given the wide scope of the potential subject matter to be covered, and the large number of indicators that might be included in the framework, a difficult trade-off would be between parsimony and completeness. The diversity that could be expected between different societies' choices of social indicators might also help to undermine the ranking of societies against each other by a single criterion, be it GNP per capita, a Human Development Index or whatever.

Making this part of the framework operational could result in some most productive social reflection and political debate, as societies sought to clarify and articulate their own perception of progress, economic and otherwise, and how that progress should be measured. However, whatever the outcome of those debates, there are certain generally valid principles in the construction and use of social indicators which are the distillation of social indicator experience over the past two and a half decades. Ian Miles's paper, starting again from the limitations of GNP, surveys those principles before making some suggestions for a social indicator framework.

Social indicators for real-life economics†

Ian Miles

1 The limits to GNP

For many years the inadequacies of the gross national product (GNP) as a measure of social – or even of more narrowly defined economic – welfare have been trumpeted. It deals with flows and not with stocks (thus it will not capture resource depletion); it deals only with monetized transactions recorded officially (and thus misses the variety of informal economic productive activities); it accepts market values of these activities (and thus counts activities that have negative impacts on the quality of life equally with those whose contributions are positive); it takes no account of economic inequalities (which have historically displayed something of a U-shaped relationship to GNP, although this must be seen to reflect political choices more than any 'iron laws' of economic development); and so on. The points are all valid criticisms of attempts to use GNP to assess welfare or the quality of life.

But GNP itself was not designed to be such a measure, however it may now be used. GNP was intended to be a measure of the scale of the output of the formal economy in a period of time, expressing this quantity in terms of the money valuations accorded it by the market (or by government bureaucracies in the case of state expenditure). Since the meaning of a GNP of a particular size is contingent upon whether this is the product of an economy with a large or small population, it is common to divide GNP data by population size to arrive at per capita GNP (GNPpc) estimates.

Of course, very poor countries display GNPpc levels much below those of the richer countries, and the people of the poorer countries typically suffer far

† The discussion below in large parts (especially the first four sections) draws on that provided by Miles (1985), in which fuller documentation and an extensive bibliography is provided.

greater hardships than their counterparts in the earlier industrialized parts of the world. Many statistical measures – such as life expectancies, literacy levels, and the like, are roughly correlated with GNPpc when cross-country comparisons are made on large samples of nations. For a country that is locked-in competitively to the international trade system in familiar ways, a slowdown in its growth of GNP relative to its competitors is liable to be reflected in problems of unemployment and related problems.

So what GNPpc does measure is in some broad way – or rather, in a complex variety of direct and indirect ways – related to things which we might consider to be aspects of social and economic welfare. Because the GNP concept has evidently now become a welfare or quality of life (QOL) concept, and because there are many instances where the broad correlation between higher GNPpc and improved welfare is empirically reversed, there have been many efforts to go beyond GNP. *Social Indicators* that are more appropriate for assessing aspects of well-being have been the focus of much attention. Such indicators, it is argued, should be useful for guiding and monitoring policies, as well as giving a better basis for assessing the costs and benefits of different strategies of economic (and social and environmental) development.

There have been a great many different approaches to providing an overview of social indicators work. One reason for this is that a great many different issues are being raised by efforts to grasp the rather ill-defined concepts of welfare, well-being and QOL. In part the reason for this is that these concepts are often deployed in contrast to narrowly economic reductions of progress to the accumulation of commodities. Important and contentious ideas, that have been forged in, and which have helped shape, social and political struggles – ideas like equality, equity, freedom, justice, solidarity – are raised here. Since the meaning of these ideas is part of the substance of political debate, it can be no surprise that they have posed a challenge which social scientists have neither been able to ignore, nor to agree upon.

Three main lines of analysis can be distinguished. First, and most prosaic in relation to the big ideas mentioned above, are efforts to modify and improve the GNP. Second, are attempts to produce a QOL alternative to the GNP: two main bodies of work are noteworthy here – combining a diverse set of relevant statistics into a single scale and using subjective indicators such as people's statements about how satisfied or happy they are. Third, are various studies producing social reports which briefly summarize aspects of welfare (but do not attempt to come up with a single statistic to replace the GNP). We will suggest that the first and third of these lines of analysis are of most value; but even so, it will be apparent that there are no quick-and-easy solutions to bring statistics to bear on questions of welfare and QOL. Using GNP has often been treated as such a solution: many of the problems that this raises are sadly encountered again when we consider most of the alternatives that have been offered.

Modified GNP

The GNP has been modified in various ways, involving more-or-less profound relaxation of the assumptions underlying its original definition. These modifications still leave us with a statistic that summarizes affairs in money terms, but typically some of the money values are not those that actual markets have provided. (The 'irregular economy' of tax evasion, some types of – usually 'victimless' – crime, and, especially in many poor countries, street trade, does involve monetary transactions which escape the observations of official statisticians. Efforts to estimate the scale of such activities have to be treated with great caution, and are often based on the flimsiest of assumptions; however, even for western European societies, it seems likely that monetary transactions equivalent to tens of percent of the official GNP figure are escaping record.)

One modification of GNP that is increasingly being used for economic comparisons among countries is based on PPP – purchasing power parity. This is the statistic used by UNDP as one component of its Human Development Index. The PPP notion starts from the fact that the same amount of money (converted to national currency at the going exchange rate) will buy different amounts of goods and services in different countries. In practice, many everyday products can be obtained more cheaply in poorer countries (because wages are lower, in large part), and when correction is made for this there is some reduction in the size of the GNPpc gap between countries.

This modification of GNPpc does move the statistic closer to one that can tell us about the meaning of variations in *average* incomes although, of course, the same average can conceal very different patterns of income distribution. There have been some experimental attempts to combine data on average levels of income and income distributions into a single measure – one attempt, the 'socially weighted real income' statistic, for example, treats a given amount of money as worth more to a poorer person. The precise way in which this is done may be open to debate, but the approach is probably worth more attention than it has so far received.

People's purchasing power is undoubtedly a significant contribution to their welfare, but the things that are omitted from monetary valuation (environmental quality, humane social relationships, etc.) are not always things that money can buy. Indeed, it may be dangerous to try to impute a monetary value to everything – this runs the risk of treating human lives, ancient monuments, unspoilt wilderness areas *as if* they can be treated for all significant purposes as really equivalent to piles of money or stocks of commodities. In practice, when planning procedures have attempted to reduce everything to monetary equivalents in order to produce cost–benefit analyses which can be used in weighing up alternative proposals, they have often floundered on the ideological assumptions implicit in choosing, for example, how to value different people's lives.

Nevertheless, there are some sorts of activity which may be more readily imputed money values, if we are prepared to accept that this is an 'as if' exercise – treating these activities as if they are governed by purchasing power, though in reality they may be also governed by, for example, power relations within the family. Informal production as discussed in this chapter by Goldschmidt-Clermont, and even leisure time have attracted particular attention. Similarly one can attempt to take account of changes in environmental conditions as discussed by Hueting.

For the purposes of comparing levels of economic welfare across countries or over time, some modifications of GNP along these lines is certainly in principle desirable. One can go on to impute monetary values to leisure time (how much could people have been earning if they had chosen to work instead), to take into account variations in the quality of goods and services which may not be captured in their prices and so on. One can take more dramatic steps yet, and subtract whole classes of expenditure from the GNP as representing wasteful and even deleterious activities (for instance, military production). The demonstration effect of such modifications of GNP can be very telling; but different modifications are required for different purposes, and the assumptions that are required to be consistent become more and more dependent on theoretical and political presuppositions. GNP was never designed to be an all-purpose measure of welfare or of progress, and efforts to modify GNP to provide such a measure fall into the trap of expressing everything in money terms – when this way of thinking may well be part of the problem.

Quality of life

Expressing things in money terms has one great advantage: the scale of measurement is a straightforward one, where we can add and subtract units without any concerns as to whether we are mixing up apples and oranges. The world, of course, is composed of apples and oranges, along with some rather more significant distinctions (such as that between guns and butter, which some of the more ambitious efforts to modify GNP do in effect try to treat separately). There are a few other common metrics that can be used to make comparisons in social and economic statistics; for example, human beings are often treated as alike for demographic analysis (or in occupational data, where one also meets with such concepts as the Full-Time Equivalent worker – who may be composed of two part-time workers!); Units of time are also a possible basis for comparison, though the difficulty and cost of generating 'time-budget' data mean that we have relatively few statistics on the time devoted to different activities by different people.

Having a common scale of measurement has the advantage that all sorts of items can be totalled up to form a summary statistic like GNP. The success of economists with GNP led many critics of its limitation as a welfare measure to seek to find ways of coming up with a similar – but more inclusive – summary indicator. Researchers have explored a number of ways of combining data derived from different units of measurement (without first transforming them all into money terms). One approach, used in the US Overseas Development Council's relatively popular Physical Quality of Life Index (the PQLI – Morris 1980) for comparing countries, is to 'stretch' different statistical scales so that their properties become more similar, and then to add them together. In the PQLI three indicators (infant mortality, life expectancy at year one and literacy levels) are each transformed so that the best-performing country's value is expressed as 100, the worst as 0, and others fall between accordingly, then the three are simply added together. The UNDP's Human Development Index, as mentioned earlier in this chapter, combines purchasing power, life expectancy and literacy. Other researchers have adopted different approaches to the same problem, some based on statistical manipulation (normalization of scores, extracting factor analytic scores, etc.), others based on personal evaluation of the relative importance of different indicators.

The problem with all of these approaches is that the new summary statistic remains in important ways very opaque. First, the user needs to refer to background material to be sure as to what discrete measures are being combined together. Second, it is unclear as to whether a change on the summary statistic is due to one or other of the contributing indicators, or to some combination of them, changing. Third, the way in which these indicators has been combined together necessarily assigns some notion of their relative importance to them, yet this is liable to be lost within the final result. Fourth, some of the problems of GNP are still reproduced here; for example, indicators of stocks and inequalities are rarely included within these composite measures, and such factors are so dissimilar from the items which are usually included that it cannot make much sense to attempt to collapse them into a single scale.

These problems have led this author to be very sceptical of the utility of these compound indicators of welfare and quality of life. The general lack of response to various efforts to come up with a new all-purpose measure suggests I am not alone in this, although I would not rule out the usefulness of, say, measures derived from factor analysis, for comparing countries or regions in terms of other concepts; for instance, if we are interested in assessing the level of industrialization, it may be more appropriate to use some composite of statistics such as the size of the industrial workforce and the value of industrial output, than to rely on any one of these figures (which are all fairly clearly assessing different aspects of a relatively narrowly defined thing).

There are also reasons to be sceptical about claims that the best measures of welfare and QOL are those based on 'subjective indicators'. Subjective indicators are based on attitude survey-type answers to questions about how happy or satisfied people are, for instance, or where they place their societies or their own lives on a scale ranging from the best to the worst possible.

Such an approach is superficially alluring. Rather than relying on experts, why not ask ordinary people to assess their QOL? But what question should one be asking? Answers to questions about overall satisfaction with one's life and with one's society may diverge (it seems that people are less prepared, incidentally, to confess dissatisfaction about things that are 'close to home' to other people, and even to themselves). Answers to questions about one's general happiness and one's experiences of feeling good and bad may diverge. Some questions are dealing with beliefs, some with feelings, some with aspirations, and so on. There is no clear case for choosing one measure above another as *the* welfare indicator; and there is no magic solution provided by subjective indicators to the problem that variations in experiences across a society can be lost when expressing things as averages. People's judgements, as expressed in such subjective measures, may be heavily influenced by factors such as the information that is available to them, the comparisons that they feel are appropriate to make, and other such factors. At the extreme, we might fantasize that objective circumstances could go to hell, as long as people continued to feel good (perhaps by consuming tranquillizers!)

There remains much research to be done as to the relationships between objective and subjective indicators. Statistics dealing with people's attitudes and beliefs surely contribute to a comprehensive account of social trends. But the conclusion must be that the search for an all-purpose welfare indicator in these statistics is doomed to failure.

Social accounts and social reports

Despite many approaches to the modification of GNP, some of which have provided more or less useful statistical innovations, they have not resulted in, and cannot result in, any single indicator which can do for welfare or QOL comparisons the sort of thing which GNP has achieved for economic output. Social indicators research has turned away from efforts to create such a rival to GNP, although modifications of GNP for specific purposes are still being developed.

Is it possible to come up with a useful statistical tool which does not fall prey to the criticisms launched against GNP? One approach is to build *accounting models* relating together different activities; perhaps the most prominent example of this, one that has been gaining a foothold in development planning in recent years, is the Social Accounting Matrix (SAM). This is restricted to monetary data in present versions, but it goes beyond conventional economic accounts in integrating the income and expenditure of different sorts of household (in different regions, different income groups, etc.), and thus allows for analysis of inequalities and the distribution of the economic gains of economic development strategies. It is possible that in the future the SAM will be further developed so as to incorporate informal production activities and their outputs, which several statisticians are also currently trying to integrate into economic accounts. However, even then it will still be vulnerable to criticisms along the lines of those launched at the GNP of reducing everything to monetary values – or of only dealing with those factors which can readily be considered in this way.

The SAM, then, is more like a better economic accounting system than a set of social accounts, let alone more general welfare or QOL accounts. More 'social' accounts include systems based on demographic flows (people's entrances and exits between states such as childhood, education, employment, unemployment, retirement and death), and rather elaborate systems based on measures of time use. These are still essentially experimental approaches; while they may prove to be powerful ways of modelling and thus of understanding and forecasting social change, they are complex and extremely hungry for data, and are not at all easy for non-experts to apply. However, there are some interesting developments underway in rendering population models in a form suitable for lay users to run on home microcomputers. In the future, it might well be that we could all access large data bases and a range of modelling tools – perhaps provided on CD-ROM – for use on powerful home computers. Alternative models could be deployed, and the assumptions and forecasts of planners comprehensively investigated in a way that is currently uncommon.

One interesting statistical summary that derives from the philosophy of these accounting approaches, but which is relatively less demanding of costly data, and which is relatively easy to interpret is the Active Life Profile (ALP). For a given social group in a given society, the ALP presents a picture of a kind of 'average life' – the duration of so many years is divided up into time devoted to sleep, formal work, informal work, illness and so on (Seers 1982). The ALP has only been used to a limited extent, but it does demonstrate that there is considerable scope for summarizing varied data in simple formats (without trying to compress everything into a single measure). Nevertheless, all of these accounting approaches are at one remove from welfare or QOL indicators: they describe people's behaviour, and the results of these activities are only captured in so far as they mean periods of recorded illness, of schooling and so on.

In contrast to social accounting stands *social reporting*. Here the goal is rather less ambitious; instead of linking a range of indicators together into an accounting model (which necessarily means restricting oneself to a limited set of indicators that can be related together in quantitative ways), and instead of trying to combine indicators together into one new summary measure, it is accepted that social life is so multi-dimensional, so rich, that it can only be illuminated (and even then only partly illuminated) by presenting different statistics alongside each other.

Social reports, such as Britain's annual *Social Trends*, are volumes that typically present statistics on major areas of social life – population change, economic affairs, work and employment, education, health and social services, crime and so on – in the form of tables, charts and graphs. Over the last twenty years, social reports have become institutionalized by the official statisticians of many countries. They generally claim to provide a well-rounded picture of social life, although the topics which they omit are significant (for instance, there is rarely much on the state's repressive activities, on civil liberties, on elite groups and on the structure of social and political power).

Nevertheless, they are extremely useful reference sources for journalists, policy-makers, researchers and others interested in social change.

Social reports do not pretend to provide a simple summary of welfare or QOL. But it is usually more or less explicitly suggested that they provide information on all of those aspects of these concerns that can be expressed statistically. As hinted above, there is reason to take issue with this, but the contribution of existing social reports to social knowledge cannot be denied. The problem is that their very size and comprehensiveness makes it a daunting task to try to extract any succinct view of what the imporant developments *vis-à-vis* social and economic progress might be. The better social reports do often contain commentaries on particular aspects of social change, or of the circumstances of specific social groups, in which certain statistics are explicated and/or amplified upon by a background essay. These are usually of studied 'neutrality'.

The challenge of producing something more like an effort to tot up costs and benefits of social trends, or a more selective social report which highlights human and ecological well-being, is one that has rarely been taken up, although an exception is the series of reports produced by the Netherlands Social and Cultural Ministry (see Ester and Nauta 1986; Mootz 1989). Sixteen variables intended to describe aspects of QOL – three to do with each of housing, health, spending power, leisure and employment, together with one educational statistic – were derived from a triennial Level of Living Survey. In much the manner described in the third section (see pp. 286ff.) (with all the problems discussed there), a single measure of well-being was derived by combining these statistics on the basis of a statistical technique (principal components analysis) which essentially assesses how far they are correlated together in the population. The Planning Office has presented results in terms of trends over time for different subgroups of the population.

Using social indicators

Only a massive compendium of statistics is going to be anything like adequate to provide information on all aspects of QOL for which statistics are available. The very size of such a compendium will doubtless appear threatening to many would-be users.

But such social reports already exist, at least in shorter versions. The task must now be to outline how a set of key indicators for assessing the ultimate outputs of social development for QOL might be identified and best presented. The matter of presentation will be taken up first, since it is more than a secondary issue. After all, the intention is to provide statistical information that can be readily understood and deployed, and where the scope for confusion or misunderstanding is minimized. However, it should be borne in mind that distinct sets of data, presented in different ways, may be more appropriate for specific types of user and types of application – even if a core of data is of wide relevance, a general-purpose QOL report is improbable, since we are liable to want slightly different sorts of information to consider, for instance, changes over time, to make cross-country comparisons, to examine the circumstances of minorities, and so on.

What sort of statistics? Averages, inequalities, thresholds

In discussing the GNP we noted that it deals with total output, and that GNP per capita figures provide us with an estimate of the average output for each member of an economy – providing no information as to the distribution of the benefits of economic activity. While averages are readily understood, however, this is not generally the case for summary measures of the level of equality or inequality of the distribution of a variable – such as the standard deviation, the Gini index, and so on. Following Galtung and Wirak (1977), a third sort of measure may often provide a useful summary: data may be presented in terms of the percentages of a population (or of major groups within the population) who are above or below a particular criterion point on a social indicator. Thus, instead of simply recording average income levels or the extent of inequality (succinct measures of the latter often proving quite difficult to grasp), we should identify the proportion of the population who fall below a poverty line.

For many aspects of welfare and QOL, such an approach can be valuable. Social progress can be measured in terms of the proportion of people falling above or below certain minimum standards. (One could go on to add maximum standards, too.) The problem then becomes one of establishing what these standards are. A 'poverty line' in Britain, in the past, for example, has often been taken to be the level of income a household would receive if on social assistance. But this is merely a level of income support determined by political fiat, and it would be preferable to work in terms of the level of income required to gain access to a quantity of goods and services sufficient to enable a healthy and unstressed life. (Ill-health and stress may be caused by other aspects of one's living conditions and life-style – an income indicator of the sort proposed is simply relevant to whether or not income is the source of one's having little choice in this matter.)

But averages and inequalities may still be important features of the quality of life. (For one thing, substantial differences among people in resources implies an unequal distribution of social power, i.e. ability to influence the direction of future development.) Data on the proportions of people below certain minima can tell us about the extent to which an economy is failing to deliver basic requirements to its members. But this proportion could remain unchanged while absolute inequality changed dramatically; for instance, the number of people below a poverty line might stay fixed at 20 per cent, say, but at the same time the difference between the richest and the poorest 20 per cent could have doubled.

The solution for usable presentation of indicators might be to provide all data in the detailed tables of a QOL report in distributional form. The report would highlight summary information on (1) average levels (2) the proportion of the population falling above or beneath key thresholds, and where relevant (3) similar information on the circumstances of specific social groups (ethnic minorities, women, regional populations, etc.). But the reader would be able to turn to background tables to examine the distribution of the population on the variable in question, which would make it possible to experiment, for instance, with different social minima or maxima, and which would make comparisons over time or between countries more meaningful.

In the discussion above we have concentrated on indicators that are relevant to individual members of the population. Some social indicators concern the collectivity rather than individuals; for instance, some statistics describe the properties or actions of social institutions or political regimes, and it makes little sense to relate these to individual members of the population. (For instance, 'concentration of media ownership per capita' or 'degree of match between voting patterns and parliamentary representation per capita' do not make very much sense.) Some commentators argue that such *global indicators* are not really appropriate QOL or welfare data, since they do not describe the circumstances of individual human beings; but in so far as the factors they describe are highly relevant to individuals, this argument (which might also lead to the exclusion of data on some classes of environmental problem) is unconvincing. Global indicators, in any case, are unlikely to pose questions of representing distributions, but since they are so dependent on institutional arrangements, they may be difficult to present in comparable terms across countries.

What set of indicators?

Certain types of statistic have cropped up again and again in discussions of QOL and welfare indicators. Even in the absence of a commonly-agreed-upon theory of human needs and welfare, the same types of item recur – educational levels, health, housing, income and expenditure, leisure time and activities (sometimes including cultural and voluntary sector activities), nutrition, political participation, quality of working life, social security (both financial and in terms of security from threats of crime and other violence). In part the selection of 'non-economic' factors reflects the organization of modern states – with their health services, ministries of education, housing departments and so on. This is not altogether unreasonable – the existence of these state bodies in turn derives in part from the expression of social needs, and demands for their satisfaction, from social movements. But in part these agencies reflect the self-interests of states, their bureaucracies, and the elite interests to whom they pay most attention. The statistics they tend to generate derive from their operating procedures in many instances, so that measures of welfare are often really statistics on *problems* as they are recognized by the state agencies (e.g. cases of illness, of homelessness, etc. that have been encountered).

An alternative approach is to group indicators less according to institutional concerns (though we should always remember that some separation of policy areas is bound to be required in practice), than according to an explicit view of what constitutes social progress. For instance, we can build on ideas originally formulated by Johan Galtung, and developed by Irvine and Miles (1982), who proposed a fourfold grouping of aspects of welfare. These are presented (with slightly different terminology) in Table 8.2 in terms of both positive and negative directions of development, of human needs and capabilities, and of the circumstances which facilitate or reduce them.

Table 8.2   Dimensions of welfare

Aspects of well-being (both 'needs' and 'capabilities')	*Material requirements* (both positive and negative)
HEALTH (versus DISEASE) physical well-being, ability to use bodily resources and basic psychological capacities	Access to food, shelter, water, basic goods Absence of disease and health-endangering conditions such as pollution
SURVIVAL (versus VULNERABILITY) low vulnerability, ability to plan	Access to resources (means of production, social security, etc.) Absence of violent disruption and threat to life and livelihood
AUTONOMY (versus CONSTRAINT) efficacy, ability to choose	Access to means of social and geographical mobility, to education and media communication Absence of repression, pressures to conformity
IDENTITY (versus ALIENATION) mental well-being, sense of self, ability to relate to self and others	Access to cultural facilities, to social support Absence of alienating social conditions

Reflecting points made earlier, we would suggest that indicators describing lack of welfare are more common than those describing positive developments, but that we will often be able to identify indicators dealing with circumstances that may promote or hinder the development of welfare.

Such broad categories are open to various interpretations, as demonstrated in the variety of implementations of a similar typology in Miles and Irvine (1982), reflecting slightly different theoretical and political orientations on the part of the various researchers. A QOL report has to avoid giving the impression that the indicators it includes are exhaustive of the meaning of terms like health, autonomy and so on. It should *open* the debate about these categories, and encourage more people to explore more ways of monitoring them, more ways of identifying and examining progress and/or problems.

Many candidate indicators can be proposed. Different sets of indicators may be appropriate for different sets of comparisons. Gross inequalities between rich and poor countries, in particular, are brought out by statistics that often say very little that is meaningful about differences across the richer countries only; for instance, such indicators of health-enabling living conditions as (1) daily diet expressed as a proportion of the WHO recommended calories per day and (2) percentage of population with access to safe drinking water; of survival circumstances as (3) levels of homelessness and geographical displacements due to refugee status or calamities; of circumstances relevant to autonomy as (4) secondary school enrolment ratios (5) availability of radios and/or TVs, and (6) literacy levels. (Where identity-relevant measures are concerned, interestingly, the same indicators would generally seem to be applicable across rich and poor countries – the problem is more likely to be non-production of relevant data for most of the Third World.).

It will be already apparent that the choice of a set of indicators involves a great many decisions as to how we understand social affairs. For example, if schooling is understood to be more of an institution of repression than of real education, then the availability of schooling will hardly increase the scope for autonomy; similar challenges may be levelled against many other 'institutional' indicators. Since we have few adequate measures of the 'output' of such institutions – literacy levels may discriminate among rich and poor countries, but tell us little about variations within the rich world – it is necessary to confront such problems, to be open to debate as to the decisions one makes. The use of a range of indicators of different aspects of each QOL category at least gives more chance of finding statistics on which broad agreement can be obtained.

Table 8.3 illustrates a range of indicators for each of the four QOL categories. The list is intended to be indicative rather than exhaustive, and is based upon the statistics presented by Miles and Irvine (1982), who set out to document trends in the United Kingdom, with much attention to disaggregation by social groups, drawing on a variety of unofficial sources as well as on official statistics. Some of these indicators are more relevant to comparisons over time, over groups within a country, or across countries (e.g. average height of the adult population may be influenced by the ethnic composition of a population).

The set of indicators shown in Table 8.3 is proposed as a starting point rather than the conclusion of analysis. Is the imbalance in suggestions across areas a product of lack of imagination or lack of available statistics? Are there more coherent groupings, within the broad categories, which can be used to relate the indicators to more conventional policy areas and allow us to move beyond simply counterposing trends on these indicators to developments in

Table 8.3   Illustrative quality-of-life indicators

Health

1. *Measures of health outputs:* perinatal mortality rates; rate of premature births; malformation rates in newborn; life expectancy at year one; average height of adult population; reported morbidity and long-standing illness; incidence of total tooth loss; level of occupational diseases, and of ill-health reasons for absenteeism from work; morbidity; causes of death and mortality ratios for major causes of death.
2. *Measures of health service inputs:* doctors, midwives per capita; hospital beds available for surgical cases; length of waiting lists for surgery.
3. *Social circumstances threatening to health:* percentage of population below poverty level; percentage of population homeless and/or without shelter at or above minimum standards; proportion of dwellings (or people living in dwellings) lacking indoor toilets and baths.
4. *Nutrition:* consumption of various foodstuffs; composition of daily diet in terms of minerals, vitamins, protein, roughage, fats, sugar, etc. (related to recommended levels); estimates of adult and infant mortality generated by own and maternal consumption of alcohol, cigarettes, etc.
5. *Environmental circumstances:* local atmospheric pollution levels (smoke, sulphur dioxide, etc.); estimates of pollution and noise levels caused by motor vehicles; noise and other pollution at work-places.

Survival

1. *Physical security:* violent and/or accidental deaths by cause (especially as related to transport accidents (and whether e.g. pedestrian, driver), occupational accidents, murder, manslaughter and infanticide; experience of violent assault.
2. *Economic security:* unemployment levels (especially distinguishing long-term unemployment); amount of discretionary income; proportion of jobs with provisions for (a) sick leave (b) maternity/paternity leave (more than minimum duration); amount of personal wealth (disposable assets).

Autonomy

1. *Social mobility:* relation between own and parent's occupational status, and other measures of occupational mobility; measures of occupational segregation by sex, ethnicity, etc; job mobility (e.g. change of employers in the past year); levels of education attained.
2. *Availability of free time:* paid holiday entitlements; holidays away from home; distribution of time between paid work, unpaid work, and leisure pursuits (ideally we should be able to correct for involuntary 'leisure' experienced by unemployed people); availability of part-time jobs at adequate pay levels.
3. *Reproductive freedom:* availability of day-care centres for pre-school children (may need to be indexed merely by the proportion of such children using such centres); births to women under 20 years of age; availability of contraceptive and abortion facilities.
4. *Institutionalization:* imprisonment of people awaiting trial; institutionalization of elderly and marginalized groups.
5. *Access to means of communication and transport:* ownership of various durables and facilities (including telephones, motor cars, televisions); availability of transport (e.g. an indicator that would represent the proportion of a person's income that

(continued on next page)

Table 8.3 — *continued*

would be required to purchase transport over a certain distance, whether by public or private transport according to national or local circumstances); number of libraries of different kinds; concentration of ownership of press and other media.
6. *Political autonomy:* voluntary participation in elections; numbers of political prisoners and prisoners of conscience (e.g. conscientious objectors); dominance of elites (e.g. those educated in particular schools) in, social mobility into, major public institutions (judiciary, senior civil service, etc.); levels of surveillance of population (telephone-tapping, letter-opening, personal data in databanks, police records, records of creditworthiness).

Identity

---

1. *Self-destructive impulses:* suicide and parasuicide levels; self-destructive consumption (opiates, cigarettes, alcohol, etc.); psychiatric hospitalizations connected with drug and alcohol abuse.
2. *Interpersonal violence:* murder and manslaughter; victimization related to suspected offender (can be used to develop indicators of family violence); fatal and serious assaults upon children by parents, assaults occasioning serious injury; crimes of violence, rape, etc.
3. *Psychiatric problems:* prescriptions of tranquillizers and related psychotropic drugs; rates of admission to psychiatric hospitals.
4. *Opportunities for growth:* levels of self-reported job satisfaction; proportions of skilled and professional jobs in labour force (or jobs offering 'fulfilling' features, as defined by job complexity and skill measures); subjective measures of quality of life (preferably not simplistic assessments of satisfaction or happiness); levels of active membership in voluntary organizations.

Source: Miles and Irvine 1982

the GNP and towards relating these trends to the style of economic growth that is being pursued?

It could be worthwhile to bring the Irvine and Miles study up to date, and take up the challenge posed by their selection of indicators. It is likely, however, that the overall conclusions reached in that study will be more than reinforced by extending analysis to the 1980s. They reported for the 1970s generally, though not universally, positive trends for the first two categories, but much more mixed trends on those indicators selected to cover the latter two QOL areas.

Conclusions

The search for a single indicator of progress is misguided. Social reality is too complex for it to make any sense to collapse its manifold dimensions into a one-dimensional scale. Indeed, this point is at the heart of many criticisms of the GNP.

The act of weighing up different components of social change to form an overall assessment of whether developments are on balance progressive or otherwise in respect of a broad set of concerns like 'health' or 'autonomy' is likewise something that cannot be reduced to a technical exercise. The evaluations involved are necessarily value-laden and political ones. This does not mean that they should not be made; but it does mean that they are contestable, and should be explicit. If an argument about social change is a good one, it can be strenthened by appropriate presentation of the individual statistics on which it is based, and allowing users to draw their own conclusions.

In Irvine and Miles (1982) the four categories chosen for their Quality of Life (QOL) Report on Britain, together with the associated indicators, were:

1. *Security*
   Physical: Life expectancy, accidental death, homicide.
   Economic: Unemployment, poverty, distribution of wealth, home-
               lessness.

2. *Welfare*
   Ownership of durables, pollution, accidents, stress at work (absenteeism), shift-work, malformation of babies, disease/illness, tooth-loss, nutrition, housing conditions.

3. *Identity*
   Suicide, alcohol/drug abuse, loneliness, psychiatric medication, mental hospital admissions, sexual/family violence, vandalism, job-satisfaction.

4. *Freedom*
   Freedom to: distribution of wealth, social/geographic mobility, equality of opportunity (e.g. education), gender discrimination (e.g. in work, education), leisure time, access to libraries, access to contraception/abortion facilities.
   Freedom from: official surveillance (e.g. telephone tapping), imprisonment, restrictive institutionalization (e.g. old people's homes).

It is striking how these categories and indicators, and those in Miles's paper based on Health, Survival, Autonomy and Identity, mesh with both the earlier discussion of human needs (Ch. 7) and Hueting's eight components of welfare (p. 257). They provide useful insights into the ethical and social dimensions of human life to complement the indicators of production.

Complementary to the QOL Report would be a Capital Report based on the four capital framework of wealth creation developed in Chapter 5. An outline of what this might entail is given below.

1. *Ecological capital*
   Covered in environmental and resource accounts (component 1).

2. *Human capital*
   Variety of health indicators, educational attainment, levels of training and skills, absenteeism from work, entrepreneurship, inventiveness and creativity (patents, scientific discovery, artistic activity).

3. *Organizational capital*

Business: profitability, industrial relations (days lost through strike action, management style, co-determination), co-operatives, employee stock ownership plans, training programmes, equal opportunities for women and ethnic minorities, parental leave, community programmes.

Government, law: participation in elections, representativeness of electoral results, representation of women and minorities, subsidiarity (decisions taken at lowest appropriate level), freedom of information, technological assessment and choice, access to the legal system, fair legal processes, freedom from official surveillance and harrassment, guarantee of human rights.

Family: divorce, lone-parent households, single person households, proportion of children living with both parents, extended families.

Community: loneliness, neighbourhood safety, racial harrassment, neighbourly help proffered or expected, frequency of change of residence.

4. *Physical capital*

Infrastructure: railways, roads, airports, cycleways, footpaths, pedestrian areas; water and sewerage; energy supply and efficiency; schools, universities, polytechnics; hospitals; health centres; communication media (concentration of ownership, variety and public access).

Buildings: homes, offices, factories.

Technology: new technologies, resource-saving technologies (materials intensity of GNP).

Investment: depreciation.

Both the Quality of Life Report and the Capital Report are important to put the production accounts in perspective. Production which is a net consumer of capital is not sustainable; production which does not contribute widely to quality of life is hardly related to social welfare. The Quality of Life Report, especially, is likely to vary greatly between cultures. The process of introspection and political debate to establish such a report could be a most valuable exercise in social self-awareness, seeking to define value, progress and development for the society in question and thus wrenching these concepts from the grip of productionism and the tyranny of GNP.

To summarize, then, what is being suggested here is a four-component indicator framework for economic and broader social progress:

1. Environmental and resource accounts, in physical units.
2. An Adjusted National Product, comprising NNP *less* natural capital

depreciation *less* defensive expenditures *less* the expenditures necessary to reach environmental sustainability standards.
3. A household production account.
4. A social indicator framework, comprising a Capital Report and a Quality of Life Report.

These statistics would, of course, also be supplemented by the other economic statistics which are regularly computed: inflation and unemployment rates, balance of payments and so on.

The framework that emerges retains production statistics as an important component, although it modifies GDP to approach more nearly the concept of Hicksian (or sustainable) income on the one hand; and includes non-monetary production on the other. However, it relates production both to the ecological base which supports it and on which it impacts; and to the wider society the benefit of which is here taken to be the purpose of economic activity in the first place. It should be clear that the framework seeks to be objective, describing the observable economic and social welfare of the society rather than the well-being of its members, which is taken to be a subjective experience with no constant relationship to external conditions.

The advantages of the described framework are self-evident. Most importantly, it once again *embeds* the economy – to use Karl Polanyi's (1944) famous phrase – in society and in nature. It allows an overview of economic progress based on a sophisticated and realistic definition of what it is an economy is meant to achieve. Moreover, for those who are so addicted to a single indicator that nothing else will do, it provides an adjusted product indicator of far more relevance to real product than NNP. But it is hoped that increasingly production would be seen and quoted in the context of the framework as a whole in which it is one and only one aspect of complex real-life economic welfare.

The second concluding point about this framework is that it is feasible. In most industrial countries at least the statistics for its first, rudimentary operation already exist. Several governments are already putting parts of it into practice, or have detailed research projects to do so. There is already a wealth of relevant, extant social and environmental data. In these countries, then, a determined programme of research and public debate could yield an operational framework within two or three years, with, of course, plenty of scope for subsequent refinements.

In Third World countries more of the necessary statistical base would have to be set up from scratch, but if this became a prime area for inter-governmental co-operation, useful results would be achieved in a few years rather than a decade. Many knowledgeable voices are already calling for better environmental and social statistics, so this is far from being an unusual suggestion. What is unusual is the call for the statistics to be incorporated into a coherent framework, which will enable their development to proceed in a more logical fashion; and the perception that the decision about which statistics to produce should be taken on the basis of profound debate in the society concerned, about the economic and social priorities to be pursued. They should not be handed down by the World Bank or the United Nations Statistical Office. In a diverse world, progress can and does mean different things to different peoples. One of the initial benefits of implementing this framework will be the public discussion of what it is the economy is trying to achieve, of what it, and human life generally, is all about. Transfixed by the ideology of production, growth and development, most societies have simply forgotten how to ask such questions. It is time to relearn, to break free of economism and democratize the definition of progress. Making this indicator framework operational would get the process underway.

From macro to micro

So far the discussion on indicators has remained at the society-wide macro level. But economic decisions have also to be taken at a micro level, to guide which indicators of outcomes at that level are required. The standard indicator used, of course, is the result of cost–benefit analysis.

For situations in which all costs and benefits of a course of action are clearly identifiable and relate to marketed or marketable goods with defined prices, cost–benefit analysis would appear to be a reasonable technique. However, most of the argument in this book has suggested that such situations are very much the exception rather than the rule.

There are, of course, ways in which 'shadow pricing', or contingent valuation, can enable non-monetary preferences to be included in a cost–benefit analysis. But even so cost–benefit analysis has a defintely limited application. The next paper concludes this chapter by describing a different analytical technique, positional analysis, through which many of the concerns which led to the construction of the macro-indicator framework can be expressed at the micro level.

Development: evaluation and decision-making

Peter Söderbaum

Mainstream neoclassical economics tends to suggest specific ideas of progress in society and business. Neoclassical economics also suggests specific approaches to decision-making and evaluation for society at large and at the level of individual organizations. These approaches are not neutral from a valuational point of view. They are, rather, value-laden in specific ways and economics is always political economics, as has been pointed out by Gunnar Myrdal among others, whose discussion of how values, ideology and socio-cultural factors influence our work as scholars is a case in point.

Values are always with us. Disinterested research there never has been and never can be. Prior to answers there must be questions. There can be no view except from a viewpoint. In the question raised the viewpoint has been chosen and the valuation implied.

(Myrdal 1978: 778–9)

Science that is objective in every sense is simply not possible.

The imperative of paradigmatic pluralism

Thus an attitude of pluralism in relation to different scientific and other perspectives seems called for. Instead of dogmatism, an open-minded attitude and a dialogue between proponents of various schools of thought seems more relevant. As a philosopher of science, Bruce Caldwell speaks about methodological pluralism, in the sense 'that no universally applicable, logically compelling method of theory appraisal exists' (Caldwell 1982: 245). Similarly, paradigmatic pluralism can be a fruitful attitude for practising economists hoping to contribute to their discipline (Norgaard 1989; Söderbaum 1990a). By this I mean open-mindedness on the part of economists (1) in relation to perspectives and traditions outside science (assuming that some kind of borderline can be drawn between science and non-science), (2) in relation to other disciplines, for example other social sciences and (3) in relation to schools of thought within economics other than the preference of the individual scholar.

An attitude of paradigmatic pluralism is very different from the idea of exclusive reliance on one theory and one truth for each area of economic study, such as consumer behaviour, entrepreneurial behaviour, international trade and so on. Especially in the social sciences, some complementarity of different perspectives on specific areas of study can be expected. As individual scholars we certainly have our own preferences for specific theories, but these should be compared systematically with competing theories, and competing theories are seldom completely worthless.

Paradigmatic pluralism can also be interpreted as a strategy for scientific endeavour. For each sub-area, such as concept of economics, development view, approach to decision-making, and so on, the scholar can systematically compare the contributions of different valuational standpoints. In this paper such a strategy will be followed.

Democracy and collective decision-making

Before we proceed to a discussion about views of development and approaches to decision-making, a word should be said about the imperatives of democracy. In my judgement, discussion of approaches to decision-making should not be reduced to a technical issue, where the analyst is expected to proceed stepwise in a particular manner to a position at which he suggests some specific alternative as the optimal one, and where the decision-maker is expected to listen to his advice.

In an attempt to reconsider this simple model of the relationship between analyst, the study that he or she carries out, and the decision-maker, I think that two facts of life have to be taken into account. First, in many cases of collective decision-making there is more than one decision-maker and decision-makers differ among themselves with respect to values and views of development. This is true, for instance, of a political assembly making decisions by majority voting. In this case politicians belong to different political parties. Each party and even each politician has been elected on the basis of a specific ideology or set of values. It can be argued, therefore, that the analyst should come up with an information base which is of use to decision-makers whose values differ. A way to proceed in this situation is to suggest conditional conclusions. Assuming values or an ideology of type B, then alternative A1 tends to be preferable among the alternatives considered. With an ideology of type C, alternative A3 is the best choice.

Second, in the case of collective decision-making, whether at the societal level or in business, the issue of participation and open access to information by those affected has to be considered. In a democracy, there is a value in participation as such, but there is also an expectation that decisions will generally be improved by an exchange of views and information with those affected by the decision, in the sense that more will be known about possible valuational standpoints, alternative courses of action and impacts. The analyst will normally learn from this kind of communication, just as he can learn from a discussion with decision-makers.

It is important that those affected and the decision-makers feel that their interests have somehow been considered in the document submitted to the latter. They may look at the way ideologies are articulated as part of the mentioned conditional conclusions or at the ways impacts on different groups and interests have been described, short-run impacts versus long-run impacts and so on. A many-sided analysis in these respects therefore seems preferable from the point of view of a working democracy.

Assuming that we are dealing with a complex decision situation rather than a simple one, preparing the way for the decision is a process of learning for the analyst and for all others involved. Contrary to the conventional view, this learning process also involves the learning of and reconsideration of values or ideologies. To the extent that journalists inform the public about the issue at its different stages, the opportunities to learn and take a stand are extended to new groups. In a sense the issue is processed in society at large. From the point of view of democracy this is a good thing, since in every society and on every issue there are normally forces that wish to avoid public debate.

From monetary reductionism to a holistic idea of economics

The history of exploitation of natural resources and other environmental deterioration indicates that something is wrong with the objectives, approaches to decision-making and accounting practices which are advocated by mainstream economists and which our societies have relied upon. Reliance on monetary control instruments does not seem enough in view of the many failures that have occurred and the difficulties ahead of us. Just as the aeroplane pilot needs more than one kind of instrument to manage his aircraft, something similar may hold for business leaders, politicians, bureaucrats and indeed anyone who cares about societal development.

In terms of the categories suggested by von Wright it can be argued that neoclassical economics is of a reductionist kind (von Wright 1986). More precisely, it is a case of monetary reductionism. It should be made clear that von Wright says that reductionist strategies in scientific work have often been successful. It is rather the one-track character or one-sidedness of the approach that is questioned. According to von Wright, especially the environmental problems now facing humankind call for a broader and more holistic approach.

In this more holistic conception of economics, non-monetary impacts (e.g. changes in the state or 'position' of natural resources) are as 'economic' as monetary impacts (Söderbaum 1986, 1987). A distinction can then be made between four categories of economic impacts (Table 8.4).

Table 8.4 Four categories of economic impact

	Flows (referring to periods of time)	*Positions (referring to points in time)*
Monetary	I	II
Non-monetary	III	IV

In addition to the previous discussion between monetary and non-monetary impacts, a distinction is made in Table 8.4 between impacts that relate to periods of time (flows) and those that refer to points in time (positions or states). The term 'position' is preferred to 'stock' because the word 'stock' tends to be interpreted narrowly as stored entities of a homogeneous kind. Position refers not only to the quantitative but also to the qualitative state or status of various objects of description.

Category I is exemplified by GNP, which is expressed in monetary terms for a year (i.e. a specific period of time). A monetary position is exemplified by the assets or debts of a firm at a particular point in time (cf. category II). The input of mercury from a pulp factory to a nearby lake exemplifies a non-monetary flow, whereas parts per million (ppm) of mercury found in fish of a particular kind at a particular place exemplifies a non-monetary position.

Table 8.4 can be used to make our arguments more explicit:

1. The reductionist idea of one-dimensional analysis in monetary terms is rejected in favour of a multi-dimensional view. In addition to monetary analysis (of a partial kind), a systematic analysis of objectives, estimated impacts and accounting in non-monetary terms is recommended.

2. Where non-monetary analysis is concerned, not only flow variables but also positional variables are of importance. These two kinds of variable are of course related, as in the case of mercury pollution referred to. The higher the discharges over a given period, a flow variable, the higher the level of mercury in fish at the end of the period, a positional variable.

Considering that much economic analysis has been an analysis in terms of flows (and more specifically monetary flows), it seems vital to point to the importance of keeping an eye on non-monetary positions. A specified reduction in mercury discharges to a nearby lake (e.g. from 300 kg per year to 200 kg per year), is an improvement in the sense that 200 kg is less than 300 kg, but 200 kg annually may still lead to further deterioration in positional terms, that is a higher level of mercury in fish. If the objective is to reduce the level of mercury in fish in ppm terms, a more radical reduction in discharges may be needed (e.g. from 300 to 30 kg).

In his classic article 'The Economics of the Coming Spaceship Earth', Kenneth Boulding argues strongly that stocks (or positions in my vocabulary) are more important than flows in economic analysis:

> The essential measure of the success of the economy is not production and consumption at all, but the nature, extent, quality, and complexity of the total capital stock, *including in this the state of the human bodies and minds included in the system.* In the spaceman economy, what we are primarily concerned with is stock maintenance, and any technological change which results in the maintenance of a given total stock with a lessened throughput (that is less production and consumption) is clearly a gain. This idea that both production and consumption are bad things rather than good things is very strange to economists, who have been obsessed with the income-flow concepts to the exclusion, almost, of capital stock concepts.
>
> (Boulding 1966: 9, emphasis added)

3. Just as non-monetary flows were related to non-monetary positions in the above argument, it is also possible to discuss relationships between monetary and non-monetary variables. Assuming that costs and benefits are different, benefit/cost ratios may be related to a number of environmental indicators in positional terms.

A benefit–cost ratio of 1.5 may, for instance, be compared to a ratio of 'only' 1.1. The state of the environment is the same at the beginning of the period in the two cases. What will the position be at the end of the period with respect to various environmental positional indicators? Whether the higher ratio will lead to more or less degradation of the environment according to different indicators depends on such things as the composition of the costs and benefits in the two cases, technology, institutional arrangements etc. (cf. Söderbaum 1980). The important point here is that analysis has been broadened from an exclusive reliance on one variable to thinking in terms of multi-dimensional impact profiles.

4. Using GNP as a proxy for welfare corresponds to a GNP growth ideology. The articulation of ideologies, i.e. conceptual frameworks and means–ends relationships, that represent alternatives to the GNP growth ideology, for instance some versions of the sustainability idea or eco-development or ecological ethics (e.g. Söderbaum 1982) will facilitate the attempt to design schemes of environmental and social indicators. Such an alternative ideology will also validate the use of alternatives to cost–benefit analysis.

In a similar manner the business concepts of entrepreneurs may be extended from profit objectives to strategies concerning environmental aspects of their operations and further to social relationships and network building. Audits that take account of environmental and social goals and ambitions could be designed and improved on the basis of practical experience. In Sweden, internal audits of the environmental impacts of company operations are already on their way. External audits are only at the discussion stage.

The decision act in holistic terms

It seems reasonable to expect that there will be many styles of decision-making rather than one, and that our ideas of rational decisions will be partly the result of a social influence. In economics the idea of rationality is connected with optimal 'solutions' based on calculations in monetary or other terms. Some variable is maximized or minimized, whereas other variables may appear as boundary conditions or restrictions.

In some simple cases of decision-making, where there are few impacts, few decision-makers and people affected, and considerable consensus about values, the idea of optimal solutions using computer programs to pick out the best alternative, and so on, seems useful. In more complex cases of decision-making some other idea of rationality is called for. Our previous discussion of democracy and collective decision-making indicates such a possibility. Decisions can be thought of as a matching procedure in holistic or Gestalt terms between the impact profiles of individual alternatives and the value profiles or ideologies of individual politicians or other decision-makers.

Here the analyst tries to identify the pattern impacts arising from the choice of each alternative and relate them to possible ideological patterns. From the point of view of a decision-maker there may be a good fit between his or her values on the one hand and some specific alternative, or a bad fit. This idea of matching and pattern recognition replaces the one-dimensional comparisons of present values supported by the conventional view. While pictures of a building, bridge or road are more or less irrelevant as part of conventional cost–benefit analysis, a picture is very relevant as part of an attempt to describe impacts in pattern terms or holistically.

Consider a case of complex decisions in private life, such as the choice between two different jobs or places and houses to live in. How do we go about making these decisions? How many of us feel that they become more rational when we include everything in a monetary or other one-dimensional calculation? How many of us think in pattern terms and limit the role of conventional calculation to estimates of the financial costs of each house and place?

It is sometimes argued that psychologists have shown that individuals can only cognitively deal with seven pieces of information at a time and that therefore one-dimensional comparison is the only realistic way to proceed. My answer is twofold. Simplification always has a price. To the extent that our societies face complex decisions in the environmental and other areas, overlooking this complexity may not be the best strategy. Second, when it comes to structure or patterns that have meaning to individuals, the restriction to seven pieces of information is no longer valid. I can recognize a friend in the street and the pattern of his face and person is not limited to seven pieces of information. Similarly, the art of reading is an example of what human beings can achieve in terms of identifying and recognizing patterns.

Positional analysis as an approach to decision-making

One possible approach to decision-making that corresponds to the recommendations made is positional analysis (Söderbaum 1973, 1987, 1990b). This approach aims to offer a many-sided illumination of the decision situation in terms of possible valuational standpoints, alternative courses of action and impacts. Depending upon the kind of decision and the social and institutional context, simplified versions of positional analysis may be considered. A more ambitious study would include the following:

- Description of the decision situation. Historical background. Relationships to other decisions (previous and simultaneous). Identification of relevant institutions (organizations and rules of the game) and interested parties.
- Identification of the problem or problems. Reproduction of problem images as stated by different actors.
- Design of alternatives and formulation of the problem (choosing a set of alternatives for further consideration).
- Identification of systems that will be differently affected depending on the alternative chosen.
- Identification of impacts (monetary and non-monetary, in flow and positional terms) and comparisons between alternatives in relation to these effect dimensions.
- A study of possible inertia and irreversibilities in non-monetary positional terms. In what way will first-step alternatives influence future options for different affected parties?
- Analysis of activities and interests in relation to the decision situation: identification of activities that will be affected differently depending on the alternative chosen. Assumption of goal direction for each activity. Activity, together with goal direction, defines an interest. Construction of

preference order from the point of view of each interest in relation to each alternative.

- Analysis of prevailing risks and uncertainties.
- Summary of information basis for decisions at the two levels of impacts and activities with related interests.
- Articulation of possible valuational or ideological standpoints in terms relevant to the study area (transportation ideologies, energy ideologies, health care ideologies, etc.).
- Conditional conclusions, relating the expected impacts of each alternative to possible valuational standpoints.

Although the approach of positional analysis was originally designed as much for use in business as in the wider society, it is only in the last few years that some interest has been shown by business consultants. More interest in the approach has been shown in relation to studies at the societal level and positional analysis is regarded by some as an alternative to cost–benefit analysis. There follows an example of such possible use related to road-planning.

Road planning and positional analysis

This case involves a decision situation ten years ago for the E18 road between Enköping and Balsta in the Stockholm region. A traffic of 15,000 vehicles per day and night was considered too much in relation to the capacity of the existing road and the number of traffic accidents was increasing. New carriageways with a higher capacity were considered. One of these alternatives, (Alternative 2 in Figure 8.3) was advocated by the responsible road planning agency and implied a new motorway 23 kilometers long that shortened the previous length by 4 kilometers.

In this case a conventional cost–benefit study was carried out by the road-planning agency. Monetary costs of construction and operation were estimated as well as monetary benefits, the latter connected with time savings of 6 minutes per individual being able to use the new road rather than the old one. The price of each hour gained during the year implied a certain level of benefits. Also the number of accidents was expected to be reduced (i.e. regarded as a benefit), and each accident was valued at 210,000 SK. Instead of estimating a benefit–cost ratio as earlier indicated, the officers of the agency pointed to an internal rate of return of 9.5 per cent for the project and it was argued that this profitability rate was higher than for any of the competing alternatives. Very little was done in terms of covering environmental benefits and costs but in principle that would have been possible using so called contingent valuation techniques as part of the cost–benefit approach.

The interested parties affected included farmers and owners of summer houses. Around 400 summer house owners were upset by the proposed development, which meant noise and pollution in a previously relatively

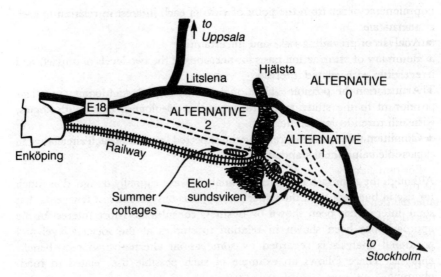

Figure 8.3   Road planning: Alternative 0 is the existing E18 road. Alternatives 1 and 2 are two possible constructions, Alternative 2 passing close to summer cottages

undisturbed area. The answer of the responsible officer of the agency to their concerns was to the effect that property owners are only considering their own interests, while the road-planning agency knows what is best from a societal point of view. His view was that the monetary calculation carried out indicated what was correct to do when all interests have been carefully balanced against each other.

A first step in applying positional analysis to this context would be to clarify the institutional context. Who is doing what as part of the decision process and what are the rules of the game? It is also important to listen to various categories of people affected or concerned by the issue. What problems do they see and what alternatives do they point to? After having written down or reproduced the variety of views, the analyst has to choose some set of alternatives for further study. One recommendation is to choose a many sided set, that is in the present case not only road alternatives that are similar in kind but also alternatives related to the nearby railway (Figure 8.3). Among road alternatives, also improvements of the existing road could be considered as well as those which involved a more limited exploitation of ecosystems and changes in the land use pattern.

Given some set of alternatives, all systems affected differently (depending on which one of the alternatives is chosen) are identified. Road systems and railway systems have already been mentioned, but in addition, for instance, homes and holiday cottages, systems for agriculture, forestry and so on are affected. This is also true of commercial systems, whose markets may expand or contract.

The systems structure will be of help in identifying possible monetary and non-monetary impacts related to different parties. Alternatives are compared systematically for each kind of impact. Differences are indicated quantitatively. Irreversible impacts especially are made as clear as possible. Building a motorway of the dimensions here discussed is a considerable and largely irreversible encroachment on ecosystems and on the initial land-use patterns. The number of hectares of each use adversely affected can be estimated. The position of flora and fauna before the exploitation can be clarified together with estimates of impact, for instance in terms of new positions after the development. Cultural artifacts along the corridor can be identified and expected changes in positional terms described.

Positional analysis entails the comparison of alternatives according not only to the level of impacts but also to the level of activities that are differently affected depending on the alternatives chosen. Emphasis is on human activities (defined for specific areas) such as housing, recreational activities, transportation, agricultural, forestry activities, hunting, commercial activities and so on. For each activity an assumption is made about goal direction in relation to the particular issue under study. When housing along the existing road is concerned, it may 'reasonably' be assumed that, when engaged in this particular activity, as low a level of disturbance as possible in terms of noise and pollution from roads is preferred.

Such assumptions make it possible to rank the alternatives considered in relation to each activity. Going through the various alternatives will make it clear that normally no alternative is best from the point of all activities. In other words, a conflict of interest is the normal case and one idea behind positional analysis is to articulate such conflicts of interest.

An attempt is then made to summarize differences between alternatives with respect to impacts and interests. This can be done in holistic terms as an impact-profile for each alternative. The information basis for decisions can be thought of as photographs from different angles. Each new photo may add something to what can be seen and understood from the previous ones.

Articulation of possible valuation standpoints together with conditional conclusions is a help to decision-makers, or perhaps something that challenges their values. In the present case, extreme 'motorist' ideologies connected with simplistic thinking in terms of growth can be one valuational standpoint, while some form of ecological ethics focusing on minimum degradation of the natural resource base is another. It is clear that the railway option would have been considered seriously as part of such ambitions to transform various human activities in a direction which is sounder from an ecological point of view.

Finally, decisions are taken in the holistic way previously suggested as a matching procedure between the impact profiles of each alternative and the ideological profiles of each decision-maker, such as politicians in the relevant municipalities.

In the event it was not possible to carry out the positional analysis in this case and the final decision (Alternative 1 plus considerable subsequent widening of the road) was taken with little reference to ecological impacts. But the case clearly illustrates how positional analysis could have given a more balanced presentation to decision-makers than the cost–benefit analysis and internal rate of return decision-basis.

Concluding remarks

Whether one likes the kind of many-sided and ethically open-ended approach to decision-making suggested here or not is, again, a matter of values. Some politicians prefer a one-sided and manipulated analysis to one that is more compatible with democracy. Other politicians do not know of alternatives to cost–benefit analysis. But there are of course also politicians, environmentalists and others who are positive to approaches such as positional analysis and Environmental Impact Statements, which attempt to make the environment and people visible. They regard it as fruitful for politicians to have to face conflicts between different interests rather than receive some end result in quantitative terms which tends to conceal any problems.

Part III

On the mechanisms of economic policy

INTRODUCTION

So far this book has sought to locate the economy within a holistic view of the human condition; to ensure that the whole economy is kept in focus; to identify the process, purpose and components of wealth creation; and to outline an indicator framework to show the economy's performance. This part briefly discusses the mechanisms that are available to economic policy-makers.

It is normally perceived that there are two such mechanisms, the market and the state, and it has unfortunately become common for proponents of one to disparage the other. Indeed, the difference between the two has been the principal political divide throughout the world.

The position to be taken here is, first, that the perceived dichotomy between the market and the state is a false one, and that the relevant policy issue is actually the balance to be struck between them. It will be argued that, second, the 'state' mechanism should be seen to have international, national and local components, which should also be used appropriately according to the issue being addressed. Third, another major mechanism will be discussed corresponding to the activity in the social economy (see Figure 5.1, p. 127).

The market and the state

It is most regrettable that confrontation has arisen between proponents of the market and the state because successful policy-making relies on achieving a dynamic complementarity between the two. The first point to be made is that there is no such thing as a 'free' market. All markets depend on an *a priori* definition of property rights (without property rights there can be no exchange); all but the simplest markets also depend on some extra-market enforcement of contract, without which most contracts would not be entered into, for fear of cheating. Thus all markets imply coercion. If someone owns something, then others can forcefully be denied the use of it. If someone agrees to something, they can be forced to abide by that agreement. The mechanism for enforcement in both cases, and for the initial definition of property rights, is not the market. It is the state. Thus the market and the state are linked in an inextricable symbiosis from the start.

What the advocates of a 'free' market are calling for is *not* the dissolution of the state's role in defining and enforcing the market. They are wanting this role to be enacted strictly on the basis of *existing private property rights*, which is a very different matter. 'Free marketeers' are simply those who propose the freedom of private property under its current distribution, to the inevitable advantage of the rich and at the inevitable expense of whose who own little or no property. The advantage and the expense will come from three sources. First, the rich will be able to use their wealth to appropriate resources whose property rights are ill-defined, or which are beyond the reach of the poor (e.g. the mineral resources of the sea-bed). Second, the rich will be able to use their wealth and power to coerce the poor into relatively disadvantageous contracts. Third, the poor tend to be worst affected by the externalities, which the exercise of property rights often produces.

As Schmid makes clear (he also discusses the wider implications of these issues most effectively), any attempt by the state to change this state of affairs is not so much a matter of 'interfering' in a 'free' market as of *changing property rights* under which the market functions (Schmid 1987). Thus laws against air pollution effectively give property rights to those who want to breathe clean air at the expense of those who have the incentive and the means to pollute it. Employment protection legislation gives property rights to the owners of labour at the expense of those who have the incentive and means to hire it. Social-security systems give property rights to people on the basis of existence at the expense of producers.

It is important (as Schmid stresses) to be clear that state action or inaction are entirely symmetrical: both favour one group over another. Action favours the beneficiaries of the change, at the expense of the *status quo*. Inaction favours the *status quo* at the expense of the would-be beneficiaries. There is nothing inherently better about a *status quo*. The case for state action (or inaction) must always be made in value-terms: the *status quo* (proposed change) must be shown to be suboptimal and the proposed change (*status quo*) shown to be preferable. The inescapable role of ethics in these decisions is obvious.

This analysis of state action in terms of the redefinition of property rights shows that, at bottom, the dispute between proponents of the 'the market' and 'the state' boils down to one between those who favour the *status quo* and those seeking change. It has nothing fundamentally to do with the mechanisms themselves, both of which are social institutions designed to achieve specific purposes: the market to organize and facilitate production and exchange; the state to define the framework and entitlements within which such organization is to be effected. The market cannot develop without the state and, as the Soviet and eastern European experience have shown, the state cannot prosper without the market. Moreover, the market as well as the state can be used to pursue social and ethical as well as economic values, as the growth of ethical investment funds and 'green' consumerism in some countries has illustrated. Of course, state policy-makers and officials can be as self-interested at the expense of social welfare as any market agent. It is most regrettable that these two potentially complementary mechanisms have become the adversarial slogans of conservatives and reformers in their dispute over the equity and validity of the *status quo*.

The practical relevance of this analysis is clear. Without exception the relatively successful economies in the world are those that have effectively integrated the functions of the market and the state: Japan, the Nordic countries, Germany, South Korea. Those with a history of perceived contradiction between the two: the United States, with an ideological bias against the state; the United Kingdom, which has tended to lurch between them; or the former eastern European bloc, with an ideological bias against the market, have performed less well both in terms of formal economic wealth (GDP/capita or production growth) and health and social indicators.

The implications for policy are obvious. It is a balance between the market and the state, a balance dictated by ethical, environmental, social and economic considerations, that should be sought, not the dominance of either of them.

9   Markets, ethics and competition

It is not only the state that frames and constrains markets and enables them to function effectively. As the next two papers show, market competition and participants themselves can and do organize their market activity in a way that is a far cry from the asocial, amoral assumptions of much neoclassical theory.

Competitive systems: a sociological view

Mitchel Abolafia and Nicole Biggart

Economic competition is widely believed to be a critical – even *the* critical – social process in market societies. From the perspective of free-market economics, the competitive pursuit of gain by individuals and firms creates exchange conditions that result in allocative efficiency, the greatest good for the greatest number. This utilitarian ideology is the foundation of modern economics and, not coincidently, numerous legal and political institutions. Economic utilitarianism even achieves moral embodiment in an esteemed social role, the entrepreneur. Competition and its outcomes approach the status of natural law – an expected, even inevitable product of human interaction.

This paper is an attempt to create a framework for understanding economic competition as social action structured by political, economic and cultural contexts. We propose a conceptualization of competition as an institutionally embedded and socially maintained form of mutual striving. Markets, we argue, are not merely the sum of the buying and selling activities of autonomous competitive individuals. Rather, we understand markets to be social arenas that structure competition according to legitimated organizing principles. Organization is manifest in the voluntary agreement of competitors to renounce certain practices and to abide by others. We will argue against the popular micro-social conceptualization of competition as the unboundedly antagonistic moves of independent actors. Rather, we believe that competition – no less than co-operation, obedience and other forms of social action – is oriented towards others, has underlying norms, and is sustained by institutional arrangements.

Recent work in economic sociology and organization theory has questioned the view of the competitive market as an atomized, unorganized mass (Abolafia and Kilduff 1988; Baker 1984a and b; Burns and Flam 1987; White 1981). An awareness that market competition is embedded in social relations is clearly emerging (Granovetter 1985; Schapiro 1987), yet little has been written about how market actors structure competitive relations or about the institutional means through which competitive action is maintained. Nor do most authors address the normative underpinnings of market arrangements (see, however, Orru *et al.* forthcoming).

In this paper we propose an institutional perspective on economic competition. We question the heuristic simplicity of the dichotomy between markets and hierarchies (Williamson 1975), suggesting that a new theory is needed to acknowledge the institutional diversity within and among capitalist systems. We argue instead for the existence of competitive systems, each with its own historically contingent form of governance. Competitive systems are institutionalized arenas for the mediation of competition. The structure of these systems varies by their historical and cultural context. Significantly, markets do not exhaust the forms of competitive system in capitalism. Recent work shows that competitive systems may also assume the form of networks (Granovetter 1985; Lindberg *et al.* 1991; Powell 1988) and associations (Lindberg *et al.* 1991). The degree of organization in competitive systems varies greatly, however. At the lowest level of organization there is little more than a normative system, agreed-on business practices such as the meaning of a handshake. Formalized institutional systems are characterized by associations with rules and a division of labour. Moreover, competitive systems vary from the transient and informal, such as a flea market, to the relatively more permanent and formalized organization of a stock exchange. Competitive systems also vary in their enforcement of competitive norms – from weak trade and professional associations to powerful self-regulated sports leagues in football and basketball, and marketing boards in agriculture. All competitive systems, however, have normative underpinnings and institutionalized means for sustaining norms of competition.

Perspectives on economic competition

Competition has been a central concept in both economics and sociology since their inceptions, and these disciplines have produced several variant perspectives. They can, however, be divided into two major types: the asocial and the political. Asocial conceptualizations are those in which actors are isolated units and social relations are as Granovetter put it, 'frictionless' (Granovetter 1985). The market is composed of actors independent and mindless of each other, or if strategically aware of competitors, this awareness is understood to be futile in altering competitive outcomes. We use the term 'asocial' to emphasize that these formulations do not have a theory of social action, or believe that the process of meaningful interaction is unimportant to competitive outcomes, not that they posit no social consequences to competition.

Competition as an asocial process

The idea of competition as an asocial process has achieved currency as part of the general domination of utilitarian thought in western society (Hamilton and Biggart 1985). There are three important variations of this mode; the classical, the neoclassical and the ecological (for an extended discussion, see Abolafia and Biggart 1990). These asocial conceptualizations of competition have been extremely powerful devices for understanding, at the abstract and aggregate level at which much economic and ecological enquiry takes place, the dynamics and organizational configurations of western market societies. We find asocial views inadequate, however, for several reasons. Asocial models, as Mark Granovetter has argued, provide an undersocialized conceptualization of human agents who everywhere act alike, rationally pursuing unspecified interests (Granovetter 1985). Asocial models cannot account for the influence of social networks, gender, class, culture, religion – those factors of social life that influence what people want and how they choose to go about getting it.

Neoclassical models assume an ideal of the world and then explain deviations from the ideal; the neoclassical model of a competitive market is transhistoric and acultural. The ecological model, despite the inclusion of a temporal dimension, is also transhistoric and acultural. Asocial theories of both the neoclassical and ecological types tend to assume that all markets, in all places and times, operate according to the same logic. Neoclassical economists and many ecologists, in an attempt to develop a general theory, envision a unitary competitive force which, like gravity, expresses itself the same way anywhere under given conditions.

It is equally possible, however, to hypothesize that competitive norms are socially constructed by actors in specific socio-cultural contexts which shape and are shaped by competitive action. Rather than explaining market and competitive differences as corruptions or imperfections of an ideal, differences may reflect varied beliefs, orientations to materialism, and the relative weakness or strength of individualism as an ethic. Western norms, for example, should not be taken for granted in a culturally sensitive theory of competition. Clearly this second hypothesis is consistent with those disciplines such as anthropology, history, and some forms of sociology which presume that social action is historically shaped and meaningful only within a cultural context. We would argue that, while asocial models may be suited to phenomena adequately described by aggregated variable analysis, that they are susceptible to a reductionist fallacy when examining intra-market relations.

A final limitation of asocial views of competition is that they are concerned only with the outcomes of competitive arrangements, not with competitive activity itself. We accept that neoclassical modelling of macro-level supply and demand, and ecological analyses of population configurations, make significant contributions to our understanding of the collective consequences of competitive action. A focus on outcomes and consequences, however, allows economists and ecologists to ignore as unimportant the social relations which are crucial to the development of competitive systems and to the understanding of the competitive process. An institutional theory concerned with the structure, content and maintenance of social action, in contrast, puts relationships at the centre of enquiry.

An institutional perspective on competition

An institutional perspective on competition is focused on the system of organizational and social constraints that structure competitive action. First, we examine the nature of social relations among participants in competitive systems and suggest a political model as alternative to the ideal type defined by the asocial model. Second, we indicate how competition comes to be embedded in institutional systems that constrain and shape it. Finally, we suggest an explanation for the observed variation between these institutionalized competitive systems.

A political model

The first step in constructing this perspective is to establish the explicitly social nature of relations in the competitive process. This theoretical requirement is filled by a political perspective on competition. In the political perspective competitors are active agents mobilizing scarce resources to shape their environment. Versions of this voluntarist view are found in conflict theory (Tilly 1978), social movement theory (Jenkins and Perrow 1977; McCarthy and Zald 1973, 1977), and some versions of strategic management (Harrigan 1985; Henderson 1984) and marketing (Kotler and Achrol 1984). Competitors attempt to shape their environment through such strategies as advertising, public relations, government lobbying, co-optation and campaign contributions. Weber, in this vein, defined competition as 'a formally peaceful attempt to attain control over opportunities and advantages which are also desired by others' (Weber 1978: 38).

In addition to seeing competitors as active agents who shape the competitive arena, the political perspective argues that actors have social orientations: actors recognize each other as contestants, although they may not be in actual contact. Rather than being atomized captives of a production function, competitors observe one another closely. It is this social orientation which most clearly distinguishes the political from the asocial view of competition.

The political perspective, moreover, views competition less benignly than the asocial perspective. While market forces and niche characteristics select winners and losers in asocial markets, in the political view it is actors who shape events. In this view, as Etzioni explains, competition is a form of conflict (Etzioni 1988). It assumes that the divergent interests of competitors are not automatically eliminated by a self-regulating market mechanism. Markets, like bureaucracies, have politics. There are wars, battles, coalitions and truces. The battlefield analogy is common in business culture and the business-strategy literature.

The institutional context

The second component in this perspective on competition indicates how competitive relations come to be embedded in an institutional context. Most asocial models simply ignore the institutional context in which competition occurs. This context includes norms, rules and enforcement structures (Abolafia 1985). When competitive relations are examined in the context of these institutions, we may speak of the whole as a *competitive system*. Laws, rules, norms and customs are the 'rules of the game' in competitive systems. As game theorists have indicated, competitive outcomes are shaped by the rules and the effectiveness of their enforcement. Unlike game theory, however, we are not concerned so much with outcomes as with the process by which the competitive system becomes institutionalized and the variations that result.

This view of the role of institutions is a familiar one in sociology (Parsons 1937), if rarely applied in the analysis of competition. Following Eisenstadt (1968), the present study goes beyond Parsons's institutionalism to develop a political perspective on the construction of competitive systems. Following from the political perspective, we believe that competitive systems are enacted by political and economic actors with a perceived stake in the outcome of the competition. We are concerned with how and why these stakeholders create and maintain competitive systems. Such systems do not precede markets, nor do they arise spontaneously from the 'needs' of the market. Rather, they are purposefully constructed and institutionalized by the competitors themselves and by interested third parties in the public sector. The institutionalization process is neither neutral nor predetermined. 'Institutionalization as a process is profoundly political and reflects the relative power of organized interests and the actors who mobilize around them' (DiMaggio 1988: 13).

The actors who mobilize mechanisms of mutual or external constraint are referred to as *institutional entrepreneurs* (Eisenstadt 1968). These actors define or redefine the rules of the game as well as establishing the enforcement structures for the competitive system. The ability to perform this role is associated with control over resources or positions of authority outside the competitive arena. Institutional entrepreneurs are most often powerful competitors or concerned parties in the public sector. These actors attempt to impose norms, rules, laws, and structures of competition to serve their own interests. Given the right set of incentives or coercive limits, competitors will observe the constraints.

Competitive systems

The final step in constructing an institutional perspective on competition is to suggest an explanation for the observed variation between competitive systems. Although competitive systems all share a common ability to constrain their participants, they differ widely in both structure and process. Farmers markets, professional associations, sports leagues, agricultural marketing boards and financial exchanges are all competitive systems. Below, we suggest five factors that, alone or in combination, constrain or facilitate relations in competitive systems. These include (1) the structure of competitive relations (2) cultural forces (3) historical era (4) level of competition and (5) degree of state intervention.

1. *The structure of competitive relations* Competitive relations are not all structured the same way. They may be structured in the form of a market, a network, a membership association or, more likely, a combination of these. The market is the most familiar and least formal structure. Markets are loose aggregations of mutually orientated competitors (White 1981, 1988). These competitors have no need to communicate. Co-ordination occurs through the price mechanism. Producers of goods and services make strategic judgements based on the actions of their competitors. In this way norms of price and quality are set and maintained. Market structures rarely, if ever, stand alone. Rather, they are sustained by network and associational structures. For example, Baker has shown that even in the highly liquid stock options market competitors are members of networks that are subgroups within the market (Baker 1984a and b). Members of these subgroups exchange information as well as resources to their mutual advantage.

Some competitive systems are more purely networks. Biggart shows that many direct selling organizations, such as Tupperware and Amway in the United States, are competitive systems structured as networks (Biggart 1989). Distributors of these products are autonomous entrepreneurs who are related to others selling the same product (their competitors). This relationship is structured through membership in hierarchical 'families' that constrain where and how competitors operate. Such informal families and clans are particularly common in Asian forms of capitalism.

The most formal structure for competitive relations is the membership association. Competitors participate in membership associations in order to pursue their common interests. In return for access to the collective goods produced by the association, members agree to abide by rules and by-laws of the association. Among the goods and services of the association are the establishment of product standards, the collection and dissemination of data on costs and prices, government lobbying, advertising and the enforcement of codes of fair competition. Although trade associations have tended to be weak in the United States, they are far more active and effective in Europe (Streeck and Schmitter 1985). In the United States, marketing boards and financial exchanges, both having anti-trust exemptions, are strong forms of association. Abolafia shows how futures exchanges actively regulate competition in an arena that is usually characterized by economists as a paradigm of the free market (Abolafia 1989).

2. *Cultural factors* Asocial models describe competition as if it is a universal natural force that takes the same form globally. Societies pursue competition

differently, putting greater or lesser constraints on it. One critical factor is the legitimacy a society places on individualism versus communalism. In communalistic societies, competition is less likely to be atomized. In Europe this may be seen in the higher tolerance in some states for corporatist arrangements in which competitors co-operate (Streeck and Schmitter 1985). Recent work on Japan has emphasized that the firm is not the crucial economic actor in their economic system. Competition is structured by a system of business groups (*keiretsu*), which are communities (networks) of firms that plan, invest, trade and act together for the good of the group (Futatsugi 1986; Kobayashi 1980; Okumura 1982). Competition is between *keiretsu*, while individual members are encouraged or restrained for the group's welfare.

3. *Historical era* Competitive systems vary by the historical period in which they are founded. This is associated with the changing organization of the capitalist system. In the era of mercantile capitalism, competition in commodity markets was often organized informally in coffee houses, curb markets and bourses. This was later formalized into exchanges in the nineteenth century with rules of trade, standardized contracts and enforcement structures for fines and suspension. At about the same time many industries were organizing trade association to set standards, share information and lobby the government. Trade associations were established in the United States by cotton manufacturers (1854), brewers (1862) and bankers (1876) among others. In the last part of the twentieth century in the United States we find competitors forming networks for research and development in a variety of high-tech industries. The institutionalization of competitive systems in any specific nation is related to each economy's process of development.

4. *Level of competition* This is what industrial organization economists have traditionally meant when they referred to competition. Level of competition refers to the number of competitors in the competitive system and the distribution of market share among them. Economists have assumed that organization arises under conditions of oligopoly or market failure (Phillips 1960; Williamson 1975). Phillips (1960) describes a pattern of parallel action similar to the behaviour found in small groups. The institutional perspective presented here indicates that organization occurs at all levels of competition. Networks and membership associations, as well as less formal norms, are found at all levels of competition, from wide open financial markets to cartels. We expect that systems with small numbers of competitors are less likely to formalize as associations. Competitive systems in which a few members hold a large part of the market share are, in turn, likely to be dominated by those members.

5. *State intervention* The extent to which government intervenes in competitive systems plays an important part in shaping them. Regulation, fair trade laws, and anti-trust laws are prominent elements in the competitive relations of most market societies. The government acts as an interested third

party to maintain the legitimacy of competitive systems. Regulatory agencies frequently use the rules and standards of informal competitive systems as a basis for the establishment of regulations. The degree of intervention varies from industry to industry and nation to nation.

Conclusion

This paper has offered a very brief introduction to an institutional perspective on competition. It has suggested a framework for understanding economic competition as social action that is structured by political, cultural and historical factors, as well as economic ones. We argue for a recognition of the diversity among competitive systems. By implication, we expect that market societies will exhibit a diverse array of competitive systems in different cultures at different levels of economic development. This argument is developed further, using detailed examples, in Abolafia and Biggart (1990).

Towards a progressive market

Paul Ekins

In the United Kingdom, and probably in Europe generally, there has been a common perception that progressive social policy is the prerogative of government. The normal view is that, in a mixed economy, the capitalist private sector creates and distributes wealth through the operation of the market, but that the state must intervene both to correct market failures, such as externalities or the inefficient provision of public goods, and to bring about such redistribution of wealth as seems called for by social justice. The market is generally perceived as being unable to pursue such progressive objectives.

In this paper I do not wish to question the role of the state, which clearly has important regulatory, allocative and redistributive functions. But I do wish to put forward the view that the market can also be organized and harnessed to exert a powerful progressive influence, and that this is fully in accordance with standard neoclassical theory and should therefore be supported even by political conservatives, who tend to believe in market solutions as opposed to government action.

The market, as is well understood, is a powerful mechanism for the expression of individual preferences in a decentralized manner. With no intermediary bureaucracy it enables people as consumers to express their preferences directly, knowing not only that their purchasing power will secure the product or service of their choice, but also that this will act as an economic vote to encourage producers to deliver more of the same. In that way resources are channelled to those who give most satisfaction, and the economists' 'efficient allocation' is achieved.

It is important to note that for the market to be able to work in this ideal fashion, several heroic prior assumptions have to be made. Consumers are supposed to possess 'perfect information' about the goods and services on offer. Markets are supposed to be perfectly competitive. The price mechanism is deemed to capture all costs and benefits. While these assumptions clearly do not pertain in practice, they are normally held to be sufficiently true for the analysis based on them to have at least approximate validity and they are reinforced by legislation where necessary (e.g. advertising standards, anti-trust laws and pollution controls).

Yet there is another pervasive assumption in market theory, as elsewhere in economics, which routinely leads to anti-social outcomes, including market failure, on a massive scale. This assumption, which is none the less powerful for being usually implicit rather than openly stated, is that people generally, and consumers in particular, do not incorporate ethical, social or environmental criteria into their individual economic decision-making. Rather the Rational Economic Man model of the economic agent most frequently depicts self-interested individuals performing isolated cost–benefit analyses on the basis of their personal pleasure and pain, profit and loss.

This is not to say that welfare economists have not made detailed attempts to incorporate altruism or the environment into their theoretical framework. But despite these sophistications in economic theory, hard-nosed analysis of economic practice, and especially the workings of the market, have until recently tended to place an exclusive emphasis on individual gain and self-interest. Consumers were deemed to be interested only in their own benefit from some purchase; firms were supposed to maximize either their profits or the power of their managers or some mixture of the two; and investors were thought to pursue some optimal mix of income, growth and security from their investments.

It would be foolish to deny the importance of any of these market objectives. However, it would be equally unrealistic to ignore the very different manifestations of market behaviour which are becoming increasingly prominent and which can together be taken to characterize a new market concept: the progressive market. The several components of this idea are the subject of the remainder of this paper.

The progressive consumer

The most cursory examination of human nature indicates that most people have strong opinions and preferences about ethical, social and environmental matters. Yet, to repeat, it has for long been routinely and inexplicably supposed that such preferences are irrelevant to people's purchasing decisions. The supposition was self-fulfilling because it resulted in consumers being given no information about these aspects of the products they were about to buy, so that they were unable to take them into account even if they wished to. Consumers therefore unwittingly endorsed the destruction of tropical rain-forests and the ozone layer through their purchase of hardwoods, hamburgers, and aerosols; connived in the blinding of young women in Mexican semiconductor factories through their purchase of personal computers; and otherwise were party to a host of other exploitations of people and planet through being unaware of the wider implications of their consumption.

Recognition of these wider implications was first effectively expressed by the International Organization of Consumer Unions (IOCU), which was founded in 1960 by a number of national consumer associations to carry out product testing and lend cohesion to the fledgling mass consumer market. By 1990 IOCU's membership numbered 170 groups in sixty-five countries and its role had broadened to turn it into an influential force for change, tackling such problems as ozone layer depletion and toxic waste dumping, the marketing of dangerous drugs and pesticides in the Third World, tobacco, baby foods, irradiation and biotechnology. To help address these and other issues, IOCU has been instrumental in setting up about twenty highly effective international networks beyond its formal membership, including the international Baby Food Action Network and Health Action International. Its monthly magazine *Consumer Currents* carries reliable information of consumer interest on a wide range of subjects, in the context of IOCU's 'five consumer responsibilities': critical awareness, action, social concern, environmental awareness and solidarity.

IOCU and its associated networks have tended to concentrate on information provision and lobbying, with a view to obtaining legislative regulation. Their advocacy of action through the market has largely been confined to calls for boycotts of offensive products. However, in several countries consumers have now begun to demand far more detailed information to guide their purchasing on a daily basis. In the United States the New York based Council on Economic Priorities (CEP) published in 1986 a landmark book entitled *Rating America's Corporate Conscience* (Lydenburg *et al.* 1986) which assessed the United States's largest companies over a wide range of social and environmental issues. In 1988 it distilled this information into a pocket-sized Shoppers' Guide to the supermarket which rated 1500 brands and producers in the same way (Corson *et al.* 1988). By 1991 over 700,000 copies had been sold, with feedback returns indicating that most purchasers had changed their buying habits as a result. Another US non-profit organization, Co-op America, runs a thriving mail-order business to tens of thousands of consumers, the catalogue only containing goods that contribute to a healthy environment or human development.

In the United Kingdom the paperback *Green Consumer Guide* (Elkington and Hailes 1988) shot to the top of the best-selling non-fiction list soon after its publication in September 1988 and the subsequent phenomenon of 'green consumerism' has reverberated round practically every board-room in the country through its in-depth coverage in management and marketing publications. The launch in September 1989 of another organization, New Consumer, sought to broaden this environmental concern to other issues, broadly on the

CEP model. In 1991 it published a detailed reference work on 130 British consumer goods companies (Adams *et al.* 1991a); a shopping guide (Adams *et al.* 1991b) which rated more or less the same companies, with 2,500 brands, over fourteen issues of social concern (disclosure, women's advancement, equal opportunities, charitable giving and community support, environment, animal testing, Third World, South Africa, political donations, involvement in alcohol, tobacco, gambling and military sales); and a consumer guide focusing on impacts in the Third World (Wells and Jetter 1991).

CEP's example has also spread to Japan where the *Asahi Journal* has done some comparative corporate ratings. It is in Japan, too, where one of the most impressive ethical consumer initiatives is to be found, the Seikatsu Club Consumers' Co-operative (SCCC). Started in 1965 by a Tokyo housewife to buy milk more cheaply in bulk, the Club has blossomed into an economic powerhouse combining Japanese efficiency with deep ecological and social concern. The heart of the business is the distribution of 400 products, all produced according to rigorous ecological and social criteria, to the 25,000 local groups of some eight member-families each. The Club's annual turnover is more than £260 million and it has over £43 million in member-investment, which it utilizes to produce its own goods when others do not meet its exacting standards.

The progressive consumer, it seems, is at last stirring from the deep sleep of commodity-fetishism and even governments have begun to notice and respond. Official environmental labelling schemes are already well-established in Germany and Japan and other countries are following suit. The potential power of progressive consumers is enormous. In the United Kingdom over £300 billion is spent each year on personal consumption with under 0.5 per cent as much going to charitable purposes. Moreover, there is ample evidence of company sensitivity to even very small swings in consumer demand. If progressive consumerism continues to intensify, the extent to which it could transform business practice is hard to overestimate.

The progressive business

In traditional business theory firms are supposed to be run for the exclusive benefit of their shareholders, although it has for some years been recognized that managers are inclined to pursue their own objectives as well. However, there is another theory of the firm founded on the concept of stakeholders. This recognizes that a firm's activity affects many parties: shareholders, customers, employees, suppliers, the local community and the natural environment. The firm therefore has an obligation to each of these parties which shoud be explicitly reflected in its policy (Goyder 1987).

It would be idle to pretend that concern for the welfare of all its stakeholders was high on the agenda of more than handful of firms, but that handful, in rhetoric at least, includes such corporate giants as NCR, Johnson Wax and IBM (which is not to say that rhetoric is always turned into reality when business pressures intensify). Nor are management techniques for handling the complexity of these issues in a competitive environment well developed. There would seem to be a clear case for government to incorporate stakeholder concepts in company law, to require companies at least to report on how they have addressed these issues in their Annual Reports and, perhaps, to provide for damages in clear cases of neglect.

As with consumption there are several straws in the wind which indicate how this area could develop: the growth in worker co-operatives, community businesses and other 'local employment initiatives' in many European countries together with supportive infrastructure such as the EC's Local Employment Development Action (LEDA) programme; organizations like Business in the Community in the United Kingdom, through which many of the United Kingdom's largest companies pledge support for disadvantaged communities; encouragement of Employee Stock Ownership Programmes – by 1990 over 10,000 US companies were estimated to have established ESOPs, making some 10 million workers shareholders in their companies (Wisman 1990); the growing awareness among many businesses and their management consultants that their most precious resource is their workforce, with all that implies in terms of employee welfare and development.

Progressive business is also illustrated by the phenomenon known as 'alternative trading', whereby Northern importing companies seek to give fair prices, market advice and technical support to small-scale Southern producers while selling their products to Northern progressive consumers. Over 300 such companies and their producer partners from forty countries with a combined turnover of some $200 million are now organized in the International Federation of Alternative Trade in Amsterdam.

While these practical expressions of the stakeholder concept are still marginal to mainstream business operation, they have become significantly less so in the last decade. It is not too fanciful to imagine that continued intensification of this trend could trigger a transformation of business culture, whereby profitability began to be seen as a signal of continuing healthy viability and stakeholder service, rather than the overriding object of maximization.

The progressive investor

Considerably more developed and sophisticated than either the progressive consumer or producer, the progressive, or ethical or socially responsible, investor is now a well-established player on the capital scene. In the United States some $625 billion is now estimated to be subject to some form of ethical screening, with professionals in this field being well organized in the Social Investment Forum. The United Kingdom has seen a veritable explosion of ethical investment funds and unit trusts, adopting a broad range of criteria and catering for a wide variety of personal and institutional investment needs. Developments in this field are closely monitored by the Ethical Investment Research and Information Service (EIRIS) which publishes a regular informative newsletter. Several ethical banks are now well-established, the best known being the South Shore Bank of Chicago and Bangladesh's Grameen Bank, both of which lend successfully to poor people in poor communities to enable them to improve their standard of living and quality of life. A more recent initiative in this field is Germany's Ökobank, launched in 1988 and specializing in loans to self-managed business and energy conservation projects, the majority of which must be in the local area. Eighteen months after its launch it had 22,000 customers and had provided loans of about DM5 million. In the United Kingdom again, several ethical share issues, appealing explicitly to altruism rather than the profit motive, have been oversubscribed, including those of the fair trading company Traidcraft and Industrial Common Ownership Finance, which finances worker co-operatives.

Promoting the progressive market

It is too early as yet to say definitely whether progressive consumers, producers and investors will fulfil in practice their evident potential for positive social and economic change. If they are to do so, it will be due to the twin action of determined individuals and enabling legislation. The individuals will need to provide the will and the independent research and information organizations to enable them to express their wider preferences with confidence. Governments will need to ensure the appropriate provision of consumer information, the incorporation of stakeholder concepts and concessions for co-operatives into company law, and the right of institutional investors to pursue non-financial investment objectives where their contributing individuals so desire.

There is no contradiction implied in this combination of individual market preferences and governmental action. All markets are defined and policed by collective consent. What will be removed is the schizophrenic anomaly whereby people in the market-place are presumed to be egotistic and selfish actors, while as citizens in the family, community or polling booth they are widely acknowledged to have powerful moral and social commitments. The progressive market concept relocates the market-place in its human, social context and, in so doing, imbues it with a powerful potential for the transformation of traditional market institutions.

10 Three levels of state action

Historically the state has meant the nation-state and this has been the forum for policy-making in economic and other fields. The situation is changing fast.

The global level

All sorts of developments are increasing international linkages and making the international level an important policy-making arena. The environmental crisis demands an international approach. Market integration such as in Europe and North America demands international coordination. The transnationalization of business and globalization of trade demands international regulation. North–South phenomena, especially the level of Third World indebtedness, call for international action.

Again the split is evident between those who seek the formation and empowerment of international institutions in response to these events, and those who favour a global 'free' market. Again it is clear that what the latter are really seeking is an entrenchment of the *status quo*, the freedom of action of the wealthy on the world stage, while the former wish to redefine property rights in favour of those threatened or disadvantaged by the present international distribution of wealth and power. As with nation-states, it is highly likely that the world market will not yield its maximum benefits unless it can be framed and defined by appropriate institutions.

The evolution of development thought: facing up to global interdependence
Paul Streeten

I have, in the past, written on the evolution of development thought from different perspectives. Three early essays are on the historical evolution of our thinking (Streeten 1979a, 1979b, 1980). A later one took various dichotomies as a starting point and examined how they fit together (Streeten 1983). A subsequent essay combined history, analysis and policy by trying to show how the successful solution of one set of problems leads to new problems to be investigated (Streeten 1985). In this paper I want to trace some ideas according to their scope and limitations of applicability.

In the early days we thought of development theory as a special field, applicable to the low-income countries of Africa, Asia and Latin America. But two tendencies have been at work to destroy this view. On the one hand, as developing countries have become more differentiated, it became clear that different principles applied to some countries from those that applied to others. One important difference is that between large economies, in which foreign trade plays a comparatively minor role, and which may be able to influence their terms of trade, and small economies, in which trade is very important, and for which the terms of trade are given; or between land surplus and land scarce economies. Such differentiation points towards the need for a typology of countries, which would depend on the purpose of the analysis and policies.

On the other hand, it was found that principles initially thought to apply only to developing countries, applied to the whole world community: to advanced and developing countries alike. In the golden days of the 1950s and 1960s, it was thought that the advanced countries knew how to eradicate unemployment and that it was largely a problem of underdevelopment. But with the rise of widespread unemployment and stagflation in the advanced countries of the North in the 1970s and 1980s, some of the employment analysis that had been conducted for underdeveloped countries seemed to apply at home. Similarly, the informal sector, first discovered in countries such as Kenya, seemed to have a parallel in the 'parallel' or underground or black economies of Europe and America. One could mention many other ideas that, first elaborated in a development context, found fruitful application in the advanced countries. To those of us who thought that neoclassical economics does not apply to developing countries, it did not come as a complete surprise to discover that it did not apply to our own, advanced countries, either.

A normative political economy

In the early days of development economics, it was regarded as one of the main functions of government and of planning to remove distortions created by the free market and to correct its failures. These were the result not only of monopoly, but also of externalities of various kinds (e.g. pollution), of indivisibilities (so that several lumpy investments have to be carried out together), and of the absence of an entrepreneurial class, so that the state has to step in. Today, the situation is reversed, and it is presumed that all distortions are the result of government intervention and only by permitting free-market forces to reign can we achieve an efficient allocation. If the earlier thinkers erred by assuming that government can do no wrong, the current fashion is to believe that government can do no right.

The now popular public-choice school attributes the 'distortions', ineffici-encies, and departures from the optimum allocation of resources to the self-interest of the governing groups, their allies, and pressure groups on whose support they depend and to whose pressures they often yield. I have criticized the thinking of this school about the 'predatory state' elsewhere (Streeten 1981b). In the present context it is sufficient to point out that the very deviations from the best allocation of resources provide the means to compensate interest groups that might lose from such reforms, and yet leave others better off. There is a need to supplement the positive theory of directly unproductive profit-seeking activities by a normative branch that would explore the avenues towards achieving efficiency. It would analyse the coalitions and the alliances that would produce the political constituencies for reform. It would replace the meaningless talk of 'political will' by the search for a political base.

Such an exploration is also necessary if we ask ourselves why the recom-mendations of the last twenty years have not been followed, in spite of lip-service being paid to their acceptability. Some of these recommendations clearly were mistaken. Others were right for their time, but the times have changed and they are no longer valid. But a third group were then and are still correct, are widely accepted in speeches and written documents, such as development plans, and yet are not implemented. Among them is the importance of meeting basic needs, of reducing absolute poverty, of creating employment, and of encouraging the productive enterprises in the informal sector. The answer has to be sought in the political constraints, the obstacles and inhibitions, to doing what leaders know to be right.

International interdependence and the case for co-operation

Many of the problems in the relations between countries arise from a combina-tion of the free-rider problem, Olson's problem and the Prisoners' Dilemma. The free-rider problem is a special case of the Prisoners' Dilemma. The free-rider problem in international relations exists because some of the solutions of international and global difficulties consist of the provision of public goods (Kindleberger 1978: 15, 1986). A public good is one from the supply of which all those who value the good benefit, irrespective of whether they have con-tributed to its costs or not. The concept can readily be extended to cover the promotion of common goals or common interests, the achievement of which benefits a group of people, irrespective of whether they have contributed to the costs of achieving these goals or interests. The enjoyment of the good or service or arrangement by one person, or group of persons, does not detract from the enjoyment by others. In this sense international co-operation that achieves joint interests, such as the prevention of international wars and the avoidance of global pollution, is a public good. So are international markets and a working international monetary order with an international central bank as a lender of last resort and a provider of international liquidity.

Scientific and technological research, except that for arms or national prestige, and the co-ordination of international investment decisions are of this kind.

These public goods will be systematically undersupplied, because any one country will not find it worth its while to take the appropriate action, relying on others to do so, even though the benefits would exceed the costs, were all to contribute. This was not the case in the past, when one dominant power, Britain in the nineteenth century and the United States for a quarter century after the last war, benefited so much from these public goods that they could tolerate the free-riding of other countries. (This is the case of Olson's small group, in which the interest of a single individual is so powerful that he will provide the public good.) But with the disappearance of a leading power in the world, their supply was reduced (inertia kept some supplies following) or disappeared. Each country, knowing that others will not contribute, lacks the incentive to contribute to something that benefits these others, including itself. The ranking of preferences by each country is the following:

1. My country does not contribute, while others do. (Free-rider, defection)
2. My country contributes together with others. (Co-operation)
3. No country contributes. (Prisoners' Dilemma outcome; disappearance of horse)
4. My country contributes while no other country does. (Sucker)

Behaviour according to 1 or the fear of 4 leads to outcome 3. Although 2 is preferred to 3, we end up with 3, unless either rewards and sanctions or autonomous motivations lead to 2. Incentives and expectations must be such that outcomes 4 and 1 are ruled out, so that if they contribute, they will not end up suckers. In their absence, the result is that peace, monetary stability, employment, environmental protection, debt relief, raw material conservation and world development will be undersupplied.

Related outcomes have also been discussed under the concept of 'the tragedy of the commons'. Each agent, acting in his self-interest, contributes to the losses of all, such as overgrazing on, and the eventual destruction of, a common pasture, or overpopulation of the world. Similarly, the concept of 'social traps' has been applied to situations when no driver has an incentive to install a gadget that reduces pollution. All these, as well as Prisoners' Dilemmas, 'collective action' problems and Olson's problem (see p. 333) are instances of 'market failure', or the impossibility of achieving preferred, 'rational' outcomes by uncoordinated self-interested 'rational' action.

But the destructive and self-destructive outcomes have been over-emphasized in the literature. Free-rider problems are not as ubiquitous as would be suggested by the theories in view of the existence of public goods and large groups. Individuals and groups may be afraid of the sanctions attached to such behaviour. Or they may act from enlightened self-interest or from habit. Or they may avoid free-riding because they believe that their contributions will induce others to contribute. Or they may be guided by moral or quasi-moral motives. Kant's categorical imperative bids us behave in a manner that can be universalized. The golden rule asks us to do unto others as we wish them to do unto us, and to refrain from doing unto them as we wish them to refrain from doing unto us. The popular wisdom tells us that honesty is the best policy.

But the application of these parables to the relations between states and their governments raises special problems. Kant's categorical imperative, the golden rule and conventional self-interested behaviour in the common interest may apply less to the actions of states than to those of individuals. We shall see that there are four reasons for this.

The Prisoners' Dilemma in the sphere of international relations arises because each country, in promoting its own natural interest, contributes to a situation in which all countries, including itself, are worse off. Just as public goods are undersupplied, so are public bads oversupplied. No single country has an adequate incentive to remove or combat them, without assurance that others will bear their share of the costs. This applies to competitive protectionism (a widely discussed public bad), beggar-my-neighbour devaluations of exchange rates or deflations, mutual impoverishment resulting from the debt crisis, the international spread of inflation, investment wars, research-and-development expenditure wars, driven, for reasons of national prestige, beyond the optimum point of national or global welfare, the arms race, global pollution of the air and sea, overfishing of the oceans and excessive exploitation of exhaustible resources to which no property rights are attached – and other, similar situations.

What is needed is either co-ordination and co-operation between states, or supra-national sanctions that force each country to act in its self-interest. Without such voluntary co-ordinated or enforced action the outcome of nationally rational actions will be collectively irrational damage and mutual impoverishment. For the damaging action is the best, whether others act similarly or not.

There are, however, also arguments against co-ordination. The Invisible Hand, which, according to Adam Smith, co-ordinates without our intentions the independent decisions of a multitude of individuals, could also be applied to the unintended co-ordination of the actions of nation-states. But the Invisible Hand that is supposed to guide the self-interest of each agent, whether individual or country, to the common good, cannot be seen in the areas of mutually destructive actions instanced above. The number of powerful countries is too small to establish working competition in the interaction of their policies, and there is no world government to set the rules.

Co-ordinated action can also be bad if it removes restraints that are in the interests of all. Thus co-ordinated policies may lead to higher rates of inflation than national policies restrained by the balance of payments. Or, alternatively, global central bankers may be more deflationary than national central banks. Co-ordinated policies based on a flawed analysis can also be more damaging than more dispersed errors. Co-ordination by governments may give rise to co-ordination of countervailing pressure groups, such as global trade unions, and frustrate the intentions of, say, an employment or anti-inflation policy.

There is another, more sophisticated, argument against the need for international co-ordination, based on Coase's theorem (Coase 1960, although as Bardhan 1989 points out, this paper contains 'only suggestions and examples' rather than the statement of a theorem). This holds that if, in the absence of transaction costs, and the presence of well-specified property rights, full information (three big assumptions) and a legal framework, one country inficts damages on another which are greater than the benefits to the first country, the injured country can enter into a contract with the injuring party (which is assumed to have the rights) and compensate it for not inflicting the injury and be better off; or, if the benefits are greater than the damage, the injuring country can compensate the injured country (if the injured country has the rights) for accepting the damage, and still be better off than it would have been, had it been prevented from inflicting the damage. Such international compensations or bribes are in fact not common, but they point to the other extreme from that of the Prisoners' Dilemma. In such a world Pareto's optimal allocations would be achieved, for any deviation would give rise to potentially joint gains, out of which losers could be compensated for forgoing the deviations or accepting the moves towards the optimum (Lipton 1985).

The distinctive features of international relations which point to the need for co-ordination are five in number. These features make it more difficult to reach Coase-type agreements and more likely to end up in Prisoners' Dilemma situations. First, there is no longer a dominant power, such as Britain before the First World War, and the United States after the Second. As already discussed, these world powers were prepared to carry a large part or the whole of the cost of providing the public goods, and of avoiding the public bads, and to exercise leadership and pressures to make others contribute. Second, the proliferation of sovereign nation-states to over 160 makes agreements more difficult than in an age when fewer governments could establish a system of mutual trust or enforcement. This is Olson's problem of the large group. According to the logic of collective action the larger the group, the weaker the incentive for any one member to contribute to the action that benefits all (Olson 1971). It is, however, true that most of these states are quite small and weak, and that co-ordination by a few large ones, such as the Group of Five or the Group of Seven, is what matters. Unfortunately, the interests of non-members are neglected in this process. Third, the rapid and accelerating pace of social and technical change makes it more difficult to evolve the stability on which trust, the importance of which in avoiding Prisoners' Dilemmas is emphasized by Lipton (1985), is built. The Prisoners' Dilemma in its pure form applies best to a single 'game'. It has been shown that repeated games of Prisoners' Dilemma in similar situations tend to lead to co-operative solutions (Axelrod 1984). But rapid change of the conditions on which co-operation is based prevents the basis for co-operation to be formed. Fourth, the absence of world government and world courts makes it impossible to establish property rights, enforce contracts and set sanctions for not abiding by agreements. There is no coercion to reinforce voluntary agreements, and ensure that a country that sticks to the agreement is not put into the position of a 'sucker'. Fifth, loyalties to the global community are, in any case, weak, and whereas individual selfishness, when it conflicts with commitments to the community, is condemned as immoral, national selfishness lays claim to higher virtue.

As Michael Lipton has said, if all outcomes were non-cooperative Prisoners' Dilemmas, no government would be possible (although some have attempted to construct the case for the state on the Prisoners' Dilemma) (Lipton 1985). If all outcomes were according to Coase's theorem, no government would be needed (except for income redistribution). The actual world of international relations is between the two extremes, but nearer the Prisoners' Dilemma end of the spectrum, for the five reasons given.

The absence of global institutions that would prevent Prisoners' Dilemma outcomes represents a lag of institutions behind technology. For technologically we have moved towards a global community. The flow of information, communications and transport of goods and people have unified and internationalized the world. But institutionally we are still stuck with the old nation-state and its boundaries. Let me give ten illustrations (a round number) of the type of institutional reform that I have in mind.

Institutional innovations

First, there is the creation of an international central bank that would be able to create and withdraw international liquidity. This would be the response to the globalization of financial private markets. A panic run on the banks would cause an international financial breakdown unless the liquidity were provided. The General Arrangements to Borrow do this now to some extent, but a central bank would do it on a more solid and reliable basis.

The central bank would also be responsible for the growth of global reserves at a pace which gives neither an inflationary nor a deflationary bias to the world economy. In the absence of such a global monetary authority the competitive actions of nation-states will tend to be either too restrictive or too expansionary. In the former case, they would transmit unemployment and unused capacity, as each country scrambles to accumulate scarce reserves, in the latter case they would spread inflation throughout the world as the reserve currency country incurs large balance-of-payments deficits to pay for economic or military ventures abroad.

Second, there is the need for an International Debt Facility. A concerted reduction in the debt of the debtor countries would probably make everybody better off. The Laffer curve applies, because both the means and the incentives to invest in the debtor countries would be raised, and a larger amount of debt could be serviced out of the resulting higher growth. Yet, because of the logic of collective action no bank has an incentive to forgive, for its forgiveness would be used only to pay interest to the non-forgiving creditors. It should be noted that the current practice of selling discounted bonds does not help the debtor countries. The buyer can still claim the whole nominal value of the debt, and if the debtor country buys the bond itself, then paying the liability is inflationary.

Two collective steps are necessary, which the free market cannot take, one by banks, the other by creditor governments and international financial institutions. The first is for the creditor banks to relieve the debtors jointly of some portion of the debt. The second step is for governments, together with the World Bank and the IMF, to arrange jointly for guarantees on the remaining debt. Without this attraction, no bank has an incentive to enter into the agreement. Normal lending and global growth can then be resumed.

Third, there is a need for an international body to provide information on decisions for fixed, durable investment with long construction periods, so that we avoid the current lurches from scarcity to excess capacity in such industries as steel, shipbuilding and fertilizers. It should obviously not be a super-cartel that allocates market shares to countries and firms, but a method of co-ordinating investment decisions.

Fourth, there is a case for an international investment trust that channels the surpluses of the surplus countries in a multilaterally guaranteed scheme to the capital-hungry developing countries. It would have guarantees against exchange rate losses and inflation for the lenders. The loans would be, in the first instance, on commercial terms. At the time of writing Japan has become the largest surplus country on current account, but Germany is also moving ahead. Rather than exhort the Japanese and Germans to expand their domestic consumption and investment, or, worse, the deficit countries to contract and spread world unemployment and lowered growth, we should recycle these surpluses to the developing countries. But this calls for institutional innovation. The new institution, a multilateral investment trust, would convert the current account surpluses into long-term loans for development. This would be in the interest of Japan, which could continue her export-led growth without having either to reduce her high rate of savings or to find domestic, lower-yielding alternatives; it would be in the interest of the other OECD countries on whose exports some of the loans will be spent; it would be in the interest of the capital-hungry developing countries, whose resources are waiting to be mobilized by such capital flows; and it would be in the interest of the world economy, which could resume its expansionary momentum. An interest-subsidy scheme could be grafted onto this for the low-income countries. In this way the current-account surpluses in search of a cause, the unemployed manpower and industrial capacity of the advanced countries, and the underutilized labour force in the developing countries would be brought together, to the benefit of all (Streeten 1988).

Fifth, there should be a better way of dealing with the energy and oil price problem than the erratic zig-zag movements that we have witnessed since 1973. Oil-producing and oil-consuming countries would get together and agree on a small, annual increase in the real price of oil, say 2 per cent per year. This assumes agreement on the best guess of the real price of oil, in, say, twenty years' time. The balance-of-payments surpluses generated by such an increase could be channelled into the investment trust proposed above. The incentives to explore for more oil, alternatives to oil and conservation would be gradual and steady. The incentives for the oil exporting countries to use their revenue for investment in alternative productive assets would be also gradual and steady. Incentives to consumers of oil would also permit a foreseeable and gradual adaptation. There would be neither debt crises nor the sloshing around of large funds in search of remunerative and safe returns. The world economy would be spared at least one major source of shocks and instability. Both inflation and unemployment rates would be reduced.

Sixth, there is a strong case for a global environmental protection agency. The global atmosphere and stratosphere and the oceans would otherwise become the receptacles for the muck of each country, and we would be continuing to destroy our natural environment, the rain forests, and already endangered species. The national environmental problems of rich countries can often be solved only at the expense of the poor countries. Those of the poor countries arise from their poverty, such as the shortage of fuel wood that leads to deforestation. But the solution of the global problems is in harmony with poverty eradication.

Seventh, a scheme for commodity price stabilization should be re-examined. In the past, the discussion of such proposals has been almost wholly confined to the micro-economic argument of improving the incomes for producers and consumers. But the macro-economic case has gone largely by default. The instability of the prices of raw materials that are used as inputs into manufactured goods has contributed to inflation and unemployment in the advanced countries, and to instability and poverty in the developing countries. A thorough re-examination of the case is in order, starting, perhaps, from Keynes's proposal for an international trade organization, which was negotiated in detail but not subsequently implemented.

Eighth, there is a need for a global anti-monopoly and anti-restrictive practices policy. As things are, advanced countries have these policies for their domestic markets, but actually encourage their firms to gang up against foreigners.

Ninth, there is the institution of an international income tax, levied progressively on GNP according to incomes per head, or, better, consumption per head, so as to encourage savings, with a lower exemption limit, collected automatically, but disbursed to developing countries according to agreed criteria. The monitoring of the fulfilment of the conditions should be done by a tenth institution.

Tenth, either the developing countries should themselves monitor one another's performance, as was done by the European countries under Marshall Aid, or a mutually accepted transnational body, such as a secretariat with global (not international) loyalties or a global commission of men and women, trusted by both contributors and recipients, should ensure that the purposes for which the aid is intended are fulfilled.

Anyone should feel free to criticize or add to these proposals, by exercising his or her institutional imagination. We should not be asking for more international bureaucrats, but for rules, procedures and norms that would replace the old world of dominance and dependence or uncoordinated chaos by one of pluralism and equality.

In the spirit of the previous paper's final paragraph it may be worth mentioning other possible global institutional innovations, both to extend the diversity of suggestions offered and to indicate the already significant foundations, theoretical and practical, for further developments in this area.

Tobin sees two possible routes for reform of the international monetary system: making currency transactions more costly, to reduce capital mobility and speculative exchange-rate pressures; and greater world economic integration, implying eventual monetary union and a World Central Bank (Streeten's first suggestion, which was also put forward by Keynes at the Bretton Woods Conference, at which he also proposed a commodity-based world currency) (Tobin 1987). Tobin favours the first route and advocates 'an internationally uniform tax on all spot conversions of one currency into another, proportional to the size of the transaction', with a tax rate of perhaps 1 per cent.

Makhijani and Browne go the other route, discussing in detail the possible role of a world central bank in administering a world reserve currency, the unit of which would be defined as the amount of money required to purchase a standard equivalent 'basket' of commodities in the different participating countries (Makhijani and Browne 1986). These countries' currencies would be related to the international currency, and to each other, through the domestic prices of these baskets, so that exchange rates would be set according to countries' relative productivity rather than by their balance of payments, currency speculation or irrelevant political considerations. The advantages of such a system would be a stable, inflation-free (because always able by definition to purchase the same 'basket' of goods) world reserve currency in place of the US dollar in this role; and exchange rates that were also both stable and reflected real economic considerations. Currencies would not be traded. The balance of payments would be controlled by different means, which the authors discuss. They also claim:

> Our proposal addresses the principal structural causes of the instability and inequality in the present system. Our system would allow for a defusing of the debt crisis, would put into its place a flexible and stable monetary instrument, and would lay an inflation-free and equitable basis for trade relations between the Third World and the industrial countries. At the same time, it would enhance internal monetary and fiscal independence.
>
> (ibid.: 75)

If a World Central Bank is still only a promising gleam in a few well-focused eyes, an existing international institution in need of considerable development and formalization to respond to globalizing forces is the International Court at the Hague. Its judgments must become binding on the international community and it must have the ability to enforce the observance of basic human rights and international non-aggression, through UN peace-keeping troops if necessary. Surely, it is now apparent that the correct time to have isolated and imposed sanctions on Saddam Hussein of Iraq was when he gassed his own Kurdish citizens. Such international action would have occupied the moral high ground untainted with the issue of who controls the Middle East's oil and, if properly enforced, would probably have forestalled the invasion of Kuwait. The International Court would also have the crucial tasks of enforcing such agreements as the Law of the Sea, the Montreal Protocol on ozone-depleting substances and the host of other international environmental measures that will be necessary if environmental sustainability is to be achieved.

On this latter point, the forms of the treaties concluded for environmental protection are crucial to their effectiveness. Goodin considers that

> the traditional structure of international law – guided as it is, by notions of autonomous national actors with strong rights which all other national actors similarly share – is wildly inappropriate to many of these new environmental challenges. A system of shared duties or, better yet, shared responsibilities is a more fitting model, given the nature of the tasks at hand
>
> (Goodin 1990: 93)

Goodin sees in the Montreal Protocol a clear shift towards such a notion of shared responsibilities.

A different approach to environmental challenges is taken by Kox (1990). Kox advocates New International Commodity Agreements (NICAs) as a means of internalizing into the price of Third World commodities the externalities associated with their production and exchange. The NICA would provide for the levy of an import tax on the selected commodities to bring their price up to that estimated for their sustainable production. The tax would provide for investment in production methods in the commodity's country of origin in order to make sustainable production methods a reality. Clearly NICAs, to be effective, would need an enforcing agency:

> It seems unavoidable to introduce auditing procedures that may run against feelings of national sovereignty, or even limit national sovereignty of producing countries . . . The auditing committee would report any irregularities to a standing committee or governing board of the NICAs.
>
> (Kox 1990: 21–2)

Again, if the problem is to be addressed, it seems inevitable that some national sovereignty will need to be surrendered to an international institution.

The increased peace-keeping role of the United Nations in the new globalism has already been mentioned, but that institution could and should play an important role in many other crucial areas including:

1. *Human rights observance* Van Boven, Professor of International Law at the University of Limburg and former Director of the United Nations Division of Human Rights, perceptively analyses the future role of the UN in this area, under the headings of Standard-Setting, Protection and Promotion (Van Boven 1989). Pietilä and Vickers suggest how the UN can develop and extend its already significant role in securing less discrimination against and exploitation of women (Pietilä and Vickers 1990).

2. *Code of conduct for transnational business* The UN Centre for Transnational Corporations (TNCs) has built up great expertise in this area in its efforts to get a code of conduct for TNCs introduced. The global market-place increasingly demands the sort of checks and balances this Code envisages if it is to operate in the general social interest.

3. *Redistribution* The attempts of the plethora of UN agencies at 'development' have, at the very best, had mixed results. Analysts like Hancock evaluate their record much more harshly:

> Whatever noble mission the United Nations may once have had has, I am now convinced, long since been forgotten in the rapid proliferation of its self-perpetuating bureaucracies – in the seemingly endless process by which empires have been created within the system by ambitious and greedy men and then staffed by time-servers and sycophants. Rather than encouraging humility and dedication, the world body's structure seems actively to reward self-seeking behaviour and to provide staff with many opportunities to abuse the grave responsibilities with which they have been entrusted.
>
> (Hancock 1989: 84)

From inside the UN system, Jolly more moderately but no less damningly writes:

> A number of problems characterise much, if not most, of the technical assistance at present provided:
>
> 1. Inadequate quality
> 2. Irrelevant focus
> 3. Insufficient local knowledge and experience and above all
> 4. Very low cost-effectiveness, when compared with alternatives.
>
> (Jolly 1989: 22)

As an example of cost, Jolly gives Tanzania, in which in 1988 some $200 million were spent on 'the salaries, pensions, housing allowances, air travel and other direct costs of 1,000 or so international experts provided as the core of technical assistance', a sum twice as much as that of Tanzania's entire civil service in the year.

Although UN staff are among the best-paid bureaucrats in the world, presumably to remunerate 'the highest standards of efficiency, competence and integrity' called for in the UN Charter, over 300 officials in New York were revealed in 1991 to 'have been involved in a tax fraud costing millions of dollars and possibly going back as long as 20 years' (Waterhouse 1991).

How this Augean stable of waste and self-aggrandizement can be cleaned out is a question to which few answers emerge. It is clear, however, that until it is, the vital redistributive function of the UN will operate at only a few per cent of its potential with enormous opportunity costs incurred on the funds it employs.

The national level

In the 1980s it became fashionable to replace the notion of 'market failure' with 'government failure'. Born-again marketeers would cheerfully concede some shortcomings of the market but would then assert that government intervention would only make them worse. The market would do the best that could be done. Given the extent of market failure, especially with regard to the environment, this is here taken to be no less than a counsel for catastrophe. But this should not blind those seeking a more balanced position to the obvious counter-productiveness of much standard government practice and the need to reform it in the direction of, in James Robertson's (1989) terms, conservation and enablement.

The enabling (and disabling) state
Geoff Mulgan and Helen Wilkinson

In the Burmese countryside farmers reluctantly deliver rice at artificially low prices to government agents. In Lima street traders ignore elaborate state regulations to survive. In western Europe small firms spend as much as a tenth of their time on paperwork for the state, and the unemployed waste hours sitting waiting in social security offices. All are victims of disabling states that make life harder by tangling people in their webs of bureaucracy.

This paper is concerned with the revolt against disabling states, and with the new interest in enabling structures that make governments more responsive and supportive: serving their people and sustaining life rather than burying it.

An interrelated set of questions about the nature of the state runs through the analysis. How can states be more successful at defining people's needs and meeting them? How can they adapt to more differentiated societies and to a new era that is sceptical of bureaucratic and technocratic solutions? What are to be the limits of the state's responsibility, and what tasks are state bureaucracies best suited for?

These questions are highly pertinent for two reasons. First because around the world there is feverish experimentation with new structures and processes which point towards new models of a more enabling state. Second because even the most enlightened and decentralized states still face traditional problems of organization and representation, problems that arise from the inescapable trade-offs between different and imperfect structures.

The Fordist state

The starting point for any twentieth century discussion of the state is that creature of the nineteenth century so perceptively described by Max Weber in his account of bureaucracy. A hundred years on it is hard to remember that it was a major organizational innovation at the time, or for that matter to recall the speed with which it grew. In the United States the federal bureaucracy expanded from 600 people in 1831 to over 13,000 fifty years later. The British state bureaucracy tripled between 1891 and 1911 and has until recently continued growing. Such is the pervasiveness of bureaucracy that in today's European Community, between 10 and 13 per cent of the employed population work in government bureaucracies. In its widest sense the public sector accounts for as much as half of all economic activity.

Despite decades of management thinking about humanization and decentralization, most states continue to be organized according to classic principles of bureaucracy. Constructed according to a hierarchy of functions, they are organized in a pyramidal structure, and bound by fixed rules and clearly defined tasks. Individuals fit the structures rather than *vice versa*. The administration of politics and decision-making itself is centred around the regular rhythm of committees and meetings. The information needed to carry out tasks is, in the language of computer science, pre-processed: forced into categories that make it easy to deal with. The census form, the national accounts, the input–output table, are the life-blood of this kind of state. Bureaucracy in the very nature of things systemizes, objectifies and depersonalizes people in order to cope with them on a mass scale.

Historically the modern state evolved in parallel to the modern corporation and the modern party. All favoured an increasingly complex division of labour, an increased dependence on rules (rather than persons) and hierarchical models of decision-making. All evolved a division of labour between representatives (whether of voters, shareholders or members) and functionaries. According to Weber the aim was to minimize discretionary decision-making and the 'politics of spoils', by transforming older forms of charismatic leadership into structures of rational-legal authority. Throughout society what the American historian Alfred Chandler (1977) called the 'visible hands' of active planning – forecasting, strategy, co-ordination – came to replace the invisible hand of the market. In theory at least chaos and arbitrary power gave way to order.

The state's expansion was double-edged. It was effective at bringing improvements on a mass scale. Transport, housing, education and health were all well-suited to the mechanistic bureaucracy. A policy could be fed in at the top, as it were, and implemented in a consistent, ordered fashion by the governmental machine. Progressives saw in the gradual expansion of this kind of state, (rational, socially aware, problem solving), a solution to the chaos, iniquities and inequalities of the past. Yet this kind of state was also often experienced as oppressive. Anomie and alienation, the emptiness of rule by numbers and of a mass society, became evident almost as soon as the nineteenth-century bureaucracies began their rapid expansions.

The benign apotheosis of the all-embracing modern state was probably Scandinavia's social-democratic model, still widely seen as an ideal of social organization despite the well-documented crisis of the Swedish economy. The Stalinist state came to be seen as its malign apotheosis, Fordist paternalism taken to a totalitarian extreme, controlling all aspects of life from culture to raw materials through the extensive bureaucracies of party and state.

These classic models of the state born around the turn of the century, are often described as Weberian or bureaucratic states. But it is perhaps better to describe them as Fordist after Henry Ford, and the analyses of Fordism which date back to Antonio Gramsci. For the essence of the modern state was the idea that policies and programmes could be mass produced in a standardized way, through a social assembly line. The word Fordist also has another virtue. It calls attention to the classic social policy of the state: just as Ford said he had to pay his workers well so they could afford his cars, the Fordist state took responsibility not only for maintaining full employment and high demand but also for the education and health of the worker.

The pyramidal state carried implications for political organization. Politics was to be carried on by national parties which would compete for state power. By winning power parties could implement their policies downwards through the impartial state bureaucracy. The individual's control over the base of the pyramid, perhaps a local official, had to pass right up the pyramid and then down again.

This is what most of us understand by the state. A mass of institutions, organized as bureaucratic hierarchies, answerable either to elected governments or to dictators: charged with putting programmes and policies into practice and with operating an enormous machinery of welfare, security and oversight.

The legitimacy of such a state comes from a range of sources. It is the means of structuring democratic politics and also the sustainer and distributor of welfare and social order. In many countries its legitimacy derives from its developmental role: like the first wave of 'late developers', Germany, France and Japan, many governments have argued the case for a strong state as a means of forcing the pace of change in a highly competitive international environment: in the absence of 'organic development', the state must step in as an accelerator and as a tool for social engineering.

Faith in this state form has consistently encouraged commentators (from James Burnham and Clark Kerr onwards) to argue that technocratic authority would come to dominate politics. East and west would become indistinguishable. Ideology would be superfluous thanks to the efficiency of the management state. Shades of the same view are still apparent today, in such writings as Francis Fukuyama's famous 'end of history' piece, which foresees a rather dull world of liberal-democratic consensus, in which debate is concerned only with technical problem-solving instead of the clash of values. Ultimately, as in Engels' intriguing vision, the state withers away leaving only the administration of things.

Yet far from reigning supreme, the last twenty years have seen an extra-ordinary shift in perceptions of the state throughout the world. Waves of anti-bureaucratic feeling, evident in the revolutions of eastern Europe, in Soviet *perestroika*, in the populisms of Latin America and the rhetoric of a Margaret Thatcher or Ronald Reagan are truly global. Hostility to bureaucracy, and to the state's presumption that it is the solution rather than the problem, is almost universal. States are now more likely to be seen as self-interested, corrupt, parasitical, burdensome controllers rather than as organs of progress.

Why is this? The obvious answer is that states have failed in their avowed missions, that they have disabled rather than enabled. It is also clear that nation states are too small for the big problems (managing the eco-sphere, regulating a multinational economy, sustaining world peace, etc.) and too large for the small problems (coping with the disintegration of communities in rural and urban environments, etc.). But the causes of the crisis of the state lie deeper. One factor has been the very success of governments in fuelling the 'revolution of entitlements' which convinced people of their rights to welfare, to employment or housing but also created expectations that states have proved unable to satisfy. The crisis was exacerbated as growing demands on the state coincided with stagnant revenues, and has often been presented as the 'fiscal crisis of the welfare state'. Questions of resource allocation were clearly crucial but the fundamental crisis was also one of service delivery. The classic state bureaucracy could not accommodate apparently limitless needs.

A second cause is the fact that the very success of state forms locked bureau-cracies into inflexible structures. The best example of this has been politicians' and administrators' obsession with through-put: the emphasis on numbers going through the system rather than the way in which the state responds to the demands being placed upon it, that is to say with quantity rather than quality. Drawing on the logistical methods of modern armies and corpora-tions, state bureaucracies became very good at large-scale standardized provision, with highly supervised workforces operating according to standard-ized procedures. But as the demands on the state become further differ-entiated, the flaws of this approach became ever more obvious. When people have diverse needs and demand different kinds of housing and different types of health care, through-put becomes increasingly redundant, particularly in societies where poverty is increasingly seen as relative and where the role of the state is to meet the needs of the few – the bottom third, urban and rural underclasses – rather than those of the many.

The third cause is more obviously rooted in structures. The pyramidal structure meant that all problems had to be passed up the pyramid. There were obvious dangers that such a structure could create overload at the top, a lower quality of decision-making and inflexibility. Other internal blockages also made states less able to respond and to adapt. The familiar compart-mentalization of bureaucracies meant that problems were shunted around, precluding more holistic solutions. 'Switchboard mechanisms' that would have made it possible to cut across divisions were structurally impossible. The result has been a pervasive perception that bureaucracies are not problem-solvers but rather manifestations of government overload.

This change in attitudes to the state has coincided with a shift in attitudes to the political forms of parties and representation, which were and are symbio-tically linked to state bureaucracies. It is no coincidence that the vanguard social movements of the 1960s, 1970s and 1980s – women's liberation, anti-racism, the Greens – all flourished in parallel with the renewed interest in markets as the principal means of resource allocation. Both were symptoms of the same causes.

Similar patterns of bureaucratic failure, and similar shifts in perception, have been apparent throughout the world, where western (and Soviet) models of bureaucracy were exported. The former colonies, whether in Africa or South-East Asia, have all suffered from the imposition of Fordist models of state organization. The absence of strong democratic cultures to keep bureau-cracies in check meant that when formal democratic structures were built up alongside older ones the latter tended to prevail. As a result third world bureaucracies often seemed to suffer from endemic malfunctioning. States seemed 'soft', serving the bureaucracy rather than the people. The dividing line between a politics of spoils (where kinship networks remain resilient) and state bureaucracies was blurred. One kind of order obscured another deeper and older order.

In many countries statism and command-led (and military) bureaucracies have often been seen as the only viable force for change, yet they too have been 'soft'. Charismatic leaders like Gaddafi, Castro and Indira Gandhi have sat astride (and repeatedly castigated) classic Fordist bureaucracies where rules are simultaneously all-pervasive and always broken. Like many others, post-colonial Zambia's bureaucracy grew by 265 per cent between 1963 and 1974, without any obvious comparable growth in its ability to solve problems. The growth is best understood not as an expansion of rule-based bureaucracy but rather as a symptom of a breakdown of rules: the increasing prevalence of a clientelist political framework and a politics of spoils.

The classic pyramidal bureaucracy is as ill-equipped to cope with difference in the First World as it is in areas of the Third World, where societies remain highly differentiated through tribal loyalties, different geographic terrains within the same country, and the different needs of urban and rural dwellers and nomads. In India, for example, central government has often used blue-prints for such things as water irrigation to impose rules appropriate for one region onto wholly different regions with disastrous results. Unfortunately, as in many other cases the ability of the state to deceive itself – to dress failure up as success, to foster 'tame' presentation villages to top officials, to massage statistics – hinders more variegated approaches. The inflexible nature of the bureaucratic state has been even more pronounced in countries such as Lesotho and Botswana which experience huge migrations in search of work, housing or land. In such societies the classic state defined by geographical boundaries of authority, is simply out of sync with more basic social realities.

Minimal states

The failures of classic state forms have fuelled a rising tide of discontent which has prompted renewed interest in the second model of the state, which predates the modern Weberian state. This is the old liberal notion of the minimal or 'nightwatchman' state, responsible for the minimal task of preserving security against invasion, and sustaining law and the conditions of free exchange. According to this model, now associated with the New Right of theorists like Milton Friedman, Robert Nozick and Friedrich Hayek, wherever possible differences and problems should be resolved through contracts and legal processes rather than arbitration or solution by the bureaucracy. Ideologies of the market and individualism are also invoked: the minimal state allows the market to function freely, and enables individuals to meet their needs and express themselves through it. States should only attempt what markets cannot do. Even then there is no presumption that the state will succeed where the market has not. Government failure is seen as inherently more likely and disagreeable than market failure.

Two key arguments sustain the 'minimal statists'. One is the overload thesis which argues that democratic systems have an inherent tendency to get overloaded with demands and expectations. State structures buckle as a result of their failure to meet the demands that the political realm generates, and must be restricted by constitutional limits on their freedom of action and their scope. Second, following the arguments of public-choice theory, it is argued that bureaucracies – and politicians – have inherent tendencies to accumulate power and wealth which must be countered by the use of competition and contracts. For the extreme proponents of this view ideals of public service and the public good are never more than cynical masks of self-interest.

The ideal of the minimal state, though hard to make operational, has become increasingly popular, not just in the First World but also in the Second and Third. It is a natural reaction for people who have lived under maximal states. In eastern Europe, the collapse of Stalinism brought a wave of support for the ideas of Friedman and Hayek, while in much of the Third World the failure of older grandiose schemes has spawned a new populism around small capital, with the state and large capital seen as twin demons, as in the inflential writings of the Peruvian Hernando de Soto (e.g. de Soto 1989). In each case the state is asked to become the enemy of bureaucracy, stripping away its own functions and using its powers to dismantle other vested interests.

The appeal of this model is evident. But it is as flawed as the Fordist models it seeks to abolish. Simply removing functions from the state can cause more problems than it solves. Remove welfare functions, and increased social unrest and crime demand greater reliance upon other elements of the state bureaucracy like the army or police. Remove educational and training functions and the result may be a less-skilled and less-employable workforce that will depend more on social security. Remove the overall security of a paternalistic state and many will be unable to fend for themselves in the bracing freedom of statelessness.

The crisis of state forms

The bureaucratic and minimal state have stood as two poles of a debate, and sometimes a battle, that has raged throughout the twentieth century; a conflict between markets and administrations, and between planning and not planning. Until recently it was a battle couched in the language of the old Cold War – a battle ultimately between the two world orders of capitalism and communism. For some the last few years have seen a resolution of the argument.

But the reality is more complex. The arguments and needs which called the Fordist state into existence have not disappeared. Famine in the horn of Africa, homelessness on the streets of wealthy cities, lack of medical insurance for nearly one in ten Americans are a symptom of the inability of markets to respond to human need. Nor is it just that the market is sometimes inadequate. Often the market can exacerbate needs, as in the case of housing markets in Britain or America or as in the case of grain hoarding in famine areas.

The need for states to be more than coercive bulwarks against a descent into nature, and more than minimal arbitrators, remains evident. The state – warts and all – remains an unavoidable party to the solution of many of the most critical problems. This is as true in eastern and central Europe, where enthusiasm for pure market solutions has been shortlived and support for socialized provision of everything from transport to education is deep rooted, as it is everywhere else.

But what is clear is that there is little prospect of a return to the arrogance of states that saw themselves as sufficient solution, and as able to define needs and their means of satisfaction. There is no longer a presumption that states are innocent until proven guilty.

Enabling states

This then is the starting point for the idea of the enabling state. Surprisingly, however, the enabling state has been to date more interesting as a set of practices than as an ideal. It is not possible either to point to any serious theory of the enabling state or to fit it within one political or philosophical tradition. As a result it can be interpreted or articulated in completely contradictory ways, as individualist and liberal or collectivist, or as corporatist and socialistic. It can view the state as best proactive or reactive.

The problems of definition also have another source. For the new political movements built around environmental, peace and women's issues have contributed little to the theory of how states work. Instead, much of their impact has come from their rejection of the familiar languages and structures of power. Sometimes, rather implausibly, they have suggested that their own internal practices provide a prefigurative form of the future state. But despite the appearance of feminists in cabinets and Greens in local councils it remains hard to define how they might organize a state, a civil service or an army.

Despite these caveats, however, there can be no doubt that there is some meaning to the idea of an enabling state, and that common themes and practices have emerged in widely differing traditions. Governments and parties of all colours have responded both to underlying pressures for reform and to the vanguard social movements of the last few decades – to feminism, anti-racism, both the Green and consumer movements, to progressive business theories and to new theories of development – all in common seeking greater decentralization, and greater end-user or citizen control.

These new concepts of the state replace mechanistic metaphors with ecological ones. They seek to be people centred rather than orientated to structure, interested more in horizontal than vertical lines of communication, with networks rather than pyramids. They emphasize learning rather than blueprints, local knowledge rather than centralized knowledge. Perhaps the best analogy is that unlike the overbearing Victorian father state, they see their role as more maternal – fostering and nurturing a society, enjoying difference and plurality in civil society rather than fearing and prescribing limits to it.

They also share three starting principles which distinguish enabling approaches from other models of the state: first, that the state remains an indispensable source of social solutions and meeter of needs; second that the state can rarely define needs well on its own, but that this must always be an active and reciprocal process with those who have needs; and third that the state is better as an enabler than as an operator or provider in its own right, so that wherever possible the means of delivery too should be organized in as reciprocal, responsive and open manner as possible.

'Co-optive states'

Given these principles there are two underlying ideal-type 'models' of the enabling state.

The first can be called the co-optive state. It draws on the traditions of corporatist organization that have formed a strong strand in the history of the Fordist state. Where older models of corporatism tended to centre around absorbing industry and trade unions, capital and labour, into the state the new forms focus as well on newer movements, on the social as well as the economic. Thus consumer, women's, arts, sports, housing, community-based, ethnic and other voluntary organizations are all brought into the orbit of the state. Professionals and consumers are placed on key committees and sometimes given grants to carry out state responsibilities (such as overseeing the quality of goods, or organizing care for the elderly, or providing information to the public). Previously independent movements and organizations become closely tied to the state and economically dependent on it.

One interesting example of this approach was the Labour administration at the Greater London Council (1981–1986) which used a radical rhetoric of 'popular planning' and enabling initiatives (see pp. 358–68 below). Incorporating representatives of ethnic communities, women's groups and other voluntary organizations onto its committees it also took on the role of funding them. The theory was that the 'true' representatives of civil society could serve both to define needs and meet them within the umbrella of the state while also remaining at one remove from its formal structures. Though often fraught, the experience showed that an outward looking, enabling state could mobilize great reserves of energy, as well as giving more substance to the democratic process. However, it also showed how hard it was to determine who really was representative of the various communities, and how disabling it was for many organizations to have to enter into a structured, funding relationship with the state.

A second example which takes the co-optive model further is the regional government of Emilio-Romagna in northern Italy, which is interesting as an example of a communist government using a more organic approach to social organization. Instead of actively planning the regional economy, the state has seen its role as one of enabling large numbers of small firms and co-operatives to work together through such things as joint marketing organizations, collaborative research and development and so forth. Driven by the historical memory of how fascism was able to organize the petit bourgeoisie, the regional state has supported and co-opted small business, enabling the economy of the region to organize itself most efficiently rather than being integrated within multinational capital. Until now the model has performed successfully. However, its potential flaw – and one that it shares with all enabling approaches – is that it lacks any strategy for dealing with large scale and multinational capital.

A third set of examples is to be found within Scandinavian social democracy, where governments have for many years used voluntary organizations as delivery mechanisms, nurturing pre-existing organizations such as housing co-ops and facilitating the development of housing for local communities by the community, providing preferential subsidies (in the case of new-build projects) and preferential mortgage loans for co-operative house building. Starting from housing some co-ops have evolved to deliver social welfare on the state's behalf, with community-based launderettes, crèches and so on, encouraged by grants from the relevant authorities. Many co-op estates have also set up their own closed circuit cable networks to develop community broadcasting. In Norway the Oslo Kommune (the capital's local authority) negotiated with one of the main housing co-operatives to take over housing provision as far back as the 1930s. It was contracted to take over the council's housing waiting list and became the dominant agency for the city. By 1947 the Kommune had sold some 5,000 homes to a Special Holding Company to be run by tenants and municipal representatives arranging and supplying preferential loans to facilitate the process. The Kommune has not discarded its responsibility to lower-income citizens; instead, it has encouraged poorer people to buy their share into a local co-op by providing loans for the deposit. Some 45 per cent the city's housing stock is now co-operative and to some extent tenant controlled.

Similar models are now becoming widespread throughout the world as non-governmental and voluntary organizations increasingly merge into the state, performing advisory, counselling and service functions, on contract from the state. In rural development, the use of non-governmental organizations is now normal, though practices vary widely from the genuinely participatory to the very bureaucratic.

A fourth set of examples use similar principles but within the state itself. Scandinavian countries are, again, a fertile source of models. There is long experience of quasi-independent bodies – like the Municipal Housing Corporations (MHCs), government agencies responsible for providing public rented housing – meeting goals set by central government. More recently similar policies of hiving off have been followed as part of the 'new managerialism', designed to bring greater clarity of goals and stricter accountability. In New Zealand for example the Labour government set up a range of semi-independent agencies to be controlled through the monitoring of their outputs, while in Britain much of the civil service is being farmed out into Executive Agencies, which are ostensibly given more autonomy as to how they meet centrally determined goals. Though best understood as a rationalization of the internal organization of state bureaucracies the parallels with enabling approaches are evident. In the best examples there is radical decentralization of operational responsibility; in Sweden, for example, public home helps have been allowed to organize their own schedules rather than depending on an office manager, while in one town in Holland roadsweepers have been allowed to upgrade their work to become household advisers on recycling.

These various models have some common features. All agree that the state is less effective as a direct provider than as enabler, financer and regulator of outputs. There is agreement that it can be more efficient to tap into pre-existing networks and organizations in civil society than to create institutions from scratch. In the best cases links are made between the need for openness in representative structures – in the ways in which needs are defined – and in the means of delivery.

Yet even the best practices have their problems. Sometimes agencies bypass or undermine democratic decision-making (particularly when national governments use them as a subtle weapon against local governments). Sometimes agencies leave out 'difficult' sections of the population – the hard to house, hard to teach or hard to care for. The more community-based initiatives also run into the problem that faces all participative structures: they are often very time-consuming, and can lead to cycles of dissatisfaction. Small groups of individuals tend to select themselves, and are not always more representative than councillors and parliamentary representatives chosen through formal routes. Finally all co-optive models cause problems for the ideal of a truly voluntary and independent sector, since they bring dependence on the state and thus an inescapable dynamic towards greater professionalism, a greater role for finance, and thus a pressure to forsake community roots. Even the most independent groups soon succumb to the rule by figures and targets and conformance to state needs.

Individual empowerment

Just as the co-optive approach has grown out of the Fordist model of the state, so too the concept of individual empowerment derives its theoretical roots from advocates of the minimal state. With roots in classical liberal political theory this approach sees the role of the state as being to create the conditions in which individuals can empower themselves. The guiding principle is that for citizens to be truly enabled all mediations between the state and the individual must be swept away. In the place of quangos, committees and commissions, consultative bodies and community councils, the state must give power – and monetary entitlement – directly to individuals. But rather than constraining the state to a minimal, 'nightwatchman' role, there is a commitment to promoting equality of opportunity.

Individuals are seen as consumers, with power to be exercised through the market-place. Thus in the case of education, where a co-opter might try and widen circles of policy debate and ensure proper representation on school boards of governors, this approach would favour giving parents vouchers with which they could choose their childrens' schools. Health consumers are expected to exercise choices about when and where to have treatment, and what this treatment will be. Similarly, states sell council houses cheaply to enable citizens to exercise their 'right to buy'. Privatization and the introduction of competition to utilities are designed to have the same effect. The principle is that just as individual consumers regulate companies in the private sector so can they regulate the state to ensure that it is responsive and efficient. Any alternative to the direct empowerment of the individual simply creates new vested interests which will ultimately work against the interests of the user. Implicit in the argument is the idea that the exercise of choice through a market-place is the most appropriate place for individual control – more appropriate even than voting for a school governor or participating through a community health council or lobbying through an MP. Voter sovereignty is replaced by the notion of consumer sovereignty.

Though originally associated with the Right, similar ideas are now becoming current on the Left of the political spectrum. In education some have argued that vouchers should give an added weight to poorer parents. Others are pursuing ideas for achieving democratization at the point of consumption: smart cards for users of health and other welfare services. Credits could be given for such things as housing (perhaps as part of a basic income) direct to consumers without the need for direct state provision.

All sides of the spectrum are trying to find ways to give a reality to the ideal of devolved power, sometimes more successfully (as in the case of housing policy) sometimes less so (as with privatizations). In the Third World the new apostles of small business like de Soto argue that the state needs to focus on upholding efficient property rights while restraining the power of large business so as to enable the small trader to trade, or shanty town dwellers to build their own houses. Again the aim is to do away with mediations.

The problems with these models of enabling are familiar ones. They can leave individuals atomized, and unable to influence the state as to if, when and how it is to devolve power. Where the co-opting and corporate models leave institutions to negotiate with the state, the elimination of mediating institutions leaves the individual with no bargaining tools, isolated and powerless. Like the referendum, another tool for bypassing mediators, such models are wide open to the most manipulative uses. The rhetoric of consumer choice can become fetishized, since real choice cannot be exercised without the means to do so. Moreover, formal rights are no substitute for substantive rights where there is an unequal distribution of wealth and power. Legal frameworks which guarantee equality of opportunity are of little use without practical mechanisms that enable people to use their opportunities.

For genuine empowerment has many dimensions. There are many limits to the use of power. For example, the millions of women in the South who bought Nestlé's milk in the 1980s in the belief that it was better even than their own breast milk lacked active and well informed states that could act as a countervailing force to Nestlé's marketing. The same lack of information makes it scarcely possible to choose which treatment to have in a hospital when one has little practical and technical knowledge on which to base that decision. Nor should it be surprising that people resist pressures to devote large amounts of time to day-to-day decision-making. The great virtue of an effective state – and of effective markets – is that they reduce hassle and leave people free to devote time to their own ends.

These are not arguments for dismissing the notion of choice. But they do suggest that there is some truth in the saying that 'people don't know what is good for them'. A truly enabling state crucially depends on policies for information and education – on impartial counsellors and bystanders – to allow for meaningful decision-making. For the same reasons true empowerment depends on effective and critical media to balance other powers, and on a lively culture that fosters democratic participation.

The exercise of choice also has one other limit. Even the most benignly enabling state, which provides the means for individuals to meet their own needs, must also offer what could be called the 'default option' – provision for those individuals who are unable or unwilling to use the means of empowerment.

Conclusions

There is as yet no unproblematic model of an enabling state. Although some of the basic organizing principles of an enabling state are evident – the flattening of the pyramid, the stress on decentralization and horizontal communication, on regulation, nurture and oversight, the emphasis on social experiment rather than social engineering and governance rather than government – the idea remains richly ambiguous.

For ultimately all systems are corruptible and none solves the problems of power in any simple way. This is particularly the case when centralization is often justified as a first step towards dismantling mediating structures in the name of decentralization (as it was by Gorbachev and Thatcher among others). Structure can be as tyrannical as structurelessness. Individuals can run into the same problems of information overload that tie up governments. Informal structures can breed corruption and nepotism. Human-orientated models that put a stress on judgement and discretion also, and inevitably, open the way for corruption and prejudice and a climate in which the politics of spoils can operate more freely.

No structure or blueprint solves problems of representation and provision. Rather the lesson of recent history is that non-structural factors are often just as important – the culture of political life, the motivation and ethos of those working in the state and in voluntary agencies.

The key for policy-makers of the future, and for those concerned to bring states and economies back under human control is to accept that control can never be placed at one sole point in the system. True democracy takes multiple forms; in work, in the locality, in civil society, even while it recognizes that an excess of democratic structures overloads the citizen by demanding too much participation.

The evolution of enabling states is an exciting process. It represents liberation from decades when the overhang of nineteenth-century bureaucratic structures stultified much of public life, constrained creativity and blocked the meeting of needs. Though the process of rethinking the state will inevitably be messy and contradictory, its successful achievement will represent an extraordinary achievement: the transformation of the state from master to servant.

The idea of the enabling state is in clear contrast to the paternalism and dependency creation that have sometimes been associated with the modern welfare state. There would appear to be a danger of a trade-off between the promotion by the state of *entitlements* to income, goods and services (e.g. through income support, subsidized housing, food stamps) and the *capability* of people to provide for their needs themselves. The state may induce a heavy and increasing demand on its services which it finds difficulty in meeting.

Proponents of the enabling state advocate that the state should move away from the direct provision of entitlements towards the enablement of people increasingly to generate the elements of such entitlements for themselves, except of course in response to or to prevent disasters, or for people who for reasons of age or disability cannot achieve such self-reliance.

This enabling of people to provide for themselves depends solely on their having access to the four kinds of capital discussed in Chapter 5: land and other natural resources to work on, tools to work with, skills to know how, and organization to increase productivity. It is universal access to these assets that it is the business of the enabling state to provide. The essence of enablement is in the facilitation of self-help, the empowering of people currently unable to meet their needs from their own resources progressively to be able to do so. As such it is concerned with increasing people's capability to provide themselves with dignified and healthy conditions of life.

It is a similar concern for increasing capabilities that lies at the heart of Drèze and Sen's important and eloquent justification of public action for social security. They write:

> The lives of billions of people are not merely nasty, brutish and short, they are also full of uncertain horrors. An epidemic can wipe out a community, a famine can decimate a nation, unemployment can plunge masses into extreme deprivation, and insecurity, in general, plagues a large part of mankind with savage persistence.
>
> (Drèze and Sen 1991: 3)

In seeking to address this situation, Drèze and Sen first distinguish between *protection* and *promotion*, the former 'concerned with preventing a decline in living standards in general and the basic conditions of living in particular', the latter having the objective 'of enhancing the normal living conditions and dealing with regular and often persistent deprivation'. They stress that there is no paternalism involved in their espousal of these objectives:

> The activism of the public, the unity and solidarity of the concerned population, and the participation of all those who are involved, are important features of public action for social security. There is no assignment of any paternalistic role to the state – or to any other body – in clarifying the plurality of the objectives involved.
>
> (ibid.: 4)

For Drèze and Sen, 'the basic idea of social security is to use social means to prevent deprivation and vulnerability to deprivation'. In evaluating what counts as deprivation, they reject the subjectivist utilitarian perspective, which could be crudely characterized as holding that people are as deprived as they feel; and the objectivist perspective that focuses on commodities and incomes in terms of what people supposedly 'need', because the satisfiers of these needs vary widely across people and situations and are, in any case, only means to well-being rather than parts of it. Instead, Drèze and Sen take *capability* as their essential focus:

> If life is seen as a set of 'doings and beings' that are valuable, the exercise of assessing the quality of life takes the form of evaluating these functionings and capability to function. . . . In the case of studying poverty, it is the failure to have the capability to achieve minimal levels of certain basic functionings that would occupy the centre of the stage. The capabilities to be adequately nourished, to be comfortably clothed, to avoid escapable morbidity and preventable mortality etc., become the appropriate focus variable. This general approach yields a policy perspective that takes us well beyond an income-centred or commodity-centred analysis, and also forces us to abandon smugness based on socially-conditioned, unreflected acceptance of traditional inequities, deprivations and vulnerabilities. The practical import of this reflective foundation, built on evaluating human functionings and capabilities, becomes clear as strategic problems in devising social security programmes are seriously considered.
>
> (ibid.: 7, 8)

In Drèze and Sen's view people's 'capability to function' is impaired both by persistent deprivation and chronic vulnerability to deprivation. They ask why social security is necessary to counter these problems, why they cannot be addressed 'through standard channels of economic growth and progress'. Part, at least, of their answer is that even in rich economies these standard channels have not been solely responsible for easing deprivation:

> Improvements in living standards in the rich economies have often been the direct result of social intervention rather than of simple economic growth. The expansion of such basic capabilities as the ability to live long and to avoid preventable mortality has typically gone hand in hand with the development of public support in the domains of health, employment, education, and even food in some important cases. The thesis that the rich countries have achieved high levels of basic capabilities simply because they are rich is, to say the least, an oversimplification.
>
> (ibid.: 11)

To illustrate this point Drèze and Sen quote statistics that show that, for both Japan and England and Wales in the twentieth century, the decades during which life expectancy increased most were the 1940s and, for England and Wales, between 1911 and 1920. These, of course, were the years of world war, during and, in the case of the Second World War, immediately after which the governments of those countries took unprecedented measures of public support for the population (including, in the United Kingdom the establishment of the National Health Service). Drèze and Sen conclude: 'No matter how exactly the credit for expansion of longevity during the war and post-war years is divided, it is extremely unlikely that the role of public support and social intervention could be shown to be inconsequential.'

Quite apart from the evidence, there are good theoretical reasons why levels of average income and capabilities could diverge. Income could be distributed unequally both between different people and with regard to the same people in different periods of their lives; and it may not always be easy to convert income into capability, because 'often the vital commodities needed for the protection or promotion of living conditions (such as public health provisions) cannot easily be individually owned, and the public sector may well be able to deliver them more efficiently than the market' (ibid.: 14).

Having established the general case for public action for social security, Drèze and Sen then explore two basic strategies for such security, which they call 'growth-mediated security' and 'support-led security', the primary emphasis in the former being on economic growth (though potentially backed up by public action), and in the latter on public action (though perhaps also needing economic growth). The ten countries (outside the OECD and Comecon) that between 1960 and 1986 achieved the highest percentage reduction in under-five mortality were Hong Kong, United Arab Emirates, Kuwait, Singapore, South Korea, Chile, Costa Rica, Cuba, China and Jamaica, of which the first five had high rates of economic growth, suggesting 'growth-mediated security', while the second five did not, suggesting 'support-led security'.

Even in the growth-mediated cases, however, there is no general evidence of state disengagement from the economy:

The constructive role of the state in these countries has in varying extents included: (1) promoting economic growth through skillful planning, (2) facilitating wide participation of the population in the process of economic expansion, particularly through the promotion of skills and education and the maintenance of full employment, and (3) utilising a substantial part of the resources generated by rapid growth for extensive public provisioning of basic necessities.

(ibid.: 24)

Thus the pursuit of growth-mediated security is quite different from the simple pursuit of economic growth.

With regard to support-led security, Drèze and Sen write:

Public support can take many forms, such as public health services, educational facilities, food subsidies, employment programmes, land redistribution, income supplementation and social assistance, and the respective country experiences have involved various combinations of these measures. While there are significant contrasts in the relative importance of these different forms of public support in the different country experiences, the basic commonality of instruments is quite striking, especially in view of the great diversity of the political and economic regimes. Underlying all this is something of a shared approach, involving a public commitment to provide direct support to raise the quality of life, especially of the deprived sections of the respective populations.

(ibid.: 26–27)

Public support of this kind need not be expensive. As Drèze and Sen say:

> The distinction of China, Kerala, Sri Lanka or other countries with a distin-guished record of support-led security does not lie in the size of financial allocations to particular public provision. Their real success seems to be based on creating the political, social and economic conditions under which ambitious programmes of public support are undertaken with determina-tion and effectiveness, and can be oriented towards the deprived sections of the population.
>
> (ibid.: 28)

Even a strategy of support-led security need not and should not exclude the operation of the market.

> A purist strategy – relying only on the market or only on state action – can be awfully short of logistic means. The need to consider the plurality of levers and a heterogeneous set of mechanisms is hard to escape in the pursuit of social security . . . In this context we have to guard against two rather disparate and contrary dangers. One is to ignore the part that the market mechanism can play in generating growth and efficiency (despite its various limitations as an allocative device), with the state trying to do it all itself through administrative devices. The other is to be over-impressed by what the market mechanism can do and to place our reliance entirely on it, neglecting those things that the government can effectively undertake (including various policies for the promotion of health and education).
>
> (ibid.: 29–30)

Drèze and Sen also make clear that it is not just the government that can and does act for social security:

> Public action must not be confused with state action only. Public action includes not merely what is done *for* the public by the state, but also what is done *by* the public for itself. We have to recognise *inter alia* the role of non-governmental organisations in providing social security (particularly in times of distress) and the part that social, political and humanitarian institutions can play in protecting and promoting living conditions.
>
> (ibid.: 28–9)

This role of non-governmental organizations is, of course, a key element of the social economy, (see p. 127), which will be discussed further in the next chapter.

What is probably Drèze and Sen's most important conclusion specifically seeks to counter exclusive neoliberalism:

It is not enormously surprising that efforts in providing extensive public support are rewarded by sustained results, and that public sowing facilitates social reaping. Perhaps what is more remarkable is the fact that the connections studied here are so frequently overlooked in drawing up blueprints for economic development. The temptation to see the improvement of the quality of life simply as a consequence of the increase in GNP per head is evidently quite strong, and the influence of that point of view has been quite pervasive in policy-making and policy-advising in recent years. It is in the specific context of that simple growth-centred view that the empirical connections between public support measures and the quality of life deserve particular emphasis.

(ibid.: 28)

The combination of Drèze and Sen's call for public action for social security focusing on increasing capabilities with Chambers's emphasis on the security that comes from sustainable livelihoods provides a powerful strategic approach to development of great relevance to policy making. It is an approach that is not only relevant for the state at national level. It is just as important with regard to local government.

The local level

Just as the sovereignty of the nation-state is being undermined at the international level, so it is increasingly being called into question from below. Neighbourhoods, localities, whole regions seem sometimes to be bypassed by national economic policies. Many different forms of local economic planning and development are springing up in response, involving some or all of local government, local business and local voluntary organizations. Many different institutional forms are under experimentation: development trusts, community businesses, enterprise agencies, local employment initiatives, community land trusts, community currencies. All these are responses by particular communities who believe that their resources – environmental, human, physically produced and social/organizational – are not being properly used or developed within the framework of a national economy. Accordingly they are seeking to develop their own mechanisms of wealth creation.

Here the possible role of enabling and supporting these initiatives is explored, through the experience of 'popular planning' in the Greater London Council from 1981 to 1986.

Popular planning in practice†

Maureen Mackintosh and Hilary Wainwright

The experiments of the Greater London Council (GLC) in shifting power were one more round in an old debate: how to extend democracy beyond the political franchise to achieve democratic control over the economy. In the process people rediscovered another old truth: where the experiment was based on popular initiative and control there was far more change than elsewhere.

A central argument of this essay is that this tension between representative democracy on the one hand (choosing political priorities, winning democratic support for them, and sticking to them) and decentralizing resources on the other hand (passing them over to people in the community to control and use) is a messy, but politically important tension, essential to achieving economic democracy.

Politicians, especially Labour ones, have a strong bias towards staying in control of what is going on. Many of the Labour Party's current proposals and policies contain neat models of how everything should have a bit of 'participation', though controlled from the top. But the great virtue of the GLC was that it let this cat out of the bag. Though it didn't democratize nearly as much as it said it did, it did demonstrate the possibilities. It showed the creativity which can be released and the pressures for innovation which can be generated when people are given a look-in, gain resources under their own control and are not immediately boxed into predetermined structures. Without that creativity and pressure – that noise and mess – not much new will be achieved.

Where do ideas come from?

The first set of arguments for democracy is about the need to go looking for information and ideas. There was an interesting tension within the last GLC administration about where ideas came from. On the one hand, the GLC itself had a strong sense of strategy, of how policies should relate to each other, which was one of its strengths. While the vision was often hopelessly over-ambitious, at least it was there, and gave people wanting the organization to do something different something to latch on to. On the other hand, in practice, many of the most creative and innovative policies came from information and ideas provided by workers, consumers, or communities resisting the economic circumstances and decisions of government, multi-national corporations and so on – which the GLC was trying to challenge. Where the GLC politicians and staff sat in County Hall or the offices of the Greater London Enterprise Board (GLEB), or shielded themselves from outside pressures, they tended to become captive to establishment ideas.

---

† This paper is a free adaptation of the final chapter of Mackintosh and Wainwright (1987), in which the GLC experience is explored in far greater detail. The GLC was abolished in 1986.

The experience of the GLC between 1981 and 1986 shows the extent to which there is a wealth of knowledge and ideas, especially about better uses of public funds, going to waste in London's economy. They also show the limited extent to which the GLC managed to draw on and build on those ideas. The GLC officers who went to talk to those working in firms and services, and living in run-down areas of the inner city, were looking for an alternative view of economic need and economic policy; an alternative to the view of managers and planners both in the private sector and in the public sector (where many are increasingly adopting the market-led assumptions of Thatcher's economics).

The extent to which they found those alternative views runs through the whole GLC story. In some cases including the in-house GLC workers, the ideas were listened to too late: the Woolwich ferry workers, for example, who could see the potential of their ship repair facility but who could not get their management to listen, and whose sense of waste from its closure was heightened by the fact that it was a public facility built up over the years on their skills and used by the local community. In other cases, the views of those who worked for a public service became crucial to the GLC's alternative plans for that service: the engineers at the Aldenham bus works, for example, who contrasted long-term viability and a socially responsible use of their skills, expertise and productive capacity with the narrow and short-term commercial calculations of London Transport management, or the community organizations who had ideas for the better use of central London land than speculative office building.

In other areas of work, GLC funding allowed people to develop and sometimes implement their own ideas of what should be done. The Health Emergency campaigners, for example, who, between fighting job cuts, developed their own ideas of what a better health service could be like. Or the Women's Employment Project workers, who developed innovative training schemes and saw the possibilities of improving and developing the school meals service, by involving workers and parents. Or the childcare workers and campaigners who developed provision for the huge variety of needs of children and parents in different circumstances. Or the furniture workers who presented a different view of their industry and of the possibilities of public funding.

The list of ideas was endless. Behind all people's judgements is a sense of the social value of their own skills and contribution; and a strong sense that public money should be spent in a socially responsible and accountable manner. For all of these people, their wasted knowledge and skills are a social waste and also an individual indignity. For many of them, the best thing the GLC did was give them the resources and encouragement to think for themselves. However critical people were of the GLC generally, they tended to come back to that: 'it's the fact that initiative is welcomed'; 'it's a different relationship, a discussion . . . a different concept of consultation'.

The GLC's attempts to draw on these ideas and this experience provide some strong lessons about the politics of this process. The most important lesson is that the learning process, if it is to be effective, has to be a genuine exchange, offering as well as listening, and returning to people the results of discussions. It sounds obvious but in practice it is not, nor is it easy. People have low expectations of local or national government. Many people, such as the bus workers, community campaigners, black groups, were rightly suspicious when the GLC arrived looking for information: would the GLC just appropriate their ideas for its own benefit, and in the end, use the ideas against them? Those actually employed by the GLC – twice bitten – were the most suspicious of all.

The GLC tried, some of the time, to do it differently: to learn but not steal, to give as well as to take. This was most complex where the GLC was itself the employer, in GLEB, or in in-house services, facing constraints of legality, finance and the market. Its ambitions looked like trying to sit on both sides of the fence at once, and some groups of workers feel that they gained nothing from the deal, especially those who participated in GLEB enterprises which have now gone under, or those who felt ignored within the GLC itself.

Too often the GLC used people's ideas without acknowledgement or return, and thereby lost support and allies. But sometimes it put its principles into practice. Again, it should have been obvious, but the genuine astonishment of trade union activists who, after the GLC had interviewed them on their ideas, got back a transcript of the discussion, plus comments and offers of collaboration, speaks for itself. At times the GLC also provided information to people which they could use in return – access to technical information, for example, from its own resources – demonstrating that the process could be a genuine exchange. There were a number of attempts to put the GLC's research skills at the service of people who wanted to research their own situation: the bus and tube workers involved in investigating the effects of one person operation felt the experience had been productive, though they had criticisms, and they certainly changed the Council's view of the issues, as well as strengthening their own self-organization.

At its best in the GLC, this process of learning and providing information both strengthened people's capacity to control their own situation, and shifted the council's conception of how it could spend its money effectively. The Aldenham workers used their knowledge of the factory, of their own skills, of the engineering needs of the transport service, *and* the information supplied by the GLC, to build up a powerful case for keeping the works open, aimed at convincing management and the Council. The energy policy workers worked with tenants' groups to learn about needs and possibilities, then provided information which the tenants could use for organization and campaigning. *Only* if people get back knowledge and resources that they can use there and then, can a local authority go on learning and asking people to give up their free time to, in effect, help it do its job properly. This will only happen if there is a conscious 'politics of knowledge' in the authority: principles to be worked from about looking for knowledge and ideas, bringing people together to develop ideas and work out what they want, providing the resources for this to be possible, encouraging criticism, and always giving back relevant information (inluding about the authority itself) in exchange.

Economic policy as process

The second major argument for democracy is that, not only is work with outside organizations essential for people in the state to work out what they want to do, it is also generally essential for getting it done. On the whole, alternative policies were not successfully implemented solely from inside County Hall; they also needed an outside base of pressure and support. The outside pressure involved people in: supporting the council against opposition; keeping the GLC to its principles and promises; and doing a lot of the actual work themselves.

In other words, strengthening the capacity for self-organization of workers, of tenants, of women's groups and black groups was not only a basis for learning, it was also an essential basis for effective intervention in London's economy.

Where there were no organized groups, outside the GLC, pressing for action and working with the Council, often little got done. An example would be the attempt to use the conditions on the lease of the GLC's industrial properties as a lever to improve workers' wages and conditions. It failed because the GLC had not found a way to work with unions and local organizations to build up a base of workers who could make use of that lever. Other property initiatives, for instance new sites developed with the involvement of organized groups, where the GLC could work with local organizations, were much more successful. Or take the example of alternative production to armaments: the achievements of the Greater London Conversion Council fell far short of its ambitions largely because of the difficulties in achieving any close working relationship with workers in any part of the arms industry.

Where the GLC supported and worked with organized groups, much more was achieved. For example, on alternative energy strategies, where the GLC and the London Energy and Employment Network established a base amongst tenants, local borough councillors and the 'alternative energy movement', the GLC's policies had a lasting impact. Where the GLC joined up with and supported groups already working on childcare and training projects for women, innovative projects mushroomed, and many are still in existence. And working to create links between trade unionists within the same transnational and thereby to increase their power was really the only way the GLC could have the slightest influence on the operation of the big transnational firms.

The support of outside organization is crucial to the lasting nature of anything achieved. Most Labour authorities will not be functioning, as the GLC was, with an axe over their heads, but they will still want their changes to last and the more their actions both bring direct benefits worth defending, *and* help create organizations capable of defending and building on them, the more likely those changes are to last. Funding the voluntary sector turned out to be an enormously effective way of getting policies implemented and work done. Where the GLC funding helped to create organizations clearly fulfilling a need, and with a strong constituency of support, renewed funding by other authorities and organizations has been common.

Political choices: women, race and popular planning

The GLC experience demonstrates that making a priority of women's work and black employment involves major changes in the conception of economic strategy, including popular planning. This is one of the most important conclusions from the GLC period.

If working with outside organizations becomes a tenet of economic policy, and if time, as always in the GLC, presses, then unless explicit choices are made about which organizations to involve, there will be a tendency for Labour authorities to work with the best organized sections of the trade-union movement and other organizations which they know or recognize. In the GLC in the early days this bias was in fact defended by some as the most efficient way of working. While this is an important part of policy-making, it precisely excludes the groups most in need, both within unions and outside them. Without an explicit effort to rectify this, popular planning will simply reinforce relative privilege and further exclude other groups from influence.

There are some strong lessons from the GLC's efforts to shift bias in employment policy. First, popular planning needs an explicit rethinking and redirection of its starting points. One of the GLC officers most involved in struggling to develop work on black employment argues that the GLC failed to recognize and start from the strong and effective organizations which do exist in the black community, for example in the struggles around education. These groups organizing against racism in education, creating links between teachers, students and parents, setting up supplementary education, were not properly valued by the GLC as one of the communities' own starting points for work around training and employment. Instead of imposing its own view of appropriate forms of organization, popular planning has to recognize and build on the existing forms of organization, and the immediate needs of the communities it wants to reach: whether women's centres, childcare or black community organizations.

This implies putting resources into supporting and helping to develop a stronger 'infrastructure' of independent organizations serving the needs of black people and women which can in turn effectively pressure the local authorities for changes in policies and use of resources. It was this which had been largely neglected by the GLC Industry and Employment Department despite the rhetoric.

To put it into practice involves new ways of working in terms of publicity, organizing help, educational work, encouragement, good 'outreach' and development work, hiring practices, pressure and sheer nerve. Many of these points also apply to working with all the less-skilled, less-organized groups in the community or at work, more generally. As someone put it, the point being made is *not*, 'Everything was perfect, we just didn't do it on women'. The point was that popular planning tends to reinforce divisions between groups unless conscious efforts are made to push the other way, hard.

However, those involved in black employment also identified a problem with this strategy of developing groups through funding. State funding and state interference can *weaken* effective and independent organizations, exacerbating political divisions and dragging the aims of the organization towards those more acceptable to the local state. This effect can be worst where the groups being funded have interests which are in sharpest opposition to the local state as presently organized, which includes many black groups. Disillusion with what the state actually delivers in these circumstances can lead to demoralization. As a result, many black groups thought long and hard before applying for state resources.

State support: democracy and accountability

It follows from the preceding argument that one of the most useful tools of GLC employment policy consisted in giving people resources so that they could do things for themselves: run projects, provide services, campaign and pressure the government, managements or the GLC itself. The expanding grants programme was a recognition of how effective this kind of resourcing was; at the same time, it raised a series of issues about democracy and accountability which are worth exploring in more detail.

We began by saying that the GLC was experimenting with what it might mean to extend democracy beyond the ballot. This was generally construed by the politicians and the new GLC officers as responding to outside pressure, and opening up the resources, information and, to some extent, the power of the Council, to ordinary Londoners.

There were a number of experiments with institutions for doing this. One, used for example by the Women's Committee (and by many other Women's Committees around the country), was to co-opt members from outside the Council. Another was to hold open meetings, and advertise widely for applicants for funding. The Industry and Employment Committee used neither of these, and was slower than the Women's Committee or the Ethnic Minorities Unit to reach people who had no initial connections with the GLC.

Industry and Employment was, however, under enormous pressure from the start to assist firms in trouble, and to fund support networks: trade-union resource centres and co-operative development agencies. There were also demands for support from a wide range of community and campaigning groups.

One of the strengths of the GLC was its flexibility in response to these pressures: work with campaigns was clearly seen as useful to employment policy, and there was no assumption that all the initiatives had to be local authority-led.

Some of the most effective resourcing was in response to popular resistance to imposed job loss or privatization. Notable examples include the campaign against the London Docklands Development Corporation (LDDC)'s decision to promote an airport in Docklands; the campaign of the National Communication Union against the privatization of British Telecom; the threat of Ford workers to strike against the closure of Dagenham foundry. Other examples were of a more diffuse discontent: the discontent of transport workers over the introduction of one-person operated buses; the anxieties of construction workers faced with the run down of Direct Labour Organizations. Or sometimes the GLC was asked for support or involvement in a joint initiative by a well-established workers' or community organization struggling for greater control over their situation: for instance, the Ford Workers Combine, or the Coin Street Action Group in Waterloo. This necessary diversity of starting points requires a flexibility on the part of the local authority, a concern to listen and investigate before deciding on priorities, and a willingness to share power and decentralize resources without being able to predict the outcome.

In the process of responding to these kinds of pressures, many of the staff working for the Industry and Employment Committee developed a strong sense of their own accountability to the people they worked with, as well as upwards to the politicians. It is worth spelling this out, because the implication of taking democracy wider than the ballot box is that the process goes wider than the politicians. The skills and commitment required of local government officers change substantially, since they come to include working with outside groups and taking responsibility for those relationships. As one of the new staff put it: 'It gives you a political validity if you can show that the people you are supposed to be representing are actually putting demands on you.' Extending democracy, creating more open government, involves hiring people who can implement that.

It also involves, as was discovered, developing clear criteria about who should be worked with and supported, what support is necessary, what rules and demands should be put on those funded and why, and what sort of relationship could and should be developed with groups once funded.

Surveying the Industry and Employment Branch's funding, some would say that the further away an issue was from the council's immediate interests, the more effective was the funding of pressure groups; some would also say cynically that this is inevitable. But it is not entirely true, especially of the GLC as a whole: politicians can set out to increase the democratic pressure on themselves. In the Women's Committee and Ethnic Minority Committees they did it to a rather substantial extent; there should have been more of it, sooner, in Industry and Employment too.

Can this kind of resourcing, then – 'popular planning' if a label is useful – be one way of developing and deepening representative democracy? This depends on the relationship built up with the groups funded by the authority.

The lessons of the GLC experience might be summarized as a tentative list of principles.

First, the funding group must *not* simply respond to pressure; the pattern of groups funded has to correspond to general political aims. This means that the pattern of funding and support (including staff time) has to be monitored, or it cannot be accountable. Where funding is not going to priority groups (women, for example) then something has to be done about it: and that means time and resources for staff to go out and help to develop the organizations which can make use of the available funding. That also means making hard choices about not funding other groups. All this constitutes a more council-led process in the early stages, with the authority actively developing a constituency.

Second, to achieve that, staff doing the funding and 'popular planning' have to be integrated into the policy-making process as a whole, rather than hived off into a corner. Recommending grants and working directly with the grant-aided groups is an immensely political job. The grants staff are those who are subject to the most direct pressure from outside, and also those whose work is most directly monitored. They need to be involved in a two-way relationship with other staff working on policy, which rarely happened in the GLC. The same applies to others involved mainly in 'popular planning' work who often did not work with other staff developing industrial policy or policy for directly-run services.

Third, to return to the issue of autonomy: while the authority may at times fund groups with whom it does not wholly agree, it will always be working within its own interests and policies. It therefore needs to be very clear about what are the demands being made on funded groups – the GLC was often muddled – and it needs to provide a lot more support to enable groups to use funds, and fulfil conditions effectively. Having done that, it needs to keep its hands off the rest of the group's activities, and leave it to develop, so long as it uses the resources as it stated that it would. There is always a risk that local authority resources or involvement undermine the independence and strength of community and trade-union organizations, making them dependent on council resources, and weakening their accountability to their real constituents who are also the essential source of their power.

Fourth, procedures have to be devised whereby the groups funded *can* influence the Council. The GLC was not very good at this. Furthermore, as things got bigger, busier, more fraught, it got worse, not better. The result was that many groups who wanted to contribute to GLC policy gave up in frustration because the GLC was so amorphous, hectic, impenetrable and unresponsive. Looking back, people feel that it should have been a specific responsibility of some staff to develop this kind of feedback, and use it. However, the implication of that in turn is probably that the GLC spread itself too wide: it could only have used feedback from groups funded if it had concentrated on fewer areas of work, and developed a much more conscious internal process of relating funding, policy, and other sorts of spending in the areas chosen.

This brings us back to the central issue. There can be no straightforward alliances between 'the people' and a part of the local state. The local state itself is a far from homogeneous entity, as the groups discovered who got caught up in internal conflict within the authority. Politicians and officers to some extent pursue self-interested ends. But there can also be a lot of genuine goodwill about extending democracy and making policy and spending effective. As a result, a more democratic economic policy is a complicated and fraught, negotiated process. Politicians have to accept that organizations they have supported turn on them; for example, trade unionists working in the City institutions disagreed with GLC policies towards these institutions, and there were arguments with the unions in the motor industry about import controls. Criticisms of their record on racism and black employment were often the hardest for some politicians to swallow.

In addition, 'popular planning' has to be flexible: the GLC moved rather rapidly away from the idea that 'an alternative plan' – on paper – was necessarily the desired product. Whether in enterprises, in sectors or localities, the work has turned out to be a continuing process with a variety of objectives, depending on the state of the organization concerned and the circumstances it faces. These might include an extension of collective bargaining; new links with people in related parts of the economy, such as for public-service workers organizing with service users as in the London Health Emergency campaigns; trade unionists on the production side making contact with workers in retailing; women and black people successfully challenging divisions arising from gender or race; an organization developing more effective means of spreading information or learning how to monitor and investigate management more effectively; and so on. Plans or written reports have proved important only under particular conditions: mainly when the campaign needs a public focus or has the opportunity of a public platform. For instance at least two 'people's plans' (for the Royal Docks and for Coin Street) were produced for public enquiries.

Finally, the resourcing must include education and self-education projects. The Industry and Employment Branch spent over £100,000 a year on explicitly educational resources. Some of this went to 'Popular Planning Projects' which were created by the Industry and Employment Branch and the Inner London Education Authority (ILEA) in several Adult Education Institutes and other centres, to provide know-how, research and support for groups not organized through the trade unions or any established campaigning or community groups; for instance young people on an estate with ideas for a service needed on the estate, homeless people wanting to put pressure on the local council, home-workers wanting to meet together and do something about their conditions. This educational work offers to a popularly based economic strategy an additional method for involving the less organized in collective initiatives about their local economy: learning democratic economic planning by trying to do it.

The aim, at least, of resourcing is now much clearer. It is to contribute to a process whereby workers and communities can gain more collective control, first over council policy and, second, over their own economic circumstances. In Britain at present, where people have such low expectations – this itself was another major lesson – of achieving either of these, that constitutes a major and important aim of economic policy.

Issues for national policy

Moves towards economic democracy are neither tidy nor peaceful. Such moves as occurred through the GLC created enormous and uncomfortable pressures, external and internal: many of the pressures, from the point of view of the local government staff who suffered them, were self-inflicted. Myths were created, accusations abounded, people got burned out; all these are problems. But those pressures were highly creative from the point of view of new directions in local economic policy-making. However, it does sound just that: very local. What does it have to do with the national level of economic policy-making? In our view, a great deal.

A good place to start to draw implications from the GLC for national policy would be the GLC's popularity. It was that rare beast in British politics, a popular Left Labour authority, and popular well beyond any natural Labour constituency, in so far as such a thing remains. There were a lot of reasons for this. Ted Heath blamed it on the government's ineptitude, especially the then Environment Secretary Patrick Jenkin. It may have had to do with GLC leader Ken Livingstone's talents on TV chat shows. Some of it resulted from plainly sensible and successful transport policies. Partly it was because the GLC did *not* run a number of the public services people most complain about, like housing and social services. But quite a bit was to do with the unprecedented openness with which the administration operated: from turning County Hall (of all places) into an accessible town hall, through the pop festivals, to the endless stream of campaigns, information and demands for participation. For all the problems, more open, and popular, it undoubtedly was, and this in itself has lessons for a national Labour government.

Labour governments may not face abolition, but they always face economic crisis and very serious opposition if they try to do anything radical. The relative weakness of the British economy, the position of the City as a financial centre potentially subject to very volatile flows of funds, the resulting vulnerability to balance-of-payments crises and the need for loans: all this has been an axe for the economic establishment to wield against successive Labour governments. Few manifesto commitments survive this process, and nor, most importantly, does the margin of support which puts Labour in power in the first place.

The Labour GLC did not succeed in holding off the hostility of national government, but it did manage to carry out considerably more of its manifesto than recent Labour governments have done. It did not lose support under attack. It left at least some changes behind it in terms of what people know and expect of government.

We think that, despite the difference in scale and the difference in function of national and local government, this history – the successes and the failures – hold some lessons for national politics.

There are lessons about public openness, information and accountability. We have a pathologically secretive national government, far worse than many other industrialized capitalist countries, and the Labour Party historically has done nothing to change this. The Labour GLC kept its electoral mandate alive by using council resources to explain and campaign for its policies. It also made the information available in the GLC accessible to a very wide range of people in the community and the London workforce. It raised people's expectations, often unreasonably high, and it opened itself more than is usual to effective criticism. As a result it made unusually available the public-sector resources that people had paid for through their rates and taxes.

A Labour government – and the Labour Party now – would gain a great deal from a much greater commitment to this kind of openness. While many of the specifics of the GLC's activity were those of local government, the benefits of more open government are more general. Labour governments, too, could raise people's expectations of the state, make its resources more available, be more open about internal conflict and conflict with the civil service and the City, open itself more to criticism by providing more information for criticism to latch on to. In the long run, despite the embarrassment at times involved, such accessibility is highly constructive – so long as the policies being proposed do genuinely bring benefits.

There has always been a current of thought in the labour movement which based socialist economic policy in the organization and ideas of working-class people in the work-place and community, from trade unionists influenced by Marx to socialist intellectuals such as William Morris and G.D.H. Cole. But this has been dominated and pushed to the margins by the more powerful rationalist tradition which considered planning to be the responsibility of specially bred professionals. As Beatrice Webb, a leading advocate and practitioner of this latter position, put it: 'It is our opinion that the average sensual man [*sic*] can only describe his needs. He cannot prescribe the remedies.'

It is the latter view which has generally dominated Labour when in power. Rarely if ever has the 'popular control' perspective had a taste of power. The Labour leadership has seen the purpose of state intervention and economic policy as being to guide the economy more efficiently than the market could do, not to lay down the conditions for increasing popular control; indeed, for them, a Labour government is itself democratic control.

It is this perspective which is challenged by the experience of the GLC. The GLC did not institute 'popular control' or anything like it. There was always a conflict within the GLC between its sweeping strategic aims for sectors of the economy and its principles of working with outside groups. But the fact that some people, reflecting on the institution from the outside, could describe the GLC's interest in and openness to the ideas and needs of ordinary people as a 'revolution' in the attitudes of the state to its citizens suggests a path for change.

This chapter has sought to illuminate some of the foundational issues pertaining to the role of government in the economy: the need for institution-building at the global level in order to match the globalization of markets; the concept of the enabling state as an alternative to both *laissez-faire* and over-extended bureaucracy; the validity of state action in such areas as social security, with it being regarded as a complement to market allocation rather than an alternative to it; the importance of the local dimension in the enhancement of people's capabilities.

Of course, these ideas do no more than scratch the surface of state action in the economy, but they do suggest a distinctive orientation to such action which can inform more detailed considerations of strategy and management at the international, macro and local economic levels. The orientation is most akin to Nielsen's 'negotiated economy' (Nielsen 1990; Nielsen and Pedersen 1991) defined

> as a structuring of society where an essential part of the allocation of resources is conducted through institutionalized negotiations between independent decision-making centers in [the] state, organizations and/or corporations. . . . Negotiation-based economic decisions are usually not subject to the possible use of sanctions. They are typically based on discursive, political or morally binding – rather than legally sanctioned – agreements.
>
> (Nielsen and Pedersen 1991: 151)

Thus the concept of the negotiated economy is rooted at the outset in three (economic, social and ethical) of the four dimensions of the tetrahedral model presented in Chapter 3 (see Figures 3.6 and 3.7, p. 87). It also goes explicitly beyond, not only the pure poles of the free market and centrally planned state control, but also formulations of the mixed economy that posit some bipolar mix of the two. It gives a clear economic role to non-market, non-state institutions, including those of the social economy, consideration of which is the subject of the next chapter.

11 Direct provision in the social economy

The market involves exchange. The state commands, enforces and enables (or disables). Direct provision involves people producing goods and services directly for themselves and other people from their own impulse. Direct provision is most obviously in evidence in households, communities and voluntary organizations. A large proportion of the activity of the world's subsistence farmers (often women) as well as much of women's other work, falls into this sector. By practically ignoring it, policy-makers have possibly missed the greatest opportunity they had to encourage wealth creation by those who often need it most.

The direct provision of wealth involves the same wealth-creation process as that for the market: the possession and appropriate combination of the four capitals (see p. 148). The principal task of those who would encourage this sort of wealth creation is to ensure that the direct providers have access to these capitals: land to grow food; skills to grow, build or make; motivation to work or participate in community or voluntary organizations; appropriate institutional forms to interact with other social actors and create a sense of purpose and solidarity; credit and income to enable both tools and other inputs to be bought which cannot be self-provided.

The household

As Marilyn Waring has stressed, the public policy implications of taking unpaid household production seriously are enormous:

> The needs for credit facilities, fertilisers, seeds would be clear for subsistence agricultural producers. . . . The needs for training and retraining the unpaid workforce would receive attention as a policy priority. Unpaid workers could make a realistic claim on the public purse as opposed to being condemned to 'welfare'. . . . Households do, and have at all times, combined labour, capital goods (land or reproducible fixed assets), and intermediate goods to produce what is required to satisfy their needs when the market fails to do so. In times of crisis, when markets are disrupted, household production largely substitutes for organised market-output.
>
> (Waring 1988: 289)

In Scandinavia a group of women researchers has been engaged for ten years on a multi-dimensional project entitled 'The New Everyday Life', which seeks a new integration of work, care and housing, on the basis of joint partici- pation by men and women in both the formal and complementary economy; equal terms for both genders in both sectors; and an understanding that the social basis for the informal economy is not the single household but co- operation between several homes and families. 'The aim is to convert the production-centred mode of thinking and acting into one that is favourable to reproduction. This means that production will serve reproduction and not the other way round' (Horelli and Vepsä undated: pp. 30–1).

In 1987 the group published a report 'The Ways to the New Everyday Life' (Forskargruppen för det nya vardagslivet 1987) illustrating the implica- tions of their approach for local housework, local care, local production and local management.

Two other Finnish researchers Pulliainen and Pietilä (1983) have dis- tinguished between the free (non-monetary), protected (home market produc- tion and public services) and fettered (determined by global competition) economies. From their assessment of the relative importance of these economies they assert:

> Revival of the free, non-monetary sector would make economic growth unnecessary. The more we can produce at home and in small communities, take care of children, the sick and each other, produce enjoyment and work together, the less need there is for the community to provide expensive public services for these purposes. And the less people need to earn money to buy these services. Both physical and mental illnesses simply decline when life becomes more humane and meaningful. Youth will be integrated into the functions and activities of the community, different age groups will help each other and enrich each other's lives. The more people's initiative and self-reliance increases, the less society's guardianship will be needed.
>
> This means that we need not enlarge the protected sector. Society does not need to increase services for health, child care, hospitals and youth. In fact, these services will be needed much less in the year 2000 than today, if the revival of the non-monetary sector comes to pass. As a consequence the fettered sector will not need to compete so keenly on the world market because the pressure in society for increasing production will decrease. In this way pressure will be released throughout society. We can save energy and natural resources, and we can reduce our dependence on the world market in general.
>
> (Pietilä 1987: 15)

The community

The bonds between people in the same locality have historically been, and continue to be in many parts of the world, a source of considerable stability, security and wealth-creation. Industrialization, the spread of markets and state-sponsored 'development' have tended to rupture these bonds, to the great cost of those who are unable to make alternative provision through the market or access to another system of social security. The pattern of disruption has been so characteristic of industrialization that it is widely regarded as industrialism's inevitable consequence. Bruyn, however, sees a new impulse in the United States which is seeking to restore the community dimension to economic development.

A new direction for community development in the United States[†]

Severyn Bruyn

The power of self-determination for people in local communities in the United States has been slowly eroded by forces in the capitalist market. The market economy has demanded that corporations expand and centralize their control in big cities in order to compete effectively with one another and with foreign competition. Communities are today less likely to contain small independent enterprises whose owners are interested in responding to local needs. They are served increasingly by business subsidiaries under the command of big corporations. Thus, the direction of local economies has become influenced to a significant degree by absentee executives living in distant cities. They decide whether to transfer local offices, move retail outlets, and shut down factories, often without regard to local needs and the economic viability of the community. Absentee executives can decide the direction of local economies on the basis of demands in the national and global markets. Thus, the corporate economy is growing and expanding while many local neighbourhoods and communities are slowly dying in America (see Bluestone and Harrison 1982).

Urbanologists argue that big corporations are not alone in being responsible for the deterioration of community life. The real estate industry operates locally within a market for profit and is not expressly interested in maintaining the well-being of community life. The constant change in the cityscape has been a function of the market system. This system has brought economic progress and prosperity to some cities, but it has also devastated many neighbourhoods and played a major role in creating social problems. These problems cost the state and federal government billions of dollars in welfare, prisons and treatment centres for residents who cannot cope with the change (Gappert and Rose 1975).

The consequences of this destruction of community life are serious for the institutional fabric of society and place a major burden on the government. The high mobility of firms and the structure of absentee ownership has its

---

[†] This paper was first published in *The Social Report* of Boston College. See Bruyn (1985) for details.

social toll. This toll is seen most easily by the public in periodic unemployment, but studies show that other problems are created, including family instability and high rates of divorce, physical disease, mental illness, crime, delinquency and drug addiction. The economic viability of local institutions, such as schools and churches, collapses when large plants relocate or businesses shut down on the basis of decisions made in distant headquarters. The local community slowly disintegrates. The result: the government then pays for the social costs of the market system. The corporate economy, lacking structures of responsibility, relies on the government to pay for its destructive impact.

The Boston Globe (11 November 1984) published summaries of conference talks given by urbanologists on the future of the city and added its own urgent messages for a new master plan with tough zoning codes to guide development. A major concern in Boston was to find new rules for architecture design and to reaffirm the capacity of the municipality to regulate the market's tendency to create a sprawling City of Cars and Towers. J. Kaufman wrote, 'Boston neighborhoods are in a flux, scarred by years of neglect . . . and torn by economic changes . . . pushing out people who made the old neighborhoods work'. But no plan was offered to create stable communities except for zoning codes, new housing, and other methods which have not worked in the past.

City planners have generally given up on designing self-reliant neighbourhoods and relatively self-sufficient communities. They argue that the idea of local control over the economy is a hopeless Utopia; self-reliant communities can no longer be a part of a practical plan of development. Instead, the megalopolis is seen as the 'future'. Vast regional formations of adjacent metropolises will stretch across the United States. This development will occur in response to market forces but without any vision of community.

My concern here is to offer a dissenting vision, emphasizing the development of local self-reliance without invoking either the market or government controls. The separate 'laws' of the market and the government are still important; in fact, their creative opposition is critical to future development. But my argument is that the continued dependence on the government-regulated market as the singular method for guiding local growth does not contribute sufficiently to the genuine redevelopment of community life.

An overview

Many scholars have claimed that we are now in an historical transition of epochal importance. The time is full of danger as well as promise and opportunity. Robert Nisbet has eloquently decried the loss of primary groups and 'community at the local level (Nisbet 1953). He describes how people in modern society become powerfully influenced by mass communications. The danger in a mass society, he says, is to look for 'community' in the nation-state. The nation-state becomes a spiritual refuge for what was lost in the locality. The flag becomes a sacred symbol, a tribal totem. The need for community – lost locally in the expanding market – is transferred with religious fervour to the symbols of the nation.

A special danger lies in the cyclic movement of the market economy. Erich Fromm documented what happened during the down-swing of the market in the Great Depression (Fromm 1941). The social conditions led to Nazism in Germany and Fascism in Italy. The search for community acquired a religious identification at the national level as local communities lost their own power of economic viability and self-direction. Thus the consequences of periodic financial crises and labour unrest can be tragic as they may lead towards solutions in 'national socialism' or towards the fascist state and world war.

The path toward establishing a new local foundation for the economy is suggested by Karl Polanyi in *The Great Transformation: The Political and Economic Origins of Our Time* (1944). It was written during the Second World War in part to correct some Marxist misconceptions of history. In effect, Polanyi claimed that the transition from feudalism to capitalism was made possible in Europe by a series of legal innovations in the economic institutions of the time. The main economic institutions involved land, labour and capital. They were legally constituted by feudal law with many people under some form of bondage. But these laws were changed from feudal controls into the market; they were slowly purchased for a price.

People began to buy and sell land, labour and capital as commodities and a market was substituted for what had been a closed, hierarchical feudal system. A new sense of freedom and individualism replaced the former oppressive conditions as the capitalist system was born. On the other hand the laws introducing capitalism were also repressive. They were designed to consolidate the power of people with property, for example, the Poor Law Amendment, Patent Laws, Enclosure Acts and so on. E.P. Thompson has said of the eighteenth-century legal environment that, in general, 'the worst crime against property was not to own any'.

The history of the capitalist system has been a record of progress and freedom heretofore unknown in the world, but it has also been marked by its own oppression of people. The business market has continued to create problems such as mass unemployment, inflation, labour–management strife, environmental pollution, consumer exploitation, corporate monopoly, runaway factories and depressed communities. The government tries to solve these problems through the labour department, welfare department, consumer protection agency, environmental protection agency, and so on. Since business is not structured to be socially accountable to its constituencies in full measure and is not chartered to operate in the public interest, it continues to require bigger government.

While the oppressive conditions of feudalism led to a quest for freedom and individuality, the conditions of capitalism have led to a quest for community and social justice. The quest has led to solutions through government controls, but these solutions have been based on false hopes. The legal alternatives in the current transition are not found in federal controls over business. The government merely adds to modern bureaucracy and to the loss of genuine community life.

To develop the legal innovations needed for free enterprise to promote a system of social justice and provide the economic foundations for a genuine community is not easy. I believe it requires a new system of self government within the business community. It calls for a system of social self-regulation among enterprises in the private sector. It also requires a corporate organization which is decentralized and socially accountable at the local level. These may seem to be radical mandates but surprisingly the business system has already begun to yield such solutions.

While local firms have tended to become 'national' and have developed under corporate command systems in the expanded market economy, new firms have also been developing to democratize and localize control over key dimensions of Polanyi's land, labour and capital. New democratic firms are developing in small numbers today to alter the market system as the new commercial firms were developing quietly in the fifteenth century to alter feudal institutions. They show promise of eliminating the oppressive conditions of the market and even suggest that social justice may combine with the free-enterprise system. They tell us that it is possible to introduce what might be called 'structures of accountability' in this period that historian Werner Sombart has described as the 'late stage of capitalism'.

The new corporations take many shapes but we can interpret this transition briefly here by their 'prototypes' in land, labour and capital. Each of the following innovative firms is designed to localize the market and help restore the economic base of the community. They are chartered to remove controls from the national and global market and reintroduce them into the hands of local people.

Land

The legal innovation in land is the land trust. The land trust is a democratic corporation designed to purchase territory in the public interest. The firm is chartered in the private sector to keep land from market speculation and exploitation. Speculation in the land market is one of the causes of community deterioration. Even though absentee owners do not always destroy local initiative and often contribute significantly to development, large numbers within a concentrated area tend to destroy local self-direction and responsibility. For example, absentee landlords in the city do not repair broken down tenements; instead they hope to sell their land at a high price in the commercial market. Gentlemen farmers let their rich soil erode by failing to attend to their property; absentee corporations in Appalachia exploit land resources while farming communities deteriorate and local residents live in poverty.

The creation of a land trust takes the land out of the market and places it

instead under local democratic controls. The land is then rented to entrepreneurs who want to use it in their own self-interest as well as in the interest
of the community. The profit motive is thus retained for lessees, but they are
kept from exploiting the land. The corporate charter of the trust expresses
certain principles which guide the use of the land in the public interest. For
example, a charter may state the necessity for renters to keep the soil from
eroding, the need to maintain an ecological balance, or the importance of
raising nutritious food in a region overly-dependent upon outside food
supplies. At the same time, the lessees are given the power to vote for their
own representation on the trustee board to reduce the likelihood that their
rights will be violated. The rent paid is used to purchase more land, and new
trusteeships are created in other locations. Separate trusteeships may then
federate to oversee regional problems (e.g. water rights) between territories.
The land trust is thus a new seedling enterprise designed to protect localities
against excesses in the capitalist market.

There are hundreds of land trusts developing in the United States –
including New Communities, Inc., in Leesburg, Georgia; the Community
Land Association in Clairfield, Tennessee; Columbia Heights, in Washington
DC; the Community Land Co-operative of Cincinnati, Ohio; the Cedar
Riverside Community in Minneapolis, Minnesota; and the Marin Agricultural Land Trust in Marin County, California. They are promising innovative ventures which require further study and the opportunity to experiment
in American real estate.

Labour

The prototype firm which democratizes and localizes control over the labour
market is the producer (or worker) co-operative. The shares of the co-op can
be taken out of the stock market and retained by the local firm. Employees
then own and manage the company and cannot be 'bought-out' by outsiders.
There are hundreds of worker co-ops developing quietly in the United States.
The numbers may seem small but there are signs that many conventional
firms are slowly moving in this direction. For example, over 6,000 firms have
adopted Employee Stock Option Plans. Even though they do not have the
essential requisites of a co-op, a few of them are gradually developing them.
The requisites are found in the informed participation of employees in the
management of the firm and in the pattern of one-vote per worker for the
board of directors.

Employee participation in management speaks to a key issue in community
economic development. The issue is in finding ways to keep a proper balance
between local and outside controls. Some outside control always comes with
trading in national-and-global markets. Communities need to retain this trade
for their own social and economic benefit, but the question is how to do it
without a major loss in local self-direction.

One solution is to cultivate employee ownership and participation in higher management as a balance wheel to the modern forces of the market. Advanced management practices in big firms are already leading in the direction of cultivating greater authority in their subsidiary system. Peter Drucker has described this trend as 'federalizing' the firm (Drucker 1973: 574). For example, Sears & Roebuck found it profitable over the years to increase autonomy in its local stores over hiring and firing of employees and the buying and selling of products. Drucker argues that Sears made an innovative management decision to do this in the face of its corporate bureaucracy. Johnson & Johnson, a multinational business, has also found it more effective to decentralize authority. It has organized local boards of directors in its subsidiaries. In both cases these firms have retained command over critical decisions but they have also provided a new authority to local management. It is a trend which is moving towards a new prototype not unrelated to the worker co-operative.

An advanced example of this decentralization is found in the structure of the *Milwaukee Journal*, which has become a democratic federation of independent subsidiaries with 2,000 employees. The journal is an employee-owned and managed firm with workers represented on the board of directors. This type of company is less likely to leave the community without a serious review of its impact on local institutions. Local participation in the top policy-making of the big firms allows a significant measure of influence in corporate decisions affecting the local community.

Capital

The 'prototype firm' designed to democratize and localize control over capital is the community development credit union (CDCU). The CDCU is a democratic bank organized by residents in their own neighbourhood. The bank is owned by its customers, who are also responsible for hiring management capable of technically investing their money in the interest of their community. There are hundreds of CDCUs organized in the United States. One example is in Roxbury, Massachusetts, where a community development corporation (CDC) has funded the South End Credit Union. Some neighbourhoods are too small to sustain a local bank; therefore local organizations have pooled their resources to meet the need. An example is Neighborhood Services, Inc., which is a coalition of organizations in Birmingham, Alabama. It has a revolving loan fund designed to finance local housing.

The CDCU arose partly in reaction to red-lining practices of conventional banks. Red-lining had been a bank policy discriminating against neighbourhoods which bank executives considered to be a high risk investment. These red-lined areas tended to be in decline and were often composed of low-income and ethnic-racial groups. Red-lining, of course, worsened the problem of community decline. Local people could not obtain loans to repair their houses, and entrepreneurs were denied funds for new construction. Residents in these declining neighbourhoods found that their own personal savings were invested by their local bank in other communities, while they were denied loans. CDCUs were then created to remedy this situation by utilizing local capital for community development. Today they are chartered as educational institutions to teach people how to manage household budgets, as well as financial institutions designed to invest in the interest of the community.

The CDC and the factor of knowledge

Finally, assistance to these democratic corporations at the local level is a function of another prototype firm whose mandate is to oversee the economic development of the whole community. This is the community development corporation (CDC). The CDC was introduced by legislation in 1967 through a coalition of Democrats and Republicans seeking to redress the grievances of people rioting in the poor neighbourhoods of cities. It is a democratic firm uniquely designed to be accountable to all the residents of the community. Residents become members for a small fee and may participate equally (each resident has one vote) in shaping its policy. The CDC is a planning and governance vehicle through which community needs are met. It is designed to establish new institutions and has begun to play a co-ordinating role in the new institutional development of land, labour and capital in the local community. Yet, it has still another role in the co-ordination of a fourth factor, knowledge. This factor was not so important in the transition from feudalism, but it is important today in the transition towards a social economy.

Knowledge has become an important part of the market in our contemporary economy. Professional knowledge is needed for local development but it exists as a scarce commodity. Expertise is bought and sold for a high price in the market-place. Professional people tend to gravitate towards big corporations and cities with wealth. Put another way, the best doctors, lawyers, accountants, teachers, engineers, physicists, architects, computer experts and so on are not attracted to small communities, declining neighbourhoods and the secondary market of small business.

The CDC could bring knowledge and expertise back into the declining community. For example, it may contract with local colleges, engineering schools and other institutions of higher education to co-ordinate their independent research and educational purposes with local development. Big corporations have already done this and benefited through contracts with universities. But CDCs can do the same. This is exactly what the Greenhouse Compact was designed to do in Rhode Island. Though not passed in a vote by state residents because of tax issues, the Compact idea of utilizing university resources for professional research and consultation represents a model for future directions in community development.

In Massachusetts there are forty CDCs capable of co-ordinating the use of professional knowledge for local development in land, labour and capital. Half of them are in neighbourhoods of Boston and include the Allston-Brighton CDC, the Codman Square CDC, the United South End/Lower Roxbury

Development Corporation, the Fenway CDC, and the Fields Corner CDC in Dorchester. These CDCs operate in a city dense with colleges and universities but have yet to make full use of their facilities and the selected expertise of their faculties.

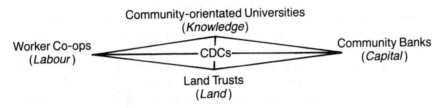

Figure 11.1   The role of the community development corporation (CDC)

Future directions

The task ahead for CDCs may be to help co-ordinate the work of these proto-type firms localizing land, labour and capital. Today, we need to know how these democratic firms all work together.

For example, the CDC will often help initiate local businesses but without organizing them under the co-op model. The employees may then become exploited because they have no representation in management policy. Also, conventional firms can then become purchased by outsiders. Their resources are lost to the community. CDCs do not generally consider land trusts to be a basic part of local planning. Local land then becomes a marketable item. The vacant lot which a CDC has helped to make productive may then be purchased by realtors and used without regard to its value to the community. This precious resource may then also be lost to the community.

Similarly, land-trust advocates do not frequently consider employee partici-pation as a charter principle in land development. A new factory may be created in the interest of the community, but the labour practices of manage-ment could be oppressive. At the same time, advocates of producer co-ops do not always see the benefits of promoting land trusts as a basic part of economic development. They see the benefit of co-ops to workers but do not see their accountability to the community. For example, if the co-op factory goes bankrupt, the land can then become purchased by outside firms. These firms may then 'speculate' on the land, and neighbourhood life deteriorates. They may also forget that workers can produce unsafe products or even try to exploit the land in their own profit-making interest. A land-trust charter, however, guides the use of the land in the larger public interest. For many such reasons, the collaboration of these firms can be in the interest of the local community.

Adding features to the democratic model: economic self reliance

These democratic firms together increase local autonomy but there is also a need to increase economic viability. A community can have a democratic economy and still be overly dependent upon outside market forces. Adding economic diversity and ecological loops to the local economy is therefore another aid in becoming independent of outside market forces.

Weirton Steel (8,000 employees) has recently become a worker-owned firm in Weirton, West Virginia, but is wholly dependent upon the market swings of the steel industry. The Weirton community can democratize its workforce and still remain dependent upon a single outside market. Thus, the local company may be forced to close because of a downswing in the steel market, even while its production is of high quality and it has no serious problems in labour relations. The Weirton community remains overly dependent upon one product and has a need to develop greater diversity in its local industry.

A greater degree of economic diversity and self reliance can be introduced in various ways. One method is by creating ecological loops in which the waste of one production system is transformed locally into productive use by another system. For example, a loop is created by converting waste heat from the operation of machinery into electricity for other uses. Another example is the recycling of throw-away tin cans into the local production of such things as bicycle handlebars. Such loops make a connection between local production and local consumption. They help remove the community from excessive dependence on the outside market.

A new movement for cultivating greater local diversity is called 'economic conversion'. The conversion process involves forming a committee composed of company management, workers, local government representatives and other community leaders. The committee collaborates with engineers and technicians in designing an alternate use plan for firms in trouble. Local CDCs can facilitate the formation of such committees in collaboration with local universities. Universities have technical personnel who can aid in the development of new products and can help local employees conduct market studies, as well as formulate business plans for the new products.

Labour unions are beginning to participate in economic conversion at local levels. For example, when General Electric recently told 450 employees that it planned to close its Charleston (SC) steam turbine generator plant, the United Electrical Workers created a list of eleven alternative products which would save jobs. The Union said that the GE plant could make a profit by producing pollution-control equipment and specialized containers for hazardous waste. Similarly, at Quincy's General Dynamics Shipbuilding Division, community groups want the company to reduce its heavy reliance on military contracts and to plan to make other products. CDCs have a role in helping to facilitate these 'conversions' in the interest of community development.

Conclusion: the international connection

Capitalist and socialist nations around the world are developing community-orientated firms and democratizing the private sector. This emergent democratic sector exists in developing countries with very different opposing ideologies such as Nicaragua, Guatemala, the Philippines, Tanzania and Sri Lanka, as well as the United States. This democratic sector is developing a new synthesis of principles drawn from competing ideologies. It has an historical role similar to the commercial sector Polanyi described as transforming the late stage of feudalism. These democratic firms are the important seeds of the new world. In our time of competition between big nation-states, leaders of these firms might well join hands across the oceans. Today they provide a basis through which a new social economy can develop beyond the dominance of the state or the market.

These democratic firms are no panacea to the problems of capitalism or state socialism. Indeed, if you look closely at them they are themselves riddled with problems of poor management, local power struggles and lack of capital, and they sometimes harbour racial prejudice. Anyone who might want to idealize these democratic companies need only ask local leaders about their problems. These prototype firms need much more experimentation and corporate self-study with professional assistance. They need many self-corrections to gain the support that some advocates would like to give them.

But, when local communities are losing their capacity for self reliance, these small, democratic firms offer a spark of hope. They are seeding themselves slowly in the territories of nation-states to provide a new path towards a humanized economy.

The voluntary sector

The failure of conventional 'development' strategies, whether driven by the market or the state, to eliminate poverty in non-industrial, and many industrial, countries, to regenerate areas of industrial decline or demarginalize so-called peripheral areas; or to change inequitable patterns of ownership and income, has led to an explosion of voluntary activity enacted by groups going under such names as non-governmental organizations (NGOs), people's development organizations (PDOs) or community development organizations (CDOs). All over the world workshops are taking place with such titles as 'Promoting People's Participation and Self-Reliance' (ILO 1989) bringing together key activists and trainers in the field of popular mobilization. Moreover, the NGOs themselves are becoming more confident, ambitious and internationally interconnected. An example is the series of sixteen international meetings convened throughout Japan in August 1989 on a very wide range of topics under the generic title 'People's Plan for the 21st Century' (PP21, 1989).

The recognition of the crucial important of the NGO phenomenon is now practically universal, in rhetoric if not in action:

> During the decade [1980s] NGOs grew significantly in importance as *grassroots development practitioners, international development cooperators, technology transfer agents, providers of technical training and development funders.* They acted as pioneers of the community-based, participatory, culturally and environmentally appropriate actions that must constitute the backbone of any move towards sustainable development – and which official development institutions are often inherently ill-suited to undertake.
>
> (ELC 1986: 5, original emphasis)

The emphasized NGO functions underline the fact that these organizations are *economic* agents, comparable in importance to the household, firm or state, which figure so largely in conventional economic analysis. Such a role has been confirmed by the World Bank's senior vice-president, Mooen Quereshi:

> [NGOs] are telling us that more involvement by grassroots NGOs in our operations will improve the Bank's impact on both poverty and environmental aspects of development. And their advice squares with our experience. It is part of our emerging practice.
>
> (UNNGLS 1989: 8)

Schneider estimates that development NGOs have directly and beneficially influenced the living conditions of some 100 million people out of the 2 billion of the world's poorest peoples they are seeking to help (Schneider 1988: 22). Schneider estimates that an investment of $13 billion per year would be required for the other 1.9 billion of this group to be reached in this way.

Money or lack of it is less likely to be the obstacle to increasing NGO success than its conflict of interest with other powerful development actors. Bodies like the World Bank, for instance, tend to see NGOs as 'cost-effective in the delivery of services' (World Bank 1989: 1), rather than accede to their demands for effective participation of affected people in the very design of Bank (and other development) projects and in changing policies that damage poor people and the environment. As Landim has written in the Brazilian context:

> The question of the World Bank in Brazil, above all, is delicate, since the NGOs have accustomed themselves, by force of circumstances, to a role of continuing criticism of the Bank's activities in terms of sustaining military regimes, co-responsibility in administrative corruption and destruction of nature. The World Bank's policy of support for NGOs – above all in the ecological field – appears contradicted by experiences which are not of the ancient past, but rather are very much current.
>
> (Landim 1990: 26)

Such confrontation between NGOs, governments and multilateral agencies is by no means universal, and happier experiences are reported in World Bank

(1990). But while 'development' strategies continue to impinge negatively on large numbers of poor people, so that their organizations are forced to spend considerable time and energy in opposition and damage limitation, it is hard for NGOs to move on to realize their positive developmental potential.

There is now much experience as to how people's organizations, especially of and/or serving poor people, can realize their objectives of achieving higher qualities of life. Much of this experience meshes with the earlier discussion of local and community economic regeneration; much of it also arises from extending the motivation and value-base of the household economy. The keyword, though now stale from ineffectual overuse in development parlance, remains 'participation'. The key question, to which enduring answers are still all too rarely found, is: how can those whose development or welfare is being sought be enabled to be active in creating it for themselves? This chapter closes with suggested answers to this question from very different perspectives: people's involvement in the services of the welfare state; neighbourhood self-development in run-down areas of an industrial country (UK); and rural self-development in South Asia.

Beyond welfare†

Peter Beresford and Suzy Croft

Welfare has a symbolic significance which has rarely been matched by the quality of its services. It is high on political agendas. But being on the receiving end of welfare is often an isolating and unpleasant experience. We speak from experience, having used income maintenance, housing and other stigmatizing social services. However, change is in the air. There is a new emphasis on people's participation and empowerment in social policy. This points the way to a different set of relationships between welfare, its users and the economic structure. It is this important new departure which we want to explore here.

One of the ironies of social policy is that it has turned 'welfare' into a term of fear and loathing. Being on 'welfare' is a fate most people dread. But if the reality is scruffy and demeaning, welfare continues to be an arena for the most important political and economic debates. Significantly these have largely been 'expert' rather than truly public discussions, confined to politicians, policy-makers and professionals. They have also tended to be fixed on ideas of 'collectivism' and 'anti-collectivism' (George and Wilding 1984).

The collectivists argue for social provision through large-scale state intervention to overcome the inequalities of the market, to meet needs which it

† This paper is based on our experience as users of, workers in and researchers of welfare services. It draws specifically on the four-year study of user involvement in UK social services funded by the Joseph Rowntree Foundation which we undertook between 1987 and 1991. Findings and guidelines from the study are reported in Croft and Beresford (1990) and in Beresford and Croft (1992).

does not meet and may have created and to ensure social justice. The anti-collectivists are opposed to such intervention. They argue it results in the growth of government, restricts people's freedom, imposes a drain on individual income through taxation, encourages dependency and undermines the market economy.

These ideologies approximate to left and right political positions. The political centre is represented by the 'reluctant collectivists'. While they accept a market economy they also see a place for state intervention to compensate for some of the rigours and inequalities they associate with the market.

Such perspectives may be less than helpful. They certainly carry with them shades of Gulliver's 'big enders' and 'little enders'. But their importance should not be underestimated. They have shadowed welfare since the days of the Poor Law. The 1980s have seen the anti-collectivists on the ascendancy in Britain. Political and economic developments in eastern Europe look like making this a continuing feature of the 1990s internationally.

There are signs though that the old analysis is becoming time-expired. New developments have unsettled it. The 1980s saw a strong revulsion from the welfare state in Britain. This was signalled by the political change that took place with the election of Conservative governments from 1979. But there was much more to it than that. Assertive organizations of people who used welfare services emerged, ranging from young people in care, to people with learning difficulties. They rejected the poor quality, paternalism and social control of welfare services. They were joined by professionals from the other side of the counter who wanted to work in different, more egalitarian and participatory ways.

The claim of collectivists to occupy the moral high ground was now disputed. Michael Ignatieff, the political philosopher, wrote:

> to continue to describe the welfare state as a 'caring institution', and to pose as the political party that 'cares' is to think of entitlements as if they were a matter of moral generosity, when in fact, they are a matter of right. Moreover, anyone who has endured social security waiting rooms will be surprised to hear that their particular combination of squalor and officiousness is an instance of 'caring'.

(Ignatieff 1989: 37)

New kinds of services appeared. By showing that things really could be different, they emphasized the deficiencies of the old ones. Women's organizations and gay women and men, for example, set up lesbian lines, rape crisis centres and buddy schemes. These established different relationships between service users and providers, met needs that had previously been ignored and were frequently run in more collaborative ways.

There was a renewed concern with issues of citizenship and the rights and responsibilities that go with it in a democratic society, echoing the demands of women, black people and members of other minority ethnic communities for equal say and opportunities.

Suddenly there was a new emphasis on the *user* of welfare services. This was reflected in the emergence of a new unifying idea of 'user-involvement'. This is being heralded as the 'buzz-word' of the 1990s. But that is not to say that everyone means the same when they use the term. A host of different ideas and agendas jostle under the heading of 'user-involvment'. They reflect the different pressures for change in welfare emerging in the 1970s and 1980s. Two important underlying approaches can be identified. These embrace different ideologies and objectives. One represents a *consumerist* approach, the other a *democratic* one (Beresford 1988). Both have their merits, but it would be wrong to confuse them.

Consumerist approaches to user-involvement tend to be service-provider led. Agencies are seeking solutions to their own problems. They want information from their users to improve their efficiency, economy and effectiveness. The talk is of 'choice' and a 'mixed economy of care', with commercial organizations playing a much larger part in providing welfare goods and services. But the longstanding ambiguity of 'consumerism' remains unresolved. Is it concerned with giving priority to the wants and needs of the consumer or with commodifying their needs and creating new markets? Can the two be reconciled, particularly when the context is people's welfare not commerce?

The consumerist approach, which in Britain has been associated with a strong shift to the private market in welfare, does not challenge existing economic arrangements or welfare's traditional relationship with the economy. Instead, what was a problem is, in one fell swoop, transformed into a solution. In our mixed economy, welfare was meant to compensate for the inequalities of the market. Now the market is supposed to humanize welfare.

If the consumerist model of user-involvement looks like being an extension of the collectivist/anti-collectivist debate, the same is not true of the democratic approach. This represents a real break with the past. First its origins lie with a new player in the game; service users and their organizations. The new organizations of disabled people, older people, people with HIV and survivors of mental-health services, do not just see their participation in terms of being an information source either for more consumer-centred service providers or the traditional fabian experts.

Their aim is *empowerment*. They want to have control over their lives. They are concerned with achieving their rights as citizens in society. They want to be producers of their own welfare instead of passive consumers of it. Their participation signals the emergence of a new domain for popular struggle. First it was the workplace, then the community and now welfare services. They have established their own democratic local, national and international organizations. They are beginning to see themselves as 'new social movements', in the same terms and alongside those of women, black people and environmentalists, with their own distinct analyses, cultures, objectives and ways of working (Oliver 1990). As a member of one organization of people with mental distress said to us: 'we are concerned with how our lives can be improved. Should we be getting involved in services at all? In many cases they are the wrong response to our needs'. Their objectives are much broader than 'user-involvement' defined by welfare services. Three strands can be identified:

1. Access to the mainstream.
2. A say in support services.
3. Securing people's civil rights.

1. *Access to the mainstream* One of the many ways in which user groups feel welfare controls people is by keeping them apart from others and restricting their access to and opportunities in the wider world. People are segregated and congregated in services like residential homes, lunch clubs and sheltered workshops. For many, welfare is too often a palliative which perpetuates their exclusion from ordinary life, instead of making it more accessible. Welfare services are almost invariably inferior and devalued.

User groups want something different. They want public transport which is truly public. They want education that does not segregate people with physical and learning disabilities in 'special' schools. Instead of being economically dependent, they want access to employment in an economy which values their skills and contribution. They want to be part of the economic and social mainstream instead of being confined to welfare services which follow from and do not compensate for the inadequacies of the economy.

2. *A say in support services* Disabled people and others who use welfare services are not saying that they don't want specialist support services. What they want are services which enable them to *keep control over their lives* and live independently. They have learnt that to get the right kind of services, they need to have a say in them. Otherwise services are more likely to match somebody else's idea of what they need, than their own.

3. *Securing people's civil rights* Users of welfare services experience all the usual discriminations of racism, sexism and heterosexism – and more. They can also expect to encounter ageism, disablism and what some users of mental-health services call 'mentalism'. These oppressions are reflected in restrictions on their rights, both within welfare services and in the wider world. Their language is framed in terms of rights and entitlements, not of care or compassion.

The whole thrust of their activities is to go *beyond welfare*. This represents a move away from the professional concern with their 'welfare' rights to their own concern with their *civil* rights. People with learning difficulties demand the right to be treated as adults, to marry and to have children. Disabled people demand the right to be born. They demand the real right to vote, instead of being debarred by inaccessible polling stations.

Organizations of users of welfare services are developing their own programmes to achieve these objectives. Disabled people, for example, highlight three priorities. These are for anti-discrimination legislation, a Freedom of Information Act and the funding and resourcing of organizations of disabled people. In his book *The Politics Of Disablement*, Mike Oliver emphasizes the importance of approaching all three in a coherent way. He says:

> None of these developments by themselves, or an incremental approach to them, is likely to prove successful. Anti-discrimination legislation without freedom of information and a supportive network of disabled people, will simply mean that the lawyers will get rich; freedom of information by itself will mean that individual disabled people will be subjected to professional mystification and sleight of hand, and support for the disabled people's movement without a framework which guarantees basic human rights will leave the movement politically (powerless). But an integrated programme . . . could provide a means of addressing the problems of dependency-creation at both political and professional levels, and hence go some way to resolving the 'crises' both in and of the welfare state at least as far as disabled people are concerned.
>
> (Oliver 1990: 100)

The route these organizations are taking to achieve their aims is to organize collectively. This is a new sense in which collectivity now figures in welfare. Welfare service users are setting up their own organizations – which *they* control. Increasingly what distinguishes the collective action of these rights movements from more traditional community-development approaches, is that people are organizing *themselves*. Disabled people are learning from other disabled people. People with learning difficulties are getting together with the support of other people with learning difficulties. In this they share the strategy of other new social movements. They have their own magazines and newsletters, from *Greypower*, 'the magazine for senior citizens and trade unionists' to *Coalition*, the journal of the Greater Manchester Coalition of Disabled People. They are beginning to get their own funding and their own workers.

The collective action of welfare-service users and their organizations brings us back to the idea of 'user-involvement'. For this collective action to be effective, it needs to be as broad-based as possible. But this poses problems. Britain, like many other western societies, does not have a strong tradition of participation. Most people do not expect to get involved. It is not something they are used to, receive support for or with which they necessarily feel comfortable. Progress in developing initiatives for user-involvement, which involve as wide a range of people as possible and challenge race, gender, disability and other discriminations, has so far been limited. Both user organizations and welfare-service providers face major difficulties in gaining such involvement despite the priority both attach to it – service providers seeking involvement so they can gain the 'representative' involvement that remains one of their key concerns and user organizations in order that people can truly 'speak for themselves'.

There are no blueprints for user-involvment. Flexibility is important. It probably makes more sense to talk in terms of guidelines than models of good practice. But there is now a significant body of experience to draw on (Beresford and Croft 1992). We no longer have to start from scratch. A range of key components for effective policy and practice are becoming apparent from our own research and other work. These include:

- *Resources* to support user-involvement
- *Training* for both service providers and service users and their organizations
- *Information* for service users to make informed choices and decisions
- *Equal access and opportunities* to ensure appropriate services reach black and other minority ethnic communities
- *Time* to enable involvement to develop
- *Appropriate forms and structures for involvement* to make possible broadbased and anti-discriminatory involvement
- *Advocacy* including citizen and professional advocacy, to ensure people have an effective voice
- *Research and evaluation* to extend knowledge and understanding of user-involvement and to involve service users in undertaking research themselves
- *The dissemination of good practice* to share and build on what is already known.

(Croft and Beresford 1992: 42)

The intervention of service users and their organizations is transforming the debate about welfare. Their analysis has broken the mould of the political squabbles of the left and right about the welfare state and offered the possibility of a real alternative for the future. It also offers the prospect of something else; of reclaiming the concept of welfare. At last its promise may be realized, as something positive in people's lives over which they have control and which gives them greater control.

Changing neighbourhoods†
Tony Gibson

The model of development that gives exclusive emphasis to either the market or the state, or some combination of the two, results in the increasing concentration of decision-making in large, centralized institutions and a culture of dependency and alienation. Such a model omits a crucial third component: the ability of ordinary people to think and act for themselves, blending the

† Tony Gibson has for many years been devising means of enabling neighbourhood participation in local change, through his 'Planning for Real' and 'Feasibility' resource packs, and his organizations Education for Neighbourhood Change and Neighbourhood Initiatives Foundation. Several of the project-processes in which his techniques have been applied have received prestigious community development awards. Gibson (1991a) is a detailed description of such a project-process funded by the UK Department of the Environment.

knowledge and experience of the experts with their own understanding of each other's needs and capacities and of their neighbourhood where they live.

It is often overlooked that the world's greatest experts on each neighbourhood are those who live and work in it. The neighbourhood is also the common ground where the effects of market forces and government intervention can be seen and felt. It is a definable patch of land – it could be as wide as a valley, or as narrow as a tower block – it includes everyone who lives and works in it, black and white, old and young, male and female – the lot.

If people are always at the receiving end of others' actions and decisions, the place soon degenerates into an anonymous dwelling area where people keep themselves to themselves for fear of each other. Confidence drains away – self confidence, reliance on each other, respect for society as a whole, trust in the future. The worst effect of this is on the younger generation who need most to be able to show their mettle. Vandalism becomes the only way of their making their mark on society which offers no other opportunities to achieve things together, and threatens a future where they are at the mercy of forces beyond their control.

The neighbourhood is the proving ground where the three ingredients of a healthy society can best be brought together – community, government and business. It is the crucible in which a new compound can be forged and tempered, with a strength and staying-power which none of its ingredients had on their own. Bringing these three ingredients together cannot be done just by words. A way has to be found in which a working relationship can be developed, which through practical co-operation can overcome the suspicions, misunderstandings and mistrust which have grown up between Us and Them. Government is seen as bureaucratic and interfering; business as greedy and self-seeking; people as ignorant and irresponsible. No one is much inclined to commit themselves to anything which the others might hijack. People must first see that things can be made to work, before they will venture further.

This non-commitment is actually an initial asset. It can be the starting point for five kinds of combined operation in which everyone is likely to feel secure. The first is a joint assessment of needs and resources as they exist, here and now. There can be all sorts of arguments about *why* things are as they are, and *who* should take the blame or the credit. But the facts as they stand about needs and resources are there for everyone to see, and the recognition that they are interlinked. Bad housing, home life under strain, boring surroundings, dead-end jobs or no jobs at all, isolated old people, footloose youngsters, dull schooling, junk food, inadequate play facilities, rising prices, flash credit schemes and loan sharks, drugs, vandalism, petty crime. They all add up.

They can be seen both as human needs, and as wasted human and material resources which could be mobilized to meet some of those needs. Checking them out is something which is best done together. A *local needs and resources survey* can bring together local residents, local government officers, and the business community on terms which allow each to contribute its own special knowledge, and all three to combine efforts to check facts, and to find out what is missing. Getting the information is non-committal. No one has to make promises about what happens afterwards. But in the process people get used to each other, find the extent (more than they usually expect) to which they can put up with each other, and begin to see eye to eye on the opportunities which are gradually revealed. Here are possibilities . . . it would be feasible to realize them . . . something could be achieved . . . it should be . . . it must be . . . let's get on and do something about it! The feasibility study becomes a confidence-building process, in which those who started out without giving any commitment become committed. Techniques and materials for undertaking such community-resource surveys have been developed and tested by Education for Neighbourhood Change, through the development of the 'Planning for Real' and 'Feasibility' resource packs (see Gibson 1991b for a guide to these packs). There is also a technique of 'Future Search' developed by Dr Alastair Crombie in association with business, community and civic groups under the auspices of the Australian National University in Canberra.

The second kind of combined operation is a joint assessment of the sort of neighbourhood our children should inherit. A generation hence, what ought people to be able to expect – homes, livelihood, environment, education, care? There are all sorts of disagreement about *how* this should be achieved, and who or what stands in the way. But beyond this people will probably have much the same picture, not unreasonably rosy, of what in the name of commonsense their neighbourhood could and should be like in twenty years time – if only they could have a hand in shaping it together.

These two pictures – of things as they are, and as they could and should be – are the common ground on which the three constituents of a healthy society can gain enough confidence in themselves and in each other to face the much tougher assignment: what could and should be done now, and how much of it can be done together.

Here, too, the first step is to share knowledge and experience. Scattered across the globe there are plenty of examples of what is being done already, although relatively few people know about them and they are often seen only in isolation – a joint planning scheme here, a self-build project there, community businesses, community care, land reclamation, home-based enterprises, each somewhere else.

This first-hand experience can be conveyed and interpreted best by the people who are themselves actually at work, and achieving results. They can say to others still teetering on the brink of action: 'We felt like you, when we started, unsure of ourselves, suspicious of each other. We made mistakes. These are the obstacles we had to remove or circumvent. This is what we learnt as we went along. This is the kick we got out of what we achieved together. This is the momentum we have built up to keep us going'.

Weighing up this experience can be a third stage in the combined operation. 'How does their starting point compare with ours? What were they up against which we are likely to have to deal with? What resources did they draw on which we could tap? What can we learn from them? What changes should we make to fit our own situation? If they could get results, why the hell shouldn't we?'.

The fourth stage in the combined operation could be to define *priorities*. 'We are roughly agreed on where we start out, and on where we want to get in the long run. We have glimpsed some of the practical ways in which others, else-where, have managed to overcome obstacles and achieve results. What should we tackle Now, or Soon, and what can be left to be decided on Later?' What steps can be taken to get some results quickly, so that everyone can share the credit, and see what can be achieved together? This is, literally, a sorting-out process, in which most of those involved can see what is urgent and imme-diately practicable, without having to reach complete agreement on what might follow later on.

Fifth, some initiatives can be taken at once, with the human and material resources which the feasibility enquiry has shown are already to hand. Others cannot be tackled until the people concerned have been able to reinforce their skills and experience and widen their horizons. This brings in the crucial element of *training*. This goes just as much for the professionals (in local government, the civil service, in business and the voluntary sector) as for residents who depend on their support. They have to understand better how to get hold of resources (money, materials, technical facilities, expert advice, personal commitment) and how to use them economically and creatively – to see to the bookkeeping and the cash flow and the stock control and public relations and good building practices; to delegate responsibilities without creating an alienating elite; to make decisions with the minimum of fuss and the maximum of accountability; to involve people without too many self-inflicted wounds. Deciding on what skills are needed, and when, and how best to draw on available resources to help provide them or reinforce them, is the final area in which both the needs and the opportunities are likely to be seen by everyone concerned as common ground.

Such training can often be done together, with professionals pooling their special knowledge and residents pooling their own first-hand experience of what really happens, and their intuitive understanding of how different sections of the community feel about it. This mutual re-education can open people's eyes to each others' backgrounds and capacities, and may reveal more in common than anyone anticipated. So it adds to the common ground, and in the exchange of experience it becomes easier to look together at the way ahead.

The neighbourhood is the level at which all three ingredients – community, business and government – can come together on the same footing. This does not mean that their powers, or their interests, are all the same. But by concen-trating on the needs and the potential of the neighbourhood they live and work in they can discover what they have in common, and through their working relationships develop enough confidence to face disagreements and survive conflicts, to become active parts of the dynamics of society, contributing to regeneration not decay. Active neighbourhoods are the living cells in society.

If they fail to function, decay sets in. But when neighbourhoods come alive, society as a whole regains its nerve, and people dare to believe in their capacity to shape the future together.

People's participation: reconciling growth with equity[†]

Ponna Wignaraja

Participatory development

Of central concern in any discussion of sustainable development in wider human terms is the issue of participation. It is a pretence to think that the crisis the South is facing can be overcome, and that the reshaping of its societies, the development of its rural areas and eradication of the worst forms of poverty can be undertaken, without the participation of the people, particularly the large numbers who are poor.

A commitment to participation implies commitment to a more egalitarian society which permits more equal access to basic resources, not only to land but also to education, health, credit and donor inputs. Where formal power is in the hands of a few and their power is grossly misused, *participation means building countervailing power which leads to a healthier democracy*, and an assertion of the right of the poor to access to resources.

People cannot be viewed as mere objects or targets of development – they are the subjects. Further, if development results from a process of releasing the creative energy of the people, particularly the poor, then they must be the final arbiters of their lives. This goes beyond merely meeting the material needs of people and beyond considerations of equity. To participate people need to raise their level of consciousness and to form their own organizations. The poor need to become increasingly aware of the socio-economic reality around them, of the forces that keep them in poverty, and of the possibilities for bringing about change in their conditions through their own reflections and collective actions. This constitutes a process of self-transformation through people's praxis where they grow and mature as human beings.

A truly participatory development process cannot always be generated spontaneously, given the existing power relations at all levels, apathy, and the deep-rooted dependency relationship between rich and poor, common in most

[†] The question of enablement in a Third World context has been considered in great detail by the group of South Asian scholars and action-researchers, whose work on village self-development in the 1970s resulted in *Towards a Theory of Rural Development* (de Silva *et al.* 1988). One of this team was Anisur Rahman, who wrote on people's self-development in Chapter 6. Another was Ponna Wignaraja, who presented a pre-edited version of the following paper to the South Commission Secretariat in 1989. Two more recent studies are Wignaraja (1990) and Wignaraja *et al.* (1991).

countries of the South. It often requires a catalyst, a new type of activist and initiator who will work with the poor, who identifies with the interests of the poor and who has faith in the people. The interaction with initiators helps people to analyse their problems, to understand their problems better and to articulate their felt needs. Their interaction sets in motion a process of reflection, mobilization, organization, action and further reflection among the poor. Through a process of awareness creation, initiators mobilize people into self-reliant action and assist in the building-up of collective strength and bargaining among the poor.

Hence, identification, selection and sensitization of such initiators becomes a central task in launching an effective participatory rural development movement. Conventional training methodology (delivering a pre-packaged basket of knowledge or skills through lectures and instruction) cannot be used for this purpose. It is a process of sensitization rather than one of formal training. It is a process of self-learning through exposure to the dynamics of actual socio-economic situations rather than learning in the abstract. Observation, investigation, group interaction, sharing and comparing experiences, criticism and self-criticism, cultivating behavioural and social skills (particularly the capacity to analyse the political economy of poverty) are the central elements of this process of sensitization. Without this awareness people cannot participate – they are merely manipulated with a pretence of consultation.

Finally, it is difficult for the poor to break away from the vicious circle of dependence and poverty individually. It is only through group effort and organization that they can reduce dependence and initiate a course of participatory, self-reliant development. Thus participation implies mobilization, conscientization and organization (for group or collective action) – in that order.

The steps in initiating a process of participatory development

While it is not possible to state the steps in a manual form, as this is too mechanistic, it is possible to outline some concrete steps which are an essential part of the participatory development process. Such a listing has been found useful when training catalysts and internalizing the process (UNU-UNDP 1987):

1. *People's creativity, the starting point* Self-initiatives of the poor form the essence of a process of participatory development, where the poor operate as conscious subjects of change. They reflect on their life-situations, and take decisions to bring about changes to improve their social and economic status. The underlying assumption is that the poor are creative and are capable of taking self-initiatives for their development, but social processes have often operated to deny opportunities for the practical expression of people's creativity. A meaningful development process must lead to a liberation of the creative initiatives of the poor and of poor women who are in the majority of this category.

2. *From objects to subjects* Conventional top–down models for development, explicitly or implicitly, treat the poor as objects of change and the relation between the intervenor and the poor often takes the form of a subject acting upon an object. It is assumed in those models that the poor have no knowledge-base or that their knowledge is irrelevant/unscientific and that they have to be told and instructed as to what they should do. The outcome is a delivery approach – that is, an attempt to bring development to the poor through deliveries of knowledge and resources from outside. Fundamental to the initiation of a process of participatory development is the break-up of this dichotomy of subject and object, and the transformation of the relation into one between two knowing subjects resulting in a creative tension between two knowledge streams, namely poor people's experimental knowledge and the formal knowledge introduced from outside. It is a dialogical process of creating change. This is also the essence of participation.

3. *Investigation and analysis of reality by the poor* Poor people can be expected to undertake self-initiatives for change when they become conscientized, that is to say when they become critically aware of their life-situation (the reality of life) and begin to perceive self-possibilities for changing that reality. Hence, the first step in the generation of a process of participatory development is to assist the poor to critically reflect upon, analyse and understand the socio-economic reality in which they live. Reality has to be posed to the poor as a problem to investigate and as a challenge to transform. The reality that the majority of the urban and rural poor face is poverty and underdevelopment – in particular, low levels of production, income and consumption and the inability even to retain a part of the surplus they generate. Hence, the problematization of the reality must lead to an investigation and analysis of the totality of life in poverty and underdevelopment. The assumption here is that there is considerable potential for the poor to improve their lives which remains underutilized. Such potential for development should form the focus of problematization and subsequent analysis by the people.

4. *Exploration of self-possibilities for actions* When the poor carry out such investigations and analysis, they also begin to perceive self-possibilities to deal with the factors in their poverty and hence to change the reality. Alternative possibilities of action will be explored and the feasibility for such actions will be examined using the poor people's own knowledge and experiences and drawing on knowledge available from outside. Resources, requirements and constraints for each action will be carefully studied. This is a process of the poor's own planning at the grass-roots. In the case of poor women, the knowledge system and internal dimension are even more relevant.

5. *Organizational consciousness* In order to initiate actions, the poor need to organize themselves in a manner (as decided by them) that best suits their purposes. They may decide to build new organizations of their choice or use

existing organizations over which they have effective control as instruments of action. The important point here is the availability of organizational mechanisms and support systems in which the poor have confidence, over which they have control and which they can use as organs for their actions. Poor women would need to build separate organizations initially to take care of the double burden (of poverty and gender-discrimination) and then link into the general organization of the poor.

6. *Initiation of actions* The poor tend to make a beginning with those actions which they can undertake with their own resources and which they feel could be implemented with success. They tend to start with fairly simple actions. The resources required for such actions are mobilized from within the community itself, through collective actions to generate funds. The success of these initial actions will give them some experience in self-initiatives and also enhance their confidence in their abilities to bring about changes in their life-situations. They then will embark upon more actions and will go into larger and more sophisticated actions which involve claiming and using resources from outside. When they reach this stage, they will begin to make claims and bargain for resources available from the social system (e.g. extension services, credit facilities, training and infrastructural facilities) so that their own resource base is now strengthened and supplemented, thereby improving their capacity to initiate more actions. There will now be an interaction between the poor groups and the socio-economic system, the poor making claims, bargaining for improving their access to social resources, while at the same time mobilizing their own resources to further the development process. As a result of this assertion, the socio-economic system will now begin to respond to the needs and requirements of the poor and to serve their interests better.

7. *From action to reflection* Reflection on actions – that is the review and evaluation of the ongoing actions, as a regular practice – is undertaken by the poor groups themselves and constitutes an important element in a participatory development process. Reflections on actions are needed to learn from experience, for early correction of mistakes, to identify problems and constraints and to seek ways to cope with them, to assess the benefits accrued from actions and to explore possibilities of improving the ongoing actions as well as initiating new actions. Reflection enhances the poor's knowledge and understanding and helps to improve the quality of their actions.

8. *Capacitation of the people* As the people's self-development process unfolds, people will begin to improve their capacities to conceive development ideas, plan, implement and manage development actions. A wide range of opportunities will be created for the practical expression and development of talents and skills that lie dormant among the poor. Leaders, intellectuals, animators, managers and so on will emerge from the action process reducing over a time the dependence on outside catalysts. The poor will tend to become increasingly

self-reliant in their thinking and action and begin to develop autonomous capacities for action. The women's movement has raised women's consciousness, and now the gender and equity issue has to be responded to not only at the philosophical level but also through concrete development actions undertaken collectively.

9. *Diversification and multiplication of actions*   Initially, poor groups will naturally tend to start with problems and issues of immediate concern to them and which they can tackle with confidence. With increasing conscientization and experience gathered in planning action, they will tend to diversify their actions to include other aspects of their socio-economic lives. Self-initiatives are educational experiences which expand people's horizons. New problems, issues and needs will be identified for investigation, analysis and initiation of actions. The success of one action creates the possibility of undertaking another, setting in motion a flow of successive actions. Furthermore, the process tends to multiply from one group to another and from one village to another. Successful actions of one group create a demonstration effect on others in a village on the possibilities of self-development. Moreover, after a point, people's groups tend to develop an urge to expand the process among others, for they begin to realize that it is only when several groups join hands and begin to act together that they will have the strength and the bargaining power to tackle larger issues of common concern to them. The logical outcome of this process is an empowerment of the poor, the development of their capacity for self-development and the emergence of poor women as a counter-power within the socio-economic system capable of asserting their rights and claims to improve their lives.

Role of the animator

A process of participatory development as described above rarely emerges as a spontaneous phenomenon. The poor, including poor women, need to be stimulated and assisted to initiate such processes. In order to undertake self-initiatives for change, the poor need to understand the socio-economic reality in which they live, perceive self-possibilities for bringing about changes in that reality, develop the capacities to translate the possibilities into concrete actions and to manage the actions. This is not a matter of 'skills' training in the narrow sense of technical skills or a manipulative process in the name of 'participation'. All categories of the poor need to develop their intellectual skills (to investigate, reflect upon, analyse and understand) as well as their practical skills (to organize, implement and manage actions). This defines the role of the outsiders, namely to assist the poor to bring out and acquire the intellectual and practical knowledge needed for their self-initiated development process (see also Tilakaratna 1985).

The role of the outsiders may be conceived as consisting of three main elements, namely animation, facilitation and progressive redundancy:

1. *Animation* is a process of assisting the poor to develop their intellectual capacity to investigate the reality of their life-situations, analyse the relevant issues, understand the factors creating poverty and deprivation and through such understanding to perceive self-possibilities for change. They are animated when they understand the reality and perceive possibilities for changing that reality. The outcome of animation is conscientization. Animation is the outcome of a specific mode of interaction between the outsiders and the poor.

The essence of this interaction mode is the evolution of a subject-to-subject relation between the two parties (replacing the conventional subject-to-object relation). The poor have a knowledge base rooted in experience, practice and living with nature and society. This knowledge has its own validity and rationality. On the other hand, outsiders bring with them knowledge derived from formal education. These are two different knowledge streams each having its own scientific basis. The delivery approach to development seeks to transfer formal knowledge to the poor and disregards the poor's own knowledge as unscientific or irrelevant. It is a subject-to-object relation. On the other hand, a participatory approach seeks to achieve an interaction between the two knowledge streams creating a mutual learning process. It is an interaction between the two worlds, capable of systematizing the knowledge of the poor, creating new knowledge and generating seeds of change. Animation seeks to break the dichotomy between subject and object and to evolve, as far as possible, a relation between two equals.

Such a mode of interaction requires the adoption of a dialogical approach and even these steps cannot be taught or applied mechanically. Teaching, instruction and transfer of skills will be replaced by discussion, dialogue stimulation of self-reflection and analysis, and sharing of experience and knowledge. The starting point for this purpose should be an attempt to initiate a dialogue with the people on the reality of their life-situations. The reality that people face (poverty, underdevelopment and deprivation) should be posed to the people as a problem for their investigation, as a challenge for them to respond to. By raising key questions such as: why do we have low incomes? Why is our production low? Why do we buy our needs at high prices and sell our produce cheap? Can we not find new kinds of work in the informal sector? What access do we have to different kinds of resources? Why do we eat certain kinds of food? The animator has to stimulate/provoke the people to come out with ideas, issues and factors that they perceive as barriers to improving their livelihood. Dialogue with the people must lead to a re-evaluation of poor people's own basic perceptions of issues pertaining to their life-situations. Hence, actions are rooted in the investigations and analysis carried out by people themselves assisted by the animator. This approach may be contrasted with the normal run of development projects where the underlying social analysis for projects is carried out by outside professionals and the poor are at best involved in the implementation phase of the projects.

2. *Facilitation*   Animation is a necessary but not a sufficient condition to enable the poor to undertake and manage development actions to transform their realities. There are a host of factors which operate to keep the poor passive rather than active. Given their behaviour patterns (often non-innovative and non-experimental in nature) and lack of experience in undertaking self-initiatives for change, it will take time before they begin to develop the confidence in their abiities to bring about changes. Hence an external input in the form of facilitation is often required to assist the poor to initiate actions for changing their conditions. Animation by breaking mental barriers begins to show self-possibilities for change. Facilitation is an attempt to assist the poor to overcome practical barriers to action. The animator's formal education, wider knowledge of socio-economic contexts, and links with the governmental machinery and service delivery personnel, should be able to assist the people to cope with their practical problems. Such facilitation can take several forms such as:

- assisting them to acquire basic management and, where necessary, technical skills, building on their own knowledge,
- assisting them to develop contacts with formal service agencies, institutions and bureaucracies of relevance to their action programmes and to develop skills and knowledge required to deal and negotiate with them,
- assisting them to improve their access to material resources such as credit available within the socio-economic system,
- assisting them to translate their development ideas into concrete activities and programmes and to work out the implementation plans (a kind of consultancy role).

3. *Progressive redundancy ('self-liquidation')*   An important characteristic of animation and facilitation roles should be their transitional character, that progressive redundancy of the animator over time as the poor develop their own capacities to initiate, undertake and manage their development. The animator's interaction with the poor must lead to capacity build-up among the people, and a crucial test of an animator's success must ultimately be their ability to render their role redundant over time within a given community or village so that they are released to start similar work in other villages. Self-liquidation (the ability of an animator to phase out from a given village) becomes important in two respects: (a) to ensure that the poor become self-reliant, that they develop the capacity to manage their actions without critical dependence on outsiders and (b) to ensure multiplication of the participatory development process such that the animator is released to move into other villages to start similar work.

This is a fundamental characteristic of the mode of interaction for participatory development as distinguished from other modes of intervention implied in the notions of bureaucracy, vanguardism and paternalism which, in one way or another, tend to perpetuate the role of the intervenors. It is the generation of internal animators from within the village communities that enables external animators to make their roles redundant over a time. Poor people's development processes create a wide range of opportunities for the people to develop their dormant skills and talents. Investigation and analysis of reality, exploration of self-development possibilities, translation of the possibilities into concrete action plans, implementation and management of actions, development of links with formal agencies and bargaining for resources and services – and reflection and review of actions – are among the many activities in which the people would be actively involved in a process of participatory development. Involvement in such a wide range of actions provides a training ground for animators and facilitators to emerge from the poor themselves. The external animators must identify those with such emerging ability, hold meetings and discussions with them and assist them to improve their knowledge and ability, so that the insiders develop the capacity eventually to replace the outsiders. The ratio of internal to external animators must progressively increase over time. This is, in fact, an indicator of the success of a project of this nature.

Evaluation

In the foregoing sections, the steps for initiating a participatory experiment whose basic objective is to enhance the status of the poor and enable them to move out of poverty has been enunciated. Irrespective of whether a government agency, a bank or an NGO initiates the experiment or whether they more spontaneously emerge, and irrespective of whether the activities start with a particular entry point, its evolution must be seen as a self-generating process where each stage is built on the collective experience of the previous stage. This is how the process is made sustainable. Thus this collective experience needs to be periodically assessed and systematized. This is the task of evaluation.

Since participation is central to both the approach and design with the poor as the subjects and not merely the objects of the process, participation is also an essential element of the evaluation process (Jain *et al.* 1986). In this sense, evaluation is part of the internal dynamics of the process, as well as an assessment of progress from the standpoint from which the objectives are derived – in this case enabling people to move out of poverty into sustainable development. To the extent that the poor have participated in the process, it is easier for them also to evaluate it. This also helps to demystify evaluation and relate it to the daily tasks and work that all participants need to undertake. This kind of evaluation also pays attention to detail.

Conventional evaluation requires an outside evaluator, who, in a sense, exercises control over the process. But in a situation of participatory development where the action-reflection process is a continuous one, internal evaluation provides the necessary control, raises further awareness and the capacity for self-management. It is this kind of evaluation which also leads to corrective actions and to subsequent development action. The internal motivational objective is to raise the poor's understanding of their experience through collective assessment, improved articulation, problem-solving and commitment to the tasks they have set for themselves. They also learn from their total experience and derive a political resolve towards collective action for achieving their objectives. This is also what is meant by empowerment.

Implications for future development policy and action

The extent of participation will depend initially on the political space that is available for the participatory grass roots processes to start and for an intervention into the existing socio-economic system. In many countries there is great potential energy and will to change. This energy needs to be harnessed, and change agents or catalysts can be found in many areas to initiate the process. In various countries there is strong support for people's causes from such groups as the radical church, various professions, students and even members of the bureaucracy, the judiciary and so on, and new coalitions can be built.

The very nature of participatory self-reliant development activities is such that they eventually attract the attention of the power structure. Some activities are co-opted, others are exterminated, some are repressed, but survive. Those which survive, existing in isolation, do not add up to much in terms of social transformation. But if they are properly linked and multiply themselves through the process of mobilization, conscientization and organization they can become a countervailing power in the societal context and help to widen the political space even further for participatory self-reliant development, opening up the possibility for governments which are trusted by the people to give this development their sensitive support.

The essence of participation is that the priorities are set by the poor themselves as subjects in the process and the process is initiated with their savings in cash or kind. A major lesson that has been learned from the experience on the ground in the past ten to fifteen years in South Asia is that a new form of accumulation can be set in motion as a result of these participatory development experiments in which 'growth' and 'equity' are not trade-offs.

A unifying characteristic of these last three contributors is that they are each based on the author's personal knowledge of and involvement in processes of participation which have brought great benefits to those involved, who were often those who were marginalized or discriminated against by other 'development processes'.

It is worth stressing, therefore, the essential practicality, achievability and relevance to both North and South of the participatory development model. Its successes have been amply documented (in addition to the sources already cited, see Bruyn and Meehan 1987; Conroy and Litvinoff 1988; Dauncey

1988; Harrison 1987; ICE 1982; Pradervand 1989; Turner 1988) and confirm that these sorts of measures cost a fraction of conventional development assistance, but unfortunately they demand other qualities with which national governments are often rather meagrely endowed: a commitment to justice, democracy and equitable resource distribution; officials whose principal task is to listen and serve rather than instruct and control; and procedures which allow people and local communities genuine responsibility for planning, deciding and executing their own development, while ensuring that they have the professional and technical advice they need both to organize themselves appropriately and make the right decisions to achieve their objectives.

Chambers makes some of the same points in terms of a resolution of the neo-Fabian/neo-liberal dichotomy:

[The new paradigm] resolves the contradiction between the neo-Fabian thesis that the state should do more, and the neo-liberal antithesis that the state should do less. In terms of this paradigm, the state has often done those things which it ought not to have done, and has left undone those things which it ought to have done. . . . The worst mistakes have been rules and restrictions which give field-level staff power to extract rents from the weak. Here a new neo-liberal agenda can liberate the poor by abolishing the regulations used to exploit them. The task is to dismantle the disabling state. In parallel, there is more that the state can and should do. Here a new neo-Fabian agenda can decentralise while providing safety nets, secure rights and access to reliable information and permitting and promoting more independence and choice for the poor. The task is to establish the enabling state. For both these new agendas, the unifying theme is reversals, to put first the diverse priorities of poor people. To understand and support these is equitable – helping people gain what they want; efficient – mobilising their creative energy; and sustainable – providing incentives for long-term self-reliant investments by the poor. The vision is then of a state which is not only protector and supporter, but also enabler and liberator.
(Chambers 1989: 20)

This is the challenge for policy-makers in a living economy: to become virtuosi on the relative strengths and advantages of the market, the different levels of the state and direct provision, and to learn how to combine them complementarily for maximum wealth (*not* output) creation. It should be a refreshing and invigorating change from the stale and fruitless continued conflicts arising from the state–market confrontation.

12 Achieving sustainability

Sustainability at its simplest refers to the ability of some function or activity to be sustained. The concern over environmental sustainability has arisen over uncertainty as to the ability of the natural environment to maintain its various functions because of the destructive impacts of human activities. Because these and other human activities depend in turn on environmental functions, their sustainability is then brought into question and, thence, that of the way of life of which they are a part.

There are several examples in history where it is likely that human activities proved environmentally unsustainable to the extent that a way of life became unsupportable, not least in the Mediterranean basin (Ehrlich and Ehrlich 1990: 53). What is different about the current economic impacts is their global scale, due to the exponential growth in both human numbers and in human production and consumption, the former now principally in the South, the latter principally in the North. Lester Brown of the Worldwatch Institute has written, 'On average, the additional economic output in each of the last four decades has matched that added from the beginning of civilization until 1950' (Brown *et al.* 1990: 3).

No one has stressed the environmental importance of economic scale in his work more consistently and effectively than Herman Daly (see especially Daly 1977; Daly and Cobb 1989). In a recent paper (Daly 1991), he has called for scale to command similar macro-economic attention to that accorded to allocation and distribution:

> The term 'scale' is shorthand for 'the physical scale or size of the human presence in the ecosystem as measured by population times per capita resource use'. Optimal *allocation* of a given scale of resource flow within the economy is one thing (a micro-economic problem). Optimal *scale* of the whole economy relative to the ecosystem is an entirely different problem (a macro–macro problem). The micro allocation problem is analogous to allocating optimally a given amount of weight in a boat. But once the best relative location of weight has been determined, there is still the question of the absolute amount of weight the boat should carry. This absolute optimal scale of load is recognised in the maritime institution of the Plimsoll line.

When the watermark hits the Plimsoll line the boat is full, it has reached its safe carrying capacity. Of course, if the weight is badly allocated the water line will touch the Plimsoll mark sooner. But eventually as the absolute load is increased the watermark will reach the Plimsoll line even for a boat whose load is optimally allocated. Optimally loaded boats will still sink under too much weight – even though they may sink optimally! It should be clear that optimal allocation and optimal scale are quite distinct problems. . . .

Optimal scale, like distributive justice, full employment or price level stability, is a macro-economic goal. And it is a goal that is likely to conflict with the other macro-economic goals. . . . The traditional solution to unemployment is growth in production, which means a larger scale. Frequently the solution to inflation is also thought to be growth in real output, and a larger scale. And most of all, the issue of distributive justice is 'finessed' by the claim that aggregate growth will do more for the poor than redistributive measures. Conventional macro-economic goals tend to conflict, and certainly optimal scale will conflict with any goal that requires further growth once the optimum has been reached. . . . As an economy grows it increases in scale. Scale has a maximum limit defined either by the regenerative or absorptive capacity of the ecosystem, whichever is less. However, the maximum scale is not likely to be the optimal scale. . . . Optimal scale is not well defined at present but one characteristic at least is known – the optimal scale must be sustainable. Our attention then naturally becomes focused on how to limit scale to a sustainable level, thereby giving the sustainable development discussion a bit more of a theoretical foundation than it has had to date.

(Daly 1991: 4, 6, 10, 13, original emphasis)

It will doubtless, be some time before the theoretical foundation of sustainability is fully elaborated but the gravity of present trends of unsustainability demands that practical policy and action proceed simultaneously with such elaboration. The next two papers discuss some of the practical implications of sustainable development and some of the key policy orientations that will be required for sustainability to become the overriding objective of economic decision-making.

The practical implications of sustainable development

David Pearce

It seems fair to say that the practical implications of the sustainable development philosophy are still being worked out. This is hardly surprising since it is only within the last year or so that economists have attempted to offer rigorous definitions of the term. But certain implications seem fairly clear, and we therefore concentrate on these. There are many others and they extend well beyond purely economic implications.

As an illustration, environmental economics establishes that environmental impacts are pervasive within an economic system. While they may be more significant in some sectors compared to others, all sectors use energy and materials and therefore generate waste. It follows that 'environmental policy' cannot really be a *separate* from other sectoral policies on energy, industry, regional development, transport, foreign aid and so on. The 'pervasiveness' of environment has *institutional* implications for design of environmental policy. It may be for example, that governmental environmental agencies need to become 'senior' ministries in the sense in which finance ministries currently are.

Precautionary policy

The existence of positive discount rates means that it *may* make sense not to act precipitately about an environmental problem such as climate change. After all, policies undertaken to deal with climate change problems are likely to be expensive, or at least more expensive than traditional environmental policy has been. We might say that it sometimes makes sense to behave in the *reactive mode* for environmental policy. This contrasts with the *anticipatory mode* in which we try to anticipate problems and incur the costs of solving the problem in advance of the problem occurring.

The issue of discounting is, however, only one aspect of the problem of choosing between anticipatory and reactive environmental policy. At least four other issues affect any choice between these policy stances.

First, by postponing a policy, we cannot be sure that it will cost the same to solve it in the future as it would cost if action was taken now. Indeed, for many problems it is highly likely that it will cost more. A particular extreme instance of such rising costs occurs when the damage done by delay is *irreversible*. For example, suppose that nothing at all had been done about the damage to the ozone layer from trace gases. There are no (feasible) technologies for reconstituting the layer once it is 'holed'. The damage done, for example through the contribution to climate warming, is irreversible. The rising cost of reactive policy, particularly where irreversible effects are concerned could easily offset the effect of time preference (discounting).

Second, the reactive stance may not be compatible with the underlying theme of sustainable development. The sustainable development idea is encapsulated in the proposition that the future has to be compensated by the past. Otherwise the future will be worse off than the present and the resulting development is not sustainable. Undertaking reactive policy towards the environment could, as noted above, result in irreversible cost to the future. The potential for irreversibility is thus sufficient for us to be highly suspect of reactive policy: it should be undertaken only if we can be sure that damage can be reversed and at a cost that can be 'afforded' by the future. What the future can afford depends on what we leave them by way of inherited wealth, natural and man-made. *The philosophy of sustainable development tends to favour strongly the anticipatory approach to environmental policy.*

Third, the reactive stance receives some support from a not always appreciated fact. This is that delay can generate better information which in turn enables cheaper and more effective solutions in the future. The implicit condition here is that the delay is accompanied by further research aimed at such cost-effective solutions. If delay is adopted simply to postpone costs without any associated research activity, then this benefit is lost. Reactive policy is not wholly bad. It can sometimes be justified by reference to the expected gains in information and improved policy cost-effectiveness. But delay is only justified if the benefits outweigh the costs: good scientific research needs to accompany delay.

Fourth, there is the problem of *uncertainty*. Environmental problems are often treated as if they are some minor deviation in the working of an economic system. But the most essential feature about environments is that their workings are *pervasive* to the economic system. This pervasiveness arises from the simple fact that all economic activity uses up materials and resources and energy, and these, in turn, must end up somewhere – in dumps, dissipated in the atmosphere, disposed of to the oceans or whatever. This pervasiveness might not be unduly troublesome but for the fact that it contributes to the uncertainty about how environmental impacts will manifest themselves. A toxic pollutant disposed of at point A may travel to point B miles away. In the process it may mix with other pollutants and the damage from the synergistic effect may be greater than the sum of the damages from the individual effects. To these kinds of uncertainties must be added the scientific uncertainty about how ecosystems function. Consider the fact that we are some way away from understanding how global carbon cycles work in detail and hence how climate change will impact regionally within the world.

How then should we behave under uncertainty? Attitudes to uncertainty vary. There are, for example, technological optimists who believe that whatever problem is generated there will be some technological solution. Such optimism is the stuff of scientific advance. The problem is one of what happens if the optimists are not right and we behave *as if* they were. Figure 12.1 shows how we might (simplistically) present such choices. What it reveals is that the cost of pursuing an optimist policy could be disastrous if in fact some form of 'prudent pessimism' turns out to be right. Prudent pessimism might well deprive society of some moderate gains and, if the optimists turn out to be right all along, then we will have sacrificed the difference between high and moderate gains.

There are really no rules for choosing which policy to undertake in the face of uncertainty. But most people are risk-averse, they do not like uncertainty. Most people would also agree that taking risks is not worthwhile when the negative 'pay-off' – what happens if they lose – is very large. Some current environmental problems risk very large losses. A risk-averse strategy favours anticipatory and not reactive environmental policy.

		Actual state of the world	
		Optimists Right	Pessimists Right
TYPE OF POLICY	Optimistic	HIGH	DISASTER
	Pessimistic	MODERATE	TOLERABLE

The pay-off matrix suggests that if the technological optimists are right and a policy of relative indifference to the environment is pursued, then society might make high gains. If the optimistic policy is pursued and the pessimists turn out to be right then some form of 'disaster' might occur. Pursuit of 'prudent pessimism' on the other hand results in moderate gains or, at worst, tolerable gains. The terminology is suggestive only, of course (substituting 'nirvana' for 'high' might alter the perception of the matrix a little). None the less, the basic idea of seeing what happens if a given policy is pursued, when in fact the state of the world is not consistent with that policy, is correct.

Figure 12.1 A pay-off matrix for approaches to environmental uncertainty
Source: Adapted from Robert Costanza (1989) 'What is ecological economics?', *Ecological Economics*, 1(1): 1–7

Importing and exporting sustainability

It is perfectly possible for a single nation to secure a sustainable development path, *but at the cost of non-sustainability in another country*. This is perhaps most easily seen by considering an extreme example in which an economy imports all its raw materials, uses indigenous technology and human skills to convert it to a final product, and then exports the final products. Because it adds significant 'value added' in the process it can then further import all its food needs as well. The nation's stock of natural resources remains intact, but the nations from which it imports may well be experiencing a decline in their natural capital stock because it is being exported.

To bring the extreme example closer to the real world, there are many countries which rely on imports of natural resources from developing countries which frequently do not have alternative products to sell in international markets. Consider the tropical hardwood market. Five countries – Malaysia, Indonesia, the Philippines, Ivory Coast and Gabon – supply some 30 per cent of the world market in tropical hardwoods. In roundwood equivalents, Japan accounts for about 50 per cent of these imports, and the EEC for just under 40 per cent. Yet it is clear that the tropical forests supplying these products are being used unsustainably. In so far as economic progress in the wealthier countries can be said to be sustainable (and this is something that needs testing with 'sustainability indicators'), it could be said that the sustainability is in part being achieved by 'importing' it through non-sustainability in other nations.

The situation may not be as bad as this. It depends first on how we define sustainability. If we take the broader view, based on total rather than natural capital only, the hardwood exporting countries may simply be converting their export revenues into investments which will sustain their future. In other words, they may be 'swapping' natural for man-made capital. Unfortunately we have little evidence that this is happening, and a good deal of evidence that no such transformation is taking place. Instead, export proceeds are often turned into consumption, not into building up the capital base, investment. A further concern about the idea of 'importing sustainability' is that the trade is 'free', and free trade should be to the mutual advantage of all participating countries since it is based on the doctrine of comparative advantage.

This suggests that a nation who could be regarded as importing sustainability should seek to compensate the exporting nation for its loss. Essentially, the exporting nation risks non-sustainability for the benefit of the importing nation. In part its failure to manage its resources sustainably is a policy choice – it chooses to 'mine' rather than 'manage' its renewable resources. But we might legitimately argue that this is not the full story and that the importing nation has an obligation to reverse the flow of sustainability benefits.

Changing the national accounting system *

It is now widely accepted that the use of GNP as a measure of 'welfare' is seriously deficient (see e.g. Ahmad *et al.* 1989 and Repetto 1988). It is well known, for example, that deductions should be made for the value of environmental damage and adjustments should be made for defensive expenditures which are undertaken in order to avoid such damages. These adjustments should occur regardless of any considerations of the underlying tenets of the sustainable development philosophy, although sustainable development thinking certainly augments the accounting reasons for these modifications.

A direct implication of sustainable development construed as non-declining capital (however defined) is the need to *value* stocks. Experience to date has largely been in terms of valuing changes in stocks (e.g. damage done by pollution, or improvements secured through environmental regulation). Valuing *stocks* involves the same kind of techniques (surveyed in Pearce and Markandya 1989 and Mäler 1989a) but is something we are less familiar with.

A further implication is the need to measure *sustainable income*. In order to calculate such a figure which was initially proposed as a definition of income by Hicks, we need to subtract from GNP the depreciation in the physical and environmental capital that has taken place (Hicks 1946). This amounts to working with a net income measure. Although the relationship between the

---

* *Editor's note*: This topic has already been extensively discussed in Chapter 5. This section is retained, however, for emphasis and completeness.

measure and current or long-term economic welfare has not been worked out so far, it is an attractive notion to work with for a number of reasons.

The notion of sustainable income captures the idea of a constant capital stock – both physical and environmental. Second, by looking at net income one is properly penalizing those economies that are generating a high current income by 'selling off the family silver', that is running down their capital stock. Third, even if sustainable income is not the same as long-term welfare for dynamic reasons, the construction of a measure of the latter is likely to be so complicated that it will never be implementable.

A measure of *sustainable income*, together with the adjustments for environmental degradation and costs of mitigation would result in the following:

SUSTAINABLE INCOME = MEASURED INCOME – HOUSEHOLD DEFENSIVE EXPENDITURES – MONETARY VALUE OF RESIDUAL POLLUTION – DEPRECIATION OF MAN-MADE CAPITAL – DEPRECIATION OF ENVIRONMENTAL CAPITAL (ECOSYSTEM FUNCTION DAMAGE, RENEWABLE CAPITAL, EXHAUSTIBLE CAPITAL)

The measures of physical and environmental capital are referred to separately because the ways in which they would be calculated could be very different, and to indicate that they are not entirely substitutable, one for the other.

Correcting prices

It is vital to ascribe the right economic values to natural resources. Two modifications are needed. First, the prices of natural resources should reflect their full value. The price of a resource is obviously linked to the cost of its extraction or harvest. The market mechanism will ensure that these costs are reflected in prices. But resource extraction and harvesting can also impose costs on others. If timber is removed unselectively from a tropical forest there is damage to the watershed through river pollution and soil erosion. Those costs are not reflected in the price of timber. The market has 'failed' because the timber price is not picking up the value of the natural environmental services it has effectively used. We can say that prices should not just reflect the extraction and harvesting costs, but also the environmental costs. There is one more adjustment to be made to resource prices. If a resource is harvested sustainably, its stock will remain broadly constant over time. If it is used unsustainably its stock will be reduced and what is lost will not be available to the next generation. This lost future benefit from unsustainable management is called a *user cost*. Obviously, there must be a user cost involved in all extraction of an exhaustible resource. There is also a user cost attached to the non-sustainable use of a renewable resource. We therefore have a basic rule for the 'proper' pricing of natural resources (see Markandya and Pearce 1987 for further discussion). Those prices should reflect extraction costs plus environmental costs plus user costs, or

$$P = MC + MEC + MUC$$

where: MC = marginal private costs of extraction and harvesting

MEC = marginal external cost

MUC = marginal user cost

The second adjustment is to the prices of commodities. Because the production of goods and services necessarily uses up environmental services which are treated as if they are free, those prices are not correct prices. The adjustment required is consistent with the 'polluter pays' principle, that is making the polluter pay for the costs of environmental clean-up or for the environmental damage done by the production of the good in question. This can be done by imposing a charge on the good for its pollution content. The charge will be partly passed on to the consumer in the form of higher prices. In practice pollution charges based on efficiency considerations are rare (for a survey see Opschoor and Vos 1989). The main way in which the 'polluter pays' principle is implemented is by making polluters pay the costs of regulations designed to achieve a given environmental standard. But it is time to begin much more imaginative policies involving pollution charges.

In terms of OECD policy, the implications of sustainable development for resource and product pricing are very familiar. The 'polluter pays' principle is well established (OECD 1975) and recent work on resource pricing has set out the fundamentals of resource pricing (OECD 1989). What sustainable development does is to reinforce OECD policy.

Project appraisal and discounting

As noted, many of the implications of sustainable development for practical decision-making are encompassed by the more general implications of environmental economics. The sustainable development philosophy, by raising further the role that environmental concerns should play in the political agenda, reinforces and underlines those implications. A similar result holds for for project appraisal, but here the precise implications do depend on the definition of sustainable development (see Conclusion below).

However, whatever definition is adopted the following implications seem to be indisputable:

1. Far more effort needs to be made in terms of tracing 'ecological linkages' in economic systems, that is the physical relationships in systems which determine the nature, scale, spatial and temporal distribution of costs and benefits. We might summarize this by saying that there is a more emphatic need for *ecological general equilibrium* work.

2. Similarly, linkages between ecological impacts, human response and economic signals need to be understood far better. Thus, if air pollution increases there will be a human health or crop damage 'response'. These 'dose–response' relationships are extensively investigated in the environmental economics literature. Less familiar are approaches which build into

dose–response linkages avertive or mitigatory behaviour by individuals and general equilibrium price changes (see Dickie and Gerking 1991 and Adams *et al.* 1982). Put generally, there is a need for economic general equilibrium analysis which can be used to assess project impacts on the environment.

3. Approaches to *valuation* need to be developed still further (see Pearce *et al.* 1989, Ch. 3, for a survey of current techniques).

More specific implications for project appraisal depend on the interpretation of sustainable development. If the narrower condition, that of conserving the natural resource base as opposed to overall capital stock, is adopted, project appraisal could be modified as follows. The basic project acceptance rule is that:

$$(B_t - C_t - E_t \,|\, d_t) > 0$$

where B and C are non-environmental costs and benefits, E is environmental cost, t is time and d_t is the discount factor. Under the normal rule project acceptance is consistent with $E > 0$. If, however, the resource-base constraint is imposed, E may be greater than zero for *individual* projects but must be less than or equal to zero for all projects. Put another way, any individual project is allowed to degrade the environment so long as the sum of all projects does not do so. This implies that there must be a set of environmentally compensating projects which may, or may not, meet the orthodox cost–benefit acceptance rule (for formal proofs see Markandya *et al.* 1990).

One attraction of imposing such a 'sustainability constraint' is that it holds out the potential for avoiding the debate about modifying the discount rate. A practical definition of sustainable development can be derived by adopting a 'Pareto sustainability' rule whereby no one generation could make itself better off at the expense of another generation. This involves actual intergenerational transfers as long as future generations can be expected to be made worse off by currently generated environmental problems. A theoretically obvious way to produce such transfers is to set aside intergenerational compensation funds. Thus, if damage E is expected at time t and the marginal rate of return on capital is r, the fund needs to be commenced with a sum of

$$E/(1 + r)^t$$

But such transfers are fraught with difficulties. In the cases of interest, we do not know E or t and r may vary with time. Indeed, as Mäler points out, r becomes *endogenous* if environmental impacts alter future real income (Mäler 1989b). Hence compensation funds do not hold out much hope for practical transfers.

Finally, adjusting discount rates has similar problems. The lowering of discount rates may simply 'drag through' the economy more materials and energy by making investment in the aggregate more attractive (see Markandya and Pearce 1988). Adopting different discount rates for environmental and non-environmental projects could result in allocative distortions, not least because determining the absolute size of a modified lower discount rate for environmental projects would be very complex.

There seems some potential therefore for investigating further the implications of sustainable development for project appraisal.

Conclusion

Practical definitions of sustainable development have necessarily had to wait for better analytical approaches to the term. These now seem to have advanced far enough for us to interpret sustainable development in terms of an integrated efficiency and equity criterion applied across generations. In turn, this can be linked to work in the growth theory context which shows that some form of 'constant capital stock' is required to achieve intergenerational equity. Two interpretations have been suggested: one based on all capital stock and a narrower one based on natural capital only. This paper has not debated which is correct because there now exists a small but significant literature on the subject. More important, we have suggested that many of the *practical* implications of sustainable development are invariant with the definition adopted. There are exceptions. The results may be summarized in Table 12.1.

Table 12.1 Implications of broad and narrow definitions of sustainable development

Implications	Sustainable development	
	Broad definition	Narrow definition
Non-declining	$K_n + K_m$	K_n
Precautionary policy	**	***
Integrative policy	**	***
Trade and sustainability	*	**
National accounts	***	***
Valuation	***	***
Pricing	***	***
Project appraisal	**	***

Notes: The stars indicate emphasis: * = significant, ** = important, *** = very important. K_n is natural capital; K_m is manufactured capital

Sustainable development may involve *departures* in conventional thinking in respect of the sustainable income concept in the national accounts and in possibly new approaches to project appraisal. Otherwise it tends to be a matter of emphasis on the environment as input and output in economic systems. Either way, sustainable development has proved catalytic in terms of modern environmental economics thinking.

Sustainability first

Paul Ekins

There is an obvious tension in the phrase 'sustainable development' which must be explicitly addressed if the debate and activity to which the phrase has given rise are to prove useful in reversing the clear threatening trends of environmental unsustainability. The tension derives from the fact that the dominant trajectory of economic development since the industrial revolution has been patently *un*sustainable. There is literally no experience of an environmentally sustainable industrial economy, anywhere in the world, where such sustainability refers to a non-depleting stock of environmental capital. It is therefore not immediately apparent that, on the basis of past experience only, the term 'sustainable development' is any more than an oxymoron. The hope implicit in sustainable development, of course, is that the future can be different. The purpose of this paper is to explore some of the conditions and instruments that could make it so.

Conditions for sustainability

It is first necessary to make operational the basic sustainability condition of a non-depleting stock of natural capital. This can be expressed in six further conditions:

1. Destabilization of global environmental features such as climate patterns or the ozone layer must be prevented.
2. Important ecosystems and ecological features must be absolutely protected to maintain biological diversity.
3. Renewable resources must be renewed through the maintenance of soil fertility, hydrobiological cycles and necessary vegetative cover. Sustainable harvesting must be rigorously enforced.
4. Depletion of non-renewable resources should proceed on the basis of maintaining a minimum life-expectancy of the resource, at which level consumption would have to be matched by new discoveries of the resources. To minimize depletion, non-renewable resources must be used as intensively as possible by designing for durability and the maximum feasible practice of repair, reconditioning, re-use and recycling (the 'four Rs'). Furthermore, all depletion of these resources should involve contribution to a capital fund to help finance research for alternatives and the eventual transition to renewal substitutes.
5. Emissions into air, soil and water must not exceed the capability of the earth to absorb, neutralize and recycle them, nor lead to life-damaging concentrations of toxins.
6. Risks of life-damaging events from human activity must be kept at very low levels. Technologies, such as nuclear power, which threaten long-lasting ecosystem damage at whatever level of risk, should be foregone.

On the basis of these sustainability conditions, sustainability standards need to be set for all environmental functions, combining best scientific knowledge and the precautionary approach (see pp. 404–5). These standards, formulated in terms of maximum sustainable yield, emission, concentration, use or carrying capacity can then be converted into policy targets. Examples of such targets are the reductions in the emissions of greenhouse gases recommended by the Inter-governmental Panel on Climate Change (IPCC): more than 60 per cent for CO_2, between 70 and 80 per cent for N_2O, over 70 per cent for CFCs (IPCC 1990). Other examples are given in the Dutch National Environmental Policy Plan, which argues for cuts in emissions of between 70 and 80 per cent for SO_2, NO_x, NH_3 and waste-dumping, 80 per cent for hydrocarbons and 100 per cent for CFCs (MOHPPE 1988: 18). The implications of such targets for different industrial sectors need to be evaluated and strategies for achieving them devised, including both timescales and budgets. To be credible, rhetorical commitments to sustainability or sustainable development should always be accompanied by commitments to targets, timescales and budgets.

On the question of the compensatory capital fund for natural resource depletion, the calculation below gives the necessary size of such a fund on the basis of the formula given in El Serafy (1989), with respect to the United Kingdom's depletion of North Sea oil, which began in 1975. This formula splits the receipts from a non-renewable resource into two streams, a capital and an income stream, the relative size of which depend on the life expectancy of the resource and the discount rate applied. The size of the capital fund from a resource like North Sea oil should be substantial. With a 10 per cent discount rate the industry should by 1989 have had a capital fund of nearly £48 billion, and the UK government a fund from royalties of nearly £25 billion. With a 5 per cent discount rate these figures rise to nearly £86 billion and nearly £43 billion respectively (see Tables 12.2 and 12.3, Figure 12.2). Ideally, these funds should be invested in the production of substitutes for the depleted resources, in this case oil. In this and in other cases, of course, no such fund exists. The oil and other non-renewable resources have simply been unsustainably consumed.

The overall result in conforming to the sustainability conditions would be to transform the dominant model of the industrial economy from a linear to a circular form (Figures 12.3 and 12.4). In the linear conception, resources – land, labour, capital – are combined in the economic process to produce goods and wastes. The model is open-ended: the resources are assumed to be supplied from, and the wastes disposed of, outside the model (the environment), with the economic process being the model's central focus. Overwhelmingly the chief objective applied to this model is growth of production, with no evident constraints because the source and sink functions of the environment are excluded from it.

In the multi-circular model (Figure 12.3), analogous to living systems, the wastes from one product or process are the resources for another, so that there is no waste and no disposal problem or pollution – just a great cycle of

Table 12.2　Production statistics for North Sea oil, 1976–89

Year	R	P	CP	R1	L	V	Rt
1976	1950	12.2	13.7	1936	160	620	81
1977	2030	38.3	51.9	1980	52	2226	238
1978	2012	54.0	105.8	1906	35	2805	562
1979	2009	77.9	183.7	1825	23	5694	2329
1980	1963	80.4	263	1700	21	8851	3743
1981	1975	89.5	354	1625	18	12340	6492
1982	1925	103.2	457	1475	14	14441	7822
1983	1950	114.7	572	1375	12	17023	8798
1984	2000	126.1	698	1300	10	20587	12035
1985	2060	127.6	825	1230	10	19760	11348
1986	2280	127.1	952	1330	10	9295	4783
1987	2360	123.3	1075	1290	10	9954	4645
1988	2380	114.4	1190	1190	10	7239	3203
1989	2480	91.8	1282	1200	13	7304	2300

R　= Total proven and probable reserves, million tonnes (mt)
P　= Annual production, mt
CP = Cumulative production, mt
R1 = Total remaining proven and probable reserves (R – CP), mt
L　= Life expectancy of reserves (R1/P), years
V　= Total value of sales, £millions (£m)
Rt = Value of royalty and tax receipts of British government, £m

Source: Department of Energy 1990 (and the corresponding publication for earlier years).

transformation. In living systems, of course, this cycle is powered by the sun. In the human economy, sustainability requires that other energy sources are increasingly replaced by solar energy and non-renewable resources by renewables. The constraints implicit in this circular, as opposed to linear, flow clearly bring into question the extent to which through-put (production) in the model can be increased.

Sustainability and growth

The relationship between sustainability and growth is one of the most disputed and intractable points in the whole environmental debate, which I have discussed in some detail in Ekins (1991a). The point at issue is whether sustainability and long-term growth of GNP (often erroneously called economic growth, but see pp. 154–5) are in fact compatible. To clarify this issue it is essential to distinguish between, especially, the first two kinds of growth described in Chapter 5 (p. 154):

I　　Growth in the economy's physical through-put of matter and energy and therefore in its generation of wastes.
II　　Growth in Gross National (or Domestic) Product.

In a physically finite world governed by the laws of thermodynamics, indefinite, let alone exponentially indefinite, Growth type I is not possible.

Table 12.3 Cumulative capital funds from North Sea oil under different assumptions

Year	Infl.	FS5	FR5	FS10	FR10
1976	17	0	0	0	0
1977	16	178	19	22	2
1978	8	634	116	108	19
1979	13	2738	821	688	254
1980	18	5884	2135	1819	728
1981	12	11114	4839	3975	1840
1982	9	18602	8836	7799	3883
1983	5	28384	13853	13123	6628
1984	5	41743	21526	20984	11171
1985	6	55290	29184	29159	15813
1986	3	62390	31958	33287	17961
1987	4	70659	35930	38102	20305
1988	5	78391	39585	42541	22441
1989	8	85825	42774	47893	24834

Application of El Serafy's formula

Formula: $X/R = 1 - 1/(1 + r)^{n + 1}$

where
X is sustainable income from resource depletion
R is total revenue from resource depletion
r is the discount rate
n is the life expectancy of the resource

FS, FR = Cumulative funds derived from investment of 'capital' proportion of oil receipts according to El Serafy formula applied to sales of government receipts at different discount rates

FS5 = Fund from sales receipts at 5% discount rate
FR5 = Fund from government receipts at 5% discount rate
FS10 = Fund from sales receipts at 10% discount rate
FR10 = Fund from government receipts at 10% discount rate

Infl. = Inflation (Source for UK inflation: Artis 1989)

Note: The cumulative capital fund totals have been derived on the assumption that the funds were invested at a rate of return equal to the discount rate and topped up annually from the revenue to compensate as far as possible for inflation.

It is in fact quite clear that it is this kind of growth that is responsible for current environmental problems.

For the business community compatibility between sustainability and Growth type II has now achieved the status of an article of faith. Thus the International Chamber of Commerce (ICC) writes:

Economic growth provides the conditions in which protection of the environment can be best achieved, and environmental protection, in balance with other human goals, is necessary to achieve growth that is sustainable.

(ICC 1990: 1)

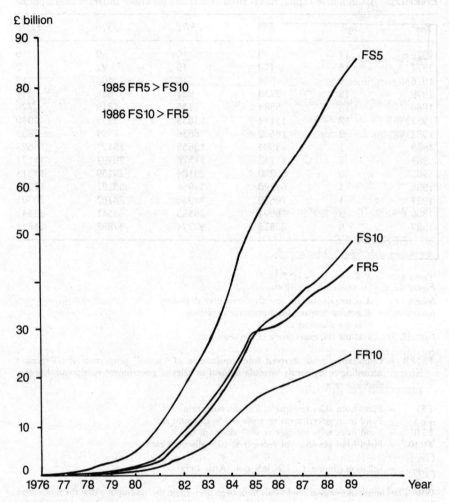

Figure 12.2 The accumulation of capital funds from UK North Sea oil according to El Serafy's formula

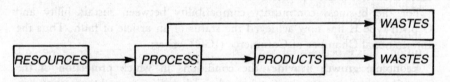

Figure 12.3 Linear economy model
Note: The dominant objectives in the linear economy model are maximization of through-put (economic growth) and increasing labour productivity, while the accounting system assumes that value equals price (unpriced considerations ignored)

ENERGY

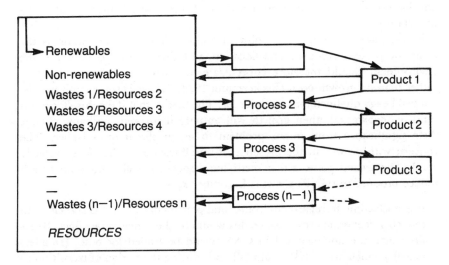

Figure 12.4 Circular economy model
Note: The dominant objectives in the circular economy model are sustainability and maximization of human welfare, while the accounting system seeks to include non-price values

Similarly Stephan Schmidheiny, Chairman of the Business Council for Sustainable Development (BCSD) said at the BCSD's launch:

> Sustainable development combines two key objectives, environmental protection *and* growth.

(BCSD 1991: 1, original emphasis)

These sorts of statements represent the extreme in technological optimism not to say wishful thinking. The crucial question such optimism begs is how Growth type II and the physically-limited Growth type I are related. Lecomber (1975) identified the three effects of technological or social change which, by reducing depletion or pollution, can decouple Growth types I and II: changes in composition of output, substitution between factor inputs and more efficient use of the same input. If these three effects add up to a shift away from the limiting resource or pollutant equal to or greater than the rate of growth, then the limits to growth are put back indefinitely. But, Lecomber warns:

> [This] establishes the logical conceivability, not the certainty, probability or even the possibility in practice, of growth continuing indefinitely. Everything hinges on the rate of technical progress and possibilities of substitution. This is perhaps the main issue that separates resource optimists and resource pessimists. The optimist believes in the power of human inventiveness to solve whatever problems are thrown in its way, as apparently it has done in the past. The pessimist questions the success of these past technological solutions and fears that future problems may be more intractable.

(Lecomber 1975: 42)

Lecomber looks for evidence in an effort to judge between these two positions, but without success. 'The central feature of technical advance is indeed its uncertainty' (ibid.: 42).

Beckermann has made the point that environmental degradation is the result of present resource misallocation and that efforts to conserve the environment should therefore concentrate on correcting this misallocation rather than on growth *per se* (Beckermann 1974). There is some truth in this, but two heavy qualifications are in order. The first is, that if the misallocations remain uncorrected, then growth will amplify them and, perhaps, change their significance from minor problem to major threat or nuisance. The concern with growth in the presence of misallocations is therefore perfectly valid. The second point is that rectifying resource misallocations may itself reduce production (GNP) growth. Lecomber says:

> It is misleading to regard environmental policies of this sort as *alternatives* to reducing economic growth since this would be their incidental effect. Benefits which are not included in GNP would be traded for other (smaller) benefits which are. GNP would fall and, during the period of transition to such policies, growth would fall, probably substantially.
>
> (Lecomber 1975: 59)

The magnitude of Lecomber's three effects which will be necessary to reconcile growth and sustainability is illustrated by an equation in Ehrlich and Ehrlich (1990: 58):

$$I = PCT$$

where: I is an environmental impact such as a potentially polluting emission
   P is the level of human population
   C is the resource consumption (or GNP) per head
   T is the environmental intensity of consumption (environmental impact per unit of consumption, or GNP)

It may be assumed that:

- I must be reduced by at least 50 per cent over the next fifty years to approach sustainability. This seems conservative in the light of the targets of the IPCC and Dutch Government quoted earlier.
- P will double over the next fifty years. This is the UN low-to-medium estimate (Sadik 1991: 3).

Under these assumptions, if C does not grow at all, then T must fall by 75 per cent; if C is quadrupled world-wide over fifty years (a growth rate of 2–3 per cent), then T must fall by 93 per cent, a factor of 16. If C is to grow by 2–3 per cent only in low- and middle-income countries, and stay constant in high-income countries, and if all population growth is taken to be in the former, then on the basis of the classification and figures in World Bank (1990), T would have to be reduced by 79 per cent (see Ekins 1991b for the calculation).

Any of these figures of reduction of environmental intensity represent an ambitious target. That of 93 per cent would only be considered feasible by technological optimists verging on the fanatic. The difference between these two figures (93 per cent and 79 per cent) is further evidence of the enormously skewed nature of current consumption patterns. If the Third World alone, with three-quarters of the world's population, doubles its population and quadruples its consumption over the next fifty years (when its average per capita consumption would still be less than 20 per cent of that currently in rich countries), then the necessary cut in environmental intensity increases from the no-growth figure of 75 per cent to only 79 per cent. Quadrupling the much larger consumption of First World countries as well raises this figure to 93 per cent.

In the light of this it is surprising that sustainable development thinking does not seem to differentiate between the need for and environmental feasibility of growth in the Third World, and the quite different situation, on both counts, of the already rich world. In particular, the now famous definition of sustainable development in the Brundtland Report as that which 'meets the needs of the present without compromising the ability of future generations to meet their own needs' (WCED 1987: 43) makes no distinction between the vastly different 'needs' in the First and Third Worlds; nor does it draw attention to the fact that the majority of First World consumption, and presumably an even greater proportion of any growth in that consumption, is far more related to satisfying consumer wants than meeting human needs.

The conclusion is clear. The best chance of achieving sustainable development lies in differentiating between North and South. In the North the concentration must be on ecologically transforming industrial production and consumption patterns. Any growth in production that this process may bring about will have to be compensated for by even greater falls in environmental intensity.

In the South there must be an emphasis on balanced, sustainable growth through pursuit of the objectives of environmental regeneration and careful industrialization using the most environmentally advanced technologies, bearing in mind the difficulties of transferring technologies between different technological and cultural milieux. Neither of these objectives can be achieved in the context of current international economic relations. As I have discussed elsewhere (Ekins 1991c), these relations, through the institutions of trade, aid and debt, are working systematically against both the development and environmental sustainability of the great majority of the countries of the South. Without thorough-going reform of these institutions, nothing approaching sustainable development in the South is likely to be achieved.

To recap therefore, with regard to sustainability and growth, the relationship between them is quite different depending on which of three variables is considered to be growing: physical production, GNP or welfare. It is clearly impossible for physical production in a finite system to grow indefinitely. Thus GNP will only be able to sustain its growth to the extent that it can be uncoupled from growth in physical production. Welfare will need to be similarly uncoupled for its sustainable growth to be possible.

The requisite uncoupling of GNP, what Daly has called 'Angelized GNP' (Daly 1977: 118), is formidable and perhaps infeasible, as indicated by the calculations from the Ehrlich equation above. In any case, the ultimate efficiency of resource use is limited by the second law of thermodynamics. The uncoupling of welfare from physical consumption is theoretically easier, because human welfare is acknowledged to have many different components apart from consumption. But it may be no easier psychologically, for such uncoupling would require a rejection of the growth ideology and the model of the consumer society which, though starting in the West, now underpin the principal aspirations of people worldwide. It will require a veritable revolution in attitudes for the current commitment to growth and consumerism to be replaced by the values of sufficiency and conservation.

Economic instruments and sustainability

In order radically to decrease the environmental intensity of consumption, many different economic instruments will need to be applied. Economic instruments can be designed to take effect either through the price mechanism or by directly regulating quantity. It is unfortunate that these types of instruments have come to be seen as competitors, with proponents of one type sometimes seeking to disparage the other. Thus Pearce *et al.* write: 'Pollution charges are generally better than "command and control". . . . Command and control policies adopt a regulatory stance which ignores the efficiencies of the market mechanism' (Pearce *et al.* 1989: 162). On the other side, Jackson and Jacobs write with regard to energy use: 'It is regulation rather than taxation that more efficiently improves the market' (Jackson and Jacobs 1991: 62).

This sort of dichotomy between the two types of economic instrument is quite unnecessary. They should properly be viewed as complements, each with benefits and disadvantages which become relatively more important in different situations. The optimal policy will seek to combine both types of instruments, using each where it is more appropriate than the other according to the following guidelines:

Price-based instruments

As the name implies, these seek to change economic behaviour through the price mechanism. The rationale for these instruments is based on the perception that, in general, the economic functions of the environment – the provision of resources and environmental services and the absorption of wastes – have been overused or abused because they have been unpriced or underpriced. The instrument seeks to increase the relevant price (or, through a subsidy, decrease the price of a substitute) in order to remedy the abuse or overuse. Examples of these instruments are environmental taxes, subsidies and tradable emission permits. The advantage of these instruments, assuming a well-functioning market, is that they enable adjustment to environmental targets to be made at least cost. Taxes can also provide revenues that can either allow the lifting of more distortionary taxes elsewhere or permit the direct promotion of other government objectives, environmental or otherwise. The revenues can also be redistributed to compensate for the possible regressive effects of, for example, taxing energy, which tends to take a larger share of the budgets of the poor than of the rich.

The disadvantage of these instruments is that they depend for their effect on the elasticities of demand or substitution, which may be sluggish, uncertain or both, or on cost-saving environment-conserving investment, which may be prevented by market failure in the form of lack of information or institutional constraints. If the elasticities are uncertain, it will not be possible to be sure *a priori* that any given environmental target will be achieved. If demand is sluggish it may be that the tax has to be so high to achieve environmental objectives that it could provide a major shock to the economy with unpredictable consequences, or be politically infeasible. Furthermore, it is not likely, for widespread and disruptive environmental effects, that an environmental tax will be able to be set exactly at the level to compensate for the social cost of the relevant negative environmental effect, as economic theory dictates.

As Hueting's contribution in Chapter 8 has shown, it is rare to be able to construct the shadow prices for environmental functions, so that taxes often have to be set intuitively at a rate calculated to achieve quantity objectives.

Quantity-based instruments

These instruments seek to achieve certain levels of environmental function or quality through regulation. They may also seek to rectify market failures of information or structure so that price-based instruments may work more effectively. These instruments are appropriate where markets are imperfect, demand is uncertain or inelastic, and it is important to be sure of achieving certain targets for reasons, perhaps, of human health or safety. The Montreal Protocol of 1990 which agreed to achieve zero emissions of ozone-depleting CFCs by the year 2000, is an example of an international quantity-based agreement. So are water quality regulations at national level. A tax on emissions into drinking water which permitted a health damaging toxic build-up somewhere, even if it achieved better than minimum quality everywhere else, would clearly be unacceptable to those affected, and probably to the wider polity.

The disadvantages of quantity-based instruments which require all agents to make the same adjustments is that they take no account of these agents' different cost functions and therefore can result in economic inefficiency in the sense of imposing more than necessary costs to reach certain environmental targets.

From this brief comparison it is clear that an effective policy response to the major environmental problems will need to make use of quantity-based targets and both quantity- and price-based instruments. The important concern is to use these appropriately to the situation in hand and according to the objectives to be achieved.

Conclusion

Even from this short discussion it should be clear that measures to achieve environmental sustainability can, and may need to, involve not only dramatic technological change but also fundamental restructuring of international economic relations (to promote the Third World development that is a pre-requisite of sustainability) and a shift in basic social values and attitudes. Of these the technological change is likely to be the easiest to bring about. The principal environmental debate of the coming years will be between those who think that this change is enough and those who emphasize attitudes and the international context. The verdict on the outcome of the debate will be given by a biosphere that reacts to continuing unsustainability in an increasingly unpleasant, disruptive and life-threatening way.

Conclusion

Before summing up it is important to be clear about what this book is not, what it does not claim to be. First, it is not the definitive statement of a new school of economic thought. Second, there are glaring omissions in the more modest task it has attempted: trade theory, the debt crisis, macro-economic and financial management, technical change, economic policy in many areas – all these areas and others have been given, if anything, only the most cursory glance.

This is hardly surprising given the book's substantial length even without these areas. But it may still be frustrating to those keen to see how some excluded topic might relate to the rest of the ideas that have been developed here.

What this book *has* sought to do is to lay out the ground-plan and describe the most salient features of what may come to be a new school of economic thought, which has here been called 'living economics'. Some elements of the plan and the features were explored in some detail, so that it is at least possible that at this point some trees are obscuring the view of the wood. The following outline of the ground-plan, though it will not say anything new, may help to put its components in perspective.

First, living economics is an economics of and for real-life. Its starting point, with which few could disagree, is the factual statement that in real-life people do put scarce resources to competing uses for the purpose of increasing their welfare. Living economics seeks to embrace the full complexity of people's actions in this regard, to gain insights into why and how people do what they do without heroic prior assumptions (e.g. individual rationality, self-interestedness, perfect competition or free markets) with a view to making recommendations as to how they could do things differently in order to be better off.

This does not mean, however, that heroic assumptions can be altogether dispensed with, but they must be the appropriate assumptions to the investigation in question. How the decision concerning appropriateness relates to the complexity of the whole can be illustrated by the well-known fable of the blind men and the elephant: each man took hold of a different part of the elephant and mistook it for the whole, proclaiming variously that the elephant was like a tree, a wall, a brush, a snake and so on. None was wholly wrong but their disagreement was total and their collective capacity for constructive action zero.

Living economics accepts, as the blind men did not, that all individual views of and schools of thought about the economy are partial. But it seeks, through fruitful communication between those who hold the views, to put the views together in a manner which makes sense of a larger whole. It never expects to have a complete picture of the totality because there will always be views that have not been included and others that have been erroneously or unsatisfactorily incorporated. Moreover, the economy is always changing. The elephant is perpetually evolving into something else, some factors staying constant, others mutating at, in the present age, increasing speed. Economics is always incomplete and out of date. Its art lies in recognizing those areas in which this is most so and then proceeding as far as possible to rectify the situation.

From this perspective, conventional neoclassical economics can be imagined to have subjected a major part of the elephant – its head, say – to exhaustive, painstaking study. It has deduced correctly how the elephant sees, thinks, eats and hoses itself. But if it also claims that the head, viewed mistakenly as the whole elephant, also walks, circulates the blood, digests the food, excretes the wastes and is responsible for reproduction, then its hubris is not merely wrong – it is ridiculous.

The acknowledgement of the partiality of any view and the urge to assemble the partial views into an ever more but never totally complete picture is for living economics what Joseph Schumpeter (1954: 41) called the 'preanalytic vision'. As this book has made clear, the analysis which proceeds from it diverges from general economics orthodoxy on many points, with the following being some of the most significant:

- The economy is not the only, and is perhaps not the most important, dimension and motivation of human life. Some aspects of life cannot be understood in terms of scarcity. The application of economic tools to these aspects is inappropriate.

- The other principal dimensions of human life are the social, ethical and ecological. These are inseparably linked to the economic dimension and it is only rarely that any dimension can be validly considered in isolation.

- The understanding of human situations in general, and economic situations in particular, can often only come from participation in the situation in question or close and sympathetic contact with participants.

- Economic choices need not be, and often cannot be, fully rational. Habits, intuition and bounded rationality are all important contributors to economic decision-making.

- Individual preferences are subject both to formation and change by social circumstances and institutions.

- The economy's physical through-put of matter/energy is subject to the absolute limits of the planet's biosphere and solar flows, and the laws of thermodynamics. These limits and laws place significant constraints both on the long-term growth of GNP and, hence, the possibility of continually increasing welfare through increased consumption.

- The motivations and outcomes of economic activity are not always commensurable and cannot always be reduced to the numeraire of money or utility. Love, altruism, duty, respect, dignity, beauty, for instance, are powerful influences on economic behaviour but cannot meaningfully be analysed only in terms of price and self-interest.

- Wants and needs are categorically different and also incommensurable.

- The contributors to human welfare are many and not all economic.

- The market, the state, households and civil society, singly or in combination, are all potential creators or destroyers of wealth.

These are some of the main features of the human condition, seen from a living-economic point of view and expressed in a way to contrast them most distinctly with the correspondingly explicit or implicit assumptions of conventional economic policy-making and analysis. The main ideas of the book can be traced to these features: the multi-dimensional approach, the inclusion of household production, the identification of four types of capital, the distinction between growth and development, the expanded indicator framework, the need to create complementarity between the economic spheres of the market, the state, households and civil society, the imperative of sustainability.

What emerges is a conceptual basis that is both richer and more realistic than the conventional economic approach. Its complexities, of course, are formidable and will need to be simplified for many analytic purposes. Often the assumptions of neoclassicism will be able to be applied without violating important aspects of the reality under scrutiny. But often they will not. And often again, the outcomes under these assumptions will be different from those produced by different, equally plausible assumptions. One of the principal benefits of this framework is that it brings the assumptions themselves under the spotlight, where they must be justified, or can be compared, as part of the analytic process. Thus economics becomes able to shed light on costs and benefits and how they are distributed, given the dominance of the assumptions and interests of different groups and ideologies. Economics can then legitimately claim to have shed its demeaning but often too apt label of 'politics in disguise', and serve as a plausible, much-needed guide to economic welfare, and how it can be efficiently created, justly distributed and ecologically sustained, in order effectively to address the pressing economic problems and failures of the modern world.

Appendix
Contacts and addresses

Living Economy Network
42 Warriner Gardens
London SW11 4DU
UK

CHAPTER 4

Addresses of organizations and publications promoting non-orthodox economic approaches

Association for Social Economics (contact: Anthony Scaperlanda)
Department of Economics
Northern Illinois University
DeKalb
Illinois 60115
USA

(publication: *Review of Social Economy* [Editor: John B. Davis], Department of Economics, Marquette University, Milwaukee, Wisconsin 53233, USA)

Human Economy Center
Box 14,Department of Economics
Mankato State University
Mankato MN 56001
USA

(publication: *The Human Economy Newsletter*)

Association of Indian Economic Studies (contact: Romesh Diwan)
6 Bolivar Avenue
Troy
NY 12180–3590
USA

Association for Evolutionary Economics (contact: F. Gregory Hayden)
Department of Economics
University of Nebraska–Lincoln
Lincoln
Nebraska 68588–0479
USA

(publication: *Journal of Economic Issues*)

European Association for Evolutionary Political Economy
   (General Secretary: Geoff Hodgson)
Department of Economics and Government
Newcastle Polytechnic
Newcastle upon Tyne
NE1 8ST
UK

(publication: newsletter)

Post-Keynesian Economics Study Group (contact: Victoria Chick)
Department of Economics
University College London
Gower Street
London WC1E 6BT
UK

Review of Political Economy (Editor: John Pheby)
Department of Economics
Leicester Polytechnic
PO Box 143
Leicester LE2 9BH
UK

Society for the Advancement of Socio-Economics
   (Secretary: Steven Helland)
714H Gelman Library
George Washington University
Washington DC 20052
USA

(publication: *Journal of Socio-Economics* [Editor: Richard Hattwick], Western
Illinois University, 519 Stipes Hall, Macomb IL 61455, USA)

International Society for Ecological Economics (Secretary: Patrick Hagan)
PO Box 1589
Solomons
MD 20688
USA

(publication: *Ecological Economics*)

International Network for Economic Method
Room 202
Hung On Mansion
179 Jaffe Road
Wanchai
Hong Kong
(publication: *Methodus* [Editor: Victor Mok], Department of Economics, Chinese University of Hong Kong, Shatin, NT, Hong Kong)

Karl Polanyi Institute of Political Economy
Concordia University
1455 de Maisonneuve W.
Montreal
Quebec H3G IM8
Canada

European Association for Bioeconomic Studies
Via Larga 11
20122 Milano
Italy

New Economics Foundation (TOES/UK)
Universal House
2nd Floor
88–94 Wentworth St
London E1 7SA
UK
(publication: *New Economics*)

TOES/Americas
PO Box 12003
Austin
TX 78711
USA
(publication: Newsletter)

TOES/France
C/o ALDEA
28 Boulevard de Sebastopol
75004 Paris
France

People Centred Development Forum
MCC PO Box 740
Makati
Metro Manila 1299
Philippines

Society for International Development
(Executive Director: Roberto Cassani)
Palazzo Civiltà del Lavoro
00144 Roma
Italy

(publication: *Development*)

CHAPTER 9

Organizations mentioned in 'Towards a Progressive Market'

Asahi Journal
5-3-2 Tsukiji
Chuo-ku
Tokyo T–104–11
Japan

Business in the Community
227A City Road
London EC1V 1LX
UK

Co-op America
2100 M Street NW
Suite 310
Washington DC 20063
USA

Council on Economic Priorities
30 Irving Place
New York
NY 10003
USA

Ethical Investment Research and Information Service (EIRIS)
401 Business Centre
71 Bondway
London SW8 1SQ
UK

Grameen Bank
Mirpur Two
Dhaka 1210
Bangladesh

Industrial Common Ownership Finance
12–14 Gold St
Northampton NN1 1RS
UK

International Federation of Alternative Trade
PO Box 2703
Amsterdam
Netherlands

IOCU (International Organization of Consumer Unions)
Emmastraat 9
2595 EG The Hague
Netherlands

LEDA (Local Employment Development Action)
c/o Local and Regional Development Planning
South Bank Technopark
90 London Road
London SE1 6LN
UK

New Consumer
52 Elswick Road
Newcastle-upon-Tyne NE4 6JH
UK

Ökobank Genossenschaft i.G.
Bornheimer Landstr. 22
6000 Frankfurt
Germany

Seikatsu Club Consumers' Co-operative
2–26–17 Miyasaka
Setagaya-ku
Tokyo
Japan 156

Social Investment Forum
711 Atlantic Avenue
Boston
MA 02111
USA

South Shore Bank
71st and Jeffery Boulevard
Chicago
Illinois 60649–2096
USA

Traidcraft plc
Kingsway
Gateshead NE11 0NE
UK

Bibliography

A Barefoot Doctor's Manual (1977) The US translation of the official Chinese paramedical manual, Running Press, Philadelphia.

Abolafia, M.Y. (1985) 'Self-regulation as market maintenance: an organisation perspective', in R. Noll (ed.) *Regulatory Policy and the Social Sciences*, University of California Press: Berkeley, CA.

Abolafia, M.Y., and Biggart, N. (1990) 'Competition and markets: an institutional perspective', mimeo, Johnson Graduate School of Management, Cornell University, Ithaca, NY.

Abolafia, M.Y. and Kilduff, M. (1988) 'Enacting market crisis: the social construction of a speculative bubble', *Administrative Science Quarterly* 33: 177–93.

Acharya, M. and Bennett, L. (1981) 'The rural women of Nepal: an aggregate analysis and summary of eight village studies', *The Status of Women in Nepal* II(9), Centre for Economic Development and Administration, Tribuvan University, Kathmandu.

Adams, J. (1980) *Institutional Economics*, Nijhoff: The Hague.

Adams, R., Carruthers, J. and Fisher, C. (1991a) *Shopping for a Better World*, Kogan Page: London.

Adams, R., Carruthers, J. and Hamil, S. (1991b) *Changing Corporate Values*, Kogan Page: London.

Adams, R., Crocker, T. and Thanavibulchai, N. (1982) 'An economic assessment of air pollution damages to selected annual crops in Southern California', *Journal of Environmental Economics and Management* 9: 42–58.

Adler, P. and Adler, P. (eds) (1984) *The Social Dynamics of Financial Markets*, JAI Press,: Greenwich, CT.

Ahmad, E., Drèze, J., Hills, J. and Sen, A. (eds) (1991) *Social Security in Developing Countries*, Clarendon Press: Oxford.

Ahmad, Y., El Serafy, S. and Lutz, E. (eds) (1989) *Environmental Accounting for Sustainable Development*, World Bank: Washington DC.

Aldershoff, D., and Kasper, H. (1986) 'Consumption levels of household based on expenditure and household production', *Journal of Consumer Studies and Home Economics* 10: 303–15, Oxford.

Anderson, D. (1987) *The Economics of Afforestation*, Johns Hopkins University, Baltimore, MD.

Anderson, V. (1991) *Alternative Economic Indicators*, Routledge: London.

Alauddin, T. (1980) 'Contribution of housewives to GNP: a case study of Pakistan', MS thesis, Vanderbilt University, Nashville, Tennessee.

Alfsen, Bye and Lorentsen (1987) *Natural Resource Accounting and Analysis: The Norwegian Experience 1978–1986*, SOS 65, Central Bureau of Statistics: Oslo.

Amanor, K. (1989) *340 Abstracts on Farmer Participatory Research*, Network Paper 5, Agricultural Administration (Research and Extension) Network, Overseas Development Institute: London.

Anker, R. and Hein, C. (eds) (1986) *Vers la mésure des activités économiques des femmes*, Bureau International du Travail: Geneva.

—— and —— (eds) (1987) *Medicion de las actividades economicas de la mujer*, ILO: Geneva/Santiago.

Aquinas, T. (1975) *Summa Theologiae, Injustice*, vol. 38, Blackfriars: London.

Artis, M.J. (ed.) (1989) *The UK Economy: A Manual of Applied Economics*, Weidenfeld & Nicolson: London.

Ascher, B. and Whichard, O. (1987) 'Improving services trade data' in O. Giarini (ed.) *Dialogue on Wealth and Welfare*, Pergamon Press: Oxford.

As, B., Harvey, A.S., Wnuk-Lipinski, E. and Niemi, I. (eds) (1986) *Time Use Studies: Dimensions and Applications*, Studies No. 128, Central Statistical Office of Finland, Helsinki.

Axelrod, R. (1984) *The Evolution of Cooperation*, Basic Books: New York.

Baker, W. (1984a) 'The social structure of a national securities market', *American Journal of Sociology* 89: 775–811.

—— (1984b) 'Floor trading and crowd dynamics', in Adler and Adler (eds) *The Social Dynamics of Financial Markets*, JAI Press: Greenwich, CT.

Bandyopadhyay, J. and Shiva, V. (1987) 'Chipko: rekindling India's forest culture', *The Ecologist* 17(1): 26–34.

Bardhan, P. (1989) 'Alternative approaches to the theory of institutions in economic development', in P. Bardhan (ed.) (1989) *The Economic Theory of Agrarian Institutions*, Oxford University Press: Oxford/New York.

Barker, T. (ed.) (1991) *Green Futures for Economic Growth*, Cambridge Econometrics: Cambridge.

Barucci, P. (1975) 'Sismondi revisited', *Revista Internazionale de Scienze Economiche & Commerciale* 22(10): 977–92.

Baumol, W. and Oates, W. (1988) *The Theory of Environmental Policy*, 2nd edn, Cambridge University Press: Cambridge.

BCSD (Business Council for Sustainable Development) (1991) 'Top world business leaders support major new initiative on environment and development', Press Release 19.2.91, BCSD, Geneva.

Becker, G. (1964) *Human Capital: A Theoretical and Empirical Analysis, with Special Reference to Education*, National Bureau of Economic Research and Columbia University, New York.

—— (1976) *The Economic Approach to Human Behaviour*, University of Chicago Press: Chicago.

—— (1981) *A Treatise on the Family*, Harvard University Press: Cambridge, MA.

Beckermann, W. (1974) *In Defence of Economic Growth*, Jonathan Cape: London.

Bentley, W.R. (1984) 'The uncultivated half of India: problems and possible solutions', *Discussion Paper Series* 11, August, Ford Foundation: New Dehli.

Beresford, P. (1988) 'Consumer views: data collection or democracy', in I. White *et al. Hearing the Voice of the Consumer*, Policy Studies Institute: London.

Beresford, P. and Croft, S. (1992) *Citizen Involvement: A Practical Guide for Change*, Macmillan: London.

Beveridge, Sir W. (1944) *Full Employment in a Free Society*, Allen & Unwin: London.

Bhaskar, R. (1978) *A Realist Theory of Science*, Leeds Books: Leeds (reprinted 1978, Harvester Press, Brighton).

—— (1979) *The Possibility of Naturalism: A Philosophic Critique of the Contemporary Human Sciences*, Harvester Press: Brighton.

Biggart, N. Woolsey (1989) *Charismatic Capitalism: Direct Selling Organisations in America*, University of Chicago Press: Chicago.

Bivens, G.E. and Volker, C.B. (1986) 'A value-added approach to household production: the special case of meal preparation', *Journal of Consumer Research* 13 (Sept.): 272–9.

Blades, D.W. (1975) *Non-monetary (Subsistence) Activities in the National Accounts of Developing Countries*, OECD: Paris.

Bluestone, B. and Harrison, B. (1975) *The Deindustrialisation of America*, Basic Books: New York.

Boulding, K.E. (1966) 'The economics of the coming spaceship earth', in H. Jarret (ed.) *Environmental Quality in a Growing Economy*, Johns Hopkins University Press: Baltimore, MD, pp. 3–14.

Bradley, F.H. (1914) *Essays on Truth and Reality*, Clarendon Press: Oxford.

Bradley, H. (1986) 'Work, home and the restructuring of jobs', in K. Purcell *et al.*, *The Changing Experience of Unemployment*, Macmillan: London.

Brandt, R.B. (1979) *Theory of the Good and the Right*, Clarendon Press: Oxford.

Breman, J. (1985) *Of Peasants, Migrants and Paupers: Rural Labour, Circulation and Capitalist Production in West India*, Oxford University Press: Delhi.

Brennan, G. and Buchanan, J.M. (1982) 'Is public choice immoral?', paper presented at the 1982 Public Choice Society meetings in San Antonio, Texas, March 5–9.

Brinkerhoff, D.W. and Zamor, J.C.G. (eds) (1986) *Politics, Projects and People: Institutional Development in Haiti*, Praeger: Westport, CT.

Brown, L. *et al.* (1990) *State of the World 1990*, W.W. Norton: New York.

Bruyn, S. (1985) 'A new direction for community development in the United States', *The Social Report* V(1): 1–4 (Boston College, Boston, MA).

Bruyn, S. and Meehan, J. (eds) (1987) *Beyond the Market and the State*, Temple University Press: Philadelphia, PA.

Bulmer, M. (1986) *Neighbours: The Work of Philip Abrams*, Cambridge University Press: Cambridge.

Bunch, R. (1988) 'Guinope integrated development programme, Honduras', in C. Conroy and M. Litvinoff (eds) *The Greening of Aid: Sustainable Livelihoods in Practice*, Earthscan: London.

Burns, S. (1977) *The Household Economy*, Beacon Press: Boston.

Burns, T.R. and Flam, H. (1987) *The Shaping of Social Organisation*, Sage: London.

Bye, T., Bye and Lorentsen, L. (1989) *SIMEN: Studies of Industry, Environment and Energy Towards 2000*, Discussion Paper No. 44, Central Bureau of Statistics, Oslo.

Cabanero, T.A. (1978) 'The "shadow" price of children in Laguna households', *Philippine Economic Journal* 17(1–2): 62–87.

Caldwell, B. (1982) *Beyond Positivism: Economic Methodology in the Twentieth Century*, Allen & Unwin: London.

Camic, C. (1986) 'The matter of habit', *American Journal of Sociology* 91(5): 1039–87.

Campbell, J., Hollingsworth, R. and Lindberg, L. (eds) (1991) *The Governance of the American Economy*, Cambridge University Press: Cambridge.

Carr, M. (1988) *Sustainable Industrial Development: Seven Case Studies*, Intermediate Technology Publications: London.

Cartwright, N. (1983) *How the Laws of Physics Lie*, Clarendon Press: Oxford/New York.

Chadeau, A. (1989) 'Measuring household production: conceptual issues and results for France', mimeo, report prepared for the United Nations International Research and Training Institute for the Advancement of Women (INSTRAW) for presentation to the Second ECE/INSTRAW joint Meeting on Statistics of Women, Geneva, 13–16 November.

Chadeau, A. and Fouquet, A. (1981) 'Peut-on mésurer le travail domestique?', *Economie et Statistique* 136, (Sept.): 29–42.

Chadeau, A. and Roy, C. (1986) 'Relating households' final consumption to household activities: substitutability or complementarity between market and non-market production', *Review of Income and Wealth* 32(4): 387–407, New Haven, CT.

Chalmers, A. (1978) *What Is This Thing Called Science?*, Open University Press: Milton Keynes.

Chambers, R. (1983) *Rural Development: Putting the Last First*, Longman: Harlow.

—— (1985) 'Putting "last" thinking first: a professional revolution' in R. Gauhar (ed.) *Third World Affairs 1985*, Third World Foundation for Social and Economic Studies: London.

—— (1986) 'Normal professionalism, new paradigms and development', *Discussion Paper* 22, IDS, Sussex.

—— (1989) 'The state and rural development: ideologies and an agenda for the 1990s', *Discussion Paper* 269, IDS, Sussex.

—— (1990) *Microenvironments Unobserved*, Gatekeeper Series, No. 22, International Institute for Environment and Development: London.

Chambers, R. and Leach, M. (1987) 'Trees to meet contingencies: savings and security for the rural poor', *Discussion Paper* 228, IDS: Sussex

Chambers, R., Pacey, A. and Thrupp, L.A. (eds) (1989) *Farmer First, Farmer Innovation and Agricultural Research*, Intermediate Technology Publications: London.

Chambers, R., Saxena, N.C. and Shah, T. (1989) *To The Hands of the Poor: Water and Trees*, IBH: New Delhi, and Intermediate Technology Publications: London.

Chandler, A. (1977) *The Visible Hand: The Managerial Revolution in American Business*, Harvard University Press: Cambridge, MA.

Chaput-Auquier, G. (1959) 'La valeur économique du travail ménager', *Cahiers Economiques de Bruxelles* 4 (July): 593–600.

Chavunduka, D.M., Huiza, G., Khumalo, T.D. and Thede, N. (1985) *Khuluma Usenza, The Story of ORAP in Zimbabwe's Rural Development*, The Organisation of Rural Associations for Progress: Bulawayo.

Clark, C. (1958) 'The economics of housework', *Bulletin of the Oxford Institute of Statistics* 20 (May): 205–11.

Clinard, M.B. and Yeager, P.C. (1980) *Corporate Crime*, Macmillan: New York.

Coase, R. (1960) 'The problem of social cost', *Journal of Human Economics*, 3 October.

Conroy, C. and Litvinoff, M. (eds) (1988) *The Greening of Aid: Sustainable Livelihoods in Practice*, Earthscan: London.

Conway, F.J. (1988) 'Agroforestry outreach project, Haiti', in C. Conroy and M. Litvinoff (eds) *The Greening of Aid: Sustainable Livelihoods in Practice*, Earthscan: London.

Conway, G.R. and Barbier, E.B. (1990) *After the Green Revolution*, Earthscan: London.

Corson, B. *et al.* (1991) *Shopping for a Better World*, Council on Economic Priorities: New York.

Costanza, R. (ed.) (1991) *Ecological Economics: The Science and Management of Sustainability*, Columbia University Press: New York.

Costanza, R., Daly, H.E. and Bartholomew, J.A. (1991) 'Goals, agenda and policy recommendations for ecological economics', in R. Costanza (ed.) *Ecological Economics: The Science and Management of Sustainability*, Columbia University Press: New York.

Coughlin, R. (ed.) (1991) *Morality, Rationality and Efficiency: Perspectives on Socio-economics*, M.E. Sharpe: New York.

Croft, S. and Beresford, P. (1990) *From Paternalism to Participation: Involving People in Social Services*, Open Services Project: London (Tempo House, 15 Falcon Road, London, SW11 2PJ).

CSE (Centre for Science and Environment) (1985) *The State of India's Environment 1984–85: The Second Citizens Report*, CSE: New Delhi.

Cutler, T., Williams, K. and Williams, J. (1986) *Keynes, Beveridge and Beyond*, Routledge & Kegan Paul: London.

Dahl, H.E. (1979) *Rural Production in Botswana 1974–75: A National Accounts Analysis of the Rural Incomes Distribution Survey*, Economic Papers No. 17, June, University of Bergen: Bergen.

Daly, H.E. (1977) *Steady-State Economics*, W.H. Freeman: San Francisco.

—— (ed.) (1980) *Economics, Ecology and Ethics*, W.H. Freeman: San Francisco.

—— (1989) 'Towards a measure of sustainable net national social product', in Y.

Ahmad, S. El Serafy and E. Lutz (eds) *Environmental Accounting for Sustainable Development*, World Bank: Washington DC.

────── (1991) 'Elements of environmental macro-economics', in R. Costanza (ed.) *Ecological Economics: The Science and Management of Sustainability*, Columbia University Press: New York.

Daly, H.E. and Cobb, J. (1989) *For the Common Good: Redirecting the Economy Towards Community, the Environment and a Sustainable Future*, Beacon Press: Boston, and Green Print (Merlin Press 1990): London.

Das, A. (1979) *Foundations of Gandhian Economics*, St Martin's Press: New York.

Dasgupta, S. (1983) 'Forest, ecology and the oppressed: a study from the point of view of the forest dwellers', ILO research report, unpublished.

Dauncey, G. (1988) *After the Crash: The Emergence of the Rainbow Economy*, Green Print/ Marshall Pickering: Basingstoke.

Department of Energy (1990) *Development of the Oil and Gas Resources of the United Kingdom*, Department of Energy: London.

De-Silva, G., Haque, W., Mehta, N., Rahman, A. and Wignaraja, P. (1988) *Towards a Theory of Rural Development*, Progressive Publishers: Lahore.

De Soto, H. (1989) *The Other Path*, Taurus: London.

Dickie, M. and Gerking, S. (1991) 'Benefits of reduced morbidity from air pollution control: a survey', in H. Opschoor and D. Pearce (eds) *Persistent Pollutants: Economics, Toxicology, Decision-making*, Kluwer Academic Publishers: Dordrecht.

DiMaggio, P. (1988) 'Interest and agency in institutional theory', in L. Zucker (ed.) *Institutional Patterns and Organizations*, Ballinger: Cambridge, MA.

Diwan, R. and Lutz, M. (eds) (1985) *Essays in Gandhian Economics*, Gandhi Peace Foundation: New Delhi.

Dobb, M. (1972) 'The trend of modern economics', first published in M. Dobb, *Political Economy and Capitalism* (1937), Routledge & Kegan Paul: London, reprinted in E.N. Hurst and J.G. Schwartz (eds) *A Critique of Economic Theory*, Penguin: Harmondsworth.

Dosi, G., Freeman, C., Nelson, R., Silverberg, G. and Soete, L.L.G. (eds) (1988) *Technical Change and Economic Theory*, Frances Pinter: London.

Douglas, M. (1987) *How Institutions Think*, Routledge & Kegan Paul: London.

Downs, A. (1957) *An Economic Theory of Democracy*, Harper: New York.

Doyal, L. and Gough, I. (1986) 'Human needs and strategies for social change', in P. Ekins (ed.) *The Living Economy: A New Economics in the Making*, Routledge & Kegan Paul: London.

────── and ────── (forthcoming) *The Theory and Politics of Human Needs*, London.

Dreyfus, H. and Dreyfus, S.E. (1986) *Mind Over Machine: The Power of Human Intuition and Expertise in the Era of the Computer*, Free Press: New York.

Drèze, J. and Sen, A. (1991) 'Public action for social security', in E. Ahmad, J. Drèze, J. Hills and A. Sen (eds) *Social Security in Developing Countries*, Clarendon Press: Oxford.

Drucker, P. (1973) *Management*, Harper & Row: New York.

Dyke, C. (1981) *Philosophy of Economics*, Prentice-Hall: Englewood-Cliffs, NJ.

Eaton, J. (1965) 'Some thoughts about mathematical models in relation to economic theory', in *On Political Economy and Econometrics: Essays in Honour of Oskar Lange*, Pergamon Press: Oxford.

Ehrlich, P. and Ehrlich, A. (1990) *The Population Explosion*, Hutchinson: London.

Eisenstadt, S.N. (1968) 'Social institutions', in D. Sills (ed.) *International Encyclopedia of the Social Sciences*, Free Press: New York.

Ekins, P. (ed.) (1986) *The Living Economy: A New Economics in the Making*, Routledge & Kegan Paul: London.

────── (1989) 'Renewable resources: what are the options?', *Environmental Conservation* 16(3): 209–16.

────── (1991a) 'Sustainable development and the economic growth debate', mimeo, paper presented to Roundtable 'The Socioeconomic Approach to the Environment', October 17–18, University of Geneva.

—— (1991b) 'The sustainable consumer society: a contradiction in terms?', *International Environmental Affairs*, University Press of New England: Hanover, NH.

—— (1991c) 'A strategy for global environmental development', *Development* 1991:2, Society for International Development: Rome.

—— (1992) *A New World Order: Grassroots Movements for Global Change*, Routledge: London.

ELC (Environment Liaison Centre) (1986) 'NGO's and Environment-Development Issues', paper presented to World Commission on Environment and Development, ELC, Nairobi.

Elkington, J. and Hailes, J. (1988) *The Green Consumer Guide*, Victor Gollancz: London.

El Serafy, S. (1989) 'The proper calculation of income from depletable natural resources', in Y. Ahmad, S. El Serafy and E. Lutz (eds) *Environmental Accounting for Sustainable Development*, World Bank: Washington DC.

Ester, P. and Nauta, A.P.N. (1986) 'A decade of social and cultural reports in the Netherlands', *Netherlands Journal of Sociology* 22: 73–6.

Etzioni, A. (1988) *The Moral Dimension*, Free Press: New York.

Evers, H.D. (1981) 'The contribution of urban subsistence production to incomes in Jakarta', *Bulletin of Indonesian Economic Studies* XVII(2): 89–96, Canberra.

Farrington, J. and Martin, A. (1988) *Farmer Participation in Agricultural Research: A Review of Concepts and Practices*, AAU Occasional Paper 9, Overseas Development Institute: London.

Ferman, L.A. and Berndt, L.E. (1981) *The Irregular Economy*, in S. Henry (ed.) *Can I Have It in Cash?* Astragal: London.

Fernandes, M.E. (1986) 'Participatory action-research and the farming systems approach with highland peasants', Department of Rural Sociology, University of Missouri, Columbia.

Feyerabend, P. (1982) *Science in a Free Society*, Verso Editions: Norfolk.

—— (1987) *Farewell to Reason*, Verso Editions: London.

Finland, Ministry of Social Affairs and Health, Research Department 1980–1986 *Housework Study* Parts I to XIV, Special Social Studies, Official Statistics of Finland, Helsinki.

Fisher, D.W. and Schweder, R.A. (eds) (1986) *Metatheory in Social Science: Pluralism and Subjectivities*, University of Chicago Press: Chicago.

Food 2000 (1987) *Food 2000: Global Policies for Sustainable Agriculture*, Report of the Advisory Panel on Food Security, Agriculture, Forestry and Environment to the World Commission on Environment and Development, Zed Books: London.

Forskargruppen for det nya vardagsivet (1987) *Veier till det nye Hverdagslivet* (The Ways to the New Everyday Life), Nord (Nordic Ministerial Council), Copenhagen (English translation envisaged).

Foster, C. and Valdman, A. (eds) (1984) *Haiti – Today and Tomorrow: An Interdisciplinary Study*, University Press of America: Lanham, MD.

Foucault, M. (1980) *Power/Knowledge*, trans. and ed. by C. Gordon, Harvester Press and Pantheon Books: New York.

Foxley, A., McPherson, M. and O'Donnel, G. (eds) (1986) *Development, Democracy and the Art of Trespassing: Essays in Honour of Albert Hirschman*, University of Notre Dame Press: Notre Dame, Indiana.

Freire, P. (1970) *The Pedagogy of the Oppressed*, Continuum: New York.

Friedman, M. (1953) 'The methodology of positive economics', in *Essays in Positive Economics*, University of Chicago Press: Chicago.

Frogan, R. and Greer, D. (1989) *Principles of Microeconomics*, Macmillan: New York.

Fromm, E. (1941) *Escape from Freedom*, Holt, Rinehart & Winston: New York.

Futatsugi, Y. (1986) 'Japanese enterprise groups', monograph no. 4, The School of Business Administration, Kobe University, Japan.

Galtung, J. and Friberg, M. (eds) (1986) *Alternativen*, Akademilitteratur: Stockholm.

Galtung, J. and Wirak, A. (1977) 'Human needs, human rights and the theories of development', mimeo, paper prepared for UNESCO, Oslo University, Oslo.

Gandhi, M. (1968) (1st edn 1927) *An Autobiography or the Story of My Experiments with Truth*, Navajivan: Ahmedabad.

——— (1984) *Hind Swaraj*, Navajivan: Ahmedabad. (First published in 1908).

Gappert, G. and Rose, H. (1975) *The Social Economy of Cities*, Sage Publications: London.

Gauhar, R. (ed.) (1985) *Third World Affairs 1985*, Third World Foundation for Social and Economic Studies: London.

George, V. and Wilding, P. (1984) *Ideology and Social Welfare*, Routledge & Kegan Paul: London.

Gershuny, J. (1978) *After Industrial Society*, Macmillan: London.

——— (1983) *Social Innovation and the Division of Labour*, Oxford University Press: Oxford.

Gershuny, J. and Jones, S. (1986) *Time Use in Seven Countries*, European Foundation: Dublin.

Ghose, A.K. (1984) 'The industrial development strategy and rural reforms in post-Mao China', in K. Griffin (ed.) *Institutional Reform and Economic Development in the Chinese Countryside*, Macmillan: London.

Giarini, O. (1980) *Dialogue on Wealth and Welfare: Report to the Club of Rome*, Pergamon Press: Oxford.

——— (ed.) (1987) *The Emerging Service Economy*, Pergamon Press: Oxford.

Giarini, O. and Loubergé, H. (1978) *The Diminishing Returns of Technology*, Pergamon Press: Oxford.

Giarini, O. and Roulet, J.R. (eds) (1988) *L'Europe face à la nouvelle économie de services*, PUF: Paris.

Gibson, T. (1991a) *Taking the Neighbourhood Initiative: A Facilitator's Guide*, Department of the Environment: London.

——— (1991b) *Making It Happen: A User's Guide to the Neighbourhood Action Packs*, Neighbourhood Initiatives Foundation: Telford, Shropshire.

Giddens, A. (1976) *New Rules of Sociological Method: A Positive Critique of Interpretive Sociologies*, Hutchinson: London.

——— (1984) *The Constitution of Society: Outline of the Theory of Structuration*, Polity Press: Cambridge.

Glaeser, B. (1988) 'A holistic human ecology approach to sustainable agricultural development', *Futures*, December, pp. 679ff., Butterworth Scientific: Guildford.

Godfrey, M. (1986) *Global Unemployment: The New Challenge to Economic Theory*, Wheatsheaf: Brighton.

Goldschmidt-Clermont, L. (1982) *Unpaid Work in the Household: A Review of Economic Evaluation Methods*, Women, Work and Development Series No. 1, International Labour Office: Geneva.

——— (1983) 'Does housework pay? A product related micro-economic approach', *Signs* 9(1): 108–19.

——— (1986) 'Le Travail non-remunéré au foyer: synthèse critique des méthodes d'évaluation économique', in R. Anker and C. Hein (eds) *Vers la mésure des activités économiques des femmes*, Bureau International du Travail: Geneva.

——— (1987a) *Economic Evaluations of Unpaid Household Work: Africa, Asia, Latin America and Oceania*, Women, Work and Development Series No. 14, International Labour Office: Geneva.

——— (1987b) 'Assessing the economic significance of domestic and related activities', *Statistical Journal of the United Nations* ECE 5(1): 81–93 (Geneva).

—— (1987c) 'Trabajo no remunerado en el hogar: un analisis de los metodos de evaluacion economica', in R. Anker and C. Hein, *Medicion de las actividades economicas de la mujer*, International Labour Office: Geneva/Santiago.

—— (1989) 'Valuing domestic activities', *Bulletin of Labour Statistics* 1989(4): ix–xiii, based on a report prepared for the International Labour Office, Bureau of Statistics, for presentation at the Second ECE/ISTRAW joint Meeting on Statistics of Women, Geneva, 13–16 November, Geneva.

—— (1990) 'Economic measurement of non-market household activities: is it useful and feasible?', *International Labour Review* 129(3): 279–99 (Geneva).

Goodin, R.E. (1990) 'International ethics and the environmental crisis', *Ethics and International Affairs* 4: 91–105.

Goodwin, N. (1991) *Social Economics: An Alternative Theory*, Macmillan: London.

Goyder, G. (1987) *The Just Enterprise*, André Deutsch: London.

Granovetter, M. (1985) 'Economic action, social structure, and embeddedness', *American Journal of Sociology* 91: 481–510.

Gregory, D. and Urry, J. (1985) *Social Relations and Spatial Structures*, Macmillan: London.

Griffin, K. (ed.) (1984) *Institutional Reform and Economic Development in the Chinese Countryside*, Macmillan: London.

Gunnemann, J.P. (1986) 'Capitalism and commutative justice', *The Annual of the Society of Christian Ethics*, Georgetown University Press: Washington DC.

Hacking, I. (1983) *Representing and Intervening: Introductory Topics in the Philosophy of Natural Science*, Cambridge University Press: Cambridge.

Hagan, P. (1991) 'ISEE workshop develops ecological economics course curriculum', *ISEE Newsletter* 2(2): 4, ISEE (International Society for Ecological Economics), Solomons, MD.

Hahn, F. (1985) *In Praise of Economic Theory*, The 1984 Jevons Memorial Fund Lecture, University College: London.

Hamilton, G. and Biggart, N. Woolsey (1985) 'Why people obey: theoretical observations on power and obedience in complex organisations', *Social Perspectives* 28: 3–28.

—— and —— (1988) 'Market, culture and authority: a comparative analysis of management and organisation in the Far East', *American Journal of Sociology* 955: S52–S94.

Hancock, G. (1989) *Lords of Poverty*, Macmillan: London.

Han Suyin (1976) *Wind in the Tower: Mao Tsetung and the Chinese Revolution 1949–1975*, Jonathan Cape: London.

Harding, P. and Jenkins, R. (1989) *The Myth of the Hidden Economy*, Open University: Milton Keynes.

Harman, W. (1988) 'The transpersonal challenge to the scientific paradigm: the need for a restructuring of science', *ReVision*, 11(2): 13–21, Washington DC.

Harrington, K. (1985) *Strategic Flexibility*, Lexington Books: Lexington, MA.

Harrison, P. (1987) *The Greening of Africa: Breaking Through in the Battle for Land and Food*, Paladin Grafton Books: London.

Haughey, J.C. (ed.) (1977) *The Faith That Does Justice*, Paulist Press: New York.

Henderson, B.D. (1984) 'On corporate strategy', in R. Lamb (ed.) *Competitive Strategic Management*, Prentice-Hall: Englewood Cliffs, NJ.

Hennipman, P. (1968) 'De externe effecten in de hedendaagse welvaartstheorie' (External effects in present welfare theory), *Economisch-Statistische Berichten*, 20 March.

Henry, S. (ed.) (1981) *Can I Have It in Cash?*, Astragel: London.

Hesse, M. (1974) *The Structure of Scientific Inference*, Macmillan: London.

Hicks, J.R. (1946) *Value and Capital*, 2nd edn, Clarendon Press: Oxford.

—— (1948) 'On the valuation of social income', *Economica*, August.

Hobson, J.A. (1889) *The Physiology of Industry* (with A.F. Mummery), Murray: London.

—— (1901) *The Psychology of Jingoism*, Grant Richards: London.

—— (1902) *Imperialism: A Study*, Nisbet: London.

—— (1914) *Work and Wealth*, Macmillan: London.

—— (1929) *Economics and Ethics*, D.C. Heath: London.

Hodgson, G.M. (1988) *Economics and Institutions: A Manifesto for a Modern Institutional Economics*, Polity Press: Cambridge.

—— (1989) 'Institutional rigidities and economic growth', *Cambridge Journal of Economics*, 13(1): 79–101. Reprinted in G.M. Hodgson, forthcoming, *After Marx and Sraffa*, Macmillan: Basingstoke.

—— (1991a) 'Hayek's theory of cultural evolution: an evaluation in the light of Vanberg's critique', *Economics and Philosophy* 7(1): 67–82.

—— (1991b) 'Economic evolution: intervention contra Pangloss', *Journal of Economic Issues* 25(2): 519–33.

—— (1991c) 'Socio-political disruption and economic growth', in G.M. Hodgson and E. Screpanti (eds) *Rethinking Economics: Markets, Technology and Growth*, Edward Elgar: Aldershot.

—— (1992) *Economics and Evolution*, Polity Press: Cambridge.

Hodgson, G.M. and Screpanti, E. (eds) (1991) *Rethinking Economics: Markets, Technology and Growth*, Edward Elgar: Aldershot.

Hollenbach, D. (1977) 'Modern Catholic teachings concerning justice', in J.C. Haughey *The Faith That Does Justice*, Paulist Press: New York.

Holmberg, A.R. (1969) *Nomads of the Long Bow: The Siriono of Eastern Bolivia*, American Museum of Science Books: New York.

Holton, R.J. and Turner, B.S. (1986) *Talcott Parsons on Economy and Society*, Routledge & Kegan Paul: London.

—— and —— (1989) *Max Weber on Economy and Society*, Routledge: London.

Horelli, L and Vepsä, K. (undated) 'The new everyday life as a goal and a way of making the future', *Tutkimos*: 30–9 (authors' contact: Ympäristöministeriö, 00120 Helsinki, Finland).

Hueting, R. (1970) 'Moet de Natuur worden gekwantificeerd? (Should nature be quantified?) in *Economisch Statistische Berichten*, 21 (Jan.): 80–4.

—— (1980) *New Scarcity and Economic Growth*, North-Holland: Amsterdam. (First published in 1974).

—— (1981) 'Some comments on the report "A low energy strategy for the United Kingdom", compiled by Gerald Leach *et al.* for the International Institute for Environment and Development (IIED)', paper prepared for the Working Party on Integral Energy Scenarios, The Hague, 20 May.

—— (1986a) 'An economic scenario for a conserver economy', in P. Ekins (ed.) *The Living Economy: A New Economics in the Making*, Routledge & Kegan Paul: London.

—— (1986b) 'A note on the construction of an environmental indicator in monetary terms as a supplement to national income', mimeo, Jakarta.

—— (1989) 'Correcting national income for environmental losses: toward a practical solution', in Y. Ahmad, S. El Serafy and E. Lutz (eds) *Environmental Accounting for Sustainable Development*, World Bank: Washington DC.

—— (1991) 'The use of the discount rate in a cost–benefit analysis for different uses of a humid tropical forest area', *Ecological Economics* 3: 43–57.

Hueting, R., Bosch, P. and De Boer, B. (1991) *Methodology for the Calculation of Sustainable National Income*, Netherlands Central Bureau of Statistics: Voorburg.

Hurst, E.N. and Schwartz, J.G. (1972) *A Critique of Economic Theory*, Penguin Books: Harmondsworth.

IBRD (International Bank for Reconstruction and Development) (1950) *The Basis of a Development Program for Colombia*, Johns Hopkins University Press: Baltimore.

ICC (International Chamber of Commerce) (1990) 'The business charter for sustainable development: principles for environmental management', ICC: Paris.

ICE (Institute for Community Economics) (1982) *The Community Land Trust Handbook*, Rodale Press: Emmaeus, PA.

IDS (Institute of Development Studies) (1989) 'Vulnerability: how the poor cope', *IDS Bulletin* 20(2), IDS, University of Sussex: Brighton.

IIED (International Institute for Environment and Development) (1989) *RRA Notes*, IIED: London.

Ignatieff, M. (1989) 'Caring just isn't enough', *New Statesman and Society*, 3 February, pp. 33–7.

ILO (International Labour Office) (1989) 'Promoting peoples' participation and self-reliance', *Proceedings of the Regional Workshop of Trainers in Participatory Rural Development*, Bulawayo, Zimbabwe, August, ILO: Geneva.

Inayatullah, S. (1991) 'Rethinking science: P.R. Sarkar's reconstruction of science', *IFDA Dossier* 81 (April/June), IFDA, Nyon, Switzerland.

INSEE (Institut National de la Statistique et des Etudes Economiques) (1986) *Les Comptes du patrimoine naturel* 535–6 des Collections de l'INSEE, série D, No. 137–138, INSEE-Ministère de l'Environnement, Paris.

IPCC (Intergovernmental Panel on Climate Change) (1990) *Scientific Assessment of Climate Change* (Report of Working Group 1, with accompanying Policy-makers' Summary), June, World Meteorological Organization: Geneva.

Irvine, J. and Miles, I. (1982) 'The dominant way of life in Britain; a case-study of maldevelopment', in I. Miles and J. Irvine (eds) *Social Indicators for Human Development*, Frances Pinter: London.

IUCN (International Union for the Conservation of Nature) and WWF (World Wide Fund for Nature) (1980) *The World Conservation Strategy*, IUCN: Gland, Switzerland.

Jackson, T. and Jacobs, M. (1991) 'Carbon taxes and the assumptions of environmental economics', in T. Barker (ed.) *Green Futures for Economics*, Cambridge Econometrics: Cambridge.

Jain, S., Jaitly, M., Srivastava, K., Nair, N. and Mathur, K. (1986) 'Women's development programme of the government of Rajasthan: a review', Report of the Institute of Development Studies, University of Rajasthan, Jaipur.

Jansen, H.M.A. and Opschoor, J.B. (1972) *De Invloed van een Enquete onder Makelaars in en rond de Haarlemmermeer* (The Influence of Noise-nuisance on the Price of Houses – Report of a Survey among House-agents in and around the Haarlemmermeer), Instituut voor Milieuvraagstukken van de Vrije Universiteit, Werknota 15, Amsterdam.

Jarret, H. (ed.) (1966) *Environmental Quality in a Growing Economy*, Johns Hopkins University Press: Baltimore, MD.

Jenkins, J.C. and Perrow, C. (1977) 'Insurgency of the powerless' *American Sociological Review* 42: 249–68.

Johansson, P.-O. (1987) *The Economic Theory and Measurement of Environmental Benefits*, Cambridge University Press: Cambridge.

Jolly, R. (1989) 'A future for UN aid and technical assistance?', *Development* 1989(4): 21–6 (Society for International Development, Rome).

Jungk, R. and Mullert, N. (1988) *Future Workshops: How to Create Desirable Futures*, Institute for Social Inventions: London.

Kaldor, N. (1978) *Further Essays on Economic Theory*, Duckworth: London.

—— (1985) *Economics without Equilibrium*, Cardiff Press, University College: Cardiff.

Kamenetzky, M. (1976) *Economia del Conocimiento y Empresa*, Paidos: Buenos Aires.

—— (1989) 'A new way of thinking', *ICIS Forum* 19(3): 11–13. ICIS (International Center for Integrative Studies): New York.

Kamenetzky, M., Maybury, R. and Weiss, C. (eds) (1986) *Choice and Management of Technology in Developing Countries*, World Bank (Projects Policy Department): Washington, DC.

Kamerschen, D.R. and Valentine, L.M. (1981) *Intermediate Microeconomic Theory*, Southwestern: Cincinnati.

Kindleberger, C.P. (1978) *Government and International Trade: Essays in International Finance*, 129 Princeton University.

—— (1986) 'International public goods without international government', *American Economic Review*, March: 1–13.

Keohane, R.O. (1986) *Neorealism and Its Critics*, Columbia University Press: New York.

Keynes, J.M. (1943) 'Proposal for an International Clearing Union', White Paper, Cmd 6437.

Keynes, J.N. (1930) *The Scope and Method of Political Economy*, 4th edn, Macmillan: London. (First published in 1890.)

Kneese, A.V. (1977) *Economics and the Environment*, Penguin Books: Harmondsworth.

—— (1984) *Measuring the Benefits of Clean Air and Water*, Resources for the Future: Washington DC.

Kobayashi, Y. (1980) *Kigro Shudan no Bunseki* (Analysis of Business Groups), Hokkaido Daigaku Tosho Kankokai: Sapporo.

Kohn, A. (1986) *No Contest: The Case Against Competition*, Houghton Mifflin: Boston.

Kolko, G. (1963) *The Triumph of Conservatism*, Free Press: New York.

Kotler, P. and Achrol, R.S. (1984) 'Marketing strategy and the science of warfare', in R. Lamb (ed.) *Competitive Strategic Management*, Prentice Hall: Englewood Cliffs, NJ.

Kotler, P. and Singh, R.A. (1984) 'Marketing strategy and the science of warfare', in R. Lamb (ed.) *Competitive Strategic Management*, Prentice Hall: Englewood Cliffs, NJ.

Kox, H.L.M. (1990) 'Third World commodity production, environment and new international commodity agreements', paper presented to VIth General Conference of European Association of Development Research and Training Institutes, Oslo, June.

Krausz, M. (ed.) (1989) *Relativism: Interpretation and Confrontation*, University of Notre Dame Press: Notre Dame, Indiana.

Kuznets, S. (1947) 'National income and industrial structure', in *The Econometric Society Meeting, September 6–18, 1947, Washington, D.C. Proceedings of the International Statistical Conferences*, vol. V, Calcutta.

—— (1948) 'On the valuation of social income', *Economica* 15: 1–16 (February), 116–31 (May).

Lamb, R. (ed.) (1984) *Competitive Strategic Management*, Prentice-Hall: Englewood Cliffs, NJ.

Landim, L. (1990) 'Brazilian crossroads: NGOs, walls and bridges', Promocion del Desarrollo Popular: Mexico City.

Lapierre, D. (1986) *City of Joy*, Arrow Books: London.

Lawson, T. (1981) 'Paternalism and labour market segmentation theory', in S.F. Wilkinson (ed.) *Dynamics of Labour Market Segmentation*, Academic Press: London.

—— (1987) 'The relative/absolute nature of knowledge and economic analysis', *Economic Journal* 97.

—— (1989) 'Realism, closed systems and Friedman', mimeo, Cambridge University.

Lecomber, R. (1975) *Economic Growth versus the Environment*, Macmillan: London.

Leipert, C. (1989) 'Social costs of the economic process and national accounts: the example of defensive expenditures', *Journal of Interdisciplinary Economics* (3): 27–46.

Lenin, V.I. (1918) 'The immediate tasks of the Soviet government', *Selected Works*, vol. 1, Progress Publishers: Moscow.

Leplin, J. (ed.) (1984) *Scientific Realism*, University of California Press: Berkeley, CA.

Levy, D.J. (1981) *Realism: An Essay in Interpretation and Social Reality*, Carcanet: Manchester.

Lindberg, L., Campbell, J. and Hollingsworth, R. (eds) (1991) 'Economic governance and the analysis of structural change in the American economy', in J. Campbell, R. Hollingsworth and L. Lindberg (eds) *The Governance of the American Economy*, Cambridge University Press: Cambridge.

Lindblom, C.E. (1977) *Politics and Markets*, Basic Books: New York.

Lipton, M. (1985) 'Prisoners' Dilemma and Coase's Theorem: a case for democracy in less-developed countries?', in R.C.O. Mathews (ed.) *Economy and Democracy*, Macmillan: London.

Lloyd, B.B. (1972) *Perception and Cognition*, Penguin Books: Harmondsworth.

Lone, Ø. (1988) *Natural Resource Accounting: The Norwegian Experience*, OECD: Paris.

Lukes, S. (1973) *Individualism*, Basil Blackwell: Oxford.

Lutz, M. (1985) 'Pragmatism, instrumental value theory and social economics', *Review of Social Economy*, October: 140–72.

—— (ed.) (1990a) *Social Economics: Retrospect and Prospect*, Kluwer Academic Publishers: Boston.

—— (1990b) 'Emphasising the social: social economics and socio-economics', *Review of Social Economy*, Fall: 303–20.

Lutz, M. and Lux, K. (1979) *The Challenge of Humanistic Economics*, Benjamin/ Cummings: Palo Alto, CA.

—— and —— (1988) *Humanistic Economics: The New Challenge*, Bootstrap Press: New York.

Lützel, H. (1989) 'Erganzung de Volkswirtschaftlichen Gesamtrechnungen um die Haushaltproduktion (Household production and national accounts)', mimeo, report prepared by the Federal Statistical Office of the Federal Republic of Germany for Presentation at the Second ECE/INSTRAW Joint Meeting on Statistics of Women, Geneva, 13–16 November, to appear in *Forum der Bundesstatistik*, Wiesbaden.

Lydenburg, S., Strub, S.O., and Tepper Marlin, A. (1986) *Rating America's Corporate Conscience*, Addison Wesley: New York.

Mackintosh, M. and Wainwright, H. (eds) (1987) *A Taste of Power: The Politics of Local Economics*, Verso: London.

Makhijani, A. and Browne, R.S. (1986) 'Restructuring the international monetary system', *World Policy Journal*, winter: 59–80.

Mäler, K-G. (1989a) 'Valuation of costs and benefits from resource use', mimeo, World Bank Economic Development Institute, Washington DC.

—— (1989b) 'Sustainable development', mimeo, World Bank Economic Development Institute, Washington DC.

—— (1991) 'National accounts and environmental resources', *Environmental Resource Economics* 1: 1–15.

Mallmann, C.A. (1973) 'On the satisfaction of human aspirations as the development objective', paper presented at the Symposium on Science, Technology and Human Values, Mexico City, 2–3 July.

Markandya, A. and Pearce, D. (1987) 'Marginal opportunity cost as a planning concept', in 'Natural Resource Management', *The Annals of Regional Science* XXI(3): 18–32.

—— and —— (1988) *Environmental Considerations and the Choice of the Discount Rate in Developing Countries*, World Bank Environment Department Working Paper No. 3, Washington DC.

Markandya, A., Pearce, D. and Barbier, E. (1990) 'Environmental sustainability and cost–benefit analysis', *Environment and Planning*, Series A, 22: 1259–66.

Marshall, A. (1969) *Principles of Economics*, 8th edn, Macmillan: London. (First published in 1890).

Martin, R. and Rowthorn, B. (1986) *The Geography of De-Industrialisation*, Macmillan: London.

Martinez-Alier, J. (1987) *Ecological Economics*, Basil Blackwell: Oxford.

Marwell, G. and Ames, R.E. (1981) 'Economists free ride: does anyone else?', *Journal of Public Economists* 15: 295–310.

Maslow, A.H. (1954) *Motivation and Personality*, Harper & Row: New York.

Mathews, R.C.O. (ed.) (1985) *Economy and Democracy*, Macmillan: London.

Max-Neef, M. (1988) 'The pruning of language', *Development* 1988 (2/3): 30–3. (Society for International Development, Rome).

Max-Neef, M., Elizalde, A. and Hopenhayn, M. (1986) 'Desarollo a Escala Humana: una opcion para el futuro', *Development Dialogue*, Dag Hammarskjöld Foundation, Uppsala, Sweden.

—— —— and —— (1989) 'Human scale development: an option for the future', *Development Dialogue*, 1989(1): 5–81. (English translation of Max-Neef *et al.* 1986.).

McCarthy, J.D. and Mayer, N.Z. (1973) *The Trend of Social Movements*, General Learning Press: Morristown, NJ.

—— and —— (1977) 'Resource mobilisation and social movements', *American Journal of Sociology* 82: 1212–41.

McCarthy, J.D. and Zald, M.N. (1973) *The Trend of Social Movements*, General Learning Press: Morristown, NJ.

—— and —— (1977) 'Resource mobilization and social movements', *American Journal of Sociology* 82: 1212–41.

McLaughlin, C. and Davidson, G. (1985) *Builders of the Dawn: Community Lifestyles in a Changing World*, Stillpoint: Walpole, NH.

McMullin, E. (1984) 'A case for scientific realism', in J. Leplin (ed.) *Scientific Realism*, University of California Press: Berkeley, CA.

McNamara, R. (1973) 'Address to the Board of Governors', Nairobi, 24 September.

McNulty, P.J. (1968) 'Economic theory and the meaning of competition', *Quarterly Journal of Economics* 82: 639–56.

Mehta, V.R. (1978) *Beyond Marxism: Towards an Alternative Perspective*, Manohar: New Delhi.

Meier, G.M. and Seers, D. (eds) *Pioneers in Development*, Oxford University Press: Oxford.

Miles, I. (1985) *Social Indicators for Human Development*, Frances Pinter: London.

Miles, I. and Irvine, J. (eds) (1982) *The Poverty of Progress: Changing Ways of Life in Industrial Societies*, Pergamon Press: Oxford.

Mill, J.S. (1844) *Essays on Some Unsettled Questions of Political Economy*, J.W. Parker: London.

—— (1968) *Principles of Political Economy*, Routledge & Kegan Paul: London. (First published in 1848.)

Mingione, E. (1985) *Social Reproduction of the Surplus Labour Force*, in N. Redclift and E. Mingione (eds) (1985) *Beyond Employment: Gender, Households and Subsistence*, Basil Blackwell: Oxford.

Mishan, E.J. (1971) 'The postwar literature on externalities: an interpretative essay', *Journal of Economic Literature* LX(1).

Mishra, P.R. and Sarin, M. (1988) 'Social security through social fencing', in C. Conroy and M. Litvinoff (eds) *The Greening of Aid: Sustainable Livelihoods in Practice*, Earthscan: London.

MOHPPE (Ministry of Housing, Physical Planning and the Environment) (1988) *To Choose or to Lose: National Environmental Policy Plan*, MOHPPE: The Hague.

Montagu, A. (ed.) (1974) *Culture and Human Development: Insights into Growing Human*, Prentice-Hall: Englewood Cliffs, NJ.

—— (1978) *Touching: The Human Significance of the Skin*, Harper & Row: New York.

Mootz, M. (1989) 'Social reporting in the Netherlands', mimeo, paper presented at conference on Social Reporting, September, Wissenschaftszentrum, Berlin.

Morris, D. (1980) *Measuring the Condition of the World's Poor: The Physical Quality of Life Indicator*, published for Overseas Development Council, Pergamon: New York.

Mulder, N. (1979) *Everyday Life in Thailand: An Interpretation*, Duang Kamol: Bangkok.

Murray, G.F. (1984) 'The wood tree as a peasant cash-crop: an anthropological strategy for the domestication of energy', in C. Foster and A. Valdman (eds) *Haiti – Today and Tomorrow: An Interdisciplinary Study*, University of America Press: Lanham, MD.

—— (1986) 'Seeing the forest while planting trees: an anthropological approach to agroforestry in rural Haiti', in D.W. Brinkerhoff and J.C.G. Zamor (eds) *Politics, Projects and People*, Praeger: West Port, CT.

Musgrave, R. (1959) *The Theory of Public Finance*, McGraw Hill: New York.

MYRADA (1990) *PRA/PALM Series*, MYRADA: Bangalore, India.

Myrdal, G. (1978) 'Institutional Economics', *Journal of Economic Issues* 12: 771–83.

Nag, M., White, B.N.F. and Peet, R.C. (1978) 'An anthropological approach to the study of the economic value of children in Java and Nepal', *Current Anthropology* 19(2): 293–306 (Chicago).

NCCB (National Conference of Catholic Bishops) (1986) *Economic Justice for All*, NCCB: Washington DC.

Nelson, R.R. and Winter, S.G. (1982) *An Evolutionary Theory of Economic Change*, Harvard University Press: Cambridge, MA.

Nielsen, K. (1990) 'The mixed economy, the neo-liberal challenge and the negotiated economy', mimeo, Institute of Economics & Planning, Roskilde University, Denmark.

Nielsen, K. and Pedersen, O. (1991) 'From the mixed economy to the negotiated economy in Scandinavian countries', in R. Coughlin (ed.) *Morality, Rationality and Efficiency: Perspectives on Socio-economics*, M.E. Sharpe: New York.

Nisbet, R. (1953) *Quest for Community*, Oxford University Press: New York.

Noll, R. (ed.) (1985) *Regulatory Policy and the Social Sciences*, University of California Press: Berkeley, CA.

Nordhaus, W. and Tobin, J. (1973) 'Is growth obsolete?', in M. Moss (ed.) *The Measurement of Economic and Social Performance*, National Bureau of Economic Research: New York.

Norgaard, R.B. (1985) 'Environmental economics: an evolutionary critique and a plea for pluralism', *Journal of Environmental Economics and Management* 12: 382–94.

—— (1988) 'Sustainable development: a coevolutionary view', *Futures*, December: 606–19.

—— (1989) 'The case for methodological pluralism', *Ecological Economics* 1, February: 37–57.

Nozick, R. (1974) *Anarchy, State and Utopia*, Basic Books: New York.

Oakeshott, M. (1962) *Rationalism in Politics and Other Essays*, Methuen: London.

Odum, E.P. (1971) *Fundamental Ecology*, 3rd edn, Saunders: Philadelphia.

OECD (1975) *The Polluter Pays Principle*, OECD: Paris.

—— (1989) *Renewable Natural Resources: Economic Incentives for Improved Management*, OECD: Paris.

Okumura, H. (1982) *Gendai Nikon Shihon Shugi no Shihai Kozo* (The Structure of Domination in Modern Japanese Capitalism), Shimpyoron: Tokyo.

—— (1989) 'Incorporate relations in Japan', mimeo, paper delivered at Conference on Japanese and US Inter-firm Relations, University of California, Davis, March.

Oliver, M. (1990) *The Politics of Disablement*, Macmillan: London.

Olsen, P. (1975) *The Future of Being Human*, M. Evans: New York.

Olson, M. (1971) *The Logic of Collective Action*, 2nd edn, Harvard University Press: Cambridge, MA.

—— (1982) *The Rise and Decline of Nations*, Yale University Press: New Haven.

Opschoor, H. and Pearce, D. (eds) (1991) *Persistent Pollutants: Economics, Toxicology, Decision-Making*, Kluwer Academic Publishers: Dordrecht.

Opschoor, J.B. and Vos, H. (1989) *The Application of Economic Instruments for Environmental Protection*, OECD, Environmental Directorate: Paris.

Orru, M., Biggart, N. Woolsey, and Hamilton, G. (forthcoming) 'Organizational isomorphism in East Asia: broadening the new institutionalism', in W.W. Powell and P. DiMaggio (eds) *The New Institutionalism in Organizational Analysis*, University of Chicago Press: Chicago.

Page, T. (1977) *Conservation and Economic Efficiency*, Johns Hopkins University Press: Baltimore, MD.

Pahl, R.E. and Wallace, C. (1985) *Household Work Strategies in Economic Recession*, in N. Redclift and E. Mingione (eds) *Beyond Employment: Gender, Household and Subsistence*, Basil Blackwell: Oxford.

Pajestka, J. and Feinstein, C.H. (eds) (1980) *The Relevance of Economic Theories*, proceedings of a conference held by the International Economic Association in Warsaw, Poland, Macmillan: London.

Panikar, R. (1984) 'Human rights: a western concept?', *Interculture* 17: 27–47, January–March.

Parquez, A. (1973) 'Sismondi et la théorie du déséquilibre macro-économique', *Revue Economique* 24(5): 837–65.

Parsons, T. (1937) *The Structure of Social Action*, Free Press: New York.

Parsons, T. and Smelser, N. (1956) *Economy and Society: A Study in the Integration of Economic and Social Theory*, Routledge & Kegan Paul: London.

PCDF (the People-Centred Development Forum) (1990) 'PCD Forum', introductory leaflet, PCDF: Manila.

Pearce, D. (1980) 'The social incidence of environmental costs and benefits', *Progress in Environmental Planning and Resource Management* 2: 63–87.

Pearce, D. and Markandya, A. (1989) *Environmental Policy Benefits: Monetary Valuation*, OECD: Paris.

———, ——— and Barbier, E. (1989) *Blueprint for a Green Economy*, Earthscan: London.

Perelman, C. (1963) *The Idea of Justice and the Problem of Argument*, trans. by J. Petrie, Routledge & Kegan Paul: London.

Perrings, C. (1990) 'Economic growth and sustainable development', paper presented to Science and Policy Working Group, Bergen Conference, Norway, 8–12 May.

Peterson, M.D. (ed.) (1987) *The Portable Thomas Jefferson*, Viking Press: New York, (Jefferson to Samuel Kercheval, 12 July 1816).

Phillips, A. (1960) 'A theory of interfirm organisation', *Quarterly Journal of Economics* 74: 602–13.

Pieters, R.G.M. and Van Raaij, W.F. (1987) 'The role of affect in economic behaviour', in W.F. Van Raaij, G.M. Van Wellhoven, T.M.M. Verhallen and K.-E. Warneryd (eds) *Handbook of Economic Psychology*, North Holland: Amsterdam.

Pietilä, H. (1987) 'Tomorrow begins today: alternative development with women in the North', paper presented to Third International Interdisciplinary Congress on Women, Dublin, July; also in J. Galtung and M. Friburg (eds) *Alternativen*, Akademilitteratus: Stockholm 1986.

Pietilä, H. and Vickers, J. (1990) *Making Women Matter: The Role of the United Nations*, Zed Press: London.

Pigou, A.C. (1949) *Income*, Macmillan: London.

——— (1962) *The Economics of Welfare*, Macmillan: New York. (First published in 1920.)

Polanyi, K. (1944) *The Great Transformation*, Beacon Press: Boston.

——— (1977) *The Livelihood of Man*, Academic Press: New York.

Polanyi, M. (1957) *Personal Knowledge: Towards a Post-Critical Philosophy*, Routledge & Kegan Paul: London.

——— (1967) *The Tacit Dimension*, Routledge & Kegan Paul: London.

Popper, K.R. and Eccles, J.C. (1981) *The Self and Its Brain*, Springer International: New York.

Powell, W.W. (1988) 'Neither market nor hierachy: network forms of organization', mimeo, Department of Sociology, University of Arizona, Tucson, Arizona.

Powell, W.W. and DiMaggio, P. (eds) (forthcoming) *The New Institutionalism in Organizational Analysis*, University of Chicago Press: Chicago.

PP21 (People's Plan for the 21st Century) (1989) 'An alliance of hope: the Minamata Declaration', *Ampo, Japan–Asia Quarterly Review* 21(2–3): 6–11.

Pradervand, P. (1989) *Listening to Africa: Developing Africa from the Grassroots*, Praeger: Westport, CT.

Prescott, J.W. (1975) 'Body pleasure and the origins of violence', *The Bulletin of the Atomic Scientists* XXXI(9): 10–20.

Prigogine, I. and Stengers, I. (1984) *Order Out of Chaos: Man's New Dialogue with Nature*, Bantam Books: New York.

Pullianinen, K. and Pietilä, H. (1983) 'Revival of non-monetary economy makes growth unnecessary', *IFDA Dossier* 35, May/June.

Purcell, K., Wood, S., Waton, A. and Allen, S. (1986) *The Changing Experience of Employment*, Macmillan: London.

Rabinow, P. (1982) *The Foucault Reader*, Pantheon Books: New York.

Rahman, Md. Anisur (1972) 'The first step', mimeo, 8 March.

—— (with G.V.S. de Silva *et al.*) (1979) 'Bhoomi Sena: a struggle for people's power', *Development Dialogue* 2, Dag Hammarskjöld Foundation, Uppsala, Sweden.

—— (1988) 'Ganogabeshana o Shwamaj Paribartan', *Lokayan*, March, pp. 41–52.

Rahnema, M. (1990) 'Swadhyaya: the unknown, the peaceful, the silent yet singing revolution of India', *IFDA Dossier* 76, Nyon, January/April, Switzerland.

Rawls, J. (1972) *A Theory of Justice*, Oxford University Press: Oxford.

Redclift, N. (1985) 'The contested domain: gender, accumulation, and the labour process', in N. Redclift and E. Mingione (eds) *Beyond Employment: Gender, Household and Subsistence*, Basil Blackwell: Oxford.

—— and Mingione, E. (eds) (1985) *Beyond Employment: Gender, Household and Subsistence*, Basil Blackwell: Oxford.

Reid, M. (1934) *Economics of Household Production*, Wiley & Sons: New York.

Repetto, R. (1988) *Resources and Economic Accounts*, OECD: Paris.

—— Magrath, W., Wells, M., Beer, C. and Rossini, F. (1989) *Wasting Assets: Natural Resources in the National Income Accounts*, World Resources Institute: Washington DC.

Robbins, L. (1984) *An Essay on the Nature and Significance of Economic Science*, Macmillan: London. (First edition 1932.)

Robertson, J. (1989) *Future Wealth: A New Economics for the 21st Century*, Cassell: London.

Ross, W.D. (1930) *The Right and the Good*, Clarendon Press: Oxford.

Roy, C. (1989a) 'Evolution des emplois du temps des citadins en France entre 1975 et 1985', mimeo, paper presented at the International Workshop on the Changing Use of Time, Brussels, 17/18 April, convened by the European Foundation for the Improvement of Living and Working Conditions, Dublin.

—— (1989b) 'La Gestion du temps des hommes et des femmes, des actifs et des inactifs', *Economie et Statistique* 233: 5–14 (Paris).

Ruskin, J. (1988) *Unto This Last*, Wiley & Sons: New York. (First published in 1864.)

Sadik, N. (1991) *The State of World Population 1991*, UN Fund for Population Activities: New York.

Sanik, M.M. and Stafford, K. (1983) 'Product-accounting approach to valuing food production', *Home Economics Research Journal* 12(12): 217–27 (Washington DC).

Sarkar, P.R. (1986–91) *Prout in a Nutshell*, trans. by Vijayananda Avadhuta, Ananda Marga Publications: Calutta, vols 1–15.

Sayer, A. (1984) *Method in Social Science: A Realistic Approach*, Hutchinson: London.

Sayers, S. (1985) *Reality and Reason*, Basil Blackwell: Oxford.

Schapiro, S.P. (1987) 'The social control of impersonal trust', *American Journal of Sociology* 93: 623–59.

Schmid, A. (1987) *Property, Power and Public Choice: An Inquiry into Law and Economics*, Praeger: Westport, CT.

Schneider, B. (1988) *The Barefoot Revolution*, IT Publications: London.

Schor, J. (1989) 'On the definition of the boundaries of an economic system', mimeo, Harvard University, Cambridge, MA.

Schumacher, E.F. (1973) *Small Is Beautiful*, Harper & Row: New York.

—— (1977) *A Guide for the Perplexed*, Harper & Row: New York.

Schumpeter, J. (1954) *History of Economic Analysis*, Oxford University Press: New York.

Schweder, R.A. (1984) 'Anthropology's romantic rebellion against the enlightenment, or there's more to thinking than reason and evidence', in R.A. Schweder and R.A. Levine (eds) *Culture Theory: Essays on Mind, Self and Emotions*, Cambridge University Press: New York.

—— (1986) 'Divergent rationalities' in D.W. Fisher and R.A. Schweder (eds) *Metatheory in Social Science: Pluralisms and Subjectivities*, University of Chicago Press: Chicago.

—— (1989) 'Post-Nietschean anthropology; the idea of multiple objective worlds', in M. Krausz (ed.) *Relativism: Interpretation and Confrontation*, Notre Dame University Press: Notre Dame, Indiana.

Schweder, R.A. and Levine, R.A. (eds) (1984) *Culture Theory: Essays on Mind, Self and Emotion*, Cambridge University Press: New York.

Scitovsky, T. (1954) 'Two concepts of external economics', *Journal of Political Economy*, 62: 143ff.

Searle, J.R. (1984) *Minds, Brains and Science*, BBC Publications: London.

Seers, D. (1982) 'Active life profiles for different social groups', Discussion Paper 178, Institute for Development Studies, University of Sussex, Brighton.

Sen, A. (1983) 'Development: which way now?', *The Economic Journal* 93(372): 745–62.

Seruzier, M. (1988) *Construire les comptes de la nation; guide d'élaboration conformé au SCN*, Collection Methodologie 21, Ministère de la Coopération, Paris.

Sherbourne, J.C. (1972) *John Ruskin or the Ambiguity of Affluence*, Harvard University Press: Cambridge, MA.

Sills, D. (ed.) *International Encyclopedia of the Social Sciences*, Free Press: New York.

Simon, H.A. (1957) *Models of Man: Social and Rational*, Wiley & Sons: New York.

Sismondi, J.C.L.S. de (1803) *De la Richesse Commerciale*, Geneva.

—— (1966a) *Political Economy*, A.M. Kelley: New York. (First published in 1815.)

—— (1966b) *Political Economy and the Philosophy of Government*, A.M. Kelley: New York. (First published in 1847.)

—— (1991) *New Principles of Political Economy*. trans. by Richard Hyse, Transaction: New Brunswick/London. (First published in 1819.)

Smelser, N. (1963) *The Sociology of Economic Life*, Prentice-Hall: Englewood Cliffs, NJ.

Smith, G.A. (1980) 'The teleological view of wealth: a historical perspective' in H.E. Daly (ed.) *Economics, Ecology and Ethics*, W.H. Freeman: San Francisco.

Smith, S. (1986) *Britain's Shadow Economy*, Oxford University Press: Oxford.

Söderbaum, P. (1973) 'Positionsanalys vid beslutsfattande och planering. Ekonomisk analys pa tvarvetenskaplig grund' (Positional Analysis for Decision Making and Planning. An Interdisciplinary Approach to Economic Analysis), Esselte Studium, Stockholm.

—— (1980) 'Towards a reconciliation of economics and ecology', *European Review of Agricultural Economics* 7: 55–77.

—— (1982) 'Ecological imperatives for public policy', *Ceres, FAO Review of Agriculture and Development*, 15(2): 139–65.

—— (1986) 'Economics, ethics and environmental problems', *Journal of Interdisciplinary Economics* 1: 139–53.

—— (1987) 'Environmental management: a non-traditional approach', *Journal of Economic Issues* 21, March: 139–65.

—— (1990a) 'Neoclassical and institutional approaches to environmental economics', *Journal of Economic Issues* 24, June: 481–92.

—— (1990b) 'Economics in relation to environment, agriculture and rural development: a non-traditional approach to project evaluation', Report 31, Swedish University of Agricultural Sciences, Uppsala.

Solow, R. (1981) 'Replies to Steven Kelman', *Regulation*, March/April: 40–1.

Sowell, T. (1972) 'Sismondi: a neglected pioneer', *History of Political Economy* 4: 62–88.

Streeck, W. and Schmitter, P.C. (1985) *Private Interest Government*, Sage: Beverly Hills, CA.

Streeten, P. (1979a) 'Development ideas in historical perspective', in *Towards a New Strategy for Development: A Rothko Chapel Colloquium*, Pergamon Press: New York/Oxford.

—— (1979b) 'From growth to basic needs'. *Finance and Development*, June, reprinted in P. Streeten, *Development Perspectives*, Macmillan: London, 1986, ch. 18.

—— (1980) 'Development: what have we learned?', in J. Pajestka and C.H. Feinstein (eds) *The Relevance of Economic Theories*, Macmillan: London.

—— (1981a) *Development Perspectives*, Macmillan: London.

—— (1981b) 'The politics of food prices', in *What Price Food?*', Macmillan: London, ch. 16.

—— (1983) 'Development dichotomies', *World Development* 11(10): 875–89.

—— (1985) 'A problem to every solution', *Finance and Development* 22(2): 14–16.

—— (1986) 'Suffering from success', in A. Foxley, M.McPherson and G. O'Donnel (eds) *Development, Democracy and the Act of Trespassing: Essays in Honour of Albert Hirschman*, Notre Dame University Press: Notre Dame, Indiana.

—— (1988) 'Surpluses for a capital-hungry world', in P. Streeten (ed.) *Beyond Adjustment: The Asian Experience*, International Monetary Fund: Washington DC, ch. 8.

Tawney, R.H. (1926) *Religion and the Rise of Capitalism*, Harcourt Brace Jovanovich: New York.

—— (1948) *The Acquisitive Society*, Harcourt Brace Jovanovich: New York. (First published in 1920.)

—— (1964) *Equality*, 4th edn, George Allen & Unwin: London. (First published in 1931.)

Tilakaratna, S. (1985) 'The animator in participatory rural development: some experiences from Sri Lanka', ILO Working Paper (WEP 10/WP .37), ILO, Geneva.

—— (1987) 'The animator in participatory rural development (Concept and Practice)', ILO, Geneva.

Tilly, C. (1978) *From Mobilization to Revolution*, Random House: New York.

Tobin, J. (1987) 'A proposal for international monetary reform', in *Essays in Economics* vol. 3 (Theory and Policy), MIT Press: Cambridge, MA.

Tomer, J.F. (1973) 'Management consulting for private enterprise: a theoretical and empirical analysis of the contribution of management consultants to economic growth in the United States', unpublished Ph.D. thesis, Rutgers University, New Brunswick, NJ.

—— (1987) *Oganisational Capital: The Path to Higher Productivity and Well-being*, Praeger: Westport, CT.

Tournier, M. (1967) *Vendredi, on les limbes du Pacifique*, Gallimard, Paris.

Trogan, P. (1988) 'Les Statistiques de production sur les services marchands et la mésure de la productivité', in O. Giarini and J.R. Roulet (eds) *L'Europe face à la nouvelle économie de services*, PUF: Paris.

Turner, B. (ed.) (1988) *Building Communities: a Third World Casebook*, Building Communities Books: London.

UNDP (United Nations Development Programme) (1990) *Human Development Report 1990*, Oxford University Press: New York/Oxford.

—— (1991) *Human Development Report 1991*, Oxford University Press: New York/Oxford.

UNNGLS (United Nations Non-governmental Liaison Service) (1989) *Newsnet* 6(1), March, UNNGLS, New York.

UNICEF (1989) *The State of the World's Children 1989*, Oxford University Press (for UNICEF): Oxford.

United Nations Statistical Office (1968) *A System of National Accounts* (Studies in Methods, Series F, No. 2, Rev. 3), United Nations: New York.

UNU/UNDP (United Nations University/United Nations Development Programme) (1987) *Refocusing Praxis*, Dossier 5.

Van Boven, T. (1989) 'The international human rights agenda: a challenge to the United Nations', mimeo, Maastricht, Netherlands.

Van Praag, B.M.S. and Spit, J.S. (1982) *The Social Filter Process and Income Evaluation: An Empirical Study in the Social Reference Mechanism*, Rep. 82.08, Centre for Research in Public Economics, Leiden University, Leiden, Netherlands.

Van Raaij, W.F., Van Wellhoven, G.M., Verhallen, T.M.M. and Warneryd, K.-E. (eds) (1987) *Handbook of Economic Psychology*, North Holland: Amsterdam.

Veblen, T.B. (1912) *The Theory of the Leisure Class*, Macmillan: London.

—— (1919) *The Place of Science in Modern Civilisation and Other Essays*, Huebsch: New York.

Vohra, B.B. (1987) 'Managing the environment', Foundation Day Lecture of the National Museum of Natural History, New Delhi, 5 June.

Von Wright, G.H. (1986) 'Vetenskapen och fornuftet (Science and Reason)', Bonniers: Stockholm.

Waring, M. (1988) *If Women Counted: A New Feminist Economics*, Macmillan: London.

Waterhouse, R. (1991) 'UN staff net millions in tax fraud', *Independent on Sunday*, 9 May, London.

WCED (World Commission on Environment and Development) (1987) *Our Common Future*, Oxford University Press: Oxford/New York.

Weber, M. (1978) *Economy and Society*, ed. by Guenther Roth and Claus Wittich, University of California Press: Berkeley, CA.

Wellman, B. and Berkowitz, S.D. (eds) *Social Structures: A Network Approach*, Cambridge University Press: Cambridge.

Wells, P. and Jetter, M. (1991) *The Global Consumer*, Victor Gollancz: London.

Wermeil, S. (1984) 'Is analysis out of touch? Scholars Blend Law, Economics', *Wall Street Journal*, 18 December.

Wheelock, J. (1990a) *Husbands at Home: The Domestic Economy in a Post-Industrial Society*, Routledge: London.

—— (1990b) 'Families, self-respect and the irrelevance of "Rational Economic Man" in a post-industrial society', *Journal of Behavioural Economics* 19(2): 221–36.

White, H.C. (1981) 'Where do markets come from?' *American Journal of Sociology* 87: 517–47.

—— (1988) 'Varieties of markets', in B. Wellman and S.D. Berkowitz (eds) *Social Structures: A Network Approach*, Cambridge University Press: Cambridge.

White, H.C., Devenney, M., Bhaduri, R., Beresford, P., Barnes, J. and Jones, A. (1988) *Hearing the Voice of the Consumer*, Policy Studies Institute: London.

Wignaraja, P. (1990) *Women, Poverty and Resources*, Sage: New Delhi/London.

Wignaraja, P., Hussain, A., Sethi, H., and Wignaraja, G. (1991) *Participatory Development: Learning from South Asia*, Oxford University Press: Karachi/Oxford.

Wilkinson, S.F. (ed.) (1981) *Dynamics of Labour Market Segmentation*, Academic Press: London.

Williamson, O.E. (1975) *Markets and Hierarchies: Analysis and Antitrust Implications*, Free Press: New York.

Wilson, J.O. (1989) 'Human values and economic behaviour: an integrative model of comparative economic systems', paper presented to Conference on Socio-economics, Harvard University, March/April. (Available from Center for Ethics and Social Policy, 2400 Ridge Road, Berkeley CA 94709, USA).

Wisman, J. (ed.) (1990) *Worker Empowerment*, Bootstrap Press: New York.

World Bank (1949) *Annual Report 1948/49*, World Bank: Washington DC.

—— (1979) *Poverty and Development*, World Bank: Washington DC.

—— (1984) *World Development Report 1984*, Oxford University Press: Oxford/New York.

—— (1987) *World Development Report 1987*, Oxford University Press: Oxford/New York.

—— (1989) 'Meeting of the World Bank-NGO Committee and recent progress in Bank–NGO cooperation', internal document ref. Sec, M89–161, February 13, World Bank, Washington DC.

—— (1990) 'How the World Bank works with non-governmental organizations', World Bank: Washington DC.

World Resources Institute (with International Institute for Environment and Development) (1986) *World Resources 1986*, Basic Books: New York.

Zucker, L. (ed.) (1988) *Institutional Patterns and Organizations*, Ballinger: Cambridge, MA.

Index